FIGHTING FOR POLITICAL FREEDOM

Across the world political liberalism is being fought for, consolidated and defended. That is the case for nations that have never enjoyed a liberal political society, for nations that have advanced towards and then retreated from political liberalism, for nations that have recently shifted from authoritarian to liberal political systems, and for mature democracies facing terrorism and domestic conflict.

This book tests for the contemporary world the proposition that lawyers are active agents in the construction of liberal political regimes. It examines the efficacy of a framework that postulates that legal professions not only orient themselves to a market for their services but frequently they are in the vanguard of actors seeking to institutionalise political liberalism. On the basis of some 16 case studies from across the world, the authors present a theoretical link between lawyers and political liberalism having wide-ranging application over radically diverse situations in Asia and the Middle East, North and South America, and Europe. They argue that it is not the politics of lawyers alone but the politics of a 'legal complex' of legally trained occupations, centred on lawyers and judges, that drives advances or retreats from political liberalism, that political liberalism itself is everywhere in play, in countries with established democracies and those without liberal politics and that it is now clear that the legal arena is a central field of struggle over the shape of political power. The case studies presented here provide powerful evidence that the nexus of bar and bench in transitions towards or away from political liberalism is a force which has universal application.

Oñati International Series in Law and Society

A SERIES PUBLISHED FOR THE OÑATI INSTITUTE FOR THE SOCIOLOGY OF LAW

General Editors

William LF Felstiner   Johannes Feest

Board of General Editors

Rosemary Hunter, University of Kent, United Kingdom
Carlos Lugo, Hostos Law School, Puerto Rico
David Nelken, Macerata University, Italy
Jacek Kurczewski, Warsaw University, Poland
Marie Claire Foblets, Leuven University, Belgium
Roderick Macdonald, McGill University, Canada

Titles in this Series

Contemporary Issues in the Semiotics of Law edited by Anne Wagner, Tracey Summerfield and Farid Benavides Vanegas

The Geography of Law: Landscapes, Identity and Regulation edited by Bill Taylor

Theory and Method in Socio-Legal Research edited by Reza Banakar and Max Travers

Luhmann on Law and Politics edited by Michael King and Chris Thornhill

Precarious Work, Women and the New Economy: The Challenge to Legal Norms edited by Judy Fudge and Rosemary Owens

Juvenile Law Violators, Human Rights, and the Development of New Juvenile Justice Systems edited by Eric L Jensen and Jørgen Jepsen

The Language Question in Europe and Diverse Societies: Political, Legal and Social Perspectives edited by Dario Castiglione and Chris Longman

European Ways of Law: Towards A European Sociology of Law edited by Volkmar Gessner and David Nelken

Crafting Transnational Policing: Police Capacity-Building and Global Policing Reform edited by Andrew Goldsmith and James Sheptycki

Constitutional Politics in the Middle East: With special reference to Turkey, Iraq, Iran and Afghanistan edited by Saïd Amir Arjomand

Parenting after Partnering: Containing Conflict after Separation edited by Mavis Maclean

Fighting for Political Freedom

Comparative Studies of the Legal Complex and Political Liberalism

Edited by
Terence C Halliday, Lucien Karpik
and Malcolm M Feeley

Oñati International Series in Law and Society

A SERIES PUBLISHED FOR THE OÑATI INSTITUTE
FOR THE SOCIOLOGY OF LAW

•HART•
PUBLISHING
OXFORD AND PORTLAND OREGON
2007

Published in North America (US and Canada)
by Hart Publishing
c/o International Specialized Book Services
920 NE 58th Avenue, Suite 300
Portland, OR 97213-3786
USA
Tel: +1 503 287 3093 or toll-free: (1) 800 944 6190
Fax: +1 503 280 8832
E-mail: orders@isbs.com
Website: http://www.isbs.com

Hart Publishing, 16c Worcester Place, Oxford, OX1 2JW
Telephone: +44 (0)1865 517530 Fax: +44 (0)1865 510710
E-mail: mail@hartpub.co.uk
Website: http://www.hartpub.co.uk

British Library Cataloguing in Publication Data
Data Available

ISBN: 978-1-84113-767-4 (hardback)
ISBN: 978-1-84113-768-1 (paperback)

Typeset by Compuscript, Shannon
Printed and bound in Great Britain by
Lightning Source UK Ltd

Acknowledgements

This book has been supported by generous funding from the American Bar Foundation and the National Science Foundation (SES-0452250). The Oñati International Institute for the Sociology of Law provided first-rate facilities and a most congenial atmosphere for our conference in May 2005. We are particularly grateful to the Scientific Director, Volkmar Gessner and Malen Gordoa Mendizabal, Convenor of Oñati Workshops. We are the beneficiaries of many constructive comments from participants in workshops and conferences where various chapters in this book were presented as earlier drafts. Finally, we thank Bill Felstiner and the Editors of the Oñati Series, the excellent and thorough comments of the referees for the volume, Stuart Scheingold, Michael McCann and Lisa Hajjar, and not least Richard Hart, Mel Hamill and our copy-editor at Hart Publishing.

Contents

Part Four: Europe

Postscript

List of Contributors

Richard Abel is Michael J Connell Professor of Law, University of California, Los Angeles.

Zühtü Arslan is Associate Professor Dr at the Turkish National Police Academy, Ankara.

Gad Barzilai is Professor of Political Science and Law, University of Washington, Seattle.

Daniel M Brinks is Assistant Professor of Government at the University of Texas at Austin.

Javier A Couso is Professor of Law and Sociology, and the Director of the Institute of Social Science (ICSO) at the Universidad Diego Portales, in Santiago (Chile).

Malcolm M Feeley is Claire Sanders Clements Dean's Professor of Law in the Jurisprudence and Social Policy Program at the University of California at Berkeley.

Carlo Guarnieri is Professor of Political Science at the University of Bologna.

Tom Ginsburg is Professor of Law and Political Science, University of Illinois, and Co-Director, Center on Law and Globalization, American Bar Foundation and University of Illinois College of Law.

Terence Halliday is Co-Director, Center on Law and Globalization, American Bar Foundation and University of Illinois College of Law, and Senior Research Fellow at the American Bar Foundation in Chicago.

Lisa Hilbink is Assistant Professor, Department of Political Science, University of Minnesota-Twin Cities.

Carol Jones is Professor, Law School, University of Wolverhampton, United Kingdom.

Lucien Karpik is at the Ecole des Mines and at the Centre Raymond Aron (EHESS), Paris.

Sida Liu is Doctoral Fellow at the American Bar Foundation, and a PhD candidate at the Department of Sociology, University of Chicago.

Setsuo Miyazawa is Professor of Law, Aoyama Gakuin University Law School, Tokyo.

Tamir Moustafa is Associate Professor in the School for International Studies, Simon Fraser University, Vancouver.

Rogelio Perez Perdomo is Dean, Faculty of Law, Universidad Metropolitana, Caracas.

1

The Legal Complex in Struggles for Political Liberalism

TERENCE C HALLIDAY, LUCIEN KARPIK AND MALCOLM FEELEY

F
IGHTS FOR POLITICAL liberalism are not dead. Nations that have never sought or accomplished a liberal political society are constrained or inspired to do so by international financial and governance institutions, international NGOs, and geopolitically influential states (Elster, Offe and Preuss, 1998). Nations that have advanced towards and then retreated from political liberalism are pressed to regain lost ground (Miller, 2003; Schmitter, 1995). Nations that have recently shifted from authoritarian to liberal political systems are encouraged to lock in the transition through institutions and constitutions (Ackerman, 1999; Ahdieh, 1997; Ahn, 1998; Gross, 2004). And nations that seemed to be mature democracies are being encouraged to recover diminished freedoms in the face of terrorism and domestic conflict.

Across the world political liberalism is being fought for, consolidated and defended. In reaction to formerly one-party or developmental states (eg, Indonesia, Taiwan, South Korea), 'Big Man' authoritarian regimes (eg, Kenya), former and current communist regimes in central and eastern Europe and Asia (eg, China), and former military dictatorships in Latin America (eg, Brazil, Chile and Argentina), internal and external sponsors of change are vigorously advocating a liberal model of politics. Everywhere, it seems, the fate of political liberalism is at stake.

It is well known that the foundations of these politics were laid down in the eighteenth and nineteenth centuries by European states and in North America. It is less well known that lawyers frequently marched at the vanguard of these movements towards political liberalism. Historical and sociological studies demonstrate that legal professions often were active builders of the institutions of liberal politics. In a variety of ways, legal professions sought the moderation of state power via judicial independence, the creation and mobilisation of a politically engaged civil society, and the vesting of rights in subjects as citizens who would be protected by judiciaries (Bell, 1994; Bell, 1997; Halliday and Karpik, 1997b; Karpik,

1998b) However, it is also clear that lawyers were both very particular kinds of liberals, for they defined their causes narrowly, and conditional liberals, because on notable occasions they failed altogether to pursue the liberal agenda (Ledford, 1996; Ledford, 1997).

Historical research on lawyers and political liberalism stimulates a wider question of major theoretical and pragmatic importance. Is the fate of political liberalism in the contemporary world also intertwined with the politics of lawyers? Put more directly, do legal professions influence the viability of political liberalism in circumstances significantly different from their historical precursors? These differences are of three kinds. First, times have changed. New conditions have emerged such as the interdependency of nation states, the growth of national and international media, and the expansion of civil society within and across countries. Second and third generation rights of political, social and economic citizenship now are institutionalised in global norms alongside the core first generation rights of civil citizenship. Secondly, legal occupations have changed. Expanding markets demand larger numbers of more sophisticated private lawyers; expanding rights attract more professional proponents; the judicialisation of politics pushes courts into the centre of the political stage; the legal academy has grown in size, stature and visibility. Law is expected to shoulder a heavy carrying capacity in the domestic politics at least of established liberal political regimes. Thirdly, the scope of lawyers' engagement with politics potentially reaches now to the full diversity of countries with markedly different histories, cultures, legal traditions and politics from their limited range of western precursors.

Moreover, it becomes increasingly clear that nation states cannot be assigned to qualitatively different categories of transitional or established democracies as if those political conditions exist in separate spheres. Countries on a path towards political liberalism, those well-established on that path, and those that have fallen off the path are confronted alike by old and new challenges of national security, by the power of executive agencies and administrative states, by threats to civil society and basic legal freedoms, by overweening states or frightened publics. The global North and South, former metropolitan societies and their colonies, countries at the top and bottom of economic development scales face challenges to political liberalism that are more similar than their other differences might predict.

This book tests for the contemporary world the proposition that lawyers are active agents in the construction of liberal political regimes. It examines the efficacy of a framework that postulates that legal professions not only orient themselves to a market for their services but can frequently be seen in the forefront of actors seeking to institutionalise political liberalism. On the basis of some 16 case studies from across the world, we present four principal findings. First, a theoretical link between lawyers and political liberalism has wide-ranging application over radically diverse situations in

Asia and the Middle East, North and South America, and Europe. Secondly, it is not the politics of lawyers alone but the politics of a 'legal complex' of legally-trained occupations, centred on lawyers and judges, that drives advances or retreats from political liberalism. Thirdly, political liberalism itself is everywhere in play, in countries with established democracies and those without liberal politics. Everywhere the problem manifests itself in one form or another. It is either being constructed or defended; it is rising or falling. Fourthly, it is clear that the legal arena is now a central field of struggle over the shape of political power. As a result the legal complex, centred on the nexus of the bar and bench, is a strategic actor in transitions towards or away from political liberalism. Our cases present mounting evidence that the theory of lawyers and politics has universal application.

I. LAWYERS, POLITICS AND THE LEGAL COMPLEX

After decades of neglect, scholarship on lawyers and politics has expanded exponentially in the past 15 years. Significant turns towards lawyers' political activism have occurred with two parallel lines of sociolegal scholarship that now overlap and creatively engage each other—cause lawyering (Scheingold and Sarat, 2004) and political lawyering (Halliday and Karpik, 2001). Cause lawyering treats lawyers' advocacy for rights of all kinds [Karpik].[1] We focus on political lawyering—the capacity and willingness of legal professions to mobilise on behalf of political liberalism itself.

(a) Political Lawyering[2]

Beginning in the early 1990s, our political lawyering project confronted a central problematic: what is the relationship between political liberalism itself and first generation rights? In confronting this problem we studied collective action by the bar as a whole rather than dissident fractions within it; we focused on the institutional structures of liberalism (the moderate state, civil society) rather than on one or another civil, social or economic right. We took a comparative-historical approach to the foundations of liberalism in four western countries only—England, France, Germany and the US (Halliday and Karpik, 1997).

  Our findings may be summarised in five propositions (Halliday and Karpik, 2001), all of which amplify the central thesis that in Europe and North America legal professions, acting collectively, have been periodic but by no means consistent agents of political liberalism.

---

[1] References to chapters in this volume are signified by square brackets around the names of authors.

[2] This section draws heavily on TC Halliday and L Karpik, 'Political Lawyering' in NJ Smelser and PB Baltes (eds), *International Encyclopedia of Social and Behavioral Sciences* (Oxford, Elsevier, 2001) 11673.

(i) *The autonomy of the judiciary and the autonomy of the bar are the principal conditions for the fight of lawyers on behalf of a moderate state.* The fight by lawyers for judicial autonomy, as an element of the moderate state, can be found in France during the eighteenth century (Bell, 1994; Karpik, 1988; Karpik, 1998a; Karpik, 1998b), in Germany during the nineteeth century (Rueschemeyer, 1997), and in the United States in the nineteenth and twentieth centuries (Halliday and Carruthers, 1997). Both as a condition of this fight and as a distinguishing feature of liberal political society, the autonomy of lawyers, and their ability to mobilise collectively on behalf of the judiciary, suggest a critical interdependence between the bar and bench for the rise of political liberalism in disparate historical contexts.

(ii) *Historically, lawyers' collective defence of civil rights does not extend to struggles in favour of economic and social rights.* With surprising continuity across history and nation, the collective action of the bar as a collectivity has been strongly defined by a 'pure' or core rights model where the 'negative rights' of freedoms of the person, speech, movement, property and association are defended against potentially oppressive states. As a collectivity, lawyers have not been champions of second and third generation rights (eg, education, welfare, voting), which is why cause lawyers who do advocate those rights more often than not are deviants on the periphery of the profession.

(iii) *The forms of lawyers' political action are principally reactive and rely on the authority of the public or civil society.* Compared to social movements, lawyers conventionally react *against* arbitrary or illegal actions by governments and repudiations of individual rights, often through trials that become *causes célèbres* (Pue, 1997).

(iv) *Courts can become the central locus of political battles around individual civil and political rights.*

(v) *Lawyers have specific resources to become* porte pârole *(spokesmen) on behalf of civil society and to act in favour of political liberalism.*

While this first wave of studies established instances of constructive relationships between legal professions and the emergence of political liberalism, it left many questions unasked, or at least, unanswered. Not least, while these findings demonstrate that the relationship between the bar and judiciary is often decisive, they neither elaborated the variability or contingency of those relationships, nor took account of burgeoning diversity of legal occupations in successive centuries.

(b) Courts as Political Actors

In earlier centuries, the alliance between the bar and bench frequently was decisive in the capacity to mobilise on behalf of political liberalism. In the twentieth century judiciaries themselves moved much closer to centre political stage and scholarly observers followed this shift from a variety of angles.

Since World War II, two developments have made the political dimension of the judiciary obvious and imposed great political responsibilities on the judiciary. The appeals of constitutional government and the limited state have taken off around the world. Although neither of these is uniquely a post-war idea,[3] nevertheless experience with fascism and communism generated immense enthusiasm for both. These ideas have in turn spawned adoptions of bills or charters of rights that provide explicit protections of individual rights, expressly limit governmental powers, and establish judicial review—the power of the courts to declare acts of the other branches unconstitutional.

In recent years countries of the European Union have adopted bills of rights. In Europe transnational courts, such as the European Court of Human Rights, have emerged as powerful policy makers that engender compliance (Zorn and Winkle, 2001). The European Court of Justice has become a significant architect in the development of a 'United Europe'. What is undisputed is that the new Europe is being constructed in part by courts (Stone Sweet, 2000; Weiler, 1991).

The idea of constitutionalism, and its incipient doctrine of a moderate state, has spread far beyond Europe and North America. Since the mid-twentieth century, it has exerted increasingly powerful appeal, in the new nations freeing themselves from colonialism, in Eastern Europe and the former Soviet Union after the fall of communism, and in the new democratisation in Latin America. Even authoritarian regimes and illiberal democracies as diverse as China and Egypt have felt unable to resist this powerful diffusion of an institutional model that on its face appears subversive to their own regimes (Ginsburg and Moustafa, forthcoming). Motives for adopting these provisions vary widely (Hirschl, 2004; O'Donnell, 1997; Epp 1998; Epstein, Knight, and Shvetsova, 2001; Moustafa, 2003), as does their strength (Ginsburg, 2003), but none dispute their importance.

The recognition of courts as political actors has stimulated multiple strains of scholarship that do not always intersect. The juridification of politics in Europe and around the world has been illuminated by research on 'political jurisprudence', a term coined by Martin Shapiro some 40 years ago, which designates studies that explore the political salience of the judicial process and the political dimensions of judicial behaviour (Tate

---

[3] In pre-war Europe some countries had adopted a version of judicial review advanced by Hans Kelsen, but after the War Germany, Austria, and France and other countries embraced it in even stronger form (Stone Sweet, 2000).

and Vallinder, 1997; Guarnieri and Pederzoli, 2002; Charles, 1998). More recently a new institutionalism is exploring the political role of judiciaries. Much of this work builds on the classic study of judicial independence by Landes and Posner (1975) which argues that judicial independence depends upon a political system with competitive political parties. While some argued that judiciaries are regularly captured and used by the dominant political regime (Dahl, 1957), other research demonstrates the significance of courts in contemporary state formation that emphasises constitutionalism, limited government and basic rights (Hilbink, 2007; Epstein, Knight and Shvetsova, 2001).

Inevitably these concerns lead to judicial review (Shapiro and Stone Sweet, 2002), a mechanism which deliberately thrusts courts into a political role. Contemporary studies of constitutionalism in Asia, Latin America, and Africa, the establishment of 'basic rights' in Israel, Canada, Australia, Europe and elsewhere, all acknowledge a political role for judiciaries (Barzilai, 2002; Ginsburg and Ganzorig, 1996; Scheppele, 2003). As a consequence students of comparative politics have finally come to discover the importance of courts (Ginsburg, 2002; Shapiro and Sweet, 2002; Stone Sweet, 2000) [Barzilai; Ginsburg; Perez Perdomo; Couso] and, more generally, the importance of law and legal institutions for political stability and political success (Van Caenegem, 1987; O'Donnell, 2001; North and Weingast, 1987; Lijhpart, 1977; Gerring et al, 2004; Wibbels, 2005).

Perhaps for the first time, therefore, in the past decade scholars of political jurisprudence, comparative politics and historical sociology have conjoined to take law, constitutionalism and judiciaries seriously. The principles of limited government, separation of powers and judicial review have transformed judiciaries, especially in the modern administrative state, into major players in many national—and international—political arenas.

Yet this burgeoning demonstration of ubiquitous constitutionalism, the juridification of politics and the integral significance of law for political stability and change have proceeded quite independently of historical and sociological research on the politics of lawyers and legal professions despite the confluence of their mobilisation to similar ends—a moderate state. In this volume we weave these strands together by positioning legal professions and courts as a putative collective actor on behalf of political liberalism.

(c) The Legal Complex

To capture the structure and dynamics of lawyers, judges and the diversity of legal occupations requires a new concept. We stipulate the system of relations among legally-trained occupations which mobilise on a particular issue as the 'legal complex'. At the core of the legal complex are lawyers[4] and judges. However, the legal complex may extend to all legally-trained personnel in a society who undertake legal work, including prosecutors and civil servants involved in the administration of justice. The legal complex, through its conflicts and coalitions, we postulate, presents configurations of relations that can fight for political liberalism. What is at stake is to explain (1) how the legal complex mobilises, and (2) when it acts on behalf of political liberalism. More ambitiously, a theory should press towards explaining (3) how political liberalism and the legal complex over the *longue durée* mutually transform each other.

Defining the bounds of the legal complex is not easy because legally-trained professionals find many niches in a society. In several countries the vitality of human rights NGOs depends upon their leadership by lawyers and thus the boundary between lawyers within the legal complex and lawyers at the head of other civil society groups is blurred [Brinks; Moustafa]. Lawyers themselves may drift in and out of politics, claiming a legal mantle while working for clients but shedding that mantle when representing voters. In several countries there is substantial mobility within the legal complex across its various segments—from private practice to government positions, from the judiciary back into private practice, from academia to the judiciary. In some countries (eg Italy) legal academics often maintain concomitantly a private practice [Guarnieri]; in others the legal academy for decades was staffed by legal practitioners [Couso; Perez Perdomo].

Something of this complexity can be observed from the relationships between lawyers and judges. In an earlier phase of this research collaboration (Halliday and Karpik, 1997b) we observed several historical instances where a unified profession collectively supported and defended independence of judiciaries from state control, thereby enabling judiciaries better to emerge as autonomous institutions and thereby moderate state power, strengthen civil society and champion core citizenship rights. Where lawyers were divided, weak or distanced from the judiciary as an institution, or when their loyalties were devoted to other centres of power in a society, then judiciaries remained undeveloped as independent institutions or their independence more easily was eroded.

A careful examination of heterogeneous cases demonstrates considerable variation in this core relationship. At one extreme, relations may be *unengaged,* where lawyers and judges are indifferent to each other

---

[4] The definition of lawyers varies markedly across legal cultures: Abel and Lewis, 1989; 1988a; 1988b. Lawyers can variously embrace practising private lawyers, all lawyers who are licensed to practise law or appear in courts, or all persons with legal training. We consider private lawyers and advocates, in particular, as the core of political lawyering.

and occupy separate worlds (cf Ledford, 1997 on the Weimar Republic, Germany). Relations may be *cooperative,* as Karpik (1998b) and Bell (1997) observe in their observations of mutual support between French *avocats* and *Parlements,* or Halliday (1987) notes more equivocally in the 'moral economy of judicial control' that existed between US lawyers and the judiciary. Relations can be *oppositional,* for this is the posture that an activist profession takes against a corrupt or captured or oppressive judiciary. Relations may be *detached* on juridical grounds, such as the posture taken by Chilean judges to maintain their non-engagement from 'politics' during Pinochet's military rule (Couso, 2005; Hilbink, 1999) [Couso]. Often relations will be more complex, whether *cross-cutting* (alliances of one faction of lawyers and judges align against another faction of lawyers and judges) or *multiplex* (they are cooperative on some issues and oppositional on others). We hypothesise that the more unified this nexus of the legal complex, the more cooperative or mutually supporting their orientations towards or against political liberalism, the more efficacy they will exhibit in moving politics to or from a liberal form.

Almost completely absent from earlier discussions of lawyers, judiciaries, and political liberalism has been the legal academy. In the twentieth century the legal academy emerged as a substantial institution on its own (Dezalay and Garth, 2002). From the late nineteenth century the modern law school attached to the university was born. Throughout the world, and particularly following World War II, universities expanded in size and scope and law became a core feature of the curriculum. Law schools, law libraries and law reviews all became features of modern legal education. Especially where law professors are full-time they have developed a strong professional identity linked to university life and not (or not only) the legal profession. This change of legal education into an academic discipline has been accompanied by the transformation of the law review which quickly emerged as a standard scholarly forum which allowed legal scholars to communicate with each other and reinforce scholarly identity.

Thus, in many places throughout the world, an independent legal professoriate emerged, dependent neither upon the bench nor the bar, but ensconced as part of higher education. But although, on one side, law professors are located in a university and committed to the culture of higher education, on the other side their educational and scholarly mission is tinged with professional training and continued association with the 'law' and the legal profession. The development of the legal training in the university further strengthened law's grounding in civil society; legal education enjoys the independence that is typically accorded to universities by the state. In this new configuration, law professors must certainly be counted as integral components of the modern legal complex. In the politics of the legal complex, therefore, we are alert to the question—does the law professoriate view itself collectively as a trustee of autonomous law, political freedom and the moderate state? If so, does it act collectively to pursue these aims? And when is it a potential ally with lawyers and civil society? Evidence from several case studies [Venezuela, Hong Kong, China] finds that legal scholars are integral to battles over political liberalism and serve as prospective allies for other segments of the legal complex (Davis and Trebilcock, 2001; Garth, 2003; Trubek and Galanter, 1974).

Prosecutors sit uneasily within the legal complex. A state prosecution service is a potential weapon in the armoury of a repressive state. In one respect, some attenuation of relations between prosecutors and police is an indicator of state moderation, a process currently underway in China where prosecutors putatively are being made more accountable to judges (Halliday and Liu, 2007). Since prosecutors are often complicit in the abuse of rights, however, several countries in Latin America have instituted the possibility of private prosecutors—representatives of victims who may press forward cases that public prosecutors neglect or disdain, as Brinks (this volume) describes in Brazil and Argentina. Prosecutors are variably integrated into bar associations which in turn will be likely to affect their responsiveness to professional norms rather than state ideology.

The complex relations that can be found between lawyers and judges are also paralleled across the entire legal complex. It may exhibit deep cleavages among its segments: private lawyers and academics on one side of the divide and judges and prosecutors on another. Or it may exhibit crosscutting alliances where a coalition of lawyers, judges and prosecutors may ally against political liberalism while another coalition mobilises collectively on its behalf. The theoretical challenge of our collective enterprise is to discover which patterns of alignments are conducive to the enhancement of a liberal polity.

It must be emphasised that the legal complex is not a static configuration of actors that is exhaustive of all legal occupations acting collectively on all issues. The legal complex constitutes the cluster of legally-trained occupations who act collectively on specific issues because that is the way actors define their own commitment. As a result, comparisons of different legal complexes are made according to (1) the different issues that organise them, and (2) the different ways in which they deal with the 'same' issue. It follows that the legal complex may be differently constituted across different issues at the same moment in time or on the same issue over time. As a result, a given country may be classified in one period as an example of lawyers-only mobilising for political liberalism, at another period as an instance of the legal complex mobilising as a whole, and at yet another as a situation in which lawyers and the legal complex failed to mobilise. The dynamism in the concept and its explanatory value lie precisely in this variability across issues, sites and time.

II. POLITICAL LIBERALISM

The concept of political liberalism is notoriously ambiguous and much contested (Voeglin, 1974). We employ a definition that has proved to be sufficiently flexible and open to withstand shifts in the meaning of the term in diverse countries over several centuries and yet is sufficiently precise for it to be meaningful in empirical inquiry (Halliday and Karpik, 1997a).[5]

First, and fundamentally, liberal political society offers and protects *basic legal freedoms.*[6] These reside in the core rights of citizenship although they often extend to residents and aliens who are not citizens. It must be underlined that we deliberately adopt a restrictive concept of citizenship rights that corresponds to those rights in the earlier European liberal polities that precede economic and social rights and those political rights concerned with suffrage. Basic legal freedoms rest upon the granting of legal personality to a citizen and the protection of all residents within a sovereign legal jurisdiction. These freedoms include the institutionalisation of juridical rights (eg, rights to due process in law, habeas corpus, legal representation and access to justice, freedom from arbitrary arrest, torture, death), which are sometimes construed as negative rights, and the protection of foundational political freedoms (eg, speech, faith, travel, association) excluding suffrage, and property rights, which are sometimes construed as positive rights.

Secondly, political liberalism encompasses a *moderate state.* The state embraces many elements, ranging from legislatures, executive agencies to courts and the military. A moderate state is distinguished by its internal and systematic fragmentation of power, such that there is ordered or constitutionally-structured contestation among elements of the state. Most importantly for our purposes, the moderate state depends upon some autonomy of the judiciary, at the very least to the degree that it can exert restraint over other elements of the state or advance claims to rights or justice.[7] State power may also be moderated by a balance of local and national political

---

[5] While the details have varied from situation to situation, historians and historical sociologists have found the definition we adopt meaningful in 17th and 18th century England and France, 19th and early 20th century Germany, and 20th century US: DA Bell, 'Barristers, Politics, and the Failure of Civil Society in Old Regime France', KF Ledford, 'Lawyers and the Limits of Liberalism: the German Bar in the Weimar Republic', WW Pue, 'Lawyers and Political Liberalism in Eighteenth- and Nineteenth-Century England', and D Rueschemeyer, 'State, Capitalism, and the Organization of Legal Counsel: Examining an Extreme Case-the Prussian Bar, 1700–1914' all in in TC Halliday and L Karpik (eds), *Lawyers and the Rise of Western Political Liberalism: Europe and North America from the Eighteenth to Twentieth Centuries* (Oxford, Oxford University Press, 1997).

[6] We shall refer interchangeably to basic legal freedoms and core legal rights.

[7] Simpson (1989) helpfully elaborates the concept of judicial independence by distinguishing between negative elements of formal independence, such as freedoms of judges from dismissal and similar pressures, and positive elements whereby judiciaries restrain executive power and champion values of the rule of law and open justice. See also Brinks (2006).

authority (Taylor, 1990). It is critical to distinguish between moderation that may result from state self-restraint and moderation that results from a fracturing and counter-balancing of powers. We do not exclude the former but emphasise the latter.

Thirdly, a liberal polity requires *civil society*. Civil society may be constituted both as a web of associations that are dependent on the state for neither their formation nor functioning (Tocqueville [1848] 1969) and as a public sphere, a realm of discourse where reason is mobilised, citizens express opinions, and ideas encounter each other and inform political understandings (Habermas, 1989). Fundamental to civil society is the notion of an autonomous sphere that stands outside and prior to the state and may act collectively to hold it accountable.[8] Civil society fills the middle ground between the state and tribe or family, yet it is not unduly penetrated or domesticated by either. Among elements of civil society we include formal groups, such as the media, unions, religious groups, business associations, professions, intellectuals, and human rights groups, and networks of connection among members of civil society that might potentially be mobilised collectively. Yet, following Weber (1978), it is well to distinguish between civil society groups that constitute themselves independently of the state but which are far removed from prospects for mobilisation on behalf of political freedom (eg, chess clubs, model aeroplane clubs, music societies) and those that are more proximate to engagement with power and law because their organising *raisons d'être* overlap with issues of freedom and the state.

Historically, there is a contingent relationship between basic legal freedoms, on the one hand, and the moderate state and civil society, on the other. Basic legal freedoms arguably are achieved through moderation of state power and mobilisation of civil society as a realm of power. Yet even here we must exercise care because a civil society cannot emerge without freedoms of association and speech, just as juridical rights will not be meaningfully implemented if rights of legal representation are not effectively enabled by relatively autonomous courts.

It must be said emphatically that we offer a *legal* concept of political liberalism rather than a *suffrage*-based model of liberalism.[9,10] Our concept

---

[8] Yet it must also be said that civil society is often, perhaps always, partially constituted by the state: Weber, 1978.

[9] Historically, of course, almost all societies that institutionalise the three elements of political liberalism we have identified also eventually institute a universal suffrage and contested electoral politics.

[10] We distinguish between *political liberalism*, which we define narrowly in terms of legal institutions, the legal rights inherent in civil citizenship, and the engagement of lawyers in civil society, and *democracy*, with its emphasis on political rights of suffrage, the contest of political parties, and representation. While we would argue that the legal dimensions of political

of political liberalism does not include political suffrage or universal voting, for four reasons. First, the inclusion of suffrage tends to overwhelm the other basic freedoms which then get ignored. Secondly, the foundational freedoms of speech and association take us a long way towards suffrage and effectively prefigure it. Thirdly, suffrage itself is nearly universal and does not enable us to distinguish among totalitarian, authoritarian, illiberal and liberal democratic societies. Fourthly, in the past, as now, the state tends to treat individual core civil rights in a different way from universal suffrage. The latter it may readily permit, under various constraints, while sharply limiting the former. In fact, it is even conceivable that a society may display most characteristics of political liberalism, *without* universal suffrage or democracy, as Jones (this volume) finds in Hong Kong. In this respect, then, 'political liberalism' is 'political' both in the sense that it is not 'economic' liberalism nor reducible to it; and in the sense that it relates to the restraint, distribution and control of power in a society.

III. ORIENTATIONS TOWARDS BASIC LEGAL FREEDOMS

The case studies reveal that lawyers and the legal complex display four principal orientations towards basic legal freedoms. First, there are many occasions on which the legal complex as a whole presses to obtain, maintain or defend political liberalism. Secondly, there are occasions where lawyers mobilise on behalf of basic legal freedoms, but not judges or other members of the legal complex (eg, Japan during much of the twentieth century, China at present). Thirdly, there are moments where a normally liberal legal complex is inhibited or selectively constrained from mobilising to defend political liberalism (eg, Israel during the Intifadas, US after 9/11, Argentina and Brazil in the face of police killings). And, fourthly, there are instances where the overwhelming majority of lawyers, judges and the legal complex fail to mobilise, indeed, are openly hostile to basic legal freedoms (eg, Pinochet's Chile, Mussolini's Italy, Japan in the 1930s).

(a) The Legal Complex Mobilises to Fight for Basic Legal Freedoms

Our cases reveal many instances when the legal complex—lawyers and judges, sometimes with academics and prosecutors—has fought for basic legal freedoms. In some historical situations that fight led to apparently

liberalism are significant for contested democracies, studies of the latter often underplay the former: GA O'Donnell, 'Democracy, Law and Comparative Politics' (2001) 36 *Studies in Comparative International Development* 7; G Sartori, 'How Far Can Free Government Travel?' in L Diamond and MF Plattner (eds), *The Global Divergence of Democracies* (Baltimore; London, Johns Hopkins University Press, 2001).

robust regimes of political liberalism (eg, Korea, Taiwan, Spain). In other cases the victories may be short-lived or battles that will need to be fought over and again (Egypt, Hong Kong). At other moments and settings the legal complex appears to be fighting a losing battle, certainly in the short term (Venezuela, Hong Kong) or possibly in the longer term (Egypt). However, historical trajectories never proceed in a straight line. The robustness we observe in Korea, Taiwan and Spain may be vulnerable to shocks we do not yet imagine. In countries where the trajectory is trending downwards at present (eg, Venezuela, Egypt and Hong Kong) a change in domestic or international circumstances may reverse the slide away from political liberalism.

(i) Korea and Taiwan

Korea and Taiwan represent two dramatic instances of regime transformations. Movements against Korea's military dictatorship during the 1980s proceeded in parallel social and legal tracks that progressively intertwined. While students and unions led protests in the streets, the law also stirred, notably in the creation of a Constitutional Court that opened up a new high level forum for litigation around rights, criminal defence and administrative law. This was joined by a new administrative court. A rump group of human rights lawyers, who had cut their teeth in defence of prisoners of political repression, in 1985 formed a clandestine society that became formalised as the *Minbyeon* in 1987 as an alternative bar association for activist lawyers. The statist-oriented legal profession opened up to more entrants and to a growing private market for lawyers who found 'dissident' activities more appealing than commercial practice. Between the lawyers and the courts a synergy developed through legal strategies for change, based on litigation, that complemented political strategies by an energised civil society. Even the formerly conservative prosecutors sought to recast themselves in the liberal opening by successfully pressing corruption charges again officials and politicians. Legal academics injected their ideas into the widening opening of liberalism. In the face of corrupted political parties, media and legal system, this re-equilibrated legal complex, in tandem with a vibrant civil society, 'had a profound impact on Korea's liberal transformation' [Ginsburg].

In Taiwan Ginsburg shows that insurgency arose from Taiwanese ethnic lawyers who were excluded from the Kuomingtang's one-party rule. In 1970 they formed a society with judges and academics to advance liberal ideas, including freedom of speech and assembly. Some of their leaders obtained notoriety by defending arrested activists and opposition figures against treason charges, relying on doctrines of human rights. Compared to Korea, however, the Taiwanese lawyer-activists pursued not a litigation campaign but channelled their efforts into political parties. A constitutional court, the Council of Grand Justices, began flexing its hitherto flaccid muscles in a series of increasingly stronger administrative rulings, thereby signalling that law might limit administrative discretion, even of a state unaccustomed to checks on its bureaucratic powers. A rapidly expanding legal profession provided manpower for a mobilisation of law. Yet success—the integration of Taiwanese lawyers into Taiwanese politics, the transition to political liberalism, and the establishment of multi-party democracy—channelled lawyers as much into party politics as towards a distinctively lawyerly politics that operates on a plane of legalism and constitutionalism. In either case, like their Korean counterparts, the Taiwanese legal complex both facilitated and constituted the institutional accomplishment of political liberalism over a period of three decades.

(ii) Egypt

From the late nineteenth century until Nasser's military coup in 1952, Moustafa argues that the prestigious Egyptian legal profession had been a bastion of liberal values. Although the regime weakened the influence of the bar and impaired the independence of the courts, it changed course in the 1970s in order to attract foreign investment with the establishment of a Supreme Constitutional Court in 1979 to protect property rights and to review and interpret legislation. This new arena for legal mobilisation provided just the forum required by a progressive number of rights lawyers who led or allied with burgeoning rights organisations in Egypt. From the late 1980s, activist lawyers and rights groups brought a succession of cases to the Supreme Constitutional Court which thereby authorised previously banned opposition political parties, ruled laws unconstitutional and restrained administrative discretion. In addition to enabling some modest expansion of pre-political freedoms, including striking down criminal law provisions that limited freedom of the press, the legal complex fought hard to strengthen due process rights, and to limit recurrent detention and torture. On these hardest of issues the legal complex lost more often than it won. Still, there were notable victories and the legal complex pressured the government relentlessly through a series of highly publicised legal actions. But eventually the regime, stung too many times, struck back against activist judges, an assertive court and their allies in civil society to narrow the liberal opening.

(iii) Hong Kong

In contrast to the preceding cases, Hong Kong neither follows the same trajectory nor is oriented to same end. A peculiar configuration of the legal complex became implicated in the construction of a rule of law regime by colonial administrators, but *without* political democracy. Jones (this volume) shows that the emergence of Hong Kong as a rule of law society occurs not until the 1970s, when the British government, confronted with a double crisis of security—the threat of Communist China on its doorstep and internal disturbances from alienated residents—directed its Hong Kong administration to embark on a double strategy: establishing a new 'social agenda' of public services and building a rule of law society. Much of the legal complex became implicated in the legal side of this legitimation project. Uniquely, most of the construction and defence of this rule of law regime came not from the private bar but from the state's in-house legal advisors, its legally-trained civil servants who had become practised at defending basic rights from abrogation by exploitative business elites. Government officials found allies in an increasingly activist bar, most notably indigenous Hong Kong Chinese lawyers who found some influential expatriate fellow travellers. The court system was strengthened and its autonomy substantially assured. In the twilight of its colonial rule, the British even introduced a Bill of Rights.

(iv) Spain

In Franco's Spain, however, only fragments of the legal complex mobilised within a broader social movement led by Catholic intellectuals and clandestine party activists. Progressive, dissident judges formed an illegal association in 1971, *Justicia Democratica* (JD), to pursue a two-fold strategy: to limit government abuses of power in particular instances and to conceive of ways in which a judiciary might be constituted in a liberal-legal democracy. JD mounted a critique of the judiciary's complicity with the regime and called not only for judicial independence from the regime, but for full jurisdiction to be restored to courts, for the restriction or abolition of military and special courts, and for wide-ranging reforms in the recruitment of judges and the organisation of the judiciary. JD dared to criticise directly those many judges who were 'complicit in the regime's arbitrariness'. With parallel support from activist lawyers, JD sharply criticised infringements on rights and the articulation of a just rights regime. It declaimed the lack of procedural protections in the penal and military justice codes, assaults on free speech and repressive activities in universities, and the criminalisation of political associations. In their place, it advocated a state whose guiding principle would be 'respect for the dignity, integrity and liberty of the human person', and that would guarantee citizens 'rights to liberty of expression, correspondence, abode, assembly and association, security, habeas corpus, due process nationality, and petition', in a word, the basic legal freedoms [Hilbink].

In two cases fractions of the legal complex also mobilised against the erosion of basic legal freedoms. In Hong Kong the handover of the colony to China in 1997 embedded a rule of law regime inside an authoritarian state. The Beijing-appointed Tung Chee-hwa administration sought repeatedly to strengthen the primacy of the National People's Congress in Beijing over Hong Kong courts, to change the Basic Law so as to limit freedom of speech (eg, Falun Gong), to ride rough-shod over property rights of the weak in preference for affluent developers, and to restrict public demonstrations. Jones shows that a rule-of-law oriented legal complex, led by vocal barristers, fought in the courts and for the courts, most importantly the Court of Final Appeal. To a substantial degree it has succeeded, compelling the administration to withdraw amendments to the Basic Law, and upholding practices of freedom of speech and association, not to mention property rights of the weak. When legal strategies failed, lawyers took to the streets.

(v) Venezuela

In certain respects, Venezuela has followed a similar trajectory. An increasing liberalism in political society over the later twentieth century was partially constituted by a large private bar, increasingly robust courts and a lively civil society. Since Chavez was elected in 1998, however, the legal complex has been in retreat, fighting an increasingly desperate battle to protect its earlier advances. The Supreme Tribunal has been packed with Chavez supporters and, with its supervisory powers, has purged approximately one-third of the country's (c 500) judges. Judges now know that they rule against the government at their peril. For all that some judges heroically are speaking out in the hope of galvanising public opinion through the media. The legal profession, while more vigorous and populous than at any time in Venezuela's history, has had minimal collective impact. Instead individual lawyers have pressed cases to nullify acts of government or protect rights in the hope of using the court as a stage from which to constrain the government. When these have failed they have turned to international forums, such as the Inter-American Commission on Human Rights, but their effects are limited within Venezuela. Judges and lawyers have been joined by some vocal eminent jurists, including law school deans, who again have sought to mobilise civil society through speeches carried in the media. Thus a rearguard action is being fought by a loosely aligned number of lawyers, judges and academics, albeit not through their formal associations and not by any coordinated mechanism. Critical for all these efforts has been a civil society that has been responsive to leadership by figures in the legal complex through newspapers, radio and television.

(vi) Modes of Mobilisation in the Legal Complex

The legal complex mobilised in diverse ways in each of these widely disparate situations. In each case a core of private lawyers and judges, seldom exhaustive of either profession, constituted the central axis of the legal complex alliance. But frequently other legal occupations joined the alliance: in Korea lawyers and judges were joined by academics and, later, prosecutors; in Taiwan, lawyers and judges obtained support from outspoken academics; in Spain lawyers and judges were joined by prosecutors; in Egypt lawyers and judges got occasional support from academics; in Hong Kong barristers and lawyer civil servants allied with judges; and in Venezuela lawyers and judges were defended by eminent law deans.

Curiously, in no case was each segment of the legal complex internally unified in its fight for basic legal freedoms. We observe at least two patterns. In the best case, the bar or bench is led by an advance guard, or substantial proportion of activist lawyers, but its remaining members are either passive or minimally resistant. The spearhead of the legal complex serves as a more rights-oriented and activist faction in a generally liberalised legal complex. In the worst case, a fault line runs through the segments of the legal complex, pitting, for instance, pro-rule-of-law Hong Kong lawyers, legal academics and officials against pro-Beijing opponents, or pro-Chavez lawyers and judges against legal liberals in Venezuela. As that balance of power shifts it can be expected that the willingness and capacity of the legal complex to advocate basic rights will also shift.

The struggle for basic legal freedoms in all these cases is inseparable from capacities given to lawyers by courts. Frequently the opening for political liberalism is associated with a restructuring of the judiciary. In Korea, Taiwan, Egypt and Hong Kong, newly established courts—constitutional courts, administrative courts, courts of final appeal—or activated courts gave lawyers a stage on which to play, opening up the prospect of mutual alliances between courts that needed legitimation and lawyers who required a forum for the airing and correcting of grievances. Into these alternative centres of state power poured lawyers intent on establishing negative and positive legal rights, including freedoms of speech and association, as well as property rights.

As Spain exemplifies positively and Egypt negatively, the programme for a progressive legal complex also extends to the breadth of jurisdiction of courts, most notably, the abolition of special and military courts and the return of all cases to the general court system. The manifesto of *Judicia Democratica* likewise reflects a broader recognition by lawyer/judge reformers—that judges must be recruited and court systems organised in ways that affirm judicial competence, independence of the executive and ruling parties, and conditions of advancement that do not rely on 'loyalty' tests. As Moustafa argues for Egypt, and we also observe in fascist Italy, a liberal legal complex ultimately cannot tolerate an 'insulated liberalism' where courts strike Faustian bargains with the state by ruling Emergency State Security Courts constitutional and limiting appeals from special and military courts to regular courts. The struggle for political liberalism thereby directs itself to delegitimate a parallel legal system erected by authoritarian states (cf Italy, Spain, Egypt).

(vii) Civil Society

In every country in which the legal complex mobilised it gained impetus from the renaissance of civil society just as lawyers, in particular, stimulated the resurgence of civic groups, often through positions of leadership. In Egypt, defence of the media gave activist lawyers' groups a significant ally. If the Supreme Constitutional Court enabled political life, it did so because of a synergy forged between the Court, which accepted test cases, and the civil society it protected. NGOs, lawyers, the media and other civil society groups in turn legitimised and protected the Court. The most dramatic effort of this coalition to undergird civil society can be seen in a proposed law (153/1999) that would have sharply limited the number and independence of civil society groups. Into this fray stepped a national NGO coalition of more than 100 organisations that led demonstrations, hunger strikes and litigation, leading to the eventual decision of the Supreme Constitutional Court to strike down the legislation [Moustafa]. In Spain, in the early days of insurgent organisation by *Justicia Democratica,* the Roman Catholic Church provided meeting places and clandestine facilities for printing publications. Liberal Catholic clergy and intellectuals joined hands with prospective reformers. In Korea unions provided the springboard for many lawyers who later widened their activism with support from labour. In Hong Kong bar leaders could often be found at the front of public demonstrations which got sympathetic coverage from the media. Lawyers articulated for the public its grievances and aspirations. In Venezuela, too, the anti-Chavez media amplified protests by legal actors against attacks on judges and the erosion of rights.

International civil society fortified internal alliances between the legal complex and domestic civil society. The vibrance of the human rights and NGO sector within Egypt depended heavily on the resources from international NGOs. European governments and NGOs provided most of the funding for Egyptian rights organisations, and well-known transnational NGOs, such as Human Rights Watch, Amnesty International and Lawyers' Committee for Human Rights, publicised human rights violations and litigation campaigns in the international media. In Spain, domestic alliances crossed the frontier to the rest of Europe, embracing foreign media and even the Council of Europe. In Hong Kong, legal liberalism obtained international protection by keeping the PRC and NPC at bay because Beijing feared being labelled as a foe of the rule of law in a business community that demanded it. Condemnations from the international media made them a potent ally for Hong Kong groups against the PRC.

Nevertheless, civil society or publics are not inevitable allies of activist lawyers. In the US the infringements on rights by the Bush Administration did not stir most of the public to protest. In Venezuela, presumably, a majority of the public supports Chavez' encroachments on core legal rights.

But in most of the cases where a cross-legal complex coalition mobilised for basic legal freedoms it appears that it received support from vocal civil rights groups and, at least, acquiescence from publics.

International influence took a geopolitical form for Korea and Taiwan. Both sheltered under a US security umbrella. Their leading scholars, lawyers and judges increasingly turned to the US for advanced education and sometimes employment. A US presence both fostered a culture of rights, especially after the Cold War, and US connections multiplied as both countries opened up their civil societies and markets to US counterparts. Geopolitics might also account for the degree of governmental support by the US for reformist movements in Egypt and Hong Kong, and certainly tacit support for resistance to Chavez' dismantling of liberal legal institutions in Venezuela.

(viii) Politics and the Market

Relationships between the legal complex and politics are more equivocal. Many movements spearheaded by the legal complex pressed for the expansion of prepolitical freedoms (eg, Egypt, Korea, Taiwan, Hong Kong, Spain) such as freedom of speech and association. In several cases essentially legal action by the legal complex crossed over to political activism through the founding or leadership of political parties (eg, Taiwan, Korea, Hong Kong) or political movements. In Hong Kong, for instance, several of the leading barristers in the vanguard of rule of law activism became leaders of a new political party, the Civic Party, in 2005. In the US Abel argues that the federal judiciary responded to legal actions and amicus briefs substantially along party lines. Yet the Spanish case indicates that while the members of the legal complex were drawn from a heterogeneous scattering of backgrounds (Communist, socialist, Catalun nationalists, liberal democrats), they found common ideological ground on concepts of 'mission', 'duty', and 'social responsibility'. In short, they found a basis of commonality that offered a *professional* solidarity that transcended partisan politics. In Korea corruption cases against politicians brought by prosecutors brought the support of the legal complex for a purification of politics through law.

We can also observe that market conditions substantially influence the ability and willingness of the legal complex to mobilise. On the one side, political leaders solicitous of foreign investment, increased trade and economic expansion may believe that a regime that secures property rights and facilitates orderly commerce must be institutionalised. Hilbink maintains that the liberalisation momentum in Spain benefited from Franco's decision to open up the Spanish economy to Europe. This led to the infusion of ideas and support for dissident groups from outside Spain. It also led to a call by technocratic economists, who themselves might be socially conservative, for a modernised legal system that enabled a thriving market.

Similarly, after Nasser's death a liberal economic turn in Egypt premised economic expansion on the need for more secure property rights, good law and courts to enforce it. Bar leaders in Hong Kong knew that alarms would go off among the business and political elites if Hong Kong's legal system was impugned as a predictable place to do business. On the other hand, Moustafa (Egypt) and Perez-Perdomo (Venezuela) maintain that an expanding market can support a prestigious and growing private bar which concomitantly is less dependent on the state for its livelihood and has more resources to commit to mobilisation. But care is necessary lest this case be overstated. In some countries a substantial proportion of commercial lawyers do not actively support a mobilised legal complex, although they may acquiesce in its activities. They are either too busy making money or nervous about political disturbances which may threaten their current economic benefits.

(b) Lawyers Mobilise for Basic Legal Freedoms

In several cases (China 2002–6; US 2002–5, Japan 1886–1920s, Japan 1980s–2005) lawyers mobilise without judges. That is, the core alliance of the legal complex is broken. Lawyers may turn from lack of support by judges to assistance from legal academics and civil society.

In China, the Communist Party (CCP) tightly controls political power and fiercely resists any threats to its one-party state, despite its protestations to the contrary (State Council White Paper, 2005). The judiciary is treated as an administrative arm of the Party-state, although the government finds itself in the contradictory situation of wanting the legal certainty and governance advantages of an effective system of commercial and criminal law (Peerenboom, 2002), while simultaneously ensuring that it does not lose its capacity for arbitrary interventions in particular cases or general interventions if a far-off autonomy should threaten Party rule. The legal profession confronts an 'iron triangle' of police, prosecutors and judges whose tight collusion to 'strike hard' at crime has been contemptuous of lawyers for most of the Communist era.

The constitution and Criminal Procedure Law purportedly institutionalise many of the universal human rights embodied in UN declarations or in rule of law societies. In practice, most basic legal freedoms are honoured in the breach, and in very few respects are core rights of citizenship respected in practice. As a telling indicator of law's fragility, provisions in the Criminal Law 1997 and Criminal Procedure Law 1996, together with interpretations and opinions issued by official agencies of the legal complex, threaten fundamentally the capacity of lawyers to defend effectively criminal suspects, and many lawyers have been jailed or their careers ruined by the most modest advocacy that is taken amiss by judges, prosecutors, police or Party officials [Halliday and Liu].

Yet there are subterranean stirrings by many lawyers. Under cover of official control, lawyers across China engaged in criminal defence are beginning to see themselves as a nascent professional community with a potential for collective action. Enabled by an electronic infrastructure, the ACLA internet forum, lawyers are wrestling with the core of an ideology that involves all three components of political liberalism. Almost universally they seek a re-equilibration of power among the agencies of justice so that courts can check the power of prosecutors and police. They are insistent on the rights of lawyers effectively to defend detainees, to meet suspects privately, to collect evidence, and to be exempt from prosecution themselves. They demand the abolition of extended detention without trial, widespread confession by torture, and sentencing before trial. Not least many advocate the autonomy of lawyers' groups themselves. So far they have had limited support from judges. In this procedural approach to liberalism, progressive lawyers receive significant support from the most vocal legal academics who variously draft new laws of criminal procedure, make public pronouncements, and seek to lead public opinion [Halliday and Liu].

In Japan, too, over a much longer period, Feeley and Miyazawa show that from the 1880s, lawyers mobilised on behalf of basic legal freedoms: defence of labour and party leaders; challenges to illegal land seizures; human rights protection; establishment of a jury trial system; and environmental defence. A stronger project can be found in lawyers' efforts to buttress not only the autonomy but also the strength of the judiciary vis-à-vis the state administrative apparatus. From the beginning, the bar supported a professionalised judiciary, but its long-time deference to the state has been much more difficult to change. A highly-qualified but essentially passive judiciary has been reluctant to use its powers of judicial review, slow to allow litigation by citizens against state agencies, and all too ready to bow to government interests [Feeley and Miyazawa]. Lawyers have fought for a larger judiciary, more responsive to citizens and needs of the market, while judges have resisted reform proposals of all sorts, including an expansion of the judiciary.

(i) Modes of Mobilisation

How is this segmented mobilisation by the legal complex to be explained? On the one side, private lawyers have been infused with liberal values. Feeley and Miyazawa state that the origins of legal modernisation following the Meiji Restoration in 1868 institutionalised the path to modernity by adopting some bulwarks of legal liberalism—adoption of a constitution (1884/1889), a civil code (1890) and the legal institutions of courts, prosecutors and a bar. This forceful push towards modernisation combined an enormously powerful state administration with a specialised but not independent judiciary and a tiny bar, supported by private law schools. For the first time public law modestly constrained bureaucratic arbitrariness and heavy-handedness and the foundations were laid of a legal complex upon which might be erected effective institutions of political liberalism. Despite its limited size, the bar adopted 'an anti-government spirit' from which came periodic resistance to infringements on basic legal freedoms. In China's long history an independent legal profession never existed except for a brief honeymoon in major cities during the Republican period (1911–49) and slight opening in the mid-1950s. It is only since the late 1970s that a private bar has emerged, and only in the last decade that it has exploded in size. In recent years large numbers of lawyers have seized upon an ideology of the rule of law. Their increased exposure to international law, UN covenants and foreign media, and their disgruntlement with obvious injustices in contemporary China, together with their capacity now to join forces via the internet, combine to produce a China-wide network of practitioners who advocate basic legal freedoms.

On the other side, the lawyers face either unresponsive or resistant judiciaries. Japan's very conservative judiciary maintained a loyalty and deference to the state apparatus. Close alliances between the bar and bench never developed as lawyers were anchored in the market and governed by their autonomous associations and judges were bound to the state. Each occupied separate social and legal spheres. China's judiciary shows signs of emerging from its historic role of being an arm of state administration. Increasingly the judiciary is professionalising. A greater proportion of judges have legal training and the proportion of judges who are former military officers is declining. The Criminal Procedure Law of 1996 sought to weaken the power of police and prosecutors over judges in criminal cases. And there is some attenuation of direct Party interventions in particular cases. But the judiciary remains subject to generalised and occasionally quite interventionist Party and official influence. There are few signs yet, although it is one plausible scenario, of a professionalised judiciary differentiated from political control or market influence that is sufficiently aligned with the rule of law ideals of lawyers that it is a potential partner in a mobilised legal complex.

In the aftermath of 9/11, US lawyers also mobilised but in the face of obduracy from the bench, argues Abel. The President claimed executive powers to detain hundreds of domestic suspects indefinitely without access to counsel or co urts, to inter prisoners from outside the US in sites that are not subject to the jurisdiction of US courts, and to abrogate international standards of human rights, such as the Geneva Conventions. The executive further claimed the right to try suspected Al Qaeda members or supporters by military commissions, using that well-trodden path of repressive governments to remove so-called security cases to special courts where protections were minimal or absent.

Lawyers and law professors, in alliance with parts of civil society, took up the cause fairly quickly. In one of many public pronouncements, the American Bar Association urged Congress in 2002 to ensure that suspects were presumed innocent, that courts would require proof beyond a reasonable doubt, and that judicial review be permitted. In spring 2004 the New York City Bar Association (ABCNY) declared that 'the holding of persons incommunicado in this country ... has nothing in common with due process as we know it. ... these detentions are alien to America's respect for the rule of law'. Bar associations and human rights groups filed many amicus briefs before federal courts. Formal bar groups were joined by ad hoc groups of lawyers and legal academics. Nearly 300 lawyers wrote an open letter to Bush, Cheney, Rumsfeld, Ashcroft and Congress, charging that the 'most senior lawyers in the Department of Justice, White House, the Department of Defense and the Vice President's office have sought to justify actions that violate the most basic rights of all human beings'. Even some lawyers from within the military joined the resistance. Many law professors also mobilised against the repressive actions of the administration, as did some retired judges.

But the federal judiciary proceeded slowly, inconsistently and inconsequentially on actions concerning habeas corpus, denial of due process and denial of legal representation, not to mention cases on the scope of executive powers. Abel concludes that 'legality has fared poorly' since 9/11 [Abel]. Individual judges have written opinions in favour of legal rights but courts as a whole have not offered protections to citizens or residents or detainees. Four years after 9/11 'the courts had yet to release a single detainee'. Concludes Abel, 'faced with the determined executive and legislature of the world's only superpower, the rest of the legal complex—lawyers, legal academics, professional associations, and judges—can do little to protect political liberalism' [Abel].

(ii) Civil Society

In part lawyers in Japan have been able to mobilise, and lawyers in China are beginning to envisage collective action, because there is support from outside the bar. Japanese lawyers partially constituted the beginnings of a hitherto absent civil society in the first two decades of the twentieth century, aided by a fledgling free press and the founding of voluntary associations. In 1921 activist lawyers, engaged in defending striking shipbuilders, formed themselves into a voluntary association, the Japanese Lawyers' Association for Freedom; a Japan Civil Liberties Union was established in 1946 to defend freedom of speech and other basic rights; a Japan Young Lawyers' Association arose in 1954 to support the new constitution; and in 1961 a group of lawyers formed the Japan Democratic Lawyers' Association, again from an activist impetus. This capacity for organisation and mobilisation propelled the bar into the leading ranks of a developing civil society in the later 1990s, precipitated by the Hanshin-Awaji earthquake in 1995. When government failed adequately to cope with the crisis, NGOs moved swiftly into the vacuum to provide relief to victims, not least the efforts of the Japan Civil Liberties Union to deal with rights issues. Out of this demonstration of an enabling civil society developed a movement for a liberalisation of laws governing the founding of civil society groups, ultimately realised in the NPO Law (1998), which by 2004 had led to 16,000 new groups, many of which are watchdogs of government agencies, often led by lawyers [Feeley and Miyasawa].

The situation is more complex in China. Civil society is carefully controlled so far as that is possible. Many official social organisations exist but they must be registered with the government and are thereby more readily subject to its control. Yet until recently a substantial grey zone of unregulated civil society has been permitted, including groups of many sorts, often connected by the internet, so long as they have stayed off incendiary topics and showed no signs of mobilising in any manner thought to be a security threat (Thirk, 2007). But lawyers can often count on support from publics, especially peasants, workers and others, who are highly disgruntled with local corruption, abuse by officials and police, and aggrieved by expropriation of what they perceive to be their property rights. Lawyers can act as spokesmen for these publics, presenting one possible outlet for grievances with a glimmer of hope for redress. Lawyers are staking a claim to leadership of a prospective civil society. That society, they say, will be protected by due process of law, citizens will be tried fairly, torture will be abolished, and the right of innocence will be presumed. Often the media, too, offer support for lawyers. Although all forms of media are controlled by the Propaganda Ministry, substantial grey zones of discretion open up in which burgeoning media can build circulation as it airs the grievances of citizens and lawyers who find common cause. In this way the market indirectly assists. Crime and corruption sells papers and advertising. So, too, do social disturbances and official misconduct. Lawyers can appear as heroes even if a deep-seated belief continues to exist among the Chinese that detainees must be guilty and lawyer representation merely excuses the rich and powerful.

In the US, lawyers found some allies in civil society. Eclectic religious and civil rights groups, Unitarians and Quakers, Churches of Christ and Reform Judaism, and the ACLU, submitted amicus briefs in court cases. The International Committee of the Red Cross sought to find 'America's disappeared', secretly interned detainees. In all this, however, the media took their cues from public sentiment for the administration rather than offering lawyers effective support in the struggle to protect rights.

(c) Lawyers Mobilise Selectively

Mobilisation on behalf of basic legal freedoms cannot be assumed, either across time or across freedoms or across attacks on freedoms. We observe several cases where lawyers and judges, with a history of commitment to political liberalism, a robust bar, a moderate state, an active legal complex and a dynamic civil society, nevertheless are inhibited from protecting basic legal freedoms in particular instances. These instances are of two kinds: either a singular moment punctuates an otherwise liberal record; or an enduring threat inhibits a legal complex from extending its habitual liberalism to every issue. In all cases these inhibitions or reservations stem from threats to security—external threats, as in the cases of Israel and the United States, and internal threats, as in the cases of Argentina and Brazil.

(i) Israel, Argentina and Brazil

On many counts, argues Barzilai, Israel can boast a liberal legal complex. Over the last 20 years there have been emerging protections of rights, an expansion of civil society, the growth of NGOs, and some fracturing and balancing of the state's internal elements. Lawyers have championed rights, led fights against corruption, become political entrepreneurs. Yet for Barzilai this is a constrained liberalism. Lawyers, he proposes, influence public discourse and politics not only by what they say when they mobilise, but what they don't say when they choose to remain silent. This silence, while ambiguous in its meaning, amounts to tacit support or acquiescence in the most illiberal policies of the Israeli State and even Supreme Court. Silence can be observed on three issues: the legitimacy of a state as a Jewish republic, the role of Arab-Palestinians in such a state, and national security issues. It is the last of these that is salient to our inquiry. By remaining silent about torture or targeted killings, the wall of separation, the military occupation, discrimination against Arab Israeli citizens, lawyers have hindered the socio-political emergence of liberalism. There are exceptions. Some anti-Zionist Jewish lawyers and some Arab-Palestinian lawyers have chosen to break the silence. But even they operate within the rules of the political game, constrained by legal institutions and strategies, neither reaching to 'political fundamentals' nor 'restructuring state power'. Thus the legal complex talks within a framework of dominant ideologies. It is silent on the hegemony of the Jewish state and national security. And in so doing it is complicit in the retardation of political liberalism in Israel.

Threats to security may also come from within. In Argentina and Brazil, the legal complex confronts fearful publics demanding protection from rampant criminality. Public security agencies have responded with deadly force—an explosion of police homicides. In Sao Paulo, the largest city in democratic Brazil, in 1992 the police killed nearly 1,500 people, 30 people a week. This amounts to about one-quarter of the homicides in the city.

In Buenos Aires the rate was about the same. Yet government prosecutors have been exceedingly reluctant to bring cases against the police, and judges have been equally reluctant to convict.

While the bulk of the legal complex implicitly condones police killings, only a small number of private lawyers mobilise unconventionally on behalf of basic legal freedoms. In several Latin American countries there exists the possibility of private prosecutions—individuals, victims, involved in a crime, can bring a prosecution if they are not satisfied with the state prosecutor. From a careful empirical analysis of hundreds of case files, Brinks shows that when lawyers mobilise on behalf of victims, often in alliance with or through NGOs, and with public support, 'the presence of a private prosecutor dramatically improves the likelihood of a successful prosecution', sometimes by 300 to 400 per cent [Brinks]. In short, lawyers can compel the justice system to live up to its ideals by limited arbitrary police actions if they can patch together the right combination of allies. But in the face of fear of crime those allies are seldom available.

(ii) Explaining Selective Mobilisation

How can we explain these inhibitions or selective disengagement of a normally liberal legal profession or legal complex? Common to them all is a deep-seated threat that precipitates fear—fear of destruction of the state (Israel) or public hysteria over internal or external threats to life and social stability (Argentina, Brazil). But this explanation is scarcely sufficient for there are instances of threat when governments refuse to abrogate their own liberal values. Can part of the explanation be found in the legal complex? Each of these countries has well developed and conventionally liberal bar associations, judiciaries and prosecutorial professions. Yet on these issues they divided or avoided engagement. Two explanations emerge from the case studies. On the one hand, public criticism itself can instil fear in lawyers, prosecutors and judges, or at least sway their readiness to act. Judges are not immune from mass demands for repressive behaviour. Legal actors may be loath to stand apart from a national consensus that gives short shrift to legal protections when confronted with national crises. On the other hand, judiciaries may be insufficiently insulated from the executive, a case that Brinks makes also for prosecutors. When confronted with mass opinion that demands social protection that law seems unable to deliver, they respond by either refusing to protect potential perpetrators and others of their class, race or religion, or acting in conformity with executive and public preferences. Moreover political appointees to the bench are more likely to align themselves with the political authorities that appointed them rather than defend ideals that transcend factional politics. Where promotion within the judiciary is based less on merit and more on conformity to the orientations of senior judges, there too is a powerful disincentive to dissent.

Broader mechanisms are at play in these cases. Argentina and Brazil have variously experienced a 'punctuated liberalism'. Moments of exceptionalism are not unknown. In Argentina and Brazil internal threats of Communism have led to military dictatorships that summarily suspended legal freedoms. What is different in the case of police killings is their co-existence with otherwise liberal orientations by the legal complex. In this sense localised emergencies inhibit mobilisation by legal protectors of basic rights. A similar kind of selective orientation to rights, less temporally punctuated than continual, is found in Israel, argues Barzilai. While the state of Israel grew through the ministrations of lawyers, they colluded from the beginning in its 'massive national endeavours' of confiscation of Palestinian lands after 1948, the creation of a *Jewish* state, and the erection of the state's 'apparatuses of collective violence and national ideology'. The kind of society that resulted, says Barzilai, has maintained illiberal elements: the intrusiveness of religion in a state that seeks simultaneously to be Jewish and Democratic; the intrusion of the state deeply into civil society; the centrality of the military as Israel's most fundamental institution; and the overwhelming of basic rights (eg, freedom of expression, movement, property rights) by national security concerns. In one respect or another, therefore, each of these states has historical precedent for contemporary limits on the scope of legal liberalism.

(iii) Civil Society, Politics and Markets

Lawyers' inhibitions, and those of judges and prosecutors, also are intertwined with civil society and publics. While each of these countries has a robust civil society, primordial social/political/racial/religious fears of Communism, anarchy, war, personal safety or existence of the nation state can temporarily or selectively silence voices that would normally be heard. Brinks shows that publics in Latin America, especially in cities such as Sao Paolo, Salvador and Buenos Aires, register high levels of fear. 'The papers editorialise about the *"ola de inseguridad"* or wave of insecurity; parents complain that their children are not safe in the street; reports of kidnappings and violent crimes make headlines' [Brinks]. In Buenos Aires, close to 50 per cent of citizens agreed that there was a need 'to put bullets into criminals' [Brinks]. These fears are translated into public resistance to protection of rights that would seem to handcuff law enforcement. Civil society becomes a vengeful public. When leaders of civil society, such as lawyers, themselves are silent, that signal is powerful, even more if reinforced by a powerful religious institution. In each case a few civil society groups do refuse to yield to hysteria or fear, but they are usually too few to sway the nation as a whole. Rather, their exceptionalism merely underlines the failure of a conventionally liberal set of legal protections to operate in these particular circumstances.

The danger of political subversion of the legal complex recurs as a threat, ironically, to political liberalism. Political partisanship offers an alternative to a trans-political ideology of legal liberalism. Both Abel and Brinks find for the US, Argentina and Brazil either an ideological affinity between judges and those who appointed them or judges and the current occupants of executive office. Whereas the growth of a substantial market for legal services often stimulates the expansion of a private bar, which in turn multiplies centres of power outside the state, each of the countries with an inhibited liberalism had a strong private bar that served a robust market. This suggests that development of a market may provide a threshold for a minimal critical mass of lawyers able to mobilise against state incursions on rights but even a market-based private profession is no guarantee against national emergencies precipitated by threats to security.

(d) Hostility by the Legal Complex to Basic Legal Freedoms

Lawyers are not only limited liberals, insofar as they seldom cohere around second or third generation rights; they capitulate in notable instances to the waves of illiberalism. In Italy (1920s–30s), Japan (1920s–30s) and Chile (under Pinochet), neither lawyers nor judges fought for basic legal freedoms, even when it was evident they were under dire threat. These are the limiting cases for our theory. Yet it must be observed that in each of these cases, and particularly those of Japan and Chile, on other issues and in earlier and later historical contexts, the legal complex did support political liberalism. The three episodes in our case studies therefore underline the point that mobilisation by the legal complex is to be analysed by particular issues at particular times. Part of the theoretical explanation then becomes to link mobilisation opportunities across time in order to explain why it is that in some circumstances the legal complex may sponsor or at least accede to political liberalism, where at others it will tolerate even abet authoritarianism.

(i) Italy, Japan, Chile

The approaches to World War II offer two instances of fascism and militarism that eclipsed potentially moderating forces. In Italy (Guarnieri, this volume), between 1926 and 1933 Mussolini's regime sought to 'corporatise' the bar by curtailing what autonomy it had, forbidding elections for positions of leadership in local bar councils, and eventually expelling as much as 10 per cent of the 25,000 lawyers in practice who resisted the authoritarian regime. Fascism advanced with neither an active bar nor a judiciary in effective opposition. As Guarnieri observes, authoritarian regimes seldom displace judiciaries but marginalise or co-opt them while transferring more politically sensitive cases to special courts that are politically vetted for correctness and conformity, as Mussolini did with special courts in Italy. Fascism might have penetrated the judiciary very little, but the price was that the judiciary, in self-protection, maintained a low profile that was not threatening to the regime. Instead 'without openly opposing the regime, [they] tried to insert the Fascist "revolution" into the tradition of the Italian state' [Guarnieri].

Neither did judges nor lawyers effectively impede the drift of Japan into a military government in the mid-1930s. While the bar could boast instances of assertiveness in the 1920s, its protests over the declining respect of government for civil rights and liberties during the 1930s could not halt its eventual cooptation by the state in the later 1930s. Feeley and Miyasawa (this volume) indicate that as early as 1932 the Tokyo Bar Association legitimated its government's foreign adventurism in Manchuria by establishing a Japan–Manchuria Lawyers' Association. And on the brink of war, in 1940 the government pressured lawyers to form a National Federation of Attorneys for the New System as part of its campaign to domesticate civil society and forestall any outbreak of opposition. Indeed with war, the strength of the military in government bypassed the Diet, weakened civil control over the bureaucracy 'virtually eliminated the "rule of law," and further weakened the already feeble institutions of civil society, including the organised bar' [Feeley and Miyasawa]. Neither did resistance spring from a compliant judiciary. Apart from occasional exceptional lawyers who raised their voices in defence of clients during the war, the legal complex was silenced as an advocate of state moderation or defender of core civil rights.

By contrast to Italy's, Japan's and Venezuela's slow drift into authoritarianism and military government, Chile's longstanding democracy was abruptly foreclosed by General Pinochet's military overthrow of the elected Allende government on 11 September 1973. In Pinochet's State of Siege, according to an observer at the time, individual liberties were suspended, the Constitutional Court was dissolved, political opponents could be deprived of citizenship, and thousands were seized, tortured and summarily executed without due process, all this in a long-time democracy. Did the legal complex resist? Couso (this volume) demonstrates just the contrary. Apart from some individual heroic lawyers who defended human rights, the organised bar as a whole remained moribund. The legal academy fared even worse, with right-wing academic supporters of Pinochet actively exposing and then expelling their left-wing colleagues. And from the outset of the military government the judiciary not only capitulated but aided and abetted the regime. In the first celebratory religious ceremony for the Junta, the Supreme Court attended en masse. While it proclaimed to Chileans and the world that 'in Chile human rights were being respected', its 'complacent attitude towards the abuses of power' was reflected in its resistance to granting large numbers of *habeas corpus* writs filed by families of political prisoners and its blind eye to the government's parallel tribunals [Couso]. The few judges who dared raise their voices in protest were disciplined and marginalised.

In all these national cases, the thread in common is the imminence of a threat to the integrity of the nation or the security of the state. These threats provide a pretext for military or authoritarian leaders to quash what legal or civil rights exist, to contain, coopt or crush lawyers and judges, and to supercede an ideology of legal protections with countervailing ideologies of nationalism, fascism or imperialism.

(ii) Mobilisation by the Legal Complex

To what extent do dynamics within the legal complex itself contribute to this inability or refusal to mobilise? It must be said that in every case the gradual or sudden slide into political illiberalism did not silence all lawyers, though it heavily muted their voices. Small numbers continued to face, for a time, the threats of the regime, even to their personal safety. We cannot yet explain what distinguished these courageous lawyers from the majority who failed to take a stand or did so ineffectually. But in all cases the collectivities of the bar were quiescent. In all cases (Italy, Japan, Chile) the judiciary offered no moderation of executive power. Ironically, in each country the courts could boast some independence from executive authority but their jurisdictions were severely bounded and in no case had they a tradition of judicial review. In Chile, autonomous courts stayed away from big questions of substantive justice and deferred to positive law, notably Pinochet's edicts and pretence of legality. The imperative structure of the courts, with their dominance by conservative High Court judges, led to a general culture of deference to executive authority by failing to protect fundamental liberties and supporting egregious national security laws. The Chilean courts under Pinochet are one of several cases in which independent courts aided and abetted attacks on political liberalism rather than came to its defence. Courts in several countries showed themselves vulnerable to two kinds of assault: on the one hand, they might be left intact so long as they did not intervene in parallel courts to enforce security laws or overturn statutes or limit administrative discretion; on the other hand, they could be transformed internally through dismissals of dissenting judges, court packing, or even dismantling of troublesome tribunals. In any event, a court suffused with a positivist jurisprudence would not be inclined to hold a government substantively accountable so long as that government could offer some patina of legitimacy for its authoritative pronouncements.

In all cases prosecutors appear to be fused indissolubly with reactionary courts. The involvement of legal academics is more complicated. There was no developed, independent, vocal legal academy in Chile. Legal education predominantly was a part time enterprise for practitioners. In any case, the left within the university was bitterly divided from the right, which moved to drive its rivals out. Defenders of political liberalism looked in vain for partners in law schools purged of defenders of liberal ideals. In Italy the highly prestigious professoriate adopted legal positivism, which understood law to be neutral and value-free. Such a doctrine, as Couso argues for Chile and Hilbink maintains for Chile and Spain, insulates professors from questions about the substantive merits of statutes and rules from authorised legislative bodies and administrative agencies. Thus professors, like most judges, were able to ride out the fascist period without either adopting fascist ideology or subjecting it to bracing critique. Japanese legal academics scarcely contested the abrogation of rights or intensifying immoderation of the Japanese state in the 1930s.

Since both courts and prosecutors aligned with executive power there was no basis for an alliance across the legal complex between lawyers and their state-employed legal counterparts. But this sharp differentiation within the legal complex mattered little since lawyers as a whole were not inclined or able to resist assaults on the core rights of citizenship.

Deeper historical and sociological roots also help explain these failures to mobilise. In Japan and Italy state-building and modernisation of political regimes were only decades old before the onset of deepening authoritarianism and militarism. In both countries with recent histories of a strong, centralised state, other potential centres of power were customarily deferential to executive authority, a deference that only intensified as threats to security were perceived or manufactured by political leaders. In none of these countries was an institutionalised regime of political liberalism already in place. Chile looks like an exception since Couso shows that presidential power, the national legislature and courts evolved somewhat independently of each other. But their ensuring relations were not governed by a doctrine of the separation of powers. Courts had neither constitutional authority nor inclination to abrogate positive law on the basis of higher order norms of justice.

(iii) Civil Society, Politics, Markets

Moreover, in these countries civil society was either non-existent, underdeveloped or assimilated to politics. From Italy's late unification as a state (1861), 'intermediary groups were distrusted: nothing had to disturb the direct relationship between the citizen and the State' [Guarnieri]. Japan's civil society was deeply distrusted and stunted, despite lawyers' efforts to defend the emergence of political parties, unions and independent groups. And in the case of Chile, one of the strongest institutions in civil society, the Roman Catholic Church, supported the executive rather than defend rights. In all cases, therefore, not only could a civil society not speak for itself, but it offered no potential ally for a potentially activist bar as existed in Japan.

Paradoxically, politics also had a corrosive effect. In Chile, as in numbers of other Latin countries, lawyers' groups were riven by party politics. Put another way, their lack of autonomy from partisanship in the political system co-existed with a failure to develop a quintessentially professional ideology that transcended party politics. Thus they had no capacity for a unified resistance on the basis of a common legal ideology in defence of basic legal rights. In Italy, and perhaps elsewhere, this impediment also coincided with class politics. Guernieri points out that Italian lawyers were drawn principally from a middle class that overwhelmingly supported Mussolini.

Finally, the market may also have exerted an indirect effect, most notably in Japan. Historically Japanese lawyers have steadfastly resisted the expansion of the legal services market, principally for economic reasons. As a result their bar, while unified and oriented towards the expansion and defence of rights, remained tiny. With little force in itself and limited allies in civil society, it could only resist ineffectually when confronted with the full force of the state.

(e) Summary

Can we conclude that there is a systematic relationship between the legal complex and fights for political liberalism? Table 1.1 shows schematically the preponderant relationships of four orientations by lawyers and the legal complex towards political liberalism across the many episodes analysed in this book.

The findings on mobilisation for a moderate state indicate that except for cases of manifest hostility in extreme circumstances (eg, war, civil war), lawyers and the legal complex generally mobilise for an independent judiciary, often in alliance with the judiciary itself. The legal complex and lawyers similarly mobilise widely for limits on executive power, but with exceptions: in several countries whose professions are normally liberal in orientation, the legal complex or lawyers are reluctant to restrain the executive when faced with internal or external threats to security.

Furthermore, across regions, history, political circumstances and legal culture, we observe repeated instances of the legal complex and lawyers mobilising against breaches of basic legal freedoms of all sorts—against arbitrary arrests, torture, indefinite detention without trial, right to legal representation, state-sponsored killings, arbitrary seizure of private property. But in parallel to the moderate state exceptions occur when an otherwise liberal legal complex tacitly or explicitly supports executive use of torture, indefinite detention, state seizure of family property, and killings in response to widespread public fears about internal disorder or threats to

Table 1.1   Orientations towards Political Liberalism

	Legal Complex Mobilises	Lawyers Mobilise	Selective Mobilisation by Legal Complex	Hostility of Legal Complex
Country Episodes	Korea, 1980s–1990s Taiwan, 1970s–1980s Spain, 1960s–1970s Egypt, 1990s–2000s HK, 1997–2000s HK, 1983–1997 Venezuela, 1998–2006 Uruguay, 1990s	China, 2002–2006 Japan, 1886–1920s Japan, 1980s–2000s U.S., 2002–2005	Israel, 2000 Brazil, 1990s Argentina, 1990s	Japan, 1930s–1945 Italy, 1920s–1945 Chile, 1973–1990
Moderate State				
Independence of judiciary	+	+	+	–
Limits on executive power	+	+	–	–
Basic Legal Freedoms	+	+	–	–
Civil Society				
For autonomy of lawyers & legal complex	+	+	+	–
Freedoms of speech, association	+	+	+	–

This table indicates the associations between the majority of cases in a category of orientation (eg, Lawyers Mobilise) towards a particular goal for which they are fighting.

+ = the mobilisation of actors towards an element of political liberalism

– = the failure to mobilise (ie, a passive stance) or opposition towards an element of political liberalism

domestic security. The extreme cases occur in war and civil war as power is concentrated or seized by political or military leaders who are prepared to jettison all civil rights, at least for a period, on grounds of national defence or national emergency.

Finally, we find a great variety of instances where lawyers and the legal complex push for their own autonomy from executive control. Characteristically, they accompany these claims with campaigns on behalf of basic political and religious rights—freedoms of speech, association and movement. In so doing they lay the foundations of active political life which can be expressed in political opposition movements and ultimately political parties.

Yet the final column of Table 1.1 also shows there are limits to the politics of lawyers and the legal complex. We previously showed that the legal complex seldom mobilises explicitly for social, economic and political rights of suffrage. The empirical evidence of this volume demonstrates moments where lawyers and the rest of the legal complex fail to mobilise against pervasive state repression either because they are coopted or because their dissent is crushed.

IV. THE LEGAL ARENA AS A DOMAIN OF STRUGGLE

Across the world in the last half century the prospect of political liberalism is everywhere in play. For countries that are variously totalitarian or authoritarian, Big Man Regimes or military dictatorships, their leaders must grapple with domestic constituencies that agitate for basic legal freedoms in a global context of advocacy for political liberalism by well-established democracies and international organisations. For countries whose liberalism seems well-entrenched, political leaders confront domestic challenges from the administrative state and international threats to national security. In all cases it is the fundaments of political liberalism—the moderate state, civil society and ultimately basic legal freedoms—that are at stake.

This volume demonstrates that a theory of political liberalism that is linked to the activism of lawyers was not simply a passing, even if foundational, phase in the emergence of western politics. In China and the US, Brazil and Argentina, Hong Kong and Venezuela, Egypt and Israel current fights are underway that reprise those of earlier decades in Korea and Taiwan, Spain and Chile, Japan and Italy. Repeatedly we discover that the fortunes of political liberalism are linked to the activism of lawyers. Often they are in the vanguard, driving for a political opening; frequently they fight a rearguard defence when established rights are threatened. On notable occasions the loss of political liberalism is also accompanied by a failure or inability to mobilise by the bar.

Yet we have shown that the theoretical link between lawyers and political liberalism is incomplete without drawing the legal complex into the explanation. Time and again—and in our cases more often than not—lawyers derive their force not from their collective action alone but from the strength of their mobilisation together with other legal occupations, most notably judges and legal academics. The legal complex has been a critical agent of political transformation, while also constituting it, at key moments in the recent histories of Korea, Taiwan, Spain, Egypt, Italy, Hong Kong, Venezuela and Uruguay. We begin to understand that dynamics within this complex and the various ways it can be structured for political action also factor into explanations of the conditions under which political liberalism will be advanced or retarded.

In sum, the fight for basic legal freedoms involves a collective political actor that hitherto has been observed without being acknowledged. The concept of the 'legal complex' gives expression to this actor. Repeatedly we have seen that the legal arena recurs again and again as a domain of struggle. It is not surprising that legally trained occupations—the various segments of the legal complex—often choose to mobilise for or against basic legal freedoms on grounds that are most proximate to their vocation and with weapons that they have acquired in training and practice. It may be more surprising, however, to discover that states, too, in the last 30 to 40 years also wage political struggles in the legal arena. And when those states resist the construction of political liberalism or seek to undermine and dismantle it, they must engage in the pretence of legality even as they undermine it. In short, even if they lose, illiberal states have no option but to fight on this terrain as well as others.

We do not elaborate here why repressive or would-be repressive states must now paint over repression with a patina of law and legality. We can suppose that the diffusion of global norms from the United Nations and other world organisations has erected a symbolic standard for comportment that all nations find difficult to ignore altogether, if they view themselves, and want to be acknowledged, as legitimate members of the international community (Meyer et al, 1997). Sometimes formal adherence to norms of legality, human rights, citizenship and rule of law may be a deliberate ideological strategy of nation states to satisfy potential allies, protectors or trading partners who insist that defence or trade must proceed hand in hand with greater respect for law and legally-constrained political freedoms. On occasions the movement by state leaders to institutionalise basic legal freedoms can be mandated by international organisations or foreign aid organisations, such as the IMF's and donor refusals to extend further aid to Kenya until it proceeded to multi-party elections. For all these reasons and others, nevertheless, it is plain that political elites in widely dispersed countries in different regions and with different profiles of politics, have in common a perceived need to resist basic legal freedoms through legality and on legal terrain so far as they can.

This implies for the legal complex that even if it loses battles for the moderate state, the defence of civil society or the defence of basic legal freedoms, it may live to fight again on this same terrain, as the cases of Japanese, Italian and Chilean lawyers well exemplify. By the same token, it offers always to would-be champions of political liberalism the prospect that a politics of liberalism can be fought with a wide variety of legal weapons alongside those other politics of mass mobilisation, suffrage or protest. The leadership of the legal complex sometimes comes from judges, sometimes from private lawyers, sometimes even from prosecutors and government lawyers. Seldom, we have seen, do all the segments of the legal complex unify completely around a coherent position. But occasionally and in diverse circumstances they do.

Yet if struggles for freedom widely recur on legal terrain, even here there are limits. They are set not only by the capacities of the legal complex, but by the intensity of repression a regime is prepared to muster. Some repression simply extinguishes the legal terrain: the brute force of the Cultural Revolution or the repression following Tiananmen Square, Pinochet's first months in the State of Siege or, in attenuated form, the effective abolition of *habeas corpus* by the US following the attacks on the Twin Towers. In these cases there may be no legal recourse at all. Indeed the legal complex itself may be a target.

Nevertheless it must be observed that the overwhelming majority of repressive states cannot themselves tolerate the abandonment of law for very long. In China and Chile, Egypt and Hong Kong, one-party and colonial leaderships sought to build legitimacy by squaring at least some of their repressive actions with law and normalising other actions by legal means.

Most commonly, therefore, the legal complex has at least some degrees of freedom to mobilise in repressive states because political elites are impelled to legitimise domestically or internationally their regimes on legal grounds. They increasingly need some kind of legal system to support expansion of the market economy. Here repressive rulers play a complicated and potentially dangerous game. While they may roll out all the soft strategies of repression, through law and alongside law, various segments of the legal complex, alone or together, may mobilise subversively through law. Moreover, law, while profoundly domestic, never is entirely domestic. It retains juridical concepts that span frontiers and it draws upon claims to universality that are embodied in jurisprudential traditions and global institutions. To legitimate their repression on legal grounds, therefore, political elites risk exposing themselves to the erosion of their repression also on legal grounds. A similar logic applies in apparently established liberal regimes that invoke emergency powers in times of crisis. To escape from the constraints of legality for a short time nevertheless confirms the centrality of legality in normal times. The deviation from basic legal freedoms is measured against a set of normative criteria well institutionalised in law and politics. In this case, too, therefore, fragments of the legal complex have an opening to close the gap between a lapsed government's practices and the core foundations of political liberalism.

REFERENCES

Abel, RL and Lewis, P (eds) (1988a), *Lawyers in Society: The Civil Law World* (Berkeley, Cal, University of California Press).

—— and —— (eds) (1988b), *Lawyers in Society: The Common Law World* (Berkeley, Cal, University of California Press).

—— and —— (eds) (1989), *Lawyers in Society: Comparative Theories* (Berkeley, Cal, University of California Press).

Ackerman, B (1999), 'The Rise of World Constitutionalism', 3 *Virginia Law Review* 771.

Ahdieh, R (1997), *Russia's Constitutional Revolution* (University Park, Penn, Pennsylvania State University Press).

Ahn, KW (1998), 'The Influence of American Constitutionalism on South Korea', 27 *Southern Illinois Law Journal* 71.

Barzalai, G (2002), *Communities and the Law: Politics and Cultures of Legal Identities* (Ann Arbor, Mich, University of Michigan Press).

Bell, DA (1994), *Lawyers and Citizens: The Making of a Political Elite in Old Regime France* (Oxford, Oxford University Press).

—— (1997), 'Barristers, Politics, and the Failure of Civil Society in Old Regime France' in TC Halliday and L Karpik (eds), *Lawyers and the Rise of Western Political Liberalism: Europe and North America from the Eighteenth to Twentieth Centuries* (Oxford, Oxford University Press).

Couso, J (2005), 'Judicial Independence in Latin America: The Lessons of History in the Search for an Always Elusive Ideal' in T Ginsburg and RA Kagan (eds), *Institutions and Public Law: Comparative Approaches* (New York, Peter Lang Publishing Group) 231.

Dahl, R (1957), 'Decision Making in a Democracy: The Supreme Court at a National Policy-Maker', 6 *Journal of Public Law* 279.

Davis, KE and Trebilcock, MJ (2001), 'Legal Reforms and Development', 22 *Third World Quarterly* 21.

Elster, J, Offe, C and Preuss, UK (1998), *Institutional Design in Post-Communist Societies: Rebuilding the Ship at Sea* (Cambridge, Cambridge University Press).

Epp, C (1998), *The Rights Revolution: Lawyers, Activists and the Supreme Courts in Comparative Perspective* (Chicago, Ill, University of Chicago Press).

Epstein, L, Knight, J and Shvetsova, O (2001), 'The Rise of Constitutional Courts in the Establishment and Maintenance of Democratic Systems of Government', 35 *Law & Society Review* 117.

Garth, BG (2003), 'Law and Society as Law and Development', 37 *Law & Society Review* 305.

Gerring, J, Thacker, SC and Morena, C (2004), 'Centripetal Democratic Governance: A Theory and Global Inquiry', 99 *American Political Science Review* 567.

Ginsburg, T (2003), *Judicial Review in New Democracies: Constitutional Courts in Asian Cases* (New York, Cambridge University Press).

—— and Ganzorig, G (1996), 'Constitutionalism and Human Rights in Mongolia' in O Bruun and O Odgaard (eds), *Mongolia in Transition* (London, Curzon Press/ Nordic institute of Asian Studies).

Gross, AM (2004), 'The Constitution, Reconciliation, and Transitional Justice: Lessons from South Africa and Israel', 40 *Stanford Journal of International Law* 47.

Guarnieri, C and Pederzoli, P (2002), *The Power of Judges: A Comparative Study of Courts and Democracy* (Oxford, Oxford University Press).

Habermas, J (1989), *The Structural Transformation of the Public Sphere: An Inquiry into a Category of Bourgeois Society* (Cambridge Mass, MIT Press).

Halliday, TC (1987), *Beyond Monopoly: Lawyers, State Crises, and Professional Empowerment* (Chicago, Ill, University of Chicago Press).

—— and Carruthers, BG (1997), 'Making the Courts Safe for the Powerful: The Politics of Lawyers, Judges, and Bankers in the 1978 Rehabilitation of United States Bankruptcy Courts' in TC Halliday and L Karpik (eds), *Lawyers and the Rise of Western Political Liberalism: Legal Professions and the Constitution of Modern Politics* (Oxford, Oxford University Press).

—— and Karpik, L (eds) (1997a), *Lawyers and the Rise of Western Political Liberalism: Europe and North American from the Eighteenth to Twentieth Centuries* (Oxford, Clarendon Press).

—— and —— (1997b), 'Politics Matter: A New Framework for the Comparative and Historical Study of Legal Professions' in TC Halliday and L Karpik (eds), *Lawyers and the Rise of Western Political Liberalism: Europe and North America from the Eighteenth to Twentieth Centuries* (Oxford, Oxford University Press).

—— and —— (2001), 'Political Lawyering' in NJ Smelser and PB Baltes (eds), *International Encyclopedia of Social and Behavioral Sciences* (Oxford, Elsevier) 11673.

—— and Liu, S (2007), 'Birth of a Liberal Moment? Looking through a One-Way Mirror at Lawyers' Defense of Criminal Defendants in China' in TC Halliday, MM Feeley and L Karpik (eds), *The Legal Complex and Struggles for Political Liberalism* (Oxford, Hart).

Hilbink, L (1999), 'Legalism Against Democracy: The Political Role of the Judiciary in Chile' (PhD thesis, University of California, San Diego).

—— (2007), *Judges beyond Politics in Democracy and Dictatorship: Lessons from Chile* (New York, Cambridge University Press).

Hirschl, R (2004), *Towards Jurocracy: The Origins and Consequences of the New Constitutionalism* (Cambridge, Mass, Harvard University Press).

Karpik, L (1997), 'Builders of Liberal Society: French Lawyers and Politics' in TC Halliday and L Karpik (eds), *Lawyers and the Rise of Western Political Liberalism: Europe and North America from the Eighteenth to Twentieth Centuries* (Oxford, Oxford University Press) 101.

—— (1988a), 'Lawyers and Politics in France, 1814–1950: the State, the Market, and the Public', 13 *Law and Social Inquiry* 707.

—— (1998b), *French Lawyers: A Study in Collective Action, 1274 to 1994* (Oxford, Oxford University Press).

Landes, W and Posner, R (1975), 'The Independent Judiciary in an Interest Group Perspective', 18 *Journal of Law and Economics* 887.

Ledford, KF (1996), *From General Estate to Special Interest: German Lawyers 1878–1933* (Cambridge, Cambridge University Press).

—— (1997), 'Lawyers and the Limits of Liberalism: the German Bar in the Weimar Republic' in TC Halliday and L Karpik (eds), *Lawyers and the Rise of Western Political Liberalism: Europe and North America from the Eighteenth to Twentieth Centuries* (Oxford, Oxford University Press).

Lijhpart, A (1977), *Democracy in Plural Societies: A Comparative Exploration* (New Haven, Conn, Yale University Press).

Meyer, J, Boli, J, Thomas, G and Ramirez, F (1997), 'World Society and the Nation-State', 103 *American Journal of Sociology* 144.

Miller, J (2003), 'A Typology of Legal Transplants: Using Sociology, Legal History and Argentine Examples to Explain the Transplant Process', 51 *American Journal of Comparative Law* 839.

Moustafa, T (2003), 'Law Versus the State: The Judicialization of Politics in Egypt', 28 *Law & Society Review* 883.

North, D and Weingast, B (1989), 'Constitutions and Commitment: the Evolution of Institutions of Governing—Public Choice in Seventeenth Century England', 49 *Journal of Economic History* 803.

O'Donnell, G (1997), *Counterpoints: Selected Essays on Authoritarianism and Democratization* (South Bend, Ind, Notre Dame University Press).

—— (2001), 'Democracy, Law and Comparative Politics', 36 *Studies in Comparative International Development* 7.

Pue, WW (1997), 'Lawyers and Political Liberalism in Eighteenth- and Nineteenth-Century England' in TC Halliday and L Karpik (eds), *Lawyers and the Rise of Western Political Liberalism: Europe and North America from the Eighteenth to Twentieth Centuries* (Oxford, Oxford University Press) 167.

Rueschemeyer, D (1997), 'State, Capitalism, and the Organization of Legal Counsel: Examining an Extreme Case—the Prussian Bar, 1700–1914' in TC Halliday and L Karpik (eds), *Lawyers and the Rise of Western Political Liberalism: Europe and North America from the Eighteenth to Twentieth Centuries* (Oxford, Oxford University Press) 207.

Sartori, G (2001), 'How Far Can Free Government Travel?' in L Diamond and MF Plattner (eds), *The Global Divergence of Democracies* (Baltimore; Mld, London, Johns Hopkins University Press).

Schmitter, P (1995), 'The Consolidation of Political Democracies: Comparative Perspectives from Southern Europe, Latin America and Eastern Europe' in G Pridham (ed), *Transitions to Democracy* (Brookfield, Dartmouth), 535.

Shapiro, M (1981), *Courts: A Comparative and Political Analysis* (New York, Oxford University Press).

—— and Stone Sweet, A (2002), *On Law, Politics, and Judicialization* (New York, Oxford University Press).

Stone Stweet, A (2000), *Governing with Judges: Constitutional Politics in Europe* (New York, Oxford University Press).

Tate, CN and Vallinder, T (eds) (1995), *The Global Expansion of Judicial Power* (New York, NYU Press).

Thirk, S (2007), *China: Fragile Superpower* (New York, Oxford University Press).

Tocqueville, A de [1848] (1969), *Democracy in America* (Garden City, NY, Doubleday).

Trubek, DM and Galanter, M (1974), 'Scholars in Self-estrangement: Some Reflections on the Crisis in Law and Development Studies in the United States', *Wisconsin Law Review* 1062.

Van Caenegem, RC (1987), *Judges, Legislators and Professors: Chapters in European Legal History* (Cambridge, Cambridge University Press).

Voeglin, E (1974), 'Liberalism and its History', 36 *The Review of Politics* 504.

Weber, M (1978), *Economy and Society* (Berkeley, Cal, University of California Press).

Weiler, J (1991), 'The Transformation of Europe', 100 *Yale Law Journal* 2403.

Wibbels, E (2005), *Federalism and the Market: Intergovernmental Conflict and Economic Reform in the Developing World* (New York, Cambridge University Press).

Part One

Asia

2

Law and the Liberal Transformation of the Northeast Asian Legal Complex in Korea and Taiwan*

TOM GINSBURG

I. INTRODUCTION

THE CAPITALIST COUNTRIES of Northeast Asia have received intense scrutiny from political economists for much of the past half century, both because of their stunning economic growth and because of their political institutions. Governance mechanisms in East Asia, we are told, were fundamentally different from those of North America and Europe, and contributed directly to rapid post-war economic growth. Indeed, the East Asian experience is often taken to offer an alternative model of capitalism to that of the West, one in which formal law was less important than long-term relationships, networks and informal contacts. A separate set of claims in the political sphere offered 'Asian Values' as an alternative to liberal democracy. Whereas liberalism emphasised individual freedom, for example, it was asserted that Asian societies had a basic preference for social order and would follow more authoritarian political trajectories.

The continuing viability of these tropes of East Asian studies must be seriously called into question when one looks at the current political leadership in Korea and Taiwan, for the presidents of both countries are former activist lawyers who challenged authoritarian rule. How these bastions of illiberal capitalism became liberal democracies with lawyer-leaders is a fascinating story with implications beyond Northeast Asia. This chapter seeks to draw attention to this story by tracing the transformation of what I call the 'Northeast Asian legal complex', a configuration of institutions that sustained strong state governance from the early post-war period

* Thanks to Elena Bayliss, Li-wen Lin, Aditi Bagchi, Julie Suk, Wen-chen Chang, Hyun-hee Kim, Kuk Cho, Salil Mehra, Whit Gray, Dai-kwon Choi, Jackie Ross, Matthias Reimann, and Michal Tamir, for helpful comments. Li-wen Lin also provided helpful research assistance.

through the late 1980s. The chapter describes the complex and traces its institutional evolution during political liberalisation, focusing on Korea and Taiwan. In contrast with accounts that emphasise the cultural specificity of Asian values as contrasted with legal liberalism, I argue that Korea and Taiwan may be the paradigm cases of lawyer-led liberal transformation, and hence offer important clues to the interaction of the legal complex and political liberalism in other countries.

The chapter is organised as follows. Part II describes the ideal type of the Northeast Asian legal complex and its component parts. Part III traces, first in Korea and then in Taiwan, the interactions between this legal complex and emergent patterns of political liberalism, drawing on a series of interviews with activist lawyers involved in the transformation. Part IV draws comparative conclusions and ties the story into the broader themes of this volume.

II. THE NORTHEAST ASIAN LEGAL COMPLEX

The legal systems of capitalist Northeast Asia for most of the last century were based around a configuration of institutions identified here as the Northeast Asian legal complex. The complex has its origins in Japan's peculiar adoption of modern Western law, and it subsequent transfer of western-style legal institutions to its colonies in Korea and Taiwan. Following the Meiji restoration of 1868, Japan embarked on a rapid programme of modernisation that included adoption of a Constitution (1884), a Civil Code (1890) and institutional structures of modern law such as courts, prosecutors and administrative agencies, all as borrowings from Western (mainly German and French) sources. As in political economy, Japan's adoption of Western legal institutions did not mean that these institutions operated in the same manner as in the West. Japan's adoption of Western law was a rearguard action to maintain independence, an 'inoculation against colonialism rather than infection by it' (Harding, 2001: 202). With the political economy organised around state intervention and late development to catch up with the West, law received much less emphasis as a means of social ordering—instead it provided a kind of formal legitimacy to demonstrate to other nation-states that Japan was a member of the club of modernity.

As Japan's colonial project swept up Taiwan and Korea, a Japanese-style government structure was put in place in each polity, including a form of cabinet government, courts, police and modern legislation (Palais, 1975; Dudden, 2005; Wang, 2000). While the details and the level of professional autonomy varied, this institutional transfer was to have an important impact long after colonialism. Japan remained a 'reference society' for Taiwan and Korean law, both public and private, for several decades after Japan's defeat in World War II. The basic 'six-law' structure of the

Constitution and Codes was retained in both countries,[1] as was the court structure. Legislation in both countries was frequently copied wholesale from Japan, though this influence was greater in Korea than Taiwan.[2] Even today, the recent Japanese experiment of establishing three-year graduate law schools is being adopted in Korea and considered in Taiwan. Local jurists continue to pay attention to developments in Japan.

The term legal complex is meant to highlight the systemic inter-relationship and integration of a set of institutions which served to complement and reinforce each other in a stable and remarkably successful way. I use the term Northeast Asian legal complex as an ideal type to describe the similar structures in place in Japan, Korea and Taiwan, although I recognise that individual countries varied and may have deviated from the type in certain ways at particular times. The Northeast Asian legal complex had three main elements: a professional, somewhat autonomous and competent court system; a small, cartelised private legal profession without much independent political influence; and administrative law regimes that insulated bureaucratic discretion exercised by developmental regimes. I treat each in turn.

(a) Semi-autonomous Judiciary

The judiciary in Japan had emerged by the 1890s as a discrete branch of government, with a strong reputation for consistency and an insistence on resisting overt political pressure. The judicial system was organised hierarchically, with effective control at the top, and developed an inter-nalised institutional emphasis on providing like solutions to like cases,

---

[1] Japanese law has traditionally had as its core 6 major laws: the Constitution and the Codes of Civil Law, Civil Procedure, Commercial Law, Criminal Law, and Criminal Procedure.

[2] One might ask why Japan would serve as a legal reference society when it had practised such a brutal form of colonialism in Korea. Theoretically, one might expect post-colonial societies to *reject* legal forms associated with the former ruling power. The answer, I think, is twofold. First, there is path dependence to adopting legal rules and especially those governing institutions. Once an institutional configuration is established, the costs of switching to an alternative are likely to be high and to increase over time. Remaining with the colonial con-figuration is easier, and provides a comfortable continuity, especially for legal elites schooled in the language of the colonial law. The second reason lies in a general point about legal trans-plants. Law derives much of its power from its universalism, its position as the embodiment of general principles and generic modernity rather than a product of its particular context. In such circumstances, as Takao Tanase (2001: 191) has pointed out, the identity of the source of the legal transplant can easily be downplayed. Indeed, close identification with Japan as the source might be a means of discrediting the law. The position of Japan as the embodiment of imposed modernity thus led to a kind of bipolar relationship with Japanese law. On the one hand, Japanese law provided a standard of what legal reforms might be appropriate in an East Asian political economy; on the other hand, Japan's adoption of particular reforms provided incentives to surpass and improve on. Just as the goal of catching up with Japan provided a popular motive for development in Korea's political economy, so keeping up with Japan became a goal of legal reform.

helping to render predictable decision-making and thereby contributing to a reasonably sound business environment (Ramseyer, 1988; Ramseyer and Nakazato, 1989; Ginsburg and Hoetker, 2006). Courts had a moderate capacity to handle civil and commercial disputes. This in turn helped to keep litigation rates low in Japan relative to those in other advanced industrial democracies (Wollschlager, 1997).

Many of the features of the judiciaries in Korea and Taiwan can be traced back to their origins in the colonial administrative apparatus. While there were greater concerns about judicial corruption in post-colonial Taiwan and Korea than have ever been observed in Japan, the basic institutional structure of a hierarchically organised judiciary operated effectively, especially when compared with judiciaries in other developing countries coming out of colonial rule. In the economic sphere, the judiciary retained autonomy. It had a distinct professional ideology and norms of neutrality in most cases.

This is not to assert a complete autonomy from political influence. The Kuomintang (KMT) and the Korean strongmen attempted to develop means of monitoring and disciplining judges, particularly in politically sensitive disputes. The Leninist KMT, with its ability to penetrate into the society, had some advantages here compared, say, to Park Chung Hee in Korea, whose interference with judicial independence was clumsier.

(b) Small Private Bar

Northeast Asia is well known for very low rates of lawyers per capita (Haley, 1991; Pratt, 2001: 156). In both Korea and Taiwan (as in Japan), legal training was generalised undergraduate education, with the bar examination treated as a separate goal for a very small proportion of those who graduated. Relatively few legal graduates would try to pass the bar, and a very small proportion would actually succeed. The bar pass rates fluctuated, but were below 3 per cent for most of the postwar period (Kim, 2002). Most bar passers devoted additional years of study to prepare for the test beyond the undergraduate degree. The few who were able to run the gauntlet to enter the legal profession were rewarded with great status and wealth. The function of the examination was no mere test of basic professional skills and qualifications; rather it was a kind of super-examination, the difficulty of which was itself the point.

One might wonder how economies as advanced as those in Northeast Asia could function without large numbers of private lawyers. The answer lies in part in the fact that law was a popular generalist education, so that many legally trained persons who were unable to pass the bar examination ended up working in quasi-legal jobs with companies and the government. This meant that background notions of legality and predictability were present throughout the system. In addition, a large amount of 'lawyer's' work is done by adjunct professions such as scriveners, paralegals and others with competence in specific arenas of practice, including tax, administrative filings, and patent applications.[3]

In Japan and Korea, passing the bar examination actually led to further training in a judicial training institute, encouraging bar–bench ties and insulation from other social forces, but Taiwan had a distinct system with separate examinations for lawyers and judges. In addition, military lawyers, judges and professors in Taiwan could gain admission to the elite and lucrative profession by means of a 'special examination' (Winn and Yeh 1995 at 575; Winn 2005.) These lawyers, especially those with the military credentials, in turn offered not so much good legal advice as connections to the judges, reinforcing personalism in the legal profession. When combined with the severe restrictions on formal 'meritocratic' admissions during the period, this system created a de facto political screen for those with wealth and connections.

In each country, the few lawyers who were lucky enough to pass the bar and enter the private legal profession had no incentive to fight for a larger profession because of the monopoly rents they collected. Nor did private business much care to push for more lawyers. Predictable courts working in a relatively small zone meant there was little pressure on the system of state-controlled legal training and rationed legal services.

The small, cartelised private bar was relatively quiet for most of the post-war period. The organised bar associations were conservative and inactive. In the 1980s, however, exogenous decisions taken by bureaucratic authorities expanded the number of bar passers. The Korean bar's growth in numbers can be traced to a 1980 decision by the Chun Doo Hwan administration to expand the number of annual passers of the bar examination from the traditional 100; in Taiwan the numbers did not begin to expand dramatically until 1989, before which only a few dozen persons might pass the examination in any given year.[4] Ministry of Examination statistics show that the Taiwan bar passage rate increased to 14 per cent in 1989, a huge jump. The rationales for the changes in policy in Korea and Taiwan remain murky. It is tempting to trace both developments in part to the contemporaneous shift toward liberalisation in economic and financial spheres, which led to greater demand for business lawyers, but there is no independent confirmation of this hypothesis, in part because of the general lack of transparency in government administration at the time.

---

[3] These include *zenrishi, benrishi, gyosei shoshi,* and *shiho shoshi* in Japan; *falu zhuli* in Taiwan, and *beop-mu-sa* in Korea.

[4] In 1988, 16 lawyers passed the regular examination, while 114 passed the 'special' examination. The next year the number of lawyers passing the regular examination swelled to 288, while those passing the special examination declined to 87. This nearly tripled the number of annual admissions and radically shifted the composition away from those with political connections toward meritocratic selection.

(c) Administrative Insulation

One of the most important parts of the Northeast Asian legal complex was the administrative law regime, which has received relatively little attention from political economists but was essential to insulate state management of the economy. Courts in all three countries took a hands-off approach to supervising administration, allowing the operation of an informal, flexible style of regulation based on broadly worded statutes (Liu, 2003: 406–7). While a large amount of administrative policy-making is inevitable in any modern state, it has been especially apparent in Northeast Asia because of broad delegation to ministries. Less precise legislation requires more making of new rules by ministries. In Japan, this proceeded under a consensual policy-making process involving *shingikai*, deliberative councils composed of the parties concerned as determined by the relevant ministry. Similar mechanisms of business–government coordination were prominent in Taiwan and Korea (MacIntyre, 1994). The emphasis was on selective, *ex ante* private participation in policy-making arenas that were structured by ministries. This system provided transparency and predictability for the most interested players, and high levels of compliance once policy was adopted (Kanda, 1997). For outsiders, however, there was no transparency whatsoever.

In implementing regulatory policy, the Northeast Asian state has operated primarily through case-by-case ad hoc determinations, made on the basis of flexible 'administrative guidance' rather than pre-announced rules. In such a circumstance, without legislative clarity or clear rules, private actors have no choice but to cultivate relationships with the bureaucrats who will in fact be making distributive decisions on a discretionary basis. Network political economy was legally constituted. The controversy concerning the extent to which administrative discretion was exercised in the shadow of political power need not concern us here. For now, it is sufficient to say that the entire structure of Northeast Asian post-war political economy was reflected in and sustained by the structure of public law.

Private parties were subject to particularistic regulation, embodied in administrative guidance, that emphasised informal business–government relationships rather than general, transparent rules applicable to all. This mode of regulation was sustained by a lack of transparency. Had regulation been transparent, the companies could have made rational calculations. But because of the flexibility and informality of the regulatory process, private information on ministerial policy became crucial for business planning, and firms had to invest in maintaining relationships with bureaucrats.

It must again be emphasised that this configuration had a particular legal construction. There were no generalised administrative procedure rules. Government information was not freely available, meaning that bureaucrats could use the regulation of information flows as an important tool in interactions with both private firms and politicians.[5] While administrative litigation was technically possible, the restricted private legal profession meant that litigation rates were fairly low. Administrative law provided some review of retail level application of law as applied to individual cases, but virtually no challenge to wholesale level rule-making, and administrative guidance was generally held to a high standard of review (Kanda, 1997; Ginsburg, 2006). Courts would intervene if and only if a private party made absolutely clear its refusal to comply with administrative guidance, a difficult feat given both the high status of bureaucrats and the myriad collateral tools government held to shape an individual firm's business environment.

(d) The Equilibrium of the Legal Complex

Each of these three elements of the Northeast Asian legal complex interacted with the others to produce a set of stable and reinforcing institutions. The predictable courts minimised pressure for private litigation (at least when compared with American 'adversarial legalism' (Kagan, 2002)). This allowed the state to maintain severe rationing of private legal services. A small private bar, in turn, minimised the possibility of social movement litigation challenging the insulated domains of policy-makers (Upham, 1987). Furthermore, the possibility of judicial and prosecutorial retirement to the bar in Korea and Taiwan led to a comfortable conservatism in those countries among the majority of legal practitioners. In Taiwan this was magnified by the ability of military lawyers to gain preferential admission to the bar without passing the examination. (Interestingly, there is no general pattern of judicial retirement to the bar in Japan, and the private legal profession tends to be more liberal as a result. Left-leaning bar passers have traditionally been more likely to select the private bar as a career in Japan than in Korea and Taiwan.)

The basic configuration of administrative discretion exercised by elite bureaucrats and a restricted supply of legal professionals meant that litigation was relatively unimportant as a means of social ordering, particularly in interactions with the state. Regulated parties, lacking legal recourse, were forced to cultivate particularistic relationships with the state, reinforcing the image of bureaucratic dominance. Long term relationships among bureaucrats and the large industrial firms provided the basic structure, reducing the need for general rules to govern arm's-length transactions. The Northeast Asian legal complex cabined law to a narrow zone.

An additional factor in Korea and Taiwan was authoritarian rule, justified to maintain security from the external threat of, respectively, North

---

[5] This point is one of divergence from the German model.

Korea and the People's Republic of China (PRC). North Korea and the PRC were not merely neighbouring communist countries, but regimes that claimed to be the sole legitimate governments of the nation; they provided a very real alternative vision of national identity and legitimacy. The resulting anti-communist ideology and Cold War imperatives meant that both the South Korean and ROC regimes needed some degree of formal legality to distinguish themselves from the totalitarian alternative. Thus the very existence of a small private bar and formal institutions of judicial independence was necessary to distinguish the regimes from the totalitarians who lacked any associational life or professional integrity. Formal constitutionalism, too, was needed to maintain US support. The presence of liberal constitutional language meant that liberal law was at least a formal ideal on which reformers and oppositionists could draw. For most of the period, however, this potential remained dormant.

III. TRANSFORMATIONS

Beginning in the 1980s, the regimes in Korea and Taiwan faced serious challenges and demands for the restoration of democracy. A key factor was the emergence of broad based social movements involving the middle class, which itself was a product of rapid economic development. In this sense, Korea and Taiwan were paradigms of modernisation theory, which posited that economic growth would lead to social and political change (Lipset, 1963).

Modernisation theory informed the law and development movement of the 1970s, which placed great emphasis on the mobilisation of law for social change. While this movement focused its attention on Latin America and Africa, this section suggests that Northeast Asia was ultimately a more hospitable environment for the dynamic to unfold. In both Korea and Taiwan, small groups of activist lawyers drew on and adapted American social activist strategies to use the law for social change. This section traces the political and legal transformations that developed in the 1980s and 1990s, with an emphasis on the interactions between activist lawyers and the dynamics of democratisation.

(a) Korea

Korea's peculiar version of authoritarianism was a series of military dictatorships that lasted virtually uninterrupted from independence in 1953 until the mid-1980s. In the mid-1980s, however, sustained challenges to the Chun Doo Hwan regime spread from activist students and labour unions to the middle class. This ultimately led Chun to resign, and his successor, Roh Tae Woo, to initiate constitutional and political reform leading to direct elections. Roh won the first election in 1987 when the two main opposition figures, Kim Young Sam and Kim Dae Jung, could not form a united front, but each of the Kims has now subsequently occupied the Blue House.[6]

The dynamics of democratisation have been traced elsewhere, but it is important for present purposes to recall that legal reform played an important role. Of particular importance was the emergence of a powerful Constitutional Court that became the focus of many reformers frustrated by the cautious and circumscribed jurisprudence of the Supreme Court. The Constitutional Court was created by the 1987 Constitution, and was not expected by its designers to play a significant role. However, the Court developed a jurisprudence that was both careful and activist, making itself available for a wide variety of claims. The Court eventually transformed criminal procedure, administrative law and many other fields, and became the prime locus of a new judicialised politics in Korea (Ginsburg, 2003).

Because it was a new organisation, the Constitutional Court did not fit easily into the traditional legal complex. Although it was staffed by judges, the process of appointment also involved the President and the National Assembly. It thus broke with the tradition of autonomous, insulated courts that eschewed politics. Instead, the Constitutional Court issued a number of decisions that were relatively generous in terms of granting standing to sue. The Constitutional Court was also a high status forum in a country where status matters a good deal. A new administrative court bench, too, attracted much attention.

A court is only useful if there are parties willing to bring cases to it (Epp, 1998). The Constitutional Court, as well as the administrative and ordinary courts, soon became a locus of activity for the several thousand new civil society organisations that exploded onto the scene after 1987 (Shin, 2003). This development was spurred in part by the election of former dissident Kim Dae Jung in 1997, who increased government support for and receptiveness to NGOs. The old account of Korea as 'strong state, weak society' gave way to a new situation wherein grass roots organisations sought to use law to check the state. Lawsuits became one of the primary channels for these groups.

One of the most visible of these civil society institutions was the People's Solidarity for Participatory Democracy (PSPD), chaired by a prominent lawyer named Park Won Soon. Expelled from Seoul National University in

---

[6] Each President entered with a reform programme. Kim Yong Sam's themes were globalisation and administrative reform, as he launched a series of administrative reforms aimed at opening up the bureaucracy, deregulating and reforming the concentration of the economy in the hands of the famous chaebol conglomerates. Kim Dae Jung furthered this agenda, along with a dramatic shift in policy toward the North in the form of the Sunshine policy of rapprochement, ultimately discredited when it was revealed that Hyundai had paid the North some $300 million for the North–South summit.

1975 as a law student demonstrating against the Park Chung Hee regime, Park had spent time in jail on political charges.[7] After leaving prison, Park passed the exceptionally competitive lawyers' examination. In keeping with the statist orientation of the legal system, the only real options for bar passers in 1980 were to become a judge or a prosecutor, and Park became a prosecutor in Taegu in 1980. He thus became an establishment lawyer, although an unhappy one, and he soon left.

Some years later, student and labour demonstrations against the Chun regime intensified. Arrests of the various demonstrators led Park and a handful of other lawyers to begin to represent political prisoners, intellectuals, labour leaders and students who had been arrested. In 1985, this handful of five or six human rights lawyers formed an informal association, which they called *Chun Bo Pae* (rights and law association).[8] They treated this as a 'kind of a secret organisation' to avoid the gaze of the late authoritarian state, coordinating and assigning cases among themselves because of the heavy workload. After the mass demonstrations of 1986 led directly to Korea's democratisation, these lawyers formalised their association as the *Minbyeon*, with 56 lawyers. This association became a kind of alternative bar association, and drew many activist lawyers with political agendas, eventually drawing hundreds of members.

After two years abroad, Park returned to Korea in 1993 and formed an alliance of lawyers, social scientists and student activists as the People's Solidarity for Participatory Democracy (PSPD). From the beginning, as the name suggests, they sought civil society participation in the sense of providing policy ideas to help consolidate Korea's democracy. Park describes the PSPD as not just a civic group, but a political party without ambition to occupy power. The existing Parties were seen as too corrupt and weak to propose laws and serve a real representative function. Law and civil society, then, played a key role in substituting for a weak party system that was perhaps unable to cope with the challenges of the constant reform.

The PSPD launched a wide range of activities, including legislative campaigns, litigation strategies, organisation of rallies and generally working for social change. Corruption grew to be seen as an issue with the potential to transform Korean governance in profound ways. Explicitly drawing from foreign models of anti-corruption legislation, including from Singapore, Taiwan, Hong Kong and the Ethics in Government Act of the USA, the PSPD drafted a statute and initiated a lobbying effort at the National Assembly that was ultimately successful.[9]

---

[7] Interview with Park Won Soon, 7 March 2005.

[8] Another lawyer with a similar biographical story was Cho Yung Nae.

[9] The lawyer-activists made legislation a primary strategy, and within 5 years, they had successfully passed more than 70 pieces of legislation: interview, Park Won Soon, 7 March 2005.

Litigation was also a component of the reform programme. The group was not focused on broad based access to justice (for example, through a legal aid strategy) so much as finding key cases to leverage broader reform programmes. The PSPD used litigation as a strategic mechanism, when it would have a broad effect on citizens' consciousness. For example, in one case, a subway accident occurred when a light was out for one hour. The PSPD brought the case claiming $1000 per person in damages, but only recovered a small fraction thereof. Nevertheless, the publicity from the case, combined with other mobilisation efforts, convinced the public transportation agency to write a charter for citizens. There were hundreds of similar examples of litigation being utilised as part of a broader strategy in diverse arenas.

The growth in civic organisations both reflected and contributed to the increasing public distrust of the Korean political establishment. Rooted in professional classes and the so-called 386 generation (30-somethings, educated in the 1980s, born in the 1960s), many of the supporters came of age around the Kwangju massacre. Distrust of the government led the civic society organisations to focus on corruption, and in this regard they have been aided by vigorous print and broadcast media as well as a prosecutor's office eager to revise its former image as a tool of authoritarian presidents. There has thus been a corresponding increase in the salience and occurrence of scandal (Johnson, 2004).

The politics of scandal, as exploited by NGOs, reached a zenith in the months before the April 2000 parliamentary elections, when a coalition of some 450 civil society organisations, chaired by Park, sponsored a blacklist of corrupt politicians.[10] Criteria for being blacklisted included corruption, participation in the National Security Council's legislative committee and other signs of being 'unfit' for support. The blacklist campaign had a significant effect on nomination processes—59 of the 86 on the final blacklist who ran were defeated (Shin, 2003; Johnson, 2004). The coalition also sought to reform the election law, which prohibited civic groups from participating in election activities.

My argument thus far is that the stable equilibrium of small bar, peripheral judiciary and strong bureaucracy was gradually eroded with democratisation in the 1990s. A key first step was the establishment of the Constitutional Court, and its willingness to grant standing to civil society organisations. The presence of a forum allowed civic groups to use litigation as a strategy which changed bureaucratic behaviour.

---

[10] 123 sitting members of the national assembly were blacklisted, roughly evenly divided by party affiliation, but including Kim Jong Pil, a fixture on the political scene who had been prime minister under Kim Dae Jung, and many other prominent politicians. Other organisations compiled similar lists.

Internal bar politics changed too. Traditionally, the bar was a minutely small group, with most graduates of the Judicial Research and Training Institute becoming prosecutors and judges. There was very little notion of a profession as an autonomous force in society, but rather a heavily statist orientation. When the Chun regime (for unclear reasons) increased the number of bar passers from the miniscule 100 per year in 1979, the orientation of the profession began to change in unanticipated ways. Since the government offices could absorb only a limited number of graduates each year, an ever-increasing percentage of bar-passers had to become private lawyers. This helped erode the statist orientation of the profession, though of course the existing bar opposed the expansion.[11] Lawyers like Park, who were quite anomalous in the 1970s and 1980s, became more common in the late 1980s with the rise of the 386 generation.

More directly, the culture of scandal forced the traditionally dominant parts of the legal profession to reform. Traditionally, prosecutors had been the highest status group in the level profession because of their close association with political power. Indeed, it was their very *lack* of autonomy that gave them prestige, as they were identified and feared as instruments of the President. The President's desire to use prosecutors for narrow political ends did not change in the democratic era: even Kim Dae Jung was seen as initiating selective prosecutions against uncooperative chaebol. But after democratisation the source of institutional prestige for prosecutors began to erode. A major factor here may have been a prominent scandal involving the Prosecutor-General, but there were lower level concerns about prosecutorial discretion. Beset by scandals, the prosecutors sought to rehabilitate their image and status through aggressive corruption investigations. Thus democratisation, while being used by activists, also triggered a reordering within the legal complex itself, toward greater autonomy from the political system.

Minbyeon's most famous former member is current President Roh Moo-hyun, who had been an activist lawyer in Pusan along with his top advisor Moon Jae In. Former Minbyeon member Koh Yong-Su is now the chair of the Korean CIA, the organisation nearly synonymous with oppression in the minds of many activists from the 1980s. Kang Kum-Sil is now the Minister of Justice. Ahn Kyung Whan, an academic, became Dean of Seoul National University School of Law and also served as an advisor to the Ministry of Justice. In short, these activist lawyers have *become* the establishment, which inevitably changed their perspectives. On the one hand, the domestication of activist lawyers has led to a

---

[11] Indeed, Ahn (1994, 123) reports that the Ministry of Justice expressed concern that expansion in the bar led to a growing number of 'dissident' lawyers because of the difficulty of finding ordinary legal work.

more cooperative relationship between government and NGOs, as civil society organisations can contribute ideas to and receive funding from government. On the other hand, there is the risk of cooptation, of which thoughtful activists like Park Won Soon are well aware.[12]

The emergence of the activist bar in Korea is a phenomenon that began in the early 1980s and has had a profound impact on Korea's liberal transformation. It adopted a kind of programme of continuous reform. When asked why lawyers took the lead, Park contrasts Korea with Japan, a country with 'real institutions' like an active mass media and an impartial prosecutor general. Korea, in his view, had no real national institutions with any credibility.[13] The political parties, media and legal system all were basically corrupt. The PSPD took over the role of setting the agenda for reform, filling a void in the polity.

Park argues that one key factor in the PSPD's success was the mix of academics, lawyer and activists, each bringing their respective expertise to the PSPD. Academics contributed ideas, but had no political or litigation experience. Lawyers had practical skills, but were elites; activists connected with citizens and thus continually shifted the agenda back to the core vision of participation. Korea's story suggests that lawyers' professional knowledge was most effective when embedded in broader networks of change agents, so that lawyers play a role, but not the only role, in the broader programme.

(b) Taiwan

Taiwan enjoyed a softer form of Japanese colonialism, and legal modernisation on the island was shaped by Chinese Republican thought as much as by Japan's legacy. After the establishment of ROC control in 1945, tensions escalated between KMT and the Taiwanese, and many thousands of local activists (and other elites) were rounded up and killed in the so-called 2–28 incident. From then on, native Taiwanese were effectively subordinated to 'mainlander' rule, which combined military efficiency with a Leninist political party. Much of the nominally democratic constitution was suspended by so-called 'Temporary Provisions' that lasted 40 years, and no effective opposition parties were allowed.

Confronted with one-party rule, Taiwanese activists focused on ending KMT rule, and channelled their efforts into securing greater political

---

[12] Park mentioned a 'time of crisis for civic groups' as government coopts their ideas: interview, 6 March 2005. Always looking forward, Park resigned as secretary of the PSPD and became a Board Member of a new institution called the Beautiful Foundation, which encourages fundraising for charities and NGOs to support civil society. The legal framework for philanthropy needs work. For example, a problem developed with tax exemption when the *chaebol* used their organisational sophistication to take advantage of the mechanism.
[13] Interview, 6 March 2005.

liberties to facilitate that goal. This differed slightly from Korea, where political parties were legal but circumscribed, and where activists focused on social and economic issues. Prevented from forming a party, Taiwanese elites eventually developed a category of *dangwai* (out of the party) politicians. Human rights and social change were a key part of their discourse, with the ultimate human right being that of self-determination. Lawyers initially were a small part of the group, with the most prominent leaders being those who favoured direct action tactics.

A crucial step came in 1970 with the founding of the Chinese Society for Comparative Law by Chen Chi-sun and other Taiwanese lawyers. They called their association the 'Chinese' society so that it would be able to be registered, for any organisation with Taiwan in the title would not be accepted by the government. The Society sponsored research and seminars on democratic legal practice, including such classical liberal issues as freedom of speech and assembly. Like the Minbyeon, this served as a kind of alternative bar association for like-minded lawyers, but also included judges and academics. Nevertheless, the society's influence in the bar remained tiny, because of the penetration of the formal associations by the effective Leninist organisation of the KMT.

Eventually, Taiwan's leaders took steps to end authoritarian rule. In 1985, President Chiang Ching-kuo appointed Taiwan-born Lee Teng-hui as his Vice President, and Lee succeeded Chiang on his death shortly thereafter. Thus began a long period of gradual democratisation, wherein political and legal reform proceeded apace.

Lawyer involvement came to the fore during the Kaohsiung incident in 1979, when lawyers from the Chinese Society of Comparative Law (including current President Chen Shui-bian) earned fame by defending arrested activists.[14] The incident began at a rally sponsored by *Formosa* magazine, one of several journals which were the early focal point for the opposition, to celebrate International Human Rights Day. Police tear-gassed the crowd, and jailed dozens of prominent opposition figures, some for several years. Chen (then 28 years old) and a small group of fellow young lawyers undertook to defend *Formosa* magazine and the activist leaders against treason charges. The most prominent leaders, including the famous democracy activists Huang Hsin-cheh and Shih Ming-teh, received sentences ranging from 12 years to life, but the trials served as a focal point for opposition, as many defendants were able to testify to their intimidating treatment in pretrial detention. Using classical liberal language of human rights and freedoms, the lawyers used the trials to call attention to the Taiwan nationalist struggle.

---

[14] Others in this category include current premier Su Tseng-Chang, who had represented Yao Chia-wen at the court martial, and former Premier Frank Hsieh, (who resigned at the end of 2006) but emerged as the DPP's candidate for President in 2008.

There followed a campaign of intimidation by the KMT, including arrests and even political murders in Taiwan and the United States. The targets extended to family members of the dissidents. Chen's own wife Wu Sue-jen was paralysed in an incident many believe was organised by KMT forces.[15] The authorities also closed 15 magazines associated with the opposition.

These strong-arm tactics that had worked in the late 1940s were no longer effective in the 1980s, however. Relatives and lawyers of the jailed dissidents ran as independents and won political office in their place; Chen himself was elected to the Taipei City Council in 1981. Political prisoners staged hunger strikes, new dissident publications grew up to replace the closed ones, and new demonstrations emerged focusing on a range of social issues rather than Taiwan independence per se. These campaigns included subjects like environmental and womens's issues, Aborigine civil rights, academic and journalistic freedom, and an end to martial law.

In contrast to the position in the United States and Korea, litigation played a relatively small role in these movements. Rather the activists focused on legislative strategies. Furthermore, the formal bar associations played little part. The Chinese Society of Comparative Law continued to operate but served as a platform for organisation around progressive Taiwanese interests rather than a locus of coordinated litigation. Attempts to change the name of the Chinese Society to the Taiwan Law Society were blocked by the Ministry of the Interior. Still, the Chinese Society continued to thrive, expanding its network to some 400 members, including many local lawyers affiliated with foreign law firms; but when these members sought to advance their positions through the formal bar associations, they were rejected. The struggles to control the formal bar reflected not just political differences, but different approaches to the role of lawyers in society. The activists wanted to eliminate restrictions on bar membership so as to expand the pool of representation; the mainstream groups sought to limit entry, as professions tend to do.

Ultimately, after the bar passage restrictions were ameliorated, the activist lawyers were able to secure victory within the bar through sheer force of numbers. Today, lawyers from the now renamed Taiwan Law Society are prominent in the bar. For example, Remington Huang of Baker and McKenzie has served as the head of both the Taiwan Law Society and the Taipei Bar Association. Once they had achieved success in the bar, the activist group ended the 'back-door' entry which had allowed military lawyers special access. This in turn consolidated their leadership within the profession.

As in Korea, one factor that played a role was the re-emergence of constitutional litigation. Although the Council of Grand Justices had had

---

[15] In the mid-1980s, Chen was jailed for libel for a magazine he was running, but his wife was elected to the Legislative Yuan.

the formal power of judicial review since the establishment of the ROC, they had been a quiescent institution under authoritarian rule. In the early 1980s, however, they began to shift away from their traditional passivity with a series of decisions expanding their jurisdiction and building up some institutional capital. Many of these decisions concerned administrative law, but did not involve particularly high profile issues. Rather the Council seemed to be signalling that legality was important and that it could serve as an instrument to constrain bureaucratic arbitrariness.

In the 1990s, the Council became much more active, systematically dismantling the tools that had been used to maintain mainlander domination. For example, the Council held that military counsellors could not be required in schools; that labour groups could organise; and that criminal procedure had to accord with international norms.

A crucial symbolic moment came when the Council was called on to resolve the question whether the Taiwan Law Society could register as an organisation, replacing the Chinese Society for Comparative Law. The long-standing policy during the authoritarian period was to deny registration to any 'social organisation' that sought to include Taiwan in the title, on the ground that this would encourage the Taiwan independence movement. In April 1999, in Interpretation 479, the Council of Grand Justices held that the constitutional guarantee of freedom of association included the right freely to choose the name of the organisation, and struck out the Ministry of Interior regulations as unconstitutional. This legitimated the role of the Taiwan Law Society and marked the decline of the authoritarian control over associational life.

What of the role of lawyers in liberal politics? Not all lawyers were members of the DPP, and not all DPP leaders were lawyers, but the correlation is significant enough to be striking (Winn and Yeh, 1995; Lu, 1992). In the mid 1990s, 30 per cent of DPP members of the Legislative Yuan were lawyers, a rate of lawyer-legislators possibly matched only in the United States Congress (Jacob et al, 1996). Today, the President, Vice-President, Premier and immediate past Premier are all legally trained, and all were involved either as defendants or lawyers in the Kaohsiung trials. Law had been an elitist profession in the one-party state, and drew ambitious and talented people for whom formal politics was foreclosed. For these young Taiwanese, law served as a vehicle to channel their considerable energies, while preparing them for the day when public office might be a real possibility.

It must also be pointed out that this development of the DPP as a lawyer-led party reflected the contingent result of struggles within the Party about tactics and strategy. A hard-line, idealist group continuously pushed for a pro-independence policy, while others sought to emphasise social policy and pragmatic accommodation to gain power. The hardliners sought to utilise direct action while the pragmatists sought a slower, more measured strategy. As the party developed, however, the lawyers gained the upper hand.

One illustration of this domestication of direct action through law was the DPP's adoption of an internal arbitration system, complete with published precedents, to deal with intra-party disputes, both personal and policy. This arbitration system utilises non-party lawyers who are close to the DPP to resolve disputes. The head of the arbitration scheme was Chen Chi-Sun, the activist lawyer whose office had served as informal meeting ground for many years of DPP activists and who had been a mentor of Chen Shui-bian. The idea of intra-party arbitration reflects the association of the DPP with law and legalistic modes of reasoning, while of course advantaging that faction of the party with those skills. It seems plausible that this internal ordering of party affairs in a legalistic way may have both contributed to and reflected Chen's emergence as the Presidential candidate of the DPP for the 2000 election.

The Taiwan story is one of lawyers advancing claims of professional autonomy at the same time as they pushed for a specific political cause. These two causes mutually reinforced each other. Asking for freedom of speech and freedom of assembly was meant to bolster Taiwan independence as well as democracy; developing a vision of a legal profession able to advance claims against the regime served this goal. It is possible, though not verifiable, that the professional goals would have been subordinated to the political ones had the lawyer-activists had to choose.

Interestingly, once the lawyers had triumphed, tensions arose with their former allies. The activist factions within the DPP have been very critical of President Chen, and Huang Hsin-cheh actually left the party after Chen was selected as the Presidential candidate. Chen's performance as President has left many disappointed, as he has neither effectively advanced the independence cause nor delivered much in the way of domestic policy. The skills needed to advance the cause in opposition have not proved to be the same ones needed to govern effectively in a complex international environment. At this writing, Chen is embroiled in a serious corruption scandal that threatens his Presidency. The liberal lawyers may have transformed Taiwanese society, but may themselves have been transformed in the process.

IV. LESSONS

The Northeast Asian story touches on a number of themes related to lawyers' roles in liberalisation. It concerns, most importantly, activist elements in the legal profession playing a crucial role in the transformation from illiberalism to liberalism, and one in which activists targeted a particularly imposing and effective administrative state complex. But the pathways of the lawyers were different in the two countries discussed here. The Korean activists mobilised a broadly based strategy for social change, but did so quite self-consciously outside the framework of party politics. Park's remark that the PSPD was a political party without aspirations to power is quite illustrative. In Taiwan, in contrast, a smaller group of activist lawyers sought and gained political power, representing themselves as the vanguard of a long-oppressed Taiwanese majority. The overtly political character of the Taiwanese lawyers may simply reflect the paramount nature of the national identity issue on Taiwan, but more likely has to do with different initial conditions. The KMT one-party regime and the suppression of Taiwanese nationalism made political party organisation a particularly attractive vehicle for change, whereas in Korea political parties were generally seen as corrupt and ineffectual. The Korean activists thus chose the 'purer' strategy of working outside the party system.

At the outset of the chapter, I suggested that many developments in transforming Taiwanese and Korean political economy reflected a kind of paradigm of modernisation theory, with political and economic liberalisation supporting each other and leading to broader cultural changes. In this regard, geopolitics are surely important to understanding the particular transformations in Northeast Asia. The United States played a key role in national defence, as a reference society, and in supplying liberal legal ideology and institutions as a model. The presence of the liberal metropole in the form of the United States meant that liberalism was present in the array of ideas available to reformers. Experiences in the United States, either in exile or in training periods, informed many of the specific strategic choices by the leading activists in Korea and Taiwan.

For example, many prominent members of the Taiwan opposition, including current Vice-President Annette Hsiu-Lien Lu, had studied in the United States, and several were lawyers. Lu has said that Champaign-Urbana, Illinois, was the 'birthplace of her enlightenment' when she observed the women's movement there in the early 1970s.[16] After her release from prison in 1985, she again returned to the US to study at Harvard, before returning to become a central member of the Democratic Progressive Party. She was elected Vice-President in 2000. Park Won Soon in Korea greatly benefited from a two year stint at the London School of Economics and Harvard Law School, followed by an internship at the American Civil Liberties Union in Washington, DC. Park attributes many of his organisational innovations to this period, when he learned about tactics and strategy while collecting legislation on human rights and corruption.

The role of the United States extends beyond providing a model and training ground to actually serving as an alternative means of entry into the legal complex. Indeed, Korean and Taiwanese students at various times

---

[16] Interview, December 2004.

have looked at US legal qualifications as an alternative degree in a context where bar passage rates have been too low to meet demand (Winn, 2005). All of this suggests why it is that Korea and Taiwan may appear to be a kind of paradigm for the process of legal liberalism in non-Western societies: both were societies that depended on the United States for their continuing viability in the face of nearby communist regimes. This is an atypical, somewhat paradoxical sense in which national security affects liberal transformation: rather than posing a threat to legal liberalism, a country's security relationship with the United States may in fact be the vehicle for liberal ideas to enter, and may provide those ideas with prestige and power.

In terms of broader links between the legal complex and liberalism, the meritocratic character of law and the social mobility offered by professions were key factors. Both Presidents Chen and Roh grew up in poverty. Chen's parents were tenant farmers; Roh did not go to college but instead passed the bar examination out of high school, a feat nearly unheard of anywhere in Northeast Asia. Law provided a field in which these young talents could demonstrate their skill and drive, and hence were able to develop reputational capital that supported political engagement. Professional and economic power was particularly important in Taiwan, where the Leninist regime coopted other channels for advancement.

Finally, it is worth recalling the dynamics by which the Northeast Asian Legal Complex was transformed. In both Korea and Taiwan, a key step was the seemingly innocuous, technical step of expanding the size of the private bar. This was undertaken by the authoritarian regime in Korea and as a technical decision of the Examination Yuan in Taiwan. This step mattered not only because of the absolute increase in the talent available to take on system-transforming tasks, but also because it shifted the proportion of the profession engaged in private practice as opposed to government lawyering and judging. In Taiwan, it allowed the 'meritocratic' elements in the profession, namely those who had passed the examination as opposed to entering the bar through one of the backdoor methods, to expand their numbers and influence in the bar. In a very real sense, the private legal *profession* emerged along with democracy in both countries. Activist lawyers were able to draw on this pool of talent to advance their agendas. In this sense the story is similar to Epp's (1998) account of 'Rights Revolutions'. A support structure of activist lawyers was needed to effectuate and channel broader demands for rights.

At the same time, the 'supply' side of the equation cannot be ignored. Had it not been for the crucial factor of constitutional courts making themselves available to claims challenging the government, the activists' strategies would have been ineffectual. The constitutional courts' willingness to constrain governmental decisions at the highest level had great symbolic importance for scaling back the previously dominant administrative apparatus. This emboldened activist elements in the legal profession to pursue their agendas more vigorously.

Korea and Taiwan have had similar histories over the last century. Colonisation by Japan introduced modern law, and established institutions that laid the groundwork for further social and economic development. After World War II, both countries were governed by capitalist authoritarian regimes confronted with communist enemies, and were part of a broader American zone of influence. As economies grew, so did pressures for liberalisation, and in both countries lawyers were well situated to take positions of leadership in democratisation. In turn, the legal systems were transformed from the classic pattern of the Northeast Asian legal complex. Passive courts, a miniscule and quiescent profession and administrative insulation have been replaced by constitutional court activism, lawyer-presidents and a new politics of transparency.

REFERENCES

Ahn, KW (1994), 'The Growth of the Bar and the Changes in the Lawyer's Role: Korea's Dilemma' in PSC Lewis (ed), *Law and Technology in the Pacific Community* (Boulder, Colo, Westview Press).

Dudden, A (2005), *Japan's Colonization of Korea: Discourse and Power* (Honolulu, Hawaii, University of Hawaii Press).

Epp, CR (1998), *The Rights Revolution: Lawyers, Activists and Supreme Courts in Comparative Perspective* (Chicago, Ill, University of Chicago Press).

Ginsburg, T (2003), *Judicial Review in New Democracies: Constitutional Courts in Asian Cases* (New York, Cambridge University Press).

—— (2006), 'The Regulation of Regulation' in E Wymeersch et al (eds), *Corporate Governance in Context: Corporations, States and Markets in Europe, Japan, and the United States* (New York, Oxford University Press).

—— and Hoetker, G (2006), 'The Unreluctant Litigant?: Japan's Turn to Litigation', 35 *Journal of Legal Studies* 31.

Haley, J (1991), *Authority Without Power* (New York, Oxford University Press).

Harding, A (2001), 'Comparative Law and Legal Transplantation in Southeast Asia: Making Sense of the "Nomic Din"' in J Feest and D Nelken (eds), *Adapting Legal Cultures* (Oxford, Hart).

Jacob, H, Blankenburg, E, Kritzer, H, Provine, D and Sanders, J (1996), *Courts, Law and Politics in Comparative Perspective* (New Haven, Conn, Yale University Press).

Johnson, D (2004), 'The Prosecution of Corruption in South Korea: Achievements, Problems and Prospects' in T Ginsburg (ed), *Legal Reform in Korea* (London, RoutledgeCurzon).

Kagan, R (2002), *Adversarial Legalism* (Cambridge, Mass, Harvard University Press).

Kanda, H (1996), 'Financial Bureaucracy and the Regulation of Financial Markets' in H Baum (ed), *Japan: Economic Success and Legal System* (Berlin, Walter de Gruyter).

Kim, JW (2002), 'American Law Schools in Japan and Korea: A Reform or Mockery?', Paper presented at Law and Society Association Annual Meeting, Vancouver, 27–31 May.

Lipset, SL (1963), *Political Man: The Social Bases of Politics* (New York, Anchor Books).

Liu, L (2003), 'Global Markets and Parochial Institutions: The Transformation of Taiwan's Corporate Law System' in C Milhaupt (ed), *Global Markets, Domestic Institutions: Corporate Law and Governance in a New Era of Cross-Border Deals* (New York, Columbia University Press).

Lu, AY (1992), 'Political Opposition in Taiwan: The Development of the Democratic Progressive Party' in TJ Cheng and S Haggard (eds), *Political Change in Taiwan* (Boulder, Colo, Lynne Rienner Publishers).

MacIntyre, A (ed) (1994), *Business and Government in Industrializing Asia* (Ithaca, NY, Cornell University Press).

Milhaupt, C (2004), 'Nonprofit Organizations as Investor Protection', 29 *Yale Journal of International Law* 169.

Pratt, JL (2001), 'The Two Gates of Taiwan National University Law School', 19 *UCLA Pacific Basin Law Review* 131.

Ramseyer, JM (1988), 'Reluctant Litigant Revisited: Rationality and Disputes in Japan', 14 *Journal of Japanese Studies* 111.

—— and Nakazato, M (1989), 'The Rational Litigant: Settlement Amounts and Verdict Rates in Japan', 18 *Journal of Legal Studies* 263.

Scheingold, S and Sarat, A (2004), 'Something to Believe' in S Scheingold and A Sarat (eds), *Politics Professionalism and Cause Lawyering* (Stanford, Cal, Stanford University Press).

Shin, EH (2003), 'The Role of NGOs in Political Elections in South Korea: The Case of the Citizen's Alliance for the 2000 General Election', 43 *Asian Survey* 697.

Tanase, T (2001), 'The Empty Space of the Modern in Japanese Legal Discourse' in J Feest and D Nelken (eds), *Adapting Legal Cultures* (Oxford, Hart).

Upham, F (1987), *Law and Social Change in Postwar Japan* (Cambridge, Mass, Harvard University Press).

Wang, TS (2000), *Legal Reform in Taiwan under Japanese Rule* (Seattle, Wash, University of Washington Press).

Winn, JK (2005), 'The Role of Lawyers in Taiwan's Democratization' in W Alford (ed), *Raising the Bar: the Emerging Legal Professions of East Asia* (Cambridge, Mass, Harvard University Press).

—— and Yeh, TC (1995), 'Advocating Democracy: The Role of Lawyers in Taiwan's Political Transformation', 20 *Law and Social Inquiry* 561.

Wollschlager, C (1997), 'Historical Trends of Civil Litigation in Japan, Arizona, Sweden, and Germany: Japanese Legal Culture in Light of Judicial Statistics' in H Baum (ed), *Japan: Economic Success and Legal System* (Berlin, Walter de Gruyter).

3

Birth of a Liberal Moment? Looking Through a One-Way Mirror at Lawyers' Defence of Criminal Defendants in China

TERENCE C HALLIDAY AND SIDA LIU

CRIMINAL PROCEDURE PROVIDES a pivotal site for observing struggles surrounding advances towards or retreats from political liberalism. Both Karpik (1997, 1999) and Pue (1997) demonstrate that a leading edge of political liberalism in France and England respectively can be found in the conjunction of legal representation and criminal defence. These both derive from and require some moderation of the state, the opening of civil society, and the institutionalisation of core rights of citizenship. Several centuries of legal development in criminal law have sought to universalise these provisions.[1]

Likewise, the relaxation and retreat from protections of criminal procedure indicate transitions away from certain foundations of political liberalism, such as denial of jurisdiction, abrogation of due process, the refusal of representation and torture. That these retreats are occurring contemporaneously in countries that led historical movements towards political liberalism and are among its most vocal advocates merely underlines the fragility of liberalism when confronted with vast putative threats from an inchoate enemy, as we have seen in Britain and the United States since 9/11 (Abel, 2005). The project of political liberalism is never complete (Halliday and Karpik, 1998b).

---

[1] The Universal Declaration of Human Rights (1948) upholds the right to a fair trial. The International Covenant on Civil and Political Rights (1966) requires that persons detained or arrested will have prompt access to counsel who should be given access to the information on which the prosecution builds a case in order to mount an effective defence. It further provides that lawyers themselves will not be subject to harassment or sanctions for representing detained persons. The Basic Principles on the Role of Lawyers (1990) further stipulate that detained persons will be given appropriate time and opportunities to consult with their lawyers and that lawyer–client communications will be confidential. Together these implicitly assert or presume each of the three attributes of political liberalism as we have specified it.

The aspect of the liberal project that centres on crime engages a complex of actors in an incessant struggle for a balance of power which embraces the central institutions of the state. The emergence of political liberalism appears to require an equilibration of power such that police and prosecutorial authority is restrained, lawyers' defensive capacities are enabled, and judicial powers are expanded. At the heart of this project lie lawyers,[2] although they are limited liberals and too often have been impediments to liberalism (Halliday and Karpik, 1998a; Ledford, 1997). Lawyers' capacity to build or defend liberalism depends upon the emergence of a coherent profession that concomitantly champions an ideology supportive of liberalism and enables collective mobilisation in its propagation and defence. To be capable of mobilisation, a profession must emerge with an identity built around a coherent ideology, a division of labour and a community of discourse. This in turn depends upon the opening of a public sphere, the creation of sites in which discourse congeals into a system of meaning and where a common identity serves as a springboard for collective action (Halliday, 1987; Karpik, 1999).

The post-Mao period in China presents a prime and rare contemporary site for the coincidental genesis of a legal profession and the making of criminal procedure law. The successive enactments of the Criminal Law and Criminal Procedure Law over the past 25 years, together with a flurry of regulations from all the main institutions engaged in the criminal process, appear to signal a sharp disjunction with China's long history of crime control in both the imperial and Maoist periods. However, these progressive legislative cycles are concomitant with the faltering steps towards formation of a criminal defence bar. The fate of criminal defence lawyers allows us to witness the difficulties in the birth of a profession, as these lawyers struggle to mobilise their ideology of representation and practice of criminal defence in the face of systemic and entrenched resistance by China's longstanding iron triangle of law enforcement—the police, procuracy and judiciary. The struggles within the legal complex that surround criminal defence signify deeper contradictions in the Chinese Party-state that go far beyond the narrower problems of professionalisation. Paradoxically, all these disjunctions and contradictions in criminal law practice have nevertheless facilitated the emergence of liberal ideologies among Chinese lawyers. This twisted development of the legal profession and political liberalism is precisely our focus in this chapter.

We shall, first, provide a thumbnail sketch of criminal procedure in China until 1996; secondly, indicate how criminal procedure reforms in China can be framed in terms of the broad contours of political

---

[2] Lawyers exist without liberalism, but liberalism without lawyers is a contradiction in terms.

liberalism; thirdly, describe our rare data source from within the All China Lawyers Association; and fourthly, analyse lawyers' self-descriptions of criminal practice and their emerging ideologies around issues of liberalism.

I. UNPROPITIOUS FOUNDATIONS: LAWYERS AND THE CRIMINAL JUSTICE SYSTEM IN CHINA

The seeds of contemporary China's encounter with legal liberalism spring from very rocky soil. Traditional Chinese culture has no concept of rights or their institutional protection. Restraint on imperial executive power relied more upon the ethical behaviour of the enlightened ruler rather than any check and balance of power. Public law was an instrument for guiding society and 'indisputably a tool to serve the interests of the state' (Pereenboom, 2001: 41). Criminal law and penal codes were retributive and relied on punishment. A primitive legal profession (the so-called 'litigation masters') not only was never established as a major player in politics, but was often suppressed and fragmented by the government (Macauley, 1998).

Following the collapse of imperial China, a brief window of legal liberalism opened up in the Republican period (1912–49) with the establishment of a nascent legal profession, the opening of law schools, and the founding of courts to interpret statutes that reflected something of a Western turn (Xu, 1998). Yet these initiatives sprouted mostly in major urban centres where they had too short a time to become institutionalised, and the fractiousness of wars and internal conflicts in China never permitted a full flowering of the seeds planted by republican reformers.

The dislocations that the Revolution brought in 1949 carried over into the legal field. Lubman (1999) has argued that the PRC criminal law has swung between two rival conceptions that arguably continue to the present: (1) the *mass line,* a largely arbitrary criminal process that relied on shifting Party priorities and local cadre discretion; and (2) the *bureaucratic model,* the Soviet model of criminal justice in which a professionalised staff (ie, police officers, procurators and judges) administer a somewhat orderly and predictable rule-governed system.[3] The 'alternation and competition' between these two models from 1949 to the Cultural Revolution were played out in the relationships among the law-enforcement triumvirate—police, procuracy and judiciary. However, in either model the process has no place for independent actors who might

---

[3] Yet this second model of routinised criminal justice confronted revolutionary cadres whose practice during the revolutionary struggle owed much to resisting law, fomenting disorder, breaking rules and mobilising masses without too much concern for harms.

Figure 3.1. Temporal Changes in Criminal Law Policy, 1949–2004

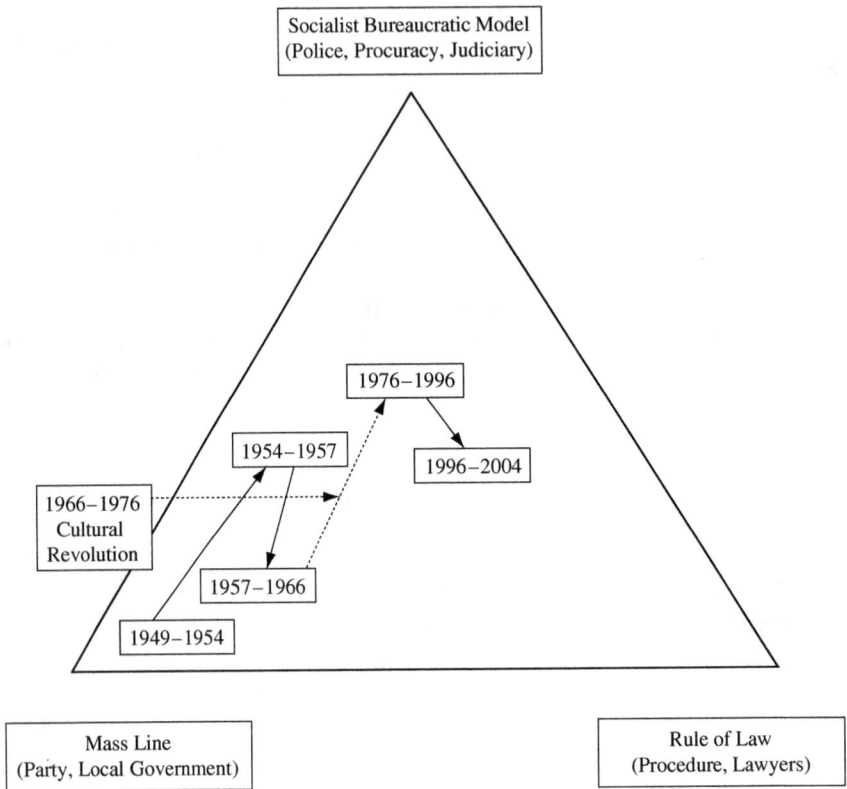

```
                    ┌─────────────────────────────┐
                    │ Socialist Bureaucratic Model │
                    │ (Police, Procuracy, Judiciary)│
                    └─────────────────────────────┘
```

Socialist Bureaucratic Model
(Police, Procuracy, Judiciary)

1976–1996

1954–1957

1996–2004

1966–1976
Cultural
Revolution

1957–1966

1949–1954

Mass Line
(Party, Local Government)

Rule of Law
(Procedure, Lawyers)

defend the accused against abuses committed by those who administer
it (Cohen, 1968), though lawyers were formally tolerated and briefly
cultivated in certain periods.

As Figure 3.1 demonstrates, following this logic, from 1949–53 the
mass line dominated and most legally-trained personnel held over from the
Nationalist period were purged. However, beginning in 1954 the pendulum
swung towards regularisation, including the passage of legislation to organise the procuracy and courts, statutes to set some guidelines for criminal
procedure, policies to differentiate functions among the police, procuracy
and judges, and tentative steps towards creating a defence bar. This brief
turn towards what was essentially a Soviet model of criminal process was
reversed sharply in 1957 when mounting criticism of the Party provoked it
to strike back in a severe 'anti-rightist' campaign that reverted to the mass
line, and called upon the police, procuracy and judiciary to act as a unified

force to implement Party policy.[4] The Cultural Revolution (1966–76) swept away even the mass line: the formal criminal process ceased to exist and the activities of police, procuracy and judiciary were variously suspended, reorganised, and disbanded, depending on the location and time. Lawyers disappeared altogether.

But the Cultural Revolution left a powerful residue. Its destructive and pervasive effects for the breakdown in law enforcement, collapse of public order, and the abandonment of any kind of regularised institutions of social control led many leaders in subsequent years to value regularised legal administration and restraints on arbitrary power so that such devastations might never recur.[5] The rise of Deng Xiaopeng to power in the late 1970s signified a revival of law, lawyers and legal institutions. But much began de novo. The bar needed to be 'invented as a profession without any guidance from Chinese tradition or China's recent history' (Lubman, 1999: 158). Taking effect in 1982, the National Peoples Congress adopted the Provisional Regulations on Lawyers that styled lawyers as 'legal workers of the state', organised in state-controlled offices and called concomitantly to 'serve the cause of socialism' and protect 'the legitimate rights and interests of citizens' (Lubman, 1999: 154). The 1997 Lawyers Law reflected the progressive expansion of civil and commercial legal practice and signalled some 'unhooking' of the profession from the state[6] (Michelson, 2003). Licensed lawyers are directly regulated by the All China Lawyers Association (ACLA), which is under close control of the Ministry of Justice. Thus slowly a revived legal profession has emerged, although it remains relatively small, highly fragmented, and of enormous variability in quality (Michelson, 2003; Liu

[4] A Chinese judge aptly summarised the relationships of the law-enforcement triumvirate in 1956 as 'three workshops in one factory', a pattern of enforcement solidarity that prevailed through the beginning of the Cultural Revolution (Lubman, 1999: 84). Meanwhile, offices of defence lawyers that had been founded in the previous 3 years were largely dismantled in this period.

[5] Cf the impact of Peng Zhen, whose suffering during the Cultural Revolution is thought to have impelled his championing of a legal system in its wake (Potter, 1998). Deng Xiaopeng similarly supported a legal system not only to aid economic development but in reaction to his persecution during the Cultural Revolution. The most dramatic sign of this shift in the Party's orientation was evident in the assignment of defence counsel to the defendants in the widely publicised trial of the Cultural Revolution's much vilified Gang of Four, including Mao's widow. There is a sharp difference of opinion about whether the appearance of obviously ineffectual defence counsel helped or hindered. Those who say it helped point to the novel concept of defendants being protected by counsel, even if the protection was minimal and ultimately ineffectual. Those who say it hindered note that the association of defence counsel with embodiments of evil may have sullied the image of criminal defence for many years.

[6] Although more progressive reformers had urged that lawyers be labelled as 'independent professionals', the NPC settled for a shift in concept from lawyers as state workers to lawyers 'as personnel who have obtained a business license for setting up practice of a lawyer in accordance with the law and who provide legal services for the public' (Art 2 of the 1997 Lawyers Law).

and Michelson, 2004).[7] A growing market for legal services has followed the tremendous wave of law-making that has been unleashed across the spectrum of public and private law, beginning in an initial cycle since 1978 and continuing in more expansive reforms since the mid-1990s.[8]

Yet the legal reforms have failed to realise many of their original goals. Until today, courts have remained clearly subservient to the Party and readily coopted by local political authorities (Lubman, 1999: 3). Lawyers have faced severe competition from several occupational groups and all kinds of unauthorised practitioners in the market for legal services (Liu and Michelson, 2004). Even in criminal defence work where no other occupations are permitted to practise for profit, the defendant still has the option of choosing a non-lawyer to represent him in the criminal process.[9] Because Chinese lawyers are usually generalists, it is hard clearly to differentiate a criminal defence bar from other sectors of the legal profession.[10]

Interwoven with the transformation of the legal profession have been cycles of reform of the criminal justice system that directly affect the capacity of criminal lawyers to present any kind of restraint on enforcement agencies. Over the past 25 years, China has enacted legislation that registers a sharp turn from its criminal law practice in history by intimating at prospects of state moderation, an autonomous bar, and rights for citizens. These ideals seemed progressively advanced through the Criminal Law (1979, 1997), the Criminal Procedure Law (1979, 1996), the Lawyers Law (1997), and numerous state regulations and notices.[11] The Criminal Procedure Law is slated for revision again within the next several years during the life of the current National Peoples Congress.

---

[7] Deng Xiaopeng estimated in 1980 that China would need some 100,000–200,000 to sustain his proposed law reforms (Pereenboom, 2002: 348). In reality, China went from 21,546 lawyers in 1986 to 117,212 by 2000 (Michelson, 2003) and over 130,000 by the end of 2003 (Liu and Michelson, 2004).

[8] From 1979 to 1997, the National People's Congress and its Standing Committee had passed 328 laws, amended laws or decisions. The State Council had issued about 770 administrative regulations, and the provincial and local governments had formulated over 5,200 provincial regulations (Cai, 1999: 136).

[9] According to Art 32 of the 1996 Criminal Procedure Law, besides lawyers, criminal suspects and defendants can also appoint relatives, friends or people recommended by their organisations as the defenders.

[10] Although a large number of lawyers consider criminal defence to be the most challenging legal work and often start their careers from criminal cases, many choose to switch to more profitable civil and commercial work after gaining a certain reputation from their criminal defence work. However, for those who stick to criminal law practice, their work and identity are inevitably politicised and are thus distinct from those of commercial lawyers working in large corporate law firms, which have become an increasingly powerful sector of the Chinese bar (Liu, 2006). As the division of professional labour becomes more specialised, this commercial versus political distinction in the Chinese bar is likely to sharpen in coming years.

[11] Major regulations since 1996 include the following: Regulation on the Lawyer's Involvement of the Criminal Process in the Phase of Investigation (Ministry of Public Security, 10 Dec 1996); Regulation on Several Issues in the Implementation of the Criminal Procedure Law

The 1979 Criminal Procedure Law, while it re-established the basic legal institutions for criminal justice, nevertheless permitted the police to detain persons indefinitely before they were charged with a crime.[12] Lawyers got access to their clients only once a case was brought before the court and they were given no more than seven days' notice before trial to prepare a case. The purpose of the defence lawyer was considered well-served if he could help the court to render a just verdict, and thus his defence was often confined to pleading for leniency without challenging the prosecution or exercising such rights as cross-examining government witnesses and calling witnesses of his own as provided by the law (Leng, 1985: 93–5). Trials were usually not open to the public and the right of appeal was strictly limited. Not surprisingly, the great majority of defendants remained unrepresented by lawyers and, for those who did get legal representation, lawyers' pleas for innocence were rarely found and highly restricted by the government (Lawyers' Committee for Human Rights, 1993).

The revision of the Criminal Procedure Law in 1996 seemed a great step forward with its goals of expanding adversarial proceedings, increasing rights of defendants, and widening the role of defence lawyers (Chen, 1995). Several procedures that severely violate proceduralism (eg, detention for investigation, exemption from prosecution, etc) were abolished, rights of appeal were expanded, and a legal aid system was established. Defendants could now obtain legal advice and begin preparation of a defence as soon as cases reached the procuracy,[13] while criminal suspects remained unable to obtain substantive representation during police investigation where most abuses occurred, although lawyers were given the right to meet the defendant as a 'representative' in the investigation phase.[14] Defendants might apply for bail. Defence lawyers had the right to collect their own evidence, inspect the prosecutor's evidence, bring their own witnesses, and cross-examine state witnesses at trial. Yet the reality of criminal defence practice

(Supreme People's Court, Supreme People's Procuracy, Ministry of Public Security, Ministry of State Security, Ministry of Justice, NPC Legal Work Committee, 19 Jan 1998); Interpretation on Several Issues in the Implementation of the Criminal Procedure Law (Supreme People's Court, 2 Sept 1998); People's Procuracy's Rules for Criminal Procedure (Supreme People's Procuracy, 18 Jan 1999); Regulation on the Protection of Lawyers' Legal Practice in the Criminal Procedure (Supreme People's Procuracy, 10 Feb 2004). There have also been a large number of notices by the 6 state and judicial agencies regarding the 1996 Criminal Procedure Law.

[12] A series of small reforms of the criminal procedure in the early 1980s weakened procedural safeguards at the same time as the government strengthened police powers and the Party initiated a series of 'strike-hard' anti-crime campaigns (Lubman, 1999:163).

[13] Art 33 of the 1996 Criminal Procedure Law stipulates: 'A criminal suspect in a case of public prosecution shall have the right to entrust persons as his defenders from the date on which the case is transferred for examination before prosecution'.

[14] Art 96 of the 1996 Criminal Procedure Law stipulates: 'After the criminal suspect is interrogated by an investigation organ for the first time or from the day on which compulsory measures are adopted against him, he may appoint a lawyer to provide him with legal advice

indicates that several provisions in the legislation may in fact have been regressive. The central contradiction in these statutes—that the Party-state would become complicit in its own self-constraint—has required cycles of clarifying regulations and notices by multiple state agencies, which generated new conflicts and ambiguities in the law. Most importantly, defence lawyers are at considerable jeopardy in criminal cases, as the sharp drop in the proportion of cases with legal representation signifies (Yu, 2002).

II. AN INTERIOR VIEW OF LAWYERS AND THE QUEST FOR LIBERALISM

Studies of lawyers and liberalism characteristically take the long view since the major reconfigurations in political regimes and the legal complex can be more readily discerned (cf Karpik, 1999; Guarnieri, 2005; Scheppele, 2005). A complementary approach observes closely those instances when a shift appears to be occurring, whether this be at the point of revolutionary transition, or constitutional reconstruction, or a regression from liberalism. In this chapter we explicate the travails of the legal complex and political liberalism through a precise focus on specific provisions in the Criminal Law and Criminal Procedure Law and their implementing institutions that are most aggravating and threatening to criminal lawyers. Two issues in particular affect defence lawyers' ability to exercise in practice the due process provisions enacted in law. The 'Three Difficulties' refer to the practical difficulties of lawyers (1) in meeting criminal suspects, (2) in obtaining access to case files, and (3) in collecting evidence to defend criminal defendants and cross-examining witnesses at trial. Together these issues encompass many of lawyers' incapacities to provide effective representation and thus stand at the front line of criminal defence against arbitrary state power. 'Big Stick 306' refers to Article 306 of the 1997 Criminal Law that makes lawyers subject to arrest and imprisonment if they are complicit with their defendants in tampering with evidence or encouraging defendants to commit perjury.

Theoretically, these two sets of issues offer empirical indicators of the general concepts of political liberalism we engage on this project. As Table 3.1 indicates, the broad contours of political liberalism as we have defined it (Halliday and Karpik, 1998) fall into four classes: the commitment of the moderate state to the rule of law and proceduralism; the structural differentiation of power within the state, most importantly through a measure of independence of courts from executive and legislative control; the opening of civil society; and the basic legal rights of citizenship. In criminal procedure law each of these four aspects of political liberalism can be specified more precisely.

and to file petitions and complaints on his behalf. If the criminal suspect is arrested, the appointed lawyer may apply on his behalf for obtaining a guarantor pending trial. If a case involves State secrets, the criminal suspect shall have to obtain the approval of the investigation organ for appointing a lawyer.'

Table 3.1.   Political Liberalism and Problems of Criminal Procedure

Major Themes of Political Liberalism	Major Issues in the Criminal Procedure	Major Problems in the Implementation of the CPL
1. Moderate State I (rule of law, proceduralism)	1.1 Meeting criminal suspects	1.1.1 Restrictions from the police and the procuracy
		1.1.2 Conditions of meeting
	1.2 Collecting evidence	1.2.1 Limitations on the rights of lawyers to collect evidence
		1.2.2 Difficulties in calling witness and cross-examining evidence at trial
	1.3 Obtaining access to case files	1.3.1 Access to evidence collected by the police and procuracy
		1.3.2 Access to case files at court
	1.4 Protection from prosecution	1.4.1 Crime of perjury in criminal defence work
		1.4.2 Leaking state secrets
2. Moderate State II (separation of power, judicial independence)	2.1 Judicial independence from Party-state influences	2.1.1 'Strike Hard' campaigns
	2.2 Power relations among the police, the procuracy, and the judiciary	2.2.1 The procuracy's supervisory power over both the police and the court
		2.2.2 Jurisdictional conflicts among the three agencies
3. Civil Society	3.1 Autonomous professional associations for lawyers	3.1.1 The Ministry of Justice's control over the ACLA
		3.1.2 Powerlessness of the lawyer associations
4. Basic Legal Freedoms	4.1 Right to legal counsel	4.1.1 (=1.1.1+1.1.2) Restrictions and conditions from the police and the procuracy
		4.1.2 Lawyers' unwillingness to represent
	4.2 Due process of law	4.2.1 Confession by torture
		4.2.2 Extended detention
		4.2.3 Sentence before trial
		4.2.4 No presumption of innocence

Key: Light grey = Three Difficulties. Dark Grey = Big Stick 306.

1. *Moderate State I.* The rule of law and proceduralism generally prescribe the representation by lawyers of individuals detained by officials of public security. Specifically, these involve access by lawyers to meet criminal suspects (see cell 1.1 in Table 3.1), the ability of lawyers to collect evidence on behalf of their clients (1.2), the right of lawyers to obtain access to case files collected by the police or procuracy (1.3), and the protection of lawyers themselves from retribution by executive authorities (1.4). Each of these aspects of criminal defence under a rule of law regime has been severely tested in China's implementation of its criminal procedure law and regulations. The 'Three Difficulties' confronted by Chinese criminal defence lawyers are exemplified by specific problems that arise from deformities in the implementation of the law (see 1.1.1, 1.1.2, 1.2.1, 1.2.2, 1.3.1, 1.3.2 in Table 3.1). Relatedly, the threat of 'Big Stick 306' directly abrogates the right of lawyers themselves to be free from arrest in court by the prosecution (1.4), which in practice has been occurring when lawyers have been accused of encouraging their clients to commit perjury (1.4.1) or of leaking state secrets (1.4.2).

2. *Moderate State II.* The separation of powers in the concept of the moderate state imply in the criminal law that a judiciary at once will obtain some degree of autonomy from the Party-state apparatus (cell 2.1) and more precisely that power relations among the police, procuracy and judiciary will re-equilibrate to enable functional and structural differentiation among these roles (2.2). In China's criminal justice system, however, the procuracy continues to hold supervisory power over the police and the court (2.2.1) and the norms formalised in the Criminal Procedure Law and subsequent regulations trigger conflicts among the three justice agencies (2.2.2). Furthermore, the Party control over the judicial agencies is not only reflected in routine activities, but strengthened during 'strike-hard' campaigns aiming at striking crimes (2.1.1).

3. *Civil Society.* In criminal law, as in law more generally, lawyers potentially anchor institutions of civil society. They do so to the extent that their own professional associations are self-governing and can mobilise a profession against the state, or ally with other groups in civil society, or variously ally with the judiciary or restrain and critique it. Autonomy of the bar is particularly acute in the criminal law, for it is here that lawyers confront most directly the coercive and potentially repressive arms of the state (cell 3.1). In China such autonomy has not been realised in general and the powerlessness of the criminal bar is manifest both in the general control exercised over the ACLA by the Ministry of Justice (3.1.1) and the ineffectiveness of the ACLA in particular instances where lawyers have been arrested for falling foul of 'Big Stick 306' (3.1.2).

4. *Citizenship.* A fundamental protection for citizens under political liberalism relies on representation by legal counsel (cell 4.1). Yet it

is exactly this primitive right that has been removed de facto from Chinese citizens because the conditions under which criminal defence lawyers are expected to serve are so threatening that they either have withdrawn altogether from criminal defence or proceed with a timidity that effectively nullifies their efficacy (4.1.1).

In practice, the 'Three Difficulties' and 'Big Stick 306' subvert each element of a legal liberalism that lies at the heart of a liberal political system. They do not exhaust the tensions between the law and practice nor the inherent difficulties in the criminal procedure statutes and the contradictions that animate them. But they do enable us to dissect in detail one part of a conflict that lies at the heart of legal liberalism's prospects in contemporary China.

Because we have access to data that are unusual, if not exceptional, in the history of any profession, we explicate the critical conjunction for liberalism between the constitution of a legal profession and the constitution of a moderate state and citizenship. We shall show that there is a curious synergy that has arisen in the confrontation of criminal lawyers with the rest of the criminal law legal complex. That synergy fuels movement towards that phase of professionalisation that is conventionally taken for granted in scholarship on lawyers and other professions—the formation of professional identity as a cornerstone of professional community and a condition of professional mobilisation. We seek to find evidence from our data in the interior of the profession of moves towards the creation of a professional identity that puts pressure on the bar association to separate itself from the controlling arm of the state.

III. NATURAL HISTORY OF A PROFESSIONAL PUBLIC SPHERE[15]

We approach the sites of criminal defence lawyers' everyday practice through a unique source—discussions of Chinese lawyers among themselves as they are recorded in the online forum of the All China Lawyers Association (ACLA). The forum was established in August 2002 and has been developed into a large internet community of lawyers, law students and other legal professionals in China. By March 2005, the forum had over 34,000 registered users who had posted 271,925 messages on 25 discussion boards with divergent topics for each board, including discussions on different legal areas, consulting services to the public, professional issues in lawyers' practice, the bar examination, local lawyer communities, and general comments on the rule of law. Messages relating to criminal

---

[15] This chapter is drawn from a larger study of criminal procedure law-making in China. The study relies upon (a) extensive interviews with law-makers, academics, practitioners and government officials, (b) primary and secondary materials, such as the publications of the criminal justice legal complex, and (c) foreign commentary and secondary research.

procedure law and the work of defence lawyers have been among the central topics and most heavily trafficked discussion sites since the beginning of the forum. Through this data source we can overhear, without contamination by outside observers, the spontaneous exchanges among lawyers about their problems in the implementation of the criminal procedure law that purport to institutionalise basic elements of political liberalism.

The online discussions are organised by threads of messages, ie, every thread contains multiple messages on the same topic. The typical length of the threads we collected is between two and 30 messages, but the longest threads on the forum sometimes contain more than 100 messages. Issues related to both the 'Three Difficulties' and 'Big Stick 306' are discussed extensively on the forum, from which we collected the most relevant 60 threads.[16] Messages take multiple forms, including: (1) descriptions of problems; (2) stories; (3) analysis of situations; (4) proposals for remedies and solutions; (5) 'voting' to support or disagree with other people's opinions; (6) emotional encouragement; and (7) explicit promotion of collective action by the lawyer community.

Participants in the forum discussions include both lawyers and non-lawyers. On the basis of some systematic evidence and qualitative analysis of content, it appears that the great majority of the forum users are lawyers and other legal professionals. As best we can tell, their geographical distribution is largely representative of the Chinese legal profession.[17] Over time, the discussion participants have differentiated into regular versus occasional users. Regular users have posted hundreds or even thousands of messages, whereas occasional users often join the forum at one time to post messages for help or participate in some specific topics and do not make many subsequent visits. Lawyers are much more frequently found among regular users than among occasional users.

In its brief three-year history, the forum has already undergone striking changes which in themselves signify the travails of an emerging professional public sphere for debate over professional identity, community and politics.

---

[16] Among the 60 threads, there are 9 threads (77 messages) directly on the difficulty in meeting criminal suspects, 12 threads (118 messages) on the difficulty in collecting evidence and cross-examining witnesses at trial, 4 threads (51 messages) on the difficulty in getting access to case files, and 22 threads (382 messages) on 'Big Stick 306' and persecution of defence lawyers. We do not claim that these 60 threads include all relevant discussions on the forum, but they provide sufficient data for the purposes of our research.

[17] According to an address book compiled by the forum administrator on 9 February 2004, there were 206 users who provided information on their real name, gender, occupation, location and contact means. Among these 206 users, 71.3% are lawyers working in law firms, 9.8% are legal scholars and law students, 5.3% work in the government (including the judiciary and the procuracy), another 5.3% work in enterprises, and the remaining 6.8% work in the bank, the military or unspecified occupations. Geographically, the 206 users are roughly proportionally distributed in China's 32 provinces according to the lawyer population, with users from only 4 provinces missing. These 4 provinces are Qinghai, Hainan, Hong Kong and Macau. There are even 3 users from Inner Mongolia and one user from Tibet, all of them lawyers.

In the first several months (August–December 2002), the discussions were among a relatively small number of users and were very loosely regulated. Around the 2003 Chinese New Year (in February), when the forum administrators were on vacation, some politically sensitive messages were posted in large numbers on one discussion board.[18] At the time, the administrators were quite benign to the users and deleted only those very radical messages that endangered the survival of the forum. There were also hot debates among the users on whether politically sensitive messages should be discussed on the lawyer forum. By summer 2003, the regulation of the forum was largely stabilised with relatively clear publicised rules of discussion.[19] Sanctions were put in place. For instance, user IDs now could be held inactive for a while as a punishment for breaking the rules of discussion. A 'Recycle Bin' was also established in 2003 for the administrators and board managers to remove inappropriate posts,[20] including a large proportion of politically sensitive messages.

Control over the discussions has been gradually tightened since then. During the 2004 Chinese New Year and the subsequent NPC meetings (February–March 2004), the forum became read-only to avoid the surge of radical posts as had happened in 2003. In June 2004, the IDs of some very active regular users were permanently deleted due to their radical posts. This generated a large number of debates on the freedom of speech in forum discussions. In September 2004, the forum was closed for about a month due to the government inspection of major internet forums.[21] At the same time, the forum administrators created an ID named 'Forum Government' to post messages for regulation, notices, and other administrative messages. They also created a discussion board named 'Forum Court' to handle disputes on deleting messages, deleting IDs, etc. From then on, forum administrators used these two IDs instead of their personal IDs for managing the forum. In short, the forum regulation was substantially formalised.

In early February 2005, the forum was read-only for about two weeks due to the Chinese New Year and then resumed. In contrast to the previous year, when the shutdown for new messages only lasted a brief time, from

---

[18] There has been no formal definition of what constitutes 'political sensitivity', but messages that criticise the Party or the central government, messages that mention banned topics like the 1989 Tiananmen incident, messages that reveal the corruption or abuse of power by the leading officials, messages that promote Taiwan independence, and messages that make radical comments on democracy or human rights are all considered 'politically sensitive'.

[19] Eg, no direct personal attack on other users, no politically sensitive comments, no duplicate posts, etc.

[20] As the second author is the board manager on the 'Legal Theory and Constitutional Law' board of the forum, we have access to this 'Recycle Bin' to observe the control of the forum. In fact, the establishment of the 'Recycle Bin' enables politically sensitive posts to be preserved from permanent deletion. Users who post such messages have the right to retrieve the messages from the administrator or the board manager.

[21] This large-scale government inspection was caused by the crackdown on a famous Bulletin Board System of Peking University because of its political sensitivity.

25 February the forum became read-only again as part of the heightened government crackdown on Bulletin Board Systems throughout the country. This time the pause period lasted for six months until 29 August 2005, a fact which generated tremendous concern among the forum participants regarding the survival of the forum. A message approval procedure was added in order to control politically sensitive posts, ie, every message needed to be approved by either the forum administrator or the board manager before being posted.[22] In spite of the long pause and strict regulatory method, most of the regular users quickly came back after the forum was resumed. A strong professional collectivity has been formed on the forum during its three-year development, which makes the users persist in their pursuit of public discourse, even when the discussions are under increasingly strict government control.

To explore the underlying reasons for the increasingly strict regulation of the forum, two informal interviews with the forum administrators were conducted in July 2004 and August 2005, respectively. During the interviews, the administrators admitted that, from time to time, they received telephone calls and orders from the Ministry of Public Security and other relevant state agencies regarding information control of the forum. Around the Chinese New Year, the annual NPC meetings and some politically sensitive dates, information control over the forum discussions would be highly strengthened. The forum's read-only periods were the direct results of such government control. In normal conditions, the administrators also have the responsibility to delete politically radical posts, but the level of control is much lower. In other words, the forum administrators assume a very delicate position between the government and the profession, which makes their work both important and difficult in maintaining the forum as a public sphere.

Overall, the ACLA forum not only provides Chinese lawyers with an unparalleled site for public discourses and the development of professional identity, but also constitutes a political site in itself. Its own history, struggles and development are indicative of the capacity of lawyers to form their intra-professional microcosm of civil society. In this sense, the institutionalisation of the discussion rules and the formalisation of forum regulation reflect the conflicts between the powerful authoritarian state and the burgeoning professional community (and civil society).

IV. DEFENCE LAWYERS IN DANGER: THREE CASES OF LAWYER PERSECUTION

Three stories capture the vulnerability of Chinese lawyers. These were reported on the ACLA forum during 2003–4 and aroused heated

---

[22] The original objective of this procedure is to establish an automatic filtre that is able to screen messages with politically sensitive key words, yet the result is a manually controlled approval system that relies on the discretion of the administrators and board managers.

discussions among the forum users. One case (the Ma Guangjun case) was also widely reported in mainstream public media, while the other two cases remained a subject of debate within legal circles only.

(a) The Lawyer SOS Case

No case has been more passionately and thoroughly discussed on the forum than the case of a defence lawyer from Anhui Province who fled from the police and posted an SOS message on the forum. The message generated 134 responses by 99 distinct users from at least 21 provinces. Here is the full text of the original message:

> I am a lawyer in Anhui Runtian Law Firm (Lawyer License Number: 128901110309). On February 15, 2004, my colleague Lawyer Yu Huakun and I were appointed by the law firm to provide legal help to the criminal suspect of a case of death by malicious injury which was investigated by the police of the Changping section of the Dongguan City Police Department of Guangdong Province. Lawyer Yu Huakun was already detained by the Dongguan City Police Department for obstructing testimony, and now I am fleeing and cannot go home.
>
> On reflection of the process in this case, we did not violate the Article 306 or 307 of the Criminal Law on the crime of obstructing testimony at all. If we indeed violated the law and committed a crime, we would have nothing to say about this situation. In fact, during the process of the case, we strictly obeyed the relevant laws, rules and regulations, not even taking half a step to the bombing area, but now the result is that one of us is in jail and the other is fleeing. I must say this is a huge grievance of the Chinese legal profession! Although this might only be an exceptional phenomenon, it clearly happened in reality. If we let things go like this, won't China's lawyers and legal system be trashed by anyone? The tragedy that happened to me and Lawyer Yu Huakun today might also happen to other lawyer colleagues tomorrow.
>
> The role of lawyers in the development of the socialist legal system cannot be substituted. Lawyers provide legal service to criminal suspects, defending their legal rights, which is the responsibility and right that the law endows to lawyers. If lawyers' right to practice according to the law could be violated, then how could the legal rights of the represented party be guaranteed? Therefore, protecting lawyers' right to practice according to the law and increasing lawyers' status in criminal cases are urgent matters.
>
> Now the ACLA is holding a conference in Huangshan, Anhui Province. I, also representing Lawyer Yu Huakun, send this message for help to all of you, please save us save yourselves, and save China's lawyers and legal system. SOS, SOS, SOS...
>
> The person crying for help: a lawyer at Anhui Runtian Law Firm (anonymous). April 8, 2004.[23]

---

[23] #440419, 8 Apr 2004, 22:56, Anhui.

The last reply to this SOS message was posted in January 2005, nine months after the original message was posted. However, the fate of the fleeing lawyer remains unknown.

(b) The Wen Zhicheng Case

The second case concerns the persecution of Wen Zhicheng, a 61-year-old defence lawyer in Ruijin City, Jiangxi Province, by the local police and procuracy. The message was posted by a lawyer from Sichuan Province in December 2004. The message started with a long case description said to be written by Wen Zhicheng himself. Here is an excerpt:

> I am a licensed lawyer in Huarui Law Office in Jiangxi Province, my name is Wen Zhicheng, and I am 61 years old this year. I was appointed by our law office to defend Zeng Hailin, the defendant of a suspected corruption case. ... Zeng Hailin was set free on September 11 this year, but I, the defender, have still been obtaining guarantor pending trial (*qu bao hou shen*)[24] as a criminal suspect. ...
>
> Zhu Dexin, the section chief of the Bureau of Anti-corruption of Ruijin Procurator's Office invited me to have a talk in the law office at 5pm on June 5 (Saturday). But at that time he promptly detained me in the name of the Ruijin City Bureau of Public Security, and then made a search of my body and my office desk. ... The alarm whistle of the police car resounded before I walked to the police car, so the crowd built up of thousands of people. ...Yang Xiaoshan, the deputy section chief of the Anti-Corruption Bureau ordered the driver to put down all the window glasses of the police car. And then the police car drove me slowly to the Procuracy with the alarm whistle resounding. It was actually to use a police car to make a parade and pillory of a lawyer under escort.
>
> Arriving at the Procuracy, two police officers and four officers of the Anti-Corruption Bureau used torture to coerce a statement from me for a period of up to 8 hours, in the 'Interrogation Room' of the Procurator's Office. ... I asked to pee for three or four times. They said: 'You may pee. But you cannot be allowed to do it until you confess the crime.' ... They forced me to confess the criminal facts of forging evidence and obstructing testimony for Zeng Hailin in the process of the Zeng Hailin corruption case. I said: 'I have practiced as a lawyer for more than 20 years, and have never forged any evidence or obstructed

---

[24] Obtaining guarantor pending trial is similar to the bail system in Western countries, Art 56 of the 1996 Criminal Procedure Law stipulates: 'A criminal suspect or defendant who has obtained a guarantor pending trial shall observe the following provisions: (1) not to leave the city or county where he resides without permission of the executing organ; (2) to be present in time at a court when summoned; (3) not to interfere in any form with the witness when the latter gives testimony; and (4) not to destroy or falsify evidence or tally confessions. If a criminal suspect or defendant who has obtained a guarantor pending trial violates the provisions of the preceding paragraph, the guaranty money paid shall be confiscated. In addition, in light of specific circumstances, the criminal suspect or defendant shall be ordered to write a statement of repentance, pay guaranty money or provide a guarantor again, or shall be subjected to residential surveillance or arrested. If a criminal suspect or defendant is found not to have violated the provisions in the preceding paragraph during the period when he has obtained a guarantor pending trial, the guaranty money shall be returned to him at the end of the period.'

testimony for any client. And similarly I have not forged any evidence or obstructed any testimony for Zeng Hailin this time. On the contrary, it is you the Procuracy who detained Zhu Jingfu, the defending party's witness on the court day of Zeng Hailin case, and detained Yang Haiping, the defending party's witness on the following day. And now you are detaining and extorting a confession by torture from the defender [me]. Your actions will be accused by the law sooner or later.' ... They afflicted me bodily, insulted me personally, and frightened me mentally, in order to compel the lawyer to surrender to their orders.

This detention and interrogation lasted from 6pm, June 5 to 2:40am, June 6.

... At 7am I was committed into No.17 prison room of the Ruijin City Detention Center and began a life living with the criminal suspects of intentional homicide, robbery, rape, theft and racketeering. ... From 9am to 11am on June 7, the Deputy Chief Procurator Zou Yuansheng picked me out of the prison room. ... He said, 'For a bad guy rotten from head to feet, why would you defend him? What you antagonise is against the nation, the laws of the nation, and the powerful state judicial agencies. If you had cooperated with the Procuracy in the evening of June 5, maybe you could have gone back home to sleep that night. But you had a hard head so you are still here today. Now if you cooperate with our Procuracy, maybe you can go back this afternoon.' I said, 'What is the responsibility of the lawyer as a defender for the criminal suspect? Do you know? This lawyer [me] practiced according to the law, but you detained lawyers. Have you estimated the outcome of this behaviour?' The talk ended in displeasure.

The Public Security Bureau stated that my criminal detention was extended to June 13. ... At 5pm of June 20, the Public Security proclaimed to me the decision of obtaining guarantor pending trial. ... Thus I had been detained for 15 days altogether.[25]

There was no further information on whether the lawyer was later prosecuted or not.

(c) The Ma Guangjun Case

In the preceding cases, the defence lawyer was either chased by the police or detained for interrogation, but neither of them was reported to be arrested or prosecuted. In Ma Guangjun's case he was prosecuted and detained for 210 days before finally being acquitted by the court. After the acquittal, the case was widely reported in local and national media. Three of these media reports were posted on the ACLA forum, including two newspaper articles from the *Southern Metropolitan News* (*Nanfang Dushi Bao*) and the *Inner Mongolia Legal System News* (*Neimenggu Fazhi Bao*), as well as a long interview with Ma Guangjun by the CCTV, the official central television station in China.

Ma Guangjun is a 50-year-old lawyer in Ningcheng County, Inner Mongolia, who defended Xu Wensheng, an impotent patient, in a rape

---

[25] #620344, 4 Dec 2004, 11:07, Jiangxi.

case in 2003. On 23 May, the next day after the court proceedings, seven key witnesses who testified in court were detained and coerced to confess that the defence lawyer advised them to commit perjury. Soon after, Ma Guangjun, the defence lawyer, was arrested for the crime of obstructing testimony and detained in the local detention centre from 22 August 2003 to 20 March 2004.[26] During his trial process, the Inner Mongolia Lawyers Association investigated the case and appointed two prominent lawyers in the province to defend Ma Guangjun.[27]

After being released, Ma was interviewed by CCTV and the programme was broadcast internationally. During the interview, Ma described the difficult situation he faced when handling the rape case:

> He [the defendant] said he had confessed three times, but all were against his will. I asked him, why did you confess against your will? He said that every time he confessed it was because the policemen had made him confess through torture for more than 20 hours. He could not put up with the torture. In order to preserve himself he had no choice but to confess. ... I didn't believe him entirely at the beginning. ... I knew that if I, as a lawyer, obtained the most crucial evidence in order to reverse the testimony in this case, I would take the risk of being caught up for committing perjury, so I decided not to take evidence by myself. ... I think that was my habit. At present it is the situation in my area that you cannot see anything, and the procuracy does not allow you to see. It only tells you that this case involves the crime of rape. ... You can only wait until the case files are transferred to the court, then you can go and see it. We have no ability, and no other means.[28]

He then proceeded to talk about his experience as a subject of the charge of perjury, starting from the moment he heard from a villager that seven witnesses had been detained by the procuracy on 23 June, the second day of the court proceedings:

> I was shocked at that moment, and I told him that the procuracy had the power to check the evidence, but if it captured someone without releasing them, at that time I absolutely would not believe it was true, because the procuracy was not only the agency for implementing the law, but also the supervisory agency. How could it do such an illegal thing? I could not believe then so I said that you had to wait in patience, they would surely be released in the evening. But in the end they had not been released by the evening of the 24th. He called me the same night and then I had the hunch that the procuracy had put its hand on the witnesses and the purpose was not only the witnesses, but also pointing at me. ... Because when we were in the court, the prosecutor and I debated very harshly. I was so aggressive and consolidated my argument step by step. So in terms of the effect in court, I think I did quite well and the prosecutor from the procuracy was placed in a very passive position. ... If the witnesses did not appear in court, nothing would happen. ... I had a feeling that, although I was clear in my mind where the trap

---

[26] #536452, 12 July 2004, 01:19, Inner Mongolia.
[27] #536448, 12 July 2004, 01:02, Inner Mongolia.
[28] #536452, 12 July 2004, 01:22, Inner Mongolia.

was, I had no choice but to jump into it. ... Because I had to maintain my dignity, I am a lawyer, so I could not escape. ... I was very ill-treated in the detention centre, and my every word and action was watched out every day. ... I got rheumatoid arthritis when I was young, and my disease was quite severe. The heating was not good in my room so my legs began to jerk when I was in bed at night. Also I was not permitted to have two cotton-padded mattresses, only one was permitted and the cotton clothes sent by my family I was not permitted to wear. ....[29]

At the moment of his own defence he wept. The moment he saw the two defence lawyers appointed by the lawyers' association to represent him in the detention centre:

I was very sad then. So I cried, really. As the defence lawyer for Xu Wensheng, I was sitting outside to meet with Xu Wensheng half a year ago, hoping to defend his innocence. I didn't expect that, half a year later, I would be sitting in the position of Xu and the Inner Mongolia Lawyers Association would have appointed two lawyers to defend my innocence. I was changed from the defence lawyer into the defendant. This kind of feeling was impossible for anyone to accept. But in front of the fact, you had no choice but to accept it.[30]

The case ended with a verdict of not guilty and Ma Guangjun's story was widely disseminated across the country. His account vividly expresses the ultimate fears of all criminal defence lawyers in China.

(d) Criminal Defence in Practice

The three cases, albeit extreme, nevertheless symbolise the yawning gap that exists between the aspirational norms promulgated in the statutes and the murky practices of everyday criminal defence. The iron triangle that has existed for 50 years among the police, procuracy and judges has proved immensely difficult to fracture and to rebalance. A culture of law-enforcement collusion that is resistant to legal representation proves highly resistant to modification. The struggles for criminal defence are pungently illustrated by lawyers' expression of their grievances with the 'Three Difficulties' and 'Big Stick 306' on the forum.

(i) Three Difficulties: 'Don't Let Lawyers Dance with their Hands "Cuffed"'[31]

Chinese lawyers complain vigorously about their difficulties in (1) meeting the criminal suspect, (2) getting access to case files, and (3) collecting evidence and cross-examining witnesses at trial.[32]

---

[29] #536452, 12 July 2004, 01:22, Inner Mongolia.

[30] *Ibid.*

[31] The headline of an article on the troubles of criminal defence lawyers in *Legal Daily*, quoted in #556167, 8 Aug 2004, 23:11, Sichuan.

[32] These problems are not only discussed within the lawyer community, but also frequently observed by legal scholars (Qi et al., 1997; Li, 1998) and media reports, including in the newspapers of the procuracy and the judiciary. See, eg: *Chinese Lawyers* (*zhongguo lüshi*), Nov 1995, Dec 1997, May 2001; *People's Daily* (*renmin ribao*), 7 Apr 2004;

Meeting the Criminal Suspect. The 1996 Criminal Procedure Law seemed to offer a significant advance in the protection of criminal suspects because it broadened the scope of legal representation from the trial phase to the phase of investigation.[33] Article 11 of the 1998 Joint Regulation on Several Issues in the Implementation of the Criminal Procedure Law by six state agencies prescribes that, except for some special occasions (eg, involving state secrets), the lawyer's application for meeting the criminal suspect should be arranged within 48 hours. In reality, lawyers complain vociferously that delay is the order of things as 'lawyers' right of meeting is often restricted "layer by layer"'.[34] Said a defence lawyer from Chongqing:

> According to my own experience, this Article [Article 11] is equal to nothing. It often happens that after the lawyer's application, the police officer would make all kinds of excuses. 48 hours is impossible, and you are a lucky dog if you can make it within 480 hours. Even if the lawyer is really pushy and can finally get the meeting settled, the officer is still reluctant.[35]

Another indicated that 'this regulation promulgated and implemented by the six agencies of authority has become a mere scrap of paper: three days, five days, ten days, a hundred days…the agencies for investigation find all kinds of reasons to refuse the lawyer's meeting'.[36]

One tactic is to broaden the exception that exists in the law and regulations: '[s]ome police agencies wilfully expand the meaning and scope of "state secret," often by rejecting the lawyer's meeting on grounds of involving state secrets'.[37] Or police will:

> Postpone the meeting with all kinds of methods, e.g., the lawyer comes and the police officer says 'I have to report to my superior but my superior is out of town,' so 2 days later he is back and the police officer says 'I have to report to the division chief and he is in a meeting.'[38]

If a meeting does take place it may be restricted to a single occasion and for only a few minutes, frequently in spaces which make conversation difficult.[39]

> During the meeting, the police officer is not just 'present at the meeting,' but sometimes 'intimidates' the criminal suspect like 'What did you say in the police

---

Procuratorial Daily (jiancha ribao), 24 July 2002; *People's Court News (renmin fayuan bao)*, 22 July 2002.

[33] Art 96 of the 1996 Criminal Procedure Law.
[34] Article from *Legal Daily*, quoted in #556167, 8 Aug 2004, 23:11, Sichuan.
[35] #618182, 27 Nov 2004, 11:13, Chongqing.
[36] #256600, 28 Sept 2003, 19:39, Jilin.
[37] Article from *Legal Daily*, quoted in #556167, 8 Aug 2004, 23:11, Sichuan.
[38] Interview B0515.
[39] #555662, 8 Aug 2004, 05:13, Shandong.

office? Why say such confusing words to the lawyer?' This is not the lawyer's meeting with the criminal suspect, but the police officer's investigation with the assistance of the lawyer.[40]

Lawyers commonly report that in meetings they may do no more than provide emotional support for the detainee and possibly inform the detainee of the suspected offence and some relevant statutes. While Article 96 of the Criminal Procedure Law states that the lawyer can 'interview the detained criminal suspect to understand the circumstances and details related to the case', as soon as the lawyer begins to do so 'the investigation officials present in the interview would immediately stop it'.[41] Lawyers across China complain that these facts-on-the-ground nullify the law. Agents of investigation use 'illegal behaviours to deal with lawyers who obey and loyally implement the law'.[42] Despite the advances in the statutory law and subsequent regulations, the meeting of lawyers with detainees remains a site of police resistance, often with substantial public support,[43] and implementation has lagged badly.

Getting Access to Case Files. The 1996 Criminal Procedure Law requires that when the procuracy decides to prosecute the case it should transfer to the court its case files with the charges and evidence which should then be made available to the lawyer for the accused.[44] Yet two policy goals in the law partially contradict each other. In order to combat a long-standing practice of police, procurators and judges agreeing on the outcome of a case before it came to court, the law reforms sought to make the trial an authentic forum in which judges heard evidence and made their decisions after the prosecution and defence could present their respective cases. A way to restrain judges from premature decision-making is to restrict the evidence they see until the trial takes place. As a result, the law reforms led to a thinning of evidence in the files transferred by the procuracy to the court. Since the evidence in these files effectively amounts to the totality of evidence available to defence lawyers, they find themselves actually in a worse situation after than before the legislation.[45]

Access to case files is also a matter of practicality. A lawyer reported that he was denied the access in a criminal case merely because the court charged a high price for xeroxing case files before and was criticised by the higher level court, so it decided not to let lawyers xerox case files any

[40] #618182, 27 Nov 2004, 11:13, Chongqing.
[41] #256602, 28 Sept 2003, 19:41, Jilin.
[42] *Ibid.*
[43] Interview 05B01, 05X05, 05B14, 05B15, etc.
[44] Art 150 of the 1996 Criminal Procedure Law.
[45] In the Nincheng County rape case, for instance, Ma Guangjun claimed that no information at all was in the case file from the police interrogation of Xu Wensheng, the defendant (#536452, 12 July 2004, 01:22, Inner Mongolia) Also see Interview B0501, B0503, B0510, etc.

more—ie, lawyers had no choice but to take extensive notes from several volumes of files, even if they got the access to them.[46] A report of the NPC's investigation on the implementation of the 1996 Criminal Procedure Law in 2000 indicates that, despite the stipulation in Article 36(1) of the law,[47] both the time and extent of the defence lawyers' access to case files are highly restricted in practice (Song, 2001).

Nevertheless, the law reforms may be producing a useful by-product. Since lawyers face significant dangers in relying on any evidence other than case files (see below), they are becoming increasingly artful in examining written materials. As a distinguished criminal defence lawyer in China picturesquely commented, 'the cross-examination in court is living people examining dead papers'.[48] Leading criminal defence lawyers report success in inducing the procuracy to withdraw charges or in persuading the court to impose lighter sentences by demonstrating inadequacies, contradictions, missing information and fabrication in the case files. Some leading defence lawyers report that this close scrutiny of police and procuracy evidence may be producing compelling investigation agencies to obtain better quality evidence.[49]

Collecting Evidence, Bringing Witnesses. The 1996 Criminal Procedure Law gives lawyers limited rights to collect evidence.[50] In practice, lawyers cannot easily gather their own evidence because they must get the permission of the procuracy or the court in order to collect evidence from victims or witnesses; and they have insufficient powers to compel the provision of evidence (there are no sanctions for failure to comply with a court subpoena) (Sheng, 2003, 2004; Yu, 2002). Collecting evidence from the victim's side needs the consent of the witnesses. And lawyers may not hire private investigators.

Witnesses are easily intimidated by authorities and are usually loath to appear in court and contradict official testimony. The Ma Guangjun case vividly illustrates the extremes of witness coercion by public security and the procuracy. As Xu Wensheng's defence lawyer, Ma Guangjun, managed to persuade several witnesses to give their testimonies in support of Xu Wensheng in court. When those testimonies contradicted the police account, the witnesses were detained by the police soon after they left the court; some

---

[46] #619075, 1 Dec 2004, 12:44, location unknown.

[47] According to Item 1 of Art 36 of the Criminal Procedure Law, 'From the date when the people's procuracy brings an indictment, the defence lawyers may look up, extract, and duplicate the bill of the indictment and the materials verified by technical experts, and may interview or communicate with the criminal suspects who are detained.'

[48] Interview B0507.

[49] Interview B0507, B0508, B0510.

[50] Art 37 of the Criminal Procedure Law prescribes: 'With the consent of witnesses, or other units and individuals concerned, defence attorneys may collect evidence concerning the case from such persons.'

were beaten, tortured and compelled to retract their testimony.[51] Witnesses may even be compelled to incriminate themselves by stating they forged evidence on the advice of defence lawyers, as Wen Zhicheng alleged in Ruijin City.[52] Because witnesses are rarely present in court proceedings, the defence lawyer has almost no chance to cross-examine on the evidence collected by the police and the procuracy.[53] It is not surprising, therefore, that the acquittal rates in criminal cases remain less than 1 per cent (Michelson, 2003: 100) and the lawyer's presence in criminal proceedings has almost no effect on case outcome (Lu and Miethe, 2002).

As a result, some of China's leading defence lawyers report that they do not even attempt to obtain evidence from witnesses or bring them into court.[54] Above all, however, they are deterred by the enactment of a draconian provision in the 1997 Criminal Law, Article 306.

(e) 'Big Stick 306'

Lawyers are at considerable jeopardy in criminal court—they confront risk to their persons, their liberty, their careers and their finances. These risks arise from a combination of provisions in the law. The reforms in the 1996 Criminal Procedure Law gave lawyers increased powers to protect their clients in the investigative phase of a criminal case. As a political tradeoff intended to meet objections of the police and procuracy, the Law prohibited lawyers from assisting their clients by concealing or destroying or forging evidence or allowing defendants to collude with each other. It further prohibited counsel from threatening witnesses or getting witnesses to commit perjury.[55] A year later the NPC yielded to intense law enforcement pressure by incorporating Article 306 of the Criminal Law, which provides that lawyers are subject to criminal penalties if they persuade witnesses either to change their testimony or to commit perjury.[56] While these provisions seem consistent with many rule-of-law norms, in practice they open up avenues for abuse which are regressive. The law itself inadequately clarifies what constitute these crimes and thus their meaning can be stretched to suit the

---

[51] #536452, 12 July 2004, 01:22, Inner Mongolia.
[52] #620344, 4 Dec 2004, 11:07, Jiangxi.
[53] #572387, 1 Sept 2004, 17:35, Chongqing.
[54] Interview B0502, B0514.
[55] Art 38 of the 1996 Criminal Procedure Law (Yu, 2002:853-54).
[56] Art 306 of the 1997 Criminal Law stipulates: 'During the course of a criminal trial, any defense lawyer or trial representative who destroys or falsifies evidence, or threatens or induces witnesses to lie, changes testimony or makes false testimony, shall be sentenced to fixed-term imprisonment of not more than three years or criminal detention. If the circumstances are serious, the sentence shall be fixed-term imprisonment of not less than three nor more than seven years.'

interests of police and prosecutors. Neither is there a satisfactory system of precedent where courts can settle the meanings of the statutory terms or where courts will hold police and prosecutors accountable.

The existence of this so-called 'Big Stick 306' makes criminal defence work in China not only frustrating but dangerous. Because the procuracy is both the opposing party of defence lawyers in court proceedings and a major executor of the criminal law, it has the unlimited power to use Article 306 to punish defence lawyers who present different evidence from that collected by the police and the procuracy. By 2002, over 100 defence lawyers all over the country, including some nationally-renowned lawyers from Beijing (eg, Zhang Jianzhong), had been prosecuted for the crime of perjury. According to Professor Zhao Bingzhi at Renmin University, 70–80 per cent of all complaint cases that the lawyers' associations have received in recent years are related to Article 306. The ACLA conducted a statistical analysis on 23 such cases and found that about half of the lawyers were wrongly detained and sentenced.[57] Li Kuisheng, a Henan lawyer, was detained for 26 months before his innocence verdict; Huang Yabin, a Fujian lawyer, was similarly wrongly detained for more than a year; Wang Yibing, a Yunnan lawyer, even decided to become a monk after being wrongly detained and tortured for two years.[58]

Not surprisingly, discussion on the persecution of defence lawyers has been one of the hottest topics on the forum. A message posted on 3 October 2002 on 'Big Stick 306' generated 73 responses from 60 users in the following five months.[59] Many cases are cited in the Forum and the ACLA magazine as first-hand testimony of the immediacy and pervasiveness of this provision:

> Last week, during the court proceeding of a criminal case at the Gansu Province Jingtai County People's Court, the defendant overthrew a confession. … But the prosecutor immediately left his seat and made a phone call outside the courtroom. During the adjournment, two policemen held up Lawyer Hu and had him hand cuffed, announcing detention for the crime of perjury.[60]

No case has been more passionately and thoroughly discussed on the forum than the SOS message from the defence lawyer from Anhui Province who fled from the police. In view of the fact that his lawyer-colleague, Yu Huakun, had already been detained by the police for obstructing testimony,

---

[57] Article from *Legal Daily*, quoted in #556167, 8 Aug 2004, 23:11, Sichuan.

[58] Article from *Chinese Lawyers*, July 2002.

[59] #268, 3 Oct 2002, 18:15, Beijing. This message is one of the earliest messages on the forum. The contrast between the relatively small number of users at the time and the large number of responses suggests the wide and deep concerns about this problem among Chinese lawyers.

[60] #39466, 15 Jan 2003, 13:29, Gansu.

this attorney rejected the charge that he had violated the same law, and fled his city.[61] Eminent lawyers have also found themselves vulnerable. In a cause célèbre:

> [T]he famous lawyer Zhang Jianzhong, the director of Beijing Gong He Law Office, who once defended Cheng Kejie and Li Jizhou,[62] was sentenced to imprisonment for two years because of the crime of assisting in the forgery of evidence in the first instance of trial.[63]

The logic of Big Stick 306 is quite straightforward. A witness gives testimony to the police. When questioned by the lawyer, the witness changes his testimony. Police allege that the change in testimony shows that the lawyer induced the witnesses to lie or present false testimony, and as a result it follows that the lawyer is obstructing justice. Or as prominent defence lawyer, Wang Haiyun, put it, when a lawyer brings evidence rebutting the police or procuracy, they may collect further evidence that leads witnesses to retract their statements on grounds that '"it was the lawyer who let me say this," or "I didn't say this, the lawyer wrote it himself"'.[64]

It is for this reason that Ma Guangjun, defence lawyer in the Ningcheng County rape case, refused to take statements from his illiterate witnesses on behalf of the defendant. He insisted that they come to court and give oral testimony. 'If I made notes and signed them, then two [witnesses] who were not able to write could break their words and say that [the statement] was written by me the lawyer. ... So I chose not to take any notes and let witnesses appear in court ... '.[65] Even then, as we have seen, Ma Guangjun did not escape Article 306 because the police forced the witnesses to retract their in-court statements and this opened the way to detention and charges of perjury and obstruction. Similarly, Wen Zhicheng in Ruijin City was detained for forging evidence and obstructing testimony in the course of his defence of the corruption case. Moreover this older lawyer with heart trouble was forced to confess to these charges under duress.[66]

One lawyer captured the sentiments of many peers with his observation that 'Article 306 ... makes the legal profession tremble'.

> ... if you want to practice law, don't become a lawyer; if you want to become a lawyer, don't do criminal work; if you want to do criminal work, don't collect

[61] #440419, 8 Apr 2004, 22:56, Jiangxi.
[62] Two famous high-ranked officials who were prosecuted for corruption and sentenced to death in 2000–1.
[63] #368312, 16 Jan 2004, 16:01, Shanghai.
[64] #256602, 28 Sept 2003, 19:41, Jilin.
[65] #536452, 12 July 2004, 01:22, Inner Mongolia.
[66] #620344, 4 Dec 2004, 11:07, Sichuan.

evidence; if you want to collect evidence, don't collect testimonies from witnesses. If you fail to follow all these, just go to the detention centre to register. ... Doesn't a system like this push the lawyer to the fire hole? ...[67]

Although some users believe that lawyers are sometimes culpable, the majority press for the abolition of Article 306. In the meantime, those who continue to practise criminal law have adopted highly defensive measures to minimise their exposure to the police and procuracy.[68] As a result, the quality of most defences is diminished to little more than careful dissection of evidence in incomplete case files. Article 306, in combination with the stolid resistance of the enforcement triangle, has driven many lawyers out of criminal defence work and significantly reduced the proportion of defendants who obtain legal counsel.[69]

In the view of some leading criminal defence lawyers, the combination of provisions adverse to lawyers in the Criminal Procedure Law, the Criminal Law, and the Lawyers Law, has actually worsened the situation for defence lawyers from that which prevailed under the 1979 Criminal Procedure Law.[70] A criminal defence lawyer from Shenzhen even described local lawyers' reaction to the implementation of the 1996 Criminal Procedure Law in the following way, 'January and February excited, March and April at a loss, May and June disappointed, July and August despaired, September out of business'.[71]

(f) Emergence of Liberal Ideology

The exchanges among lawyers on the Forum go beyond specific complaints about particular grievances and incidents. Frequently the language of protest emanates from underlying premises about the nature of law, professionalism and the state. These are not often articulated expressly or systematically, but a loose coherence of ideas can be perceived across a variety of discussion threads. The ideological integration of these ideas or the degree of consensus around them must not be overstated for they exist as fragments across many conversations. It is impossible to ascertain how well they either cohere in the minds of the lawyers or represent widely held views that span lawyers and reach across the provinces of China. Yet they occur with such frequency and in various combinations that they cannot be

---

[67] #268, 3 Oct 2002, 18:15, Beijing.

[68] Interview 05B02, 05B14, etc.

[69] In 2000, eg, all 5,495 Beijing lawyers only handled around 4,300 criminal cases, with an average of 0.78 cases per lawyer. In 1999, this average number was 2.64 cases. Data from *Chinese Lawyers*, July 2002.

[70] Interview 05B02, 05B10.

[71] Article from *Chinese Lawyers*, Jan 1998.

ignored. We see them as mutually and contingently constituted out of the interaction between the circumstances in which the lawyers find themselves and their preferences for professional autonomy and the rule of law.

(i) The Rule of Law

Most striking are rudiments of an ideology of the rule of law. On one side lawyers call for restrictions on state power and for restraints in the abuse of public power. 'As long as the phenomenon of power substituting for law exists, the law made by the state could never be properly implemented and executed.'[72] State power is illicitly manifest in corruption and judicial injustice.[73] On the other side law must protect private rights. Citizens must be tried fairly, be guaranteed a right to a defence, and prescribed punishments should be publicised for specified crimes. Academic criminal procedure specialists call for defendants to have the right of silence and to be presumed innocent before conviction.[74] Furthermore, the due process of law and its procedural meanings are frequently mentioned in the discussions of extended detention, confession by torture, judgment before trial, and the police and procuracy's obstruction of lawyers' work.[75] These concepts have an affinity with a legal ideology that emphasises proceduralism, equality and balance of power that has rarely appeared before in China's long history of criminal justice.

The rule of law stands against its opposite, 'the profound history of the rule of man' in China. In his interview on national television, lawyer Ma Guangjun from Nincheng County states repeatedly that the law, the court, cannot be reduced to the 'will of an individual person, a certain department or a certain leader'. The criminal process cannot stand 'for the face of some leader' and will not 'permit any individual to outmatch law, wilfully ride on law, or act as if human life is not worth a straw'. Says a lawyer from Suzhou City, Anhui Province, even the Lawyers Law must be held against a higher standard for it 'goes against the ideology of rule of law in the ideal state! The right in name can deprive/threaten democracy at any moment!! This is still the society under rule of a human being, isn't it!!' The promise of law rises as a new ideal. Why did Ma Guangjun persist in proclaiming his innocence, despite months in a local jail? Because 'I believe in law ... I believe that the dark clouds cannot block the sun for ever even in the small district of Nincheng County'.[76]

---

[72] #256611, 28 Sept 2003, 19:51, Jilin.
[73] #368312, 16 Jan 2004, 16:01, Shanghai; #536448, 12 July 2004, 01:02, Inner Mongolia.
[74] #450228, 16 Apr 2004, 16:06, Hebei; #368312, 16 Jan 2004, 16:01, Shanghai.
[75] #455014, 21 Apr 2004, 10:46, location unknown.
[76] #555785, 8 Aug 2004, 11:22, Anhui; #536452, 12 July 2004, 01:22, Inner Mongolia.

But the concept sits uneasily alongside the belief that good law comes from a pristine state. While courts should not be subject to the will of a person, the court does 'stand for the will of the state ... for the dignity and law of the state'.[77] Here and elsewhere the barrier blurs between the rule of law and rule by law. The court, while standing against one sort of power, nevertheless also expresses and executes state power, as if it is not the state itself but some perversion or transcendence of it, possibly in the form of a local leader or national figure, that is to be feared.

(ii) Professional Community and Mobilisation

More emphatically can be found the presumption among lawyers on the Forum that the rule of law is meaningless without a role for lawyers. It is not only that lawyers ensure the right of a fair trial. Most fundamentally, in the final analysis lawyers are the only weapon to fight against the abuse of state power. Indeed, the status and level of influence by lawyers in a society is indicative of the extent of democracy and the rule of law.[78]

To build the rule of law requires that lawyers must be able to defend themselves. They readily acknowledge their weakness. Ma Guangjun characterised lawyers' position in relation to the courts, procuracy and police as a 'feeble' colony-like status. 'The unity of lawyers is a feeble, vague, weak and flabby power', says a lawyer from Anhui Province.[79] Another lawyer agrees that 'in front of the powerful public power lawyers are actually too feeble'. China has never witnessed lawyers objecting collectively to injustice, he said.[80]

Yet, protecting clients demands self-protection. 'In our country, if we cannot protect the rights and interest of the lawyers themselves, how can you expect that we can protect the legal interest of the clients?' In reply to the cry of SOS, a lawyer from Shandong Province asked, 'Is it the case that Chinese lawyers only have the responsibilities to protect the rights of the clients, but no right or capacity to protect ourselves?' And with a touch of sarcasm he continues to wonder if this state of affairs is 'the goal of the socialist system of lawyers with Chinese characteristics?!':[81]

> Yes, lawyer colleagues, we should unite to protect our own legal rights. Lawyers are the protector of rights but we cannot protect our own rights, this is the tragedy of China's rule of law! ... To unite is the only way out for lawyers![82]

---

[77] #536452, 12 July 2004, 01:22, Inner Mongolia.
[78] Chen Ruihua, quoted in #368312, 16 Jan 2004, 16:01, Shanghai; Ma Guangjun, #536452, 12 July 2004, 01:22, Inner Mongolia.
[79] #536976, 12 July 2004, 19:17, Anhui.
[80] #537209, 13 July 2004, 08:42, location unknown.
[81] #576076, 7 Sept 2004, 00:38, Shandong.
[82] #612439, 13 Nov 2004, 10:15, Shandong.

Over and over again, lawyers call each other to collective action. In response to the SOS plea, one lawyer writes, 'What to do? There is never any Christ nor any immortal emperor. The key is our lawyers' collective cohesion and the fighting spirit.'[83] Lawyers cannot expect others to do what they will not do themselves. 'Every lawyer needs to stand up and fight to do his/her duty, otherwise they will all go down one by one.'[84] And in an echo of a classic cry from internal opponents to National Socialism:

> If we still tolerate this, the next victim might be ourselves. If lawyers cannot protect their own rights, how would you make people believe that you could protect the rights of the clients? Gentlemen, if we tolerate all this just because we haven't got hurt, just to guarantee our own good lives, then we would not be qualified as lawyers.[85]

One course of action offers little prospect. We 'can't rely on leaders of the lawyers' association because they are appointed by the government'. Lawyers' associations are 'more interested in collecting dues than 'obtaining justice for lawyers', more committed to 'collecting money' than doing anything. Lawyers' associations, the 'parental home of lawyers' must be condemned for they 'are parents who eat dishes without managing anything ... the parents did not fulfil their responsibilities, our brothers and sisters got hurt'.[86] Even the Lawyers Law regulates rather than protects.[87]

However, the rare exception proves that collective action, even by an official association, can produce dramatic results. Upon Ma Guangjun's arrest in Ningcheng County, the Inner Mongolia Lawyers Association appointed two lawyers to defend him. Hundreds of lawyers from every part of the county and Chifeng City attended the court hearing. Ma Guangjun told CCTV that he would still be in jail today if the lawyers' association had not mobilised.[88]

To protect themselves, many Forum participants propose that lawyers build a collective identity and capacity for collective action. We need to forge 'our own destiny by ourselves' in order to counter the 'powerful state machine of the public law'. 'Lawyers should unite together in consciousness and respect for other in the profession. When we meet with difficulties we should support, aid and cry for each other.'[89] A theme of mutual support

---

[83] #526705, 28 June 2004, 12:07, Hubei.
[84] #460363, 25 Apr 2004, 22:35, location unknown.
[85] #528094, 30 June 2004, 09:36, location unknown.
[86] #528094, 30 June 2004, 09:36, location unknown; #634726, 8 Jan 2005, 14:33, location unknown.
[87] #450228, 16 Apr 2004, 16:06, Hebei.
[88] #536452, 12 July 2004, 01:22, Inner Mongolia.
[89] #536976, 12 July 2004, 19:17, Anhui.

rings across the Forum threads. In response to the SOS appeal another lawyer stated:

> For Whom the Bell Tolls? For you, for me, for everyone of us. When we see the misfortune come to other people and feel lucky, we would eventually find out: when the catastrophe comes, there is already nobody to save us. I cry to every lawyer who still has some conscience, stand up, stand together, do our best to save our colleague.[90]

In this way a professional community, united through a common consciousness, can mobilise through their collective organisations to protect their own. And in protecting their members they will shape civil society and the consciousness of the masses since a vulnerable lawyer is 'a misfortune for China's rule of law, a misfortune for the Chinese people!'[91]. By not relying on lawyers' associations or the government, lawyers in China must 'unite together and dominate our own destiny by ourselves'.[92]

It follows that there is a direct contingency between a rule of law society and lawyers' collective action. The lawyer who posted the tragic story of lawyer Wen Zhicheng of Ruijin City understood its lessons precisely:

> Our nation should obtain the cultivation of law and establish a legal professional community. But from this case, how far away we are from the establishment of the legal professional community! How far away from the establishment of the rule of law society! Every lawyer should have the spirit of sacrifice to realize the cultivation of law. All the lawyers should unite together to protect our rights! The rights of lawyers should be respected, the social status of lawyers should be improved, the legal community should be truly established, the law practitioners should be universally respected in the society and the rule of law should be realized. It is really a multi-benefit thing. Why do I, we, and all the people not stand up to strive for this goal?![93]

Constructing a lawyers' collective consciousness can be exemplified through the individual lawyer who risks his/her safety by speaking on behalf of the collectivity. In a notable case, lawyer Shen Zhigeng defended his colleague Zhang Jianzhong, the director of Beijing Gong He Law Office, against accusations of forging evidence, with the words, 'I was here at present to defend for Zhang Jianzhong not only on behalf of myself, but also expressing the collective voice of all the lawyers'.[94] Ma Guangjun saw his trial and

---

[90] #460363, 25 Apr 2004, 22:35, location unknown.
[91] *Ibid.*
[92] #537209, 13 July 2004, 08:42, location unknown.
[93] #620344, 4 Dec 2004, 11:07, Sichuan.
[94] Quoted in #368312, 16 Jan 2004, 16:01, Shanghai. Zhang Jianzhong was sentenced to two years in prison.

vindication as a kind of test case: 'I think that because this case not only related to me, an individual named Ma Guangjun, but it related to the issue of a professional environment for a lawyer which was related to when a lawyer is fulfilling his duty in a justified and legal way.'[95]

Yet several lawyers acknowledge that even together they cannot stand alone against the power of the state or the arbitrariness of unrestrained local officials. Their natural allies are the media. In the SOS case, Tao Mujian from Chengdu, Sichuan Province stated that because the government was not trustworthy he recommended creating 'big publicity' and media support.[96] A persistent reporter helped vindicate Ma Guangjun's miscarriage of justice. CCTV carried his tale across China. *Southern Weekend* magazine in Guangzhou hosted a forum on lawyers and the rule of law in China in which one case after another was recounted of lawyers' travails in the justice system. Nevertheless, the media, too, is susceptible to official, Party and government control, and therefore must exercise its own restraint in order to forestall restraints on its reporting of lawyers' troubles. Government regulation rests on both their shoulders.

We must again reiterate that this portrait of the rule of law being advanced by a unified professional community, coherent in its identity and willing to act collectively, must not be overstated. Although many strong voices express these themes in one thread after another, not all lawyers agree that the government cannot be trusted. More than one person advised the fleeing SOS lawyer to go to the Ministry of Justice, to the local Bureau of Justice in Anhui Province, to 'trust the government and the Party', to rely upon the All China Lawyers Association.[97] Still, these are minority voices on the Forum, surprisingly unrepresentative given that these conversations are taking place on a site organised by the ACLA which in turn is regulated and constituted by the Ministry of Justice.

(iii) Institutional Analysis and Critique

Throughout the threads that relate to political liberalism there are direct institutional and structural critiques of the system of justice and state power more generally. These lead to calls for fundamental institutional changes that go beyond the system of justice to impinge upon the structure of state power.

The plight of Chinese defence lawyers results from the continuing imbalance of power in the PRC criminal justice system. Because the procuracy has supervisory power over the administration of justice by the judiciary,[98]

---

[95] #536452, 12 July 2004, 01:22, Inner Mongolia.
[96] #441476, 9 Apr 2004, 20:16, Sichuan.
[97] Various voices in the discussion of #440419, 8 Apr 2004, 22:56, Anhui.
[98] Arts 181 and 205 Criminal Procedure Law.

when the procurator gets an unfavourable result in a criminal case, he can either protest against the sentence made by the judge to the upper-level court or start a special procedure for prosecutorial trial supervision. Since the police, procuracy and judiciary regard themselves as an integrated system for striking crimes, officials and staff in these three agencies often are hostile to defence lawyers. Li Xuan, a legal scholar and experienced part-time lawyer in Beijing, put it this way:

> In fact, the judicial practice in the recent 20 years suggests that Chinese lawyers have absolutely no status facing all kinds of judicial officials. This is because in the whole judicial system, the judicial agencies [the police, procuracy and judiciary] control the state power and make final decisions for cases, and lawyers are only powerless legal service providers among citizens and speak for one party in cases. As the bad consequences of the official-centred conception and the conception of the rule of men, the judicial personnel have strong sense of superiority in status regarding lawyers. In such conditions, lawyers have to be very careful in face of judges, procurators, and police officers ... . [I]t frequently happens that the judge directly uses state coercive power to drive the lawyer out of the courtroom or charge them with crimes . ... [P]olice officers and procurators ... use the state coercive power more directly and frequently, and their tough behaviours to lawyers are sometimes even worse than the behaviour of judges.[99]

The root of this imbalance of power in the criminal process lies in the power structure of the Chinese state. The three judicial agencies (the Ministry of Public Security, the Supreme People's Procuracy and the Supreme People's Court) are more powerful actors in both legislative and administrative activities than the Ministry of Justice—the state regulatory agency for lawyers. Li Xuan argues that this power was reflected in the reform of the 1996 Criminal Procedure Law which the three judicial agencies used 'to consolidate and expand the scope of their power'. By contrast, 'lawyers had almost no opportunity to speak and protest during the legislative process'. The role of legal scholars was largely 'ornamental'.[100] Lawyers' low status in the criminal process is further undermined by the fact that the ACLA and local lawyers' associations are subject to the regulation of the Ministry of Justice and the local Bureaus of Justice and thus enjoy very limited professional autonomy.

Much criticism is directed at the courts. Lawyers defend the accused in the courtroom but the decisions are made too often in places invisible to lawyers, either before the trial, or after the court hearing by higher level judges, or the Adjudication Committee composed of court leaders, or the Political Legal Committee through which the Party exerts its influence over courts, particularly in sensitive cases. This makes lawyers 'dispensable'

---

[99] #551554, 2 Aug 2004, 23:28, Beijing.
[100] *Ibid.*

and calls into question how and where decisions are being made. Many lawyers support the assertion that 'if the administrative relations between the upper and lower courts have not been replaced fundamentally', then 'it is impossible to realise the so-called rule of law in China'. Too often it seems to Forum participants that decisions are made outside the courts altogether by 'powerful people' or by 'local authorities' through one channel or another.[101] The recruitment of judges also still leaves much to be desired. Too many former soldiers still occupy seats in basic-level courts. So do 'people who have entered into the court by their varied relations with some certain authorities'.[102] The implication is that personnel recruited in this way have neither the training nor the loyalty to the court as an institution.

As fundamental is the attack on the distribution of power within the legal complex. A lawyer from Zibo, Shandong Province, maintains that:

> [L]awyers have an extremely unequal position compared with the police, procuracy and judiciary. In such conditions, relying on the self realization of the police, procuracy and judiciary to promote the change in lawyers' status is like looking for fish in the forest (*yuan mu qiu yu*).[103]

Similarly, 'seen from the cases happening in every place in the whole country and in every year, lawyers have been prosecuted repeatedly, and the condition has always been that the three agencies such as the public security office, the people's procuracy, and the court all located themselves in a commanding status' over lawyers. An article posted on the Forum from *Lawyer World* (*lüshi shijie*) magazine sums up the view of many criminal defence lawyers that 'the status of the prosecutor and the defender is imbalanced. The "power for prosecution" is easy and skilful, but the right of defence is nice but hollow'. Self-restraint by the law enforcement authorities offers no solution. 'In the design of our legal system, the public prosecutor is both the athlete and the referee.' Reform of the judicial system has been talked about for years, but there will be little change unless it is 'supported by fundamental forces'.[104]

The problems for lawyers are indicative of the wider problem that the judiciary is not insulated from executive power; indeed, is embedded within it. 'There is no place for all civil rights to exist when the judicial power has not been independent of the administrative power.' Not only does the weak Ministry of Justice offer little protection from more powerful executive agencies, but it is part of the problem. Ultimately, power trumps law in China. 'It is always power that is higher than law.' Power substitutes

[101] #256574, 28 Sept 2003, 19:14, Jilin; #368312, 16 Jan 2004, 16:01, Shanghai; etc.
[102] #616652, 23 Nov 2004, 10:16, Shenzhen.
[103] #556170, 8 Aug 2004, 23:21, Shandong.
[104] #555662; 8 Aug 2004, 05:13, Shandong.

for law which is not independent. The corruption of the judiciary is only a part of the corruption of power in China. Repeatedly lawyers identify the problem as one of structural inequalities, judicial integrity and independence, and institutional imbalance. 'Unless the institutional problem is solved fundamentally, it is impossible that this kind of circumstance can be altered radically.'[105]

In part, the slow pace of reform reflects public opinion. The notion that all criminal suspects should receive legal representation, let alone presumption of innocence, has been hard for the public to swallow. 'The basic evaluation of the lawyers in the peoples' minds' is that 'lawyers are defending the bad guys ... , lawyers are opposing the judicial agencies ... , lawyers are defrauding common people for money.'[106] Tian Wenchang, a distinguished Beijing criminal lawyer, points to a 'contradiction between the professional morality of lawyers and the social morality'.[107] There is a 'vast sea of the demos mass', a 'demos ideology', that suspects must be guilty; a profession that stands between criminal suspects and their punishment offends public morality.

As a result lawyers are vulnerable on two sides. From one angle they must protect themselves from the 'Big Stick' wielded by the procuracy and police, knowing they have few defenders from the official establishment of professional regulation. From another angle they have little support from the masses and no allies in a non-existent civil society except, occasionally, the press.

(iv) The Spirit of Sacrifice

In view of this tenuous institutional position in an authoritarian society, why do lawyers take such risks? How do they sustain a vocation in the face of implacable resistance and manifest weakness? We may quickly dismiss the economic hypothesis. It is true that large numbers of lawyers take criminal work because they exist in a fiercely competitive environment and have little choice in order to make a living (Michelson, 2003; Liu and Michelson, 2004). It is also true that a handful of lawyers at the top of the criminal defence bar do well financially by representing wealthy clients in anti-corruption and other cases where the death penalty is an imminent fear.

Overwhelmingly in the Forum, however, lawyers enunciate heroic values that capture something of the revolutionary zeal of earlier generations of Chinese. There are more than a few hints that the zeal for the rule of law substitutes for the loss of faith in an earlier revolutionary ideology. The heroes of the criminal defence bar are animated by their belief that they are the last bastion between abusive public power and helpless individuals.

---

[105] See responses to #536448, 12 July 2004, 01:02, Inner Mongolia; #256574, 28 Sept 2003, 19:14, Jilin; #440419, 8 Apr 2004, 22:56, Anhui.

[106] #555662; 8 Aug 2004, 05:13, Shandong.

[107] Quoted in #368312, 16 Jan 2004, 16:01, Shanghai.

Reflecting on his nine-month battle with Nincheng County authorities, Ma Guangjun proclaimed that 'the only weapon to fight with and the only barrier to guard against the public power, especially the abuse of power, is the institution of lawyers':

> the fact this kind of thing could happen ... involves a problem concerning the public power of the state. When this kind of public power was out of control, when this kind of public power was abused, what would the final result lead to? In these circumstances, you must take certain risks.[108]

For this in fact he was prepared to make himself a martyr, to establish a precedent for all of China. He was the first lawyer to be arrested without preliminary procedures and the first to be held for several months before the court proceedings began. 'My example was the first for the entire country', and while it was a course of action he would not have chosen, when the challenge came he met it at great risk to himself.

Yet it was not the heroic image of the lawyer as the last redoubt against unbridled power that brought Ma Guangjun into the case, nor the 1,000 yuan[109] the poor person could pay. It was to correct one injustice and prevent another. In an interview on CCTV, he was asked what relationship he had with the defendant.

> Reporter : Have you known the defendant before?
> Ma Guangjun : I have never met him, never heard of the case before.
> Reporter : Why did you accept the case?
> Ma Guangjun : Because having been a lawyer in practice for so many years, I have adopted the principle that the more unjust the case, and the more it is the kind of case where common people are eager to receive legal aid, then the more willing I am to undertake the case. And at the same time, because this was the kind of case in which unjust judicial actions existed, I was eager to deal with it as well. This is my personal commitment.[110]

For others it is the dignity of law that has its own calling. Invoking martyrs from Chinese history, a lawyer from Anhui Province writes:

> After reading the article written by Liu Lu, I have thought of the sentence of one ancient poem that 'the wind is rustling and the river is frozen, the heroic man has gone and will not return forever!' (*feng xiaoxiao xi yishui han, zhuangshi yiqu xi bu fuhuan*) Now that we have chosen to be lawyers, we shall be prepared to devote all our lives to the dignity of law, just like the Wuxu Six Men of Honour (*Wuxu Liu Junzi*).[111]

---

[108] #536452, 12 July 2004, 01:22, Inner Mongolia.
[109] About $US125.
[110] #536452, 12 July 2004, 01:22, Inner Mongolia.
[111] #556732, 9 Aug 2004, 21:54, Anhui. Both the poem and the Wuxu Six Men of Honour are stories of famous martyrs in Chinese history.

Above all, lawyers are harbingers of democracy, heralds of the rule of law. From China's far west, a lawyer from Xinjiang calls upon heroes from recent democratisation movements:

> It is because the profession is filled with danger that we are the tower of strength in the society. Think about Chen Shui-bian in Taiwan who passionately defended the people of Meili Island in his early life. And think about Roh Moo-hyun in Korea who pled for the students in the democratic movement under the tyranny ruled by Park Chung-hee. So that now Taiwan and Korea have accomplished democracy and prosperity at the present time. It is just that we should pay the cost for democracy!![112]

Despite his torture and humiliation at the hands of the police, the old lawyer, Wen Zhicheng from Ruijin, could still cry, 'Every lawyer should have the spirit of sacrifice to realise the rule of law ... . Why do I, we, and all the people not stand up to strive for this goal?!'[113]

A revolutionary rhetoric can be found in many of these hundreds of messages. It is as if a fervour for an abandoned ideology is being transferred to a new set of hopes. The spirit of sacrifice, the call to unite for the common good, the responsibility to defend the weak and oppressed all have revolutionary resonance. And some find it in the rule of law. In response to the appeal, 'SOS, the fleeing lawyer is crying for help!', another lawyer appropriated the opening words of the Chinese national anthem to the plight of lawyers: 'Rise, all people who are not willing to be slaves. Use our flesh to build our new Great Wall.'[114]

(g) Public and Private Faces of the Legal Profession

The viewpoints of lawyers we have analysed were expressed within the relative privacy of a dedicated electronic space. That space, however, is created by a public professional association that is controlled by the Ministry of Justice. How then does the private expression of issues by lawyers compare to the public presentation of self by the All China Lawyers Association? We collected data from the *Chinese Lawyers* (*zhongguo lüshi*) magazine (the official professional journal of the ACLA) and conducted interviews with leading lawyers in the ACLA and the Beijing Municipal Lawyers Association (BMLA).

Reports in the *Chinese Lawyers* magazine have covered most major issues concerned with lawyers' criminal defence, including the 'Three Difficulties', 'Big Stick 306' and the hostility of judicial agencies towards

---

[112] #556755, 9 Aug 2004, 22:33, Xinjiang.
[113] #620344, 4 Dec 2004 11:07, Jiangxi.
[114] #546617, 27 July 2004, 12:39, location unknown.

lawyers. However, the tone of the magazine articles is much more restrained and there is almost no direct criticism of the judicial agencies or the political system. Many articles advise lawyers how to adapt to the status quo (eg, CL1999_12, CL2001_05) and some discuss the possibilities of ameliorating the conditions for defence lawyers' practice by institutional or legal changes without describing the current problems in detail (eg, CL1998_12, CL1999_01, CL2003_0224). Titles like 'Lawyers' Risks and Self-Protection in Criminal Defence' (CL1999_12) and 'The Way Out for Lawyers' Criminal Defence' (CL2003_0224) are typical for such reports. This conservative attitude of reporting the problems in criminal defence work indicates that the ACLA's caution in not offending the powerful actors in the legal complex, namely, the police, procuracy and judiciary.

In recent years, there have been a few articles in the journal that directly address the severe problems in practice and report of specific cases. A July 2002 article titled 'Chinese Lawyers Who Dare Not to Defend for Criminal Suspects' (CL2002_07), for example, started with the substantial decrease of criminal defence work for Beijing lawyers and then reported five major Article 306 cases all over the country, including three cases in which the defence lawyer was detained for over a year. It also cited comments from legal scholars, leading lawyers, and even some procurators in regard to Article 306. Generally speaking, however, such a detailed overview of the difficulties and problems in criminal defence is quite rare in the ACLA journal articles and other media reports.

Furthermore, the *Chinese Lawyers* magazine also frequently reports on symposiums held by the ACLA or other agencies on criminal procedure law and criminal defence work. Distinguished scholars, lawyers, judges and procurators were invited to these symposiums to discuss various problems in criminal defence lawyers' practice, including: (1) the impact of the 1996 CPL revision on lawyers' work (CL1996_06a, CL1996_06b); (2) the implementation of the law and the judicial interpretations (CL1998_04); (3) protection for criminal defence lawyers (CL1998_01, CL1999_01); and (4) relationship between the procuracy and the defence lawyer (CL2004_0309, CL2004_0719). Compared with the messages on the Forum, the discourse in these symposiums is highly constrained by the presence of multiple actors of the legal complex.

Furthermore, discourses regarding the weak position of the Ministry of Justice in the state structure and the powerlessness of the ACLA, both widely discussed on the Forum, have never appeared in the magazine. The tight regulation of the ACLA by the Ministry of Justice makes it impossible to state its own weakness in public channels. Moreover, while discourses of political participation and collective action are prevalent in the Forum responses to the plight of defence lawyers, we find little such discourse through public channels. There is, accordingly, also no thoughtful analysis of the political and institutional constraints on lawyers' collective action. Even detailed descriptions of the torture and ill treatment of defence lawyers in Article 306 cases are avoided by the *Chinese Lawyers* magazine.

Interviews with bar association leaders from both the ACLA and the BMLA show similar patterns regarding the problems in criminal defence. Although all of these leading lawyers we interviewed are specialised in criminal defence, most of their cases are highly profitable white collar crimes, especially cases related to the corruption of government officials. Compared to the public writings in the magazine, the interviewees provided rich accounts and thoughtful analyses of the difficulties in criminal defence work and the underlying problems, some even strongly proposing the abolition of Article 306.[115] However, as bar association leaders they rarely mentioned the powerlessness of the ACLA or the weakness of the Ministry of Justice in the political system. Instead, a few of these leading lawyers suggested that the lawyers' associations were getting stronger and playing an increasingly important role in both law-making and implementation.[116] This is in sharp contrast to the condemnation of the lawyers' associations by the Forum users when discussing the same problems in criminal defence work. Furthermore, none of these leading lawyers indicated the importance of the profession's collective action, which is another major theme on the Forum. Instead, they prefer to use official channels (eg, the Ministry of Justice and the NPC Legal Work Commission) to push for potential changes.

Overall, although the publications of the ACLA and interviews with lawyers' association leaders treat similar topics to the Forum discussions, we find surprisingly different discourses between the public and private discussions of the legal profession. This difference is particularly interesting considering that the Forum administrators are also editors of the ACLA journal, and comments of those leading lawyers are frequently being posted on the Forum and followed up with discussions. This indicates that under an authoritarian political regime and facing hostile judicial agencies the legal profession has developed two faces, namely, a public face that appears obedient to the state and conservative towards sociopolitical changes, and a private face that reveals an increasingly strong collective identity and emerging liberal ideologies.

IV. CONCLUSION

We have proposed that the enactment and implementation of law to protect alleged criminals presents a key research site in any country to take the pulse of movements towards or away from political liberalism. Until

---

[115] Eg, Interviews INB0507, INB0510, INB0512.
[116] Interviews INB0507, INB0508.

the last 25 years, the rights of criminal detainees and defendants and the ability of lawyers effectively to represent alleged criminals advanced relatively little beyond the almost complete absence of those protections in China's long history. Since 1979 a series of law reforms and since 1996, a flurry of court interpretations and administrative rules have placed some semblance of criminal procedure law on the books. In practice, however, the struggles of Chinese criminal lawyers with the 'Three Difficulties' and 'Big Stick 306' demonstrate that practice is far removed from precept and that the much-vaunted reforms of the later 1990s provide defendants with scarcely effective legal representation.

These procedural barriers follow from barely differentiated structures of law-enforcement power, where the police, procuracy and judiciary maintain an inertia sustained by an ideology that conceives of them as a closed fist of government executive authority. In the face of sustained efforts by the police and procurators to maintain their institutionalised hold over the criminal process, a struggling criminal bar, fortified with fragments of legal liberalism, seeks to expand its domain of work and seize domains of activity from exclusive control by law enforcement authorities. The contest is waged on very narrow fronts—a gain of private audience with clients, a glimpse into police files, a right to contest the way evidence is gathered or to bring independent evidence or to enlist other witnesses—but with the prospect that a foothold might simultaneously open up a viable area of practice and create a bridgehead for legal liberalism.

Nevertheless, the combinations of Articles 38 of the Criminal Procedure Law and Article 306 of the Criminal Law effectively take away on one flank what had been gained on another. If the capacity of representation shrinks to a defence of a lawyer's own personal safety from prosecution, then the lawyer remains a hostage to the very arms of the state that representation is intended to resist. Not only does a lack of differentiation fail to fracture internally the striking power of the criminal law enforcement apparatus, but the intimidation of the only part of the legal complex that might oppose it, the criminal bar, effectively reduces the agent of a nascent liberalism to a cipher. In this struggle criminal lawyers cannot look to judges because their natural allies in other national and historical contexts are the enforcement arms of the state security apparatus in the Chinese situation.

To whom can criminal lawyers turn? Apparently only to each other. And herein lies an irony of criminal law and enforcement in contemporary China. If a civil society is to emerge in China, or if legal liberalism is to gain perceptible ground, it is arguable that lawyers might be candidates for such agency as they have been in some other societies. Emergence of a nascent profession begins with the forging of a collective identity. Since identity formation is about boundary demarcation, the coalescence of a collective 'us' is enabled by the opposition of a collective 'other'. Thus the police, procurators and judges present a formidable 'them' that at once has cultural and organisational force. In their coordination, as state agencies and as long-standing allies, the criminal enforcement complex precipitates lawyers to forge their own forms of social organisation that will protect the vulnerable individual attorney from the clenched fist of a fused law enforcement apparatus.

It is another irony that the very organisation that criminal lawyers berate for its perceived impotence, the All China Lawyers Association, controlled as it is by the Ministry of Justice, nonetheless enables criticism by providing the Forum where criminal lawyers can forge a China-wide identity and a springboard for collective action. The ACLA Forum effectively offers an infrastructure for communication which functions as a 'public sphere' for lawyers, enabling them to discover their identity and to craft an ideology that solidifies it. This source of lawyers' experiences in criminal practice more importantly is a social structure that permits, even encourages, a national lawyerly identity to be created, that stimulates the practice of civic discourse with relative impunity, and that creates in microcosm a public square that might later be imitated by or embrace other occupations and fractions of society. In this sense, it presents an early twenty-first century analogue to the eighteenth century salons of France, the early modern Inns of Court in England, and the late-nineteenth century elite bar associations in the United States. The roots of an embryonic profession are grounded within the double shelter of a state agency and an official association.

But the semblance of an emerging professional solidarity may be illusory. The 'profession' that is regulated via the All China Lawyers Association is one of many legal occupations, several in severe competition with each other (Liu and Michelson, 2004). More significantly, however, within the ACLA-regulated profession, the success of a criminal defence bar in defining itself in terms of political liberalism may put it at odds with the commercial bar. Already, at the top end of the profession, China has flourishing and affluent commercial law firms, especially in cities that have led China's burgeoning economic development (Liu, 2006). To the extent that the criminal bar articulates a vision of political lawyering that brings it into confrontation with the Party and Party-state apparatus, the comfortable existence that commercial lawyers enjoy as they ride the economic waves to personal fortune may be threatened by closer regulation, less autonomy in the work-place or firm, and more government oversight.

This incipient cleavage returns us to inherent clashes between economic and political globalisation, economic and political lawyering, that were raised in the Postscript to our earlier studies (Halliday and Karpik, 1998b). A coincidence of interest may well unite the Party-state, in its bid to deliver economic liberalisation without political liberalisation, and the commercial bar, in its aspiration to market control without the disturbance of political engagement. The Party-state will prefer the profession, like the populace, to appreciate the benefits of economic liberalism in order to distract it from claims for political liberalism. Ironically, again, the weakest part financially and reputationally of the Chinese profession—the criminal lawyers—may, in working against the commercial interests of their fellow professionals, endow on the profession as a whole an ideology that defines its core values. It is precisely such a relationship of ambivalence that Scheingold and Sarat (2004) find in the relationship between cause lawyers, who are deviants within a profession, and mainstream lawyers, who define themselves in part by their difference from cause lawyers and yet draw upon the ideology of engagement on behalf of the weak that animates the cause lawyers.

In view of the marginalisation of criminal lawyers within the bar, and in light of the failure of implementation to deliver the promise of procedural protections, it is easy to compare present-day China adversely to rule-of-law societies, against whose practices China compares badly, and to global norms, against whose standards China falls short. Taking the view of the *longue durée*, however, where concepts of rights and fracturing of power have never been manifest, the steps of the past 25 years seem like giant strides. In this small window of time, China has enacted criminal and procedural law which bears resemblances to legal liberalism, it has laid the foundations of a legal profession and a regulatory framework, and it has permitted lawyers an electronic space in which professional identity is being crafted and the foundations of collective action are being laid. It is surely necessary to admit that the formal law is not descriptive of practice, that professional regulation is scarcely self-regulation, or that collective action boasts major triumphs. A nascent legal profession may appear to be a hapless victim in a larger drama where long traditions, hostile ideology and powerful institutions may permit a veil of political liberalism that disguises its unreality. Yet history shows that even hollow law, which in the short term is subversive of liberal politics, may in time and changed circumstances become a solid foundation for the construction of political liberalism. We can only now observe a time of trial and await history's verdict.

REFERENCES

Abel, R (2004), 'Lawyers Legalizing Torture', Biennial European Conference of the Working Group on Comparative Studies of Legal Professions, July 2004, Berder, France.

Cai, D (1999), 'Development of the Chinese Legal System Since 1979 and its Current Crisis and Transformation', 11 *Cultural Dynamics* 135.

Chen, G (1995), 'Lun Xingshi Susong Fa Xiugai de Zhidao Sixiang. ['On the Theory of the Criminal Procedure Law Revision.']', 4 *Fazhi yu Shehui Fazhan* [*Law and Social Development*] 43.

Cohen, JA (1968), *The Criminal Process in the People's Republic of China, 1949–1963* (Cambridge, Mass, Harvard University Press).

Guarnieri, C (2005), 'Lawyers and Statist Liberalisms in Italy', Conference on The Legal Complex and Political Liberalism, 1–5 May, Onati, Spain.

Halliday, TC (1987), *Beyond Monopoly: Lawyers, State Crises and Professional Empowerment* (Chicago, Ill, University of Chicago Press).

—— and Carruthers, BG (2004), 'The Recursivity of Law: Global Norm-Making and National Law-Making in the Globalization of Corporate Insolvency Regimes', Working Paper, American Bar Foundation.

—— and Karpik, L (eds) (1998a), *Lawyers and the Rise of Western Political Liberalism: Europe and North America from the Eighteenth to Twentieth Centuries* (Oxford, Oxford University Press).

—— and —— (1998b), 'Politics Matter: A New Framework for the Comparative and Historical Study of Legal Professions' in TC Halliday and L Karpik (eds), *Lawyers and the Rise of Western Political Liberalism: Europe and North America from the Eighteenth to Twentieth Centuries* (Oxford, Oxford University Press).

—— and —— (1998c), 'Postscript: Lawyers and the Globalization of Liberal Politics' in TC Halliday and L Karpik (eds), *Lawyers and the Rise of Western Political Liberalism: Legal Professions and the Constitution of Modern Politics* (Oxford University Press, Oxford and New York).

He, W (1998), *Sifa de Linian yu Zhidu [The Concepts and Systems of Judicature]* (Beijing, China University of Politics and Law Press).

Karpik, L (1998) 'Builders of Liberal Society: French Lawyers and Politics' in TC Halliday and L Karpik (eds), *Lawyers and the Rise of Western Political Liberalism: Europe and North America from the Eighteenth to Twentieth Centuries* (Oxford, Oxford University Press).

—— (1999), *French Lawyers: A Study in Collective Action, 1274–1994* (Oxford, Oxford University Press).

Lawyers Committee for Human Rights (1993), *Criminal Justice with Chinese Characteristics: China's Criminal Process and Violations of Human Rights* (New York, Lawyers Committee for Human Rights).

Ledford, KF (1997), 'Lawyers and the Limits of Liberalism: the German Bar in the Weimar Republic' in TC Halliday and L Karpik (eds), *Lawyers and the Rise of Western Political Liberalism: Europe and North America from the Eighteenth to Twentieth Centuries* (Oxford, Oxford University Press).

Leng, SC (1985), *Criminal Justice in Post-Mao China: Analysis and Documents* (Albany, NY, State University of New York Press).

Liu, S (2006), 'Client Influence and the Contingency of Professionalism: The Work of Elite Corporate Lawyers in China', 40 *Law & Society Review* 751.

—— and Michelson, E (2004), 'Chinese Lawyers and Their Competitors: State-Mediated Jurisdictional Conflicts', The Law & Society Association Annual Meeting, Chicago, Ill.

Lu, H and Miethe, TD (2002), 'Legal Representation and Criminal Processing in China', 42 *British Journal of Criminology* 267.

Lubman, S (1999), *Bird in a Cage: Legal Reform in China After Mao* (Stanford, Cal, Stanford University Press).

Macauley, M (1998), *Social Power and Legal Culture: Litigation Masters in Late Imperial China* (Stanford, Cal, Stanford University Press).

Michelson, E (2003), 'Unhooking from the State: Chinese Lawyers in Transition', PhD dissertation, University of Chicago.

Peerenboom, R (2002), *China's Long March toward Rule of Law* (New York, Cambridge University Press).

Potter, PB (1998), 'Curbing the Party: Peng Zhen and Chinese Legal Culture', 45 *Problems of Post-Communism* 17.

Pue, WW (1997), 'Lawyers and Political Liberalism in Eighteenth- and Nineteenth-Century England' in TC Halliday and L Karpik (eds), *Lawyers and the Rise of Western Political Liberalism: Europe and North America from the Eighteenth to Twentieth Centuries* (Oxford, Oxford University Press).

Scheingold, S and Sarat, A (2004), *Something to Believe In: Politics, Professionals and Cause-Lawyering* (Stanford, Cal, Stanford University Press).

Scheppele, KL (2005), 'We Are a Nation of Lawyers: The Role of Lawyers in Hungarian Political Transformation' Conference on The Legal Complex and Political Liberalism, 1–5 May, Onati, Spain.

Sheng, Y (2003), 'A Promise Unfulfilled: The Impact of China's 1996 Criminal-Procedure Reform on China's Criminal Defense Lawyers' Role at the Pretrial Stage (Part 1)', 4 *Perspectives* 1.

—— (2004), 'A Promise Unfulfilled: The Impact of China's 1996 Criminal-Procedure Reform on China's Criminal Defense Lawyers' Role at the Pretrial Stage (Part 2)', 5 *Perspectives* 27.

Song, B (2001), 'The Difficulties in Criminal Lawyers' Practice After the Implementation of the New Criminal Procedure Law', 3 *Chinese Lawyers* 41.

Xu, J (1998), *Zhonghua Minguo Lüshi Zhidu Shi* [History of Lawyers in the Republic of China] (Beijing, China University of Politics and Law Press).

Yu, P (2002), 'Glittery Promise vs. Dismal Reality: The Role of a Criminal Lawyer in the People's Republic of China after the 1996 Revision of the Criminal Procedure Law', 35 *Vanderbilt Journal of Transnational Law* 827.

Zhang Q (2003), 'The People's Court in Transition: The Prospects of the Chinese Judicial Reform', 12 *Journal of Contemporary China* 69.

4

'Dissolving the People': Capitalism, Law and Democracy in Hong Kong

CAROL JONES

'The government, having lost the confidence of the people, has decided to dissolve the people and form a new one'.[1]

O RTHODOX THINKING AMONGST international institutions claims a mysterious link between capitalism, democracy and the rule of law. The development of one somehow inexorably leads to the other. Yet Hong Kong, the world's eighth largest trading economy, one of its top five international financial centres and a recognisably liberal society based on the rule of law has never developed democracy (Chan and Postiglione, 1996). Hailed by Friedmanites as the epitome of classic laissez faire capitalism, and rated by the Heritage Foundation as one of the most competitive and open economies in the world, it shares the core values and rights of a liberal state—protections against the arbitrary exercise of power (such as arbitrary arrest and detention), habeas corpus, due process, the right to silence, to public trial and to legal representation, as well as the core freedoms, such as freedom of speech and freedom of association associated with the moderate state. But it is not a 'liberal democracy', nor has it ever had universal suffrage or a representative government. In both colonial and post-colonial times, the state has instead been moderated by legal channels of accountability, and constrained by a legal complex which has, paradoxically, often included the state's own lawyer-officials.

Hong Kong's distinct concatenation of law and liberalism, capitalism and democracy, thus raises several questions: How did an authoritarian colonial society become so liberal without the moderating role of democracy on capitalism? Did the legal complex help fashion Hong Kong liberalism, and if so how? Were lawyers simply the handmaidens of trade

---

[1] Berthold Brecht, cited in M Turner, *60s/90s* (Hong Kong, Art Installation, Hong Kong Arts Centre, 1996).

and commerce, enforcers of stability and order? Did they help restrain the illiberal tendencies of the Hong Kong government and its ruling elite? How did Hong Kong's retrocession to the People's Republic of China (PRC) in 1997 change its legal complex?

Hong Kong's trajectory post-1997 shows an ongoing shift from liberalism to authoritarianism. This retreat is being fought by liberally-inclined members of the judiciary, the bar and legal academia, in alliance with various groups in civil society. Their mobilisation arose largely as a reaction to the state's abrogation of first-generation legal rights (eg freedom from arbitrary arrest and detention, right to privacy, freedom of association, freedom of expression, etc). At the end of colonial rule, a small (but elite) group of barristers managed a rare achievement in forming successful coalitions with other groups and activists in civil society in defence of liberal and democratic values. In the 10 years since the 1997 handover, they have come to stand at the very centre of the struggle over Hong Kong's identity, that which most demarcates it from Mainland China. Indeed, post-1997, moderation of the territory's governance has been most articulate and most effective in the courts of law, rather than Hong Kong's unrepresentative Legislative Council (LEGCO).

In the run-up to 1997, the rule of law became the lightning rod around which anxieties about the depredations of the Mainland authorities clustered. Attacks upon law, lawyers and legality were seen as signs that the handover was already eating away at the territory's foundations. Though no blatant crackdown followed 1997, a creeping authoritarianism has heightened popular vigilance in defence of liberalism. Calls to uphold the rule of law, defend the courts, and protect judicial independence have prompted mass demonstrations on a far greater scale than calls for democracy. But if Hong Kong people now see the law and lawyers as their best chance of moderating the state, what does this imply for the future of politics (and democracy) in the territory?

Freedom of speech and association may, as Halliday, Karpik and Feeley argue, 'take us a long way towards suffrage and effectively prefigure it',[2] but Hong Kong's experience gives us reason to suspect that, instead of being the 'natural' ally of democracy, they may also delay or disarm it (Dowdle, 2005). From the 1970s onwards, law and lawyers relieved the pressures for social and political change, stifling indigenous demands for democracy. When, in the mid-1980s, a more representative government was finally proposed, the idea came from above, from government civil servants, not from 'below' or from tussles with a liberal legal complex. Historically, such colonial officials had opposed constitutional change on the basis that self-government for Hong Kong would allow a rapacious colonial elite to

[2] See the introduction to this volume.

exercise rule over the indigenous Chinese. In the 1980s, however, it was they who proposed democratic reform. This was immediately opposed by most of Hong Kong's ruling elite (Chinese and European), who regarded democracy as an unwelcome constraint on power. The solicitors' branch of the legal profession (the business lawyers, the largest segment of the Hong Kong legal complex) shared this preference for the status quo, consistently opposing the Bar's championing of liberal values.

Beijing, too, opposed democratic development in Hong Kong. Deng Xiaoping instead promised that after 1997 the territory would have a high degree of autonomy, with 'Hong Kong people ruling Hong Kong'. The two societies—Communist and capitalist—would re-unite, but as 'one country, two systems'. Ten years after the handover, however, and despite a widespread expectation that Hong Kong people would soon be able to elect their leaders, no agreement had been reached about when they would be permitted to do so. The loyalties of the ruling business and political oligarchy lie with property, business and Beijing, rather than Hong Kong people. The structure of LEGCO ensures a permanent government majority, rendering opposition parties powerless. Changes introduced by the PRC in 1997 disenfranchised large sections of society, leaving the post-colonial government even less representative than under British rule. Channels of consultation between the colonial government and the people have been systematically dismantled to re-establish a strong central executive. In this re-colonisation process, education and culture increasingly valorise patriotic values.

The liberal opposition which emerged in the 1980s comprised political activists, civil society elements, and a few members of the liberal legal complex. A small and disparate group, they nevertheless scored some spectacular victories, both against the outgoing British administration and against the post-1997 government, providing a focus around which more widespread dissatisfactions and aspirations have coalesced. From this fragmented core, a more conscious mobilisation in support of liberalism has developed post-1997 amongst more substantial fractions of the bar, academe, the bench, and even prosecutors.

This engagement of lawyers with political and social movements represents a significant departure from the past. With a few notable exceptions, the Bar and the Bench made no attempt during the colonial period to constrain the state or rein in the excesses of Hong Kong's merchant elite. Though weak and fragmented, they sometimes found support, however, amongst colonial lawyer-officials (eg government legal advisers) as well as other liberally-inclined groups, such as missionaries, educationalists and doctors. Against the odds, they established a 'little tradition' of liberalism.

Here, I provide only a brief overview of Hong Kong's complex politics of colonialism and liberalism from 1841 to the 1960s, focusing instead on the critical juncture in the 1970s and 1980s, when the liberal ideal of the rule of law became central to the governance of Hong Kong. I also explore the post-1997 emergence of a pro-Beijing legal complex, which has self-consciously mobilised against the liberal coalition. Comprising members of the private bar, of academe, and state, this has articulated with other pro-Beijing groups in Hong Kong to form a 'united front', demonstrating their 'love of China' by mobilising in support of Beijing whenever Hong Kong courts have conflicted with the government. To date, they have, however, proved unable to mobilise on the same scale as the pro-liberal, pro-democracy legal complex.

I. FROM EARLY COLONIALISM TO POST-WORLD WAR II COMMUNISM AND COLD WAR *REALPOLITIK*[3]

The 'Hong Kong story' is not one of linear 'progress' from nineteenth century authoritarianism to twentieth century liberalism. Hong Kong's history is scattered with episodes of repression *and* political liberalism, of an illiberal *and* a moderate state, of oscillations towards and retreats from liberalism, of a state at times restrained by forces in civil society, but mostly not. These periodic swings indicate that the development of liberalism (and democracy) is never 'inevitable', and that the presence of a legal complex by no means guarantees that either will flourish.

Until recently, the independent sector of the Hong Kong legal complex was an ineffective check on the state. That job was done by others—liberals, evangelicals and humanitarians—within the colonial elite—who challenged the discriminatory practices of Hong Kong's elite. 'In-house' government legal advisers (part of the legal complex hidden from view) also intervened to check the predations of the state. In the early colonial period (from 1841 to the 1880s), for example, highly repressive anti-Chinese legislation was moderated by such individuals:[4] educated members of the British middle classes, some trained in Chinese language and culture to become Cadets, key administrators serving liaising between the Hong Kong government and the Chinese. Their immersion in Chinese culture and their adherence to liberal legal ideals made them the awkward conscience of Empire. They reminded Governors of the need to balance self-interest against the moral and humanitarian projects of colonialism and, with limited success, acted as a brake on the state and ensured that the Hong Kong government operated within the rule of law. Such dissenting voices were to remain part of colonial governance.

By contrast, the bar and the judiciary hardly ever tried to check state power. Between the 1880s and World War II, the legal complex almost

[3] For a detailed description of this period see Jones, 2005.
[4] See eg Munn, 1995.

invariably associated itself with the status quo. The main opposition to government and capital came from organised labour, whose interests brought it into direct conflict with the European and Chinese elites. Their wealth and position were tied to the preservation of the existing oligarchy, the Chinese elite having more in common with the Europeans than with the 'coolie' class. Though the Hong Kong government in theory adhered to a policy of non-interference in economic affairs, this invariably translated into support for capital against labour. But far from being politically apathetic (as often alleged) the Chinese working class forced government and employers into concessions, checking their otherwise unbridled pursuit of wealth. In this period, therefore, it was organised labour, not lawyers or courts, which moderated state power.

The subsequent use of law to suppress trade unionism—and, in the 1920s and 1930s, to deport and detain political activists—led to the emergence of a new fraction of the legal complex, a small clique of Chinese lawyers (trained in the UK). During the 1930s, these 'leftist lawyers' provided a weak but significant corrective to the exercise of government power. Seen as suspect and dissident, they stood at the periphery of the legal profession, whose core remained solidly conservative, pro-government and pro-capital.

This remained the case for most of the twentieth century. The end of World War II—associated elsewhere with the view that colonial peoples should be assisted towards self rule (what Tsang, 2004 calls 'the post 1946 outlook')—were in Hong Kong marked by the return of the old guard and unreconstructed attitudes. Initial plans for representative government (the Young Plan) were supported by one or two leading members of the local bar (notably Brook Bernacchi, a barrister) as well as members of the Reform Club and labour activists, but were opposed by the European and Chinese elites, and eventually stymied by the Governor, Grantham, during the early1950s (Tsang, 1988: 32).

In the 1950s, Communism became the main threat. In the 1930s, the Hong Kong government had permitted both Nationalists and Communists to base themselves in the territory (though it collaborated with the Nationalist government in China to detain and exile its communist opponents).[5] Post-war, the exodus from Maoist China brought partisans of both sides to Hong Kong, as well as leading triads. The colony's geopolitical position meant that it now became part of the 'Bamboo Curtain' and the Allies' post-war strategy against communism. Law curbed Communist and Nationalist activities but, because these laws applied equally to both, the Government earned a reputation for even-handedness whilst simultaneously employing Emergency Regulations to detain without trial and to deport 'undesirable aliens'.

---

[5] For details see LKC Chan, 1999.

These Regulations made the Hong Kong of the 1950s and 1960s a highly repressive society, an oligarchy of tycoons and property developers with no effective political or legal opposition. It was also deeply corrupt and socially divided. Bribery and 'connections' governed one's life-chances; Dickensian working conditions prevailed in factories and sweatshops; the grievances of ordinary people went unaddressed by an indifferent colonial government. The refugees of the 1950s had by the 1960s given birth to a new generation of 'born in Hong Kongers'—by 1966, half the population was under 21; 40 per cent was under 16. This youth engaged in mass rioting in 1966, producing a 'legitimacy crisis' for the government (Scott, 1989). More serious rioting in 1967 brought the Cultural Revolution to Hong Kong, as local Communist cells waged a prolonged and violent war against foreign imperialism. These were years of bombs, curfews, Maoist rallies. Armed force, tear gas and water canon were deployed against thousands of Hong Kong people. Concomitantly, however, other areas of Hong Kong society were enjoying a high tide of 'Western' liberalism—the Beatles toured the colony; girls wore Mary Quant mini-skirts, boys sported 'Teddy Boy' hairdos and generated a distinctive *ah fei* subculture. Economic liberalism was credited for Hong Kong's 'miracle' take-off and the boom in consumerism and prosperity. Social liberalism thus flourished in certain sectors of society, whilst repression characterised its laws, courts and regulations.

In the 1950s, the government's own legal advisers and law officers had argued between themselves about whether, and how, to restrain Government's use of its extraordinary powers of deportation and detention without trial. When, in 1956, Taiwan and the PRC refused to accept certain types of deportees, Emergency (Detention Orders) Regulations were introduced allowing those earmarked for deportation to be detained indefinitely without trial. Between 1953 and 1960, 32,258 were detained, and another 2,304 (mainly political prisoners) were put up for 'Confidential Banishment'. Since the system remained shrouded in secrecy, it was left to 'in-house' lawyer officials to restrain what they saw as an unreasonable exercise of state power. The Attorney General mooted ways in which 'we could get rid of the Emergency Regulations [and] limitless detention'.[6] The Chief Justice, Sir Michael Hogan, favoured a tribunal system subject to judicial oversight, with the deportee legally represented. Internal legal advisors argued that a system which detained people indefinitely and forced people to return to a country where they might be punished for their political beliefs left the UK government open to the most searching criticism by international human rights bodies.[7]

---

[6] See Hooton to Chairman, Committee of Review, 18 Jan 1960 CO/1/425/59.
[7] Memo 25, *Report of Working Party in Deportation and Detention Without Trial* 1961; HKRS 179 1/5.

By the mid-1960s, this system of deportation and detention without trial had attracted scrutiny from the International Commission of Jurists. It argued for a system in which the detainee would be brought before a magistrate within 48 hours of being detained, have the right to cross-examine witnesses and the right of appeal. In 1965, further controversy arose when the judge appointed to oversee the tribunal system, Mr. Justice Briggs, resigned in protest at the Governor's overruling of the tribunal's recommendation that six male detainees be released. The six then embarked on a hunger strike. Government lawyer-officials suddenly found themselves aligned with a small number of barristers and judges, as well as various sectors of civil society (such as the media) in opposition to the system. The UK government instructed its own lawyer-officials to examine the situation. Their enquiries raised the alarming possibility that some detainees had died whilst in detention. Reports from Hong Kong activists (such as Elsie Elliott) that corrupt policemen were using the threat of deportation and detention to silence critics also underlined the chilling effect of the system on social reformers. In LEGCO, Mr. Cheong-leen argued that Hong Kong law violated the UN Universal Declaration of Human Rights, and the Human Rights Council of Hong Kong's own Declaration of Human Rights and Fundamental Freedoms.[8] In London, Labour MP John Rankin argued that Hong Kong people lived in constant fear of being deported to China.[9] Despite these misgivings, however, the system remained unaltered.

Hong Kong's independent lawyers had remained silent throughout this debate. In the late 1960s, however, a small number of leading barristers and academics did mobilise against the government's use of Emergency Regulation 31, which enabled the government to detain people not only without trial but without reasons. In 1967, Regulation 31 was extensively deployed to detain without trial the thousands of people involved in the 'anti-imperialist' riots. It remained 'on the books' well after the rioting subsided. This prompted the first real alliance between fractions of the bar (notably Henry Litton, for the Bar Association, and Brook Bernacchi, for the Reform Club), the judiciary, legal academia (John Rear and Brian St Clair), liberal segments of civil society (*Justice*, Elsie Elliott, the media) and leftist groups whose members had been detained. Unbeknownst to them, Regulation 31 was simultaneously being hotly debated by lawyer-officials within the colonial administration. Other Regulations—against the spreading of rumours, for example, and permitting secret trials—were equally robustly attacked as inimical to justice, totalitarian, and indicative of an 'absolutist state'. The arbitrary power of detention exercised by the Hong Kong government was castigated as 'contrary to one of the cardinal

---

[8] LEGCO Annual Convention Debate, 6 and 7 Dec 1965.
[9] *Tiger Standard*, 6 Oct 1966.

rules of ... justice', and a violation of 200 years of British efforts to 'advance the legal standard of international behaviour'.[10] The Bar Association, representing some 50 barristers, voiced its misgivings in private in 1967, but in 1968 openly criticised the government. By contrast, the Law Society, representing the 200-strong solicitors' branch of the profession, distanced itself from the bar's position, some publicly 'deploring' the bar's stance and arguing that Regulation 31 was a 'political matter' in which the Law Society ought not to get involved. The legal complex was, thus, not unified in its opposition.

These intra-professional fault lines were to resurface before and after 1997 when, once again, the bar led the opposition to the government's erosion of basic freedoms and rights. By then, some of the 1960s critics had themselves become members of the judiciary. They were, perhaps, less likely than their predecessors to be captured by the state. By 1997, too, Hong Kong's legal complex included a number of 'home-grown' lawyers related to each other and to elite families. The barristers and judges who were to become what Feeley, Halliday and Karpik term '*porte parole*' (liberal spokespersons on behalf of civil society) were thus themselves fractions of the ruling elite.[11]

The spate of legal activism seen in the 1960s was soon forgotten, its decline due—paradoxically—to the wider entrenchment of liberal values by the government itself in the 1970s. The legitimacy crisis which the 1960s riots provoked was resolved (Scott, 1989), not by introducing democracy, but by engineering a sophisticated hegemonic restructuring designed to renew the government's 'right to rule'. Success in this endeavour disarmed the government's critics and thoroughly disabled the nascent legal-political mobilisations of the 1960s.

II. 1970s–1980s: 'DISSOLVING THE PEOPLE'

The 1970s (the 'Golden Years') ushered in a decade of unprecedented liberalism and colonial welfarism. The goal of the administration was to defuse conflict, renegotiate its relations with the population and depoliticise what had, in the 1960s, become a society difficult to govern. The early 1970s saw a continuation of sporadic bombings, demonstrations against the Vietnam War, student activism, and the proliferation of subversive groups (Communist and Koumingtang). Social, political and economic inequities remained intact, and thus retained their potential as triggers of discontent. A people made prosperous and content would hopefully prove less receptive to Communist calls to overthrow the state.

---

[10] *South China Morning Post*, 16 Nov 1968; *Sunday Post*, 17 Nov 1968; *Hong Kong Standard*, 18 Nov 1968, in response to Rear's attack on the government's continued use of detention without trial in a letter to *The Times*, Nov 1968.

[11] See Feeley, Halliday and Karpik, this volume.

Hong Kong's internal security forces were honoured for suppressing the riots but, in the long run, outright repression was socially costly and less reliable than a compliance willingly granted by a people convinced that the command-giver is morally entitled to expect obedience (Poggi, 1990). The exercise of state power is more secure and more effective if it 'can appeal to principles establishing such an entitlement and such an obligation' (*ibid*). The liberal ideal of rule of law thus became a central plank in the government's renegotiation of its relationship to the ruled. This simultaneously involved disrupting particularistic loyalties (to family, clan, triad) and replacing them with more universal ones, improving the lot of labour, co-opting the unions, and erasing their 'long tradition of resistance' from the history books. In an extraordinary exercise in social engineering, government 'dissolved the people'. A new unity was formed around new organisations and new values. By the end of the 1970s, Hong Kong people were citizens, enjoying formal equality and a wide range of social and economic freedoms, providing a more stable basis of social solidarity.

So extraordinary was the degree of government intervention in Hong Kong society in the 1970s that Rabushka (1973) accused the Hong Kong government of betraying its laissez faire principles. Its agenda for remaking Hong Kong society consisted of 10 principal measures:

   (i)   state intervention to improve housing, health care and other welfare;
   (ii)   the provision of extensive legal rights and channels for calling government to account, such as legal redress, legal aid, judicial review, the Ombudsman's Office, mediation, arbitration and tribunals;
   (iii)   the establishment of 'clean', fair and open administration, principally through the elimination of corruption by a new legal body, the Independent Commission Against Corruption (ICAC) with extensive legal powers;
   (iv)   the provision of multiple channels of consultation to convey grassroots grievances up to the government bureaucracy, disseminate government policy down to the grassroots, and smooth acceptance of policy at local level;
   (v)   the provision of some semblance of self-determination, principally at local level through District Board elections;
   (vi)   the intensification of neighbourhood policing as well as the secret surveillance of political activists;
   (vii)   the creation of annual mass campaigns (eg Keep Hong Kong Clean and Fight Crime) to mobilise the public in support of government policies;
   (viii)   the establishment of a rolling programme of community building designed to increase people's sense of belonging and identification with Hong Kong;

(ix) the provision of subsidised secondary education for all; and
(x) the promotion of a 'Hong Kong identity' and civic pride through local fashion, design, music, architecture and literary culture.

Hong Kong was to be remade as the finest, most modern and most advanced city in Asia, with new cultural forms as well as social (but not political) institutions. 'Home-grown' Hong Kong styles (such as 'canto pop') and fashion design were officially encouraged. The Government Information Service (GIS), established in 1971 to disseminate government propaganda, changed the word 'colony' to 'territory' and coined the phrase 'Hong Kong people'. In 1972, on their return from Singapore, Hong Kong officials copied Lee Kwan Yew's populist (almost Maoist) state-building campaigns to mobilise the community around enemies within, such as crime and disease. The Annual 'Fight Crime' and 'Keep Hong Kong Clean' campaigns ran alongside the Hong Kong Festival and the Miss Hong Kong beauty pageants. This accompanied a 'rose garden' strategy to cultivate civic pride and a sense of citizenship amongst those who in the 1960s had felt alienated, with no sense of 'belonging'. A huge increase in public spending (on civic amenities, such as playgrounds, sports centres and parks) and major infrastructure projects (new roads, tunnels, railways and hospitals) changed the very look of the city. A 10-year housing plan was announced to provide cheap public housing for all, alongside universal education, free primary—and compulsory secondary—schooling. Health care was to be free at the point of care for those whose incomes fell below a certain level. Legal aid increased exponentially—by the late 1970s, over 60 per cent of the population were eligible. Hidden subsidies supported the production of cheap rice, cheap transport and cheap car parking.

The result was a real rise in living standards for the majority of the population. Many moved from rooftop dwellings and squatter huts into public housing, where rents were subsidised. The worst excesses of the labour market were mitigated by legislation—wages were still subject to the market, but working hours, holidays and labour conditions all improved markedly. Child labour was officially banned.

The tacit consent of the population was additionally secured through a marriage of expanded public consultation (King, 1975) and law's promise of formal equality. A new law enforcement agency—the ICAC—launched a major offensive against bribery and corruption. Hong Kong was to be a 'clean' society open to talents. Social and economic inequality would continue but simply reflect 'just deserts' (Morrison, 1995). Everyone could live the 'Hong Kong Dream' of the 'bootstrap capitalists', the refugees who had arrived in Hong Kong with nothing but had risen to become millionaires.

Official publications now depicted Hong Kong as an economic (rather than a political) city, and Hong Kong people as politically apathetic, self-seekers after wealth. Both the academy and the polity talked of a 'refugee mentality', of a population willing to subsume individual rights and freedoms to the maintenance of social stability, of a Confucian culture which valorised harmony, stability, and of traditions of conflict avoidance and subservience to authority. Hong Kong people were represented to themselves in official reports as *homo economicus*, living in a 'depoliticised economic society ... separated from a bureaucratic state' (Habermas, 1987: 37). 'Utilitarian familism' was a Hong Kong 'ethos'(Lau and Kuan, 1988) which encouraged individuals to place familial interests before their own or the interests of society as a whole (*ibid*). This indifference to their rulers, along with rising prosperity, explained the passivity of the masses even as they experienced the upheavals of modernisation. It militated against political engagement, encouraged quiescence, and emphasised traditional attitudes such as benevolent, bureaucratic paternalism. Political powerlessness generated an emphasis on materialistic needs, short-termism and a preference for a socially stable (even if unjust) society. This all discouraged socially disruptive behaviour, a disinterest in the affairs of society, or in changing it. It produced minimal integration, but integration nonetheless.

Hong Kong's alleged stability was also explained in terms of the colonial government's successful 'absorption' of nascent political tensions through a plethora of consultative and administrative decision-making bodies (King, 1975: 422). These lent legitimacy, functioning as a channel for upward transmission of grassroots grievances. The key was 'synarchy', a form of 'elite consensual government ... [whereby] the British consciously or unconsciously governed the colony ... by allowing, though limiting, non-British participation in the ruling group' (*ibid*) However, without more positive steps to encourage identification with Hong Kong, there would be less stability (Lau and Kuan, 1988: 216) and if political instability were ever to erupt, it would 'spell the doom of the colony'. Hong Kong would become ungovernable (*ibid*). It was important, then, that the Hong Kong Chinese remain content—and politically apathetic.

This restructuring of the colonial state in the direction of liberalism was thus *state*-led but also state-limited. It required the suppression of interests antithetical to the state, both by coercion and by the manufacture of consent. The criminal justice system helped eradicate cronyism and *guanxi*, weakening old ties and loyalties. Established communities, often based on native place associations, were literally demolished. New organisations were created to harness the loyalty of Hong Kong 'citizens'. City District Officers (CDOs) replaced *kaifongs* as 'mothers and fathers' of the people.

History was now represented to Hong Kong people as a stable, 'peaceful past', their political apathy a product of centuries of Chinese culture. Given the seismic quality of Mainland Chinese politics,[12] this is quite extraordinary, but the erasing of politics from history meant that there was no

---

[12] Eg, the Tai-ping Rebellion, the Boxer Rebellion, the May Fourth Movement, the 1911 Republican Revolution, the 1949 Communist Revolution, the 1966–76 Cultural Revolution, and the 1989 Pro-Democracy Movement.

collective memory to counter it. Past disturbances were dismissed as 'blips' on an otherwise tranquil colonial history. The Hong Kong story was officially one of progressive unity, a city of law where order was only interrupted briefly by the antics of a few political zealots. It was a society remarkable for its social stability and prosperity, with one of the lowest rates of crime in the world, a place so successful, peaceful and harmonious that no challenge to its hegemony should be tolerated (Barzilai, 2005: 15). State law was 'conceived and generated as the rule of law' (*ibid*). Law formed an articulated elite and public consciousness as to what type of citizen was the most essential for the maintenance of the political regime to the point where the state dominated communal consciousness, identities and legal practices (Barzilai, 2005: 59; 285). Law was valid not because it was just, nor simply because it was commanded, but because it served the common interest, defined as the opportunity to prosper (Poggi, 1990: 29). Law had, indeed, replaced politics:

> The balance between, so to put it, the jurisdiction of politics and the politicization of law is an unstable one; but whatever its vicissitudes, clearly the mutual involvement of these two phenomenon, politics and law, becomes deep … and impinges significantly on the nature of both phenomenon. This is indicated among other things by the ideological charge attached to expressions such as rule of law … It is by means of law that the state articulates its own organization into organs, agencies, authorities … attributes to individuals the capacities, entitlements and obligations of citizenship … and so on … The state, thus 'speaks the law' in almost all aspects of its functioning [Poggi, 1990: 29–31].

By the end of the 1970s, Hong Kong people lacked political accountability but had gained legal accountability; in place of political redress, they had the possibility of legal redress; in place of political transparency they had legal transparency; and instead of political rights, they enjoyed basic rights and social freedoms. Undemocratic, the state was nevertheless accountable to law and open to legal challenge by any citizen (Fine, 1984: 21). Rule of law, hitherto a minority interest, became state ideology. What followed was a decade of a 'security-oriented liberalism' (Barzilai, 2005: 95) which promised Hong Kong people equal access to state organs, an enhanced voice in decision-making, the freedom and opportunity to pursue social mobility and economic success, the fair allocation of public goods, and a procedurally just administration of society by an impartial civil service. It did not offer them a democracy or a redistribution of political power, since the state itself was supposed to be administered in the interests of all, free from distortion and capable of maintaining a level playing field (Barzilai, 2005). This, in turn, would give everyone, regardless of birth or 'connections', the same life chances.

It might have been expected that, with the opening of the territory's first law school in 1969, lawyers would become more involved in the defence of these new rights. However, they concentrated instead on servicing the needs of the economy. Most ordinary Chinese still avoided the police, lawyers and courts, where the persistence of English as the official language made the system seem mostly indifferent to the lives of ordinary people. Only one magistrate (Miller) acquired a reputation as a judge who stood up for the little man against the government. Lawyers generally concerned themselves with property and the doings of Hong Kong's wealthy elite; 'law for the poor' was marginal, unpopular work.

Thus, when the Attorney General increased prosecution powers, or extended state control over freedom of assembly, sedition, public order, and criminal procedure he faced no opposition. The 'velvet glove' of social improvements thus hid an 'iron fist' only marginally more accountable than before. Special Branch kept a close watch on university students (suspected of being Maoists) and a group of middle class intellectuals (the Hong Kong Observers) who, along with bar, called for the adoption of an Ombudsman system. Counter-insurgency agents were recruited from Malaya, Vietnam, Korea and Singapore, where 'winning hearts and minds' was a standard tactic. The strength of the police force increased from fewer than 20,000 to over 30,000, as did its penetration of Hong Kong society. By the end of the 1970s, Hong Kong had the largest per capita force in the world. A small number of defence lawyers left a trace of resistance (an increase in *voire dire* hearings in criminal trials suggest an attempt to curb the predations of the police), but their weakness was reflected in their low rate of success.

At the same time, however, numerous bodies had been created to provide greater transparency, public accountability and channels of complaint—a Complaints Against Police Office was founded in 1973, and a Police Public Information Bureau in 1968. Summer Youth Camps, started in1968, mobilised youth in support of state agencies; a Police Community Relations Office was established in 1974, alongside Neighbourhood Policing Units, the Unofficial Members of Executive and Legislative Council Police Group (UMELCO), and the Mutual Aid Committees (MACs) in private housing blocks (designed not simply to listen to owners' grievances but to 'stop grey blocks turning Red').[13]

Nor were the new legal rights empty rights—the vast expansion of legal aid made it feasible to prosecute them and bring government to account. New institutions enabled people to have their grievances heard. The Administrative Tribunals (eg the Lands, Small Claims and Labour Tribunals) were established in 1973 and 1974 as Chinese language tribunals, to provide a fast, cheap and simple means of settling disputes. In 1976, a separate Court of Appeal, with its own permanent justices of appeal, was established. In the same year, an independent Judicial Services Commission was set up to advise the Governor on judicial appointments. Mediation and

---

[13] Walden J, cited in I Scott (1989).

arbitration were officially encouraged. The Labour Department promoted a new Conciliation Service to resolve labour disputes. When this failed, the trades unions increasingly took their disputes to the courts rather than the streets.

The government also embarked on a frenzy of legislative activity. In 1970 alone, LEGCO dealt with more legislation (105 new ordinances) than in the entire previous decade. The laws it passed upheld a kind of 'neo-liberal' mix of just deserts, traditional family values, conservative Chinese and patriarchal British culture. Law touched all areas of life.[14] Hong Kong had never witnessed such legislative activity. It created what Cottrell calls the universal legal subject, 'a free and equal possessor of himself', a government of fairness, the review and restraint of state power, protections for the individual, fostering consensus in what remained a patently unequal society:

> Whatever the real economic and social differences between individuals, capitalist law tends towards the idea that all are equal in its eyes. Special determinants of legal status based on property, religion, nobility, race, sex or other qualifications tend gradually to disappear ... on its face—in legal doctrine and legal ideology— capitalist law tends to treat all as equals, so disguising the structures of real inequality which it maintains ... . [Cotterrell, 1984: 124].

Procedural justice and the new provision of legal aid promised an 'equality of arms' between individuals and the state. A government which predominantly operated to benefit the powerful represented itself as an impartial referee in a game which benefited all.[15] Nevertheless, bringing the state to account was much more achievable than at any other time in Hong Kong's history.

Paradoxically, however, few legal challenges arose, partly because so few lawyers were willing to engage in 'cause-lawyering'. The judiciary, too, still remained silent on controversial state/individual issues. Dominated by expatriates, many of its members came to Hong Kong after circulating, in peripatetic fashion, around the Commonwealth. This transience meant the judiciary lacked cohesion, unity, strength and any real identification with Hong Kong society. It may have subscribed to a professional ideology of rule of law, but it appeared unable or unwilling to speak up in its defence.

But the lack of any challenge to state power was equally due to the success of the state's own liberalising project. By accommodating *some* of political liberalism's demands for social justice and law, an essentially autocratic regime was able to govern with legitimacy. The government itself, by encouraging communities to mobilise, facilitated a new type of civil society with which it felt able to engage, and some social movements did

---

[14] Eg Public Order, Chinese Customary Marriage and Concubinage, Public Health, Adoption, Children's Playgrounds, Employment, Country Parks, Gambling, Public Housing.
[15] H Collins, cited in Cotterrell (1984): 115.

arise to challenge the status quo (Butenhoff, 1999: 3). This, at last, looked a little like Habermas' 'public sphere' where something approaching public opinion could be formed. However, transformative social movements were stunted by the limited political space permitted them. The regime, always anxious about 'change from below', arrested housing workers who took the call for community building too literally by helping tenants organise anti-government protests. In 1977, when the ICAC did its job too well, the police mutinied and the government granted corrupt officers an amnesty. Grass roots pressure groups advocating political reform were also:

> carefully monitored by the Government and the Special Branch of the HK Police, and where possible their activities were discretely obstructed or frustrated, sometimes by the use of highly questionable tactics. This deliberate and active discouragement of the growth of the democratic processes by the Government continued right up to 1980 [Walden, 1983: 74].

Purporting to welcome such groups, the government quietly did 'everything it could behind the scenes to immobilise them [either by] fraternization and reasoning to win them over to the official point of view'; or by absorption; or if that did not succeed by 'damaging their credibility' (Walden, 1983: 41).

Such incidents mapped the parameters of the moderate state. Government was prepared to tolerate political participation, but only at local level and only on non-partisan matters. The government did not wish to see the emergence of popular local leaders capable of mobilising the population from below. At the same time, the success of its social engineering projects meant that it could plausibly argue that there was, in fact, no popular demand for democracy. Its CDOs 'listened to the people'. They had no real power, but they did convey public grievances up the political hierarchy, channel government policy down to the grassroots, ease the acceptance of unpopular policies, and act as antennae for signs of unrest and political agitation. As such, they were sometimes part of the legal, sometimes the 'political', complex. Since they were also JPs, they could provide simple legal services (the Hong Kong Law Society used a CDO to run its first free legal advice scheme). CDOs thus extended the reach of the colonial state but, at the same time, worked to mitigate policies detrimental to 'their' local communities. It was, indeed, crucial to the regime's hegemony that they sometimes succeeded. However, their evolution into UK-style Citizens' Advice Bureaux was never realised.

This style of governance owed much to the regime's continuing fear of the 'Red Menace', but was also driven by the belief that a developmental state needed to be a strong state, capable of driving through its policies unhampered by opposing views. Policy implementation had to be seen as procedurally fair, even-handed, and impartial (Poggi, 1990: 32; Held et al, 1984). In the liberal democratic state, this would involve citizen representation via formal electoral procedures.[16] In Hong Kong, however, the authorisation of state power flowed not from the ballot box but from the state's delivery of fair procedures, rising prosperity, and a responsive government. Legality became the *leimotif* of state/society relations. Procedural justice—the *way* things were done and goods distributed—became more important than its substantive results. If the state erred it could be challenged by judicial and administrative means.

By the 1980s, Hong Kong was a 'city of law'. Its Law Faculty was producing its first home-grown lawyers; LawTel provided a free legal hotline; the Criminal Procedure Ordinance finally granted legal aid in criminal cases to persons committed for trial in the High Court or charged in the District Court, or convicted in any court. Those rendered most unequal and disadvantaged by the economic and political systems were reassured that an independent judiciary could protect them against the arbitrary exercise of state power. It was possible to challenge the government through the courts and win (Cain and Harrington, 1994; Bankowski and Mungham, 1976; Morris, Lewis and White, 1973). Even when it lost cases (as it occasionally did) the government was obliged to accept the verdict. As in an earlier age in England:

> [The] Authorities ... chose to limit themselves in order to acquire greater effectiveness: they traded immediate power for legitimacy ... popular grievances often took the form of complaints about authority's failure to execute the letter of the law ... grievances were more likely to be expressed in terms of authority's dereliction of duty than as an explicit challenge to authority itself ... if all men were subject to the law, then those in authority were accountable for their actions—accountable both in law and to the law [Brewer and Styles, 1980: 14].

But, as the UK, these kinds of rights never really altered the fundamental form of the liberal state, though they substantially modified it (Held, 1989). Though legal rights became so synonymous with political accountability that, by the 1980s, many locals in practice saw Hong Kong as 'democratic', the composition of the colony's main decision-making bodies—LEGCO and EXCO—remained largely unchanged. None were directly elected; LEGCO still lacked the power to set or alter the government's agenda. Government chiefly comprised prominent citizens and representatives of large companies, though some of these were now Chinese. Access to power continued to be highly stratified and inegalitarian, flowing from the cultivation of relational links. The civil service, previously riddled by corruption and cronyism, acquired a reputation for professionalism and neutrality, but never fully succeeded in its shift towards universalism. Up to and beyond 1997, it retained features of patronage, paternalism and patrimonialism.

---

[16] See D Held (ed), *Prospects for Democracy* (Stanford, Cal, Stanford University Press, 1993); D Held and G Scott, *Models of Democracy* (Cambridge, Polity Press, 2006).

Entry was barred to those who had attended Communist schools and expatriates still dominated the top jobs. The prospects of officials lower down the hierarchy were tied to the fortunes of departmental heads who, in turn, cultivated their own coteries of supporters. The governing elite still shaped public policies to suit the requirement of the dominant socio-economic interests (Poggi, 1990).

Thus, though the state had successfully 'dissolved' the people and had itself become moderate (on its own initiative rather than through struggles by, or with, the legal complex) it had become only partially 'modern'. The relationship between rulers and ruled remained only slightly less paternalistic and authoritarian than before. Hong Kongers were still said to be 'children', commercially savvy but lacking the capacity to elect their own rulers. The legal complex remained as quiescent as ever, producing lawyers not for the people but for the wealthy. The mantle of liberalism, fleetingly donned by a few members of the Bar in the 1960s, now cloaked the regime itself.

III. 1983–90s: LIBERALISM IN RETREAT

In the 1980s, Hong Kong underwent a (re)politicisation triggered by Sino-British negotiations over the future of Hong Kong. The lease on the New Territories expired in 1997, prompting the question whether Hong Kong would remain a British colony. When it transpired, in 1983, that she had agreed the handover of Hong Kong without consulting Hong Kong people, the British Prime Minister, Margaret Thatcher, was decried for 'selling Hong Kong down the river'. In 1984, the Joint Sino-British Declaration, setting out the terms and process of the 1997 retrocession, was presented to the Hong Kong people as a *fait accompli*. Riots during this period (in 1981 and 1984) were blamed on anti-Westernism and avaricious taxi drivers, but they also reflected a more generalised anxiety about life after 1997. The possibility that Hong Kong would become 'ungovernable' between 1984 and 1997 now surfaced in official and academic circles.

In 1980, the administration published a Green Paper, 'A Pattern of District Administration in Hong Kong,' mooting the possibility of limited, gradual reform of LEGCO and EXCO to increase popular participation in government. It followed this in 1984 with a Green Paper, 'The Further Development of Representative Government in Hong Kong' which suggested increasing popular representation at the lower, local level of government (the District and Urban Councils) and making the 'central institutions of government' more representative and accountable. This 'set off a chain of events which led to the emergence of a movement to promote greater reform' (Tang, 1995: 94). At the time, only a small group of activists was interested in political development but, subsequently, the

1980s became 'marked by debates, sometimes heated, over the pace and direction of political reform in Hong Kong' *(ibid)*. Political parties began to emerge; new leaders arose, amongst them Martin Lee, a barrister, who later assumed the leadership of the Democratic Party. The Liberal Party formed around a loose coalition of business interests, professionals, lawyers and academics. The system of functional constituencies, introduced in the 1980s, meant that neither could hope to become the 'official opposition' to the government; even alliances between various groupings could not defeat the government's in-built majority in LEGCO. At the same time, however, the government made public funding available to political parties enabling them to draw up proposals and present their manifesto to the public in more organised fashion.

According to a senior civil servant of the time, these moves were designed to persuade the UK Parliament that it was not 'handing 6 million people to the direct control of a Communist state' (Walden, 1983: 76). They would 'make the community feel a greater sense of identity with its government' without producing any real accountability (Walden, 1983: 40). The 1984 White Paper was intended to give 'the impression that Hong Kong was being put on the democratic road, with the consent of the Chinese government ... the British [were] ditching the Hong Kong people with dignity. And it worked' *(ibid)*.

Although Hong Kong had a 'gigantic consultative system for feeding back to the Government the views of the citizens' *(ibid)* there was still no way of checking whether these grievances were accepted or rejected. The reasoning behind government decision-making remained opaque. Nor was there any way of ensuring that the civil service did not 'become a law unto itself' *(ibid)*. Indeed, Walden argues that it was top civil servants who blocked democracy:

> Without democracy ... top civil servants had the freedom to respond quickly to situations where urgent government action was needed; businessmen and the industrious public could get on with doing what they were best at, working hard, making money and pocketing most of it, and Hong Kong's export-oriented economy was not lumbered by an inflexible cost-price structure supported by politically organised labour [Walden, 1983: 75].

Later events justified Walden's cynicism. When, after 1984, China called for the abandonment of the constitutional reform proposals, Britain capitulated. Subsequently, the New China News Agency (NCNA, China's unofficial embassy in Hong Kong) established 'its own embryonic organisations to determine the structure of and control the future government of the HKSAR' (Walden, 1983: 87). There would be no self-government. Instead, Hong Kong would get a slightly modified version of what it already had. This would be supported by 'captains of commerce, industry and finance [who made] no bones of the fact that they consider the development of democratic politics in Hong Kong a greater threat to HK's prosperity and stability than its takeover by Communist China' (*ibid*).

Amongst the elites, then, anti-democratic attitudes were still deeply entrenched and democracy still seen as 'the quickest way to ruin Hong Kong's economy and create social and political instability ...' (*ibid*). However, the emergence of high-calibre activists (many of them lawyers) in the late 1980s raised the possibility that Hong Kong might, after all, form something like a 'loyal opposition' (*ibid*).

Within the administration, a few civil servants (who, Walden says, were regarded as disloyal or even dangerous) continued the push for self-government. But those who now shaped Hong Kong's future still saw 'Hong Kong Man' as incapable of, and uninterested in, self-rule. He was 'motivated by a desire to gain pleasure or happiness by acquiring and consuming wealth', a 'utility maximiser' bent upon material acquisition (Heywood, 1992: 26). He would be content if he could continue to work long hours, eat well, shop, gamble at Happy Valley, and bet on the Mark Six lottery. Hong Kongers were 'rootless opportunists', 'short term residents with expensive tastes' (Turner, 1996: 7), consumers of a 'lifestyle' rather than citizens with a culture, history and rights. The Basic Law (BL), which became Hong Kong's 'mini-constitution' after 1997, embodied this view of the people. Its Hong Kong was not a polity but a 'lifestyle'. It envisaged a 'non-political system of administration' within which Hong Kong people could pursue their economic, personal and family advancement beneath a benign authoritarian regime which would continue to provide them with the prosperity, security and the freedom to consume what goods and services they chose, pursue their own interests and make what they wanted of their own lives (Heywood, 1992: 40).

This was the vision, not of Hong Kongers as they were, but of how the BL drafters wished them to be. Ironically, the very process of drafting the law itself aroused competing visions of the HKSAR. The Basic Law Drafting Committee (BLDC) was viewed with suspicion, its built-in pro-China lobby being strengthened by the very public resignation of two local leaders. There were also widespread misgivings about 'the PRC leadership's real understanding of, and official stance on, such fundamental principles as constitutionality, jurisprudence, administrative control, elections, autonomy, public accountability, human rights and, above all, representative democracy' (Chan and Postiglione, 1996: 11). Deng Xiaoping's famously vague 'One Country, Two Systems' depiction of the relationship between Hong Kong and China after 1997 left the major differences between them unaddressed. Anxious for greater clarity, liberal members of the elite, as well as lawyers and grassroots activists, pressed for greater detail. From the mid-1980s onwards, they began to mobilise around a handful of leaders, including leading lawyers such as Martin Lee, Allen Lee, Simon Ip, Margaret Ng, the 'Ombudsman', Mr A de Sales, activists such as Szeto Wah, and members of the Hong Kong Observers, such as Christine Loh.

It was not until the 1990s that legal academia entered the fray. Hong Kong lawyers were either too politically apathetic, too materialistic, too indifferent, or too afraid of China to take on politically sensitive issues and cases (Li, 1994: 89). Echoing their stance on Regulation 31, the solicitors' branch (represented by the Law Society) argued that Martin Lee tarnished the reputation of the profession by politicising it (Li, 1994: 92). This attitude reflected the leadership of the profession, which many saw as weak, tending to represent 'certain sectoral interests only', excluding 'progressive' views, and failing to serve the community's needs.[17]

The majority of solicitors were locally-born Chinese with families less able to flee Hong Kong than their expatriate colleagues, should a 'sensitive' issue have negative repercussions. The bar, however, included not only a greater percentage of expatriates but also many overseas-educated Chinese, often graduates of prestigious UK universities where they had been exposed both to the values of a liberal education and the 'noblesse oblige' ethos of the UK bar. The 'cab rank' rule by which barristers are allocated cases also determined that unpopular clients and sensitive cases could not be turned away. Some members of the bar, clearly imbued with the sense of duty derived from these values, felt obliged to offer their services in cases where injustice threatened to flow from lack of proper representation or inequality of arms.

This difference between the bar and the solicitors helps explain why only part of the legal complex ever mobilised around political issues. Amongst solicitors, the law was widely regarded as a means to an end, not an end in itself. Mostly, they remained indifferent to the unmet legal needs of ordinary citizens and concentrated on elite legal problems. An immense social distance existed between the masses and this, the vast majority of the legal profession. Moreover, locals remained under-represented within the legal complex itself. Localisation, supposedly accelerated in the run-up to 1997, had in fact come to a standstill. Majorie Chui, the first Chinese female magistrate in Hong Kong, noted that instead of grooming locals in time for the return of Hong Kong to China, there was a rapid increase in the employment and promotion of expatriates, to the point where they held over 90 per cent of the higher judicial postings (Chui, 1999: 18). The Chief Justice stated publicly that maintaining a substantial expatriate element in the judiciary was essential to the preservation of confidence in Hong Kong's system (Chui, 1999: 22). Other 'unhealthy developments' included the extension of the Chief Justice's retirement age, as well as that of his High Court judges

---

[17] In 2002, barrister Margaret Ng called on the government to replicate Hazel Genn's 1999 UK study of unmet legal need (*Paths to Justice*) in Hong Kong.

and Supreme Court Registrars, thwarting the promotion of local candidates (Chui, 1999:19). Patronage of expatriates was pervasive:

> It was not difficult to see that those who had a particular connection with or friendship with important people rose quickly up the judicial ladder ... connections mattered more than personal integrity ... The judiciary was plagued by a whole catalogue of scandals in the 1980s involving High Court judges, District Court judges, magistrates, coroners, and Supreme Court registrars. Some, including several high Court judges, had to resign amid the scandals. Fresh scandals continued to plague the judiciary right up to the handover of the colony to China in 1997 [Chui, 1999: 24–5].

At one point, expatriates were promoted to fill all five senior judicial vacancies (what Chui calls 'Five devils knocking on the door'). Another nine expatriates were promoted to fill other judicial vacancies ('Nine big devils having a feast') (Chui, 1999: 21). As Chui notes:

> the clearest indictment of the appointments in this period is the fact that at the handover 13 years after the signing of the Sino-British Joint Declaration, the judiciary was still dominated by expatriates. Even now, after the resumption of Chinese sovereignty, the judiciary still suffers from a shortage of experienced locals, particularly for the higher bench. Hence even now, expatriates still dominate the High Court and the Court of Appeal, which is why the vast majority of cases in these courts are still conducted in English [Chui, 1999: 20].

Chui rapidly shed her 'naïve belief that I would be expected to administer justice fairly and independently at all times, without fear or favour' (Chui, 1999: 3). Magistrates were appointed on contract terms. When several were not re-appointed, the rumour within legal circles was that they had delivered judgments unfavourable to the administration (*ibid*).

A blurring of roles also undercut the separation of powers—when Sir Denys Roberts was appointed Chief Justice in 1979, he had just retired as Chief Secretary, the head of the colonial civil service. Second in command after the Governor, he had acted as Governor from time to time and served as Attorney General. He had, therefore:

> been a key official behind many of the government's policies. For that reason, his move to the judiciary aroused much controversy, as it was seen to blunt the separation of power between the judiciary and the Executive branch of government. In particular, there was concern over Sir Denys' previous posting as AG, in effect the head of the Crown's prosecution service, and the effect that might have on his policies as head of the judiciary. It was amidst these fears over the continued independence of the judiciary that Sir Denys became Chief Justice [Chui, 1999: 16].

Roberts' term of office was characterised by complacency. When he retired in 1988, he commented that 'I received the judiciary in good health in 1979 and I leave it in 1988 with virtually nothing achieved, save that to my credit

I leave two tennis courts fully restored'.[18] His power to appoint the Registrar of the Supreme Court gave him great influence over the administrative controller of the judiciary's finances and resources. The body which served as the government watchdog on staff expenditure in the judiciary (the Departmental Establishment Committee) was disbanded, making the Registrar and his administrative deputy 'the two most powerful persons in the judiciary ... so powerful that the locals in the judiciary referred to them as "the eunuchs," comparing them to the palace officials of imperial China, while more Westernised members of the legal profession referred to the Registrar's Chambers as "the Fuhrerbunker"' (Chui, 1999: 18–19).

The Judicial List was also withdrawn from publication on the ground that publishing it as part of the Government Staff List might be construed as indicating a lack of independence from government. As Chui says, 'one wonders how its removal could enhance judicial independence in the eyes of the public, while judicial officers remained on the civil service payroll, were housed in government quarters with civil servants, and were subject to the same Civil Service Regulations and Conditions of Service as civil servants' (Chui, 1999: 17). The Movement Order, informing judicial officers of new appointments, promotions, and postings, also ceased to be circulated and 'all information about appointment, promotion, transfer and seniority of judges and magistrates was removed from the scrutiny of members of the public as well as judicial officers' (*ibid*).

Public confidence in the legal system was also damaged by scandals within what should have been a bastion of official propriety, the Attorney General's Chambers (Legal Department). At one point, four senior Crown Counsel (Reid, Egan, Chandler, Harris) were all questioned by the police on criminal matters. A culture of 'Ozzie mateship' was said to obtain in the Department and '[t]he conviction and imprisonment of a top crown counsel and Acting Director of Public Prosecutions on corruption charges revealed that even in these times of progress in democracy and public accountability, justice in the colony could still be bought and sold' (Chui, 199: 27).

One of these senior counsel was tried for attempting to procure an under-age girl for sex and rape. His close friendship with the Chief Justice was well-known; his marriage was 'performed by the Chief Justice by special license at the Chief Justice's official residence only a short time before his arrest' (*ibid*). Such lapses of judgement had provoked muted public criticism in the old days, but social attitudes had changed, and greater probity in public administration was demanded. Thus when, in the mid-1990s, the first Chinese Chief Justice (Sir Ti Liang Yang) used his official residence as his campaign headquarters during his bid to become the first Chief Executive of the HKSAR, his transgression drew stinging criticism. Laxity in the Legal

---

[18] Cited in *South China Morning Post*, 6 May 1995.

Department was also brought to an end by the appointment of a new head from the UK's Serious Fraud Office. The Coroner, accused of sub-letting his government apartment to his girlfriend, was forced to resign. The Legal Department was described as a 'shambles' and the Attorney General, Jeremy Matthews, as the 'classic bureaucrat ... the kind of guy who would pick up a spelling error rather than punch through an obstacle when a major issue confronts him'.[19] He remained in post partly because '[i]f the Attorney General had to resign every time there was a major problem, we would go through two a year'.[20] The BL's requirement that such senior law officers should be Chinese meant that Matthews had to be replaced in 1996, but no-one locally wished to take up the post.[21] Delays in localisation meant that there were also to be problems replacing the Director of Public Prosecutions (Peter Nguyen) and the Solicitor General (Daniel Fung). Amongst the names thrown into the ring were those of liberal members of the bar, but none were appointed.

Though little is known of how the Chinese members of the legal complex viewed the system at the time, Chui argues that the main problem was the lack of an effective watchdog, giving the government 'power without accountability':

> Politics at times took control over the law. There were wrongful and unfair prosecutions. There was detention without trial. People who should not be in prison were, while people who should be in prison were not. That such things happened could not remain a secret, but those in a position to correct the injustice merely closed ranks and minds [Chui, 1999: 27].

Given this dismal account, why did the rule of law assume such potency for Hong Kong people in the 1990s? Part of the explanation lies with China's 'ten years of turmoil' (the Cultural Revolution) and the quashing of the Chinese pro-democracy movement on 4 June 1989 (the 'Tiananmen Square Massacre'). Both provided Hong Kong people with examples of the unrestrained, capricious and arbitrary exercise of power. However unworthy the British were otherwise, it was acknowledged that Hong Kong had the rule of law. When, in 1989, the tanks of the PLA turned against China's proletariat, the contrast between Beijing and Hong Kong, 'city of law', was compelling. Over a million Hong Kong people marched in support of the 4 June protesters. The orderly and peaceful nature of the demonstrations reflected well on the local police and reinforced the administration's reputation as a respecter of basic rights and freedoms.

---

[19] Legal Department lawyer quoted in *South China Morning Post*, 6 May 1994.
[20] *Ibid.*
[21] Simon Ip Sik-on, solicitor and Chair of LEGCO's legal services panel, *South China Morning Post*, 6 May 1994.

4 June 1989 produced one of the most significant changes in Hong Kong's legal system, a Bill of Rights (BOR). The Government hoped that this would reassure people that their rights would survive the 1997 handover to China and halt the flight of capital. Until it was enacted in 1991, human rights had always taken 'second place to laws made by the colonial government' (*ibid*). The legal landscape now changed quite dramatically. The number of laws which had to be amended to accord with the BOR was so extensive that government departments needed a 'freeze' period to revise all the legislation. Thereafter, the BOR became a highly effective restraint on the exercise of state power. A free press, the appointment of an independent Ombudsman, the presence of a few committed lawyers willing to act *pro bono*, and a small band of high calibre judges, all played their part. Real power still lay with senior civil servants, but they became much more aware of the 'judges on their shoulder'.

Throughout the 1990s, BOR litigation proved especially effective in criminal and immigration cases, where state/individual relations were pivotal. A small coterie of academic and professional lawyers began to help litigants challenge these departments. As a result, the government, wholly unused to such well-informed opposition, received some nasty shocks. Certain litigants (such as the 111 Vietnamese Boat People who, in 1990, challenged the lawfulness of their detention[22]) were not especially popular in Hong Kong, but their spectacular wins against the government in the courts attracted immense publicity and left a lasting impression that the rule of law could force the government to change its ways. In the *Pham Van Ngo* case, the judiciary, in the form of Sears J, was finally seen to call government to account. Sears criticised the Immigration Service for detaining the 111 Vietnamese Boat People fleeing Vietnam for Japan,[23] describing the fact that they had been deprived of their liberty for 18 months (on the basis of a telephone call) as 'an affront to the rule of law':

> The power to detain must be for a reasonable period of time; what that should be depends on the particular facts, on which as I have said earlier, I was being kept in the dark ... The Evidence of Mr. Asprey [Secretary for Security] does not justify the conduct of the Government in depriving these persons of their liberty for such a long period of time ... there was a clear and unequivocal promise by the Government that they would repair the boat, and the person were 'free to leave Hong Kong'; instead, the boat was destroyed and the persons found themselves in a detention centre. Any right minded democratic society should be appalled at

[22] *Re Pham Van Ngo* [1991] 1 HKLR 499; see also *Thang Thiueu Quyen and others* CFA No 2 of 1998 (Civil); *Long Quoc Tuong and 111 others* CFA Civil Appeal No 200/97, 23 July 1998.

[23] The migrants were detained when their boat broke down in Hong Kong waters. They were promised repairs to the boat before being allowed to proceed to Japan. The boat was in fact destroyed and they were detained in a detention camp.

these events ... Fortunately, the law ... recognises that Governments cannot behave in this matter ... The Government, in my judgment, must have thought that ... it was far cheaper and easier just to lock these people up, rather than help them ... I am in no doubt that the standard of the Government's conduct fell woefully short of what would be expected in a civilised community ... These 111 ... have been treated as if they were an unwelcome nuisance rather than as human beings ... not one word of apology has ever been offered to [them] ... I must restrict myself to moderate language. Being as fair as I can to the Government ... they should be ashamed at the way they have treated these 111 persons.

Asprey's suggestion that, whatever happened in court, the 111 would be sent back to Vietnam appeared to Sears to be a direct challenge by the executive to the judiciary. This was:

not only independent of the Government, it is strong enough to resist any attempt that the rule of law should be weakened because a judge's order causes embarrassment, or inconvenience, or extra financial burden on the Government. I find it disconcerting to be told by a high official that if I grant this order, these 111 persons, who have been so shamefully treated, will be deported to Vietnam ... perhaps on more mature reflection, Mr. Asprey and the other high Government officials, might like to reconsider this statement ... I trust that the high officials of the Hong Kong Government would not wish to give the general public the impression that an order of a High Court judge can be brushed aside lightly, because if they do, they tarnish and weaken the rule of law. At this time in Hong Kong's history, it is of vital importance that the rule of law not only prevails but is seen to be supported by the Government.

The BOR and the Basic Law now gave constitutional and public interest law a significance which few members of the legal complex were competent to address. However, in 1989, the University of Hong Kong (HKU) appointed a leading constitutional lawyer, Yash Ghai, to a new Chair in the Law Faculty. During the transition years, he was to play a crucial role, criticising the dominance of the executive, the weakness of the legislature, and emphasising the role of the judiciary in articulating the rights and freedoms under Hong Kong's new constitutional order. Ghai's expertise and international standing gave him symbolic authority. This meant that, however irritated members of the bench, bar and government became, his arguments were difficult to dismiss. Somewhat fortuitously, his appointment coincided with that of other academics, from jurisdictions where human rights and public interest lawyering were well-developed. Some had links to networks of academics and non-governmental organisations (NGOs) around the Commonwealth and in the UK; others were able to tap into US and UN human rights organisations. As members of the territory's elite university, they also had access to the legal elite—many members of the bar either were fellow alumni of Oxbridge and Ivy League universities, or had trained at familiar London-based Chambers. Such contacts provided useful resources upon which they could draw in their mobilisations around local issues.[24]

By the mid-1990s, the Faculty of Law at HKU could reinvent itself as a public law faculty. Its students, exposed to a much more 'public interest' syllabus than hitherto, also saw some of their high status professors engage with low prestige groups and law firms to fight 'rights-type cases' for no remuneration, activities which suggested an alternative value-system to that which dominated the profession generally.

Never a unified group, these academics nevertheless contributed to the formation of a critical mass in the liberal legal complex. They proved a force for change, especially since the government itself lacked their expertise—indeed, it temporarily 'borrowed' some of these scholars from academia on short-term contracts, in an effort to remedy its own deficiencies. This not only provided the legal academics with a powerful entrée into Government policy-making, it also established an elite social network across which alliances could be formed between lawyer-officials and like-minded lawyers on the 'outside'. A small number of Chinese scholars already in academia also enjoyed closer connections with local grass-roots organisations. Thus, at both the top and bottom ends of the social scale, academics were able to give 'rights lawyering' wider social credibility, their personal networks linking them to both elite and non-elite groups.

Their influence did not, however, spread throughout the entire legal complex. Mobilisation was limited by two countervailing forces. First, the majority of solicitors favoured the status quo. Secondly, an emerging group of Mainland Chinese scholars had, since the mid-1980s, found appointments in local law schools. Sometimes referred to as the 'forward party' (preparing for the 1997 handover), their connections to PRC bodies in Hong Kong[25] made them influential members of the PRC's politico-legal complex.

One of the key 'battles' around which members of this reconfigured legal complex mobilised in the early 1990s was the establishment and composition of the Court of Final Appeal (CFA) which would replace the Privy Council as Hong Kong's highest court after 1997. The CFA was regarded as the acid test of whether the rule of law would survive the handover. The number of foreign judges allowed to sit on the CFA was regarded as crucial to Hong Kong's continued membership of the 'common law world', whilst interpreting Hong Kong's new constitutional position required experienced, independent judges of the highest calibre. In 1991, the Joint Liaison Group agreed that a CFA should be established before 1997; the number

---

[24] Eg 5 expatriate female law professors helped local groups lobby the UN to end discrimination against women in land inheritance matters.

[25] Such bodies include Xinhua, Provisional LEGCO, the BLDC and its successor the Basic Law Committee, as well as leading Mainland jurists.

of overseas judges would be restricted to one in every sitting, the other four members of the bench being local judges. However, between 1992 and 1997, the CFA fell victim to conflicts between the Hong Kong Governor, Chris Patten, and the Chinese leadership, following Patten's 1992 proposals to widen the electorate. The Chinese side in the Sino-British negotiating team accused the UK of trying to 'set up a British designed CFA' to prolong its influence in Hong Kong after the handover. An alternative CFA, based on a Chinese model, was mooted.[26] Members of Hong Kong's liberal legal complex, along with journalists and political groups, thought that China was taking 'sinister measures to jeopardise the power and authority of the CFA by putting it under a higher authority in Beijing', scuttling the territory's judicial autonomy.[27] Two years before the handover, the issue remained unresolved, raising the prospect that post-1997 Hong Kong would face a 'judicial vacuum'. The Chinese side argued that there were no guaranteed places for British-appointed judges after the transfer of sovereignty—it would be up to the post-1997 administration to decide whether they retained their places on the CFA.[28]

The government attempted to introduce its own CFA bill to LEGCO but, whilst the Law Society supported it, the bar opposed it, arguing that there was no assurance that Beijing would allow those appointed to the CFA to continue as judges after 1997.[29] Some cynical civil servants maintained that 'the whole CFA talks were merely a political show. Everyone knows the result (no CFA before 1997) though the show has to go on'.[30]

Few, however, were prepared to express such opinions publicly—as 1997 drew closer, critics became more muted and self-censorship more widespread. Leading lawyers and political activists had already been declared 'subversives' and 'criminals' by the Mainland authorities. Though a few at the Bar continued to speak out in fearless fashion, liberalism was generally on the retreat.

The CFA was eventually established after the handover. Ironically, in its eagerness to demonstrate the international standing of the court, the administration appointed some of the Common Law world's most prestigious, but also activist, constitutional lawyers to its bench. Together with their local counterparts, they were later to prove a thorn in its side.

Hong Kong's out-going Governor (Chris Patten) also left a thorny legacy for the post-1997 administration. His popular standing owed much to his championing of grassroots interests against the alliance of Hong Kong's business elite and the Mainland government. Making the rule of law the

---

[26] *South China Morning Post*, 3 June 1995.
[27] Chris Yeung, *South China Morning Post*, 6 May 1994.
[28] *Ibid.*
[29] *South China Morning Post*, 11 Dec 1994.
[30] See Chris Yeung, *South China Morning Post*, 6 May 1994.

leading trope of his Governorship, he impressed upon the population its centrality to Hong Kong's liberal 'way of life'. Hong Kong was:

> A success story almost without parallel. A community with a pretty good government ... Low crime. Excellent police. Competitive businesses. The rule of law. It's argumentative and free. Open and responsible. Moderate and fair.
>
> The bedrock, the bedrock of your way of life is the rule of law that guarantees fair and equitable treatment for everyone. It governs all your dealings, personal and financial. You have an independent judiciary in which every individual can have confidence. Because no one is above the law. No politician, no business leader, no Governor. Because no one is above the law, the law serves everyone [Chris Patten, cited in Flowerdew, 1998].

Under Patten's regime, rule of law came into its full ideological glory. Opinion polls rated it the most important aspect of life in Hong Kong. By 1 July 1997, it had become the ruling idea of the time. Television stations broadcast *Judge Pao* on two of Hong Kong's four channels at peak times, reflecting public demand for the judge who administered justice without fear or favour. The public was on high alert for any attack on law, courts and lawyers. When, on the eve of the handover, a PRC General insisted on crossing the border without the requisite papers, aggrieved Immigration officers complained to a radio talk-in programme that the law was not being applied equally to everyone. Such incidents were seized on as signs that China's arrival was already undermining Hong Kong's 'bedrock'. Law students emblazoned the phrase 'no-one is so high as to be above the law' on their jackets. The rumour that China was to going remove the word 'Independent' from the title of the ICAC aroused fears that, post-1997, Mainland-style corruption would contaminate Hong Kong.

At midnight on 30 June 1997, when Hong Kong ceased to be a British colony, Martin Lee addressed a crowd from the balcony of LEGCO, before leading a symbolic exit of the Democratic Party from the building. The legality of the new Provisional LEGCO was tested in the courts,[31] where the Court of Appeal was accused by human rights groups of abdicating its role as guardian of law and liberty. Fresh elections in 1998 finally ushered in an elected body. New electoral rules, however, marginalised the democrats and hampered the development of a single majority party.[32] The new administration also progressively dismantled the 1970s channels

---

[31] See *HKSAR v David Ma and Others* [1997] HKLRD 761. The Basic Law held that the post-1997 LEGCO should be an elected body but Provisional LEGCO was an unelected body appointed by the PRC. At its pre-1997 meetings (in the PRC), it repealed labour protection and human rights laws, altered the electoral rules (disenfranchising almost 1 million people) and changed the Public Order Ordinance.

[32] Although the democrats captured the same two-thirds of the popular vote in the 1998 elections as in 1995, post-1997 arrangements meant they were entitled to only one-third of LEGCO seats.

of consultation, closing down routes whereby local political leaders could emerge, reintroducing old-style colonial practices, and generally recreating a strong centralised executive (Chan, 2002: 8).

The new regime quickly polarised the population. It harmed political pluralism and compromised social harmony (Chan and So, 2002). It responded poorly to a series of crises, including the 1997 Asian Financial Crisis, the avian flu emergency, the 1998 opening of the new airport, a corruption scandal which exposed the unsafe construction of public housing estates, the SARS epidemic, a drop in property values, and 'other glaring cases of serious misdeeds by government personnel, agencies and public bodies' (Chan, 2002: 4). The 1970s settlement had promised competent (if unrepresentative) government which would govern in the interests of all. The 'sheer incompetence of the post-1997 leadership and civil service' (*ibid*) and the re-emergence of patronage demonstrated the limits of this settlement.

Hong Kong's Chief Executive (Tung Chee-hwa) blamed this series of fiascos on the old-style colonial civil service inherited from the British. A new structure was introduced, making civil servants more accountable to the public for their policies. However, Tung selected 'personally loyal and politically "patriotic" talents from the private sector to fill two of the top three portfolios' (Chan, 2002: 9). Appointments were made on the basis, not of 'professional expertise, public service experience, administrative skills, political wisdom or developmental visions,' but of personal loyalty and ideological compatibility (*ibid*) strengthening Tung's direct command over the entire political machinery. His administration lost legitimacy precisely because '[a] disproportionately large number of government appointments' were given to tycoons and big business elites (Chan, 2002: 15). The Grand Bauhinia Medal—the highest official honour awarded by HKSAR government—was also awarded to a former head of the pro-Beijing Federation of Hong Kong Trade Unions, a well-known leader of the 1967 riots in Hong Kong (*ibid*) reopening 'the far from fully healed old wounds and pained memories of the 1967 leftist rampant violence' (Chan, 2002: 16). Chan argues that:

> Such very deliberate and obviously partisan criteria—patriotic and big business— monopolization of the communal or sectoral representation and interest articulation channels, as well as public affairs participation mechanisms under the Tung regime, can only further intensify the already worsening under-currents of political tensions and the sharpening social class schism. Is the very worst kind of the politics of exclusion and divisiveness [Chan, 2002: 10–11].

Post-1997, unemployment and the Gini Coeffcient reached record levels. The havoc caused by the attack on Hong Kong's currency in 1999 was staunched only when the Financial Secretary, abandoning the mantra of laissez faire, intervened to protect the economy.

This all added up to a 'depressing combination' of loss of confidence in the administration, deteriorating social cohesion, a widening of the gap between rich and poor, sharper class divisions, a frail and fragmented social fabric, threatened livelihood, economic insecurity, and the constant threat of mainland authoritarianism and political culture coming to Hong Kong (*ibid*). The government responded by trying to reinvent Hong Kong as a 'world city' of high-tech industries, information networks, knowledge-based, high value-added economy, an economic superhub with a Disney theme park and a Cyberport (*ibid*). But none of these grand projects addressed the 'livelihood demands and dire poverty of the deprived grass-roots and alienated middle class' (*ibid*). Neither did they meet any of the popular demands for social justice. Instead, they boosted the fortunes of local property tycoons and provided what Chan describes as an ineffectual response to Hong Kong's declining economic fortunes.

Tung's preferencing of big business reawakened memories of the 1960s. Allegations of special treatment for the oligarchs undermined public faith in the fairness of institutions and officials. Revelations emerged about the administration's failure properly to scrutinise and regulate developments by leading tycoons (such as the Discovery Bay and LINK-REIT schemes).[33] According to Chan, Tung's 'grand capitalist origins' inclined him towards policies which saved the economy 'for the big businesses not for the victims of the market, the unemployed, those afflicted by wage freeze, salary reduction, and negative equity' (Chan, 2002: 6).

The legal profession and the judiciary—so pivotal to moderating the state—were also thought to be coming under political pressure. A series of questionable decisions by the Legal Department prompted accusations that tycoons were above the law.[34] The Financial Secretary, accused of dishonesty for buying a luxury car just before he raised the vehicle registration tax, was controversially allowed to keep his position (Cheng, 2005: 9). The 'Big Spender' case raised grave doubts about the Legal Department's willingness to withstand executive pressure to return suspects to China.[35] Most

---

[33] Discovery Bay, a luxury housing complex, appears to have escaped planning laws governing housing by being developed as a holiday resort. On the Linkreit case see, eg, *South China Morning Post*, 19 Apr 2005.

[34] The prosecution of media tycoon, Sally Aw Sian, was said not to be in the 'public interest' because it might endanger her business and lead to unemployment. Locally, it was taken to indicate that powerful people were exempt from the law. The Secretary for Justice's poor explanation for her decision led to a motion of no confidence, led by Margaret Ng, legal sector representative. When, during the debate, Liberal Party chairman, Ronald Arculli (a solicitor) left LEGCO in tears, colleagues said he was 'crying for the rule of law': see *South China Morning Post*, 23 Mar 1999.

[35] 'Big Spender' Cheung Tze-keung and his associates were tried under Mainland law and executed in Guangdong for crimes committed in Hong Kong, including the kidnap of the son of a Hong Kong tycoon known to have strong links to the PRC leadership. In this and the

damaging of all, the government asked the National People's Congress (NPC) to intervene in CFA judgments which went against it. Repeated recourse to the NPC in this fashion prompted foreign commentators to observe that the rule of law in Hong Kong was dead. The new regime, 'in its search for administrative expedience or political correctness ... seriously undermined judicial independence and the rule of law' (Chan, 2002: 7).

In the first of these cases, the *Ng Ka ling*[36] case, the right of abode for Hong Kong residents' children born in Mainland China was the issue. When the CFA decided in favour of the children and against the government on 29 January 1999, the decision was hailed as a victory for the rule of law, proof that the post-1997 courts remained independent. However, the government (supported by Mainland jurists) asked the NPC to reinterpret Articles 22 and 24 of the Basic Law to invalidate the CFA's decision. The government argued that allowing the children into the territory would over-stretch public services and be detrimental to society. Others saw the administration's invitation to the NPC as tantamount to:

> opening the front gate to invite Beijing's direct judicial interference in order to save the SAR executive arm from certain defeat on purely legal grounds in vital matters of great consequence.' [The regime] looked to Beijing to save it from the unwelcome practical consequences of due legal process as administered by the SAR's supposedly independent judiciary system or in an anticipatory attempt with political correctness to seek Beijing's approval on controversial matters ... (this would) ... erode the independence of the judiciary and hamper the fair administration of justice for all, which are the key pillars supporting Hong Kong's rule of law to guarantee basic freedoms and economic air play [Chan, 2002: 7].

Beijing's influence was also thought to lie behind Tung's public condemnation in LEGCO of the Falun Gong. His depiction of the group (as 'definitely a devious cult', and 'an evil cult') were so strange to Hong Kong ears that they were taken to prove that he had been 'looking North' (ie to Beijing). His calls to ban it were greeted as lacking legal justifications regarding 'the probable unlawfulness in the Falun Gong's activities according to HKSAR law' (*ibid*). The Falun Gong, outlawed in Mainland China in 1999, remained lawful in Hong Kong. Further government attempts to clamp down on the group in 2002 eventually provoked a legal challenge in 2005, when the CFA quashed the convictions of eight protesters on charges of

'Telford Gardens' murder case, there was much local speculation about what considerations influenced the Secretary for Justice's failure to request the return of the suspects for trial in Hong Kong.

[36] *Ng Ka ling and another v Director of Immigration* (1999) 2HKCFAR 4; *Cheung Lai Wah and others v Director of Immigration*, Court of Appeal, Civil Appeal 203 of 1997, CACV216/1997.

wilfully obstructing and assaulting the police.[37] This decision was taken to uphold the right to protest and sent a message to the police that they could not arbitrarily remove this right.[38]

The case was one of several in which the CFA judge gained a reputation for being unafraid to render decisions against Hong Kong's powerful. In May 2005, they allowed an elderly woman to seek judicial review to block a Housing Authority plan to sell off public housing, car parks and shopping malls.[39] That the planned real estate investment trust (described as the world's largest property trust listing) was brought to a halt by one tenacious old lady was seen in the local press as an ignominious retreat by one of Hong Kong's most powerful institutions. Her legal advisers belonged to a small coterie of lawyers with a reputation for *pro bono* work and defending the 'little person' against the might of government.[40] The government, it was alleged, tried to pressure the courts to put aside established legal procedure to rush the case through. The courts responded by stressing the importance of due process rights and 'the right of the rich and poor alike to have equal access to the courts.'[41] Another 84-year-old female 'squatter' won her claim against Henderson Land, one of Hong Kong's largest property developers, when the CFA ruled in favour of her title to a New Territories plot. Hong Kong's tycoons, so favoured by the Tung administration, thus found their influence checked by the courts.

The state itself also faced repeated legal challenge. When protesters tested the constitutionality of the Public Order Ordinance provisions regarding the regulation of public processions (specifically the discretionary power of the Commissioner of Police to restrict the right of peaceful assembly for the purpose of 'public order'—ordre public) the CFA, in a landmark case,[42] described the freedom of peaceful assembly as a

> fundamental right ... clearly associated with the fundamental right of freedom of speech. The freedom of speech and freedom of assembly are precious and lie at the foundation of a democratic society. These freedoms are of cardinal importance for the stability and progress of society ... A democratic society is one where the market place of ideas must thrive. These freedoms enable citizens to voice criticisms and seek redress. This is relevant not only to institutions

[37] The defendants' lawyer, John Clancey, was a leading human rights lawyer and member of the Asian Human Rights Commission, which was spearheading an Asian charter on the rule of law.

[38] *South China Morning Post*, 6 May 2005.

[39] This was the so-called *Link-reit* case. Lo Siu-lan petitioned the High Court for the right to have the plan judicially reviewed by the CFA. See *South China Morning Post*, 19 Apr 2005 for summary.

[40] The lawyer in this case was Mark Daly, of Barnes and Daly.

[41] *South China Morning Post*, 21 July 2005.

[42] *Leung Kwok Hung and Others v HKSAR*, CFA Final Appeal Nos. 1 and 2 of 2005 (Criminal); 8 July 2005.

exercising power of government but also to organisations outside the public sector which in modern times have tremendous influence over the lives of citizens. Minority views may be disagreeable, unpopular, distasteful, or even offensive to others. But tolerance is a hallmark of a pluralistic society. Through the exercise of these freedoms, minority views can be properly ventilated ... If there is one type of law more in need than any other of being clearly and carefully circumscribed it is the type that places or permits restrictions on the exercise of fundamental rights and freedoms and criminalises exercising them beyond those restrictions.[43]

The CFA found the Commissioner of Police's power of prior restraint unconstitutional, cementing the public perception of the judiciary as defender of freedom and check on government.

Despite its activism, there was no direct attack by China on the CFA itself. The NPC's insistence in 1999 that the CFA 're-visit' its right of abode decision was the closest the two came to a head-on collision. The government's decision, to invite the NPC to override the CFA, provoked a local and international outcry. Whilst such tactics strengthened executive power, they damaged international (especially business) confidence in the HKSAR.

The Mainland's own development depended partly upon its leadership demonstrating to the international community that it was a responsible global citizen who upheld the rule of law. Outright attacks on Hong Kong's troublesome lawyers and judges were, therefore, counter-productive. For example, when leading barrister and LEGCO member, Margaret Ng, was prevented by the Mainland authorities from attending an international conference of jurists in Beijing, the CCP scored a spectacular own goal. China's actions were condemned by the high-profile lawyers attending the conference, resulting in damaging media coverage.

Since 1997, the development of an independent stance amongst leading lawyers and the judiciary contributed to a growing sense that it is possible to challenge Hong Kong's powerful elites and survive. The masses, for example, gradually began to do what Patten had exhorted them to do: stand up for their rights. From 1999 onwards, street demonstrations became larger and more frequent, often led by lawyer-activists. On 1 July 2001, for example, a 700-strong group led by Martin Lee, representatives of grass-roots bodies (Szeto Wah for the teachers' union, Lau Chin shek, veteran of the free labour movement), Emily Lau, and six other pro-democratic legislators demanded direct elections for Hong Kong's next Chief Executive (CEO). Members of the legal complex (students, academics and, particularly, barrister Margaret Ng) also led a mass silent demonstration through

---

[43] *Ibid.*

the streets against the NPC's interference with a judgment of the CFA in the right of abode cases.

In a democracy, the failures of the Tung administration would have resulted in his being voted out of office. This avenue being closed to them, Hong Kongers took their discontent to the streets. In 2001 and 2002, 'politically apathetic' Hong Kong witnessed so many demonstrations that it earned itself the title 'City of Protests'. The demonstrations continued in 2003, 2004, 2005 and 2006, particularly against the government's repeated requests for the NPC to interpret the Basic Law.

The most significant protest occurred on 1 July 2003 against proposals to enact Article 23 of the Basic Law, providing for new anti-subversion laws. Over half a million people took to the streets in one of the largest popular demonstrations ever seen in the territory. The scale of the protest shocked the government and alarmed Beijing. It left those who had taken part with a sense that an historic shift had occurred (Cheng, 2005: 2). Led by lawyers, social activists and union leaders, the march attracted support from all sections of society, including cleaners, hawkers, and religious groups. As the government refused to drop the draft legislation, further demonstrations followed on 9 and 13 July.

As Cheng says, these demonstrations made it clear 'that the majority of Hong Kong people wanted him [Tung] to stand down' (*ibid*). However, it was the implications of Article 23 for the rule of law which brought them out on the streets. Whilst some of the leaders voiced demands for Hong Kong people to have a say in government, for most people the demonstrations were about stopping government encroaching on their basic rights and freedoms. As Fletcher says, 'of all the dreams that drive men and women into the streets, from Buenos Aires to Budapest, it is this popular defence of the "rule of law" which is the most puzzling'(Fletcher, 1996: 4). In the face of such hostility, and fearing that the mood of protest might spill over into the Mainland, the government was prevailed upon to set aside its Article 23 proposals. The whole episode had, however, undermined a chief PRC objective, that of depoliticising the territory and remaking its citizens into people who 'loved China'.

Many of the grassroots community organisations involved in these protests sought concrete solutions to their problems and did not see the political parties as especially helpful. According to a 2001 survey, most people felt that groups other than politicians were better at addressing their grievances (Cheng, 2005: 15–16). People were 'tired of political shows'.[44] Even so, a pro-democracy protest in January 2004 attracted about 100,000 people, whilst in the 2003 District Council elections voter turnout reached record levels, with the pro-democracy camp 'winning handsomely' (Cheng, 2005: 18).

---

[44] Letters to the Editor, *South China Morning Post*, 17 Nov 2005.

At a New Year's Day 2004 rally, and another on 1 July 2004, tens of thousands called for universal suffrage for the CEO and LEGCO elections. It may be that they felt that, if they 'owned' the government, they would not have to worry about it introducing laws such as Article 23 (*ibid*).

At the same time, however, in an opinion poll in August 2003 the independent legislator and barrister, Audrey Eu, topped the ratings, followed by members of the Liberal Party. The Democratic Party (Martin Lee and Szeto Wah) came next, whilst other pro-democracy legislators occupied fifth, sixth, seventh and ninth places (Cheng, 2005: 18). Even pro-democracy politicians, it seemed, were losing ground to independently-minded lawyers. Newspaper editorials also worried when, in June 2005, a swathe of departures began amongst legal academics. Among those leaving were public and constitutional law experts,[45] seen as an important independent voice in Hong Kong's constitutional, human rights and public law controversies.[46]

Whilst Hong Kong's political structure had always hobbled opposition parties, however large their popular mandate, law and lawyers were in a different position. Successful challenges to government in the courts had shown the bar to be a more effective opposition than pro-democracy politicians, whilst the independence of judges and lawyers also made them more popular. The relatively poor public rating of all political parties indicated that 'the existing institutions of governance ... [were] not gaining enough public trust or the capacity to inspire the population' (Cheung, 2005: 45).

Thus, though public confidence in the integrity of institutions had generally declined under the Tung administration, the institutions of the law had managed to retain public trust. This seems to have been understood by some senior lawyer-officials for, in 2002, they took up the initiative (begun by barrister Margaret Ng and members of legal academia) to expand ordinary people's access to justice.

In 2005 and 2006, lawyer-activists finally turned their social capital into political power. Merging with academics and leading members of the Bar (the Article 45 Concern Group) they formed a new political party—The Civic Party. The lawyers in the Party's vanguard were 'core' members of the bar and members of Hong Kong's elite. Its main support came from other groups in civil society which had fought against Article 23.

Though the new party had representative government as part of its manifesto, it was seen as altogether more moderate than existing pro-democracy parties. Four of its members were elected to LEGCO, and the party enjoyed a higher public rating than most others (Cheng, 2005: 44). One member, Wong Yan-lung, became something of a trailblazer when he replaced

---

[45] Including Yash Ghai, cited by CFA judges in several judgments.
[46] *South China Morning Post*, 8 June 2005.

Elsie Leung Oi-sie as Secretary for Justice, joining what had hitherto been regarded as a largely 'pro-Mainland' government legal complex. The new appointee was not drawn from an elite background, being born into the poorest section of society. He had, however, studied at Cambridge and, as such, had gained elite credentials. As a government lawyer, he might have been expected to lack integration with the local bar, but as a private practitioner he had participated in the bar's silent march against the government's decision to seek an NPC (re)interpretation of the Basic Law. This was all a sharp contrast with Ms. Leung, widely regarded as someone with good contacts and political credentials with Beijing, but 'loathed by many as the justice secretary who failed to defend the rule of law'.[47] In 2005, when Tung finally resigned,[48] she had further alienated the public by suggesting that yet another interpretation of the Basic Law by the NPC was required on the term of office to be served by the new CEO; the government, she argued, could not afford 'the luxury of letting things run their natural course in the courts'.[49] The former Chair of the Bar Association, Alan Leong Kah-kit, described this as a blatant disregard for the rule of law:

> There is never a guarantee that the court will deliver as the executive requires—that is the whole point of the court process ... My impression is that the Government is trying to avoid any ... risk by seeking an interpretation from the NPC Standing committee, but that it not right ... Without the executive taking that risk, where has the rule of law a place in our system?[50]

Leong was supported by another former Chairman of the Bar Association, Rony Tong Ka-wah (a member of the Article 45 Concern Group). Another lawyer-led silent march followed.[51]

The Democrats' more radical stance and their wider grassroots support gradually led to their demonisation by the Hong Kong establishment. By contrast, members of the Civic Party, with their more elite backgrounds, were welcomed as the acceptable face of democracy.[52] Thus, 10 years after the handover, Hong Kong's public seems to regard the rule of law as a more or less acceptable equivalent to democracy, and lawyers as more effective than politicians as a check on the state. The things which once made

[47] *South China Morning Post*, 21 Oct 2005. Leung had attracted fierce criticism for her role in inviting the NPC to interpret the Basic Law in 1999, as well as for the weight she attached to the opinions of Mainland lawyers.

[48] In 2005, Beijing finally gave up trying to support Tung Chee hwa and he resigned. Replacing him provoked another constitutional crisis and the administration sought another 'interpretation' of the Basic Law from the NPC.

[49] *South China Morning Post*, 19 Apr 2005.

[50] *Ibid.*

[51] *Ibid.*

[52] I am grateful to Ian Scott for this observation.

Hong Kong a vibrant, successful city—'its socio-political values, mentalities, institutions, processes, and procedures buttressing and empowering a free, fair, open, liberal, pluralistic and cosmopolitan community'—are closely associated with its enjoying 'basic freedoms under the rule of law' (Chan, 2002: 14).

For all their elitism, then, the liberal legal complex commanded wider popular support than any part of the political system. Paradoxically, however, the very strength of its rule of law ideology weakened the democratic movement and democratic development.

IV. CONCLUSION

The relationship between liberalism and the legal complex in Hong Kong is a story of oscillations towards and away from liberalism, but also of ideological hegemony. It is a story of how the rule of law became the ruling idea of the time, how it became a source of political culture, 'produced and reproduced by the ruling elite for purposes of control ... achieved through inculcation of therapeutic social symbols of justice and state impartiality ... state law, state ideology, and legal ideology significantly construct political cultures in liberal and non-liberal settings' (Barzilai, 2005: 3, 5 and 7).

Hegemony, however, is always unstable. The liberal legal complex remains an important check on the authoritarian tendencies of the new regime, but legal liberalism and democracy now occupy increasingly separate spheres. As people lose faith in politics and turn to law, they face a liberal legal complex that is itself fragmented between the Civic Party and the Democratic Party, and which can no longer depend for support upon lawyer-officials. The small number of committed lawyers who emerged as leaders of pro-democracy political parties in the 1980s took their lead from government officials, who first introduced the idea of greater representative government. Though government had its own cynical reasons for doing this, once let loose, the idea took on a life of its own. In the 1990s, these lawyers became significant players in the political process. They remain at the forefront of the post-1997 battle against liberalism's retreat. Until this point, however, the profession played virtually no part in the championing of rights and freedoms. It was generally left to lawyer-officials within the state itself to act as a moderating force. However, lawyer-officials in Hong Kong must now be seen to be loyal to China, whilst lawyer-officials in China are equally clear about their subordinate role.

Moreover, though the new political leaders champion democracy, the cause which has rallied mass support since 1997 has been the rule of law, the signifier of the Hong Kong way of life. Lacking the formal political power to moderate government policy, Hong Kong people have taken to the streets and to the courts with astonishing success. Given the mediocrity of the legal system for most of the colonial period, what is remarkable is that so many have rallied around lawyer-leaders to defend basic freedoms against the predations of the state.

Alongside the liberal legal complex, however, has emerged a strong pro-China legal complex. Comprising a highly influential legal academia in both Hong Kong and the Mainland, this offers a competing (if unpopular) vision of Hong Kong's future, backed by powerful forces. It has helped shepherd in an era of legal authoritarianism, offering the government illiberal interpretations of disputed laws, regulations and powers, and mobilising the pro-Communist media to press their case. Coming from a civil law system in which the writings of jurists carry greater weight than in the common law tradition, their opinions hold sway amongst the CCP leadership and the Hong Kong administration. With other pro-China organs, they have mobilised to promote the CCP line. Problematically, however, actions regarded by the PRC legal complex as desirable are viewed in Hong Kong as contrary to the rule of law.

Liberalism in Hong Kong is therefore on the retreat. It is, in any event, uncertain whether the legal complex ever really fostered the democratic impulse. For most of Hong Kong's history, it simply prolonged the life of non-democratic regimes by lending them a liberal face.[53] Hong Kong—and PRC—oligarchs remain resolutely opposed to democracy, which they see as inimical to their interests. For them, as for many Asian regimes, there is no natural affinity between capitalism and democracy. History suggests that, when they could get away with it, they did their best to thwart democracy and ignore the rule of law. They would have succeeded more often were it not for a few troublesome liberals—at the bar, in the courts and within the state itself—who effectively acted as a check on power.

REFERENCES

Bankowski, Z and Mungham, G (1976). *Images of Law* (London, Routledge and Kegan Paul).

Barzilai, G (2005), *Communities and Law: Politics and Cultures of Legal Identities* (Ann Arbor, Mich, University of Michigan Press).

Brewer, J and Styles, J (1980), *An Ungovernable People: the English and their Law in the Seventeenth and Eighteenth Centuries* (London, Hutchinson).

Cain, M and Harrington, CB (1994), *Lawyers in a Postmodern World* (Milton Keynes, Open University Press).

---

[53] Is Hong Kong's experience unique? Does it augur an alternative 'path to modernity'? Clearly, it has been shaped by idiosyncratic forces, but something like it prevailed for centuries in 18th and 19th century England, where the rule of law operated as a powerful ideology for authoritarian regimes. This has been captured by Marxist historians of law such as Hay (1975), Thompson (1975) and Hobsbawn (Hobsbawn and Rude, 1969).

Chan, A (2002), 'The Constitution and the Rule of Law' in SK Lau (ed), *The First Tung Chee-hwa Administration* (Hong Kong, The Chinese University Press).

Chan, J (2002), 'Civil Liberties, Rule of Law and Human Rights: The HKSAR in the First Four Years' in SK Lau (ed), *The First Tung Chee-hwa Administration* (Hong Kong, The Chinese University Press).

Chan, LKC (1999), *From Nothing to Nothing: The Chinese Communist Movement in Hong Kong* (Hong Kong, Hong Kong University Press).

Chan, MK (1991), 'Democracy Derailed: Realpolitik in the Making of the Hong Kong Basic Law 1985–1990' in MK Chan and DJ Clarke (eds), *The Hong Kong Basic Law: Blueprint for Stability and Prosperity under Chinese Sovereignty?* (Hong Kong, Hong Kong University Press).

—— (1994), 'Hong Kong's Precarious Balance: 150 years in an Historic Triangle' in MK Chan (ed), *Precarious Balance: Hong Kong becoming China* (Hong Kong, Hong Kong University Press).

—— (2002), 'The Hong Kong SAR in Flux' in MK Chan and AY So (eds), *Crisis and Transformation in China's Hong Kong* (New York, ME Sharpe).

—— and Clarke, DJ (1991), *The Hong Kong Basic Law: Blueprint for Stability and Prosperity under Chinese Sovereignty?* (Hong Kong, Hong Kong University Press).

—— and Postiglione, GA (eds) (1996), *The Hong Kong Reader* (New York, ME Sharpe).

—— and So, AY (eds) (2002), *Crisis and Transformation in China's Hong Kong* (New York, ME Sharpe).

Cheek-Milby, K (1995), *A Legislature Comes of Age* (Hong Kong, Oxford University Press.

Cheng, JYS (2005), 'Causes and Implications of the July 1 Protest Rally in Hong Kong' in JYS Cheng (ed), *The July 1 Protest Rally* (Hong Kong, City University of Hong Kong Press).

Cheung, ABL (2005), 'The Hong Kong System under One Country Being Tested: Article 23, Governance Crisis and the Search for a New Hong Kong Identity' in JYS Cheng (ed), *The July 1 Protest Rally* (Hong Kong, City University of Hong Kong Press).

Chui, M (1999), *Justice Without Fear or Favour* (Hong Kong, Ming Pao Publishing).

Clark, DJ (1991), 'The Basic Law: One Document Two Systems' in MK Chan and DJ Clarke (eds), *The Hong Kong Basic Law: Blueprint for Stability and Prosperity under Chinese Sovereignty?* (Hong Kong, Hong Kong University Press).

Cotterrell, R (1992), *The Sociology of Law* (London, Butterworths).

Davis, MC (1995), *Human Rights and Chinese Values* (Hong Kong, Oxford University Press).

Dowdle, M (2005), *Constitutionalism in the Shadow of the Common Law* (Hong Kong, draft paper presented to University of Hong Kong, Faculty of Law, November 2005).

Edwards, GE and Byrnes, AC (eds) (1993), *Hong Kong's Bill of Rights The First Year* (Hong Kong, Faculty of Law, University of Hong Kong).

Endacott, GB (1958), *A History of Hong Kong* (Hong Kong, Oxford University Press).

—— (1964), *Government and People in Hong Kong 1841–1962* (Hong Kong, Hong Kong University Press).

England, J and Rear, J (1981), *Industrial Relations and Law in Hong Kong* (Hong Kong, Oxford University Press).

Faure, D (2003), 'In Britain's Footsteps: The Colonial Heritage' in D Faure (ed), *Hong Kong: A Reader in Social History* (Hong Kong, Oxford University Press).

—— (2005), *Colonialism and the Hong Kong Mentality* (Hong Kong, Centre for Asian Studies, University of Hong Kong).

Faculty of Law, University of Hong Kong (1990), *Hong Kong's Bill of Rights: Problems and Prospects* (Hong Kong, University of Hong Kong).

Fletcher, GP (1996), *Basic Concepts in Legal Thought* (New York, Oxford University Press).

Fine, B (1984), *Democracy and The Rule of Law: Liberal Ideals and Marxist Critiques* (London, Pluto Press).

Flowerdew, J (1998), *The Final Years of British Hong Kong* (Basingstoke, MacMillan Press).

Genn, H (1999), *Paths to Justice: What People Do and Think about Going to Law* (Oxford, Hart).

Ghai, YP (1999), *Hong Kong's New Constitutional Order* (Hong Kong, Hong Kong University Press).

—— Chen, W and Fu, HL (2000), *Hong Kong's Constitutional Debate* (Hong Kong, Hong Kong University Press).

Goodstadt, L (2005), *Uneasy Partners* (Hong Kong, Hong Kong University Press).

Habermas, J (1987), *The Philosophical Discourse of Modernity* (trans F Lawrence, (Cambridge, Mass, MIT Press).

Hay, D, Thompson, EP, Linebaugh, P, and Rule, JG (1975), *Albion's Fatal Tree* (Harmondsworth, Peregrine).

Heywood, A (1992), *Political Ideologies* (London, MacMillan).

Held, D (1983), *States and Societies* (Oxford, Robertson in association with the Open University Press).

—— (1989), *Political Theory and the Modern State* (Cambridge, Polity Press).

—— (ed) (1991), *Political Theory Today* (Cambridge, Polity Press).

Held, D, McLennan, G and Hall, S (1984), *The Idea of the Modern State* (Milton Keynes, Open University Press).

Ho, A (1997), *Quotations from Chris Patten* (Hong Kong, Sub-Culture Ltd).

Hobsbawm, EJ and Rude, G (1969), *Captain Swing* (London, Penguin).

Hong Kong Government, (1966–7), *Report of Commission of Inquiry into the Kowloon Disturbances 1966* (Hong Kong, Government Printer).

—— (1968), *Hong Kong Disturbances 1967* (Hong Kong, Unpublished Report, Colonial Secretariat).

Hong Kong Observers (1981), *Pressure Points* (Hong Kong, Summerson Eastern Publishers Ltd).

Jones, C (1990), *Promoting Prosperity; The Hong Kong Way of Social Policy* (Hong Kong, The Chinese University Press).

—— (2005), 'Dissolving the People', paper delivered at the conference on 'The Legal Complex and Struggles for Political Liberalism', Onati, Spain, 5–9 May.

Jaschok, M (1988), *Concubines and Bondservants* (Hong Kong, Oxford University Press).

Justice (1969), *On the Feasibility of Instituting the Office of Ombudsman in Hong Kong* (Hong Kong, International Commission of Jurists).

King, AYC (1975), 'The Administrative Absorption of Politics in Hong Kong' 15:5 *Asian Survey* (May) 422.

Lau, SK (1982), *Society and Politics in Hong Kong* (Hong Kong, The Chinese University Press).

—— (ed) (2002), *The First Tung Chee-hwa Administration* (Hong Kong, The Chinese University Press).

—— and Kuan, HC (1988), *The Ethos of the Hong Kong Chinese* (Hong Kong, The Chinese University Press).

Li, P (1994), 'Hong Kong Lawyers in Fear of China?' in R Wacks (ed), *The Right to Representation: Problems and Prospects* (Hong Kong, The University of Hong Kong, Law Faculty).

Litton, H (1978), 'Colonial Regulation 55: the Fragile Iron Rice Bowl', 8 *Hong Kong Law Journal* 137

Liu, BTM (2000), *How We Are Judged* (Hong Kong, City University of Hong Kong Press).

Lock, ACS (1993), *To Live and Work in Peace and Contentment: The Political Attitudes of Hong Kong Chinese from the late 1940s to the late 1950s.* (Hong Kong, unpublished PhD thesis, University of Hong Kong).

Mathews, G and Lui, TL (eds) (2001), *Consuming Hong Kong* (Hong Kong, Hong Kong University Press).

Morris, P, Lewis, P and White, R (1973), *Social Needs and Legal Action* (London, Martin Robertson).

Morrison, W (1995), *Theoretical Criminology: from Modernity to Post-modernism* (London, Cavendish).

Munn, C (1995), 'Scratching with a Rattan: William Caine and the Hong Kong Magistracy 1841–44', 25 *Hong Kong Law Journal* 213.

—— (1999), 'The Criminal Trial under Early Colonial Rule' in TW Ng (ed), *Hong Kong's History* (London, Routledge).

—— (2001), *Anglo-China: Chinese People and British Rule in Hong Kong 1841–1880* (Richmond, Curzon).

Ng, TW (ed) (1999), *Hong Kong's History* (London, Routledge).

Norton-Kyshe, JW (1898), *The History of the Laws and Courts of Hong Kong* (London, TF Unwin).

Penlington, VA (1986), *Law in Hong Kong* (Hong Kong, Federal Publications).

Poggi, G (1978), *The Development of the Modern State* (London, Hutchinson).

—— (1990), *The State: its Nature, Development and Prospects* (Oxford, Polity Press).

—— (2001), *Forms of Power* (Cambridge, Polity Press).

Rabushka, A (1973), *The Changing Face of Hong Kong* (Washington, DC, Hoover Policy Studies).

—— (1979), *Hong Kong: A Study in Economic Freedom* (Chicago, Ill, University of Chicago Press).

Scott, I (1989), *Political Change and the Crisis of Legitimacy in Hong Kong* (Hong Kong, Oxford University Press).

Shuwen, W (ed) (2000), *Introduction to the Basic Law of the Hong Kong Special Administrative Region* (Beijing, Law Press China).

Simpson, AWB (2001), *Human Rights and the End of Empire* (Oxford, Oxford University Press).

Tai, BYT (1999), 'The Development of Constitutionalism in Hong Kong' in R Wacks (ed), *The New Legal Order in Hong Kong* (Hong Kong, Hong Kong University Press).

Tang, JTH and Ching, F (1984), 'The MacLehose-Youde Years' in MK Chan (ed), *Precarious Balance* (Hong Kong, Hong Kong University Press).

Thompson, EP (1975), *Whigs and Hunters* (Harmondsworth, Peregrine).

Tsai, JF (1993), *Hong Kong in Chinese History* (New York, Columbia University Press).

Tsang, S (ed) (1995), *Government and Politics: A Documentary History of Hong Kong* (Hong Kong, Hong Kong University Press).

—— (1988), *Democracy Shelved* (Hong Kong, Oxford University Press).

—— (1997), *Hong Kong: An Appointment with History* (New York, IB Tauris).

—— (2004), *A Modern History of Hong Kong* (Hong Kong, Hong Kong University Press).

Turner, M (1996), *60s/90s, Dissolving The People* (Hong Kong, Hong Kong Arts Centre Installation).

Wacks, R (ed) (1989), *The Future of the Law in Hong Kong* (Hong Kong, Oxford University Press).

—— (ed) (1993), *Hong Kong, China and 1997* (Hong Kong, Hong Kong University Press).

—— (ed) (1999), *The New Legal Order in Hong Kong* (Hong Kong, Hong Kong University Press).

Walden, J (1983), *Excellency, Your Gap is Showing!* (Hong Kong, Corporate Communications Ltd).

—— (1987), *Excellency, Your Gap is Growing!* (Hong Kong, All Noble Company Ltd).

Welsh, FA (1997), *History of Hong Kong* (London, Harper Collins).

Wesley-Smith, P (1998), *Unequal Treaty 1898–1997: China, Great Britain and Hong Kong* (Hong Kong, Hong Kong University Press).

Yu, PSS (1998), *The Seventh Child and The Law* (Hong Kong, Hong Kong University Press).

5

The State, Civil Society, and the Legal Complex in Modern Japan: Continuity and Change

MALCOLM M FEELEY AND SETSUO MIYAZAWA

I. INTRODUCTION

THROUGHOUT MUCH OF its history, the Japanese state has not distinguished between law and administration, and until late in the modern era did not even permit the development of a separate legal profession. However the domination of the legal process by the state was unwittingly weakened by government reforms initiated at the outset of the Meiji Restoration in the late 1860s. As a separate legal profession emerged, it not only sought to establish its own independence, but also championed the idea of the autonomy of the law and a liberal social order. Slowly and steadily both the bar and the bench have gained greater independence, and in so doing have contributed to the emergence of a moderate state. A conservative judiciary has gained a degree of bureaucratic independence from other branches of the government, but it has not sought to align itself with the organised bar or championed the idea of an autonomous rule of law. In contrast, the organised bar has consistently tried to extricate itself from governmental controls, and aggressively promoted the idea of autonomous law and the liberal state.

The short history of the Japanese bar conforms to the counter-revisionist views of the legal profession that has been advanced by Terrence Halliday and Lucien Karpik (1997). They argue that one of the classic characteristics of the organised legal profession is its sense of civic duty, its attachment to liberal principles, and its promotion of the moderate state. In challenging much of the recent scholarship on the legal profession, Halliday and Karpik point out that, '[w]ith few exceptions, lawyers were and still are considered as homo socius or homo economicus, but never as homo politicus,', They then go to assert, 'we challenge the neglect of politics and show that ... politics may become the dominant principle of lawyers' collective action' (Halliday and Karpik, 1997: 15–16). From the outset the activities of lawyers in Japan have conformed to this model. From their beginning, lawyers in Japan have viewed their profession in the classic terms suggested by Halliday and Karpik. They are quintessentially homo politicus. However, despite this strong sense of 'calling' and intense organisational efforts to reinforce it, lawyers and the organised bar in Japan have had only a limited impact in shaping public affairs and in contributing to the development of civil society and a moderate state. Its successes have been limited because of its small size (tiny in comparison to the legal profession in Western industrialised societies) (Miyazawa, 1999: 21–6).

Still, by most measures discussed by Halliday and Karpik (1997: 15–16), Japan is a moderate and liberal state. Freedom House consistently ranks Japan high, among the highest in the world, on political and civil rights (Garon, 2003: 43). Thus the questions: What accounts for these developments? And what roles have the bar and the bench played in bringing them about? This chapter explores these questions in historical context.

II. THE STATE, CIVIL SOCIETY AND THE LEGAL COMPLEX IN PRE-WORLD WAR II JAPAN

(a) Overview

In perhaps the single most well-known essay on the Japanese legal process, Takeyoshi Kawashima (1963) argued that even in contemporary Japan, people lack a 'rights consciousness' and that social relationships are characterised by a desire for 'harmony'. As a consequence instead, he continued, the Japanese are reluctant to resort to law and litigation to resolve disputes; they prefer conciliation and mediation. At one level Kawashima is undoubtedly correct. Disputing in Japan is characterised by relatively low rates of litigation; there are a myriad of less formal government-sponsored dispute resolution mechanisms; and the legal process is distinguished by how few judges and lawyers there are in comparison to most other industrialised countries. But it is questionable whether this system is a 'natural' consequence of a weak 'rights consciousness' as Kawashima argued. Rather, it may be a deliberate policy imposed by a strong state to assure that legal process independent of the state does not develop.

We argue, following a number of revisionist scholars since Kawashima (eg Ramseyer and Rasmusen, 2003; Ramseyer and Nakazato, 1999; Upham 1987; Haley, 1978; Feldman, 2000), that at crucial junctures throughout its long history, the Japanese government has taken direct action to restrict the nature and development of the legal process. Until the 1870s, the state prohibited the development of a distinct legal system and legal profession, and even when they were established in the 1870s, the government took steps to limit the independence of the judiciary and restrict the power of the bar. It is these conscious political decisions and not any generalised cultural resistance to law, lawyers or litigation that has led to low levels of formal disputing in Japan. In the legal process, as in many arenas of civil society, the state has sought to restrict development of autonomous institutions, and when such institutions have been established, they have been placed under the watchful eye of the state. Indeed, only in Post-War Japan is it possible to speak meaningfully about an independent and autonomous bench and bar. And indeed, even today this idea remains highly contested (Miyazawa, 1991; Ramseyer and Rasmusen, 2002; Haley, forthcoming).

The history of the Japanese legal process is largely a history of Japanese public administration. Until the modern era, there was no distinct or autonomous legal system or even a 'myth' of one (Shapiro, 1981). Law was widely understood as an aspect of 'administration', not a distinct form of social ordering. Throughout the long period of Tokugawa rule (1603–1867), the government forbade the establishment of a separate legal profession. Despite various efforts to skirt round this prohibition, the state was largely successful in insisting that litigants appear before its administrators without aid of legal representation. Indeed, in many walks of life laws governing behaviour were not even published or circulated. They were invoked after the fact by administrators who thought of them as but one of many tools they had at their disposal to secure order. The consequence of this was, of course, to concentrate power into the hands of state bureaucrats.

When finally Western-style law and legal training were introduced, they were imposed for purposes of state. Western-style law was adopted to head-off Western imperialism, and law schools were established to train government officials. Although these plans did not unfold precisely as planned—Western liberal ideas sparked many social movements, and a desire to be part of an independent legal profession drew many new law graduates into private practice—Meiji officials were vigorous in trying to prevent the emergence of a robust civil society and an autonomous legal order. In the following sections of this chapter, we describe the long-standing connection between law and state administration, and then chart the slow but steady development of a separate legal system and a distinct legal complex up to the twenty-first century.

This chapter is intentionally descriptive at many parts, although the space available makes it inevitable to present only condensed description. That is because the chapter interprets the historical development of the legal complex and its interaction with the state from a theoretical perspective that has been developed outside Japan, largely based on historical experience of the West. We believe that this approach will make it easier for readers better to appreciate theoretical implications of the Japanese experience.

(b) The State, Civil Society and the Legal Complex in Tokugawa Japan

It is conventional to start a historical analysis of modern Japan from the Meiji Restoration in 1868, the abrupt beginning of modern Japan. However, we begin with an examination of the legal process in the Tokugawa period in order to show continuities between that period and modern Japan. Many developments that are associated with the Meiji era were in fact extensions of practices rooted in the earlier era, and many of the factors that have limited the development of a more robust civil society and legal complex reflect continuities with the pre-modern past.

The Tokugawa era commenced in the early sixteenth century. The new national order was a colonial regime. It consolidated central power by either conquering or co-opting *daimyo*—samurai war lords—who previously had exercised considerable independence from the weak central government, and by establishing an effective and efficient administrative system that extracted tribute from local fiefdoms but at the same time maintained their loyalty. Its power rested upon a delicate balance between central authority in Edo and the powerful *daimyo* who ruled in the provinces. Within their domains these regional warrior families exercised near total control over a great many matters, maintained their own army of loyal samurai, established codes, exercised civil authority, and stimulated regional economic development. Villages were organised hierarchically, from village headman down to heads of families (Ooms, 1996), by means of an elaborate and clearly understood system of status ranks based upon occupation, land ownership and birth. But all of this was done under the watchful eye of the powerful central government ruled by the Shogun, whose authority was nominally based on recognition by the Emperor.

Great warrior families built castle towns which by the mid-seventeenth century had developed into vibrant regional commercial centres that accelerated the pace of urbanisation. During the eighteenth century, great merchant families established a flourishing commercial system. Edo, Kyoto and Osaka emerged as three great cities administered directly by the central government. A prosperous society thrived. By 1770, 5 to 7 per cent of the population resided in cities, in contrast to 2 per cent in Europe at the same time (McClain, 2002: 54). Japan was transformed into a country of artisans, traders and day labourers, with a large, prosperous and literate middle class (McClain, 2002: 85). This 'golden age' did not come about, however, because a moderate state permitted citizens in a vibrant civil society freely to pursue their own interests. Rather, commerce, the economy and cultural life were 'guided', albeit loosely and somewhat benignly, by the state (Holt and Turner, 1966). Despite the robust economy and vibrant social and artistic accomplishments, and a thriving urban commercial class, Japan remained a feudal society characterised by great land-owning families whose heads exercised vast powers over their dominions. People of all ranks were above all else not citizens but 'subjects' to be ruled. Peasants were bound to the land. People had to petition the authorities for permission to marry, to change their residences, to acquire or sell real property. Status differentials were divided and divided again, so that villages and cities were comprised of groups differentiated by minute degrees of status that were symbolised by dress, weaponry, housing, forms of address, and rights and duties. Despite widespread literacy, economic prosperity, urbanisation, and an advanced commercial economy, in many respects *Gesellschaft* rather than *Gemeinshcaft* linked people of Tokugawa Japan together. To guard against competing sources of allegiance, the Shogunate required all powerful regional warlords—potential challengers to central authority—to spend alternate years in Edo under its watchful eye. To ensure they would not emerge as competing sources of allegiance, the government embraced an amalgamation of all three of Japan's religions, Buddhism, Shintoism and Confucianism, maintaining them as state-sponsored enterprises. The bitter history that pitted church against the state throughout European history is virtually unknown in Japan. Almost from the outset, the different religions, which might have fostered competition and conflict within Japanese society or emerged to challenge temporal authority, were coopted and domesticated, used by the state to reinforce its legitimacy (McClain, 2002: 30). And to guard against the idea of 'citizens' with rights, the state forbade development of a separate legal system and legal profession. In this tightly controlled feudal society, there was little room for the institutions of civil society, and no room for autonomous law or an independent legal profession.

But this does not mean there was no conflict in traditional Japan. In his wonderful study of civic life and power struggles in Tokugawa villages Herman Ooms (1996: 8) describes vibrant communities rife with conflict, whose residents seethed with envy and resentment, were possessed of a refined legal consciousness, and were quick to name and blame and claim. 'To change unwanted situations, the peasants relied far more frequently on suits and petitions than on mass protests or uprisings', he notes, though he goes on to show how the distinction between law 'suits' and personal 'petitions' was blurred. Village judge and headman were one and the same person. Both petitions and law suits used a supplicatory form of address that appealed to the 'good will' of the official decision-maker, and outcomes were routinely 'not verdicts but conciliations or compromises without clear cut winners or losers'(Ooms, 1996: 8–9). And the types of petitions and their solutions were affected by the status of the parties involved. Still, Ooms observes, 'One cannot avoid the impression that lawyerless Tokugawa Japan was far more litigious than the Japan of today' (Ooms, 1996: 8). But then, like today, there was a concerted effort to channel disputes through government controlled institutions, not an autonomous legal process.

At the national level, the Tokugawa shogunate developed a sophisticated form of commercial law to facilitate a robust commercial economy. Codes were developed. Judges handed down decisions. Rulings were written down and established as precedents. A complicated legal order capable of dealing with problems arising from an advanced commercial life—bills of exchange, banks, clearing houses and produce-exchanges, promissory notes and cheques, chain-stores—was created. To facilitate its operation, an elaborate judicial system was created, with national courts in Edo, the capital, under the direct control of the central authorities, and a far flung system of local courts staffed by members of local daimyos. Village headmen and other officials handled local disputes. However, all the courts ultimately derived their authority from the shogunate and reflected its policies. 'Going to Edo' (to lodge a complaint) was a common expression in the Tokugawa period.

Although it was sophisticated—at both the local and national levels—the legal system reflected the feudal structure of Japan. It was thoroughly paternalistic. There was no clear distinction between judge and administrator, or petition and litigation. Rulings were rarely clear-cut. In Weberian terms, Tokugawa justice was a system of substantive justice, not rational justice familiar to modern legal systems in the West. The closing article of the Code of 1615 symbolises this spirit. Quoting Confucius, it states: 'Let the people abide by the law, but not be instructed in it'. One well-known Tokugawa dictum held that,'Unreason is less than Reason; Reason is less than Law; Law is less than Authority; and Authority is less than Heaven' (Ooms, 1996: 312). Accordingly, many codes and judicial decisions were never published (Hiramatsu, 1981). Furthermore, law was not universally available. 'Whether they were family or feudal, the rule was that suits brought by inferiors were not accepted' (Henderson, 1965: 118). Still at the village level, regulations requiring residents to fulfill their civic duties were required to be read aloud annually to assembled villagers. Criminal punishments were specified in detail, and elaborately graded by the status of both the offender and the victim (Ooms, 1996: 39). But within these strictures, people could and did complain to authorities and in theory everyone—men and women—had a voice (Ooms, 1996: 34).

For all this subtlety and sophistication, law in Tokugawa Japan was not autonomous; it was not independent of the state or administration. Indeed, as was noted above, there was no distinction between administrator and judge. The judiciary is best understood in terms of division of labour and specialisation within the well-developed bureaucracy, not as a separate or distinct 'branch' in Montesquieu's sense. Law may have been formal in a great many ways, and it possessed a high degree of consistency and regularity. Certainly judges were celebrated for their wisdom and lack of bias. But there was never any doubt that at some level law was an instrument, a tool used by officials to facilitate social order and not (also) a restraint upon officials themselves. The judicial process was inquisitorial; wise and knowledgeable judges were expected to investigate matters and affected parties were expected to cooperate in the quest for substantive justice. Administrators, like wise parents, were capable of sorting out conflicts, imposing responsibilities, and acting decisively but fairly. To suggest otherwise was to insult their capacities.

Nor was there a position that could conventionally be understood as the functional equivalent of today's lawyer. Judges were deemed capable of understanding the interests of the parties, and thus advocates for parties were thought to be unnecessary. Still, in at least some areas of the law, there were those who came to act in behalf of litigants and even receive fees for doing so. Known as *kujishi*, they were proprietors of inns at which parties to actions lodged while awaiting a hearing before a judge in a regional centre or in Edo (See, eg, Ooms, 1996; Matsui, 1990: 3; and Ch'en, 1981: 73). However, the role of *kujishi* did not eventually evolve into that of a professional advocate. *Kujishsi* were not required to have legal training, nor did they ever receive any form of professional recognition. The popular literature of the times portrays them as shysters; there is no counter-narrative that portrays even a tiny fraction of them as champions of the underdog, or as defenders of 'rights'. People were not 'citizens', they were 'subjects'.

However, there is a large and robust popular literature of the Tokugawa era that celebrates the wise administrator-judge who capably investigates matters and crafts Solomon-like judgments. The moral is clear: Justice flows from rulers who have the wisdom to ferret out truth and the insight to discover true character (Matsui, 1990: ch 1). Subjects should submit to an authority, law was 'administration', and the extent to which it was moderate had more to do with benevolent paternalism (Foote, 1992) than with limits guaranteed by the rule of law. Law had no anchor in civil society. Indeed, civil society did not even exist in Japan in any meaningful form (Garon, 2003: 43).

(c) The Meiji Restoration

The Edo government eventually fell for a great many reasons—inefficiency, ineffectiveness, corruption. But two factors loom large. First, there was the perceived failure of Japan's rulers to stave off the forces of Western imperialism; in the early 1860s, some of Japan's leading daimyo families, particularly those in western Japan, came to believe that a weak central government had capitulated to Western imperialists, and withdrew their support for it, and eventually rebelled against it. Secondly, the expanding commercial classes sought to break loose from the rigid traditions of the land-based forms of aristocracy.

More of a coup d'etat than a revolution, the Meiji Restoration was not animated by any bold new vision. The new leaders came from that part of the samurai class which felt that their interests had not been sufficiently represented by the old regime. Indeed, their success was based largely upon their appeal to 'traditional' Japanese values and not any vision of a bold new order. Despite this, the new regime did develop something of a 'good government' agenda and promoted it aggressively: strengthen the state in order to ward off imperialist forces, provide more effective and efficient public administration, and enter more fully into the modern industrialised world. But beyond this, it was not a change brought about by an expansive vision of a more democratic future as were the upheavals in Europe at roughly the same time. Unlike the political activity in Europe, the 1868 'revolution' in Japan cannot be seen as a call for a more energised civil society or expanding liberal reforms. It was one group in the ruling class replacing another in the name of more efficient and effective government.

Still, the new government unleashed forces that precipitated unprecedented change. In their effort to fend off Western imperialism, Meiji leaders adopted Western institutions with a vengeance—but, as they emphasised, on Japan's own terms and not at the end of a gun barrel. The effects of this effort were staggering. Within 25 years Japan was transformed from a feudal society whose economy was based upon agriculture and light manufacturing into one of the world's major economic and colonial powers whose slogan was 'Rich Nation, Strong Army' (Samuels, 1994). By the early twentieth century, its industrial output ranked fourth world-wide, behind only the United States, Great Britain and Germany (Holt and Turner, 1966). And its colonial holdings on mainland Asia and throughout the Pacific islands made it one of the world's great colonial powers. Even as these developments broke down traditional caste and status structures, and produced rapid economic development, they also precipitated enormous social dislocations. The change came with all the problems associated with rapid industrialisation: urban slums, exploitation, alienation, political protest, violence. Japan condensed into a quarter of a century a transformation that had taken well over 100 years to accomplish in England: the displacement of the feudal, land-based aristocracy by the rising new commercial and industrial elite.

To consolidate this change, the leaders began to establish many of the features of modern Western governments, including in 1889 the adoption of a modern Western-style constitution (although some of its provisions—a cabinet system, a judicial system—had been put into place some years earlier). Despite this Japan continued to be ruled by an oligarchy. Although sovereignty formally resided in the emperor, he was in fact 'little more than legitimating façade ...' (Abe, Shindo, and Kawato, 1994: 7). Real authority resided with the Prime Minister and his cabinet of ministers, all drawn from the families victorious in the Meiji revolution. Popular suffrage was more apparent than real; the 1889 'reforms' permitted only a tiny fraction—around 2 per cent—of the adult male population the right to vote. Unlike modern parliamentary democracies, the prime minister was responsible to the emperor and not the legislature, and the emperor in turn was a figure-head for an entrenched oligarchy. In effect this meant rule by a self-perpetuating elite. The elected legislature had limited powers; it could only ratify—and occasionally modify—proposals originating from the Cabinet and the ministries it dominated, but could not introduce legislation. As Robert Scalapino has observed, the new and seemingly liberal constitutional structure rested on a weak democratic foundation (Scalapino, 1967: 42). Nevertheless this abrupt change did foster expectations for greater democratisation and more robust civic engagement.

Throughout the 1870s, there was considerable interest in and debate about how best to structure the new social and political order. Debate gave rise to a number of popular movements that were the forerunners of modern political parties and civic associations of all sorts, which was unprecedented in Japanese history. One movement, the Freedom and Popular Rights Movement (*jiyu minken undo*), took inspiration from the French Revolution and advocated a broadly representative legislature and expansive constitutional protections of individual rights (McClain, 2002: 189; Feldman, 2000: 27–31). Another advocated a British-style constitutional monarchy. And still others took inspiration from Prussia, which like Japan was a newly founded nation cobbled together from a collection of separate fiefdoms, and which like Japan contained a mixture of modern industrial cities and feudal-like rural areas. Many such efforts foundered because Japan lacked any meaningful tradition of civil society. It lacked religious institutions, labour organisations, guilds and professional associations which in some countries provided fora for debating and advancing such ideas. In the early Meiji era, for the most part, debate about these and other related ideas took place under the direction of the state. Still, one of the first civil society institutions to emerge with a separate and distinct identity to play a role in the debate was the legal profession.

(d) The State, Civil Society and the Legal Complex in the Meiji-Taisho Periods

Immediately after the establishment of the new government, vast numbers of delegations fanned out from Japan to learn about Western institutions. The impetus was to gather information about technology and manufacturing, but the effort quickly spread to all areas of Western culture, from philosophy to the fine arts to popular culture, and to Western-style law and government.

There was a special interest in learning about Western law. The pretext for invasion by imperialist powers in the 1850s was that Japan lacked a legal infrastructure—contract, credit, commercial transactions, a system of courts—that would permit it to conduct trade with the West. The new regime's response was a pledge to develop a Western-style legal system in order to facilitate trade. Thus emissaries to the West came back with knowledge about Western law, legal training and courts, and the government set about establishing Western-style legal training (for a history of legal education in Japan see Miyazawa and Otsuka, 2002) (for a history of legal profession in Japan see Hattori, 1963; Haley, 1991: ch 5; and Matsui, 1990). A Ministry of Justice was established, and it promptly founded its own legal training school (Matsui, 1990: 66). Law was to be taught as and conceived of as a branch of public administration. The expectation was that the new law trained specialists would join the Ministry to draft laws, serve as administrators, and work as judges and prosecutors.

But those who received the Western-style legal education at the new law schools learned more than officials had bargained for. Many of their teachers had been trained in England and the United States, and came back not only to teach law but to extol the virtues of an independent legal profession and the nobility of private practice rather than government service (Hattori, 1963: 127). In the 1870s and the 1880s, this development was facilitated by the establishment of a number of private law schools, some free-standing and others that eventually developed into large universities (such as Waseda and Chuo) whose faculties were recruited from among the newly trained lawyers (Matsui, 1990: 6).

The government had not anticipated this development, and quickly responded by imposing tighter controls over legal training, and restricting the roles of lawyers and the size of the bar. An 1872 statute specified the roles of judges and prosecutors, and prescribed a very limited role for private lawyers (who were initially called *daigennin* until they obtained the new title of *bengoshi* in 1893) (Matsui, 1990: 4). But even as it sought to restrict the roles of these new lawyers, the government's actions legitimated the new profession. Indeed, the 1872 law was revolutionary. For the first time, the Japanese government recognised a distinct legal profession— law-trained judges and prosecutors and lawyers in private practice. The genie was out of the bottle. Unwittingly a legal profession had been established. However, from the outset, the bar was defined by what its members were *not*; they had rejected careers in government and thus were not judges, prosecutors or ministry officials; they stood outside and somewhat in opposition to the state. Recognising this, the state in turn developed something of an adversarial relationship with the new profession, and sought to restrict its role and impact.

Despite demand, the government continued to limit the size of the new legal profession, and law schools came under ever tighter scrutiny from the Justice Ministry (Takayanagi, 1963). Between 1874 and the mid-1880s, the Ministry of Justice enacted regulations that established high barriers for entry into the profession, restricted activities of lawyers (initially, they could address courts only on behalf of clients in civil cases) (Matsui, 1990: 76), and placed the emerging profession under progressively tighter supervision (eg judges and prosecutors rather than bar were responsible for supervising lawyer disciplines) (Matsui, 1990: 5, 7–8). In 1895, after finding that up to two-thirds of law graduates preferred private practice, the government dramatically revised the content and the structure of legal education. It replaced Anglo-American law and legal training, which had unwittingly fostered the ideal of private practice and legal autonomy, with German law and legal training, which was thought to be more in line with stronger state control. For a while defections to the private bar by new graduates declined (Hattori, 1963: 127), though private practice continued to beckon substantial numbers of new law graduates.

Not withstanding these obstacles, the bar continued to grow. Perversely government efforts to restrict it helped define and reinforce the profession's anti-government ethos. In order to keep them under its thumb, the state required *daigennin* to form local associations (*kumiai*) that were government-approved organisations (Matsui, 1990: 9). Lawyers joined, but then used these associations to advance their own professional interests and to promote a liberal political agenda. Although by western standards the number of lawyers in Japan was tiny, the numbers gradually expanded and the influence of the bar increased proportionately. Indeed, by the 1930s, the lawyers per capita were higher than they were in 1970 (Haley, 1991: 97). And in 1928 the bar was even powerful enough to convince the government to introduce a limited form of jury trial along Anglo-American lines for criminal defendants (Matsui, 1990: 148). Although this innovation was ultimately suspended by the military government in 1943 (Matsui, 1990: 154), nevertheless it does reveal the power of the bar before militarisation took firm root in the mid-1930s.

From the outset the bar was at the forefront of challenging a government not accustomed to being openly opposed. In the 1880s, lawyers challenged the illegal land seizures which the new Meiji leaders had used to punish enemies and reward supporters (Matsui, 1990: 44). Throughout the Meiji and Taisho periods (from 1868 to the 1930s), the bar regularly defended labour leaders and political activists who had been subject to politically motivated prosecutions. Throughout the 1880s and 1890s, lawyers played leading roles in the formation of new political parties that challenged the entrenched regime (Matsui, 1990: 30). Such efforts often involved not just individual action by single lawyers, but collective action by bar associations. Indeed, the various local bar associations were organised into a seemingly endless number of committees to address specific issues, almost all of which dealt with the protection of rights or the expansion of civil society institutions in the face of governmental opposition.

The bar's anti-government ethos that characterised its early years still holds today. In 1990, Yashuhiro Matsui (1990: 31) wrote that the 'origins of the anti-government sprit (*zaiya seishin*) of present day practicing attorneys' can be found 'in the defiant spirit (*hankotsu seishin*) of *daigennin* who defended activists of the Freedom and Popular Rights movement in cases where the government persecuted that movement'. Although he clearly romanticises the idealism of the Meiji-era lawyers, most present-day attorneys would probably agree with Matsui's basic claim.

Meiji-era lawyers not only directed their complaints against Justice Ministry officials; they also criticised the courts as well. The Court Organisation Law of 1890 created a separate career judiciary, but placed it under the supervision of the Ministry of Justice. Ministry officials thus controlled recruitment, selection and promotion of judges, and in so doing effectively made judges junior partners in the Ministry, and in so doing distanced them from lawyers and the organised bar. Most litigation involved commercial disputes or family matters, so only occasionally did cases raise issues of direct interest to the state, but when they did, Ministry officials were quick to apply their influence over the judges. Cooperative judges were rewarded with rapid promotions and prime postings; uncooperative judges found their careers at a standstill or were exiled to the provinces. Above all, Ministry officials had the prerogative of selecting the 'right' judges at the outset so as to minimise the likelihood of conflict (Hattori, 1963: 123). The bar campaigned vigorously against all this, arguing that judges should be selected from among practising lawyers and be wholly independent of the justice ministry (Matsui, 1990: 143). But its efforts were to no avail.

Still, by most accounts the Japanese judiciary developed into a well-regarded institution, certainly more professional, more even-handed, and more independent than the heavy-handed administrators of the Tokugawa era whom they had replaced. For example, in a highly publicised case in 1891 involving the attempted assassination of the Crown Prince of Russia (later Czar Nicholas II), the case was transferred from a district court to the Great Court of Judicature, the highest court, and the Court refused to punish the defendant by death despite government pressure (Hattori, 1963: 121–2). This account is frequently cited as evidence of judicial independence, however, it is the exception rather than the rule. More typically courts were quick to punish defendants in politically-charged cases (Matsui, 1990: 113–16).

(e) The State, Civil Society, and the Bar in the War Period

The government's response to the Great Depression took two forms. In the 1930s, the government accelerated colonial expansion in Korea, Manchuria and the Pacific islands, and it asserted greater control over the economy. These programmes reinforced each other; they responded to right wing populists and military officers who felt that Japan had not done enough to assume its rightful place in the world, and to workers and farmers who were clamouring for protection against unbridled capitalism. As the crisis deepened, the government reverted to ever more traditional Japanese form. *Jushin*, 'senior statesmen', consisting of former prime ministers and other leading public figures, embraced the idea of replacing the emerging party government with a national unity government that was 'above politics'—a return to oligarchy. Eventually, the National Mobilization Law (*Kokka Sodoin Ho*) was enacted in 1938, the Great Politics Participation Association (*Taisei Yokusankai*) was formed in 1940, political parties and labour unions closed themselves, and most politicians and civic leaders joined the Association. This national unity government cracked down on dissent and, as the international crisis deepened, quashed opposition.

This started even before the formation of the wartime political structure. Indeed it began in 1925 with the enactment of the Public Security Preservation Law (*Chian Ijiho*), although this Act was not regularly invoked until the 1930s. Under its sweeping provisions critics of the regime were charged with and convicted of criminal offences, and as such it gave the government a new and effective means of control. Although much of the organised bar had opposed this new legislation and other laws like it, and valiantly attempted to defend those charged under them, lawyers who did so had to worry that they too would be regarded as disloyal simply because they represented critics of the regime in court. Increasingly, dissidents either remained silent or fell into line (McClain, 2002: 429; Matsui, 1990: ch 3), and those lawyers who represented them became more circumspect. By the time the war was in full swing, open criticism had all but disappeared. In 1941, when the Public Security Preservation Law was amended and strengthened, the organised bar expressed no objection, in sharp contrast to what it had done with the original Act (Matsui, 1990: 210).

Although lawyers and their organisations were among the most actively opposed to these 'emergency' measures, eventually they, too, were either cowed into silence or fell into line. Only a tiny handful of lawyers continued to stand firm in opposition to developments and to defend those charged with disloyalty. In the early 1930s, the Japan Attorneys Association (*Nihon Bengoshi Kyokai*) and other professional organisations formally protested the decline of respect for civil rights and liberties (Matsui, 1990: 207–8), but their efforts diminished throughout that decade and all but disappeared during the war. At times lawyers' associations even became champions of government policies (Matsui, 1990: 211–25). Indeed as early as 1932, for example, the Tokyo Bar Association at the urging of the government established the 'Japan-Manchuria Lawyers Association' as part of the government's effort to legitimate the 'annexation' of Manchuria.

Pressure to line up behind the government extended to cover civil society institutions. For instance, Tatsukichi Minobe, a retired Tokyo Imperial University professor of constitutional law, was bitterly attacked in 1934 by the press and by government officials for articles he had written a full decade earlier that questioned whether the emperor was the source of state sovereignty, and escaped criminal prosecution only by agreeing to withdraw from public life (Takayanagi, 1963: 11). Members of opposition parties and groups, most especially the Communist Party, were ruthlessly persecuted from the late 1920s. This persecution subsided only because it was so successful; countless numbers of government opponents— communists and liberals alike—publicly recanted their views and were commended for doing so at government staged events (Matsui, 1990: 169–72; McClain, 2002: 429). A handful of lawyers and a few organised groups of lawyers, such the Japan Lawyers Association for Freedom (*Jiyu Hosodan*) described below, stood up against government-sponsored oppression in the 1920s and 1930s, but as a group the organised bar mounted no campaign against the repressive powers of the state in the midst of war, in the 1940s.

The 'consensus' approach to ruling culminated in 1940 with the establishment of the 'Preparation Committee for the New Order'. Created by Prime Minister Fumimaro Konoe, this committee consisted of 37 people representing different segments of society. The result was the Great Politics Participation Association described above. The regime hoped to use it to establish the core of a mass-based political movement that would galvanise support for the government and allow it to by-pass the Diet, the ministries and the established political party system (McClain, 2002: 451). Although this movement did not fully materialise and did not usher in a fascist-like political party, it did expand the influence of the military in governmental affairs, weaken the authority of the civilian bureaucracy, and virtually eliminate the idea of the 'rule of law'. In so doing, it enfeebled both the bench and the bar. Indeed the Japan Attorneys Association established the National Federation of Attorneys for the New System in 1940, whose announced mission was to join with the government in furthering the war effort (Matsui, 1990: 218). Although a few lawyers bucked the tide and offered spirited defences of dissidents in the face of overwhelming odds, they are the exception (Oppler, 1976: 107–8). Most lawyers capitulated, and at best when they did represent dissidents offered mitigating excuses rather than direct challenges lest they themselves be associated with the offences for which their clients were charged. Towards the end of the War, military police started to replace lawyers as providers of legal advice to bereaved families of deceased soldiers. Furthermore, the practice of criminal defence, never a high prestige activity, declined still further in status and acceptability. One famous and well-reported incident in this vein, involved a military officer who asked a lawyer, who had gone to register for conscription, why he did not have an 'honest job' (*seigyo*) (Haley, 1990: 104; Matsui, 1996: 225).

In light of its history and ethos as a challenger of government authority, as well as its early opposition to militarisation in the 1930s, one might wonder why the organised bar so rapidly and completely joined the war effort in the late 1930s and throughout the war. Matsui (1996: 215) hypothesises that, like many ordinary people in Japan at that time, most lawyers accepted the prevailing ideology of the state under the Emperor, and could not resist policies that were declared in the name of the Emperor, particularly at a time of national crisis and in the face of some duress. This may be the case. For instance, Hashimoto has written a case study of a well-known lawyer in Shizuoka who was active on human right issues in criminal justice both before and after the War (Hashimoto, 2005). Even this lawyer, Hashimoto notes, joined the Great Politics Participation Association in 1941 and indeed became an officer of and active in its local office, so much so that in 1946 he was purged from public office. He apparently did not find any contradictions between his aggressive pre-War human rights activism and his 'wartime' service in the name of the Emperor. His experience was not an isolated case; it was not the exception, it was the rule throughout wartime Japan.

Increasingly during the years leading up to the War, Japan's legal system failed; the rule of law was abandoned in the name of security and safety. But it would be wrong to conclude that this return to oligarchic rule and the substitution of administration for law was essentially a return to Tokugawa era practice. Despite the crises brought on first by the Depression and then the period of militarisation and the War, there was a distinct difference between the government action in pre-Meiji Japan and pre-World War II Japan. Not even the 'emergency' and the establishment of the military government in the 1930s could fully eradicate the minimum commitment to the rule of law. A good example is the Public Security Preservation Act. It was first enacted in 1925. And again in 1941, when the government wanted to tighten control over dissidents and speed up their processing in the criminal process, it did not ignore legal formalities, it amended them. Changes in 1941 made it still easier and faster to charge and convict those charged with dissident behaviour. In one sense this does show the power of the rule of law—officials felt obliged to maintain the appearance of legality rather than simply acting summarily. This is, we suppose, some sort of achievement for the rule of law, and it may have been the best that liberal lawyers and judges were able to obtain under the circumstances. That is, even in the face of national emergency, some judges and lawyers—enough to make a difference—continued to insist on fidelity to the rule of law. Still, the state was able to concentrate its powers within this constraint and run rough-shod over those who opposed it.

(f) Comparing Tokugawa and Post-Meiji Japan

Although militarisation in the 1930s brought a halt to liberalisation, the Meiji-era reforms were substantial and lasting. The 1889 constitution and the series of enabling statutes establishing the legal system adopted in the following year permanently transformed the legal process. A professional judiciary was established. Legal training was mandated for all judges and prosecutors. Courts began publishing opinions. Laws were published and adhered to. Although these laws granted vast powers to the state and neither offered strong protections against government powers nor made provision for judicial review of governmental actions, nevertheless the *public* nature of these new policies forced the government to follow prescribed procedures, something that would have been wholly alien to officials in the Tokugawa era. Furthermore, in an effort to establish a modern legal system, the government had inadvertently created a modern legal profession as well. It had in essence embraced 'the rule of law'. in the sense that the governmental action itself had to be based on law. For the first time in Japanese history, the idea of a moderate, liberal state had a strong basis in government policy.

By the early twentieth century civil society was beginning to develop as well. A free press was established. Labour organised and unions were growing. Political parties sprung up. And with respect to the legal complex, an independent bar, albeit small and weak, had been established, was active and was growing. Furthermore law schools provided a source of independent knowledge about law and government. Despite its small size, the bar was cohesive and effective. Although all of these new institutions operated under the watchful eye of the state, nevertheless they represented a distinct break with the past, and the emergence of a real civil society in Japan.

Lawyers played a significant role in this development. Garon (2003: 45–54), for instance, has traced their role in pressing for the expansion of the sphere for public discourse outside the government from the mid-1890s to the 1920s. They lobbied for new laws expanding freedom of expression and organised to protect these new-found rights. Most of the leaders in the important Freedom and Popular Rights movement in the early Meiji era were attorneys. The Japan Lawyers Association for Freedom (*Jiyu Hosodan*) was established in 1921 by attorneys who met in Kobe to organise the defence of striking workers in that city's shipbuilding industry and who had been prosecuted for trumped-up offences against public order. With approximately 1,600 members nationwide and a formal international relationship with the National Lawyers Guild in the United States, this association is still active today. It represents something similar to 'Movement lawyers' in the United States of the 1960s (Scheingold and Sarat, 2004: 118–19; for an account of its recent activities, see Jiyu Hosodan, 1998: 2002). In early twentieth century Japan, it was nearly impossible for ordinary individuals to be autonomous from the state, but the professional status of attorneys accorded lawyers a shield against government. As a consequence lawyers and their organisations became major allies of other fledgling civil society groups as well.

III. THE STATE, CIVIL SOCIETY AND THE LEGAL COMPLEX
IN POST-WORLD WAR II JAPAN

(a) The Judiciary in Post-World War II Japan

In his history of the post-War judicial system published in 1963, Hattori Takaaki , a Tokyo District Court Judge who later became Chief Justice of the Supreme Court, wrote that 'the Judge has been completely freed from the supervisory power of the Minister of Justice, who had exerted an undesirable influence over the prewar judiciary. Now the judiciary is subject only to the general supervision of the Supreme Court, a group of their own professional seniors' (Hattori, 1963; see also Oppler, 1976: ch 8). Hattori went on to describe how, under the Constitution of 1947, the courts were granted the power of judicial review, and gained independence from the legislative and executive branches, including the Supreme Court's powers to manage such matters as judicial recruitment, promotion and assignment.

Not everyone agrees that this system of self-management overseen by the Supreme Court has led to a robust independent judiciary (see, for instance, Miyazawa, 1991; Ramesyer and Rasmusen, 2003). However, it has clearly led to a system of career judges who are selected from among the best and the brightest of the graduates from the Supreme Court-supervised Legal Training and Research Institute (LTRI or *Shiho Kenshujo*), a programme which all those who pass the bar must undertake if they wish to practise law, whether as assistant judges, prosecutors or practising attorneys. The Court also controls the initial selection process for 'assistant judges', as well as placement, rotation and promotion, and subsequent reappointment every 10 years thereafter. It thus creates a high sense of dependency upon the judicial bureaucracy.

Critics maintain that this system creates institutionally-dependent judges who are far removed from the real-world concerns of the practising bar and its clients, and that it produces conformist judges who are both conservative and biased towards the government. A mountain of evidence supports this proposition. Miyazawa (1991) has documented numerous instances of lower court judges being passed over for promotion because of their political views and memberships of some outside organisations. Such practices are more than isolated rarities; they show up as distinct statistical patterns. In their nation-wide study of judicial rotation and promotion, Ramseyer and Rasmusen (2003) found that judges who dissented from Supreme Court precedents or otherwise made rulings against the government or joined an allegedly left-leaning organisation faced ostracism or worse. Typically they were reassigned to posts in out-of-the-way places or assigned to handle less prestigious matters; occasionally they were not reappointed. But, Rameyer and Rasmusen found, the vast majority of judges quietly went along with the system. John Haley (Haley, 1998; and forthcoming), a vigorous defender of the Japanese judiciary, has conceded the accuracy of this account, but goes on to defend the practices they describe, arguing that such actions ward off even more aggressive political intervention into the affairs of the judiciary and thus are necessary to assure the integrity and autonomy of the judiciary. (For an account of the Ramseyer and Haley debate, see Upham, 2004.)

Furthermore, despite the establishment of judicial review, the Supreme Court has been reluctant to use this power. Between 1949 and 2005, the Supreme Court held laws and governmental actions unconstitutional only *seven* times. In two of these cases, the Court found flaws in the election process (malapportionment) but nevertheless allowed the election results to stand (Luney and Takahashi, 1993; and Higuchi, 2001); the other four cases did not raise issues of any real political significance; only the most recent decision in 2005 about limited voting right of Japanese nationals living abroad actually awarded compensation of 5,000 Japanese yen each to 13 plaintiffs. Using judicial review of the constitutionality of laws and governmental actions as a standard for measurement, the Japanese judiciary is definitely passive.

The passive judiciary—and by extension the limited effects of litigation and lawyers—is seen in any number of other ways as well (Feeley, 2002). Citizens have difficulty suing governmental agencies. Indeed, according to the judiciary's own statistics, only 1,790 cases of administrative litigation were filed in 1999, and the government prevailed 84 per cent of the time. These numbers pale in comparison to other advanced industrial societies. (Comparable figures for the United States are 34,376 cases against the government in federal courts in 1999; Germany, 201,543 cases in 1998; and France 106,985 cases in 1997.) (CD-Rom, *Jurisuto* [Jurist], No. 1208, 2001.) Furthermore, the situation has been getting worse. The number of authorised judges in 1890 was 1,531; the figure in 1998 was 2,896, a dramatic decline per capita, when one considers that the population of Japan increased over threefold during this period, from 40 million in 1890 to 123 million in 1990, and commercial activity and government regulation expanded exponentially (Sources: up to 1960: Hattori, 1963; Report of the Justice System Reform Council, 2001). The judiciary has been consciously trying to reduce public access to itself, hardly a sign of an activist judiciary.

However, the view that the Japanese courts are passive and reactive is not universally accepted. Perhaps the most stringent critic of this view is Tokyo University Law Professor, Daniel Foote. In a 2006 book, he argued that while historically Japanese courts may have been timid, since the 1960s they have become both more independent and more aggressive. He marshals considerable evidence to support his claim (Foote, 2006: chs 5, 6 and 7). Foote (2006: ch 1) rejects the concept of judicial activism as too vague, and proposes in its place the concept of 'judicial policy-making', as developed by Feeley and Rubin (2000). His argument: at least since the 1960s Japanese courts have been engaged in policy-making in at least several important areas, and indeed at times have been as aggressive as their American counterparts (Foote, 2006: ch 6).

Foote identifies four areas where judicial policy making has been most pronounced: (1) the creation of new norms by the Supreme Court under the leadership of individual justices; (2) the creation of new norms by trial courts, from the bottom up as it were in response to new problems; (3) the creation of new norms by lower courts in order to protect the stability of personal relationships; and (4) the creation of new norms by an organised effort of the judiciary. He supports his argument by pointing to examples of each type of policy-making.

Foote identifies two examples to support his thesis that the Supreme Court has been an innovative policy making body. One area involves two cases—a 1975 and a 1976 decision both handed down by the First Petty Bench of the Supreme Court—that liberalised the grounds for retrial under Article 435 of the Code of Criminal Procedure. He attributes this change to the concerted efforts of two Justices on the Court who had been seeking such liberalisation since 1938. The other example of policy-making involves a 1969 decision by the First Bench of the Supreme Court that for the first time pierced the corporate veil and thereby expanded corporate liability. Again, Foote attributes this decision to the leadership of two justices who had come to appreciate this doctrine while studying in the United States.

Foote identifies three sets of cases as examples of 'bottom-up' policy-making by trial courts. The first is a very famous group of lower court decisions in the late 1960s and the early 1970s that dealt with pollution, most notably the 'Big Four Pollution Cases' involving the Kumamoto Minamata disease (mercury poisoning), the Niigata Minamata disease, the Toyama *Itai-Itai* (hart-hart) disease (cadmium poisoning), and the Yokkaichi asthma. Foote argues that the decisions in these cases dramatically expanded tort liability. Specifically, they expanded a polluter's duty of care, lowered the requirements to prove foreseeability, shifted the balance of proof to polluters who now have to disprove causality, and created joint tort liability of multiple polluters. Taken together, he argues, these cases have to be understood as something more than decisions by individual judges; they constitute a dramatic instance of judicial policy-making that revolutionised Japanese tort law and established a new policy with respect to mass toxic torts. Although initiated by the lower courts, this approach quickly became part of an organised judicial effort that was let by the Supreme Court General Secretariat that convened conferences of lower court judges to encourage just such interpretations. The second set of cases deals with equal employment opportunity. Here Foote identifies two important cases handed down by judges in the Tokyo District Court: a 1966 decision that nullified the dismissal of a female worker upon her marriage, holding that such an action violates a provision

(Article 90) of the Civil Code which prohibits state action that is contrary to public order and good morals. The other was a 1990 decision that nullified a business's policy that provided different salaries for males and females doing the same work. A third set of two cases expanded protection against sexual harassment. And finally a fourth set of cases—one by the Shizuoka District Court in 1990, and another by Fukuoka District Court in 1992—expanded tort liability under Article 709 of the Civil Code.

Foote identifies another group of cases that he argues established significant new policy regarding the protection of 'personal relationships' in several different settings, extending them far beyond what was provided by statute. These cases dealt with employees' rights to job security; tenants' rights against termination of contract by the landlord; the rights of wives against husbands seeking divorces; and the rights of smaller and weaker parties against larger parties in issues involving termination of contracts. In other words, Foote argues, the Japanese courts made significant policies that enhanced the protection of several types of 'have-nots' or 'one-shoters' in the legal process.

Finally, Foote identifies two areas where the courts have aggressively and effectively innovated in changing their own structure and case load in ways that have important consequences for litigants. The first effort involved judges in the Tokyo District Court who developed creative ways to deal more effectively with dramatic increases in their case load. In the 1960s and 1970s, the Court established a special division to respond to the increase in cases involving motor vehicle accidents. They created a simplified process for finding facts, allocating responsibility, and calculating damage awards. In doing so, they successfully lobbied police, prosecutors, attorneys and insurance companies to accept their policies. The results were stunning: contested traffic accident cases plummeted—from the peak of 2,300 in 1970 to fewer than 600 in 1977, and indeed the alternative process was so successful that the special division was soon closed down altogether. Since then this alternative has been implemented nationwide (Ramseyer and Nakazato, 1999: 90–9). A second judicially-initiated reform dealt with bankruptcy. After the burst of the economic bubble in the early 1990s, bankruptcies mushroomed. In the 1980s there were on average fewer than 4,000 bankruptcy cases per year; by 2001, the figure was over 170,000. The Tokyo District Court responded to this crisis by establishing a separate bankruptcy department and creating a streamlined procedure to handle the vast numbers of small cases, using court clerks to screen cases and appoint receivers. As with the traffic accident innovation, the court sought and obtained support from all interested parties, including the three major bar associations in Tokyo. Within a year, 95 per cent of bankruptcy cases at the Tokyo District Court were handled by this simplified procedure, and again the procedure was adopted nationally. By all accounts, Foote concludes, it has been successful.

Foote (2006: ch 7) admits that this power cannot be exercised across the board, but that within significant areas the courts have considerable independence to make policy. This is because, he argues, each of the three branches of the government has its own 'field' (*hatake*) in which—within well-understood limits—they are free to innovate and to make policy. Foote argues that in all the areas of judicial policy-making he examined (and that are summarised above), the courts' actions remained within their acknowledged 'field'. He then goes on to explore the boundaries of these fields and how they are established. The zone of freedom to make policy within the judicial field is not, he maintains, a simple issue of public and private (with judges possessing greater freedom to innovate in private law areas); the Big Four pollution cases indicate otherwise since they clearly involved government actors. Nor is it an issue of deference to the legislature, or an matter of great political sensitivity. The ruling Liberal Democratic Party (LDP) has clear and continuing interests, and indeed the government was party to several the cases he reviews—those involving pollution, labour relations, landlord and tenant relations, issues involving the corporate veil, and the like. Landlords and big business, both of whom had their powers trimmed by the courts, have long been active supporters of the LDP. Even as he argues for the idea of 'fields' and argues that the idea is widely acknowledged and agreed upon, Foote concedes that apart from the issues involving administrative reforms in the operations of the courts (streamlining procedures to handle traffic accident and bankruptcy cases), it is as yet impossible to identify the boundaries or the rationale for these fields.

On its face Foote's analysis flies in the face of our argument that the Japanese judiciary, even in its modern post-war form and even since the activist 1960s, remains largely passive and reactive. Should we change our evaluation of the Japanese judiciary in light of it? We think not. The central reason is that the questions we have asked are somewhat different from those addressed by Foote. Our concern in this chapter is whether and to what extent the judiciary acts in concert with the bar and legal academics as a self-conscious part of an autonomous or semi-autonomous legal complex to promote and protect political freedoms and a moderate state. The most relevant areas for our concerns, therefore, are those where the state appears as a party.

In this regard, Foote (2006: 287–8) readily acknowledges that Japanese courts have never relied on their powers of judicial review forcefully to confront the other branches of government, and have only occasionally been forceful in matters pertaining to administrative law. That is, a politically weak judiciary or one that contributes but little to the liberal agenda of the legal complex need not be an altogether weak judiciary. As he suggests, within its 'field' it can aggressively make policy. Although he is frustrated in his efforts to define this boundary with precision and the reasons for it, nevertheless he is clear about some of the actions that fall outside the boundaries of the judicial field. He writes, 'the judiciary still appears to take the position that strict scrutiny of actions of the executive and legislative branches is not its role', and that 'policy making by Japanese courts has been done in areas where damage awards are provided, and they have been reluctant to engage in policy making concerning injunctive relief'. Further, he acknowledges that 'such a stance is in a striking contrast to the United States', and with 'what Feeley and Rubin chose as a typical example of policy making was prison litigation' that directly challenges the executive branch of the government.

Thus when placed in this context, the instances of judicial policy-making that Foote has documents may not be as significant as he suggests. Two of his examples—dealing with motor vehicle accidents and bankruptcy—involve the courts in voluntarily reducing their jurisdiction in order to reduce their case loads and access to them. While this is certainly innovative policy-making, it is hardly a dramatic exercise of judicial power. There is no doubt that the innovative use of judicial conferences in the pollution cases helped deal effectively with an issue of tragic proportions, but still it may not be the innovation Foote suggests it is. As Upham (1987: ch 2) noted 20 years ago, this scandal precipitated a tremendous 'moral momentum'—tens of thousands of people were affected by the tragedy—and no judge could have failed to provide some compensation to the victims in those cases as long as there was some reasonable basis for doing so (Upham, 1987: 44). Indeed, Upham's analysis suggests that the government was more than willing to take the lead in dealing with the matter in hopes that this would reduce publicity of its own responsibility for the catastrophe. Furthermore Miyazawa (1990) has reported that although these actions were innovative, they also restricted the power of the lower courts to devise innovative legal interpretations expanding the liability of the government, and in fact that in these cases none of the courts ever held any government body—local or national—liable as many of the plaintiffs had urged (Miyazawa, 1991). These judicial actions were a delicate balancing act that provided some relief in one of the world's first mass toxic tort cases but at the same time limited the exposure—legal and political—of the government which, in the view of many, had been negligent in regulating the industries involved. Support for our view is found in the fate of a case handed down in 1987. There for the first time in a tort case, a judge in the Kumamoto District Court held national and local government legally liable only to have his decision reversed upon appeal. Furthermore, he soon found himself reassigned to a post in the provinces, and soon resigned to take a less prestigious position in a lower court nearer his home, a pattern that Rameseyer, Miyazawa and others have found repeatedly.

In short, the judicial policy-making that Foote has undeniably pointed to is nevertheless more restrictive and limited than he suggests. And in light of the themes of this volume, the innovative judicial decisions cannot easily be understood as efforts to advance political freedoms or moderate government. At best they are technocratic innovations, valuable but not necessarily evidence of judicial effort to confront the state. Furthermore, as Upham has documented (1987: 62), after the burst of judicial innovation and activism of the 1960s and 1970s, the government took decisive action to reduce legal challenges directed at it. As he writes, the government co-opted potential challengers through 'the dramatic turnaround in regulatory policy, the creation of extrajudicial avenues for compensation for pollution injuries and the resolution of pollution disputes, and the systematic inclusion of environmental concerns and limited citizen participation in governmental planning'. Thus, by the early 1980s 'environmental litigation has largely disappeared as a major political or legal factor in national policy, and the central government has recaptured the initiative in environmental planning' (Upham, 1987: 63). As evidence, Upham contrasts the celebrated but ultimately unsuccessful tort claims in the Osaka Airport noise case of the 1980s with the earlier and more successful tort claims in the pollution cases. Miyazawa's (2005) updated survey of environmental litigation cases found much the same thing; although plaintiffs can often gain something in pretrial settlement, they virtually never win in court when making claims against government. Most scholars now agree that it is not worthwhile to look to the judiciary for new and innovative doctrine and approaches, especially in efforts to challenge the discretion of government officials. Since the 1980s, there has been a decline in liberal expectations; by the turn of the century even some formerly radical sociologists of social movements began to argue that antagonistic social movements are ineffective, and that their best hope is to work collaboratively—rather than through legal confrontation—with the government, even though access to ministries and the legislative process is often beyond the reach of marginal groups. Some scholars studying social movement remain somewhat optimistic about using litigation (Otsuka, 2005), but even they acknowledge that social movements are not likely to win any significant cases. Their goal is to use litigation as a means of mobilising social movements in ways that have been described by Scheingold, McCann, and others. But even here, this appears to be more hope than reality.

The one partial exception to this clear pattern is that the courts have continued to be somewhat aggressive and successful in cases involving environmental issues. In a 2000 air pollution case near Kobe, the district court handed down a decision 12 years after an initial filing that held the government and the highway corporation liable. The court ordered them to pay 332 million Japanese yen to 50 plaintiffs, and issued an injunction requiring them to reduce the level of pollution (Kidder and Miyazawa, 1993). Unlike some other decisions for the plaintiff, this judgment stood up on appeal—though only barely. The higher court did not forthrightly uphold the decision and award, but it did quietly send a signal to the government that it might lose its appeal. Subsequently the government settled but on terms much less generous than the plaintiffs had wanted and than the trial court had awarded. Other environment cases have met similar fates.

An even more significant court decision, again involving environmental issues, was a 2004 Supreme Court decision holding the government liable in an offshoot of seemingly endless litigation involving the Minamata cases begun in the 1960s. It was filed by a number of Minamata disease victims who had moved from Minamata to the Kansai area shortly after the scandal broke in the late 1960s, and had separated themselves from the bulk of the victims who had ultimately agreed to a government-brokered settlement in 1995. Because of problems in obtaining certification as victims after their move, this case dragged on and on. In yet one more case, the Supreme Court in 2004, handed down a major victory for the victims. A panel of the Supreme Court found that both the national government and local governments possessed authority to have tackled the problems well before 1960, and that they were negligent in not having done so. The Court's decision may have been influenced by the fact that one of the justices had previously been an attorney active in environmental litigation, but it is more likely that this liberal decision, like some others since 2000, was a result of the politics of judicial reform that was begun in the late 1990s (see the discussion later in this chapter).

Still, not too much should be read into this 2004 high court decision. By the time the Court acted, some 40 years after the incident, all of the principals had retired from office and indeed most of them had died! Ruling against living defendants might be a different matter. Furthermore, the victory for the plaintiffs is more apparent than real; as of this writing, the government continues to ignore the court order, declaring that it will adhere to the old standards for finding liability, and further no one in the government has agreed to serve on the board to certify people as victims, something has is also required under the court order. As a result 1,000 people who thought they had achieved a victory in the Supreme Court have not yet been formally certified as participants in the process. To date the Court seems uninterested in forcing the government to comply with its orders.

There is still more evidence of judicial timidity. A judge in the Osaka High Court hanged himself in December 2006, three days after he had handed down a decision holding that a new government system that collected information on individuals was unconstitutional if it included data on those who had indicated they did not want to be included in it. It was the first High Court decision to hold this new system unconstitutional. He left no note and no one knows the reason for his suicide. Several years earlier he had been severely criticised for holding another law unconstitutional. In light of this, it is not unreasonable to suggest that judges who declare laws and administrative regulations unconstitutional are under tremendous strain.

In sum, although there are some instances of 'judicial policy-making', and even some dramatic instances of it, the cases are few and far between, are consigned to a few areas (mostly environmental issues), and even then they usually lack bite in terms of forcing government compliance. As a consequence, it is fair to characterise the Japanese judiciary as fundamentally passive vis-à-vis the other branches of the government. At best, the relationship between the judiciary and the other branches of the government follow something of a zigzag; the level of passivity of the judiciary appears to fluctuate depending on various factors. However, Foote (2006: 290) is undoubtedly correct when he says that the judiciary has become more assertive because 'zealous and creative attorneys carry out litigation' in spite of tremendous odds against them and their clients. Thus, we move to an analysis of the bar in post-World War II Japan.

(b) The Bar in Post-World War II Japan

Immediately following the War, the Japanese bar emerged as if from hibernation. It quickly regained and significantly expanded its sense of independence, its autonomy and anti-government ethos (*zaiya seishin*). One reason for its immediate resuscitation was its compatibility with the American occupation forces. For the most part, the occupation forces took an independent bar for granted, though eventually American officials clashed with left-wing members of the bar over their defence of alleged communists, and others opposed to the American policy of complete Japanese disarmament. Writing in 1976, years after the Occupation, Alfred Oppler (1976: 47) , a lawyer working with American occupation officials, recalled that Japanese lawyers welcomed American support in their continuing battle with the justice ministry and the Supreme Court officials, who wanted to impose severe restrictions on lawyers in the proposed Practising Attorney Act of 1949, and attributes the liberal nature of the law to American support.

Despite this new-found support, the bar did not grow appreciably in numbers in the aftermath of the War, nor indeed has it since. Like the judiciary, the bar chose to remain small. Not until the 1990s did the bar take any steps to increase its size. But what is lost by small size is partially offset by cohesiveness. The Practising Attorney Act, enacted in 1949, required attorneys to join local bar associations (*bengoshikai*) as well as a national organisation, the Japan Federation of Bar Associations (JFBA) (*Nihon Bengoshi Rengokai*) (www.nichibenren.or.jp/en/). When the bar was re-established as an independent organisation after the War, local bar associations and the JFBA rather than the justice ministry were given power to discipline attorneys. Furthermore, the status of lawyers was enhanced; post-war examination training of future attorneys was now combined with that of future assistant judges and prosecutors. All now take the same national bar examination (*Shiho Shiken)*, and those who pass spend a total

176 Malcolm M Feeley and Setsuo Miyazawa

of two years together (in 2002, this period was reduced to one and a half years, and in 2006, it was reduced to one year) as trainees at the Supreme Court's Legal Training Research Institute (LTRI) and in field placements in local courts, prosecutors' offices and attorneys' offices (Hattori, 1963). All trainees are paid salaries by the state. Despite the fact that the Supreme Court controls this training, attorneys have welcomed the arrangement, believing that it accorded them equal status with judges and prosecutors. Furthermore, the bar is well-organised, and has organised a great many committees that pursue a variety of public interest causes, often in the face of government opposition.

Article 1 of the Practising Attorney Act of 1949 proclaims that 'A practising attorney is entrusted with a mission to protect fundamental human rights and to realize social justice'. In Japan this is more than an empty slogan. It reaffirms the bar's longstanding sense of responsibility, central to its ethos from the outset. This sense of responsibility has shaped its postwar efforts (Miyazawa, 1999: 21–6). In 1952, the JFBA established the Japan Legal Aid Society to provide legal aid in civil cases (Ichiki and Ohishi, 1999), and has continued to sponsor it to the present. In the 1960s, during the upsurge in popular political protest and political activism, the Japanese bar was active in representing those charged with politically motivated crimes and other activists. Some 'new left' lawyers adopted aggressive, hyper-adversarial styles and had some considerable success. As such they contributed to an increase in aggressive litigation practices more generally. Other lawyers organised public interest actions dealing with environmental concerns that were also successful, at least at the outset (Upham, 1987: ch 2). The intense political activism of the 1960s did not sustain itself, but it did have some lasting effects. The numbers of public interest organisations dedicated to the amelioration of social problems increased markedly, as did the bar's commitment to using its resources to challenge governmental arbitrariness (Garon, 2003).

As we discussed in the preceding section, the judiciary has been unwilling legally to challenge the legislative and executive branches, and when the occasional brave judge has, more often than not, he has paid a high price for his independence. On an institutional level the government can and on several occasions has trimmed the jurisdiction of the courts rather than risk conflict with the judiciary. In his interviews with cause lawyers in the Kansai area in 1994 and 1995, Miyazawa (1999: 33–8) found that they were well-aware of their situation; even in very strong cases, they felt they had to accept meagre settlements since victory at trial was unlikely. Only occasionally did any of them pursue the latter course, and almost always in order to use litigation as a means of fostering public awareness of their cause (Kidder and Miyazawa, 1993). Eric Feldman (2000) has documented a similar process: the have-nots often pursue legal rights, but they rarely win. At best they hope to obtain a modest settlement. In Japan, there is no 'myth of rights' (Scheingold). Both social movement activists and 'cause lawyers' have realistic expectations of what the judiciary can and cannot do; both have low expectations.

Still, the many lawyers and the bar, as the institutional arm of lawyers, have a strong sense of civic commitment. The bar's contribution to civil society includes more than representing interests in court. Its civic commitment is also revealed in the numbers and the types of organisations it sponsors. The JBFA sponsors the Human Right Protection Committee, and nearly 100 other special committees. These committees provide networks of back-up resources for attorneys handling novel issues on criminal justice, international human rights and environmental protection. They also serve as think-tanks, through which the JFBA both formulates and publicises its own positions on issues.

Some of these organisations predate the War, but most were established after the War. The Japan Lawyers Association for Freedom (JLAF) was established in 1921 and has long been affiliated with the National Lawyers Guild in the United States. After the War, the bar members, with the bar's blessing, established still other types of associations. In 1947, the Japan Civil Liberties Association (JCLU or *Jiyu Jinken Kyokai*) was established with assistance provided by the American Civil Liberties Union (ACLU). (McArthur actually invited ACLU's Roger Baldwin to Japan to establish the JCLU, and Eleanor Roosevelt visited the JCLU in 1952.) While the JCLU also has lay members, its officers and members are almost all lawyers or legal academics (www.jclu.org/index_e.shtml). Like the ACLU with which it is affiliated, the JCLA has been particularly active on policy issues related to the freedom of expression and other human rights (Jiyu Jinken Kyokai, 1997). Another group, the Japan Young Lawyers Association (*Seinen Horitsuka Kyokai*) was established in 1954 to promote the new Constitution (www.seihokyo.jp/). It is one of the few legal organisations in Japan whose membership includes attorneys, judges and legal academics. We have seen in an earlier section that judges who belonged to this organisation were persecuted in the late 1960s and the early 1970s. In 1961, those attorneys who participated in the movement against the US–Japan Security Treaty of 1960 organised to form the Japan Democratic Lawyers' Association (*Nihon Minshu Horitsuka Kyokai*), which continues to be engaged in a wide range of environmental, consumer and labour issues (Takahashi and Tsukahara, 1996). There are any number of smaller associations of activist attorneys. Memberships tend to overlap among associations with similar ideological inclinations.

There is also a distinctive group of 'cause lawyers' in Japan (Scheingold and Sarat, 2004). A 1999 study (Miyazawa, 1999: 27–38) of lawyers in Kobe, Osaka and Kyoto found that they spent more than 30 per cent of their time working as 'cause lawyers'. They handle a host of cases, ranging from criminal cases with single defendants to massive environmental cases involving several hundred complainants and more than 100 lawyers (Kidder and Miyazawa, 1993; O'Brien and Okoshi, 1993). In most instances they work on 'cause' cases for little or no pay, and support themselves from fee-paying clients in ordinary civil cases. As radical as some of them are, almost all of them tend to support themselves in this way. Most support severe restrictions on the number of lawyers, believing that these limits provide them with the economic security that enables them to take on pro bono work. This stance reveals the underlying tensions in the bar's position regarding expanded access to legal rights. If the bar were to achieve its objectives of greater access to the law, especially for the poor, its size would need to be increased dramatically. Yet, as committed as they are, Japanese lawyers are reluctant to press for a larger bar.

This position is certainly not for lack of talent or interest in the legal profession. Each year after long periods of university and cram-school courses, tens of thousands of young men and women take the state-controlled bar examination. However until the late 1990s only about 500—from 2 to 4 per cent of those taking the examination—passed it each year. The numbers grew after that, but not dramatically. 'Passing' is not determined by obtaining some minimum score in the examination; rather the the pass rate is set in advance by the Bar Examination Committee of the Ministry of Justice. In 2005 over 25,000 applicants took the bar examination, and 1,500 passed. This number is scheduled to increase over the next few years and to reach 3,000 by 2010. Despite liberalisation and expansion, the Ministry of Justice will continue to administer the bar examination, and the Supreme Court will continue to administer legal apprenticeship at the Legal Research and Training Institute. In fact the JFBA has never tried to increase the numbers of private lawyers; all expect that the additional numbers of those passing the bar will move into public service, as assistant judges or prosecutors. In our view, this clearly suggests short-sightedness on the part of the bar. If suddenly it were to accomplish the many legal reforms it has long called for, it would be unable to implement them because of a lack of lawyers.

However, two developments in the 1980s and 1990s generated substantial pressure for major changes in civil society, including the legal complex. The extended period of prosperity throughout the 1980s and 1990s fostered both greater internationalism and a reduction in traditional social constraints. New volunteer groups sprang up particularly after the great earthquake in Kobe in 1995, and contributed to the enrichment of civil society. This trend was reinforced by increasing internationalism. As Japan continued to absorb Western influences, an increasingly liberal populace imposed new pressures for change on the government.

On 17 January 1995 an earthquake that struck the Kobe area resulted in the deaths of more than 6,000 people. It was the impetus for major changes in civil society state relations as both the national and state levels proved to be incompetent in responding to the crisis. Government officials were unable to provide even basic relief immediately after the earthquake (Schwartz, 2003: 14–19). In sharp contrast, a great many non-governmental organisations (NGOs) responded immediately, sending trained personnel and supplies. In their quick and effective response, NGOs demonstrated their value with crystal clarity. Belatedly, the ruling political party and business leaders acknowledged their value and incorporated this insight into their evolving new policy of privatisation. One result was a 1998 Act that made it much easier to establish not-for-profit organisations (NPOs) (Kingston, 2004: 70–85). Prior to this, the law required would-be NPOs to obtain governmental permission to operate, and this permission was usually granted only to organisations which promised to be 'guided' by a supervising government agency, or were staffed by retired personnel from that agency. In essence, agencies in the various ministries had strangleholds over NPOs. (One of the few NPOs that has avoided this form of subservience is the JCLU. It was established in the early 1950s during the Allied Occupation and with strong support from Occupation officials and its sister organisation in the United States, the ACLU.) However, the earthquake broke this government stranglehold; the new law transferred authority to authorise NPOs from the central government to prefectural governments, and greatly simplified the process for application and approval.

In short order, 16,000 new NPOs of all sorts were established (Kingston, 2004: 75; Tsujinaka, 2004). Many of them are small organisations that provide supplementary services for local governments. Some serve as citizens' watchdogs of central and local governmental agencies. Others are shareholder organisations that monitor practices of businesses and environmental government agencies. Leaders of these organisations are often attorneys, and the organised bar has formed relationships with many of them. However there are remaining impediments that restrict the continued growth of such organisations. Concerned with tax fraud, the Finance Ministry makes it difficult for individuals to claim tax deductable contributions to these organisations despite a law that permits them. As a consequence NPOs face substantial challenges obtaining financial support. Still, there has been a dramatic increase in NPOs, and the since the mid-1990s they have become a public force to be reckoned with.

Activist lawyers provided two types of help in the wake of the earthquake. With financial support from the bar, they established legal advice centres for those who had suffered in the earthquake. In the first four years after the earthquake, the Japan Legal Aid Association spent 892 million Japanese yen on the programme. This programme not only helped to provide immediate relief for a great many victims of the earthquake, it also helped to set in motion a move to establish still more self-help institutions. Many of them also were successful in framing the losses in terms of human rights. They had some considerable success in arguing that the loss of shelter and the failure of the government to provide relief to earthquake victims were a denial of human rights. For example, Katsuyuki Kumano, an Osaka lawyer who had long been involved in human rights cases (for a discussion of his work see O'Brien, 1996: ch 4), drew on language in the International Covenant of Civil and Political Rights (ICCPR), Article 11(1), to argue that the continued homelessness of many victims of the 1995 earthquake violated the Covenant's 'right of everyone to an adequate standard of living ... including food, clothing and housing ...' (Asahi newspaper, 22 January 2007, evening edition, 1). Accordingly, he invited leading lawyers of the Habitat International Coalition, a UN NGO, to Japan, and together they began lobbying on behalf of the victims who had lost their housing. The mission of this group also expanded as it got more deeply involved in local matters; it successfully opposed city plans to build a highway through a devastated area on the ground that it would increase pollution. As this case illustrates, providing legal relief to quake victims led to a natural expansion of interests and objectives. What began as legal advice was transformed into broadly based social action.

Japanese corporation law makes it difficult for NPOs to form, and so many of the lawyers who responded to the legal needs of earthquake victims soon found themselves helping new social groups to seek legal incorporation. In the aftermath any number of new NPOs dedicated to environmental protection, relief activities after disaster, human rights protection, the promotion of peace, promotion of equal opportunities and consumer protection were formed, and many of them not only required lawyers to help them incorporate but needed lawyers to advise them on their activities. Cause lawyers often stepped forward to help. However, we should not overestimate these developments. Per capita there are still far fewer NPOs in Japan and far fewer public interest law firms than there are in the United States. Furthermore while Japan has a much higher percentage of lawyers engaged in public interest work, almost all devote only part of their time to it. There are only a handful of lawyers—most employed by JCLU as staff lawyers—who devote all their time to public interest work. Unlike in the United States, there are no law school-based clinics or 'alternative' public interest law firms. Indeed, it is for this reason that the normally liberal bar defends its small size: although many lawyers devote some time to public interest work, they must subsidise this work by high fees that are guaranteed by the small size of the bar. There are some signs that this is changing, but at the time of writing few concrete steps have been taken. They are discussed later in this chapter.

Ironically the recession of the 1990s reinforced some of these same developments. The government's response to the economic crisis was a form of Thatcher and Reagan-inspired neo-liberalism; denationalisation, deregulation and privatisation. In a society that had long been accustomed to state 'guidance', this retreat of government provided new-found opportunities for business and civil society institutions, including the bar. It also led business to call for a more responsive legal system, including a more informed and independent judiciary and a larger and more specialised bar. They were necessary, business leaders felt, to fill the void that had been vacated by ministry officials in the 'guided' economy, to help them survive in a more competitive environment.

In June 1999, a self-proclaimed neo-liberal government under the Liberal Democratic Party (LDP) established the Justice System Reform Council to develop plans for a more responsible and responsive legal system. The Council received a broad mandate: to consider changes in size, recruitment and training of the judiciary, as well as the size and nature of the bar (Justice System Reform Council, 1999; Miyazawa, 2001). Seeing this as a rare political opportunity, other groups including the organised bar, which had long campaigned for legal and related reforms, joined the bandwagon for re-reading judicial and legal reforms that the Council had been charged with formulating. This unlikely coalition then joined forces to press its agenda for legal reform. The result was the most far-reaching set of legal reforms since the Occupation (Miyazawa, 2001; Kingston, 2004: 3).

The Council's central question was, 'Do the bench and the bar provide sufficient access to justice?' Its answer was a resounding 'no'. Its final report published in June 2001 (Report of the Justice System Reform Council, 2001) proclaimed that bold steps must be taken to transform both the spirit of law and the rule of law into 'the flesh and blood of this country'. In uncharacteristically blunt language for a Japanese government-sponsored report, the Council acknowledged that in a very real sense the rule of law had not taken root in Japan, despite its 130-year experience with a modern legal system, and its 50-year experience with its American inspired post-war constitution. Despite the changes, according to the Council, law in Japan remained an instrument of government administration, and had not developed into an autonomous system which could be used by members of the public as a means of holding government officials accountable for their actions. To support its claims, the Council pointed out that the number of lawyers and judges per capita, which had never been high compared to that in other industrialised states, had in fact declined markedly since the 1930s. Accordingly, the Council recommended that the government triple the number of new lawyers and add a minimum of 500 new judges by 2010, and add still more if court case loads continued to increase (Report of Justice System Reform Council, 2001: 45).

From the outset, the Supreme Court's General Secretariat was vigorously opposed to the Council's work. The Secretariat resented the parliamentary-created Council, dug in its bureaucratic heels, and embraced the status quo. Once the Council started its deliberation, officials in the Secretariat challenged the Council's findings and presented its own views. The Secretariat steadfastly maintained that the courts were not overburdened and that citizens had ample opportunity to gain access to justice through the courts or other forms of government-sponsored dispute resolution programmes.

True to bureaucratic form, the Secretariat acceded to some modest changes, but stood firm against all the proposals for major changes. It agreed to slight increases in the numbers of judges, but rejected proposals that called for the appointment of judges who had substantial prior experience as lawyers in private practice. It acceded to the long-standing request to 'reintroduce' the jury trial, but agreed only to a watered-down form of jury trial—not the Anglo-American-style jury that had existed in the Japan of the 1920s and 1930s, but a European-style mixed system of lay assessors and professional judges, who were restricted to sitting in only a tiny number of serious criminal cases (Miyazawa, 2002). Some other proposals were accepted as well: national and regional boards were established under the Secretariat to review the qualifications of judicial candidates nominated by the Secretariat; new judges will now spend roughly two years in principle during their 10-year tenure as assistant judges working in law firms or some other outside organisation; the Secretariat is to cooperate more closely with the Japan Federation of Bar Associations and is supposed to recruit more attorneys with backgrounds in private practice into the judiciary; and the Secretariat agreed to establish and publicise standards and procedures for evaluating sitting judges. With the possible exception of the introduction of mixed courts, most of these changes do not constitute a substantial break with past practices. However, even the new mixed court system may be limited because it can be dominated by professional judges. Furthermore, the new programmes will all be managed by the Secretariat, so that it will continue to maintain near total control over judicial selection and judicial administration. Outsiders must closely watch how these 'reforms' will actually be implemented.

Some of the Council-inspired reforms built on longstanding concerns of the bar. In 1990 local bar associations instituted a British duty solicitor-like system to provide pretrial detainees with a free meeting with counsel. The bar has also been solicitous of legal needs of the poor who reside in small towns and rural areas, and developed a creative programme to open legal aid law offices for these areas. The first such office was opened in 2000, and met with such success that the programme expanded rapidly. Young lawyers were specially recruited and subsidised by the bar according to certain standards in addition to whatever income they might generate on their own, to serve in remote areas for periods of two or three years, with an option of remaining. These offices are flooded with clients, thereby refuting conservatives' claims that rural people do not want or need law and lawyers to resolve their disputes. However, demand for lawyers has outstripped supply and the bar's resources to support the programme, and the bar has argued for an expanded responsibility of the government for legal aid.

The Council's report provided impetus for securing expanded government funding for these programmes and other similar ones. Even as the Council was still deliberating, the government agreed to increase financial support for the Legal Aid Society. The Civil Legal Aid Act of 2000 stipulated for the first time a governmental responsibility for civil legal aid to the poor, and accordingly significantly increased governmental support for such programmes. A second major reform expanded the court-appointed defense counsel in criminal cases. While the present system provides free counsel only after indictment, the new system will make counsel available to indigent suspects who are detained beyond 72 hours after arrest. This new system of criminal legal aid was introduced in stages beginning in 2006, covering approximately 10,000 suspects a year, and it will be expanded in 2009 to cover approximately 100,000 suspects. Furthermore, the third and most far-reaching change in legal services for indigent people was the establishment of a public corporation, the Japan Legal Assistance Centre (*Nihon Shiho Shien Centre*), in 2006, which administer civil and criminal legal aid programmes. The Centre is supervised by the justice ministry. Functions and staff once provided by the bar's much smaller programme have been moved to the Centre, the Japan Legal Aid Society will be closed in March 2007, and all civil and criminal legal aid in Japan is provided by this Centre's staff attorneys as well as private attorneys working on contract with the Centre.

Furthermore, in agreeing to compromises in the wake of the Council's recommendation, the bar made something of a Faustian bargain with the government. The 2001 report of the Justice System Reform Council embraced the bar's call for more support for legal aid, and as well, was responsive to the bar's complaints that judges lacked practical experience as lawyers. On the whole the bureaucracy resisted the recommendations, but it did make the bar an offer it could not refuse. The bar agreed to accept a modest increase in the numbers of lawyers up to 3,000 new lawyers per year by 2010. In return the government agreed to support legal aid and require new judges to obtain some modicum of experience in legal practice. However, the result was not what the bar would have wanted: although there will be more expanded legal aid, the Japan Legal Assistance Centre, supervised by the Ministry of Justice, not the bar, now controls it. Furthermore, the Centre can staff the programme with young judges and prosecutors who will serve brief stints as legal aid lawyers during their training period if the bar fails to recruit a sufficient number of staff lawyers. This fulfills the Supreme Court's promise that judges will be required to obtain practical experience, but is hardly likely to ensure robust legal defence for the poor. Here again, one sees traditional governmental practices at work, inserting their influence over institutions of civil society to ensure their domestication.

Overall, these reforms are something of a mixed bag. Certainly civil society institutions have expanded. But the bar's gains have been purchased at a price. The Supreme Court General Secretariat and Ministry of Justice were successful in keeping the expansion of the judiciary to a minimum. The bar could not effectively challenge them on this because the bar itself was reluctant to increase the numbers of new lawyers. The bar's rationale for this was that a small highly paid bar is necessary in order for lawyers to have the resources to devote a substantial portion of their time to public interest causes (Miyazawa 1999: 23–6). Although this position was explicitly rejected by the JFBA in 2000, many attorneys and local bar associations do not agree with the JFBA's new position. Furthermore, the JFBA has started to argue that 3,000 lawyers should not be produced before 2010, and 3,000 should be the ceiling of new lawyers even after 2010. The bar also continues to accept the practice of government-administered bar examinations and the training institute on the ground that it places lawyers on an equal footing with prosecutors and judges in the legal world. Whatever truth there may be to this, the arrangement virtually guarantees that judges and prosecutors will never have any experience in private practice, something that practising lawyers complain about at length.

Still, on balance over the past 60 years, the bar has made substantial gains, and has continued to maintain its sceptical stance towards the government, becoming even more assertive and independent. Although decidedly a mixed bag, the recent reforms represent an important expansion of the bar's power. The sorts of accommodations described above are not unique to the bar; students of civil society in Japan underscore the close connection— and the cooptation—between organisations in civil society and the government (Garon, 2003; Pekkanen, 2003). The government permits them to function, but monitors their activities or devises joint ventures that keep them under watchful bureaucratic eyes. Such is the case even with the bar, an institution with perhaps the longest history of challenging the state and one that has carefully guarded its prerogatives.

IV. CONCLUSION

This chapter has surveyed the history of the relation of the legal complex and the state from the Tokugawa period to the present. We have found a consistent pattern: a strong state reluctant to relinquish power and thus to permit growth of civil society institutions, including the legal complex. Even when such institutions have been established, the state seeks to 'guide' them. The Meiji revolution provided an unanticipated opportunity for the establishment of an independent bar. Once a legal profession and the principle of legality took root, the drive for autonomy of both the profession and the law emerged as something of an independent force. Slowly and steadily both bench and bar gained greater degrees of independence, although they have never formed a shared identity or common mission. An inward-looking judiciary with few formal ties to the private legal profession has been able to gain a degree of bureaucratic independence from other branches of the government, but it has not aligned itself with the bar or fostered the idea of autonomous law. In contrast, the bar has carefully fostered its own independence and established itself as something of a watch dog of the state. This effort has been partially successful. The organised bar has a considerable degree of autonomy, and has consistently sought to check the state. In periods of political unrest—in the immediate aftermath of the Meiji restoration, in the Taisho period, immediately after World War II, and again in the 1960s and 1990s—the organised bar has championed civil liberties and advocated liberal reforms. But like other civil society institutions facing the military regime just before and during World War II, it caved into pressure, rarely even speaking out to defend the occasional lawyer who was brave enough to represent a politically unpopular client.

Furthermore by consistently supporting the idea of a small (tiny, by Western standards) bar, it has guaranteed that at best it will remain a vibrant but small and weak institution, that the bar will never become an influential profession. Developments since the late 1990s may change this, but we doubt it. There are serious proposals to triple the size of the bar, remove most professional legal training from the Supreme Court, and expand opportunities for lawyers to work as in-house counsel of business corporations and government agencies. These and related developments are the most far-reaching changes since the initial reforms of the Meiji era, and if realised they may change the relation of the state and the bar, result in a more adversarial legal culture, and perhaps even a more autonomous judiciary. However, if past experience is any indication, only a small portion of these proposals will be realised. And even if they are, it is probable that the state will find a way to extend its influence over the newly expanded legal profession.

Still the bar is a robust and active institution in civil society, a consistent champion of liberal ideals and of the moderate, limited state. The Allied Occupation in post-war Japan permitted the bar to reassert this tradition, and more generally to foster the expansion of civil society institutions. Although Japanese institutions continue to exercise a traditional form of 'self-censorship' in which civil society institutions look to the state for 'guidance' and approval, post-war developments have fostered a great many civil society institutions—political parties, labour unions, a free press, the rule of law. The disturbances of the late 1950s and again in the late 1960s helped produce two separate cohorts of social activists, including activist lawyers, who have had a significant influence on the development of civil society institutions. Group-based, rights-oriented litigation is now part of the landscape of Japan in a way that did not exist in pre-war Japan (Feldman, 2000), and the numbers and variety of civil society institutions have increased.

Internationalisation has further loosened traditional constraints on Japanese society and fostered more robust civil society institutions, including the bar (Reimann, 2003). Similarly, both economic boom and bust have also contributed to an increased role for the legal complex. During the boom years of the late 1800s and again in the 1920s and yet again in the post-war period, rapid economic expansion generated social problems, and non-governmental organisations rose up to respond to them. The bar was one such organisation. The economic down-turn of the 1990s that led the government to turn to its own form of Thatcherism—downsizing government, denationalisation, deregulation, privatisation and increased reliance on the market—also had an important unanticipated effect. Civil society institutions, including the legal complex, have expanded to fill the vacuum created by a downsized government. Deregulaton has led to an increase in business support for legal reform, including reforms in legal education and the judicial process, and increases in the size of the bar. As we have seen, the bar has taken advantage of this in any number of ways. To date, however, most serious proposals for change have all been made within the context of government committees, and thus government bureaucrats have been able to shape and limit the nature of the change and the proposals for still more change. Nevertheless the net result has been an increase in opportunities of organisations in civil society, including a somewhat expanded and more activist bar. Though it is still too early to tell, these changes may also lead to a somewhat more independent judiciary and autonomous legal system.

To return to our working hypothesis: the legal complex, and particularly the bar, has contributed to the gradual expansion of the rule of law and civil society. From its founding in the late nineteenth century, the bar has maintained an oppositional stance towards government. Although this role was interrupted during World War II, it was immediately re-established at the war's end, and has since expanded. The bar is still dependent on the state in many ways and at times has had to struggle to preserve its autonomy; nevertheless it is a mainstay of civil society.

REFERENCES

Abe, H, Shindo, M and Kawato, S (1994), *The Government and Politics of Japan* (trans and with an Introduction by JW White, Tokyo, University of Tokyo Press).

Ch'en, P (1981), *The Formation of the Early Meiji Legal Order* (Oxford, Oxford University Press).

Duus, P (1988), *Modern Japan*, 2nd edn (Boston, Mass, Houghton Mifflin).

Feeley, M (2002), 'The Bench the Bar and the State: Judicial Independence in Japan and the United States' in M Feeley and S Miyazawa (eds), *The Japanese Adversary System in Context* (London, Palgrave Macmillan).

—— and Rubin, E (2000), *Judicial Policy Making and the Modern State: How the Courts Reformed America's Prisons* (Cambridge, Cambridge University Press).

Feldman, E (2000), *The Ritual of Rights in Japan: Law, Society, and Health Policy* (New York, Cambridge University Press).

Foote, D (1992), 'The Benevolent Paternalism of Japanese Criminal Justice', 80 *California Law Review* 367.

—— (2006), *Litigation and Society: Reconsidering a Commonsense on Judiciary [Saiban to Shakai: Shiho no Joshiki Saiko]* (Tokyo, NTT Shuppan).

Friedman, L (1975), *The Legal System* (New York, Russell Sage Foundation).

Garon, S (2003), 'From Meiji to Heisei: The State and Civil Society in Japan' in F Schwartz and S Pharr (eds), *The State of Civil Society in Japan* (New York, Cambridge University Press).

Haley, J (1978), 'The Myth of the Reluctant Litigant', 4 *Journal of Japanese Studies* 359.

—— (1991), *Authority Without Power: Law and the Japanese Paradox* (New York and Oxford, Oxford University Press).

—— (1998), *The Spirit of Japanese Law* (Athens, Ga, University of Georgia Press).

—— (forthcoming), 'The Japanese Judiciary: Maintaining Integrity, Autonomy and the Public Trust' (forthcoming in the Festschrift for Dan Fenno Henderson).

Halliday, T and Karpik, L (1997), 'Politics Matter: a Comparative Theory of Lawyers in the Making of Political Liberalism' in T Halliday and L Karpik (eds), *Lawyers and the Rise of Western Political Liberalism* (Oxford, Clarendon Press).

Hattori, T (1963), 'The Legal Profession in Japan: its Historical Development and Present State' in A von Mehren (ed), *Law in Japan: The Legal Order in a Changing Society* (Cambridge, Mass, Harvard University Press).

Henderson, D (1965), *Conciliation and Japanese Law: Tokugawa and Modern* (Seattle, Wash, University of Washington Press), i.

Higuichi, Y (ed) (2001), *Five Decades of Constitutionalism in Japan* (Tokyo, University of Tokyo Press).

Hiramatsu, Y (1981), 'Tokugawa Law', 14 *Law in Japan* 1.

Holt, R and Turner, J (1966), *The Political Basis of Economic Development: An Exploration in Comparative Political Analysis* (Princeton, NJ, D Van Nostrand Co).

Ichiki, G and Ohishi, T (1999), 'Current Issues for Legal Aid in Japan: Reform Perspective' in L Tribe and J Cooper (eds), *Educating for Justice Around the World: Legal Education, Legal Practice, and the Community* (Aldershot, Ashgate).

Jiyu Hosodan (ed) (1998), *Creating Constitutional Precedents [Kenpo Hanrei wo Tsukuru]* (Tokyo, Nihon Hyoronsha).

—— (ed) (2002), *A Tale of the Japan Lawyers Association for Freedom [Jiyu Hosodan Monogatari]* (Tokyo, Nihon Hyoronsha), i and ii.

Jiyu Jinken Kyokai (1997), *Defending Human Beings [Ningen wo Mamoru]* (Tokyo, Shinzansha).

Justice System Reform Council (1999), *The Points at Issue in the Justice Reform,* available at www.kantei.go.jp/foreign/policy/sihou/singikai/991221_e.html.

—— (2001), *Recommendations of the Justice System Reform Council: For a Justice System to Support Japan in the 21st Century,* available at www.kantei.go.jp/foreign/policy/sihou/singikai/990612_e.html.

Kawashima, T (1963), 'Dispute Resolution in Contemporary Japan' in A von Mehren (ed), *Law in Japan: The Legal Order in a Changing Society* (Cambridge, Mass, Harvard University Press).

Kidder, R and Miyazawa, S (1993), 'Long Term Strategies in Japanese Environmental Litigation', 18 *Law & Inquiry* 605.

Kingston, J (2004), *Japan's Quiet Transformation: Social Change and Civil Society in the Twenty-First Century* (London, Routledge Curzon).

Luney, P and Takahashi, K (eds) (1993), *Japanese Constitutional Law* (Tokyo, University of Tokyo Press).

Matsui, Y (1990), *A Study of Japanese Practicing Attorneys [Nihon Bengoshi Ron]* (Tokyo, Nihon Hyoronsha).

McClain, J (2002), *Japan: A Modern History* (New York, WW Norton).

Migdal, J (1998), *Strong Societies and Weak States: State-Society Relations and State Capabilities in the Third World* (Princeton, NJ, Princeton University Press).

Miyazawa, S (1991), 'Administrative Control of Japanese Judges' in P Lewis (ed), *Law and Technology in the Pacific Community* (Boulder, Colo, Westview Press).

—— (1999), 'Lawyering for the Underrepresented in the Context of Legal, Social, and National Institutions: The Case of Japan' in L Trubek and J Cooper (eds), *Educating for Justice around the World: Legal Education, Legal Practice, and the Community* (Aldershot, Ashgate).

—— (2001), 'The Politics of Judicial Reform in Japan: The Rule of Law at Last?', 2 *Asian-Pacific Law & Policy Journal* 89.

—— (2002), 'Summary of and Comments on Recommendations of the Japanese Judicial Reform Council (2001)' in M Feeley and S Miyazawa (eds), *The Japanese Adversary System in Context* (London, Palgrave Macmillan).

—— (2005), 'The Present Situation of Policy-Oriented Contemporary Litigation and the Need for Further Reforms of Justice System in Japan [Seisaku Shikoteki Gendaigata Sosho no Genjo to Shiho Seido Kaikaku Keizoku no Hitsuyousei]', 67 *Ho Shakaigaku [Sociology of Law]* 46.

—— and Otsuka, H (2002), 'Legal Education and the Reproduction of the Elite in Japan' in Y Deale and B Garth (eds), *Global Prescriptions: The Production, Exportation, and Importation of a New Legal Orthodoxy* (Ann Arbor, Mich, University of Michigan Press).

Murayama, M (2002), 'The Role of the Defense Attorney in the Japanese Criminal Process' in M Feeley and S Miyazawa (eds), *The Japanese Adversary System in Context* (London, Palgrave Macmillan).

Nihon Saibankan Network (ed), *Saibankan datte Shaberitai [Judges Do Want to Talk, too]* (Tokyo, Nihon hyoronsha).

O'Brien, D and Okoshi, Y (1993), *To Dream of Dreams: Religious Freedom and Constitutional Politics in Postwar Japan* (Honolulu, Hawaii, University of Hawaii Press).

Ooms, H (1996) *Tokugawa Village Practice: Class, Status, Power, Law* (Berkeley, Cal, University of California Press).

Oppler, R (1976), *Legal Reform in Occupied Japan* (Princeton, NJ, Princeton University Press).

Otsuka, H (2005), 'The Effects of Legal Mobilization Toward the Policy Making Process [Sosho Doin to Seisaku Keisei/Henyo Koka]', 67 *Ho Shakaigaku [Sociology of Law]* 75.

Pekkanen, R (2003), 'Molding Japanese Civil Society: State-Structured Incentives and the Patterning of Civil Society' in F Schwartz and S Pharr (eds), *The State of Civil Society in Japan* (New York, Cambridge University Press).

Ramseyer, M and Rasmusen, E (2003), *Measuring Judicial Independence: The Political Economy of Judging in Japan* (Chicago, Ill, University of Chicago Press).

—— and Nakazato, M (1999), *Japanese Law: An Economic Approach* (Chicago, Ill, University of Chicago Press).

Reimann, K (2003), 'Building Global Civil Society from the Outside In? Japanese International Development NGOs, the State, and International Norms' in F Schwartz and S Pharr (eds), *The State of Civil Society in Japan* (New York, Cambridge University Press).

Samuels, R (1994), *'Rich Nation, Strong Army': National Security and the Technological Transformation of Japan* (Ithaca, NY, Cornell University Press).

Scalapino, R (1967), *Democracy and the Party Movement in Prewar Japan: The Failure of the First Attempt* (Berkeley, Cal, University of California Press).

Scheingold, S and Sarat, A (2004), *Something to Believe In: Politics, Professionalism, and Cause Lawyering* (Stanford, Cal, Stanford University Press).

Schwartz, F (2004), 'Introduction: Recognizing Civil Society in Japan' in F Schwartz and S Pharr (eds), *The State of Civil Society in Japan* (New York, Cambridge University Press).

Seinen Horitsuka Kyokai Bengosi Gakusha Godo Bukai (ed) (1990), *Japan Young Lawyers Association [Seihokyo]* (Tokyo, Nihon Hyoronsha).

Shapiro, M (1981), *Courts: A Comparative and Political Analysis* (Chicago, Ill, University of Chicago Press).

Takahashi, T and Tsukahara, E (eds) (1996), *Document Contemporary Litigations [Document Gendai Shiho]* (Tokyo, Nihon Hyoronsha).

Takayanagi, K (1963), 'A Century of Innovation: The Development of Japanese Law, 1868–1961' in A von Mehren (ed), *Law in Japan: The Legal Order in a Changing Society* (Cambridge, Mass, Harvard University Press).

Tsujinaka, Y (2003), 'From Developmentalism to Maturity: Japan's Civil Society Organizations in Comparative Perspectives' in F Schwartz and S Pharr (eds), *The State of Civil Society in Japan* (New York, Cambridge University Press).

Upham, F (1987), *Law and Social Change in Postwar Japan* (Cambridge, Mass, Harvard University Press).

—— (2004), 'Political Lackeys or Faithful Public Servants? Two Views of the Japanese Judiciary', 30 *Law & Social Inquiry* 421.

Part Two

Middle East

6

Mobilising the Law in an Authoritarian State: The Legal Complex in Contemporary Egypt

TAMIR MOUSTAFA

T HIS CHAPTER FOCUSES upon the struggle for individual rights and
the rule of law in the Egyptian context. The Egyptian legal profession has a long history of political activism characterised by a deep
commitment to liberal political institutions and the rule of law. Lawyers
played a particularly strong role in political life in pre-revolutionary Egypt,
dating all the way back to the late nineteenth century. Fourteen of the 19
prime ministers who served between 1919 and 1952 had their formal training in law and nearly all cabinets through the period featured a majority of
lawyers (Reid, 1981; Ziadeh, 1968). Indeed, the most famous and venerated
personalities in early twentieth century Egyptian history—among them Sa'd
Zaghlul, Mustafa Kamil, Mustafa al-Nahas and Tawfik al-Hakim—were
all lawyers. The Lawyers' Syndicate and the Judges' Association were, as
they are now, two of the most important focal points for political life in
Egypt. The Egyptian national courts, established in 1884, also enjoyed a
high degree of independence, particularly in comparison to those of other
non-western countries during the same period. Much like the Western
experience, judicial independence and the strength of the legal profession
were intimately tied to the country's free market economy and the relative,
if imperfect, balance of power between the main political factions in
pre-revolutionary Egypt.

The 1952 Free Officers' coup d'etat that brought Gamal 'Abd al-Nasser
to power marked a sharp departure from this liberal, democratic order.
For the past five decades the Egyptian legal complex has struggled to
protect individual rights within an authoritarian state. Scholars generally
assume that the legal complex is non-existent or impotent in such political

contexts; courts are assumed to have no autonomy, judges are assumed to be pawns of their regimes, and groups in civil society are thought to have no protection from the law. However, the Egyptian case illustrates that the legal complex is engaged in continual and meaningful struggles for individual rights, even in authoritarian states. This chapter explores the specific dynamics and challenges of legal mobilisation in such a constrained political environment.

I. AUTHORITARIAN RULE, SOCIALISM, AND THE DECLINE OF THE EGYPTIAN LEGAL COMPLEX (1952–70)

Following the 1952 military coup, the constitution was annulled by executive decree, political parties were forcibly disbanded, and legal institutions were weakened significantly.[1] 'Abd al-Raziq al-Sanhuri, one of Egypt's greatest legal scholars and the architect of the Egyptian civil code, was assaulted by Nasser supporters and forced to resign in 1954. Another 20 prominent members of the *Majlis al-Dawla* (the Administrative Court) were forcibly retired or transferred to non-judicial positions. The regime further consolidated its control by circumventing the regular court system and establishing a series of exceptional courts throughout the early 1950s including *Mahkmat al-Thawra* (The Court of the Revolution) in 1953 and *Mahakim al-Sha'ab* (The People's Courts) in 1954. These courts had sweeping mandates, few procedural guidelines, no appeals process, and were staffed by loyal supporters of the regime, typically from the military. The final and most significant blow to Egyptian judicial institutions came in the 1969 'massacre of the judiciary'. There were extensive purges of judicial officials, the Judges' Association was dissolved, and a new Supreme Council of Judicial Organisations was formed, giving the regime greater control over judicial appointments, promotions and disciplinary action.

The legal complex also suffered in less direct, but equally profound ways by the transition to a socialist economy. Paralleling the political transformation of Egypt, Nasser steered the country in a new economic direction by nationalising virtually the entire private sector. With private sector activity reaching a near standstill, the most profitable commercial cases supporting the legal profession were lost. Lawyers were left to work on civil or criminal cases that generated only a fraction of the revenue of commercial cases, and commercial lawyers were folded into the state's bourgeoning public sector. As a result, the legal profession fell from being perhaps the most lucrative and respected profession in pre-revolutionary Egypt to one of the least desirable career paths. The strength of the Lawyers' Syndicate,

---

[1] For a more detailed discussion of this period see Brown (1997), Ubayd (1991).

the Judges' Association and the courts themselves were weakened by this economic transformation as much as the direct political assaults that were administered by the regime.

II. REBIRTH: SYNERGY WITHIN THE EGYPTIAN LEGAL COMPLEX (1970–98)

(a) Judicial Institutions

By the time of Nasser's death, the Egyptian economy was in a state of extreme disrepair. Faced with economic stagnation, massive foreign debt, and escalating pressure from international lenders, Anwar Sadat increasingly pinned his government's political survival on attracting foreign direct investment. However, given the regime's record of nationalising the majority of the private sector, it was difficult to convince private investors that their assets would not be subject to adverse legislation after they entered the Egyptian market. Foreign investors did not return despite extensive tax incentives through the 1970s, and even Egyptian citizens themselves continued to move $40 billion offshore because of insecure property rights (Moustafa, 2007).[2]

The regime eventually established an independent Supreme Constitutional Court (SCC) as a commitment to investors that property rights would be protected through an independent process of judicial review.[3] The SCC enjoyed a surprising degree of institutional autonomy, with an independent appointment process and full control over its own financial and administrative affairs.[4] A few years later, the regime additionally restored substantial independence to the administrative courts in an effort to address a crisis of internal discipline (Rosberg, 1995).[5] Independence was granted to these judicial institutions for purely instrumental purposes, but they proved to be a double-edged sword within a few short years.

---

[2] This period is documented extensively in ch 3.

[3] The SCC played an extensive role in the economic reform programme, as examined in Moustafa (2007), chs 4–6.

[4] New appointments to the Court are made by the President from among two candidates, one nominated by the general assembly of the Court and the other by the Chief Justice, but in practice these nominations were always the same. The Chief Justice of the SCC is formally appointed by the President of the Republic, but for the first two decades following its establishment, the President selected the most senior justice serving on the SCC to the position of Chief Justice. A strong norm developed around this procedure, although the president always retained the formal legal ability to appoint anyone to the position of Chief Justice who met the minimum qualifications as defined by the law establishing the court.

[5] When it became clear that centralised monitoring strategies were failing to produce reliable information on the activities of the state's own institutions, the regime enhanced the independence and capacity of administrative courts to serve as a neutral forum for citizens to voice their grievances and to expose corruption in the state bureaucracy.

(b) Opposition Parties

In one of its earliest political rulings, the SCC enabled hundreds of prominent opposition activists, such as Wafd Party leader Fu'ad Serag Eddin, to return to political life.[6] Another ruling in 1988 forced the legalisation of the opposition Nasserist Party against government objections.[7] The SCC even ruled national election laws unconstitutional in 1987 and 1990, forcing the dissolution of the People's Assembly, a new electoral system, and early elections.[8] Two similar rulings forced comparable reforms to the system of elections for both the Upper House (*Majlis al-Shura*) and local council elections nation-wide.[9] These rulings undermined the regime's corporatist system of managing opposition parties, and enabled independent candidates to compete in elections. Simultaneously, judicial activism in both the SCC and the administrative courts allowed opposition activists successfully to challenge decisions of the regime-dominated Political Parties Committee and to gain formal opposition party status. By 1995, 10 of Egypt's 13 opposition parties owed their very existence to court rulings.

Opposition parties and independent activists continued to score dozens of victories in the Supreme Constitutional Court throughout the decade, most notably in the area of press liberties.[10] For example, in February 1993, the SCC struck down a provision in the Code of Criminal Procedure that required defendants in libel cases to present proof validating their published statements within a five-day period of notification by the prosecutor.[11] Following this legal victory, the Labour Party successfully challenged Article 15 of Law 40/1977, holding heads of political parties jointly responsible for all publications in party newspapers, along with the reporter and the editor-in-chief of the newspaper, in cases of libel claims against public officials.[12] The SCC ruling was a landmark case because it broke one of the most important regime controls on the opposition press, and it was one of the first cases in which the SCC explicitly invoked international

---

[6] SCC, 26 June 1986, *al-Mahkama al-Dusturiyya al-'Ulia* (hereafter *al-Mahkama*), vol 3, 353.

[7] SCC, 7 May 1988, *al-Mahkama*, vol 4, 98.

[8] SCC, 16 May 1987, *al-Mahkama*, vol 4, 31; SCC, 19 May 1990, *al-Mahkama*, vol 4, 256.

[9] SCC, 15 Apr 1989, *al-Mahkama*, vol 4, 205; SCC, 15 April 1989, *al-Mahkama*, vol 4, 191.

[10] For an extended review of Supreme Constitutional Court activity during this period see Moustafa (2007: chs 4–6).

[11] SCC, 6 Feb 1993, *al-Mahkama*, vol 5(2), 183.

[12] SCC, 3 July 1995, *al-Mahkama*, vol 7, 45. This provision essentially formed a corporatist system of control over the opposition press. Since the heads of opposition political parties were held directly responsible for all publications, Law 40/1977 pressured the leadership of opposition parties to practise self-censorship and to rein in their staff and writers.

human rights frameworks and treaties.[13] With each ruling, it became more apparent that constitutional litigation was the most promising avenue to challenge NDP legislation and induce further political reform. By opening the political arena and empowering opposition activists, the SCC cultivated a support network that began vigorously to support judicial independence. This pattern of SCC–civil society synergy was simultaneously under way with two other groups engaging the court: legal professional associations and the human rights movement.

(c) Legal Professional Associations

The Lawyers' Syndicate reemerged as an outspoken advocate for political and judicial reform through the 1980s. Its journal, *al-Mohammah*, became an important forum for intellectuals and activists to publicise their calls for further judicial and political reforms. Numerous conferences were also held under the auspices of the Lawyers' Syndicate, drawing intellectuals, academics and opposition activists to discuss the important issues of the day, including avenues for effective political reform. Moreover, the Syndicate began to provide free legal representation to the poor as a way to lodge cases against the regime. Similarly, the Judges' Association continued to play an assertive role throughout the 1980s. In its 1986 National Justice Conference, the Judges' Association issued a formal call for the comprehensive reform of Egyptian judicial and political institutions. *al-Qada'*, the official publication of the Judges' Association, became an important forum for judges and academics alike to address issues concerning the administration of the courts as well as the rule of law and political reform in general. Administrative court judges sounded out their own proposals for reform in their publication, *Majalat Majlis al-Dawla*.

However, all was not well within the legal profession. Ideological fault lines began to emerge within the Egyptian legal complex. As suggested earlier, the legal profession fell from being the most lucrative and respected professional career path in pre-revolutionary Egypt to one of the least desirable professions during Egypt's socialist transformation. Even with the return to a mixed public/private sector economy, the legal profession never regained its previous status. Much of the problem was related to a tremendous overproduction of lawyers, partly as a result of the state's commitment to offer advanced education to every Egyptian family, free of charge.[14] From 1970 to 1980 alone, university enrolment jumped threefold,

---

[13] For more on the 'internationalisation' of SCC legal doctrine see Boyle and Sherif (1997) and Moustafa (2007).

[14] It is important to note that the overproduction of lawyers was a problem even before the vast expansion of the public education system under Nasser and Sadat. From 1917 to 1960,

from nearly 180,000 students to over 550,000 students. Law schools that were once highly selective, attracting the best and the brightest of Egyptian youth, became the easiest faculty to enter at the university. The quality of legal education declined quickly and law schools produced an ever-increasing number of new lawyers each year, further diminishing the prestige of the profession.[15]

The expansion of private sector activity and the increased need for legal services strengthened segments of the profession that were best positioned to take advantage of the regime's economic reform programme. Leading Egyptian law firms entered into joint operations with American and British firms to service new, transnational trade ventures.[16] However, at the same time that a small segment of the legal profession was experiencing the biggest boom in decades, a vast surplus of lawyers, most with poor training and coming from disadvantaged socioeconomic backgrounds, continued to form the bulk of the profession. Sharp cleavages between old-school liberals, on the one hand, and disadvantaged but highly motivated Islamist lawyers, on the other hand, soon took shape within the profession. By 1985 these cleavages were evident not just in the Lawyers' Syndicate membership but also in the formal programmes organised at the Syndicate.[17] In the 1990s, Islamist lawyers began to initiate an aggressive campaign to challenge the secular foundations of Egypt's civil code.

Islamist candidates won a majority in the Doctors' Syndicate elections in 1986, the Engineers' Syndicate in 1987, the Pharmacists' Syndicate in 1990, and, most importantly, the Lawyers' Syndicate in 1992. This final victory in the Lawyers' Syndicate stunned the country because of its longstanding role as a bastion of liberalism. But changes from inside and outside the legal profession—the overproduction of lawyers, the decades-long slump in private economic activity, the decline in the prestige of the profession, and hence the change in its socioeconomic composition—combined with the Islamist revival sweeping the country to produce a strong Islamist mandate in the Lawyers' Syndicate.[18]

---

the Egyptian population doubled in size but the number of lawyers increased twelve-fold (Reid, 1981: 131).

[15] The overproduction of lawyers reduced the cost of legal services and encouraged litigation as a means to solve disputes. This contributed to the tremendous backlogs and long delays in court proceedings.

[16] For more on the transformation of the branch of the legal profession engaged in transnational commerce see Dezalay and Garth (1996).

[17] *Shari'a* committees were established in all syndicate branches across the country to offer social and cultural services to lawyers and their families. Conferences and seminars were also organised around various themes related to Islamic law. Finally, these *shari'a* committees were charged with drafting legislation that would be submitted to the People's Assembly for consideration with the aim of bringing contemporary laws into conformity with the *shari'a*.

[18] Islamists took 18 out of 24 seats in the September 1992 election.

The regime decided that the Lawyers' Syndicate, long a thorn in its side, could be brought under its control under the guise of combating radical Islamists, who were waging armed attacks against the regime by 1992. The government quickly pushed through a new law requiring a minimum 50 per cent turnout in syndicate elections in order to prevent future Islamist victories based upon low voter turnout. Perhaps more ominous was a provision in the new law stating, 'syndicates shall not engage in activities other than those for which they were formed'.[19]

Within days, a conference was held bringing together representatives of 17 syndicates. The syndicates issued a joint statement condemning the legislation, contending that the legislation was unconstitutional, and demanding its annulment. Ahmed Seif al-Islam Hassan al-Banna, a prominent member of the Muslim Brotherhood and the new spokesperson of the Islamist majority on the Lawyers' Syndicate board, illustrated both the level of constitutional consciousness among the opposition and the degree of awareness of the utility of litigation in the SCC when he publicly demanded that the regime retract the law or 'we will take the matter to the Supreme Constitutional Court to prove that the law is unconstitutional'. Indeed, over the next year, 12 syndicates launched court cases attempting to transfer their constitutional challenges to the SCC.[20] Their efforts were encouraged in public statements by activist judges. Ahmed Mekki, vice-president of the Court of Cassation and an outspoken activist judge, went on the record to state that he believed Law 100/1993 was unconstitutional and that if a petition contesting the law reached his court, he would immediately transfer it to the SCC for consideration.[21]

Tensions between the regime and the Lawyers' Syndicate increased to unprecedented levels when an Islamist lawyer and EOHR member, 'Abd al-Harith Madani, was abducted by state security forces, tortured and killed in custody in April 1994. Madani's death provoked a direct confrontation between state security forces and hundreds of lawyers assembled in protest at the syndicate headquarters. After a day of rioting, dozens more lawyers

---

[19] At the same time, the regime attempted to undermine the Lawyers' Syndicate from the inside. In 1993, one of the remaining NDP members on the syndicate board, Muhammad Sabri Mubadda, launched an administrative court case demanding the board's dissolution based on a technicality. Mubadda contended that the 1992 elections were not conducted in line with Law 95/1980, which stipulates that the names of all candidates be provided to the Socialist Public Prosecutor at least one month before elections are held. Mubadda's request was denied but the legal wrangling in the administrative courts illustrated the governments attempt to undermine the Islamist board on technical grounds, without producing an overt confrontation.

[20] This legal strategy was combined with more traditional strategies. On 21 February 1993 the Lawyers' and Engineers' syndicates held a one day strike which reportedly included well over 100,000 lawyers and engineers, according to opposition estimates: *al-Wafd*, 21 Feb 1993, 1.

[21] *al-Wafd*, 3 Nov 1997.

were taken into detention. The case focused international attention on the Egyptian regime, with detailed reports compiled by Human Rights Watch, the Centre for the Independence of Judges and Lawyers, and the Lawyers' Committee for Human Rights.[22]

The regime eventually succeeded in bringing the Islamist dominated Lawyers' Syndicate under sequestration, not through the new syndicate law, but by manipulating the Syndicate's internal factions. In 1996, a Syndicate member initiated a court case accusing the board of financial irregularities. The administrative court hearing the case placed the Syndicate under sequestration.[23] The failed attempt to undermine the Lawyers' Syndicate from within in 1993 and the successful bid to do the same in 1996 illustrate the way that the regime can manipulate internal cleavages for its own advantage, in much the same way that it exploits internal divisions within opposition parties. The sequestration order paralysed an important component of the Egyptian legal complex at a time when a number of crucial confrontations were being fought out between the regime and its opponents.

(d) Human Rights Groups and Public Interest Litigation

The most dynamic component of the Egyptian legal complex throughout the 1990s was a new breed of human rights organisation that went beyond simply documenting human rights abuses to confronting the government in the courtroom. The most aggressive group engaged in public interest litigation was the Centre for Human Rights Legal Aid (CHRLA), established by the young and forceful human rights activist, Hisham Mubarak, in 1994. CHRLA quickly became the most dynamic human rights organisation, initiating 500 cases in its first full year of operation, 1,323 cases in 1996, and 1,616 by 1997. CHRLA documented human rights abuses and used the cases that it sponsored to publise the human rights situation. As with every other human rights group in Egypt, CHRLA depended almost completely upon foreign funding, but throughout the mid-1990s foreign funding sources proved plentiful and CHRLA quickly expanded its operations, opening two regional offices in Alexandria and Aswan.

In hopes of emulating the model provided by CHRLA, human rights activists launched additional legal aid organisations with different missions. The Centre for Women's Legal Aid was established in 1995 to provide

---

[22] For more details on the Madani incident and regime-syndicate relations during this period see *Clash in Egypt: The Government and the Bar* (Centre for the Independence of Judges and Lawyers, 1995).

[23] Opposition activists contended that they were not able to get a fair hearing in this case and in subsequent appeals because the government interfered with court dockets to ensure that cases would be heard by pro-government judges. The Islamist dominated Engineers' Syndicate was similarly brought under sequestration in 1995 for alleged financial irregularities.

free legal aid to women dealing with a range of issues including divorce, child custody and various forms of discrimination.[24] The Land Centre for Human Rights joined the ranks of legal aid organisations in 1996 and dedicated its energies to providing free legal aid to peasants.[25] The Human Rights Centre for the Assistance of Prisoners (HRCAP) similarly provided legal aid to prisoners and the families of detained individuals by investigating allegations of torture, monitoring prison conditions, and fighting the phenomenon of recurrent detention and torture through litigation.[26] Opposition parties began to offer free legal aid as well, with the Wafd Party's Committee for Legal Aid providing free representation in over 400 cases per year beginning in 1997.[27] Similarly, the Lawyers' Syndicate was active in providing legal aid, and it greatly expanded its legal aid department until the regime froze its functions in 1996.

By 1997, legal mobilisation had unquestionably become the dominant strategy for human rights defenders not only because of the opportunities that public interest litigation afforded, but also because of the myriad obstacles to mobilising a broad social movement under the Egyptian regime. Gasser 'Abd al-Raziq, director of the Centre for Human Rights Legal Aid explained that 'in Egypt, where you have a relatively independent judiciary, the only way to promote reform is to have legal battles all the time. It's the only way that we can act as a force for change.' A strong and independent judiciary was so central to the strategy of the human rights movement that activists institutionalised their support for judicial independence by founding the Arab Centre for the Independence of the Judiciary and the Legal Profession (ACIJLP). The ACIJLP set to work organising conferences and workshops that brought together legal scholars, opposition party members, human rights activists, important figures from the Lawyers' Syndicate and Judges' Association, and even justices from the Supreme Constitutional Court itself. The ACIJLP also began to issue annual reports on the state of the judiciary and legal profession, extensively documenting government harassment of lawyers and exposing the regime's interference in the

---

[24] The Centre initiated 71 cases in its first year, 142 in 1996, and 146 in 1997 in addition to providing legal advice to 1,400 women in its first 3 years of activity.

[25] With the land reform law, Law 96 of 1992, coming into full effect in October 1997, hundreds of thousands of peasants faced potential eviction in the late 1990s and legal actions between landlords and tenants began to enter into the courts by the thousands. Between 1996 and 2000 the Land Centre for Human Rights represented peasants in over 4,000 cases and provided legal advice to thousands more (Interview with Mahmoud Gabr, Director of Legal Unit, Land Centre for Human Rights, 18 Nov 2000).

[26] In each of its first five years of operation, the Human Rights Centre for the Assistance of Prisoners launched over 200 court cases and gave free assistance (legal and otherwise) to between 7,000 and 8,000 victims per year (Correspondence with Muhammad Zare'i, Director of the Human Rights Centre for the Assistance of Prisoners, 24 Jan 2002).

[27] Interview with Muhammad Gomm'a, vice-chairman of the Wafd Committee for Legal Aid, 17 Dec 2001.

normal functions of judicial institutions. Like other human rights groups, the ACIJLP established ties with international human rights organisations including the Lawyers' Committee for Human Rights in order to leverage international pressure on the Egyptian government.

Human rights activists engaged in public interest litigation also began to understand that *constitutional* litigation in the Supreme Constitutional Court was potentially the most effective avenue to challenge the regime. CHRLA's executive director, Gasser 'Abd al-Raziq recalled that 'we were encouraged by [Chief Justice] 'Awad al-Murr's human rights language in both his formal rulings and in public statements. This encouraged us to have a dialogue with the Supreme Constitutional Court. CHRLA woke up to the idea that litigation in the SCC could allow us to actually change the laws and not just achieve justice in the immediate case at hand.'[28]

The change in legal tactics paid off handsomely when CHRLA successfully challenged Article 195 of the Penal Code in cooperation with Egypt's main opposition parties.[29] Pleased with their swift success, CHRLA attorneys initiated a campaign systematically to challenge repressive legislation in the SCC starting in late 1997. Their first target was Law 35 of 1976, governing trade union elections. CHRLA initiated 50 cases in the administrative and civil courts, all with petitions to challenge the constitutionality of Law 35/1976 in the Supreme Constitutional Court. Ten of the 50 cases were successfully transferred, and within months the SCC issued its first verdict of unconstitutionality against Article 36 of the Law.[30] CHRLA also successfully advanced three cases to the SCC challenging sections of the Penal Code concerning newspaper publication offences and three additional cases dealing with the Social Insurance Law.

CHRLA was further encouraged by activist judges in the regular judiciary who publicly encouraged groups in civil society to challenge the constitutionality of regime legislation. Some activist judges went so far as to publicise their opinion of laws in opposition newspapers, and vowed that if particular laws were challenged in their court, they would transfer the relevant constitutional question to the SCC without delay.

The rulings of unconstitutionality and the additional 14 pending decisions in a three-year period represented a tremendous achievement, given the slow speed of litigation in Egyptian courts and the relatively meagre resources at the disposal of the human rights movement. Until this campaign, activists, opposition parties and individuals initiated cases in an ad hoc fashion, but CHRLA's successful strategy of coordinated constitutional

---

[28] Interview with Gasser 'Abd al-Raziq, director of the Hisham Mubarak Legal Aid Centre, formerly the Centre for Human Rights Legal Aid, 16 Apr 2000.

[29] SCC, 1 Feb 1997, *al-Mahkama*, vol 8, 286. CHRLA filed appeals with the SCC in 5 additional cases in which it had been representing journalists prosecuted under Art 195.

[30] SCC, *al-Mahkama*, vol 8, 1165.

litigation prompted the rest of the human rights community to initiate similar litigation campaigns directed towards the SCC.[31]

This brief review of opposition and human rights activism illustrates how the new Supreme Constitutional Court provided institutional openings for political activists to challenge the state in ways that fundamentally transformed patterns of interaction between the state and society. For the first time since the 1952 military coup, political activists could credibly challenge the regime by simply initiating constitutional litigation, a process that required few financial resources and allowed activists to circumvent the highly restrictive, corporatist political framework. Most importantly, constitutional litigation enabled activists to challenge the regime without having to initiate a broad social movement, a task that is all but impossible in Egypt's highly restrictive political environment.[32] Through its rulings, the SCC facilitated the reemergence of opposition parties, human rights groups and legal professional associations. Moreover, the SCC continued to shield opposition parties and human rights groups when under attack by the state, essentially becoming their main guardian.

The SCC facilitated the reemergence of a legal complex with the ability to monitor and document human and civil rights violations. Moreover, the SCC made itself the focal point of reform efforts, thus attracting constitutional petitions that enabled the court to expand its exercise of judicial review. Finally, in return for providing protection and access to political participation, the SCC forged a vocal support structure that would defend SCC independence if its mandate were threatened by the regime. Opposition parties, human rights groups and legal professional associations vigorously supported SCC independence because the court actively defended them from government interference and it provided one of the few avenues available to challenge government legislation. A tacit partnership was built on the common interest of both defending and expanding the mandate of the SCC.

III. THE LIMITS OF LITIGATION: STATE SECURITY COURTS AND 'INSULATED LIBERALISM'

Although the Supreme Constitutional Court took startlingly bold stands on most political issues, there were important limits to mobilisation through the courts. These limitations, I contend, are critically important

[31] Several other human rights groups, such as the Land Centre for Human Rights, successfully transferred cases to the SCC for consideration.

[32] The ability to circumvent collective action problems is one of the most significant benefits of legal mobilisation even in consolidated democracies where civil liberties are relatively secure (Zemans, 1983), but the possibility of initiating litigation in lieu of a broad social movement is even more crucial for opposition activists in authoritarian systems where the state forcefully interferes with political organising.

to understanding why the regime did not act more forcefully to suppress the SCC sooner. At odds with its strong record of rights activism, the SCC ruled Egypt's Emergency State Security Courts constitutional and it has conspicuously delayed issuing a ruling on the constitutionality of civilian transfers to military courts. Given that Egypt has remained in a perpetual state of emergency for all but six months since 1967, the Emergency State Security Courts and, more recently, the military courts have effectively formed a parallel legal system with fewer procedural safeguards, serving as the ultimate regime check on challenges to its power.[33]

By 1983, dozens of cases had already been transferred to the Supreme Constitutional Court contesting a legal provision denying defendants the right to appeal rulings of Emergency State Security Courts in the regular judiciary. Plaintiffs contended that the provision violated the right of due process and the competence of the administrative courts, but the SCC ruled the Security Courts constitutional the following year.[34] The SCC reasoned that since Article 171 of the Constitution provided for the establishment of the State Security Courts, they must be considered a legitimate and regular component of the judicial authority. Although this ruling was based on legal reasoning that many constitutional scholars and human rights activists found questionable at best, the Supreme Constitutional Court never looked back and refused to revisit the question of State Security Court competence. Six months after this landmark decision, the SCC summarily dismissed 41 additional cases contesting the jurisdiction of the State Security Courts.[35] The SCC dismissed another 30 cases petitioning the same provision over the course of the following year.[36] The flood of cases contesting the competence of the State Security Courts in such a short period of time reveals the extent to which the regime depends upon this parallel legal track as a tool to sideline political opponents. The large volume of cases transferred to the SCC from the administrative courts also underlines the determination of administrative court judges to assert their institutional interests and to fend off encroachment from the State Security Courts. Finally, the Supreme Constitutional Court's reluctance to strike down provisions denying citizens the right of appeal to regular judicial institutions, despite the dozens of opportunities to do so, illustrates the SCC's reluctance to challenge the core interests of the regime.[37] The SCC assumed a similar stance when it

[33] For more on the structure, composition and procedures of the Emergency State Security Courts and the Military Courts see Brown (1997), 'Ubayd (1991) and The Centre for Human Rights Legal Aid (1995).
[34] SCC, 16 June 1984, *al-Mahkama*, vol 3, 80.
[35] See *al-Mahkama*, vol 3, 90–5.
[36] See *al-Mahkama*, vol 3, 108–13, 152–7, and 189–94.
[37] In an interview, former Chief Justice 'Awad al-Murr described the Egyptian political system as a 'red-line system', where there are implicit understandings between the regime and

received petitions requesting judicial review of the regime's increasing use of *military* courts to try civilians in the 1990s.[38]

Even outside the military courts the regime effectively detains its political opponents for long periods of time through a procedure known as 'recurrent detention'. Under Article 3 of the Emergency Law prosecutors can detain any citizen for up to 30 days without charges. Once a subject of administrative detention is released within the required 30 day period, he is sometimes simply transferred to another prison or holding facility and then registered once again for another 30 day period, essentially allowing state security forces to lock up anyone they wish for months or even years at a time. Human rights organisations first brought the phenomenon of recurrent detention to light through extensive documentation in the 1990s. The Egyptian Organisation for Human Rights (EOHR) noted that the problem became particularly prevalent after 1992 when the regime began to wage a protracted campaign against militant Islamists.[39] Between 1991 and 1996 the EOHR documented 7,891 cases of recurrent detention, and the number of actual cases is almost certainly much higher (EOHR, 1996). Ninety per cent of EOHR investigations revealed that detained subjects suffered from torture, and most were denied the right to legal representation or family visits.

Article 3 of the Emergency Law permits the President of the Republic, or anyone representing him, to 'detain persons posing a threat to security and public order'. However, the Emergency Law does not define the terms 'threat', 'security' and 'public order', leaving it to prosecutors to apply the provision with its broadest possible interpretation. Administrative courts issued a number of rulings attempting to define and limit the application of Article 3, but their rulings landed on deaf ears.[40]

Ironically, the regime's ability to transfer select cases to exceptional courts and even to detain political opponents indefinitely through the practice of recurrent detention unquestionably (and ironically) facilitated the emergence of judicial power in the regular judiciary. The Supreme Constitutional Court and the administrative courts were able to push a liberal agenda and maintain their institutional autonomy from the executive largely because the regime was confident that it ultimately retained full control over its

the opposition over how far political activism will be tolerated: personal interview, 11 June 2000.

[38] Even outside the courts the regime effectively detains its political opponents for long periods of time through a procedure known as 'recurrent detention', further undermining the relevance of the judicial system (Moustafa, 2003: 906–7).

[39] The problem of recurrent detention was further aggravated by the 'anti-terrorism' law, Law 97/1992, which expanded the authority of the public prosecutor's office and weakened the oversight of the administrative courts.

[40] For examples of administrative court rulings concerning administrative detention and recurrent detention see EOHR, 1996: 41–5.

political opponents.[41] Supreme Constitutional Court activism may therefore be characterised as 'insulated liberalism'. To be sure, court rulings had
a deep impact upon state policy, but the SCC was ultimately bounded by a
profoundly illiberal political system.

IV. THE LEGAL COMPLEX UNDER SIEGE (1998–2002)

Despite these limitations, human rights groups and opposition parties
continued to score impressive political victories through the Supreme
Constitutional Court, and the regime grew uneasy about the potential for
more serious political challenges through the Court in the future. Groups
active in civil society had begun to formalise their strategies of constitutional litigation, and by 1998 human rights groups in particular were
raising dozens of petitions for constitutional review every year. Intent on
reasserting control, the regime began to tighten its grip on opposition activists and the SCC itself. The ensuing struggle illustrates both the productive
synergy within the Egyptian legal complex and their ultimate inability to
withstand the pressures of regime retrenchment.

The first concrete assault on the SCC came in July 1998. Mubarak issued
a presidential decree amending the law of the Supreme Constitutional Court,
effectively limiting compensation claims in taxation cases. Opposition
newspapers were filled with editorials insisting that the decree was
unconstitutional on both procedural and substantive grounds.[42] NGOs,
such as the new Arab Centre for the Independence of the Judiciary and
the Legal Profession, also joined the fray, printing extensive critiques in
opposition papers.[43] Prominent members of the legal profession, such as
the head of the Cairo branch of the Lawyers' Syndicate, also criticised

---

[41] Brown similarly finds that 'having successfully maintained channels of moving outside
the normal judiciary, the regime has insured that the reemergence of liberal legality need not
affect the most sensitive political cases … The harshness of the military courts, in this sense,
has made possible the independence of the rest of the judiciary' (1997: 116).

[42] The procedural argument for the unconstitutionality of the law was that it was unnecessary for Mubarak to circumvent the People's Assembly and issue an executive degree. The
substantive arguments were based upon constitutional provisions protecting property rights
and protecting access to justice. Eg, see N Gomm'a, 'The Legislation is Contradictory to
the Constitution and an Aggression on the Function of the Court', *al-Wafd*, 12 July 1998;
'Amending the Law of the SCC is an Aggression on the Rights of Citizens', *al-Ahali*, 15 July
1998; M Hilal, 'Three Reasons Behind the Attack on the Supreme Constitutional Court', *al-
Sha'ab*, 4 Aug 1998; M Shukri, 'Abd al-Fatah, 'Remove Your Hands from the Constitutional
Court', *al-Haqiqa*, 8 Aug 1998.

[43] See the extensive report by the Arab Centre for the Independence of the Judiciary and
the Legal Profession printed in *al-Wafd*, 14 July 1998. Also see the extensive critique provided
by The Legal Research and Resource Centre for Human Rights, printed in *al-Wafd*, 17 July
1998. The Centre for Human Rights Legal Aid issued its own report a few days later in *al-
Wafd*, 20 July 1998.

the decree.[44] Minister of Justice, Seif al-Nasr, and other regime supporters attempted to justify the legitimacy and legality of the amendment.[45] The ensuing debate, which lasted in both the state press and opposition papers for months, illustrated how the SCC had become a focal point of contention, simultaneously adjudicating and structuring state–society interaction. Moreover, the debate in the press underlined the extent to which the SCC had altered the rhetoric that both the regime and social actors employed, with both sides building the legitimacy of their positions upon constitutional arguments. Finally, the vigorous responses from opposition parties, the human rights community and legal professional associations were sure signs that Egypt's political landscape had been transformed significantly from the late 1970s when the Supreme Constitutional Court was established. This new political landscape was no mere coincidence; the legal complex that rushed to support the SCC during its encounter with the regime had been rehabilitated and empowered as a direct result of SCC rulings.

(a) Returning the Favour—The SCC Defends the Human Rights Movement

The government also launched a fully fledged campaign to undermine the human rights movement by issuing a new law that cut their access to foreign funding and forced all human rights organisations to apply for a licence with the Ministry of Social Affairs (MOSA) or face immediate closure. The new law forbade civil associations from engaging in any political activity and gave MOSA the right to dissolve associations 'threatening national unity or violating public order or morals'.[46]

---

[44] See the article by 'Abd al-'Aziz Muhammad, 'Treasonous Amendment to the Constitution and to the Law!', *al-Wafd*, 16 July 1998.

[45] S al-Nasr, 'Three Reasons behind Amending the Law of the SCC', *al-Ahram al-Misa'i*, 13 July 1988; M Morsi (Chair of the Legislative Committee in the People's Assembly), 'I Agree with the Law of the Government to Amend the Law of the Rulings [*sic*] of the Constitutional Court and Here are My Reasons!', *Akhbar al-Youm*, 18 July 1998; M Badran, 'The Decree is a Step in the Right Direction', *al-Ahram*, 27 July 1997.

[46] As with other laws restricting political rights, Law 153/1999 does not define what constitutes a threat to national unity or a violation of public order, giving the regime maximum leverage liberally to apply the law and to deny activists the ability to seek protection from the law. The new law also struck at the Achilles heal of the human rights movement by further constraining its ability to receive foreign funding without prior government approval. Additionally, Law 153 prevented non-governmental organisations from communicating with foreign associations without first informing the government. These new regulations were clear attempts by the regime to place new constraints upon human rights groups that were effectively leveraging international pressure on the Egyptian regime through transnational human rights networks.

The human rights movement mobilised considerable opposition to the new Associations Law in a short period of time. Within a week, human rights groups organised a press conference where they contended that Law 153/1999 violated the constitution and they vowed to fight it in the Supreme Constitutional Court if it was not repealed. At the same time, human rights groups met with the major opposition parties and professional syndicates and secured their support. Days later, a national NGO coalition was convened, bringing together over 100 associations from across the country. NGOs committed to mobilise domestic and international pressure on the regime through a demonstration in front of the People's Assembly, a week-long hunger strike, and litigation in the courts. International pressure came quickly with statements from Human Rights Watch, Amnesty International, the International Federation of Human Rights, the Lawyers' Committee for Human Rights and the US State Department.

By 3 June 2000, the Supreme Constitutional Court struck down this single most important piece of legislation governing associational life in decades.[47] The ruling was a bold move by the SCC not simply to defend the freedom of association for its own sake; the ruling also saved the most loyal supporters of SCC independence as well as one of the most critical support structures initiating the litigation that fueled the SCC's drive to expand its mandate. Moreover, the ruling came at a critical time for human rights activists and pro-democracy reformers because national elections for the People's Assembly were just months away and human rights activists planned to document electoral fraud across the country, which would enable opposition candidates to fight election results in the courts, as they had done following the 1995 elections.

(b) The SCC and Opposition Politics

In the lead-up to the 2000 elections, the topic of electoral reform emerged once again and the convergence of interests between opposition parties, non-governmental organisations and judicial personnel was never more clear. Sa'ad Eddin Ibrahim and other human rights activists initiated work to build a network of human rights organisations to monitor the 2000 elections, as they had done with great success in 1995.[48] But the regime proved its determination to derail the effort and to rein in the human

---

[47] Case 163, judicial year 21, issued 3 June 2000.

[48] Ibrahim was the driving force behind the civil society election monitoring campaign that in 1995 exposed the methods and the sweeping extent of electoral fraud, both to Egyptians and to the international community, for the first time. This documentation provided the basis for opposition candidates to challenge electoral fraud in the administrative courts, casting a constant shadow on the legitimacy of the People's Assembly for its entire 5-year term.

rights movement with or without the Associations Law that the Supreme Constitutional Court had struck down just weeks earlier. On 30 June 2000, Ibrahim was arrested on charges of 'accepting funds from a foreign party with the purpose of carrying out work harmful to Egypt's national interest and disseminating provocative propaganda that could cause damage to the public interest'.[49]

Just days after Ibrahim and his colleagues were taken into detention, the Supreme Constitutional Court retaliated once again with another bombshell ruling, this time demanding full judicial supervision of elections for the first time in Egyptian history. The SCC ruling stated unequivocally that Article 24 of Law 73/1956 was unconstitutional because it allowed for public sector employees to supervise polling stations despite the fact that Article 88 of the Constitution guaranteed that 'the ballot shall be conducted under the supervision of members of the judiciary organ'.[50] Once again, what opposition parties were unable to achieve through the People's Assembly over the previous three decades, they were eventually able to bring about through constitutional litigation. The Wafd Party's Ayman Nur acknowledged that the Supreme Constitutional Court had virtually replaced the role of opposition parties in driving the reform agenda when he stated that 'this ruling and the previous others will unquestionably affect the future of domestic politics. ... the judiciary has nearly taken over the role of the political parties in forcing the government to take action in the direction of greater democracy'.[51]

As with previous rulings on the electoral law, the Supreme Constitutional Court ruling on judicial monitoring did not dislodge the regime from power, but it did have a significant effect on the means by which the regime maintained its power. The regime was once again forced to resort to ever more extreme forms of extra-legal coercion to ensure that the SCC ruling would not undermine the NDP's grip on power. Yet, despite the increased reliance on extralegal coercion, the regime took every opportunity to capitalise on the SCC ruling. President Mubarak addressed the opening session of the new People's Assembly and hailed both the SCC ruling and full

---

[49] The Egyptian human rights community again mobilised international pressure. Within days, 9 international human rights organisations including Amnesty International and Human Rights Watch issued a joint statement condemning Ibrahim's detention and calling for his immediate release. Pressure also came from the US embassy once again when it reportedly raised concerns at 'the highest levels' with the Egyptian government. The international pressure proved effective, as Ibrahim was released after two months of detention. As with the detention of Hafiz 'Abu Sa'ada, however, the charges against Ibrahim were not dismissed. Instead, they were simply suspended, which allowed for the resumption of a trial at any time.

[50] The case was raised 10 years earlier by Kamal Khaled and Gamal al-Nisharti, both candidates who ran for seats in the People's Assembly elections of 1990, in coordination with opposition parties, which recognised the full importance of constitutional litigation as an avenue to challenge the regime after the dissolution of the People's Assembly in 1987 and 1990.

[51] *Al-Ahram Weekly,* 3–9 Aug 2000.

judicial monitoring as a great step forward in the march of democracy. The televised speech was intended to showcase the legitimacy of the voting process in the 2000 People's Assembly elections and to assure the public that the widespread electoral fraud, which had reached unprecedented levels for the 1995 People's Assembly, was a thing of the past. But the continued shift from pseudo-legal to extra-legal control increasingly exposed the hypocrisy of the regime; the growing disparity between the regime's constitutionalist rhetoric and its repressive measures was untenable. While Mubarak publicly praised the Supreme Constitutional Court for its service to democracy, the regime was arranging to deal a blow to SCC independence behind closed doors.

(c) The Legal Complex on the Brink of Collapse

With the retirement of Chief Justice Galal in late 2001, the regime made its move to rein in the SCC. To everyone's surprise, including that of SCC justices, the government announced that Mubarak's choice for the new chief justice would be none other than Fathi Nagib, the man who held the second most powerful post in the Ministry of Justice. Opposition parties, the human rights community and legal scholars were stunned by the announcement. Not only had Fathi Nagib proved his loyalty to the regime over the years, but he was the very same person who had drafted the vast majority of the regime's illiberal legislation over the previous decade, including the oppressive Law 153/1999 that the SCC had struck down only months earlier. Moreover, by selecting a Chief Justice from outside the justices sitting on the Supreme Constitutional Court, Mubarak also broke a strong norm that had developed over the previous two decades. Although the president of the republic always retained the formal ability to appoint whomever he wished for the position of chief justice, constitutional law scholars, political activists and justices on the court themselves had come to believe that the president would never assert this kind of control over the court and that he would continue to abide by the informal norm of simply appointing the most senior justice on the SCC.[52] Mubarak proved them wrong.

Nagib defended his appointment by contending that there were 'technical deficiencies' in SCC rulings that he was charged with remedying. 'It was important for me to be selected to take care of technical deficiencies in the rulings of the court. These are not political deficiencies—there was simply a problem with the level of the court rulings'. But when pressed, Nagib was astonishingly candid about what he meant by the 'technical deficiencies' of Supreme Constitutional Court rulings:

---

[52] The only *formal* restrictions on presidential appointments of Chief Justices concern the age, formal legal training and experience of candidates.

They [SCC justices] were issuing rulings that were bombs in order to win the support of the opposition parties. They were very pleased with the rulings, but the rulings were not in the interests of the country. This needed to be corrected. Now the President [Mubarak] can be assured that the court will make rulings that are in the interest of the country and yet still maintain its independence.[53]

The prominent political role that the SCC had assumed in Egyptian political life through the 1980s and 1990s was recognised by everyone, but Nagib's blunt recognition of the political objectives motivating his appointment was truly remarkable. Given the SCC's crucial role in opposition reform efforts, political activists were not willing to accept the presidential decree without a fight. Just one month after the appointment, long-time political activist 'Essam al-Islambuli raised a case in the administrative courts challenging President Mubarak's executive decree. Islambuli contended that Nagib's appointment not only went against the informal norms of internal recruitment and promotion, but contravened constitutional guarantees of judicial independence and represented a conflict of interest since Nagib himself had authored so many of the laws that were being contested in front of the SCC. Government lawyers attempted to claim executive sovereignty, and they further argued (ironically) that the administrative courts were not empowered to rule on the appointment since Article 174 of the Constitution guarantees SCC independence. The administrative court rejected the government's contentions, agreed with the merits of the constitutional claim raised by Islambuli, and referred the case to the SCC. Once again, the Supreme Constitutional Court was put in the terribly awkward position of having to arbitrate between the regime and political activists at loggerheads over the SCC's own powers and degree of autonomy.

It was inconceivable that the SCC would rule in favour of Islambuli's challenge to Nagib's appointment, not only because of the political sensitivity of the case, but also because Nagib had assumed control of the court in the meantime. But Fathi Nagib's sudden death from a heart attack in August, 2003 made it a moot point. Or did it? In the wake of Nagib's passing, the question of SCC autonomy in appointments resurfaced once again. Instead of a reversion to the prior norm of the most senior justice on the court becoming chief justice, as many had hoped, Mubarak surprised political activists once again by appointing Mamduh Mar'ai, head of the Cairo Court of Appeals. Not only had Mar'ai spent much of his career in the inspection department of the Ministry of Justice, a post informally charged with exerting government control over judges, but most lawyers, judges and political activists did not think of him as a candidate with sufficient experience and education to head the most important court in Egypt.

[53] Interview with Fathi Nagib, 27 Mar 2002.

At the same time that the regime was exerting control over the Supreme Constitutional Court through outside appointments, the government continued its assault on the human rights movement. Human rights advocate Sa'ad al-Din Ibrahim's trial captured the world's attention and brought Egypt's judicial system into the international spotlight. Ibrahim was accused of accepting foreign funding without government approval as required by Military Decree 4/1992, embezzling money from an EU grant, and 'spreading false information and vicious rumors abroad, dealing with internal conditions in the country which would weaken state's prestige and integrity'. Despite an extensive campaign by international human rights groups, a vigorous legal defence, and testimony from some of Egypt's most respected figures, Ibrahim was eventually found guilty and sentenced to seven years in prison by the Emergency State Security Court.

The initial sentence was contested in the appellate level Emergency State Security Court and, despite a constitutional challenge to the emergency law by none other than 'Awad al-Murr, former Chief Justice of the Supreme Constitutional Court, the Emergency State Security Court refused to grant Ibrahim access to the SCC and reaffirmed the seven year sentence handed down by the lower level Emergency State Security Court. Ibrahim and his colleagues were abruptly transferred from the courtroom to an undisclosed location in downtown Cairo, and finally to the infamous Tora prison, to begin serving their terms. Amid intense international criticism and scrutiny, Ibrahim's lawyers approached the Court of Cassation requesting a retrial. The court agreed and the government presumably relented as a way to end the embarrassing international attention.

Knowing full well that the case had attracted international attention, Ibrahim's lawyers skilfully used the Court of Cassation as a forum to air the regime's dirty laundry. The defence team argued that the Ibn Khaldun Centre was simply conducting social scientific research with the intent of helping the country advance rather than acting as a treasonous fifth column. Defence lawyers reproduced a number of mainstream publications that came to similar conclusions concerning political corruption, sectarian tensions and the like. Court transcripts reveal that the judges were clearly receptive to this airing of the regime's dirty laundry.[54]

The Court of Cassation acquitted Ibrahim and his colleagues on all charges of treason and ordered their release in March 2003. However, there was little to celebrate. The two-year ordeal was the final assault on a movement that had endured years of government harassment, crippling new legislation regulating NGO activity, and financial strangulation through the closing of foreign funding sources. By the time of Ibrahim's release, little remained of a human rights movement that just a few years

---

[54] Prosecution docket No 39725/2002, court docket No 39725, judicial year 72.

earlier had promised to be the most effective force for political reform in the Arab World.

Moreover, during Ibrahim's trial the government issued a new Associations Law (84/2002) to replace Law 153/1999, struck down by the SCC two years earlier. The government addressed the procedural problems of Law 153/1999 that had been grounds for the SCC's ruling of unconstitutionality when it routed the new legislation through the Shura Council and provided NGOs with the right to appeal decisions of the Ministry of Social Affairs in the administrative courts. Law 84/2002 proved to be just as draconian by maintaining the power of the Ministry of Social Affairs to reject or dissolve any association threatening 'public order or public morality'. [55] This time around, the human rights movement and opposition activists had been so weakened by the government's continuous assaults that they could do little to block the new legislation.[56]

V. CONCLUSIONS

What are the broader theoretical insights that we can take away from this study of the struggle for rights and the rule of law in the Egyptian legal context? The first is the relationship between market economies and the vigour of the legal complex. Market economies provide the economic base that is essential for a vibrant legal profession, since lawyers are necessary for business transactions of all kinds. It is striking how the legal profession suffered in post-revolutionary Egypt with the shift to a socialist-oriented economy. Pressure from the regime constituted a direct constraint on the Lawyers' Syndicate, but the nationalisation of private sector firms into public sector holdings constituted even more formidable, indirect challenges by draining the lifeblood from the legal profession. Additionally, authoritarian rulers are more likely to empower courts when they pursue market-led growth strategies in order to provide a more secure environment for investment. It should be noted that some of these dynamics mirror earlier developments of rule-of-law systems in the West (Halliday and Karpik, 1997).

The Egyptian experience also indicates that the legal complex is most effective when the profession is ideologically cohesive. The split between liberals and Islamists that emerged in the Lawyers' Syndicate starting in the late 1970s brought the Syndicate to gridlock by the early 1990s. It also made it far easier for the regime to manipulate the internal cleavages in the Syndicate for its own advantage. Government sequestration effectively

---

[55] The regime proved its intent to apply the full force of the law when it refused to grant legal recognition to the New Woman Research Centrr, the Land Centre for Human Rights, and the Egyptian Association against Torture in the summer of 2003.

[56] The period 2002–6 is documented in Moustafa (2007).

sidelined the Lawyers' Syndicate during the late 1990s when the Supreme Constitutional Court was making its boldest moves to rein in the government. The sequestration prevented the Syndicate from playing a more active role in protecting the independence of the Supreme Constitutional Court when it soon came under fire from the regime.

The legal complex was also made vulnerable by violence between the police and radical Islamists through the 1990s. Although clashes only involved a tiny radical fraction of the Islamist movement, they gave the regime the pretext continually to renew the emergency laws, clamp down on the Lawyers' Syndicate, and try civilians in state security and military courts. The regime would have undoubtedly found other pretexts to enact the same measures, but the spectre of all out Islamist/regime violence in Algeria and incipient clashes in Egypt made the regime's justifications that much easier, both for domestic consumption and vis-à-vis the international community. The Egyptian case, as well as the global roll-back of rights provisions in the post 9/11 world, underlines the fact that 'national security' rhetoric trumps most efforts to defend individual rights protections.

The Egyptian case also illustrates that the legal complex makes the most headway where there are dense networks of interaction between domestic human rights organisations and the international human rights community. This is particularly crucial for groups operating in countries of the Global South, because they can tap into the financial resources of international human rights networks and leverage international pressure on their regimes from the outside. The legal complex is also at its strongest when it has the financial and institutional capacity to sponsor coordinated public interest litigation campaigns (Epp, 1998). Assistance from international human rights networks is not costless, however, since it makes rights groups vulnerable to accusations of foreign interference and treason. For this reason, it is absolutely crucial that rights groups be enmeshed in the broader society, and not simply come to life through the assistance of Western rights organisations. Indeed, it is this indigenous link between rights groups and the people that the regime wishes to disrupt.

Of course, the legal complex must also have access to a judiciary with sufficient independence to shield human rights groups, opposition activists, and other groups in civil society from regime assaults *and* vice versa. In the Egyptian case, the Supreme Constitutional Court provided an effective avenue for activists to challenge the state through one of its own institutions. Success in battling the regime's restrictive NGO law as well as successful litigation forcing full judicial supervision of elections illustrated how rights groups and opposition parties had become increasingly adept at using judicial institutions successfully to challenge the regime and defend their interests. However, just as the SCC and Egypt's civil society coalition built a movement based upon the converging interests of the court, opposition parties and human rights organisations, so too was the regime able to incapacitate this cooperative effort by successively undermining each element of the legal complex through legal and extralegal tactics. Rather than neutralising the Supreme Constitutional Court outright in the mid-1990s, the regime instead adopted the subtler strategy of simply moving against the SCC's supporters. The Lawyers' Syndicate was neutralised by 1996, human rights associations faced near total collapse by 1999 due to intimidation and restrictions on foreign funding, and opposition parties were progressively weakened throughout the period, despite SCC rulings on political rights. By undercutting each element of the legal complex, the regime effectively killed two birds with one stone; it impaired the ability to monitor the regime's increasingly aggressive violations of civil and human rights while at the same time disabling their capacity to raise litigation and mount an effective defence of the SCC when it came under attack.

Intensified regime backlash in the wake of the rulings on the NGO law and election monitoring also makes clear one of the central ironies of legal mobilisation in authoritarian contexts: When judicial institutions defer to the executive on core political issues, they can take a more assertive role in advancing less consequential rights issues. But when they challenge core regime interests, on the other hand, they risk confrontation. Ironically, the legal complex is best able to advance individual rights by leaving core regime interests uncontested. The Supreme Constitutional Court and the administrative courts were able to push a liberal agenda and maintain institutional autonomy from the executive largely because the regime was confident that it ultimately retained full control over its political opponents through state security courts, military courts and the process of recurrent detention. The advances of the legal complex can therefore be characterised as a case of 'insulated liberalism'. To be sure, the legal complex was able to advocate for individual rights with some surprising successes, but they were ultimately bound by a profoundly illiberal political system.

REFERENCES

Arab Republic of Egypt, *al-Mahkama al-Dusturiyya al-'Ulia*, i–x.

Baker, R (1990), 'Fighting for Freedom and the Rule of Law: The Bar Association' in R Baker, *Sadat and After: Struggles for Egypt's Political Soul* (Cambridge, Mass, Harvard University Press).

Beattie, K (2000), *Egypt During the Sadat Years* (New York, Palgrave).

Bernard-Maugiron, N and Dupret, B (eds) (2002), *Egypt and Its Laws* (London, Kluwer Law International).

Boyle, K and Sherif, A (eds) (1996), *Human Rights and Democracy: The Role of the Supreme Constitutional Court of Egypt* (London, Kluwer Law International).

Brown, N (1997), *The Rule of Law in the Arab World: Courts in Egypt and the Gulf* (Cambridge, Cambridge University Press).

Centre for Human Rights Legal Aid (1995), 'al-Qada' al-'Askiry fi Misr: Qada' Bighayr Damanat … Quda bidoun Hasana Mathamoun bila Haquq '[The

Military Judiciary in Egypt: Courts Without Safeguards, Judges Without Immunity, and Defendants Without Rights].

—— (1996), 'Saying What We Think: CHRLA's report on Freedom of Opinion and Expression in Egypt'

—— (1997), 'After the Defeat of Law 93/1995: The Current State of Freedom of the Press in Egypt'

Cotran, E and Sherif, A (1999), *Democracy, the Rule of Law, and Islam* (London, Kluwer Law International).

Dezalay, Y and Garth, B (1996), *Dealing in Virtue: International Commercial Arbitration and the Construction of a Transnational Legal Order* (Chicago, Ill, University of Chicago Press).

Egyptian Organisation for Human Rights (1996), *Recurrent Detention: Prisoners Without Trial* (Cairo, Egyptian Organisation for Human Rights).

—— (2000), 'EOHR Statement no. 3 on Monitoring the Parliamentary Elections for 2000–2005'.

Epp, C (1998), *The Rights Revolution: Lawyers, Activists, and Supreme Courts in Comparative Perspective* (Chicago, Ill, University of Chicago Press).

Halliday, T and Karpik, L (1997), *Lawyers and the Rise of Western Political Liberalism: Europe and North America from the Eighteenth to Twentieth Centuries* (Oxford, Oxford University Press).

Hill, E (1979), *Mahkama! Studies in the Egyptian Legal System* (London, Ithaca Press).

Kienle, E (2000), *A Grand Delusion: Democracy and Economic Reform in Egypt* (London, IB Tauris).

Merryman, JH (1985), *The Civil Law Tradition: An Introduction to the Legal Systems of Western Europe and Latin America* (Stanford, Cal, Stanford University Press).

Moustafa, T (2003), 'Law Versus the State: The Judicialization of Politics in Egypt', 28 *Law and Social Inquiry* 883.

—— (2007), *The Struggle for Constitutional Power: Law, Politics, and Economic Development in Egypt* (New York, Cambridge University Press).

Nosseir, A (1992), 'The Supreme Constitutional Court and the Protection of Human Rights', unpublished manuscript.

Rifa'i, Y (2000), *Istaqlal al-Qada' wa Mehna al-Intikhabat [The Independence of the Judiciary and the Ordeal of Elections]* (Cairo, al-Maktab al-Misri al-Hadith)

Reid, D (1981), *Lawyers and Politics in the Arab World, 1880–1960* (Chicago, Ill, Bibliotheca Islamica).

Rosberg, J (1995), *Roads to the Rule of Law: The Emergence of an Independent Judiciary in Contemporary Egypt*, PhD dissertation, Massachusetts Institute of Technology.

Rutherford, B (1999), *The Struggle for Constitutionalism in Egypt: Understanding the Obstacles to Democratic Transition in the Arab World*, PhD dissertation, Yale University.

Sherif, A (1988), *al-Qada' al-Dusturi fi Misr [Constitutional Adjudication in Egypt]* (Cairo, Dar al-Sha'ab).

—— (1999), 'The Supreme Constitutional Court of Egypt and Vicarious Criminal Liability' in E Cotran and A Sherif (eds), *The Role of the Judiciary in the Protection of Human Rights*.

Tate, CN (1995), 'Why the Expansion of Judicial Power' in CN Tate and T Vallinder (eds), *The Global Expansion of Judicial Power* (New York, New York University Press).

—— and Vallinder, T (eds) (1995), *The Global Expansion of Judicial Power* (New York, New York University Press).

Ubayd, MK (1991), *Istiqlal al-Qada': Darasa Maqarena* (Cairo, *Dar al-Nahda al-'Arabiyya).*

United States Department of Commerce (1981), 'Investing in Egypt', *Overseas Business Reports*, OBR 81-08.

Volcansek, M (1994), 'Political Power and Judicial Review in Italy', 26 *Comparative Political Studies*, 492.

Waterbury, J (1983), *The Egypt of Nasser and Sadat: The Political Economy of Two Regimes* (Princeton, NJ, Princeton University Press).

—— (1993), *Exposed to Innumerable Delusions: Public Enterprise and State Power in Egypt, India, Mexico, and Turkey* (Cambridge, Cambridge University Press).

Zemans, F (1983), 'Legal Mobilization: The Neglected Role of the Law in the Political System', 77 *American Political Science Review* 690.

Ziadeh, FJ (1968), *Lawyers, the Rule of Law and Liberalism in Modern Egypt* (Stanford, Cal, Hoover Institution on War, Revolution, and Peace, Stanford University).

7

Reluctantly Sailing Towards Political Liberalism: The Political Role of the Judiciary in Turkey

ZÜHTÜ ARSLAN

I. INTRODUCTION

THERE IS HARDLY any theoretical or empirical study on the political role of the legal complex in establishing or consolidating political liberalism in Turkey. This is not merely a matter of negligence on the part of Turkish scholars. In fact, two main reasons can be discerned for the lack of such studies. First of all, the concept of political liberalism is not very familiar to the society in general and academics in particular. With a few exceptions, legal academics who are familiar with political liberalism refer to it as a pejorative term, and use the general term of democracy instead to express the core features of political liberalism. This does not mean however that there are many studies on the relationship between the legal complex and the development of democracy or on the politics of the Turkish judiciary.[1] Secondly, the lack of such studies is partly due to the deeply embedded belief that the members of the legal complex, particularly judges, are quasi-sacred human beings. Discussing and criticising the judgments of the courts as well as the qualifications of the judges is generally considered as a risky business which may end up in prosecution and conviction for contempt of court.

This chapter is intended partly to remedy the lack of study on the role of the judiciary in transition to or retreat from political liberalism. It argues that the Turkish judiciary alongside the other elements of the legal complex (ie lawyers and legal academics), usually adopts a negative approach to political liberalism and particularly to the political rights of individuals.

---

[1] For some exceptions see Özbudun, 2006; Belge, 2006; Shambayati, 2004; Erdoğan, 2003; Ünsal, 1980.

The judiciary has impeded the development of political liberalism. The main reason for this impediment may be found in the self-declared mission of the courts in Turkey, which is to protect the state and its official discourse rather than the individual and his/her rights and liberties. The adoption of such a mission inevitably brings about the politicisation of the judiciary according to which the political convictions of judges play an increasingly important role in deciding the cases. The negative effect of the politicisation of the judiciary has been accelerated by the expansion of judicial power to cover more social and political issues, and by the judicial involvement in politics which is generally known as the judicialisation of politics.

In order to substantiate this argument, I shall first discuss the conceptual and empirical relationship between the judiciary and political liberalism. In this part of the chapter, the basic components of political liberalism are briefly explored and the idea of judiciary as 'the least dangerous branch' is subjected to a critical reading. The second part of the chapter deals with the role of the Turkish legal complex in the development of the basic components of political liberalism. Although this chapter is mainly concerned with the judiciary, this section will also refer to the position of lawyers and legal academics as regards the development of political liberalism. At this point, one must distinguish between the roles of the Bar Associations and individual lawyers. While the former, with the National Union of Bars at their centre, adopts a more or less similar approach to that of the courts, the latter contributes to a certain extent to political liberalism through cause lawyering and civil society organisations. This part is followed by a section on the approach of the judiciary to basic rights and liberties. The analysis in this section will amplify the main thesis that the judiciary has impeded the establishment and consolidation of a liberal political society. The politics and judgments of the Constitutional Court and the Court of Cassation concerning the freedoms of expression, association and religion will be critically evaluated to reveal the negative approach of the judiciary to the core features of political liberalism.

The chapter finally takes up the adaptation problem of the Turkish judiciary in the process of Turkey's membership of the European Union. Turkey is the principal heir to the Ottoman Empire, which reigned over three continents for about six centuries. The Ottomans have left a very strong legacy to the Republic of Turkey in terms of social and political culture. This legacy has shaped the identity of modern Turkey, despite the fact that the young Republic introduced a great many institutions to break with its past. One cannot however escape one's past; the spectres of history insistently haunt its children. We are the product of history as well as the current age. As Amin Maalouf, a French writer of Lebanese origin, put it eloquently, 'each one of us has two heritages, a "vertical" one that comes to us from our ancestors, our religious community and our popular traditions, and a "horizontal" one transmitted to us by our contemporaries and by the age we live in' (Maalouf, 2000: 86). With the advent of globalisation, the 'horizontal' inheritance has become more decisive in determining our identities.

The European Union (EU) is surely one of the most influential 'horizontal' heritages for the people living in Turkey. The EU constitutes the source of not only the recent legal and political changes in Turkey but also a new politics domestically. A series of so-called 'Harmonisation Packages', adopted by the Turkish Parliament with a view to meeting the Copenhagen Political Criteria, introduced ground-breaking statutory and constitutional changes such as making the judgments of the European Court of Human Rights a reason to reopen the cases before the criminal, civil and administrative courts, repealing some provisions of the Prevention of Terrorism Act to expand the freedom of expression, and narrowing the jurisdiction of the military courts. After briefly explaining these legal and constitutional changes, we shall take up the issue of the ability of the courts to enforce and adapt themselves to the structural and functional changes. It will be argued that the Turkish judiciary is perplexed about the adaptation to the new situation imposed by the changing rules.

The concluding paragraphs of the chapter draw attention to the potential limits and internal tensions of political liberalism. They will reveal, for instance, that there is no necessary connection between the existence of 'autonomous' legal complex and political liberalism. In a state where there exists a comprehensive official ideology and a judiciary with a mission of consolidating this ideology, the judicialisation of politics will inevitably bring about more restrictions on certain rights of political opposition.

II. POLITICAL LIBERALISM AND THE JUDICIARY

Political liberalism can be defined as a set of idea(l)s and institutions which aim to accommodate different and often conflicting lifestyles and comprehensive doctrines of free and equal individuals in a constitutional democracy. This concept of political liberalism requires at least three components, namely a limited (moderate) state with the independence of the judiciary at its centre, a civil society, and the protection of basic rights of citizenship (Halliday and Karpik, 1997). The last feature of the liberal political society seems to suggest that the legal concept of political liberalism is mainly applicable to the modern nation-states based on citizenship. However, in a liberal political society it is the individual, rather than the citizen, who is the subject of the basic rights such as the rights to free speech, religion, association and property. The use of terminology is important, simply because some states tend to deny certain rights for non-citizen individuals.

The consolidation of a moderate state and the protection of basic rights require the effective restriction of the political power. 'A free society', as Friedrich Hayek put it, 'certainly needs permanent means of restricting powers of government, no matter what the particular objective of the moment may be' (Hayek, 1976: 182). The legal complex may play a significant role in restricting political power and protecting basic rights. Indeed, Halliday and Karpik argued that '[w]estern legal professions have historically been engaged in "political projects" that constitute political liberalism. They have been among the builders of the liberal state and society' (Halliday and Karpik, 1997: 16). This perspective reflects, among others, the traditional view of the judiciary as a bulwark of the basic liberties against arbitrary political power. In other words, courts are supposed to play a very essential role in a liberal political society, because they are the institutional devices through which public reason can find its expression and the basic liberties of individuals are protected (See Rawls, 1996: 213–16, 231).

Halliday and Karpik's perspective also appears to assume that the independent judiciary as a part of the legal complex cannot pose any threat to basic rights and liberties. This idea has been deeply embedded in the western political and legal tradition. For instance, in *Federalist* number 78, Alexander Hamilton explicitly rejected the argument that judicial review of legislative acts will make the judiciary superior to the legislative. Hamilton reached a number of conclusions as to the position of the judiciary vis-à-vis the legislative and executive powers as well as the individual liberties. First of all, referring to the views of Montesquieu, he argued that 'the judiciary is beyond comparison the weakest of the three departments of power; that it can never attack with success either of the other two'. Secondly, he rejected the possibility of any persistent danger to liberty deriving from the courts, and ensured that 'liberty can have nothing to fear from the judiciary alone' (Hamilton, 1961: 465–6).

These optimistic and somehow naïve predictions or rather wishful thinking of the founding fathers about the judiciary proved wrong over time. Some scholars have argued that the courts in Hamilton's country and all over the world have turned out to be 'the most dangerous' threat to the liberties of individuals. Whatever the merits of these arguments, one thing is certain beyond any doubt: at both national and international levels the judiciary is playing an increasingly important role in settling the political questions. This raises the eternal question of how to guard the guardians.[2] Judicial expansion at the expense of legislative and executive powers inevitably creates the fear that 'judicial power could become political power without democratic responsibility' (Guarnieri and Pederzoli, 2002: 13). This is exactly what has happened in Turkey. Aided by the principle of judicial independence the courts themselves have turned out to be the political power that has denied or restricted some basic rights introduced by the legislature.

---

[2] In his *Panopticon* Jeremy Bentham describes this question (*quis custodiet ipsos custodes?*) as 'one of the most puzzling of political questions' (Bentham, 1995: 46).

In the following sections, I will argue that the Turkish judiciary, as the leading element of the legal complex, contributed to the establishment of a moderate state by restricting the powers of democratically elected governments. However, the judiciary as well as the other parts of the legal complex has done little to develop and consolidate the third element of the political liberalism, namely the protection of basic rights and liberties.

III. THE POLITICS OF THE TURKISH LEGAL COMPLEX

The legal complex plays a significant role in the political life of Turkey. The members of the legal complex influence politics through not only judicial decisions on controversial issues but also direct participation in the law-making process. The serving President of the Republic is the former Chief Justice of the Constitutional Court. Similarly, ever since it was established great numbers of the deputies in the Parliament have been elected from among lawyers. Ninety-eight out of 550 members of the current Parliament are lawyers by profession.[3]

Ever since the establishment of the Republic of Turkey, the Turkish legal complex has been mobilised to consolidate the regime by both eliminating the potential threats and providing legal justifications for the authoritarian behaviour of the regime. Thus the legal complex has functioned as part and parcel of both the repressive and ideological state apparatus, to use Althusser's terms. The Turkish legal complex, the judiciary at its centre, has consistently sought to align itself with the ruling stratum of the Republic, namely the military and civilian bureaucracy. The liberalisation of the regime has been a process which involves a political struggle between the state elites and the political elites. In this struggle, the judiciary alongside the military appears to be one of the most conservative state apparatuses that resist the liberalisation and democratisation of the legal and political life of the country.

The primary objective of the builders of the Republic was to create a westernised society, an objective which was already initiated by the rulers of the late Ottoman Empire. To this end, they introduced radical reforms concerning the daily lives of the people as well as the legal and political structure of the state. The reception of the western laws was among these reforms. Turkey received the Swiss Civil Code, the Italian Penal Code and the German Code of Criminal Procedure. Although the legal system was westernised through reception of these laws, the adoption of liberal democratic ideals and institutions such as multi-party politics, freedom of expression, and the political opposition took a significant time. In fact, the establishment of a liberal polity was not among the short-term

---

[3] *TBMM Albümü 22.Dönem*, (Ankara: TBMM Yayınları, 2003), p.xxvi.

objectives of the founding fathers of the Republic. Their priority was to create a culturally modernised nation by breaking peoples' ties with history and traditional/religious values. From the very beginning, the state-building enterprise called for the orientation of authoritarian measures towards the potential opposition. The Turkish legal complex, particularly the judiciary, played an instrumental role in implementing such authoritarian measures.

In Turkey, the politics of the state elites has been grounded on the 'friend/foe' division granting the state the power to define the latter. This antagonistic politics is the direct result of the political conditions under which the Republic was created. 'The republican state', as Heper pointed out, 'was born in the midst of external as well as internal conflict and in a rather heterogeneous milieu'. The new state emerged from the ashes of the Ottoman Empire which was dismantled at the end of World War I, and it faced great challenges such as Armenian irredentism and Kurdish nationalism (Heper, 1985: 48). These challenges, complemented later by 'fundamentalist Islam', helped to keep the state more or less permanently on a security footing in which aspects of political liberalism are secondary to internal order and maintenance of the political regime. In short, the political and sociological conditions of the period in which modern Turkey was born imposed an authoritarian nation-state politics, and this has frequently been reproduced by the subsequent state elites.[4] In order better ro understand the contribution of the Turkish legal complex to this politics, we should first briefly review the position of the legal complex as regards the principal aspects of political liberalism, namely moderate state, civil society and basic rights.

(a) The Legal Complex and the Moderate State

The Turkish legal complex is to a large extent autonomous from the executive and legislative powers, and therefore has the capacity to resist the arbitrary decisions of these powers that violate basic rights and liberties. The Bar Association has operated as an independent institution since its establishment in 1969. Legal academics are independent of the executive power and enjoy a certain degree of academic freedom. Finally, the Constitution provides the principle of the independence and impartiality of the judiciary. According to Article 138 of the Constitution, 'no organ, authority, office or individual may give orders or instructions to courts or judges relating to the exercise of judicial power, send them circulars, or make recommendations

---

[4] Toynbee and Kirkwood described the political idea that permeated the Turkish state as follows: '[t]he political idea on which the Turkish state is constructed derives from a conception of a nationally homogenous, administratively centralized, absolutely sovereign state which must be served by its citizens as a jealous God intolerant of variety and autonomy in any form' (Toynbee and Kirkwood, 1927: 4).

or suggestions'. Similarly, Article 140 of the Constitution stipulates, 'judges shall discharge their duties in accordance with the principles of the independence of the courts and the security of tenure of judges'.

There is however an ongoing debate about the independence of the judiciary in Turkey. Some constitutional provisions concerning the inspection, appointment and promotion of judges and pubic prosecutors are construed to undermine the principle of the independence of the judiciary. Article 40 provides that 'judges and public prosecutors shall be attached to the Ministry of Justice where their administrative functions are concerned'. More controversy arose over the composition of the Supreme Council of Judges and Prosecutors, which is responsible for the admission, appointment, promotion, transfer and discipline of almost all judges and prosecutors. The Supreme Council is presided over by the Minister of the Justice and the Undersecretary of the Ministry of Justice is an ex officio member of the Council. Five other members of the Council are appointed by the President of the Republic from among the top judges (Article 159). Furthermore, the Council is dependent on the Ministry of Justice concerning the secretariat, budget and premises. In its most recent report on Turkey, the European Commission has emphasised the shortcomings that undermine the principle of independence of the judiciary. It suggests that 'Turkey should ensure the independence of the judiciary, in particular as regards the High Council of Judges and Prosecutors and the appointment of new judges and prosecutors'.[5]

Despite these relatively minor obstacles, the courts operate independently of executive and legislative powers and play a significant role in checking and restricting the democratically elected governments. In this sense, the judiciary has contributed to the establishment and consolidation of a moderate (limited) government in Turkey. One must particularly mention the role of the Turkish Constitutional Court as the 'negative law-maker', to use the words of Kelsen. The Constitutional Court was established by the 1961 Constitution, which was the direct product of the 27 May 1960 military intervention. The Court was created as a counter-majoritarian organ with a view to protecting the political regime against the potential threats of democratically elected powers. The prevailing 1982 Constitution followed in the footsteps of the 1961 Constitution by designing the Constitutional Court 'as an instrument that will protect the fundamental values and interests of the state elites'. As Özbudun put it eloquently, 'the Constitutional Court has behaved essentially in the direction of the expectations of the state elites that created and empowered it' (Özbudun, 2006: 218).[6]

---

[5] European Commission, *Turkey: 2005 Progress Report*, Brussels, 9 Nov 2005, SEC (2005) 1426, 16 and 103–4.
[6] On this point see also Belge, 2006; Erdoğan, 2003.

(b) The Legal Complex and Civil Society

Civil society, as Halliday and Karpik argue, 'complements the internal moderation of the state by forming an expansive social basis for modern political liberalism' (Halliday and Karpik, 1997: 34). It is therefore a *sine qua non* of political liberalism. Some students of Turkish politics rightly argue that the lack of civil society in its functional sense as *intermediatory* groups between the society and the state has been one of the most serious obstacles to the establishment of the liberal/moderate state in Turkey. This 'missing link'[7] has impeded the development of organised social groups and facilitated the domination and control of the state elites over society.

Ironically, the lack or weakness of civil society is also the product of the strong state which aims to control society. It is difficult, if not impossible, to cultivate a real civil society in a political culture which deems the state a 'father' and 'sacred' entity. The paternalist state prevents the emergence of autonomous realms like civil society. The fact that the Turkish state has a comprehensive official ideology also impedes the development of a functional civil society. The adoption of an official ideology prevents the state from becoming politically neutral towards different and incommensurable conceptions of 'good' in society. As a result, the state favours or even collaborates with some civil society organisations, while suppressing others. It simply 'responds on a selective basis; it does not react in an egalitarian fashion to the different demands coming from the diverse institutions of civil society' (Karaman and Aras, 2000: 44).

The last two decades nonetheless have witnessed a flourish of civil society organisations mainly due to the relatively liberal economic policies. The liberal policies in the fields of law, politics and economics have triggered the formation of numerous non-governmental organisations in Turkey (Çaha, 2001). Some lawyers and legal academics have participated in a number of civil society organisations which have been mobilised to protect basic rights against the state. Some Turkish lawyers have played and still continue to play a very important role in the campaign and activities of human rights organisations such as the Human Rights Association (*İnsan Hakları Derneği*), The Turkish Human Rights Foundation (*Türkiye İnsan Hakları Vakfı*), the Organisation of Human Rights for Oppressed People (*Mazlum-Der*), the Human Rights Agenda Association (*İnsan Hakları Gündemi Derneği*)

---

[7] The term 'missing link' was used by Mardin to describe the lack of intermediate groups in the Ottoman Empire between the rulers and the people. He explained this idea as follows: 'all Ottoman citizens stood in a direct rather than a mediated relationship to the supreme authority. This missing link we call "civil society". It could be expected that Turkey would encounter difficulties in the development of modern democracy to the extent that this depends on this missing link. Marx's emphasis on the "empirically real contradiction" of state and society is still difficult for Turkish thinkers to understand, for the contradiction is not a datum of the Turkish experience' (Mardin, 1969: 279).

and Amnesty International-Turkey. There are also some lawyers' associations founded by lawyers with an aim of fostering the ideals of democracy, rule of law and human rights.

The mere existence of non-governmental organisations is not enough to assure the flourishing of a civil society in a liberal political regime. The Grand Lawyers' Association (*Büyük Hukukçular Birliği*), which was established by some ultranationalist lawyers and claims currently to have 800 members, has mobilised to restrict freedom of speech by initiating legal charges against some writers and novelists, including Nobel Prize winner Orhan Pamuk, on the ground of 'insulting Turkishness'. The Association 'skilfully exploited the remaining illiberal traits of Turkish criminal legislation, as well as the failure of judicial authorities to readjust the interpretation and implementation of existing legislation on liberal lines' (Grigoriadis, 2006: 15). We will return to the readjustment problem of the Turkish judiciary in the last section of this chapter.

(c) The Legal Complex and Basic Rights

There is undoubtedly a close connection between the political ideologies of the members of the legal complex and their contribution to the development of political liberalism. We have unfortunately no empirical data to reveal the political ideologies of the Turkish legal complex. However, we may infer some conclusions as to the ideological positions of judges, lawyers and legal academics by looking at the case law of the courts and public statements and political expressions made by lawyers and legal academics. Although the Turkish legal complex contains a limited number of 'liberal' and 'socialist' judges, prosecutors, lawyers and legal academics, it cannot be classified as a group of liberal minded people. The majority of judges, lawyers and legal academics seem to have adopted an authoritarian interpretation of Kemalism that comprises the ideas and principles laid down by Kemal Atatürk, the founder of modern Turkey.[8] Among the Kemalist principles, statism, nationalism and secularism remain the ruling passions of the legal complex. The legal complex has always been conservative in its peculiar sense that it has supported the prevailing status quo based on the principles of Kemalism.

The conservative nature of the legal complex has impeded the development of political liberalism. Let me take the bars first. Bar associations are expected to spearhead a wave of mobilisation for the protection of basic rights of individuals against the state. The autonomy of the bars helps them

[8] In Turkey, a few prominent judges defend relatively 'liberal' ideas while at the same time describing themselves as 'Kemalist' or 'Atatürkist'. Sami Selçuk, the former Chief Justice of the Court of Cassation, is a leading example. See Selçuk (2000).

to realise this expectation, because 'bar autonomy is a weapon that, in certain circumstances, can defend the interests and liberty of itself, other intermediate groups, and citizens more generally' (Halliday and Karpik, 1997: 21). The Turkish bars have occasionally mobilised to improve the human rights situation by organising seminars, publishing books and leaflets, issuing public declarations, etc. The Izmir Bar Association's endeavours to combat torture are particularly worth mentioning. It established the Torture Prevention Group in 2001 for the purpose of providing legal aid to the victims of torture and arranging public campaigns to raise consciousness as to the prevention of torture. Until its closure in 2004 the Group had received hundreds of applications alleging torture, and had organised workshops throughout Turkey to share its experience with other lawyers. The Group was, however, closed down by the new president of the bar on the basis that it was receiving funds from the European Commission and working to damage national interests.[9]

Apart from this kind of individual example, most of the bar associations and the National Union of Bars usually seek to align themselves with the state in restricting certain rights and freedoms. A typical example of this attitude of the bars may be found in the headscarf issue. The headscarf ban, which will be examined in more detail in the following section, is by no means limited to the universities. Most members of the legal complex believe that it is applicable to all places which constitute the so-called public sphere. The term public sphere is widely interpreted to include the office building of the President of the Republic, the VIP lounges of airports, plenary sessions of the parliament, and hearings of the courts. In 2003, the President of the Fourth Chamber of the Court of Cassation removed from the hearing a female lawyer who was present as a defendant before the court. The President of the Court declared that the courtroom was a public sphere to which a lawyer with a headscarf, even if she stood as an accused person, could not enter. This decision was supported by the Chief Justice of the Court of Cassation at that time and also by the bar associations. In a press release, the President of the National Union of Bars together with the presidents of the bars of İstanbul, Ankara, İzmir and Antalya declared that the right to a fair trial is a natural right for everybody provided that everyone acts in accordance with the laws, court decisions and rules of

---

[9] Amnesty International published a public statement on 14 January 2005 condemning the closure of the Torture Prevention Group. It emphasised, among others, that '[t]he Group had been engaged in groundbreaking work in bringing justice to torture victims and its closure is a step-back in the struggle against torture... The tireless and groundbreaking work of the Torture Prevention Group is a model not just for lawyers in Turkey but around the world': Amnesty International Public Statement, 'Turkey: Closure of Torture Prevention Group Shocking', 14 January 2005, available at http://web.amnesty.org/library/Index/ENGEUR 440012005?open&of=ENG-2U5, retrieved on 30 January 2007.

hearing order. The bars also recalled that the headscarf was a political symbol against the principle of secularism.[10] The bars further prohibited female lawyers from wearing the headscarf even during their apprenticeship. The Council of State (*Danıştay*), the highest administrative court, upheld the decisions of the bars to invalidate the apprenticeship of female lawyers with headscarves. It stated that the wearing of a headscarf by trainee lawyers was contrary to the principles of the secular state and incompatible with the occupation of lawyer.[11]

Another example of the negative approach of lawyers to political liberalism can be found in the public declarations of some bars relating to the ratification of the United Nations International Covenants on Civil and Political Rights and Social, Economic and Cultural Rights. Turkey signed these so-called twin covenants in 2000 and ratified them in 2003. In this process of ratification, there were campaigns against the Covenants mainly because of their first articles which guarantee the rights of people to self-determination. Some political parties and non-governmental organisations argued that these covenants would violate the principle of the 'territorial integrity' of the Turkish state. The Istanbul Bar Association, the biggest bar in Turkey, was among these protesters. In its public statement, the bar declared that the UN Covenants has 'threatened our nation-state and sovereignty', and therefore called the President of the Republic to refrain from approving the law passed by the Parliament to ratify the Covenants.[12] Nevertheless, the President approved the law and the Covenants became part of Turkish domestic law.

The Turkish bench is by no means better than the bars in defending basic rights and freedoms. Schwartz's following assertion about the position of federal judges in the United States also appeals to the Turkish judiciary: 'for most of American history, the federal courts have been a bastion of conservatism rather than a leader in protecting human rights' (Schwartz, 2004: 10). The conservatism of the Turkish judiciary is not used in the western sense of the term conservatism as a political ideology or position which stands for traditional and religious values. The judiciary in Turkey does not seek to conserve the traditional and religious values of the society. Its conservatism has two aspects. It (a) supports the existing political and legal order established by the state elites who also include the members of the legal complex, and (b) restricts individual rights and freedoms more than necessary to preserve the status quo.

---

[10] 'Son Günlerde Yargıya Yönelik Türban Odaklı Eleştiriler ve Yurt Sorunları' (Headscarf-Based Critiques of the Judiciary in Recent Days), 18 November 2003, available at www.istanbulbarosu.org.tr/Detail.asp?CatID=1&SubCatID=9&ID=370, retrieved on 5 April 2005.

[11] *Danıştay*, Sekizinci Daire (Eight Chamber), E. 1992/3342, K.1993/2611, K.T. 05/07/1993.

[12] See 'İstanbul Barosu Yönetim Kurulu'nun Kamuoyuna Açıklaması', Public Statement of Istanbul Bar's Executive Board, 13 June 2003, available at www.istanbulbarosu.org.tr/Detail.asp?CatID=1&SubCatID=6&ID=283, retrieved on 8 December 2005.

The recent public survey conducted by the Association for Liberal Thinking to examine the attitudes of the general population and judiciary towards human rights issues, particularly freedom of expression, sheds light on the role of the courts in protecting rights. According to the result of this public survey, 48.4 per cent of judges and prosecutors believe that human rights violations are common in Turkey. 46.1 per cent responded affirmatively to the question whether their basic rights and freedoms are restricted. As to the independence of the courts, 33.2 per cent believe that the state exerts influence on trials involving freedom of expression, whereas 56.3 per cent reject the existence of such an influence.

The members of the judiciary appear to adopt a restrictive approach to freedom of expression. 46.6 per cent of them said the following expression must constitute a crime: 'they (judges) are closed to knowledge, not open-minded, and they don't implement their duties carefully and don't care about it. It is the Constitutional Court that does not feel any uneasiness about being systematic destroyer of freedoms'. Only 42.9 of the judges and prosecutors said this expression should not be a criminal offence. 47.1 per cent said the expression that 'eight-year (uninterrupted) education is certainly irreligious' should be a criminal offence, while 44.5 per cent responded negatively. The overwhelming majority of judges and prosecutors (62 per cent) responded negatively to the question whether 'instruction-education in Kurdish should be allowed in schools'. The answers to the questions concerning religious liberties also reveal the restrictive approach of the judiciary. 73.8 per cent of the respondents said 'No' to the question whether 'the Islamic sects and communities should conduct their activities freely'. 62 per cent are against the free propaganda of Christianity and Judaism in Turkey. 49.7 per cent believe that there should be free choice whether or not the Islamic headscarf can be worn in universities, whereas 44.8 per cent are in favour of the ban on the headscarf. However, 63.6 per cent of the judges and prosecutors endorse the ban on the wearing of the headscarf by female civil servants (ALT, 2003: 46–56).

The opinion of the general population seems to be in contrast to that of the members of the judiciary on certain issues. 63.2 per cent of people believe that there is state pressure on courts deciding free speech cases. 70 per cent of respondents said that whether or not to wear the headscarf in universities must be a matter of free choice. The majority of the people (61 per cent) also support the idea that civil servants should be allowed to wear the headscarf (ALT, 2003: 33).[13]

---

[13] Other public surveys conducted also by secular organisations have verified the findings of the ALT survey as to the popular objection to the headscarf ban in universities and state buildings (for civil servants). The public survey carried out by the Turkish Economic and Social Studies Foundation (TESEV) in 1999 revealed that 76.1 per cent of people supported the idea that the headscarf should be free in universities. Only 16 per cent supported the headscarf ban. 74.2 per cent of people said that female civil servants should also be allowed

This public survey also reveals a certain degree of distrust toward the judiciary. While the majority of judges and prosecutors (68 per cent) think that the judiciary implements the laws fairly and impartially, 65 per cent of people said the courts in Turkey are not fair and impartial in applying the laws. Only 21 per cent said the courts implement laws in a fair and impartial way. Almost half of the people (47.8 per cent) said the courts themselves violate human rights. Only 32 per cent did not mention the courts as violators of the rights (ALT, 2003: 20–2). Another recent public survey has revealed that only 3 per cent of the respondents found the judiciary a credible institution.[14] The findings of these surveys suggest, inter alia, that the judiciary has little credibility in the eyes of the public.

IV. THE POLITICS OF THE TURKISH JUDICIARY AND BASIC RIGHTS

Under the current constitutional order, initiated by the 1982 Constitution, the storms of controversy have swirled about two basic issues: the protection of secularism and the maintenance of the territorial integrity of the country. The judiciary, and in fact a large part of legal complex, did its best to eliminate the real and potential dangers to these basic principles of the republic. The legal struggle against the 'enemies' of the regime consolidated the understanding of so-called 'militant' or 'combatant' democracy, and thus impeded the development of political liberalism.

(a) The Judiciary and the Headscarf Issue

The approach of the judiciary to the so-called headscarf problem[15] may reveal the basic parameters of the current culture war between the legal elites and the general population. Since the headscarf affair has become the subject of heated debate in most European countries, its examination enables us better to grasp the common attitudes of the judges in national

---

to wear the headscarf. In another survey, the results of which were published by *Milliyet* daily in May 2003, 75.5 per cent of respondents said the headscarf should be free in the universities, and 62.6 per cent said civil servants should be free to wear the headscarf. These results are consistent with the answers to the question 'is there anybody in your house who wears the headscarf?' 77.2 per cent of people responded affirmatively to this question. According to this survey 70 per cent of the respondents believe that the headscarf was not a symbol of a move against the principle of secularism. The most recent survey, conducted by the TESEV, reveals that 71.4 per cent of respondents support the freedom of university students to wear headscarves (Çarkoğlu & Toprak, 2006: 71).

[14] See *Politika Merkezi* (Political Centre) Survey, *Milliyet*, 5 Dec 2005.

[15] For a brief story of the legal and political aspects of the headscarf ban in universities see Human Rights Watch, 'Memorandum to the Turkish Government on Human Rights Watch's Concerns with Regard to Academic Freedom in Higher Education and Access to Higher Education for Women who Wear the Headscarf', available at http://www.hrw.org/backgrounder/eca/turkey/2004.

as well as international courts like the European Court of Human Rights. In Turkey the headscarf problem has been one of the watershed cases which may reveal the reason for the limited role of the legal complex in developing political liberalism. The religious headscarf worn by Muslim women is seen by the bulk of the Turkish legal complex as a symbol of 'political Islam'. It seems to cause deep fear in members of the legal complex who regard it as a threat to the basic principles of the republic, notably secularism. On the other hand, the Turkish people overwhelmingly support the headscarf as part and parcel of religious freedom, which is itself one of the fundamental aspects of political liberalism. These conflicting approaches to the headscarf problem not only create legal controversy at both national and international levels but also intensify the traditional power struggle between the state and society. The apparent 'victory' of the state elites in this power struggle with the decisive help of judiciary has increased the democratic deficit, which is generally seen as a source of legitimacy problem. The headscarf ban supported by the judiciary has also very much restricted the public sphere by excluding certain individuals from participating in it while maintaining their own identities as religious believers. Since the public sphere guarantees the autonomy of individuals, its inaccessibility to those with religious identities inevitably impedes the process of social development in civil society.[16] In short, the headscarf ban in Turkey restricts not only the autonomy of certain individuals and thus endangers healthy participation in the public realm, but also hinders the development of political liberalism by limiting the freedom of religion and education of a certain part of society.

We may now turn to the very interesting narrative of the headscarf and law in Turkey. In 1988, an Act of Parliament (Law 3511) was passed to remove what was known as the 'headscarf ban' in the universities. Until the enactment of the Act, female students in the universities had not been allowed to wear a headscarf. Some students who insisted on wearing the headscarf were removed from the universities, and their legal actions ended in failure. The Council of State (*Danıştay*) upheld the acts of the universities banning the headscarf. It held, inter alia, that:

> Without any specific intention or purpose, some of our less educated girls (and women) cover their heads under the influence of traditions and costumes of social environment in which they live. It is known, however, that some educated girls have covered their heads with the intention of opposing the principles of the secular Republic, and of advocating a political order based on religion. For them, the headscarf is not an innocent habit, but rather a symbol of a world view- a symbol against the freedom of woman and the basic principles of the Republic.[17]

---

[16] For the relationship between the public sphere and civil society see Halliday and Karpik, 1997: 35.

[17] *Danıştay* 8. Daire: 20.12.1983, E. 1983/142, K.1983/2788; 23.2.1984, E.1983/207, K.1984/330; 13.12.1984, E. 1984/636, K.1984/1574.

This Act was invalidated by the Constitutional Court in 1989.[18] The Parliament passed another Act in 1990 stating that 'no prohibition shall be imposed on modes of clothing and external appearance in the universities, unless it contravenes the laws in force'. An application was lodged once more with the Constitutional Court on the ground that the Act was unconstitutional. The Court this time found the Act constitutional, but declared that it did not invalidate its previous decision which banned wearing the headscarf in the universities. The most controversial part of the annulled Act read as follows: '[within the buildings of the universities] it shall be permitted to cover for religious reasons their heads and necks with a headscarf or turban'. The basic question, according to the Constitutional Court, is whether an Act of Parliament can be enacted on the basis of religious rules.[19] The Court responded to this question in the negative, and found the Act to contravene the Preamble, and Articles 2, 24, and 174 of the Constitution.[20]

The Constitutional Court first declared that the principles of secularism and Kemalist nationalism guaranteed in the Preamble and Article 2 of the Constitution made it impossible to view this Act as constitutional. The Court explicitly ruled out the possibility that there may be some 'democratic rights' which are in conflict with the principle of secularism. It held that:

There is no doubt that secularism is the core and foundation of the Turkish Revolution, the Republic, and national life... The freedoms are constrained by the Constitution. The actions against the constitutional principle of secularism and the rules of secular education cannot possibly be considered as democratic rights. The principle of secularism, which has constitutional privilege, is compatible with democracy. It is also a principle according to which all rights and liberties must be evaluated. [21]

The Court reluctantly conceded that secularism might in fact be incompatible with the protection of rights and freedoms. In the Court's view, the Constitution is extremely vigilant to protect the principle of secularism against freedoms; 'it does not sacrifice this principle for the sake of liberties'.[22] It is obvious that the Court conceived secularism as an 'ultra-constitutional norm' that determines the boundary of the rights. However, a certain definition of secularism was not given by the Court, though it said that the principle of secularism could not

[18] 25 *Anayasa Mahkemesi Kararlar Dergisi* (The Constitutional Court Reports)150. (E.1989/1, K.1989/2) (hereinafter *AMKD*).
[19] *Ibid*, at 142.
[20] *Ibid*, at 158.
[21] *Ibid*, at 150.
[22] *Ibid*, at 158.

be seen as a mere separation of religion and the state, and must be interpreted according to the social and political conditions in Turkey.

The Court previously attempted to justify the priority given to the foundational principles of the state. In interpreting laws, the Court emphasised, 'it is inevitable to regard the foundational principles of the state [eg secularism and Kemalist nationalism] as superior to other provisions of the Constitution'.[23] This is an acknowledgement of these principles as constituting what may be called the 'main legal paradigm' within which the Court operates.

Whilst this paradigm exists independently of the members of the particular interpretive community (the Court in this case), one must bear in mind that interpretation of this main paradigm is crucial for its application. The members of the interpretive community frequently read their own conception and understandings into the main paradigm. By arguing that wearing a headscarf is in conflict with the Article 174 of the Constitution, which guarantees the reforms of Atatürk, the Court behaved in this way. A dissenting judge stressed that none of Atatürk's reforms in fact provides any prohibition on women with respect to wearing certain clothes. In a word, the Court used an irrelevant aspect of the main-paradigm to justify its decisions. Furthermore, the very wording of the Act itself did not provide unequivocal support for the Court's assumption. The covering of heads for 'unreligious' reasons was not prohibited by the Act, as the dissenting judge pointed out.[24] The Act did not mention the term Islam as a religion. Although in a predominantly Muslim populated country 'religious reason' may refer to Muslims, it still does not prevent persons other than Muslims from covering their heads with a headscarf.

The fundamental flaw in the judgment of the Constitutional Court lies in its reading of this Act. The Court obviously misread the Act by assuming that it was nothing but an indication of the desire to create a 'theocratic state'. It appears that the Court has based all its reasoning on this wrong assumption. It is wrong for two reasons. First of all, the Act emerged to remove a clear violation of freedom of religion and conscience, a freedom which can be found in every human rights document. Secondly, the issue of headcovering is primarily a religious (not political) matter; a matter of belief deriving from the authoritative sources of Islam.[25] It constitutes a personal religious obligation which must be freely allowed in a liberal constitutional system. Even if it were true that individuals wear headscarves for merely political reasons, the Court had to produce convincing arguments

---

[23] E.1972/56, K.1973/11, 11 *AMKD* 2, 141.

[24] 25 *AMKD* 000, at 163.

[25] See, eg, *The Holy Qur'an: Text, Translation, and Commentar*, (trans A.Yusuf Ali, Beltsville, Mld, Amana Corp, 1983) at 904–5.

for the justification of the ban on the 'political' headscarf. In any case, the Court did not and could not possibly produce any criteria to distinguish between the 'religious' headscarf and the 'political' headscarf. The intention of headcovering, in fact, is not very important from the perspective of individual rights and freedoms. It is obviously a religious obligation, and constitutes a subject of freedom of religion and conscience. A 'rights-based' approach entails handling the case in this way. The Constitutional Court, however, misinterpreted the problem, and misread the Act simply because it adopted an 'ideology-based' approach towards the protection of individual rights and freedoms.

More interestingly, the Constitutional Court asserted that the Act has nothing to do with freedom of religion and conscience as protected by Article 24 of the Constitution. It made it clear that:

> Freedom of dress in a particular manner creates disparity between believers and disbelievers. Freedom of conscience is the right to believe whatever you want. By obfuscating freedom of conscience with secularism, liberty of religious dress cannot be defended. The issue of dress is restricted by the Turkish Revolution and Kemalist principles; it is not a matter of freedom of conscience.[26]

This is perhaps the only point in which the European Court of Human Rights differs from the Constitutional Court. The former conceives the wearing of the Islamic headscarf as a matter of freedom of religion, but finds the restriction on this freedom necessary in a democratic society. The Strasbourg Court's endorsement of the ban on the headscarf for university students has by no means ended the controversy in Turkey. Those who insistently defend the ban were delighted by the decision. On the other hand, all public surveys indicate that a clear majority of the people are against the headscarf ban in universities.[27] The party in power, which identifies itself as a 'conservative democrat', desires to remove this ban by obtaining social and institutional reconciliation. By 'institutional reconciliation' the government seems to mean reconciliation with the state elites including the courts and the Council of Higher Education, which impose the headscarf ban despite the fact that there is no law in force preventing female university students from wearing headscarf within university buildings.

(b) The Judiciary and Political Rights

Discussing the human rights policy of the Turkish judiciary with special reference to freedom of expression and freedom of association will reveal the nature and extent of the judicial impact on Turkish politics. In this

[26] 25 *AMKD* 000, at 154.
[27] See n 13 above.

section, we shall look at the judicial settlements of some cases involving the freedom of expression and association of political parties. These cases will explain the extent of juridification of Turkish politics. The human rights problem in Turkey is political in the sense that ruling elites have always engaged in a political struggle with self-declared dissidents. The basic aim of the state elites is to eliminate political opposition to the status quo. The composition and colour of the political opposition changes from time to time; in the 1970s it was the Marxists who were considered as a real threat to the political regime. However, after the collapse of the Soviet Union and the defeat of so-called 'existing socialism' the colour of the political threat turned from red to green. Since the beginning of 1990s, 'political Islam' has been perceived as the main threat to the secular nature of the political regime. On the other hand, the separatist movements based mainly on Kurdish nationalism have been considered as enemies undermining the territorial integrity of the republic. The courts in Turkey played a very effective role in eliminating these dangers. The State Security Courts, which have recently been abolished and replaced by Assize Courts, have condemned many writers and politicians for inciting people to hatred on the basis of either race or religion. Almost all of these judgments have been upheld by the Court of Cassation.

Until the end of 2002, a conviction for incitement to hatred under Article 312/2 of the Penal Code had a significant political result. Those who were convicted under this Article were prohibited from participating in politics. In this respect, many politicians, including the current Prime Minister, were victims of the decisions handed down by the State Security Courts and upheld by the Court of Cassation. These judicial decisions served to eliminate 'unwanted' political figures from politics with a view to shaping the actors of the political arena.

The Constitutional Court has also played a leading role in eliminating the 'religious' and 'separatist' threats to the regime. It has generously used its power to dissolve political parties. The Turkish Constitutional Court has adopted an 'ideology-based' paradigm in deciding political party cases. This paradigm reflects a positivist, one-dimensional, monolithic and authoritarian outlook. While the liberal legal paradigm gives priority to individuals and their rights vis-à-vis every kind of social and political association, the 'ideology-based' paradigm favours the state and society over the individual (Arslan, 2002: 11).

Since its establishment in 1961, the Court dissolved so many political parties, turning the country into a 'graveyard of the parties'. The Court has generally invoked two basic principles of the official ideology in order to dissolve political parties. They are (a) the principle of the indivisibility of the state with its country and nation, and (b) the principle of secularism. For example, on 16 July 1991, the Constitutional Court dissolved the United Communist Party of Turkey (TBKP) on two grounds. First, the

Party's incorporation of the word 'communist' into its name was found to be contrary to Article 96(3) of the Political Parties Act. That article states: 'No political party shall be formed with the name "communist," "anarchist," "fascist," "theocratic," or "national socialist", the name of a religion, language, race, sect or religion, or a name including any of the above words or similar ones'. Secondly, statements in the TBKP's constitution about the 'Kurdish question' were construed as encouraging separatism and the division of the Turkish nation, both of which are prohibited by the Constitution. The Constitutional Court next dissolved the Socialist Party (on 10 July 1992) on the basis that the activities of the Party violated certain principles set out in the Constitution and the Political Parties Act that prohibit separatism and every kind of endeavour to create minorities within the country. The Court found unacceptable the party's statement concerning the existence of the 'Kurdish nation' as separate from the 'Turkish nation'. On 14 July 1994, the Constitutional Court dissolved the Freedom and Democracy Party (ÖZDEP) on the grounds that its objectives encouraged separatism by defending self-determination for the 'Kurdish people' and for conducting judicial and educational services in their own native language. Ironically, the Court ruled that ÖZDEP's programme violated, among other things, the principle of secularism, which is the core principle of the official ideology, even though this Party is known as a purely secular organisation. According to the Court, the statement in ÖZDEP's programme that 'the State shall not interfere in religious affairs, which must be left to the religious communities' was incompatible with secularism and Article 89 of the Political Parties Act. The Court also dissolved the Peoples' Labour Party (HEP), the Democracy Party (DEP), and more recently the People's Democracy Party (HADEP) for violating the national and territorial integrity of the country. The Welfare Party (RP) and the Virtue Party (FP) were dissolved for becoming a centre of activities against the principle of secularism. The former was the major party in a coalition government, when the Principal State Counsel initiated the application for an order to dissolve it on 21 May 1997. The Virtue Party was the main opposition party when it was dissolved by the Constitutional Court (Arslan, 2002: 15–17).

Under the 1982 Constitution, the dissolution of political parties has drastic conclusions for both the legal personality and the rulers of the party concerned. The order of the Constitutional Court dissolving a political party requires *ipso jure* the liquidation of the party and transfer of its assets to the Treasury. The founders and rulers of the party are banned from holding similar office in any political party for five years. The Constitutional Court's judgments on political parties therefore have shown a typical example of the 'judicialisation of politics', that is, 'a definite tendency for an increasing number of decisions formerly taken exclusively within the overtly political branches of government to be taken, instead, by unelected judges answerable to no electorate' (Hodder-Williams, 1996: 2).

(c) The Role of the European Court of Human Rights

It would be helpful to mention briefly the approach of the European Court of Human Rights to the decisions of the Turkish judiciary on certain political freedoms. In almost all cases, involving the restriction of the applicants' right to free speech in inciting hatred among the people on the basis of race or in promoting the terrorist and separatist organisation, the Strasbourg Court found a breach of the Convention.[28] It is equally true that all political parties that were dissolved by the Constitutional Court for violating the territorial integrity of the country have won their cases in Strasbourg. The Strasbourg Court has perhaps remedied some negative aspects of the political system arising out of the adoption and application of the militant democracy (Arslan, 2002).

It is however wrong to say that the Strasbourg Court has also contributed to a liberal understanding of secularism in Turkey. In the case of the Welfare Party (*Refah Partisi*), both the Chamber and the Grand Chamber upheld the judgment of the Turkish Constitutional Court and found no violation of Article 11 of the Convention.[29] Similarly in the case of *Leyla Şahin*, in which the applicant complained about the ban on wearing a headscarf in universities, the Chamber and, more recently, the Grand Chamber of the Court did not find a violation of freedom of religion, despite the fact that no European university has such a ban on headscarves.[30] In these judgments, the Court indulged in a categorical and negative assessment of Islam and its imperatives. In the *Refah* judgment, the Grand Chamber invoked the terms such as 'Islamic fundamentalism' and 'totalitarian movements' which should not be used in a judicial decision, as Judge Kovler put it in his concurring opinion. In the *Leyla Şahin* case the Court described the Islamic headscarf as a political symbol which has been contrary to the principles of plurality and gender equality. Given the fact that many Muslims conceive the headscarf as a precept of their religion, the European Court of Human Rights or indeed any state organisation is not in a position to decide

---

[28] In most of these cases the Strasbourg Court also found a violation of Art 6 of the Convention on the ground that the existence of military judges in the State Security Courts contravenes the independent and impartial judiciary which is part and parcel of the right to a fair trial. See, mutatis mutandis, App no 22678/93, *Incal v Turkey*, 9 June 1998.

[29] App nos 41340/98, 41342/98 and 41344/98, *Refah Partisi (The Welfare Party) and Others v Turkey*, Grand Chamber, 13 Feb 2003. See www.echr.coe.int.

[30] App no 44774/98, *Leyla S,ahin v Turkey* (Chamber), 29 May 2004; *Leyla S,ahin v Turkey* (Grand Chamber), 10 Nov 2005. In an almost identical case against Uzbekistan, the UN Human Rights Committee found a violation of Art 18 of the ICCPR. It held that '[t]he Committee considers that the freedom to manifest one's religion encompasses the right to wear clothes or attire in public which is in conformity with the individual's faith or religion. Furthermore, it considers that to prevent a person from wearing religious clothing in public or private may constitute a violation of article 18, paragraph 2, which prohibits any coercion that would impair the individual's freedom to have or adopt a religion': Communication No 931/23000, *Raihon Hudoyberganova v Uzbekistan*, Uzbekistan. 18 Jan 2005, CCPR/C/82/D/931/2000. (Jurisprudence), para 6.2.

theological questions like 'what the headscarf should mean to Muslims' (Gunn, 2004: 472).[31]

The willingness of the Strasbourg Court to endorse the militant secularism of Turkey is partly due to the globalisation of the fear created by 9/11. 'It is difficult', as Kevin Boyle points out, 'to suppress the thought that the endorsement by a European-wide court of such a radical intervention in the democratic process [dissolution of *Refah*], as a result of which the choice of a significant percentage of the Turkish electorate was removed from power, was influenced by the events of "9/11" and the world we have lived in since then' (Boyle, 2004: 9). In short, the Strasbourg Court's political approach in the cases like *Refah* and *Şahin* encouraged the state elites to suppress political rights and religious liberties.

The failure of the Turkish judiciary, aided partly by the Strasbourg Court, to protect political freedoms derives mainly from the politicisation of the judiciary. The judges routinely prioritise the established political discourse. The rights and liberties of individuals are protected only to the extent that they are compatible with this official discourse. The judiciary has a self-proclaimed mission to curb the rights of those whose views are considered or perceived as a threat to the political ideology it seeks to protect. This inevitably ends up in the judicialisation of politics which refers to the expansion of judicial power vis-à-vis the executive and to judicial intervention in politics. The expansion of the judiciary is generally seen as a 'positive development, since it can often reinforce individual rights and responsibilities' (Guarnieri and Pederzoli, 2002: 13). The historical experience in Turkey does not seem to verify this assumption. On the contrary, 'the Turkish case obliges us to abandon the notion that rights "increase" as executive power "decreases"' (Belge, 2006: 686).

V. ADJUSTING THE TURKISH JUDICIARY TO THE NEW LIBERAL ORDER

In the process of becoming a full member of the EU, Turkey has undergone a radical change which is sometimes called a 'silent revolution'. In fact, a number of constitutional and legal amendments have been made in the last couple of years to liberalise the constitutional and political system. Some of these changes are concerned with the political and legal structure of the state, while some others are about the protection of individual rights and liberties. I just want to outline a brief sample of these changes introduced to meet the so-called Copenhagen Criteria of the EU for prospective members.

---

[31] For a comprehensive and critical analysis of the *Leyla Şahin* case see also Altiparmak and Karahanoğullari, 2006.

First, significant, albeit inadequate, steps have been taken to demilitarise the political and legal structure. The 2001 constitutional amendments as well as recent harmonisation laws have radically modified the structure and function of the National Security Council, which played a central role in the militarisation of politics. These amendments increased the number of civilian members of the Council and limited its powers to make it merely an advisory body. The 2004 constitutional amendments also contributed to the demilitarisation policy by excluding the military member from the Higher Education Council, and subjecting the fiscal transactions of the military to review by the Court of Audit. Secondly, the controversial National Security Courts were abolished by the Turkish Parliament in May 2004. The existence of these special courts, which included military judges and prosecutors until 1999, has been seen as a violation of the rule of law. The Criminal Procedure Law was also radically changed to transfer important police powers to the judiciary, namely the public prosecutors and judges. The powers of the prosecutors have been increased in the policing process such as search, seizure, investigation and interrogation.

Thirdly, the Turkish Constitution and the Political Parties Act have been amended to make the dissolution of political parties more difficult. Amended Article 69 of the Constitution has introduced an alternative sanction to the dissolution of political parties. Accordingly, the Constitutional Court is empowered to prevent the political parties, instead of dissolving them, from temporarily or permanently receiving state aid. Finally, the Turkish parliament has also introduced positive changes removing restrictions on basic rights and liberties. The death penalty was completely abolished by the 2004 constitutional amendments. The harmonisation packages included a number of provisions aimed at preventing torture and maltreatment. Some important amendments have been made to expand the scope of freedom of thought and expression. Article 26 of the Constitution was amended in 2001 to remove the ban on the use of any language legally prohibited in the expression and dissemination of thought. Similarly, amendments to the Law on Foreign Language Education and Teaching removed the restrictions on the learning of different languages used by Turkish citizens in their daily lives. It is also significant that the state television stations started to broadcast in native languages other than Turkish.[32]

---

[32] The changes in economic, political, constitutional and cultural areas are welcomed by liberal pro-Europeans. On the other hand, these reforms created a tension among some Eurosceptics who argue that the reforms will inevitably undermine the foundational principles of the republic, namely the indivisibility of the state and the secularism. Ironically the Eurosceptic group includes some Kemalists, the Kurdish nationalists and certain groups of Islamists. Although they are against Turkey's membership of the European Union from different perspectives, they appear to have developed common policies towards particular issues such as Cyprus and the role of the military in politics. See Polat, 2004.

Changing the Constitution and the laws is however not sufficient to advance to political liberalism. The implementations of these reforms are far more important than their introduction. The Turkish judiciary seems to be perplexed about the implementation of political reforms. Under the influence of highly statist political and legal culture, judges have generally been hostile to the policy of political and economic liberalisation. In 2001, when the draft bills were introduced to amend the Constitution with the aim of expanding the freedom of political parties, the Constitutional Court publicly denounced this attempt. In a press release, which was also called a 'memorandum' directed to the government and the parliament of the time, the Court recalled the necessity of dissolving political parties to protect the indivisibility and democratic foundations of the state. The Court warned that making difficult the dissolution of political parties would leave the democratic republic without protection.[33] On 14 March 2005, the Constitutional Court unanimously struck down Article 19 of Law 4916 which paved the way for the sale of immovable property to foreigners. This decision seems to reflect the nationalist sensibilities of some groups who presented the legislation as 'selling off the country' to foreigners. All in all, this decision of the Constitutional Court is consistent with the negative attitude of the Turkish judiciary towards economic liberalism, particularly the policy of privatisation (Erdoğan, 2003: 179–84). The judiciary is believed to 'form the most formidable resistance to change by refusing a swift implementation of the reforms on democracy and human rights, and by turning the economic privatization initiatives of the pro-European government into a debacle' (Polat, 2006: 527).

The reluctance of the judicial organs to adapt themselves to the changing legal/political climate of the country is by no means limited to the Constitutional Court. The Court of Cassation, the highest appeal court in Turkey, insists on interpreting the provisions of the new Penal Code in such a way as to restrict freedom of expression. On 23 November 2004 the Court of Cassation delivered a significant judgment applying the amended Article 312/2 of the Penal Code which punishes 'incitement to enmity and hatred' if it endangers the public safety.[34] The Court quashed the conviction of a journalist for expressing ideas contrary to principle of secularism. This decision was widely covered by the national media, some of which presented it as a 'revolution'.[35] Although the Court majority regarded secularism as an 'unalterable truth for all times', it argued that mere expression

---

[33] 'Anayasal Muhtıra' (Constitutional Memorandum), *Milliyet*, 23 Jan 2001.
[34] *TC Yargıtay Ceza Genel Kurulu* (*Grand Chamber of the Court of Cassation*), E. 2004/8-130, K. 2004/206, K.T. 23.11.2004.
[35] İ Berkan, 'İfade Özgürlüğünün Sınırları Genişlerken [Expanding the Scope of Freedom of Expression]', *Radikal*, 5 Feb 2005; anon, 'Devrim Gibi Karar [Judgment Like a Revolution]', *Dünden Bugüne Tercüman*, 5 Feb 2005.

of thought contrary to secularism should not be proscribed. This groundbreaking decision was fragile because it was taken by a majority of 14 to 13. Indeed, eventually, in an almost identical case, the Court of Cassation (sitting as the General Assembly of Criminal Chambers) over-turned its earlier decision by quashing the judgment of the Chamber which acquitted a journalist accused of inciting people to enmity and hatred on the basis of religious discrimination under Article 312 of the Penal Code.[36]

The Court of Cassation has also interpreted Article 301 of the new Penal Code in a very restrictive way. Article 301, which replaced Article 159 of the former Penal Code, stipulates that 'public denigration of Turkishness, the Republic or the Grand National Assembly of Turkey shall be punishable by imprisonment of between six months and three years'.[37] The Court of Cassation upheld the suspended conviction of journalist Hrant Dink for 'insulting Turkishness' in an article on Armenian identity. The Court noted, inter alia, that Dink denigrated Turkishness by saying that 'the clean blood that will replace the poisonous blood spilling from Turk exists in the noble vein of Armenian that will be constructed with Armenia'. The Court held that Dink's 'insulting' remarks constitute a skilful modification of Mustafa Kemal's words in his address to the Turkish youth that 'the strength you need exist in your noble blood'.[38] Hrant Dink's assassination on 19 January 2007 outside the office of *Agos*, the Armenian-Turkish weekly newspaper that he founded and edited, also sparked a heated debate on the role of Article 301 and the judicial process in his murder.[39]

VI. CONCLUSION

One may draw three main conclusions from the above analysis of the rela-tionship between the Turkish legal complex and political liberalism. First, the legal complex in Turkey, unlike in most of the democratic countries, has not contributed significantly to the development of political liberalism.

---

[36] *TC Yargıtay Ceza Genel Kurulu* (*Grand Chamber of the Court of Cassation*), E. 2004/ 8-201, K. 2005/30, K.T. 15.03.2005.

[37] The second para of Art 301 criminalises the denigration of the Turkish government, the judicial, military and security institutions of the state.

[38] *TC Yargıtay Ceza Genel Kurulu* (*Grand Chamber of the Court of Cassation*), E. 2006/ 9-169, K. 2006/184, K.T. 11.07.2006.

[39] See, for instance, MA Birand, '301 killed Hrant Dink', *Turkish Daily News*, 23 Jan 2007. In his last article entitled 'The "pigeon skittishness" of my soul', Dink himself expressed his disappointment with the attitude of the judiciary in the following terms: 'I have largely lost my confidence in the "justice system" and the notion of "Law" in Turkey ... The judiciary does not protect the rights of citizen but the State. It is not on the side of the citizen, but under the strict control of the State. In fact I was completely sure that even though it was said that the judgment about me was delivered "in the name of the Turkish people", it was actually taken "in the name of the Turkish State"'.

This is partly due to the authoritarian nature of the official ideology adopted by the legal complex, and partly to the conservative characteristics of the judiciary. Moreover, the political conditions to which the judiciary has always reacted swiftly must also be taken into account in order better to understand the reason why the legal complex has played an influential role in stalling political liberalism. As argued before, the Republic of Turkey has created its own friends and foes from the very beginning, and the legal complex has defined its role as a protector of the regime against its enemies. In the continuing power struggle between the state and political elites, the legal complex has allied itself with the former. A significant number of law professors, lawyers and judges have contributed to the justification of periodic military interventions that impeded the development of political liberalism by leading to the suspension of the rule of law and gross violations of human rights.

Secondly, we should perhaps reconsider the relationship between the components of political liberalism in the light of the Turkish experience. Although moderate state, civil society and rights are *sine qua non* conditions of political liberalism, there is no automatic link between these components. The Turkish judiciary, as an independent and powerful branch, has played a substantial role in curbing the powers of the legislative and executive branches of the state, and thus created a moderate state. The establishment of independent judiciary and bar associations does not however necessarily guarantee the development of civil society and the protection of individual rights. In fact, the expansion of judicial power resulted in less protection for basic rights and liberties.

Finally, the potential internal tensions and paradoxes within the concept of political liberalism may be reduced by transnational factors like the European Union that exert a considerable influence on the liberalisation of Turkish legal and political structure. In the process of becoming a full member of the EU, Turkey has been in transition from bureaucratic authoritarian regime to more liberal state and society, even though some parts of the legal and political complex clearly resist this transition. Turkey is changing and the legal complex will have to adapt to this changing climate. This adaptation requires the Turkish legal complex to abandon its old habits, fears, alignments and long practised ideological approaches.

REFERENCES

ALT (2003), *Human Rights and Freedom of Expression in Turkey* (Ankara, ALT and the European Commission).

Altiparmak, K and Karahanoğullari, O (2006), 'After Şahin: The Debate on Headscarves is not Over', 2 *European Constitutional Law Review* 268.

Arslan, Z (2002), 'Conflicting Paradigms: Political Rights in the Turkish Constitutional Court', 11 *Critique: Critical Middle Eastern Studies* 9.

—— (2005), *Anayasa Teorisi (Constitutional Theory)* (Ankara, Seçkin Yayıncılık).

Belge, C (2006), 'Friends of the Court: The Republican Alliance and Selective Activism of the Constitutional Court of Turkey', 40 *Law & Society Review* 653.

Bentham, J (1995), *The Panopticon Writings* (ed M Božoviè, London, Verso).

Boyle, K (2004), 'Human Rights, Religion and Democracy: The Refah Party Case', 1 *Essex Human Rights Review* 1.

Çaha, Ö (2001), 'The Inevitable Coexistence of Civil Society and Liberalism: The Case of Turkey', 3 *Journal of Economic and Social Research* 35.

Çarkoğlu, A and Toprak, B (2006), *Değişen Türkiye'de Din, Toplum ve Siyaset [Religion, Society and Politics in Changing Turkey]* (İstanbul, TESEV Yayınları).

Dworkin, R (1985), *A Matter of Principle* (Cambridge, Mass, Harvard University Press).

Erdoğan, M (2003), *Anayasa ve Özgürlük [Constitution and Freedom]* (Ankara, Yetkin Yayıncılık).

Grigoriadisi, IN (2006), 'Upsurge amidst Political Uncertainty: Nationalism in Post-2004 Turkey', Stiftung Wissenschaft und Politik (SWP) Research Paper, Berlin, October 2006, available at www.swp-berlin.org/de/common/get_document. php?asset_id=3380.

Guarnieri, C and Pederzoli, P (2002), *The Power of Judges: A Comparative Study of Courts and Democracy* (trans CA Thomas, Oxford, Oxford University Press).

Gunn, TJ (2004), 'Religious Freedom and *Laïcité*: A Comparison of the United States and France', 2 *Brigham Young University Law Review* 419.

Halliday, TC and Karpik, L (1997), 'Politics Matter: a Comparative Theory of Lawyers in the Making of Political Liberalism' in TC Halliday and L Karpik (eds), *Lawyers and the Rise of Western Political Liberalism* (Oxford, Clarendon Press).

Hamilton, A, Madison, J and Jay, J (1961), *The Federalist Papers* (New York, A Mentor Book).

Hayek, FA (1976), *The Constitution of Liberty* (London, Routledge & Kegan Paul).

Heper, M (1985), *The State Tradition in Turkey* (London, The Eothen Press).

Hodder-Williams, R (1996), *Judges and Politics in the Contemporary Age* (London, Bowerdean).

Karaman, M and Aras, B (2000), 'The Crisis of Civil Society in Turkey', 2 *Journal of Economic and Social Research* 39.

Maalouf, A (2000), *On Identity* (trans. B Bray, London, Harvill Press).

Mardin, Ş (1969), 'Power, Civil Society and Culture in the Otoman Empire', 11 *Comparative Studies in Society and History* 258.

Özbudun, E (2006), 'Political Origins of the Turkish Constitutional Court and the Problem of Democratic Legitimacy', 12 *European Public Law* 213.

Polat, N (2004), 'Realignment in Turkey', 4 *Internationale Politik*, Transatlantic Edition, 35.

—— (2006), 'Identity Politics and the Domestic Context of Turkey's European Union Accession', 41 *Government and Opposition* 512.

Rawls, J (1996), *Political Liberalism* (New York, Columbia University Press).

Schwartz, H (2004), *Right Wing Justice: The Conservative Campaign to Take Over the Courts* (New York, Nation Books).

Selçuk, S (2000), *Longing for Democracy* (trans K Başlar, Ankara, Yeni Türkiye Publications).

Shambayati, H (2004), 'A Tale of Two Mayors: Courts and Politics in Iran and Turkey', 36 *International Journal of Middle East Studies* 253.

Toynbee, AJ and Kirkwood, P (1927), *Turkey* (New York, Charles Scribner's Sons).

Ünsal, A (1980), *Siyaset ve Anayasa Mahkemesi: 'Siyasal Sistem' Teorisi Açısından Türk Anayasa Mahkemesi [Politics and Constitutional Court: The Turkish Constitutional Court from the Perspective of 'Political System' Theory]* (Ankara, SBF Yayınları).

8

The Ambivalent Language
of Lawyers in Israel: Liberal Politics,
Economic Liberalism, Silence
and Dissent*

GAD BARZILAI

I. BETWEEN SILENCE AND SPEECH—LAWYERS AND
THE POLITICAL SPHERE

CONTRARY TO NUMEROUS other professionals, lawyers are political
agents in their daily professional practices. They habitually act
through legalistic struggles to alter allocation of public goods
(Halliday and Karpik, 1997). Frequently, they either function in politics
and/or have meaning in politics (Abel, 1989, 1995; Barzilai, 2005; Eulau
and Sprague, 1964; Feeley and Krislov, 1990, Feeley and Rubin, 2000;
Haltom and McCann, 2004; Kagan, 2000; Lev, 2000; Sarat and Scheingold,
1998, 2001; Scheingold, 2004; Scheingold and Sarat, 2004; Shamir and
Ziv, 2001). By definition of their profession, lawyers incline to legitimate
the nation-state. Their professional ideology presumes crucial public constitutive functions of the legal complex and it relies on perceived state's
abilities to respond rather effectively to public needs and expectations.

When lawyers practise in the legal complex—even those who voice
political dissent—they act through the formal legalistic rules as those

* I would like to express my deepest thanks to Malcolm Feeley, Terry Halliday and Lucien
Karpik for their very helpful and insightful comments on earlier drafts of this chapter. Lisa
Hilbink sent me the notes of the Onati conference around this volume. Clark Sorensen and
Patti Goedde guided me on lawyers in South Korea. The Israeli bar and the management of the
Israeli courts were very cooperative and enabled me to access valuable original information.
Lee Varshavsky, my research assistant from Tel Aviv University, was very helpful in assisting
me to accumulate figures regarding lawyers in Israel. Gerhard O'Neill and Dan O'Connor
provided me the data on Australian lawyers. Stuart Scheingold and Joel Migdal offered me
their helpful comments on an earlier draft. Finally, the comments of three anonymous referees
were very helpful in improving the chapter. The generosity and wisdom of all these people
notwithstanding, the responsibility is all mine.

of jurisdiction, standing, justifiability, adjudication, procedures, rules of ethics and rules of evidence. Hence, both legitimisation and legalisation of the nation-state through lawyers seem to be fundamental and expected functions of lawyers through the legal complex. These two functions of lawyers may even be empowered in liberalism since it advances two foremost normative principles. The first principle is the preference rendered to individual rights over any other type of collective good. The second principle is the state's 'neutrality' and its ability to produce a procedural justice. Presumably, lawyers exercising professional knowledge of the legal complex may have a singular role in advancing these two liberal visions.

However, this chapter does not portray lawyers in the course of conventional democratic politics. Rather, it is devoted to another aspect concerning lawyers, the legal complex, and political liberalism—it argues that lawyers in a diversity of sociopolitical and economic sites in state and civil society are crucial agents of the formation and signalling the sphere of deliberations in democracies. In other terms, when lawyers talk and furthermore when they are silent in the political sphere, and yet practise as lawyers, they actually determine the boundaries of the political discourse and political deliberations. Rather than using categories of 'private lawyers', 'government lawyers' and 'cause lawyers', this chapter adds a different and yet a complimentary theoretical vantage point for better understanding the legal complex. This chapter does not look into a specific type of lawyer. Instead it is interested in comprehending the overall population of lawyers, and how the bar has mobilised, effected and affected sociopolitical forces. It focuses not only on the functions of empowering and challenging legalisation of the state but also on how lawyers are meaningful in shaping the boundaries of political discourse. More contextually, this chapter also looks into the Israeli experience and in turn it invites a few generalisations that are comparable to other case studies around our globe.

II. THE COMPARATIVE SETTING

(a) Lawyering in Proportions

With more awareness of liberal rights and individualism, significantly associated with capitalism, industrialisation and economic expansion, the number of lawyers especially in Western societies has increased. It is both important and striking to offer a comparison between those countries and Israel, which was established in 1948 subsequent to different waves of Zionist immigration mainly from East Europe and Russia to Palestine, beginning in 1882. It is important to put Israel in a comparative perspective, since if its number of lawyers is comparatively diminutive, what does it entail for lawyers' contribution to political liberalism and its absence? Alternatively, if the number of lawyers is considerable in comparative perspective, how does it affect political discourse and how do lawyers contribute to framing it amid liberalism? The cross-national comparison may be striking, since Israel does not have historical roots of liberalism, and from this perspective its historical backdrop is significantly different from those of Western and European countries.

About 60 per cent of the Israeli demographic increase and composition since 1948 is due to immigration from non- liberal countries; North Africa and Middle East Muslim countries (mainly in 1951–61), East European countries (mainly in 1919–23; 1946–8); and from the republics of the former Soviet Union (mainly 1989–91). With no significant demographic origins of a Western liberal culture, and even considering some liberal experience since the end of the 1960s, we may hypothesise that the number of lawyers in Israel might have been rather low in a comparative perspective, and especially in comparison with Western liberal states. The praxis is counter-intuitive, however.

I have gathered a data set about lawyers in 39 countries; some are western liberal democracies and others non-liberal settings. My observation is that among European and most Western nation-states and most democracies, Israel has the highest number of lawyers per population size. In 2005 the country had one lawyer per 211 citizens, a figure which is significantly higher than in most liberal societies like the US (one lawyer per 434 citizens), United Kingdom (one lawyer per 489 citizens), Germany (one lawyer per 619 citizens), Australia (one lawyer per 672 citizens), Holland (one lawyer per 1,251 citizens), and France (one lawyer per 1,281 citizens).

As Table 8.1 below exhibits, in comparative terms and considering population size, Israel had in 2005 204 per cent more lawyers than in the US, 232 per cent more lawyers than in United Kingdom, 293 per cent more than in Germany, 593 per cent more than in Holland, and 601 per cent more lawyers than in France. Not only do West European and North American countries share a more historically entrenched political liberal tradition, but all of them (with the exception of relatively newly established democratic Portugal) have a more prosperous economy with higher GDP per capita than Israel. And yet, Israel has the highest number of lawyers per population size. It would have been plausible to assume that the number of lawyers in Israel may resemble that in a country like South Korea. Both Israel and South Korea have experienced an intensive economic development of the private sector, both do not have liberal origins and traditionally entrenched political liberalism. Further, both are under massive American political influence, and both are characterised by strong feelings of national security siege mentality. Yet, the relative number of lawyers in Israel is 30,13 times more than in South Korea, per population size.

Table 8.1 Lawyering in Comparison (2005)

Country	Population	No. Lawyers	GDP per Capita	No. Citizens per Lawyer
Israel	6,869,500	32,600	20,800	211
Spain	40,341,462	148,543	23,300	272
Liechtenstein	33,717	112	25,000	301
Greece	10,668,354	35,000	21,300	305
Iceland	296,737	690	31,900	430
US	295,734,134	681,000	40,100	434
Italy	58,103,033	128,000	27,700	454
Portugal	10,566,212	22,575	17,900	468
Luxembourg	468,571	979	58,900	479
United Kingdom	60,441,457	123,500	29,600	489
Canada	32,805,041	67,000	31,500	490
Cyprus	780,133	1,577	20,300	495
Ireland	4,015,676	7,500	31,900	535
Germany	82,431,390	133,113	28,700	619
Bulgaria	7,450,349	11,353	8,200	656
Australia	20,090,437	29,887	32,000	672
Belgium	10,364,388	14,529	30,600	713
Norway	4,593,041	5,770	40,000	796
Switzerland	7,489,370	7,289	33,800	1,027
Hungary	10,006,835	8,900	14,900	1,124
Denmark	5,432,335	4,635	32,200	1,172
Holland	16,407,491	13,111	29,500	1,251
France	60,656,178	47,354	28,700	1,281
Czech Re,	10,241,138	7,947	16,800	1,289
Slovakia	5,431,363	3,994	14,500	1,360
Macedonia	2,045,262	1,379	7,100	1,483
Turkey	69,660,559	44,221	7,400	1,575
Croatia	4,495,904	2,706	11,200	1,661
Austria	8,184,691	4,678	31,300	1,750
Poland	38,635,144	21,500	12,000	1,797
Slovenia	2,011,070	992	19,600	2,027
Sweden	9,001,774	4,321	28,400	2,083
Lithuania	3,596,617	1,382	12,500	2,602
Ukraine	47,425,336	18,000	6,300	2,635
Latvia	2,290,237	833	11,500	2,749

(*continued*)

Table 8.1   Continued

Estonia	1,332,893	447	14,300	2,982
Finland	5,223,442	1,735	29,000	3,011
Japan	127,417,244	21,208	30,400	6,008
South Korea	48,422,644	7,617	19,200	6,357

Sources:

1. For European countries data was gathered from CCBE (Council of Bars and Law Societies of Europe).
2. For Israel data was collected from the Bureau of Statistics and the Bar.
3. For South Korea the numbers were collected from the South Korea Bar Association.
4. For the US, data was collected from Internet Research Group.
5. For Canada data was collected from Trust Canlaw. www.canlaw.com/lawyers/membership.htm.
6. For Australia the data was collected through the help of the Australian Bar.
7. For Japan the data was gathered in the Japanese Bar.

Now, knowing that the number of lawyers in Israel is so high in comparison to that in many other countries invokes a crucial question. What does such a large professional group mean to political liberalism, the legal complex and political power? Accordingly, the next section attempts to explore why Israel has had such a high number of lawyers. Then I argue that while lawyers have been agents that propelled some facets of political and economic liberalism, they have also constituted a structure of a limited political discourse, which has legitimated and legalised the silence of dissent against some fundamental narratives of the nation-state.

How may we explain the existence of a large professional body of lawyers that is rather passive in the political discourse? How are lawyers meaningful, if at all, to political liberalism, the legal complex, and state–society relationships? If my solution to the puzzle is correct, we need to introduce the concept of *silence*, alongside *voice* for better understanding of collective action, state–society relations, and lawyers. In other words, this chapter invites one to look at lawyers not only as agents of mobilisation, legislation, regulation and litigation. Additionally, we are best advised to comprehend and theorise lawyers as framers and markers of voice, silence and political absence. If my argument is solid, it should assist in further exploring why lawyers may be both agents of social changes and agents of social maintenance in the very same legal complex. However, my solution may constitute an imagined community of lawyers. To avoid that methodological and epistemological slope this chapter distinguishes between various types of lawyers. In politics like in any space of language and behaviour there are different types of voices and silences.

(b) A Word on Legal Words

Language is a sociopolitical construct, with no in-depth meanings to its rules, unless mythical social certainty and deceptive social consent are investigated as lingual sources (Wittgenstein, 1958: 225–9; Wittgenstein, 1969; Wittgenstein, 1974: 188). Law is an epiphenomenological constitutive language that has its structure of norms and a grammar, ie, rules of interpretations and rules of logic (Wolcher, 2005). I narrate lawyers as structures and agents of the legal language; lawyers are embedded in legal words as their world. They create it, generate it, and often present it as certain and consensual. Lawyers may talk and they may be silent and use these lingual facets of silence and talking as types of collective action towards the state and within its power foci.

III. LAWYERS AND THE STATE BEYOND ISOMORPHISM

At the outset of the twenty-first century, most nation-states are non-liberal, yet most democratic nation-states have some liberal characteristics as part of their institutional arrangements and national cultures. In comparative perspective, liberalism means a civil society, including political opposition groups, that somewhat moderates the state and may replace its governing bodies through practices that are based on individual rights, NGOs' activities, a relatively limited state intervention in society, state protection that significantly guarantees individual rights, and plurality of recognised religious practices, even if the state, like in Spain or England, renders preference to a specific religion. In various contexts various states would be characterised by different degrees of liberalism.

Israel falls into the category of a nation-state that is deeply involved in society and strongly promotes a republican interest of being prominently a 'Jewish and Democratic State'. Notwithstanding, it is experiencing strong effects of mainly an American liberal culture, among both its Jewish (81 per cent) and Arab-Palestinian (19 per cent) citizens. Israel is a mixture of non-liberal and liberal characteristics of the nation-state and its legal complex.

It is non-liberal in a few facets. First, the state prefers constitutionally and practically one religion (Judaism) as its state formal religion. While the state's preference of one religion is a common phenomenon in world politics, including in Western Europe, in Israel such a Jewish republican preference also constitutes the dominant legalistic basis of allowing immigration into the country and bestowing citizenship. Furthermore, Judaism as state religion is also the basis of constituting differential expressive and implicit, formal and informal, public policy treatments of various groups and imposing constitutional and practical thresholds on access to electoral procedures, political rights, cultural rights, socioeconomic rights and land acquisition.

Secondly, through blocking and elevating the costs of using alternative channels of personal and collective fulfillment, the state compels non-Orthodox Jews to practise Orthodox habits in a diversity of facets of life like marriage, divorce, conversion, daily religious practices of worshiping, and burial. Thirdly, the state is highly involved in its citizens' lives, and is very central in most civil activities. Such an active state facilitates itself through an extensive maze of economic regulation and high taxation, centralised national education, a wide range of compulsory military service, and strong disciplinary ideological mechanisms around the legal ideology of Israel as a 'Jewish and Democratic State'. Fourthly, the Arab-Palestinian minority in Israel and the Palestinians in the 1967 occupied territories have significantly and systematically been discriminated against Israeli Jews in various legal, political, socioeconomic, and cultural dimensions. Thus, public goods have discriminatorily been allocated for Jews against Arab-Palestinians, despite some liberal adjudication and involvement of the judiciary. Fifthly, national security symbols are so salient and the military is the most central institution in social life, as to infringe upon basic human rights such as freedom of expression, freedom of movement, and property rights. Beyond the issue of state-sanctioned religion, Israel has not fully responded even to a minimal definition of liberalism (Halliday and Karpik, 1997). It neither allows equal expression of voices and practices, nor has it been characterised by equal tolerance towards various minority groups and non-ruling communities.

However, Israel has also experienced some significant liberal characteristics and therefore it should be denoted as a country that has experienced political liberalism. First, there has been an increasing legal construction and exercise of basic freedoms and individual rights within procedures of electoral democracy. While there is almost no written entrenchment of individual rights and human freedoms in constitutional legislation, heretofore, there is a constitutional judicial review of those (mainly judge-made) rights by the Supreme Court. The Supreme Court project of developing individual rights has been intensified following the legislation of Basic Law: Human Dignity and Freedom 1992, and Basic Law: Freedom of Vocation in 1992 (later reenacted in 1994). Secondly, after the mid-1990s more than ever before, national public policy towards minorities has somewhat recognised individual rights, primarily in issues such as budget allocations, land distribution, language and social and medical welfare. Thirdly, civil society has been expanded including among Israeli Arab-Palestinians, a process characterised, inter alia, by increasing the number of NGOs. Thus, as will be exhibited, the numbers of law offices and lawyers have increased and, as will be analysed, below, the engagement of lawyers in various venues of public debates has been enlarged, as well. Fourthly, some privatisation of economy and religion has further been generated, and it has incited more practices of non-state economic organisations and pluralisation of religious practices. Fifthly, especially after the mid-1980s, the state has become more restrained, more moderate, as far as its direct intervention in the society is concerned, and its power structures have become more fragmented and in conflict with each other.

Akin to other nation-states, the contribution of lawyers to national experiences of political liberalism has thus far been more central than merely importing and exporting liberal values that lawyers are presumed to advance. While Israeli lawyers, even in the early 1950s, had argued in courts and outside the judiciary for implementing some liberal legal rights as freedom of expression and freedom of association, only to identify Israeli lawyers with promoting liberal values might be irreducibly simplistic, as is the case in other nation-states. Theoretically we should better comprehend lawyers not merely as individual agents who promote liberalism; rather we should conceptualise lawyering as a site of collective action in the context of dynamics in political power and public discourse.

Israeli lawyers, like lawyers in some of the post-Soviet republics, were using their professional knowledge in order to be engaged in politics towards and during the establishment of the state in 1948. There is no way to comprehend the formation of the 'Jewish state' and processes towards its legalisation and legitimisation—both domestically and internationally—without considering the contributions of Zionist lawyers to the legal construction and approval of the Zionist political project (Likhovski, 2002; Shamir, 2000). The interactions between the legal profession and the political founders of Israel were intimate and intensive as part of structuring and engendering the state's political power. The legal complex was a constitutive epiphenomenological entity that had reflected and generated a Zionist collective desire to establish a Jewish state. Some of the state's political founding fathers (eg, David Ben-Gurion, Itzhak Ben-Zvi, Moshe Sharett) studied law. Later, they were significantly assisted by government and private lawyers in order to advance three massive national endeavours that took place, primarily, between 1939 and 1954. These projects were the confiscation of lands inhabited by Palestinians untill the 1948 war over Palestine/Eretz-Yisrael; the construction of Israel as essentially Jewish; and the creation of the state's apparatuses of collective violence (Barzilai, 2003).

We should better understand how legal knowledge is immersed in processes of constituting state power foci. All these efforts to consolidate the state's national power were embedded in legislation and regulations that were aimed to legalise the new state and to entrench its professed essence as a Jewish republic. In this context, the legal complex had been crucial. Government lawyers were responsible for legalistically engineering these projects, while private lawyers were mostly with no aspiration systematically to challenge the mobilisation of professional knowledge for national purposes. Lawyers submitted only very few appeals to courts against these national projects. Generally, in the 1950s lawyers were either agents of the state or silent about its policies. Most Israeli legal scholars, mainly concentrated in the only law school in the country until 1958, the Hebrew University, Jerusalem, were occupied with issues concerning preparing drafts of a possible written constitution. Alternative models for the legal construction of the state were not debated in professional legal venues, and critical challenges to massive confiscation of Palestinian lands were almost never raised. Legal challenges to military rule over the Arab-Palestinian minority (1948–66) had been rare and rather futile.

While the trend of absence of lawyers from public debates had continued well into the 1960s, another characteristic of Israeli lawyers has evolved since the 1970s, as part of alterations in state political power foci. At the same time as lawyers were involved in shaping the state's political power, they also became more engaged in politics as agents of liberal economy and have significantly contributed to the economic liberalisation of the state and afterward to its interactions with the global economy. Economic privatisation of currency, financial institutions, governmental agencies, public services, and the labour market has altered the basic relations between state power foci and lawyers, since the liberal maze of economic transactions requires the veil of certainty that legal knowledge may provide. Hence, under conditions of more economic pluralisation, the legal profession may expand in numbers, as in England, the US and Russia (after the end of the Cold War), or it may incite strong states to limit the number of lawyers who are registered at the bar so as to coopt a smaller number of lawyers. This was the case in Japan and South Korea until the 1990s. Amid economic liberalisation the state may conceive lawyers as a menace to its domination and in turn suppress the growth of the profession, or it may use lawyers as vehicles of economic entrepreneurship in order to have a better economically developed, but not disobedient, civil society. Lawyers may be perceived by a state's power foci as a challenging professional elite or as a vehicle further to boost the economy.

Israeli lawyers were perceived by the political elite as an obedient professional group of entrepreneurs. Mainly since 1967, and the colonisation of the 1967 occupied territories, lawyers have become agents of liberalism in the state and through it. The number of private law offices and their gradual expansion in Israel and abroad has increased. Since economic growth and economic transactions require legalisation, and since the legal profession may economically benefit from such an economically legalised growth, lawyers have enjoyed the expansion of the Israeli economy that was blooming partly due to the exploitation of Palestinians in the Israeli labour market. Accordingly, lawyers have taken a rigorous role in the liberalisation of the Israeli economy and have transformed legal knowledge into economic and political strongholds. Thus, traditionally, the established law schools at the Hebrew University, Jerusalem, and Tel Aviv University, have been antagonistic to the establishment of private law colleges. They have used the elitist argument that the level of studies might be severely diminished once the criterion of admittance was associated with luxurious private tuition. Yet, under the market pressures of an increasingly liberal economy, which created a perceived need for more lawyers, private law colleges have been established since the mid-1980s, and the number of lawyers has dramatically increased since the 1970s.

Table 8.2   Lawyers' Growth in Israel (1968–2005)

Population	No. of Lawyers	Year
2,841.1	2100	1968
2,929.5	2300	1969
3,022.1	2500	1970
3,120.7	2800	1971
3,225.0	2900	1972
3,338.2	3100	1973
3,421.6	5000	1974
3,493.2	5200	1975
3,575.4	6100	1976
3,653.2	6300	1977
3,737.6	8400	1978
3,836.2	6900	1979
3,921.7	7300	1980
3,977.7	7600	1981
4,063.6	8400	1982
4,118.6	8400	1983
4,199.7	9000	1984
4,266.2	10400	1985
4,331.3	10300	1986
4,406.5	10900	1987
4,476.8	12500	1988
4,559.6	13000	1989
4,821.7	10764	1990
5,058.8	11054	1991
5,195.9	11164	1992
5,327.6	11687	1993
5,471.5	12300	1994
5,612.3	14480	1995
5,757.9	16080	1996
5,900.0	17530	1997
6,041.4	19100	1998
6,209.1	20848	1999
6,369.3	23127	2000
6,508.8	25415	2001
6,631.1	27574	2002
6,748.4	29509	2003
6,869.5	31311	2004
6,990.7	32600	2005

Lawyers' Growth (1968–2004)

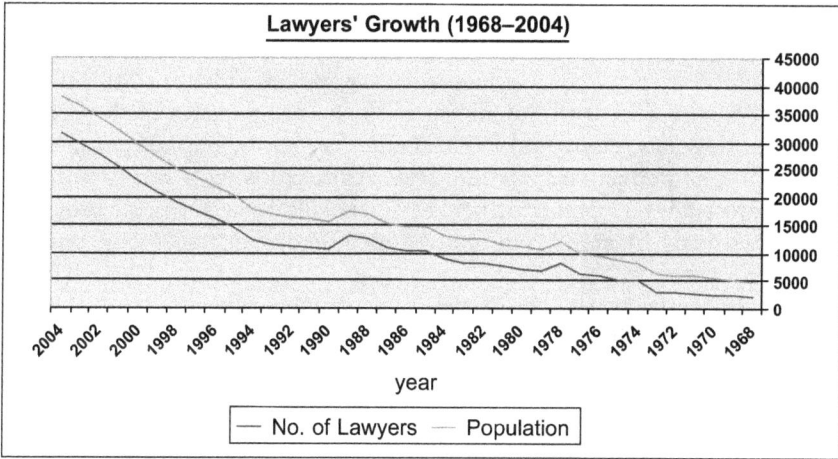

No. of Lawyers

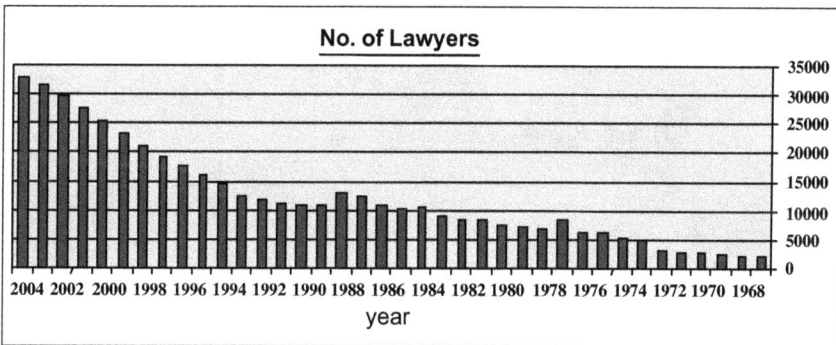

As Table 8.2 above and the Figure demonstrate, the number of lawyers during the years 1968 to 2005 has increased by 1552 per cent, while the population growth has increased by 246 per cent. Accordingly, demography may explain some of the growth in number of lawyers, however the increase in number of lawyers has been five times larger than what may be statistically expected based solely on population growth. Most of that dramatic increase, as shown above in Table 8.2 and the Figure, was absorbed by legal departments in commercial banks, insurance companies, municipalities, and by the state attorney general and general prosecutor offices, which have employed many lawyers. Yet, the private market of lawyers has noticeably been expanded as well. Since the late 1980s, as part of international capital flow onto and from Israel, a phenomenon of mega law offices (law offices that have included several dozen lawyers) has been developed. Several law offices have established branches overseas, eg, in London and New York City. Indeed, the Israeli economy has become more liberal and lawyers have been one major vehicle to incite it and to benefit from it.

As Table 8.3 and the Figure below demonstrate, most lawyers in Israel in 2005 have defined their main legal expertise in private commercial and civil law (about 55 per cent), while only very few have identified themselves as lawyers who deal with human rights. Since the statistics of the bar are based on how lawyers would like to be defined in the market place, commercialised and advertised, the statistics exhibit to what a very significant degree most lawyers prefer to benefit financially from a liberal economy and accordingly be engaged in and be identified with issues of economic aspects in state law.

This condensed genealogy of the legal complex unveils only one facet of the story about liberalism and lawyers in Israel and beyond. Until this

Table 8.3   Lawyers' Fields of Expertise (2005)

Lawyers' Fields of Expertise (2005)	
Civil and Commercial Law	16,911
Public Law	9,907
Criminal Law	1,773
Human Rights	7
General	2,219
Total	30,817

Source: Israeli Bar

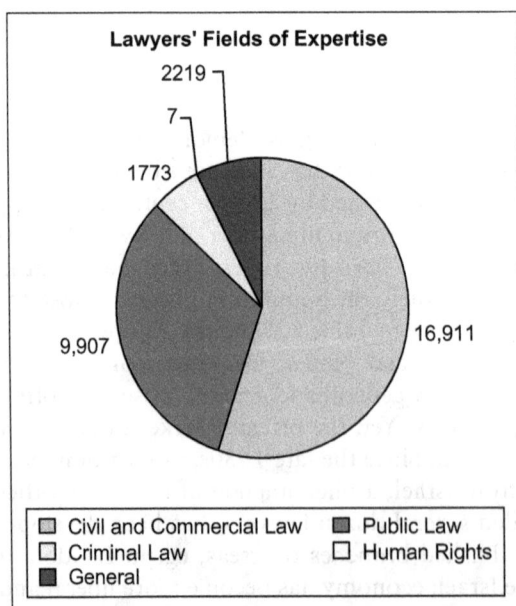

Lawyers' Fields of Expertise

point, my research demonstrates the strong association between *economic liberalism* and the increase in number of lawyers. We are still required to explicate the interactions between lawyers and *political liberalism*. We have to look more circumspectly into the legal complex not as a unified space, but rather as a field in which different institutions, and various trends, even dialectical trends, have been interlinked to create a compound phenomenon. More specifically, we have to investigate how the liberal economic ontology and expansion of the legal profession have affected the political role of lawyering in shaping the boundaries of the public discourse. Lawyers have been an important component of economic liberalism, since they have been propelled into politics by it and stimulated it. But they have also been an important part of political liberalism, engaged in shaping its boundaries. Correspondingly, the rest of this chapter explores how lawyers have *talked* and have been *silent* concerning public issues of democracy, individual rights and human rights, and what role they have played in claiming and disclaiming the state.

IV. VOICES OF AMBIVALENCE: TALKS, SILENCE AND DISSENT

(a) On Speech and Silence: Lawyers as Sociopolitical Markers

While silence is a behavioural form of language, it may be a central mode of voice in the generation of public discourse and collective action. Thus, Wittgenstein has pointed out that silence is a very meaningful part of language (Ostrow, 2002: 13–15). Silence is a politically meaningful facet of absence from expressive lingual formation and generation of the public discourse. Nevertheless, despite its being an articulation of absence, silence may be more meaningful for legitimisation than an expressive voice. The meaning of silence is essentially contextual. Thus, if lawyers refrain from litigation but encourage their clients to disobey the law, their silence has a meaningful voice of dissent. Absence from actively and rhetorically constructing the public discourse might be a form of dissent through which opposition is aired. Alternatively, if lawyers have passively supported a public policy and governmental actions, their silence has had a legitimating consequence. If silence is a form of accepting a norm of status quo with no challenging hermeneutics, it becomes a functional absence, since the dominant norm is being legitimatised with no political opposition.

While talks engender some confidence around the contents of discourse (Baker and Hacker, 1985: 243–51; Wittgenstein, 1969), silence may undo a space of uncertainty as around one's attitudes. Hence, silence inclines to perpetuate the dominant attitudes and norms in a given public discourse. It may not defy hegemony and it may hinder counter- hegemonic forces. If a lawyer litigates an issue s/he may challenge hegemony, however futile and confined it may be in the public discourse. Litigation may be only one type among various facets of collective action that may confront hegemony and public policy. Moreover, if a government is expecting an explicit consent of the public, silence may be a voice of opposition. Silence may constitute a strong articulation of dissent, amid a discourse in which one's expressive consent is being required or expected.

Notwithstanding these exceptions that are rare in public debates and political discourse, silence induces, whether intentionally and unintentionally, the generation of support of hegemonic attitudes and public policy. Silent lawyers, who are defined not through their formal professional positions and expressive professional functions, but through their practices as lawyers in the public discourse, are important agents of marking the public discourse. However, they are not always conscientious of their social responsibilities. Their silences legalise and legitimatise hegemonic attitudes concerning issues of human rights and the 'rule of law'. Since lawyers are by definition political actors, the phenomena of professional silence and silent lawyers should be further elucidated as a major issue in collective action and liberalism.

Analytically we may distinguish between several origins of silence. First, one may be unaware of a specific topic in public discourse. Lack of awareness of an explicit topic or significant lack of information regarding a topic and its various facets may often result in silence. In the context of this chapter, unawareness of legal political issues is a rather implausible variable to explain silence among lawyers, especially since the topics that I discuss below have acquired a high public profile and their saliency in the media has been high. Secondly, absence of social consciousness may be another independent variable that explains silence. Lawyers may be aware of a specific problematic issue concerning human rights and the 'rule of law', and still they may not be aware of the meaning of their silence and its ramifications on the public discourse. In Israel, legal education, especially until the mid 1990s, has ostensibly neglected to emphasise the sociopolitical role of lawyers and their social responsibilities.

Thirdly, indifference and alienation towards the state or its political establishment may be another source of silence. Lawyers may know of a problematic issue in a certain public policy but be alienated towards the state and its political establishment or they may be indifferent as to possible ramifications of their silence. Fourthly, lawyers may oppose a specific policy and be aware of possible negative ramifications of their silence in the political sphere, and yet they impose upon themselves censorship for various reasons. Inter alia, they may presume that professional criticism concerning national security affairs is unpatriotic or may inflict damage on their ties with the political establishment. Such considerations may be powerful in silencing private and government lawyers. Fifthly, lawyers may also agree with government policy, above being loyal to the regime's national narratives, and conceive silence as the intentional legalisation of a concrete public policy. I typify such conformity as silence, not because it is necessarily a wicked phenomenon, but due to the fact that silence hinders lawyers from having an active role in publicly debating and forming issues linked with human rights.

The subsequent parts of this chapter drill into spheres in which lawyers have been vocal and talkative in public life, and spheres in which they have been silent. This nexus of silence's talk explicates how lawyers have formed and marked the public sphere, beyond being agents of economic liberalism. I explore how lawyers were framers and markers of the public sphere without dramatically altering state and society relations. Thus, lawyers have propelled expansion of liberalism and have hindered its transformation into sociopolitical criticism of the nation-state. Through silence and speech they have been both the reformers of sociopolitical order and the guardians who have maintained some structured antinomies of liberalism in a non-liberal nation-state.

(b) A Liberal Symphony

The legal profession—with its multifaceted functions in the legal complex—has been a vehicle to affect public discourse and to somewhat moderate the state, primarily concerning issues that have not been considered as 'national security' and have not challenged the Zionist state to reconstruct its basic essence and ideology. Until the early 1990s such a professional monopolisation of public civil debates had largely been a characteristic of Jewish lawyers, who have constituted the ruling hegemonic group in the legal complex. Then, with the graduation of more Arab-Palestinian Israeli lawyers in Israeli and US law schools their expressive partaking in public discourse has also become more prominent. Accordingly, lawyering, that has aimed to dominate and shape public discourse through talkative rhetoric of legal knowledge, has had several aspects.

First, the scope of civil society, both Jewish and Palestinian, has been expanded and institutionalised due to the dramatically rising number of NGOs that have been watching, reporting, educating, lobbying and litigating human rights in Israel and its 1967 occupied territories. Lawyers have established NGOs to struggle against governmental corruption and to force upon the government more transparency and accountability. Other lawyers have become prominent members and leaders of NGOs that have focused on litigation for human rights in the occupied territories and civil rights in Israel in its pre-1967 borders. Furthermore, lawyers have become leading figures in NGOs that have struggled for social justice, some of whom have been affiliated with legal clinics in law schools. These extra-parliamentary activities through NGOs and legal clinics have been embedded in US liberal experience and have been imported into Israel by US law school graduates, both Jews and Palestinians. Those lawyers were trained in US law schools such as Harvard, Yale, Stanford, Columbia, NYU and the American University, returned from the US to Israel and applied their legal education. Hence, it is hardly conceivable to imagine how the setting of human rights NGOs could have been developed without the major contribution of lawyers. In this context, legal knowledge has certainly been politicised and mobilised through NGOs.

It is barely comprehensible how such a trend of litigious and legalistic advocacy in the legal complex could have been generated without basic liberal beliefs in individual rights, such as individual equality, human dignity, property rights, freedom of expression, freedom of religion and freedom of information. These beliefs and the legalistic presumption that litigation may be an effective type of political action have resulted in numerous salient issues that were litigated in courts through legalistic NGOs. One may mention, inter alia, affirmative action for minorities, gender equality in military service, torture, prohibitions on unification of Palestinian families, civil supervision of the security services, military actions in the occupied territories, political appointments, budget allocations, political partisan corruption, the status of the Arabic language, land distribution, the status of internal Palestinian refugees and unrecognised Palestinian villages, religious conversions, and civil marriage. These issues were constructed, framed and conveyed through lawyers as salient topics in the public sphere and the mass media. Lawyers have been both agents and the structure. They have reflected liberal beliefs and constituted legalistic venues for debates and action framed through the media as crucial for decision-making processes.

Secondly, in addition to the hectic facet of NGOs' actions in the legal complex, lawyers have become prominent in public bodies, eg, governmental agencies, political parties and state institutions, like the State Comptroller. The legal profession has expanded itself beyond the more apparent functions of representing clients, either private or public. Based on a somewhat transnational and intergenerational myth about the virtues of their legal profession, lawyers have assumed managerial and leadership positions, outmatching any other professional group in the Israeli public sphere, with the exception of senior military officers. There is a strong causal relationship between changes in social stratification amid economic liberalism, fragmentation of political power, and lawyers' talk. Lawyers have benefited from the mounting liberal trust in legal knowledge that has incrementally replaced the declining confidence in dwindling legislative and governmental agencies. They have further been empowered through enlargement in the scope of the middle class that has conceived lawyers as agents of dispute resolution in the protection of property rights and privacy, while the parliamentary and partisan political setting has dramatically become polarised and fragmented.

Thirdly, alongside being economic entrepreneurs via their involvement in constructing economic transactions, lawyers have also become political entrepreneurs. Identified with the idea of political stability as conducive to economic equilibrium and prosperity, lawyers have hectically voiced public expectations, especially since the late 1980s, for reforms in the parliamentary system and have vociferously demanded direct elections for the prime ministership. A public presumption constructed by leading lawyers asserted that a fragmented parliament with severe polarisation of attitudes cannot ensure stability. Lawyers have vigorously voiced the argument as if political stability through a semi-presidential system is preferred over political representation through the parliamentary system.

Throughout public debates and parliamentary deliberations concerning electoral reforms and possibilities of enactment of a written constitution, the US political model was influential, though not carefully studied. On the one hand, it may be sensible to anticipate lawyers' participation in deliberations on enacting a constitution, especially since Israel is perceived as one of the very few democracies that does not have an all-encompassing written constitution that entrenches human and individual rights. On the other hand, in the process of these debates lawyers marginalised all other professional experts, such as political scientists and sociologists. They have constructed fundamental issues of state and society relations as if those are formalistic legalistic matters that may be resolved solely through relying on legal knowledge. Those lawyers were significantly empowered in a legal complex dominated by a very adjudicative, assertive, rather liberal Supreme Court, which after 1986 has repeatedly enunciated its aspiration to expand its judicial constitutional review, and has systematically articulated that nurturing individual rights is its main vision.

Fourthly, the status of the Israeli bar has been altered. Since all Israeli lawyers must be examined and licensed by the very same national bar, it has acquired national, monopolist, and almost unchallenged public power of exclusive professional authorisation of lawyers. Traditionally, the bar has had four main functions in exerting its monopoly and aiming to discipline lawyers: examination, authorisation, and annual registration of lawyers; ethical supervision over lawyers' professional conduct; informing lawyers and providing them with professional complementary education; and finally, nominating the bar delegates to the Judicial Appointment Committee (JAC) that selects all judges and justices to the Israeli judiciary. Until the end of the 1990s, however, the Supreme Court justices were the most saliently important dominant institution in the legal complex, and the more the parliament has lost its political power, the more sway the justices have radiated.

Through letters of recommendation in professional academic committees, justices were involved in academic promotions in law schools, their concepts of the 'rule of law' generated the education of jurists in law schools, and they were the most significant body in the JAC. But since the end of the 1990s, the bar has somewhat altered the balance of power in the legal complex and beyond. The mounting esteem of lawyering has made the bar an important venue of political struggles. Elections for the bar's governing bodies have gained high public visibility, a national media event, and often a platform to those lawyers who were looking for political careers in the parliament, the government and the bureaucracy. The bar has always been of some political significance for political parties, but the growth in the number of lawyers, its complete monopolistic status and its affluence have made it more ambitious regarding its public rank. A very assertive and adjudicative Supreme Court has further encouraged litigation as a mode of political action at all levels of the Israeli judiciary.

Table 8.4   Litigation in Israel Judiciary

HCJ	Circuit	District	Year
N/A	35271	4715	1948
N/A	54938	5719	1949
N/A	70925	7462	1950
316	89348	10461	1951
339	112353	13292	1952
238	108398	14334	1953
238	133907	13909	1954
197	143140	13249	1955
222	156093	16436	1956
236	161394	18112	1957
221	190288	20845	1958
221	181324	23129	1959
331	211015	26124	1960
377	190122	26996	1961
340	222012	29969	1962
334	220644	35815	1963
334	241180	34219	1964
382	272654	39992	1965
382	302195	46078	1966
404	294143	47584	1967
342	295688	50375	1968
359	257128	50711	1969
381	246329	54668	1970
502	259805	55210	1971

(*continued*)

Table 8.4   continued

534	278288	57311	1972
487	238604	54221	1973
536	243652	60122	1974
657	334166	65142	1975
633	378407	61926	1976
714	368346	60500	1977
897	402805	61377	1978
760	447726	65539	1979
827	467749	70526	1980
707	443077	75860	1981
726	435211	75244	1982
808	498140	82929	1983
958	557139	90695	1984
1139	613390	101798	1985
1483	553613	101189	1986
1466	599639	99108	1987
1438	585846	96438	1988
1642	652131	98301	1989
1577	665501	99807	1990
1785	653744	106055	1991
1727	656753	106115	1992
2059	725381	109099	1993
2059	730822	114211	1994
2059	742870	114988	1995
1578	835755	110289	1996
1732	796118	102229	1997
1847	795962	163347	1998
1691	819994	169262	1999
1688	851377	190156	2000
1866	846836	196566	2001
2094	902475	205350	2002
2564	852500	198498	2003
2338	925132	232054	2004
2110	798993	228353	2005

Remarks:
1. HCJ—High Court of Justice
2. District Courts—including Family Courts
3. Circuit Courts—including Transportation Courts
4. Data above does not include Labor Courts

The figures in Table 8.4 above summarise data on litigation in the Israeli judiciary between the years 1948 and 2005. Litigation in circuit courts has grown by 2265 per cent, in district courts it has increased by 4843 per cent, and in the High Court of Justice (HCJ) by 667 per cent. In all categories of the judiciary, litigation has increased more rapidly than the pace of demographic growth. It points to the expansion of litigation associated with economic and political liberalism, and with fragmentation of political power foci. Based on my research, in a country of 6,869,500 citizens (2005), the number of files in active litigation has reached about 1,127,226, in all branches of the judiciary, including the branches of the Supreme Court (not just the HCJ), and labour courts. Namely, as part of a general proclivity over time, one in every six citizens in Israel has litigated a case in the courts. The military occupation of the 1967 territories has certainly inflamed part of the litigation, since Palestinians from the occupied territories could and in fact did litigate in Israeli courts. The occupation was embedded in Israeli economic expansion and also in the fragmentation of its political power foci.

Vigorous litigation has been constituted, constructed, articulated and generated through popular commercialisation and further politicisation of legal knowledge as instrumental know-how to resolve public issues. Lawyers have been empowered by the state civil bureaucracy and civil society as articulated political and economic agents, and they aspired to have their public voice heard more compellingly. Accordingly, the bar representatives in the JAC have become more vocal in expressing their stance on public issues, even in opposition to the attitudes of the Justices and Justice Minister. From 2004 until 2006 the bar had conducted a national survey among all Israeli lawyers who were asked in structured questionnaires for their evaluations of the judges and justices' efficiency and judicial faculties. The survey referred to all courts, including the Supreme Court. Since 2004 the detailed results have been published in the media noting the lawyers' evaluations of each one of the judges and justices, identified by their names. Yet, once the eminence of the bar in the legal complex had been transformed into a straight institutional challenge to the Supreme Court, a conflict erupted. The reaction of the Supreme Court was infuriated and an institutional crisis was unfolding.

The President of the Supreme Court, Aharon Barak, had ostensibly and abruptly cancelled all his commitments to meet with the bar's governing bodies. He further cancelled his traditional speech to the bar's annual meetings (2004 and 2005). Barak overtly criticised the bar for what he had regarded as an undemocratic move that was intended to contravene judicial independence and inflict biased pressures on the judiciary, particularly the Supreme Court. The institutional crisis in the legal complex has finally been resolved by a new equilibrium. Only after Barak's consent to set up a public Ombudsman to scrutinise public complaints against judges/justices, and under intense pressure from all branches of the judiciary, did the bar announce its abandonment of the feedback questionnaire. As in most other democracies, the Israeli judiciary has dominated the legal complex, but the bar has acquired significantly more public voice as part of political and economic liberalisation.

Having about 32,600 registered lawyers (2005), supported by affluent law offices, being at the core of a bourgeoisie ideology and economic interests that form the legal profession as of great virtues and power, the bar has aspired to have new and improved political strongholds in political life. A striving Supreme Court that has inflated its jurisdiction and accumulated institutional power through challenging the government, its bureaucracy, the religious establishment, the security services, political parties, and the parliament, has incited a coalition between the bar and partisan politicians (some of whom were bar members) who have desired to tame the Court.

These characteristics of a talkative lawyering point to the effects of political fragmentation and experience of liberalism on making Israeli lawyers, both Jews and Arab-Palestinians, more saliently and vocally engaged in political life. However, their voice has predominantly been raised concerning possible reforms in the political rules of the political game. Most lawyers in Israel, with the exception of only a few, have allowed the status quo in some major issues of public policy. While lawyers have been active as liberal agents in the economic sphere, they have largely been advocates of the basic legal ideology and national narratives. The stillness of Israeli lawyers has been particularly prominent regarding 'national security' issues. Hence, lawyers (including Arab-Palestinian lawyers) have shaped the political discourse through legalising the state and its ideology and by advancing public debates about the rules of the political game. In practice, however, it was a rhetorical veil to the silence regarding national ideology, legal ideology and national security. Below, I elucidate the political language of silence as constructed by lawyers.

(c) The Clamour of Silence

The political proclivity of lawyers, as agents who mark public debates, has been very supportive of the political establishment and its Zionist ideology. It has prevailed even when a public policy might have been abusive of human rights. Generally, lawyers have not questioned the fundamental ideological principles of the state. It was mainly evident in the absence of debates initiated by lawyers around the legitimacy and legality of Israel as a Jewish republic, the place of the Arab-Palestinian minority in this context, and national security issues. Thus, despite international protest against torturing Palestinians who were under suspicion of planning terrorist activities, the bar has never warned the Israeli government of the legal and humanitarian problems surrounding tortures, even once those very questionable tortures were widely reported by salient human rights NGOs such as Amnesty International. The declared government policy of targeted killings incited debates in the bar but most lawyers supported that policy of extra-judicial killings. In a survey conducted during April 2004 among Bar members (N = 767), 69 per cent responded that the policy of targeted killings was legal, 11 per cent thought that it was legal under very specific conditions, and only 20 per cent considered the policy unlawful.[1]

The general tendency among lawyers has been to settle economic liberalism with some political conservatism. When surveyed about the International Court of Justice's ruling (July 2004)[2] on the illegality of the 'wall of separation' along the West Bank (N = 283), 40 per cent argued that the International Court had no jurisdiction to decide the issue, while 27 per cent defined the ruling as discriminatory against Israel. Only 33 per cent justified the ruling.[3] Lawyers have not challenged the status quo and have not raised criticism concerning problematic issues on the junction of national security and human rights. Generally, they have been silent regarding the military occupation as a whole. Referring more specifically to the bar, denoting itself as a professional body it has stayed remote from any public criticism of the military occupation.

Government lawyers have had a foremost role in that context of silence. On the one hand, in internal debates, far from the public eye, some government lawyers protested against the continuation of the military occupation that has created an intolerable situation in which lawyers were compelled to advocate massive abuse of human rights. Officially, however, government lawyers have censored themselves and as part of state power foci they have continued to legalise the military occupation with only a few instances of a public protest.[4]

Merely two groups of lawyers have constituted an exception to silence. They have both utilised liberalism to contest prevailing public policies. One group is composed of Jewish lawyers who are dissenters to the Zionist enterprise. The other group includes Arab-Palestinian Israeli lawyers who have opposed Zionist ideology and its emphasising of the Jewish hegemonic essence of the state. The first group consisted of a few lawyers and NGOs who charged fees from their clients, and yet selected 'proper' legal cases in

---

[1] See www.israelbar.org.il/survey.asp?catId=263 (in Hebrew).

[2] See www.icj-cij.org/icjwww/idocket/imwp/imwpframe.htm.

[3] *Ibid.*

[4] One of the exceptions was the special report written by Attorney Talia Sasson, Head of the Criminal Division in the General Prosecution Office, who has criticised the phenomenon of illegal settlements in the 1967 occupied West Bank. However, Sasson was nominated by the government to write the report. Later, in March 2005, it was formally adopted by the government. Sasson could have talked since the government allowed her to raise a voice in a way that had served Ariel Sharon's governmental policy at that time.

order to break the silence and dispute some of the Zionist regime's political fundamentals and prevailing public policies. Inter alia, they litigated cases against non-separation between the state and Jewish Orthodoxy (in issues such as marriage and religious conversions), discriminatory state and corporate ownership of lands, unfair employment conditions of foreign workers, compulsory military service in the 1967 occupied territories, human rights abuses in the 1967 occupied territories, illegality of Jewish settlements in the West Bank, strict restrictions on the unification of Palestinian families, military censorship on the development and deployment of nuclear and biological weapons, and torture.

Those lawyers and NGOs have presumed that criticism of the state through litigious efforts to de-legalise its distortions may legalise alternative modes of public policy and generate public discourse around them. Being expressive dissidents amid silence, those lawyers have not aspired to incite a sweeping sociopolitical mobilisation. Rather, they have conceived that relying on legal liberal arguments and instigating adjudication may result in dismantling some discriminatory public policies. Thus, liberal legalistic terminology was employed to de-legalise state policies and unveil their discriminatory essence through arguments such as freedom of/from religion, gender equality, sexual preference equality, distributional justice, human dignity, equal citizenship, and freedom of expression. Accordingly, dissident lawyers have stimulated the Supreme Court judicially to frame and reconstruct individual rights.

Nonetheless, since litigation is a court-centred collective action, which relies on the judiciary as state agent, the aspiration of lawyers with different political affiliations to reform the political regime and its underlying concepts and policies has resulted only in very limited success. Being somewhat receptive to liberal arguments, and obedient to the state's narratives, the courts have been careful not to alter state ideology and the basic principles of its public policies. Since litigation is an in-power activity, ie, within the framework of the established political power arrangements (Barzilai, 2005), state political power has prevailed, especially and predominantly where state ideology has particularly been immersed alike in issues concerning national security and the social, religious and national boundaries between Jews and Palestinians. Liberal litigation has rendered a few legal victories for liberal proponents but could not have altered fundamental public policies and legal ideology. Thus, an Israeli Arab-Palestinian family was allowed by the Supreme Court to settle land registered under the ownership of the Jewish Agency. The HCJ, however, has emphasised in its ruling the Jewish essence of the state, and Jewish control over its resources, including its lands. The judiciary has intensified the state's non-Orthodox supervision over religious councils and it has pluralised religious services and religious conversions. Yet, it has underscored the special legal status of the Jewish religion as the state's formal national religion. Namely, fracturing the silence has had a meaning of equalising only some localities of discrimination. Similarly, the Supreme Court has adjudicated appeals regarding the military actions and rule in the 1967 occupied territories, but has also legalised government authority to rule over these territories. Hence, defying silence through litigation has also further legitimated the state, its main narratives, and state courts as markers of state and society relations.

Israeli Arab-Palestinian lawyers have been another group to rupture the silence. The phenomenon of Arab-Palestinian lawyers publicly litigating in predominantly Jewish courts for political purposes has existed in Israel for many years. However, only from the mid-1990s an organisation of ideologically motivated Palestinian lawyers named *Adalah* (Justice based on equality) has commenced operation. It has institutionalised Israeli Arab-Palestinian appeals to the courts in order incrementally to recover the socio-economic political conditions of the minority. This proclivity of litigation among the minority has been deployed by relatively young Arab-Palestinian lawyers, who grew up in Israel under the military rule imposed upon the minority (1948–66), and later were educated in Israeli and American universities (Barzilai, 2003, 2005; see also Ziv, 2000). They prefer to speak Arabic, but they are fluent in Hebrew and English. Personally, they have been affiliated with Arab-Palestinian political bodies in Israel. They are critical of the Jewish-Zionist regime for excluding Arab-Palestinians from national power foci, notwithstanding that as lawyers they believe, with some doubts, in their professional calling and its ability to challenge the silence around formal and informal discrimination against the minority (Barzilai, 2003).

Adalah lawyers have had some faith in the power of legal talks and rhetoric of liberal rights to render some significant legal alterations in the status quo, which in turn may impel some sociopolitical reforms. Their litigious tactic has been to apply liberal terminology of equality that compels the state either overtly to acknowledge entrenched established discrimination or to offer legal remedies for minority members. Strategically, in the context of political liberalism, litigation has been perceived as political collective action that may turn a series of individual rights into a reality of group rights, even cultural and national autonomy for the minority. With some economic liberalisation and a growing middle class, the Arab-Palestinian community, partly more attentive to potentialities of litigation, partly more confident in its economic and political power (Ghanam, 1997), has become more acquiescent to activities of NGOs in the legal complex.

The quandary among Arab-Palestinian lawyers, in between lights and shadows of political liberalism, has not been whether an appeal to court might be upheld or dismissed, but whether breaking silence through adjudication by Jewish Zionist state institutions may not result in de-legitimacy of the minority's national identities. Indeed, litigation is not necessarily considered in terms of achieving legal victories (Feeley, 1992; McCann, 1994;

Barzilai, 2005). In the case of Israeli Arab-Palestinians, litigation has been aimed at realising political, socioeconomic and symbolic benefits, other than being perceived triumphant in the narrow litigious manner.

Talking liberalism in state courts has been a contentious issue among minority members. What Robert Kagan coined as 'adversarial legalism' (Kagan, 2000), namely—a prevailing norm of resolving sociopolitical, cultural and economic issues through litigation, has been a disputable matter among minority lawyers and minority human rights activists (Esmeir, 1999; Jabareen, 2000). Thus, Arab-Palestinian feminist organisations, which have constituted a prominent portion of Arab-Palestinian NGOs, have inclined to another type of language, as a venue of negotiating society and state relations. They have searched for other avenues to shatter silencing forces around domestic violence and multifaceted social subjugation of Arab-Palestinian women, who have suffered from intersectional discrimination in Jewish society as Palestinians and Arabs, particularly as Muslims, and in their own community, as women. Such NGOs have initiated grassroots activities, like assistance to raped and battered women and rescuing women from being murdered due to 'family honour' (Barzilai, 2003).

Litigation in state courts, on the other hand, has often been considered superfluous and costly action with no tangible sociopolitical, cultural and economic benefits for the community. Silence should be shattered not through articulating in state courts isolated events of abuses of power. Those isolated events would be legalised and transformed into narrow issues of rights and obligations Instead, collective action should be focused on de-constructing the status quo, and forming an egalitarian social consciousness via daily grassroots practices. Even following the *Kaadan* affair,[5] in which the Supreme Court ruled that discrimination against Israeli Arab citizens in matters of land allocation is unlawful and prohibited, many Arab-Palestinian activists have perceived state law as Jewish, Zionist, and in turn discriminatory against the minority.[6] Though some Arab-Palestinian grassroots organisations have not completely negated litigation in state courts, but rather have conceived it as secondary and only complementary to their grassroots activities.

Adalah has voiced expectations to benefit from the emerging liberal rhetoric in the judiciary, particularly among Supreme Court justices. The polarised and fragmented *Knesset,* with significant Jewish Orthodoxy and nationalist effects has not been considered as conducive to attaining equality, while judicial professionalism has been perceived as less discriminatory and more attuned to liberal talks around egalitarianism. During the 1990s, *Adalah* lawyers were professionally socialised in a more open Israeli society,

---

[5] HCJ 6698/95 *Kaadan v The State of Israel* (8 Mar 2000) 57 *Dinim* 573.
[6] See debates at the Hebrew University, Jerusalem, Minerva Centre for Human Rights, Apr 2000; Debates in the Association of Public Law, Jerusalem, June 2000.

networking with Jewish NGOs and the academia, under some cultural effects of liberal discourse of civil and human rights. Hence, they have conceived state law not merely as a set of coercive restrictions and regulations, but as a potentially dynamic and fragmented fabric. The fact that nation-states are fragmented aggregations of power foci is central for understanding state and society relations (Migdal, 1988, 2004). Lawyers have aspired to take advantage of the fragmented state and the dominance of its Supreme Court in the legal complex for generating some individual rights, and in turn to produce opportunities for minority members to redeem their socioeconomic and political predicaments within the complex boundaries of the state's political power.

Adalah has acted in resemblance to Western policy-oriented NGOs, which have mobilised liberal law by litigating in state courts and submitting their grievances to the state's political power (Epp, 1998; McCann, 1994). Those organisations have not been revolutionaries but rather pragmatist. They have accepted the prevailing legal terminological environment, and opted to utilise it for their needs and interests. *Adalah*'s Founder and General Director, Hassan Jabareen, explained to me, in a personal interview, how liberal rhetoric of rights may be relevant for the minority: 'The Israeli Supreme Court has already recognised the existence of women and reformist Jews as groups in Israeli law. There is no such acknowledgement of Israeli Arabs. We have tried to change the Court's language.'[7] It should be underscored that the *Kaadan* ruling, as explored above, did not conceive Arab-Palestinians as a community, as well. It articulated a liberal perspective of individual (citizen) rights in the Jewish state and accordingly recognised Arabs in Israel as equal individuals but not as a distinct non-ruling community (Barzilai, 2003).

In its appeals to the Supreme Court, *Adalah* neither addressed a plea to reform the structure of the political regime, nor directly criticised national narratives of Judaism and Zionism. The appeals used conventional and very concrete liberal legal causes, such as discrimination between citizens, within the rules of the political game. The organisation has aspired to break the silence and to narrow the spaces between Israeli Jews and Arab-Palestinians by using the liberal experience in state law. Among others, *Adalah*'s appeals have included demands to produce road signs in Arabic as an additional formal public language; to provide public transport for Arab students from their villages to their schools; to render state assistance to Arab students with learning difficulties in accordance with formal criteria applied on Jewish students; and to allocate budgets for the minority in proportion to its share in the overall population, (for more details see: Barzilai, 2003). In this respect, *Adalah* has significantly assisted in breaking the silence around systematic state discrimination against Arab-Palestinian citizens

---

[7] Personal interview with Attorney Hassan Jabareen, 25 Jan 1999.

of Israel. It has employed a liberal language of equality in rights to unveil discriminatory citizenship.

By using the same language of equality and discrimination as Jewish litigants have exercised in courts, *Adalah* could have constructed and generated state law as equally applicable to the minority. Subsequent to Iris Young's distinction between challenging the state's power and challenging its allocation of resources (Young, 1990), *Adalah* has not contended for reforming and restructuring the state's political power, as it might have been expected facing its political affiliations with national Israeli Arab-Palestinian groups. Rather, since *Adalah*'s lawyers have appealed to state courts, and have conceived litigation as a main means of collective action, they have challenged policy, not meta-narratives, which incited discriminatory allocations of public resources. As Hassan Jabareen explained to me: 'we are using legal terminology in a way that the justice will feel that s/he may be seen as politically incorrect [if the appeal is dismissed]'.[8]

Such an approach of talking liberalism through litigation has been effective to some extent. Thus, in the period between 1997 and 2000, *Adalah* had submitted 25 appeals to the Supreme Court. Its rate of success was 50 per cent if all legal cases, including pending appeals, were taken into account; and 67 per cent of success if only 18 legal cases that had already been decided were being considered. Yet, in most legal cases (75 per cent of the successful appeals that were upheld in Court) the final legal result was based on out-of-court settlements.[9] In these legal settlements, the organisation achieved some of its requested legal remedies, whilst state organs (eg, the courts, government, public bureaucracy, the military, police, and the legislature) did not conceive those arrangements as substantial alterations in the status quo. For both political actors, the state and *Adalah*, out-of-court settlements have been a rather utilitarian means to preserve legitimacy.

For the state, out-of-court settlements, framed within the legal terminological environment, have been better options than granting a complete formal equality through acknowledgement of the community's rights. Dotan and Hofnung (2005) explored several hundred legal cases of out-of-court settlements in other matters, in which the Supreme Court had preferred some narrow compromises, with no or minimal publicity, over salient and sweeping rulings. Thus, the Court could deliver some limited legal remedies according to some expectations of minority members, without endangering the hegemonic political culture of the Jewish majority.

For *Adalah*, out-of-court settlements have been an avenue to moderate discriminatory practices of the Jewish state. These legalistic settlements have also delivered a symbolic success, which has been functional for

---

[8] *Ibid.*
[9] For details see G Barzilai, *Communities and Law: Politics and Cultures of Legal Identities* (Ann Arbor, Mich, University of Michigan Press, 2003).

its organisational maintenance in the community as an organisation of lawyers. As neo-institutional studies have shown, organisations, particularly professional organisations of lawyers have constructed law as their symbolic capital in order to survive and to generate themselves in the legal complex and public life in general (Edelman, Uggen and Erlanger, 1999; Sarat and Scheingold, 1998). *Adalah* has aspired to exhibit some degree of legal success in its adversarial strivings. Such a legal success in moderating the state through exercising liberal language has assisted *Adalah* in framing itself as an effective communal organisation that operates in the intersection of sociopolitical and legal complexities.

Additionally, these litigious achievements have given rise to concrete (albeit very restricted) public benefits, such as an incremental process of formally framing more equality, and possible grounds for the good reputation of *Adalah* in the hectic spheres of human rights activists and competitive Israeli NGOs. Since 2000, *Adalah* has demonstrated its organisational abilities to monopolise parts of the minority discourse through advocating for the families of 13 Israeli Arab-Palestinians who were killed by the Israeli police during violent demonstrations by Israeli Arab-Palestinians in October 2000 in reaction to the then opposition leader, Ariel Sharon's visit to the Temple Mount. *Adalah* coordinated the legal defence of hundreds of detainees under police custody, and the communal demands that policemen who were responsible for the killings would be criminally indicted.

Breaking the silence does not necessarily have practical ramifications. In practice, however, litigation in the context of political liberalism has had only a minor effect on the mobilisation of Israeli Arab-Palestinians. None of *Adalah*'s appeals to courts incited the mobilisation of parliamentary and extra-parliamentary forces. *Adalah*'s appeals neither have incited the community's political struggles against the political establishment, nor have they fostered large internal reforms inside the community. *Adalah*'s relative legal effectiveness in gaining confined legal remedies and moderating the state notwithstanding, its ability to generate sociopolitical changes has been very doubtful.

The main realisation of *Adalah*'s litigation up to the end of 2006 has been in forcing the Jewish state's institutions to equalise some individual rights between Israeli Arab-Palestinians and Israeli Jews. Such a not insignificant reform, with all its limitations, could not have been attained through silence and without an expressive tactic of liberal rights talk in the legal complex and beyond.

V. CONCLUSION

This chapter theorises lawyers as agents of collective action who mark boundaries of state and society relationships through silence. It has analysed and theorised double-edged ramifications of liberalism on lawyers and how they have shaped public discourse as both political agents of liberalism and its generators. It is theoretically and empirically explicated why and how lawyers as political actors in the legal complex who use political liberalism may shape through silence and talks the boundaries of the political sphere. On the one hand, while doing so lawyers challenge allocation of public goods and often promote privatisation and even more legal pluralism. On the other hand, lawyers in the liberal age not only localise global neo-liberal markets through maintaining and legalising capital flows. They also legitimate state legal ideology that is carried through the legal profession and lawyers. Lawyers are a constitutive part of narrations and neo-institutional arrangements in the legal complex that enable them to dissent, but only to a limited degree.

They generally talk in the framework of dominant ideologies and not less often they are silent regarding prevailing public policies. In Israel they are mainly silent concerning the hegemony of the state as Jewish and regarding national security issues. Once they are choosing vocally to raise a dissent as part of their profession they are trapped in their own mythologies and constraints and have to challenge the status quo only to a limited degree. As in Greek legends they may use their profession and fly, but not too high lest their power be melted and dissolved. They can talk, but their talks are limited within the institutional and cultural boundaries of the very same ideology that enables them to have a voice. The Israeli experience of Jewish and Arab-Palestinian lawyers invites some comparable insights into the wonders and paradoxes of the legal profession as a means of political rhetoric and practices.

REFERENCES

Abel, RL (1989), *American Lawyers* (New York, Oxford University Press).

—— (1995), *Law in the Struggle against Apartheid: 1980–1994* (New York, Routledge).

Baker, GP and Hacker, PMS (1985), *Wittgenstein: Rules, Grammar and Necessity* (Oxford, Basil Blackwell).

Barzilai, G (2003), *Communities and Law: Politics and Cultures of Legal Identities* (Ann Arbor, Mich, University of Michigan Press).

—— (2005), 'The Evasive Facets of Law: Litigation as Collective Action', 10 *Adalah Newsletter,* available at www.adalah.org/newsletter/eng/feb05/feb05.html.

Dotan, Y (1999), 'Judicial Rhetoric, Government Lawyers, and Human Rights: The Case of the Israeli High Court of Justice During the Intifada', 33 *Law and Society Review* 319.

Edelman, LB, Uggen, C and Erlanger, HS (1999), 'The Endogeneity of Legal Regulations: Grievance Procedures as Rational Myth', 105 *American Journal of Sociology* 406.

Epp, CR (1998), *The Rights Revolution* (Chicago, Ill, University of Chicago Press).

Esmeir, S (1999), 'Litigation, Legal Discourse and Identity', 1 *Adalah Newsletter* 12.

Eulau, H and Sprague, D (1964), *Lawyers in Politics: A Study in Professional Convergence* (New York, Bobbs-Merrill).

Feeley, MM (1992), 'Hollow Hopes, Flyerpaper, and Metaphors' in *Symposium— The Supreme Court and Social Change, 17 Law and Social Inquiry* 745.

—— and Krislov, S (1990), *Constitutional Law* (New York, HarperCollins).

—— and Rubin, EL (2000), *Judicial Policy Making and the Modern State: How the Courts Reformed America Prisons* (Cambridge, Cambridge University Press).

Ghanem, A (1997), *Israeli-Arab Political Participation* (Haifa, Haifa University Press) (in Hebrew).

Halliday, TC and Karpik, L (eds) (1997), *Lawyers and the Rise of Western Political Liberalism* (Oxford, Clarendon Press).

Haltom, W and McCann, M (2004), *Distorting the Law: Politics, Media and the Litigation Crisis* (Chicago, Ill, The University of Chicago Press).

Hofnung, M and Dotan, Y (2005), 'Legal Defeats- Political Wins: Why do Political Representatives Go to Court', 38 *Comparative Political Studies* 75.

Jabareen, H (2000), 'Toward a Critical Palestinian Minority Approach: Citizenship, Nationalism and Feminism in Israeli Law', 9 *Plilim—Israel Journal of Criminal Law* 53 (in Hebrew).

Kagan, RA (2000), 'Adversarial Legalism: Tamed or Still Wild?', 2 *New York University Journal of Legislation and Public Policy* 217.

Lev, DS (2000), *Legal Evolution and Political Authority in Indonesia: A Study in the Political Bases of Institutions* (The Hague, Kluwer Law International).

Likhovski, A (2002), 'Colonialism, Nationalism and Legal Education: The Case of Mandatory Palestine' in R Harris, A Kedar, P Lahav and A Likhovski (eds), *The History of Law in a Multi-Cultural Society* (Aldershot, Ashgate Dartmouth).

McCann, M (1994), *Rights at Work: Pay Equity Reform and the Politics of Legal Mobilization* (Chicago, Ill, University of Chicago Press).

Migdal, J (1988), *Strong Societies and Weak States: State Society Relations and State Capabilities in the Third World* (Princeton, NJ, Princeton University Press).

—— (ed) (2004), *Boundaries and Belonging: States and Societies in the Struggles to Shape Identities and Local Practices* (Cambridge, Cambridge University Press).

Ostrow, MB (2002), *Wittgenstein's Tractatus: A Dialectical Interpretation* (Cambridge, Cambridge University Press).

Sarat, A and Scheingold, SA (eds) (1998), *Cause Lawyering: Political Commitments and Professional Responsibilities* (Oxford, Oxford University Press).

—— (2001), *Cause Lawyering and the State in Global Area* (New York, Oxford University Press).

Scheingold, SA (2004), *The Politics of Rights: Lawyers, Public Policy, and Political Change*, 2nd edn (Ann Arbor, Mich, The University of Michigan Press).

—— and Sarat, A (2004), *Something to Believe In: Politics, Professionalism, and Cause Lawyering* (Stanford, Cal, Stanford University Press).

Shamir, R (2000), *The Colonies of Law: Colonialism, Zionism, and the Law in Early Palestine* (Cambridge, Cambridge University Press).

—— and Ziv, N (2001), 'State-Oriented and Community Oriented Lawyering for a Cause: A Tale of Two Strategies' in A Sarat and S Scheingold (eds), *Cause Lawyering and the State in Global Area* (New York, Oxford University Press) 287.

Wittgenstein, L (1958), *Philosophical Investigations* (London, Basil Blackwell).

—— (1969), *On Certainty* (Oxford, Basil Blackwell).

—— (1974), *Philosophical Grammar* (Berkeley, Cal, University of California Press).

Wolcher, LE (2005), *Beyond Transcendence in Law and Philosophy* (London, Birkbeck Law Press).

Young, IM (1990), *Justice and the Politics of Difference* (Princeton, NJ, Princeton University Press).

Ziv, N (2000), 'Group Rights, Identity and Equality: Lawyering for Palestinians in Israel', paper presented at the Law and Society meeting, Miami.

Part Three

The Americas

9

The Legal Complex and the Response to Police Violence in South America

DANIEL M BRINKS

I N THIS CHAPTER I examine the legal response to the continuing high level of police violence and impunity that afflicts many of the countries of the region and poses an important challenge to political liberalism in Latin America. The chapter focuses especially on the work of lawyers, prosecutors and judges in the context of criminal prosecutions of police officers accused of murder. I use this empirical material to examine the role members of the legal complex are playing in preserving or establishing the institutions that protect basic legal freedoms—due process, personal integrity, freedom from arbitrary killing—in the face of a strong challenge. The challenge comes from a widespread perception that forceful police action is necessary to stem a perceived wave of violent crime.

The 'political liberalism' project singles out members of the legal complex for separate treatment in an analysis of the processes and actors that contribute to the establishment of political liberalism. This is based on the notion that these actors have a special interest in establishing the legal freedoms and institutions that undergird political liberalism (Bell, 1994; Halliday and Karpik, 1998; Karpik, 1998). Simplified and summarised, the idea is that legally trained professionals have a bias in favour of the rule of law, which, in turn, has an affinity with political liberalism and the moderate state. The editors note, however, that this bias does not always produce consistent progressive behaviour, and one of the goals of this volume is to examine the sources of this variation.

I will argue that at least some of this variation occurs when legal professionals' long-term professional interest in the moderate state, the rule of law and the autonomy of courts clashes with more immediate, perhaps client-based interests. A lawyer in São Paulo once related to me a particularly pointed instance of this dilemma. Her client begged her to become the conduit for a bribe that would gain him release from a brutally overcrowded jail to the (slightly better) facility where by law he was supposed to be transferred in any event. She refused on the premise that, in the long run, the legal system would function better and her clients would be better served if lawyers did not contribute to corruption. Her client then promptly retained another attorney with fewer scruples. In this chapter I will argue that prosecutors face a similar dilemma when they operate in a political environment that is tolerant of (indeed demands) extrajudicial executions. The process of strengthening legal processes and the rule of law can be expected to benefit all members of the legal complex (and many of their clients) eventually, but it may on occasion conflict with the desired outcome of a particular legal process or class of legal processes. As a shorthand, I will refer to these outcome preferences as substantive preferences, in contrast to the more universal, long-term professional preference for the rule of law. Lawyers' substantive preferences may be the product of client demands or simply individual ideology.

When the preference for a strong, clean legal process aligns with substantive preferences, of course, members of the legal complex may well become 'consistent agents of political liberalism'. But when this progressive agenda is at odds with their substantive preferences we should expect less consistent behaviour. In fact, we might expect that the professional progressive bias will more often yield to contrary substantive preferences than the reverse, since the former is subject to coordination difficulties and free ridership, as illustrated in the foregoing example. Under what conditions, then, may we expect that lawyers will be pulled away from the liberal project by their substantive preferences?

The first distinction we can draw is between state-based and non-state members of the legal complex. State-based members, such as prosecutors and judges, have the state or, more broadly, the general public as their client. When the leadership of the state is legally dismantling or de facto subverting political liberalism, as in the case of Buenos Aires during the time of this study, or when there is strong popular demand for a disregard of liberal protections, as in São Paulo, it is likely that the legal professionals it employs will be a part of that process, rather than a part of the resistance. Insulating these professionals from political pressures, by crafting autonomous judicial and prosecutorial institutions, might help to attenuate the pressure to join in the repression, but is not likely to eliminate it altogether. When the leadership of the state is, on the other hand, fully supportive of the liberal project, as in Uruguay, then state-based sectors of the legal complex are more likely to be supportive as well.

Private lawyers who represent those targeted for repression, on the other hand, will find their professional and substantive preferences typically aligned in favour of the liberal project. Sometimes it will be easier for these targets of repression to find and fund legal representation. Thus in India, during the state of emergency, when the middle class and intelligentsia were the targets, the result was strong legal mobilisation, including by mainstream legal organisations and judges, in defence of the rule of law and liberal freedoms (Epp, 2003: 96–9). When the repression is focused on weak and marginalised sectors, however, as in the cases I examine here, it will be more difficult for these sectors to sustain large numbers of lawyers whose substantive, client-based interests place them in opposition to the repressive project. The activity of these segments of the legal complex will then be contingent on civil society support (in the cases I examine here, the Catholic Church in Brazil, or the Ford Foundation in Argentina), fee shifting or contingency fee arrangements and similar mechanisms allowing them to earn a living while representing the marginalised.[1]

My analysis confirms some of the expectations laid out here and in the introduction to this volume. I find that lawyers who have the state as a client—primarily prosecutors in my case, but also judges, when they are insufficiently insulated from political actors—tend to respond quite readily to popular and especially to elite demands for more (or less) repression. The results are evident, as judicial and prosecutorial enthusiasm for these cases varies quite dramatically in response to political conditions. On the other hand, private lawyers, especially those members of organised civil society, can often be found acting on behalf of the victims of repression. In association with strong civil society actors, including the Catholic Church in Brazil, these lawyers can work to exert powerful political and legal pressure in favour of moderation and the rule of law. When the victims are uniformly poor, as in São Paulo, the result is less intervention by private lawyers and a lower overall level of rights protection. When the victims include some more affluent individuals and the attorneys are privately funded, as in Córdoba, effective prosecutions are more numerous but the results are marked by socio-economic inequality.

This disparate conduct means that I observe both segmental divisions and cross-cutting cleavages within the legal complex. At least in the cities I examine, segmental divisions seem most likely when strong political currents run against the liberal project. Under those conditions, state-based and non-state sectors of the legal complex, groups of dissident lawyers representing the marginalised and elite lawyers representing the powerful and

---

[1] Epp (Epp, 2003) might add that the organisation of the bar into large firms, freeing up some members of the firm for *pro bono* activity, is an important part of this process. We could also imagine that a vibrant private bar, offering strong alternatives to government service, might also free state-based lawyers from client demands. Neither of these appears to be prominent in my cases, however.

influential, view each other with distrust or contempt. In addition to cleavages and divisions, however, we also occasionally see nefarious alliances among segments—judges and prosecutors (and the police) in Buenos Aires, for example, uniting in the repressive project. As one judge in São Paulo ruefully told me, 'the police pretend to investigate, prosecutors pretend to prosecute and we pretend to judge. That way we all get along.'

I. THE CASES TO BE ANALYSED

The analysis is based on sub-national and cross-national comparisons of five cities in Argentina, Brazil and Uruguay, specifically, Buenos Aires and Córdoba in Argentina, São Paulo and Salvador in Brazil (both federal systems with separate state or provincial judiciaries), and the national courts of Uruguay (a unitary system). These three countries are, as many would be in Latin America, appropriate subjects for this volume. All three have recently made transitions back to electoral democracy. After a series of authoritarian episodes, including one of the most violent dictatorships in South America, Argentina returned to electoral democracy in 1983; Brazil and Uruguay returned to democracy in 1985 after less brutal but longer authoritarian periods. All three are struggling with increasing crime and rising demands for an effective response to crime.

Despite the advent of democracy, most observers point out the weakness of legal institutions in at least two of these three countries. Critics have been especially harsh with the high courts in Argentina (Verbitsky, 1993; Larkins, 1998; Miller, 2000) though the Buenos Aires provincial courts fare no better (Fucito, 1999; Fucito, 1999). By reputation at least, the courts in Córdoba are better than those in and surrounding the capital (FORES and Colegio de Abogados de Buenos Aires, 1999). Like Argentina's, Brazil's courts are often the target of domestic and foreign critics (Faria, 1988; Faria, 1994; Faria, 1996; Prillaman, 2000). The police in Buenos Aires are the most violent in the country (Dutil and Ragendorfer, 1997), while those in Brazil generally, and São Paulo in particular, are also viewed as extremely violent (Barcellos, 1992; Cano, 1999; Amnesty International, 2005). Salvador is the capital of Bahia, which, as Ames notes, '[f]or many years, ... has been the strongest bailiwick of the Brazilian Right' (Ames, 2001: 129), and has a reputation for neither an independent judiciary nor a restrained police force. Uruguay, on the other hand, is said to have an effective and egalitarian legal system (O'Donnell, 1999: 311).

As the editors point out, political scientists who worked on these countries were deeply concerned with their transitions into and out of authoritarianism (see, eg, O'Donnell, Schmitter and Whitehead, 1986), but the problem of establishing deeper, intra-electoral, political liberalism once electoral democracy was in place was largely neglected, at least until recently. Nor, as we see in the next section, is this a trivial matter for these countries. By examining the work of legal institutions on the front lines of the defence of political liberalism in these countries we can perhaps draw out some lessons for the establishment and maintenance of truly moderate states in other recent democracies.

II. CRIME AND POLICE VIOLENCE AS A THREAT TO THE MODERATE LIBERAL STATE

Some incidents of police violence can be written off as uncontrolled excess, perhaps the work of a few bad apples. These incidents might even be rationalised as a predictable if unfortunate response to a violent crime epidemic. But at some point police violence attains sufficient magnitude to call into question the existence of political liberalism and a truly moderate state (Mainwaring, Brinks and Pérez-Liñán, 2001; O'Donnell, 2001). In 1992, in São Paulo, Brazil, *under a democratic regime*, the police killed nearly 1,500 people, an average of four people every day of the year. The police accounted for 27 per cent of the homicides in the city that year (Holston and Caldeira, 1998), and over the course of the 1990s killed more people in this one Brazilian state than Pinochet's regime did in all of Chile, during its entire term. In the second half of the 1990s, the per capita rate of police killings in Buenos Aires was nearly identical to that of São Paulo. The per capita rate of police killings is twice as high in Salvador da Bahia as in São Paulo.[2]

As importantly, the courts appear to be impotent in the face of this epidemic. As seen in Figure 9.1, the higher the rate of police violence, the lower the conviction rate for police officers who kill.

As noted in the introduction to this volume, political liberalism is built on the protection of basic legal freedoms, including 'the institutionalisation of juridical rights (eg, rights to due process in law, habeas corpus, legal representation and access to justice, freedom from arbitrary arrest, torture, death)', and on a moderate state in which the judiciary 'can exert restraint over other elements of the state'. Moreover, the criminal justice system, with its due process component, is one of the key arenas in which lawyers work toward the creation of political liberalism (Halliday and Harpik, 1998), and one of the places in which we might first observe a retreat from a moderate state (Abel, 2004 and Halliday and Liu's contribution to this volume). The existence of a police force that ignores due process and flouts the rule of law through the extensive use of extra-judicial executions and arbitrary violence, and over which the criminal justice system appears powerless, strikes at the very heart of political liberalism.

---

[2] For details on and sources of these figures see Brinks (2008).

Figure 9.1   Police homicides and conviction rates in South America, selected locations, during the 1990s

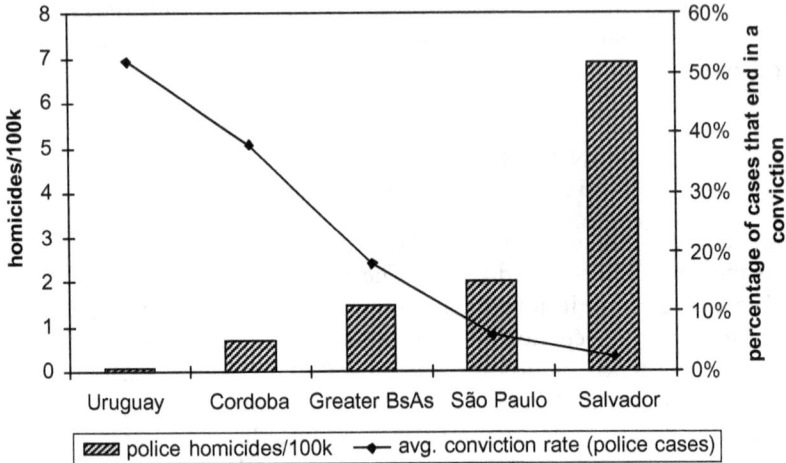

Sources: Brinks (2008). Figures are averages for the 1990s except in the case of Salvador, where data are available for only four years in the middle of the decade. Conviction rates for São Paulo are also based on four years in the second half of the decade.

If these polities in general, and their legal complexes in particular, were actively involved in institutionalising political liberalism, then we should observe the gradual reform and strengthening of a network of institutions that act to prevent, and where that fails punish, extrajudicial executions and other forms of arbitrary police violence. Unfortunately, political liberalism has too often been presented purely as a web of restraint cast over the state, as a set of institutions that impede and limit the range of action of state actors. This is exactly what has led to a dangerous retreat from political liberalism and democracy in many countries in Latin America. When security concerns seem to call for a more effective state, restraint can seem more vice than virtue. This was true in the 1960s and 1970s, when the national security doctrine swept democracy aside in the interest of protecting Latin America from communism, and it is becoming true today, as democracy is eroded from within to protect citizens from each other. If the state is imagined as immobilised by liberal rights protections, then under the threat of terrorism, violent crime or other threats to citizens' personal security, the first reaction is to begin snipping the lines, loosing the giant to destroy the enemy.

As we will see, in Buenos Aires and São Paulo, in particular, any attempt to curb police violence is set against popular demand for an effective—even if violent and repressive—response to crime. In this context, what role can members of the legal complex play in creating, maintaining and operating the institutions that offer a state response to the problem of state violence? Do they act consistently to preserve and protect due process and the rule of law, or do they simply act like members of the public, going along with demands for draconian responses to crime? Do different actors within the legal complex consistently respond in different ways to similar situations and constraints, or is their response idiosyncratic and unshaped by membership of the legal complex? As we will see, substantive preferences originating in political pressures can contradict and override state-based actors' more general interest in an effective rule of law.

III. MEASURING THE PERFORMANCE OF VARIOUS SEGMENTS OF THE LEGAL COMPLEX

Since the focus in this chapter is on the criminal prosecution of homicides committed by the police, the key actors are judges, prosecutors, private attorneys and some lawyer-led non-governmental organisations that focus on police violence. The analysis will centre on their role in individual investigations and prosecutions of police misconduct. In addition, I will make passing reference to the position that some professional associations have taken in connection with the problem of police violence. In this section I evaluate each of these actors, in each of the cities in the study, to see whether they are engaged primarily in knitting and maintaining liberal institutions, or snipping through them.

One might expect judges and prosecutors to be in the forefront of protecting the boundaries of due process and the integrity of the criminal justice system, both of which are threatened when the police become judge, jury and executioner. But in three of the cities, with some important variations we will explore in more detail, the 'iron triangle' of police, prosecutors and judges (Halliday and Liu, in this volume) remains relatively intact, even when the police officer is a defendant in a murder case. By cooperating in a pro forma investigation and exoneration of the police officer who kills, judges and prosecutors de facto incorporate the extrajudicial execution of a suspect into the criminal justice process. The only figure consistently supporting the victim's rights is the private attorney, retained for this purpose and often drawing support from organised civil society.

Supporting this statement with evidence requires some background. As is relatively common in Latin America, Brazilian and Argentine criminal procedure provides an opportunity for those directly affected by a crime to participate in the prosecution of the alleged perpetrator through the intervention of a private attorney. This figure, variously called the *assistente do Ministério Público* or *assistente de acusação* (prosecutor's assistant) in Brazil, and *querellante* or *particular damnificado* (harmed private party) in

Argentina, acts as a second prosecutor in the case. To simplify, I refer to all those acting in this capacity as 'Private Prosecutors'. The attributes of the Private Prosecutor (in terms of his or her capacity to introduce evidence, seek a higher charge or sentence, or continue with a prosecution the prosecutor wants to drop, and the like) vary considerably across jurisdictions and even, over the course of the 1990s, within jurisdictions. In general terms, until nearly the end of the decade, this figure was stronger in the federal courts of the capital city in Argentina and in São Paulo than in the provincial courts in Buenos Aires. In Uruguay, this figure does not exist (except in defamation cases which are not, of course, at issue here).

We can use the presence and impact of this Private Prosecutor, who is retained by the victims' relatives and has primarily their interests to protect, as a first indicator of the relative enthusiasm of public prosecutors for these cases. If the presence of a Private Prosecutor greatly increases the odds of a successful prosecution, it is likely that public prosecutors are not doing an effective job, for whatever reason. Private parties must, in essence, step in to supplement, replace or, in the worst case, counteract the actions of the public prosecutor. A second indicator of the self-motivation of judges and prosecutors is the impact of popular demonstrations around the time of the trial. If these demonstrations are irrelevant, we might conclude that state actors are largely self-motivated, acting in response to a pro-legality impulse or the legal characteristics of the case rather than reacting to popular opinion. But if convictions occur only in those cases in which there were demonstrations, then we can infer that judges and prosecutors are responding primarily to pressures to convict in particular cases, rather than to a constant imperative in favour of individual rights and the rule of law.[3]

To evaluate these indicators I use a sample of cases I compiled from lists of people killed by the police. In each jurisdiction I gathered lists of victims of police violence from either NGOs or government offices. I then used court records and attorneys' files to track the cases through the courts,

---

[3] I will concede that these are not perfect indicators, but I believe they come reasonably close to measuring what they are intended to measure. Demonstrations might be triggered by more egregious violations, eg, which would at least partially account for higher conviction rates, but that would not explain the dramatic cross-country variation in their impact, especially since all the cases are selected to include only likely rights violations and therefore all cases are roughly legally comparable (see Brinks, 2008, for a detailed explanation of the sampling). Moreover, it is more often the case that a demonstration coincides with extra-legal characteristics of the victim (age, gender or social class) than with the legal characteristics of the event. They are, therefore, a more faithful indicator of political importance than of legal merit. Finally, the conclusion from this individual case-level analysis—that legal professionals in public office tend to reflect their political context at least as much as a professional imperative in favour of political liberalism—is broadly confirmed by the aggregate, cross-national analysis (Figure 9.1) and the discussion of legal actors in each city (below). For additional discussion of possible alternative explanations and a detailed discussion of individual cases see Brinks (2008).

reviewed journalistic accounts of their progress and interviewed participants wherever possible. The result is a database of more than 500 cases
from Uruguay, Buenos Aires, Córdoba and São Paulo. Table 9.1 presents
the impact of the Private Prosecutor, with or without popular demonstrations, on conviction rates in cases in which someone dies at the hands of the
police.[4] The difference in conviction rates across categories in Buenos Aires,
Córdoba, and São Paulo is significant at levels higher than .001.[5]

Table 9.1 Impact of Private Prosecutor and Popular Demonstrations on conviction
rates in Uruguay, Buenos Aires, Córdoba, and São Paulo

	No Private Prosecutor		Private Prosecutor		
	No Demonstrations	Popular Demonstrations	No Demonstrations	Popular Demonstrations	Average (total n)
Buenos Aires	6.67% (n = 45)	–	13.64% (n = 44)	41.43% (n = 70)	23.9% (n = 159)
Córdoba	13.33% (n = 30)	0% (n = 2)	20% (n = 10)	80% (n = 30)	41.66% (n = 72)
São Paulo	1.68% (n = 179)	–	35.14% (n = 37)	–	7.41% (n = 216)
Uruguay	50% (n = 22)	37.5% (n = 8)	n/a	n/a	46.67% (n = 30)

All differences, except for Uruguay's, statistically significant (p < .01), numbers in parentheses
represent total number of cases in that category.

The difference is not significant in Uruguay (and, in any event, runs in
the opposite direction). Even without the assistance of Private Prosecutors,
the courts manage a conviction rate that is higher than the average for any
other jurisdiction, and higher than any individual cell except those cases in
Córdoba that have both Private Prosecutors and popular demonstrations
running in their favour. Since Uruguay retains, to a greater degree than any
of the other systems analysed here, the old inquisitorial Civil Law model
of criminal procedure, the investigation is in the hands of the judge, and
prosecutors play a relatively minor role. Given this institutional arrangement and the results obtained, we can conclude that in Uruguay judges are
performing their task effectively, with all the assistance they require from
prosecutors. Both judges and prosecutors, then, are engaged in protecting
the institutions that moderate the state.

---

[4] Slight differences between this table and Figure 9.1 are the result of dropping some cases
with missing data, which typically increases the conviction rate, as there is more information
available about cases that go all the way to trial, rather than being dismissed early on.
[5] I run a 2 × 2, 2 × 3, or 2 × 4 table for each city and use Pearson's chi[2] to test the likelihood
that the variables are independent of each other.

In each of the first three cases, in contrast, the presence of a Private Prosecutor dramatically improves the likelihood of a successful prosecution. In São Paulo, the presence of this figure increases the likelihood of a conviction by a factor of 20. In Buenos Aires they double the likelihood of a conviction, while in Córdoba they add about 50 per cent to the odds of a conviction. In each of these three cities, therefore, state-based members of the legal complex are at minimum failing to secure the institutions that restrain the state's repressive hand. Indeed, even if we do not assume they act with the intent of casting off restrictions on police behaviour, repeated failures to prosecute or convict broadcast a message of impunity, encouraging the perception that the police are not accountable for their violations. In Buenos Aires, Córdoba and São Paulo, then, non-state lawyers are taking over prosecutors' responsibilities in the prosecution of state actors who violate basic civil rights. These private lawyers often, especially in São Paulo and Buenos Aires, work with (or lead) legal NGOs, as we will see.

Popular demonstrations are frequent in Buenos Aires, Córdoba and Uruguay; in São Paulo they are so rare they do not appear in my sample at all, though there have been demonstrations in some very prominent cases. In Buenos Aires and Córdoba they have a strong effect in addition to the effect of the Private Prosecutor, raising the conviction rate by three and four times, respectively.[6] In Uruguay, on the contrary, they show no statistically significant effect, though there is a higher conviction rate in cases in which there is no demonstration (if this means anything at all, it might mean that the demonstrations are a reaction to a perceived lack of response by the courts). In other words, in Uruguay prosecutors and judges do their work without taking into account public opinion in particular cases;[7] and in São Paulo, interested parties do not even bother putting together a demonstration in these cases. In Córdoba and Buenos Aires, on the other hand, state actors—either judges or prosecutors, or both—often need the additional goad of public outrage before they will take the steps required to produce a conviction (note, however, that Córdoba has a substantially better record than Buenos Aires even without public demonstrations).

In summary, then, it is quite evident that, in the absence of private intervention, public prosecutors in São Paulo, Buenos Aires and Córdoba are not effectively prosecuting state violence. The state's lawyers do a better job

---

[6] While there are many cases in Buenos Aires in which a Private Prosecutor is present that do not include demonstrations, there are none in which we find demonstrations in the absence of a Private Prosecutor. For this reason, and to remedy some of the missing data problems, I assumed the presence of a Private Prosecutor in 20 Buenos Aires cases that had demonstrations but were missing data on the Private Prosecutor variable. In other words, in 20 of 70 cases the presence of a Private Prosecutor is imputed from the presence of demonstrations. If I exclude these 20 cases the results show the same tendencies but the difference in conviction rates is less marked.

[7] Detailed case studies of particular prosecutions in Uruguay confirm this impression. See Brinks (2008).

in Uruguay, though their role there is limited by the procedural code, which gives the investigative judge primary responsibility for preparing the case for decision. Judges in Uruguay and São Paulo are less influenced by public demonstrations than those in Córdoba or Buenos Aires, but Uruguay's judges manage to convict in a dramatically higher percentage of cases than those in São Paulo.

Despite a high conviction rate, Córdoba's judges and prosecutors appear to be very influenced by public opinion. Their high overall conviction rate is in part a function of a larger number of cases in which private parties step in to remedy the deficiency of the prosecution, and in which popular pressure to convict rises to the level of popular demonstrations. Judges and prosecutors in Buenos Aires, meanwhile, bring up the rear, being quite susceptible to public pressures and incapable of convicting in a high percentage of cases. If we assign each of these actors a positive (+), negative (−), or neutral (=) role in moderating the state by vigorously pursuing the prosecution of police officers who violate restrictions on the arbitrary use of force, our final evaluation may look something like Table 9.2.

Table 9.2   Evaluation of the role of Judges, Prosecutors and private lawyers in the Prosecution of Police Officers in Buenos Aires, Córdoba, São Paulo and Uruguay

	Buenos Aires	Córdoba	São Paulo	Uruguay
Judges	−	=	=	+
Prosecutors	−	−	−	+
Private Prosecutors	+	+	+	n/a

IV. ACCOUNTING FOR THE DIFFERENCES AMONG SEGMENTS OF THE LEGAL COMPLEX

Who are these Private Prosecutors, and why are they always favourable to greater legal protections from state violence? Why are judges and prosecutors in general not more inclined to defend the rule of law and the integrity of the criminal justice process, their very milieu and raison d'être? In this section I explain the findings from the previous section. I show that state-based members of the legal complex fail to act consistently in favour of the liberal project when their substantive preferences for a particular outcome in the case at hand—driven by client demands—conflict with a call for greater legality. Judicial and prosecutorial institutions can be designed to ameliorate but not eliminate the consequences of these pressures. Lawyers based in organised civil society, on the other hand, are freer to pursue the defence of the marginal populations that bear the brunt of state rights violations.

When it functions well, the criminal justice system relies on what we might call endogenous incentives. The police will investigate, prosecutors will prosecute, judges will judge, because that is what they are paid to do, by the state and ultimately by society. But what if a particular prosecution runs contrary to the dominant state project? We cannot ignore the exogenous incentives that derive from the social and political context in which these actors operate. They filter into individual judges' or prosecutors' actions through the institutions that define their careers. These institutions can be more or less autonomous from their political context, thus passing on or filtering out political and social pressures. But we should expect all state-based legal actors to serve a 'client' of sorts—individual political actors, in cases in which these institutions are captured by partisan interests, or broader societal interests, if the institutions are more autonomous. Only rarely would we expect state actors to take positions that run consistently against long-standing and deeply felt popular sentiment.

In relation to police violence in particular, a political context that is hostile to restraining police violence will tend to produce judges and prosecutors who are at best, if they are sufficiently autonomous, neutral toward these cases. At worst, it will produce judges and prosecutors who actively collaborate with the project of undermining restraints on police misconduct. Halliday and Liu's contribution to this volume, for example, illustrates how judges and prosecutors can collaborate with the state's project, and how that project itself can become so pervasive and coercive as to reshape even the actions of defence attorneys, despite the latter's assigned roles.

In addition to incentives we must consider capabilities. Regardless of their inclinations, Private Prosecutors will be constrained by their ability to obtain funding and support. State actors, on the other hand, depend on state support. By definition, they work within the state's legal apparatus, the bottom rung of which is the police force. Prosecutors and judges are, to different degrees in these different systems, dependent on the police for the information and services they need to function at all. This dependence limits their ability to challenge the police even when they are inclined to do so. Those who, like judges and prosecutors in São Paulo, are relatively independent of pressures from above can still be hamstrung by their dependence on the police for the basic stuff of which prosecutions are made. In the following sections I offer a brief overview for each jurisdiction of the institutional and contextual features that affect the incentives and capabilities of judges and prosecutors.

(a) Buenos Aires

As noted in the earlier discussion, judges in Buenos Aires, whether federal or provincial, are known for their submission to political forces. Prosecutors, meanwhile, are expressly subjected to the directives of the politically appointed head of the prosecutor's office.[8] Thus we would expect both of these actors to be especially influenced by the political context surrounding police behaviour. Unfortunately, this is also the jurisdiction in which political leaders have been the most vocal in calling for the use of deadly force in policing. Most political pressure, therefore, is in favour of a less accountable police force. Occasionally, as we saw in the previous section, a particular case prompts sufficient public outrage that demonstrations ensue. In these cases, predictably, these politically subject judges take a less lenient view. Results thus seesaw between the norm of impunity and the occasional conviction in response to public outrage.

One of the constant refrains heard in Argentina in recent times is the concern over *seguridad ciudadana* ('citizen security', the preferred term for addressing issues of crime and personal safety). The newspapers editorialise about the *ola de inseguridad* or wave of insecurity; parents complain that their children are not safe in the street; reports of kidnappings and violent crimes make headlines. The concern is especially acute in the Metropolitan Buenos Aires area, and its shantytowns are especially singled out as the source of much of this crime. Ruth Stanley (2003) has done an extensive analysis of the rhetoric and politics surrounding the question of violent crime in Argentina. Her paper is replete with statements by elected leaders suggesting that the courts are ineffective in controlling crime, and that the only way to combat the 'wave of insecurity' is to shoot those who are threatening society with anarchy. Ruckauf, governor of Buenos Aires province at the end of the 1990s, Hugo Patti, a notorious police chief associated with kidnappings and torture during and after the last dictatorship, and Aldo Rico, the leader of a military rebellion during the first civilian administration, have capitalised on this concern to seek political office at the municipal and provincial levels (Seligson, 2002).

A statement from Ruckauf during the 1999 gubernatorial campaign exemplifies this approach:

> It is necessary to enter into all the shantytowns with all the police officers necessary to put an end to crime. The police are capable, it's simply necessary to give them proper instructions and rules of engagement [*reglas de combate*]. But let us give them the norms they need: we can't have a situation where a policeman enters one of these places and kills someone and then some lawyer of the criminal appears and says it's the policeman who is the murderer [Stanley, 2003, quoting from Página 12, 5 August 1999].

The rhetoric suggests a war—and in war there is no due process. When the police kill inhabitants of shantytowns or criminal suspects, these acts are

---

[8] This may seem unexceptional, but in São Paulo, eg, prosecutors are required to exercise their independent prosecutorial judgement and are expressly exempted from any obligation to follow the directions of the head of their office.

repeatedly presented as the legitimate exercise of police powers in the course of open combat against crime. Popular support for these 'law and order' political figures extends to the use of violent and repressive police methods. In a poll taken in 1999, 5.7 per cent were more or less in agreement, 44.9 per cent were in agreement, and 4.6 per cent were strongly in agreement when asked if there was a need to put bullets into criminals (*'meterle bala a los delincuentes'*) (El Cronista, 9 August 2000, cited in Stanley, 2003).

This general political environment at times becomes quite focused on judicial and prosecutorial actions. In a northern suburb of Buenos Aires, for example, when the policeman who killed a minor was arrested, there was a demonstration in front of the prosecutors' office demanding his release. When a judge sought to interrogate Patti in connection with the torture of two suspects and Patti refused to obey the court order, the judge's insistence prompted widespread popular demonstrations in support of Patti. Then-governor Duhalde later commended Patti as 'the best police chief' in the country. Only rarely will a judge or prosecutor score political points by aggressively pursuing a case of police violence, and, if anything, these attitudes have only hardened from the beginning of the 1990s to their end.

This is not to suggest that the question of police impunity can never gain political traction in Buenos Aires. The frequent disclosures that the police are behind notorious kidnappings and murders, or release state prisoners to go and rob for them, and periodic events like police complicity in the murder of a young woman, occasionally galvanise public reaction. Smulovitz and Peruzzoti (2002) document this phenomenon, in which a community organises to demand a response from the justice system. But this reaction has been more focused on perceived criminality and corruption in the police force than on due process and abuses in the course of policing operations.

The excessive use of force triggers a mainstream reaction only when the victim can be defined as one of 'us'—that is, it requires an 'innocent' victim or visibly criminal actions on the part of the police. The 1991 death in custody of Walter Bulacio, a high school student arrested at a concert, has prompted annual mass demonstrations, benefit concerts and other popular protest. The killing of innocent bystanders can prompt a popular outcry—a schoolteacher in the Boca neighbourhood of Buenos Aires in 2000, a music teacher in the northern suburbs of Buenos Aires in early 2001. The murder of three middle class youths in Floresta in late 2001 led to a neighbourhood revolt. And the disappearance of two youths in La Plata in 1990 and 1993, all too reminiscent of the 'dirty war' period that characterised the last dictatorship, prompted political and popular reactions that led to exhaustive forensic investigations and, ultimately, convictions. But the near daily killings and outright executions of marginalised youths do not cause an outcry beyond their immediate family and friends.

In summary, Buenos Aires has experienced an extreme form of what Garland (2001) called a 'culture of order' in which the criminal is construed as an irredeemable other, and in which the only way to manage risk is to eliminate the evildoer—if necessary, by summary execution. Police homicides are politically and socially construed as the response to violence and crime, and the victims are viewed as the casualties in an active war between the forces of crime and the forces of order. Attempts to reform and restrain the police have foundered in the face of public demands for more effective policing—which is interpreted and presented by elected officials as a licence to use *mano dura* or iron fisted methods of law enforcement. Electoral formulas advocating increased police use of lethal force are by far more common and more successful than those advocating restraint in law enforcement and greater protections for crime suspects. 'Client' interests, in the form of demands from politicians and society, are too strong for judges and prosecutors to do anything more than simply acquiesce, except in those cases in which a Private Prosecutor does the work of preparing a prosecution and popular demonstrations suggest a more favourable political construction of the case.

By default, then, it is often up to the Private Prosecutor to take on the case with true prosecutorial zeal. As noted earlier, the legal attributes of the Private Prosecutor can vary. Until late in the decade, in the province of Buenos Aires the Private Prosecutor was truly a secondary figure, dependent on the goodwill of the prosecutor and the judge. She could not seek a conviction, for example, if the prosecutor refused to do so; she could not independently introduce evidence that the prosecutor did not present; she could not ask for a sentence greater than what the prosecutor had requested. Some of these limitations remain in place, but in 1998 the National Supreme Court ruled (in the case known as *Caso Santillán*) that it was unconstitutional to deny an interested party, known in the provincial legal code as the *particular damnificado*, the ability to request a conviction when the prosecutor would not do so. This recent expansion of attributions brings the provincial *particular damnificado* much closer to the federal analogue, the *querellante*, giving both the attributes of a state prosecutor. Even if the prosecutor argues in favour of an acquittal, the judge is required to rule on the *querella*'s request that the defendant be convicted.

CORREPI (*Coordinadora contra la Represión Policial e Institucional*— Coordinator Against Police and Institutional Repression) is probably the most important of the organisations in the metropolitan Buenos Aires area that includes lawyers who routinely serve as Private Prosecutors in police violence cases. CORREPI was created in 1992 as an association of relatives of victims of police violence. The staff not only comb newspapers for information about cases that might otherwise go unexplored and unreported, they also contact relatives of victims offering both social and legal support. Its lawyers clearly take a leadership role in what is otherwise a grassroots organisation, though they would argue they are merely members. CORREPI's lawyers are involved in everything from conducting a parallel investigation, to protecting witnesses, to organising (and marching in) demonstrations, to speaking to the media. Between cases they work on educating people about their rights, and do more academic work, presenting papers at human rights conferences, and carrying out other public education functions.

The organisation holds regular meetings of relatives of victims to plan popular mobilisations, talk about the progress of legal actions, and offer encouragement and support. CORREPI has branches in such places as Matanza, just outside Buenos Aires—a populous and largely poor urban municipality—and among the poor sectors of the northern suburbs of Buenos Aires, like the Tigre area and the shantytowns beyond San Isidro, as well as in the interior of the province of Buenos Aires and in other provinces, like Córdoba, as we will see. Members and contacts live in shantytowns and poor neighbourhoods.

CORREPI is truly, as the introduction might put it, an 'insurgent, rump group' rather than broadly representative of the profession as a whole. Freed from public prosecutors' ostensible allegiance to a greater social interest, its lawyers are free to adopt the victim's preference for a conviction at all costs. Moreover, CORREPI's ideological stance is clearly not rooted in political liberalism. In all its publications, the organisation is careful to present police violence as part of an inevitably repressive state project. In this view, the state uses its security forces to repress the poor in the service of capitalism, and judges and the law are equally complicit in this repressive project, which will only come to an end with a mass revolution. Needless to say, this procedural and ideological stance very often puts CORREPI at odds with both judges and prosecutors, generating sharp intersegmental cleavages. One Buenos Aires trial court judge, for example, confided that she had held the trial in her own office (with not even enough free chairs for all the members of the victim's family) rather than in the courtroom, because otherwise CORREPI would turn her trial into a circus.

CORREPI's radicalism also generates crosscutting cleavages. There are other non-governmental organisations with similar missions that are not as radical in their rhetoric, including the Centro de Estudios Legales y Sociales (Centre of Legal and Social Studies—CELS), Centro de Profesionales por los Derechos Humanos (Centre of Professionals for Human Rights—CeProDH), and the Public Interest Law Clinic of Palermo Law School, among others. These groups are clearly closer to the professional mainstream. Many fulfil a very important function, by educating the public and officials and shaping policy, although it is CORREPI that intervenes in the vast majority of actual prosecutions for police violence and has the closest contacts with the marginalised population that bears the brunt of the violence.

These organisations occasionally cooperate with each other and with CORREPI, but the latter can often be heard excoriating its potential partners as tools of a foreign neo-liberal project and little more than a veneer for an oppressive capitalist system: the CELS, CORREPI has said, represents 'the fullest expression of the liberal and pro-United States vision of human rights, both on the ideological and financial plane, since it is no secret that the Foundation established by the Nazi-phile Henry Ford and his son is its patron (with all the conditionality this implies)' (Informative Bulletin No160, 30 March 2002). It is perhaps worth quoting at some length from a CORREPI statement when its cooperation with CELS on a case before the Inter-American Court of Human Rights was brought to light, in what it considered a misleading way:

> 'The profound ideological, political and methodological differences between CORREPI and CELS are public and notorious. ...
> In connection with our collaboration with the CELS, we wish to emphasize that CORREPI considers that the authentic struggle for human rights is not found behind the swiftest computers or behind the comfortable seats at the OAS but in the streets, next to the people [*el pueblo*] that resist and fight. ... Finally, we must highlight that CORREPI is not an NGO ... but rather a humble expression of the class struggle in Argentina.'[9]

While the more mainstream organisations draw funding and support from foreign foundations or educational institutions, CORREPI's lawyers are sustained by their criminal defence work, their representation of the victims of abuse in civil damages cases, and in particular by the relatively recent legalisation of contingency fee agreements. In contrast to China, they derive their freedom of action from the robust measure of political liberty available in Argentina since re-democratisation. They depend, therefore, on the development of a viable professional career on behalf of marginal populations, and on the (albeit imperfect) realisation of a substantial degree of political liberalisation. Their work would surely be easier if the Buenos Aires courts were more autonomous.

(b) Córdoba

There is not a great deal of available data on the level of social support for repressive public safety policies in Córdoba, but all indications are that it is lower than in Buenos Aires. Polls show a slightly higher concern for crime than in Buenos Aires (Polling by Centro de Estudios de Opinión Pública, April 1999, reported in the principal daily, *La Voz del Interior*). But the issue of public safety did not dominate politics in Córdoba the way it did in Buenos Aires province for much of the decade. Leaders' platforms do not include the aggressive statements found in Buenos Aires in the middle and end of the decade, and in São Paulo at the beginning of the decade.

---

[9] Excerpts from CORREPI Informative Bulletin (*Boletín Informativo*) No 121 (26 May 2001), available at www.correpi.lahaine.org/articulo.php?p=174&more=1&c=1.

The Radical Party (Unión Cívica Radical) held the governorship from democratisation in 1983 until 1999, when a governor from the Justicialist (Peronist) Party was elected. The Radical governors were more or less in the centre of the Radical party, itself a centrist party, and neither of them used strong law and order rhetoric. During the Justicialist administration, public safety became more of an issue, but the main policy proposals still centred on community policing rather than more repression—the position has hardened somewhat in recent years. In some instances, the leadership's reaction to these events suggests less support for police officers who kill and attempt to hide the facts. In no more than two or three cases, to the best of my knowledge, the political leadership has taken steps to intervene in a case by removing high ranking police officers from their positions after a killing. All the cases of which I have knowledge, moreover, required widespread popular demonstrations before a political response was forthcoming. Over all, political leaders in Córdoba have not distinguished themselves by exerting pressures too far in either direction on the issue of police abuses, except in cases that trigger popular outrage.

Data on popular support for repressive tactics are also equivocal. There is no firm public opinion data on the point, although polls show a relatively high level of support for mainstream human rights organisations. Although the NGOs organised around this issue are fewer and smaller than in Buenos Aires, 33 per cent of the cases in the Córdoba sample trigger popular demonstrations—the highest percentage of any of the locations studied. Córdoba is a highly mobilised city in any event. In my experience, it is a rare week that passes without a demonstration of some kind taking place in its downtown area. In summary, then, the political leadership is mostly neutral, awaiting public reaction before taking a stance, while public pressure in favour of prosecutions is more common here than in Buenos Aires.

Given the strong impact of popular demonstrations on the outcome, the greater prevalence of public reactions partially explains the high conviction rate in Córdoba. But that conviction rate masks prosecutorial weaknesses and at best a certain agnosticism on the part of judges, as noted in the earlier discussion. What lies behind this lackadaisical attitude on the part of prosecutors? How can we explain a conviction rate as low as 20 per cent when a Private Prosecutor appears but there are no demonstrations? Why does this jump to 80 per cent when demonstrations take place?

Public prosecutors are organised in a strictly hierarchical model, with politically appointed leadership, in sharp contrast to the more autonomous design of Brazil's Ministério Público. Throughout the 1990s, the head of the office was appointed to a renewable five year term by the governor, with the consent of a simple majority of the Senate. Front line prosecutors, meanwhile are admonished: 'a prosecutor that receives instruction regarding the exercise of his functions shall comply with them, though he may express his personal opposition. ... If the Attorney General ratifies the questioned instruction, the prosecutor must obey and the Attorney General will assume responsibility for the act' (Article 4 of the Organic Law of the *Ministerio Público* (Prosecutor)). As a result of these institutional features, individual investigations readily respond to social and political pressures for or against more aggressive action. Indeed, local attorneys complain that these features have politicised the prosecutorial function to a significant degree.[10] Córdoba's institutional arrangements thus tend to encourage sharp fluctuations in prosecutorial attitudes in response to short term external pressures.

On the other hand, according to close observers, the Courts are rule-oriented and have a strongly formalistic propensity. A research project based on a series of in-depth interviews of non-judicial officers in the courts of Córdoba city indicates that the political appointment process, dominated by centre-right, socially conservative local politics, produced a largely conservative, hierarchical, rule-oriented judiciary, free from direct political interference but attuned to prevailing political winds and the interests of powerful social and economic actors (Scarponetti et al, 2000). Importantly, judicial employees unanimously denied the presence of overt corruption or favouritism, or direct political meddling in case outcomes (Scarponetti et al, 2000: 405–6, 409). The overwhelming impression is of a cautious, conservative judiciary, drawn primarily from elite families (411), with judges more devoted to preserving the existing order than interested in doing 'justice' (410). The researchers conclude, in part, with a description that will be familiar to students of even the better functioning judiciaries in Latin America:

> Córdoba's tribunals show a conservative structure, with bureaucratic features that are visible in the organizational culture. The dominant features are the emphasis on administrative functions, a pyramidal working structure and the priority of formalism in procedures (Scarponetti et al, 2000b: 394).

Despite the emphasis on conservatism, formalism and hierarchy, however, judicial staff told researchers that 'complicated' cases are handled directly by the judge, with less intervention by the staff. They defined 'complicated' most often in political terms: having to do with important interests, having public prominence, or otherwise being in the public eye. Importantly for our purposes, they agreed that public opinion and social pressures can cause a case to be treated with special care (410).

This squares with the results of the previous analysis. Córdoba has a judiciary that is, by and large, willing to convict a police officer of homicide, and more inclined to do so in cases that garner public attention. But because of their legalistic orientation and non-investigative role, judges

---

[10] Interview with Silvia Osaba, 20 Feb 2001.

demand and expect adherence to formal rules and a high standard of evidence. In routine cases, judges depend entirely on prosecutors or claimants to build the record on which they will judge the case, and prosecutors (who depend on the police for an investigation) are a weak link in the system. Only when Private Prosecutors supplement the work of public prosecutors, or a 'complicated' case prompts judges and prosecutors to take a more active role, are prosecutions more likely to succeed.

Some of the Private Prosecutors active in Córdoba are also members of CORREPI or a similar organisation. But the intervention of attorneys not affiliated with any NGO, who ordinarily earn a living through criminal defence, is quite common. Much more than in Buenos Aires or São Paulo, the lawyers acting as Private Prosecutors in Córdoba are private attorneys, working for a fee, rather than members of an NGO, drawing on charitable funding. Partly this is because there are far fewer cases of police violence, so that it would be difficult to dedicate a substantial portion of time to this kind of work, and partly it is because the victims in the Córdoba sample are somewhat more affluent than those in Buenos Aires. This confirms the idea, anticipated earlier, that mainstream lawyers will find it easier to oppose a repressive project when it affects a more mainstream population. On the negative side, this produces a strong pattern of socio-economic inequality in legal outcomes, in which one of the key determinants of a conviction is the affluence of the victim (Brinks, 2008). But it also means that these Private Prosecutors are less likely to earn the hostility and distrust of other members of the legal complex.

(c) São Paulo

In recent years, the leftist Workers' Party (PT) has accumulated important victories across Brazil at the municipal, state and national levels. In the state of São Paulo, the PT ran the mayor's office of the capital city until recent interim elections. And yet this strong showing by the left coincides with accounts that attribute 'massive support for illegal and/or authoritarian measures of control' to the population as a whole (Holston and Caldeira, 1998: 267). Holston and Caldeira argue that 'shooting to kill not only has broad popular support but it is also 'accepted' by the 'tough talk' of official policy' (271). As in Buenos Aires at the end of the decade, during the early 1990s in São Paulo electoral formulas that emphasised civil rights protection routinely lost to those that adopted explicit shoot-to-kill policies. Thus, Franco Montoro, the first governor of São Paulo after the dictatorship, preached a restrained police force and instituted various police reform measures. But he was followed by Orestes Quércia and Luiz Antonio Fleury Filho, both of whom hindered the implementation of Montoro's reforms and adopted an approach strongly reminiscent of the *mano dura* discourse seen in Buenos Aires (Chevigny, 1995).

A series of surveys led by José Murilo de Carvalho in 1996, exploring knowledge of and support for civil rights in Rio de Janeiro, suggest that these rights are relatively weakly rooted in Brazilian society (Murilo de Carvalho, 1997). In connection with police activities, about 70 per cent of those surveyed agreed with the statement that criminals (*bandidos*) do not respect the rights of others and therefore do not deserve to have their own rights respected. Fully 63 per cent strongly agreed with this statement (*concordo totalmente*). Forty five per cent agreed that the use of violence by the police to obtain confessions is sometimes or always justified. And while 46 per cent flatly stated that those who lynch criminals are wrong to do so, 11 per cent thought they were right, and another 41 per cent thought that their actions, while wrong, were understandable.

There appears to be consensus among operators and observers of the justice system that the population continues to accept the use of lethal force as an instrument to fight crime. In interviews in 2001, a series of public officials agreed with this assessment.[11] Interestingly, Mário Papaterra also argued that prosecutors are often further to the right than many of his police officers. These prosecutors, he said, use the same metric as the rest of the population to determine who is entitled to full legal protection: a *marginal* may not be, but a *homem de bem* (an upstanding person) is.

Interestingly, elected representatives after the middle of the decade shifted policies back toward a more restrained police. Governors Mário Covas and Geraldo Alckmin, who took office in 1994 and 1998 respectively, did not follow the strong-arm rhetoric of Quércia and Fleury. In 1996, under Covas's auspices, São Paulo became the first of several states in Brazil to create an *Ouvidoria da Polícia*, an ombudsman specifically designed to address police abuses. Covas offered strong institutional and political support for the monitoring activities of the *Ouvidoria*.[12] Alckmin has de-prioritised the issue somewhat, but he did not completely back off on this support and has not adopted the law and order rhetoric of Covas's predecessors.[13] Thus from 1994 on elected officials at the state level were

[11] Interviews with Luiz Eduardo Greenhalgh, a PT national senator from São Paulo (São Paulo, 30 Apr 2001); Hélio Bicudo, a former national congressman, vice-mayor of São Paulo, the primary sponsor of the law subjecting the military police to civilian justice, and a member of the Inter-American Human Rights Commission (São Paulo, 27 Mar 2001); Benedito Mariano, first director of the Ouvidoria da Polícia (São Paulo, 21 Mar 2001); Mário Papaterra, São Paulo's Adjunct Secretary of State for Public Security, a former prosecutor who was, when I spoke to him, the civilian in charge of the civil and military police forces for the state ministry of security (São Paulo, 23 Mar 2001); Antônio Carlos da Ponte, a prosecutor in the jury division (which has jurisdiction over homicide cases)(São Paulo, Apr 2001); and Norberto Joia, another prosecutor in the jury division (São Paulo, 16 Apr 2001).
[12] Interview with Benedito Domingos Mariano, first director of the Ouvidoria (São Paulo, 21 Mar 2001).
[13] Interview with Fermino Fecchio, Director of the Ouvidoria da Polícia (São Paulo, Apr 2001).

less supportive of violent methods than those in the province of Buenos Aires at the end of the decade, and less so than governors at the beginning of the decade.[14] In summary, it appears that there is strong public support for draconian police actions, on the part of elected officials, however, the situation has improved.

Coupled with a significant degree of independence on the part of both judges and prosecutors, we might expect this to produce at worst a neutral judiciary and prosecutorial force. At minimum, we would expect them to perform somewhat better than their peers in Buenos Aires, who are subject to more intense pro-police pressures on the part of actual political leaders, and are more open to political pressure in any event. To what might we attribute the truly dismal conviction rate in São Paulo, then?

The key problem in São Paulo is the limited capacity of the judiciary to overcome police obstructionism. The investigation of cases involving excesses by the Military Police is assigned to the Military Police itself.[15] This institutional characteristic means that the Military Police essentially controls the information that is made available about cases involving its own members, often resorting to forging confrontations, planting guns, intimidating witnesses, threatening lawyers, and preparing false forensic reports to create an information blackout.[16] By carefully targeting politically and economically marginalised populations, the police simplify their task considerably. In the sample of cases I tracked, only four out of more than 200 cases involved middle class victims (compared to 32 per cent of those for whom I have this information in Córdoba), 77 per cent of the victims lived in a shantytown, and fully 72 per cent were unemployed. Even if a prosecutor should attempt to investigate more thoroughly—something we would not necessarily expect from what is at best a neutral actor—he or she would be stymied by police control over the factual record.

Private Prosecutors are the principal means for overcoming this institutional opposition. The most important civil society actor on this issue in São Paulo is the Santo Dias Centre for Human Rights (the *Centro Santo Dias de Direitos Humanos*). Under the leadership of Cardinal Paulo Evaristo Arns, a noted human rights defender, the Archdiocese of São Paulo established

---

[14] The municipal government does not have any policing responsibilities, but at this level there is also a shift to the left. The beginning of the decade finds Paulo Maluf (a well-known figure of the Brazilian right, governor of São Paulo during the military regime) as mayor, followed by his designated successor, Celso Pitta, also on the right. But at the end of the decade, paulistanos elected Marta Suplicy, from the PT, to the post.

[15] In general, Brazil has a separate investigative force to assist prosecutors, the Civil Police. The single exception to this is in cases involving crimes committed by the Military Police. The political history of this exclusion is rather complicated, having its roots in an authoritarian era statute creating a separate justice system to judge the actions of the military police (Zaverucha, 1999; see, eg, Pereira, 2001).

[16] I have presented more complete descriptions and statistics on the use of these methods elsewhere (Brinks, 2003; Brinks, 2008).

the Centre in 1980. It is named after a catholic worker murdered by the São Paulo Military Police while leading a strike in October 1979. From the beginning, its primary mission has been to work on behalf of the victims of police homicides. Over the last 20-plus years, the Centre has acted on behalf of the victims in over 300 cases of police violence (not limited to murder). It offers legal assistance in both civil and criminal actions. It files claims for compensation in the former, and acts as the Private Prosecutor in the latter. The Centre's attorneys call witnesses, obtain experts' reports, and generally bring information into the courtroom that would otherwise not come to light.

While it fills the same niche in the legal ecosystem, channelling demands from victims of repression to the courtroom, Santo Dias is different from CORREPI on a number of levels. First, it is not a grassroots organisation with an extended non-legal membership. It is run by the Archdiocese, and has a small staff of lawyers and their assistants who do the typical work of lawyers, filing papers and requests with the courts, while clients come into the office to talk to the staff. It does not organise and participate in political demonstrations in the streets of São Paulo or at the doors of the courthouse, though it has organised conferences and public acts in support of human rights, published studies and lobbied for public policy changes.

In contrast to CORREPI, moreover, the Centre does not appear to suffer the suspicion and distrust of judges and prosecutors. Several reasons can be offered for this. First, of course, is its association with the Catholic Church, an organisation with a great deal of legitimacy in Brazil. More importantly, however, it limits its political activity to lobbying for new legislation rather than attempting to influence the way a judge decides the case at hand. As a result, it is viewed as a more mainstream human rights organisation than its Argentine counterpart with its Marxist rhetoric, confrontational politics, and courtroom door demonstrations. It has more informal links to the official bar association than CORREPI, and many of its lawyers have moved on to public service at the city, state and national levels—Beatriz Sinisgalli in the state police oversight entity, Fermino Fecchio as director of that entity, Benedito Mariano in that same capacity first and then in charge of security policy for the mayor of São Paulo, and Hélio Bicudo as a senator and national and international human rights figure. It would be hard to characterise the Centre as a dissident organisation within the profession.

There are other entities in the São Paulo area that work on the problem of police violence or on human rights more generally. Examples are the Commissão Teotônio Vilela and the Human Rights Commission of the Brazilian Bar Association (the *Ordem de Advogados do Brasil*, known as the OAB). The Commissão Teotônio Vilela and the OAB, for example, intervened in the prosecution of Ubiratan Guimarães, the Military Police colonel in charge of the operation that ended in the massacre of 111 inmates of São Paulo's house of detention in 1992. These NGOs do the important work of putting together human rights reports, bringing media attention to bear on the problem, lobbying for legal change, and participating in the prosecution of high profile cases, but they rarely intervene directly in routine criminal prosecutions of rights violators. In that sense, they are more like the CELS in Buenos Aires. Their political work is primarily bent on changing the legal framework, the sociopolitical context and the social construction of these cases, and less inclined to the prosecution of individual cases.

(d) Uruguay

The critical distinction between Uruguay's sociopolitical context and what we have seen in Argentina and Brazil is the lack of repeated calls on the part of the public and the elected leadership for more draconian and repressive responses to crime. A decade-long study concluded that while murder rates had remained stable from 1990 to 2000, armed robbery had increased almost threefold, from just fewer than 17 per 10,000 inhabitants to nearly 45 per 10,000. As a result, Uruguay shows much the same pattern as all eight countries included in the 1996 Latinobarómetro: 87 per cent of respondents felt that crime had increased, and Uruguayans were second only to Venezuelans in the percentage of respondents (8 per cent) naming crime as the principal problem in the country. But the social and political response to these crimes is palpably different in Uruguay than in Argentina or Brazil. There is a complete absence of political platforms and public statements by elected officials comparable to Ruckauf's, Patti's or Rico's *mano dura* and *meta bala* arguments; and opinion polls and interviews find no statements comparable to the *marginal tem que morrer* (criminals must die), or *bandido bom é bandido morto* (the only good criminal is a dead criminal) heard in Brazil.

In Uruguay moderate statements are common even when we might expect the opposite. In July 2000, an armed robber shot and killed a taxi driver. The taxi drivers' association released a statement in response that read, in part, as follows:

> We ask ourselves: what could lead someone to kill for a few coins, other than the most atrocious poverty, the greatest degradation of the basic values of a human being, the lack of employment, of a just wage, a fraternal education [*educación solidaria*], and dignified living conditions? ... We are convinced that this is one more murder committed by the reigning economic and social model, and that those who promote policies that marginalise and exclude the immense majority are just as responsible for this crime as the individual who pulled the trigger ending the life of this worker [La República, 12 July 2000].

This opinion, attributing crime to social conditions and the solution to social change, is widespread, as we will see.

Uruguay's political leadership began the 1990s relatively agnostic on questions of civil and human rights but then shifted toward more support. Uruguay's first two presidents after re-democratisation were centre-left on most issues, resisting market reforms and the neo-liberal impetus. Both de-emphasised human rights accountability for the abuses of the previous regime (Skaar, 2002), but had a more pro-rights approach under democracy. The third president, Batlle, on the other hand, is an old fashioned political liberal with a social democratic rhetoric when it comes to crime and a more proactive stance on the human rights question. Once he took power in 2000, he immediately took steps to uncover information in some of the most notorious cases associated with the dictatorship (Skaar, 2002). Throughout the decade, police violence was consistently low, and official government responses to individual events were typically critical of police violence. All three of these presidents probably fall on the progressive side of the governors of Córdoba during the same period.

Meanwhile, the electorate was steadily moving to the left, as the ever-greater success of the Frente Amplio in local and national elections demonstrates. The political climate is therefore quite different from the climate of social control (Garland, 2001) observed in Buenos Aires or São Paulo. While in São Paulo it appears that the electoral success of the left was divorced from public opinion regarding the use of lethal force and due process guarantees for criminals, in Uruguay, polls show what might be termed a more social democratic view of crime and the proper response to it: 46 per cent blame social conditions, only 35 per cent moral decay; and 48 per cent oppose the death penalty compared to 43 per cent in favour (Latinobarómetro results reported in *El Observador*, 19 May 1996). Bayce, relying on a series of polls by Gallup, Factum, Vox, Equipos and Marketing, also reports less support for repressive measures: in 1995, he shows only 31 per cent favoured the death penalty, while 61 per cent opposed it (Bayce, 1996: 101).

As in Córdoba, there are no polls directly addressing the question of the use of deadly force by the police. But some of the polls reported by Bayce indirectly suggest disapproval: in 1989, 46 per cent opposed while 36 per cent favoured a *mano dura* approach (referring to a repressive style of policing); in 1990, only 10 per cent favoured the use of 'more repression' to control crime; in 1993, only 20 per cent agreed that *más vigilancia* (more vigilance) was needed on the part of the police, and only 8 per cent agreed that more *persecución* (which translates as pursuit or prosecution) was needed. In 1995, an absolute majority of respondents (54 per cent) stated that the solution to crime does not lie in repressive measures, whether harsh or soft, but rather in addressing the social causes of crime (Bayce, 1996).

I asked Juan Faropa, who runs a police training programme established with UN and local funding, why the police in Uruguay kill so much less than the police in other countries in the region. I expected to hear something about superior training, more civilian control over the police, or perhaps even lower levels of violent crime. Instead, he said only that 'our society would not tolerate it. People will tolerate moderate levels of violence [moderate beatings, for example, which have been a persistent problem in Uruguay] but not killings' (author interview, 19 December 2000). In summary, the political reaction to crime in Uruguay is not a call for giving the police more latitude in the use of deadly force, but rather a focus on resolving the perceived social causes of crime. If Juan Faropa is right, judges and prosecutors in Uruguay face strong 'client' pressures to prosecute police homicides effectively. Indeed, in Table 9.1 we see that in Uruguay demonstrations are common exactly in those cases in which the courts *fail* to prosecute a violation.

Complying with these exogenous pressures requires judges (and prosecutors) to overcome a relative scarcity of resources. Uruguayan judges cannot count on an independent investigative force, but the drastically lower number of cases (30 over the course of a decade, compared to thousands in Buenos Aires or São Paulo) and a more inquisitorial system give Uruguayan judges greater capacity to respond. Uruguayan judges rely extensively on low-tech devices such as re-enactments of the crime, personal questioning of the police officers and eyewitnesses, and the like. Judge-run techniques are all the more effective if the same judge who ordered them and carried them out is in charge of evaluating their sufficiency. Uruguayan judges are truly investigative judges in the old Civil Law tradition (see, eg, Merryman, 1985 for a description of investigative judges in the Civil Law tradition), and thus can become quite prosecutorial, applying a rather lower standard of proof than the formalistic adversarial judges of Córdoba. In short, in Uruguay political pressures and a stance in favour of political liberalism tend in the same direction, and join with the capacity to overcome police resistance, producing a high level of convictions.

IV. CONCLUSIONS

What can we learn from this brief review of state and non-state members of the legal complex in three different countries in Latin America? From the conduct of judges and prosecutors, it appears that state actors have a difficult time defending the moderate state in the face of mass demands for a more repressive response to crime. This should not be too surprising, since it is the state itself that channels demands for a more repressive approach to policing. If there is a strong move toward lifting the restraints on the state, judges and prosecutors will sooner or later feel the pull. Depending on their institutional autonomy, they experience stronger or weaker 'client' incentives that conflict with the defence of a moderate state. To insulate them from this repressive impulse and allow them to exercise a counter-majoritarian role would require, at minimum, such measures as a less political manner of appointment and removal, meritocratic advancement and the like, similar to what we observe in São Paulo. Even so, in a political context hostile to claims of due process, a high degree of independence may well neutralise hostility but it will seldom produce an aggressive defence of liberal rights on the part of state actors.

Explaining the consistently progressive stance of the Private Prosecutors in these cases, of course, is easier. Private attorneys self-select for ideological compatibility with the cause at hand: a lawyer with a strong affinity for repressive state tactics will tend not to seek employment with a human rights NGO, and is less likely to accept a case inconsistent with her beliefs. Moreover, these attorneys serve clients—the relatives of victims of police violence—whose interest in punishing perceived police misconduct is unalloyed. Many of them also earn a portion of their living doing criminal defence work, and their clients often end up on the receiving end of police abuses, including murder. These personal and client-based incentives line up with narrow and broad professional incentives—they make a living prosecuting these cases, or working within NGOs whose main mission is to limit police violence, and they share in the overall lawyerly interest in strengthening the rule of law (Halliday and Karpik, 1998).

We might in any event expect private lawyers, in comparison to state based lawyers, to be especially solicitous of the rule of law. Their power derives principally from the operation of the rule of law, and their primary weapon to oppose state power is the law. Without the rule of law, they have no response to the coercive power of the state, applied either to their clients or to themselves. Without a liberal rule of law, in fact, criminal defence attorneys can become merely ornamental if not personally endangered, as the experience of defence attorneys in China suggests. State lawyers who are doing the state's bidding, on the other hand, can always fall back on state power, even if the law does not support them.

Does this mean, then, that private lawyers will always align against the erosion of political liberalism and the moderate state, while state lawyers will only do so when its protection is already part of or congruent with the mainstream political project? The conduct of some government lawyers in the United States (Abel, in this volume) suggests that this latter segment of the legal complex may not always bow to regressive client pressures. And in my own cases, it appears that the more autonomous judges (such as those in São Paulo and perhaps Córdoba) seem to act in a more progressive way, to the best of their ability. We might venture the conclusion, then, that (a) state-based members of the legal complex attempt to balance the demands of their client with a general interest in strengthening the rule of law, but (b) there is reason to believe they will more often find it difficult to do so than private attorneys (at least when the latter are not faced with outright repression).

The Public Prosecutor in Brazil is probably the best example of a state-based member of the legal complex that is protected from political 'client' pressures: it is constitutionally guaranteed the same level of autonomy as the courts and charged with defending the democratic legal order. Indeed, if the Military Police did not have such a chokehold on information about their own misconduct, it is entirely possible that these prosecutors would be the one exception to the rule stated just above. And yet even here we see a decided lack of zeal given a socio-political context marked by concern with violent crime, in which the Prosecutor's office can garner very little political capital—indeed may lose it—by aggressively pursuing police excesses.

A detailed study of the São Paulo prosecutor by the Centre for the Study of Violence of the University of São Paulo (the *Núcleo de Estudos da Violência, or* NEV) fleshes out this observation. This study concludes that, after the constitutional reforms of 1988, 'the institution was quite influenced by the constitutional changes, so that its actions became oriented toward social interests and independent of the government and political leaders' (Cardia, Adorno, and Pinheiro, 1998: 206–8; see also, Bastos Arantes, 1999; Batista Cavalcanti, 1999; Bastos Arantes, 2000). NEV investigators further conclude 'the central preoccupation of the institution is the political struggle—internal and external—to confer *status and power* on the *Ministério Público*' (Cardia, Adorno and Pinheiro, 1998: 208, emphasis in original).

This central preoccupation is perfectly congruent with the liberal project, insofar as strengthening the rule of law is an essential step toward enhancing the Prosecutor's power. And, indeed, the Public Prosecutor has in many ways acted to enhance legality in Brazil. Over the last decade, for example, the *Ministério Público* has successfully prosecuted for corruption dozens of officials at the state and local levels, including both Paulo Maluf and Celso Pitta, former mayors of the city of São Paulo, and has intervened on behalf of the environment and consumers in many prominent actions. It has generally focused on high profile political scandals and corruption, environmental issues, and consumer protection (Mello de Camargo Ferraz, 1997; Paulina, 1999; Pereira da Silva, 1999; Bastos Arantes, 2000).

But here is where we see client demands enter the picture. However valuable its actions may be in these areas, and however proactive the institution may be in areas that garner a high institutional priority, its undoubtedly high qualities do not translate into effective action in the prosecution of police homicides. Reducing the number of these homicides does not, evidently, rank as a sufficiently compelling social interest. The little political capital to be derived from an investment in controlling police violence—especially violence apparently taking place in the course of policing activities rather than outright police criminality—means that police homicides do not receive sustained attention from the institution as a whole. Career-oriented prosecutors, hewing closely to institutional priorities, de-emphasise these prosecutions. Even in this best case scenario state-based actors are strongly influenced by the political context from which they derive institutional support and, indeed, their very existence. They are not likely, therefore, to be a long-term barrier to political movements away from a moderate state.

In Uruguay, the one jurisdiction in which state actors are clearly imposing limits on arbitrary police action, it is because they enjoy the support of political leaders and society. There, a relative shortage of due process protections for accused police officers translates into a more level playing field and a higher conviction rate.[17] Even there, then, state-based members of the legal complex are carrying out social imperatives, not so much striking out in a radically different direction from the rest of society.

What about private attorneys, then? Private Prosecutors in particular experience relatively little conflict in promoting greater accountability for a violent police. Under the proper conditions, there is no shortage of lawyers willing to make a living by defending the rights of those who have been abused by the state. These lawyers tend to have a strong ideological basis for doing the work they do, but the material conditions must also permit them to earn a living doing so. Relaxing the rules on the use of contingency fees in Argentina, for example, allowed lawyers to earn fees by suing the state on behalf of those who cannot afford to pay. This was a crucial change in the context of police violence cases, which overwhelmingly affect the poor. A Catholic Church that has embraced social justice in Brazil and is willing to fund the effort allows the Centro Santo Dias to do its work in São Paulo. The support of the Ford Foundation, among others, allows the CELS to continue with its work. These actors can respond directly to the concerns of the victims of an immoderate state, even if those concerns run counter to broader political trends.

However, if we look a little deeper at the Private Prosecutors and glance to the sides at other legal groups, we can see how private attorneys are also balancing ideology and substantive preferences against their professional interest in protecting the structure of the rule of law. In the case of CORREPI, for example, they advocate on behalf of the poor and demonstrate for greater judicial control over the police, but that does not prevent them from following their ideology and condemning political liberalism as an oppressive capitalist project. Similarly, we often see the cause of human rights generally supported by members of the organised bar, as in São Paulo, even in the face of strong popular sentiment against the victims of police abuses.[18] This support, however, is typically channelled to organisations

[17] I should note that these judges are not singling out police officers for especially harsh treatment. In contrast to all the other cases, in which police officers are treated with especial delicacy, in Uruguay they are subject to the same procedures as any other defendant.

[18] The Centro Santo Dias has enjoyed considerable support from the local and national bar associations (the OAB, Ordem de Advogados do Brasil, and OAB-SP, Ordem de Advogados do Brasil—São Paulo), and the OAB's human rights committee sometimes intervenes directly in litigating prominent cases.

that had their genesis in the repression of the authoritarian period, which targeted many of the leftist intellectuals who are now part of the legal mainstream—the OAB, CELS, CeProDH, and the Santo Dias Centre are all examples.

Even what is probably the most conservative legal association in Argentina, the Colegio de Abogados de la Ciudad de Buenos Aires, with strong ties to big firms and big business, speaks out frequently in favour of stronger and more autonomous courts. A review of its official pronouncements over the last two years shows 11 out of 28 statements protesting some government action that is interpreted as detracting from judicial independence or the rule of law.[19] These protests are, however, critiques of a government which its membership, in general, opposes. More striking, perhaps, is the fact that interspersed among these calls for more judicial autonomy are less purely progressive statements: condemnations of popular protests (for impairing the rule of law), and especially strongly voiced support for the pardons and amnesties for human rights violators from the previous dictatorship. Its support for individual rights, justice and the rule of law is not unaffected by the political allegiances of its members.

How might we summarise the response of the legal complex to the challenge posed by current concerns about violent crime in Latin America, then? It should be obvious by now that Brazil's or Argentina's state was never immobilised by an effective web of restraint—not in 1985 or 1983, and not at any time since. If anything, a lack of restraint led to a corrupt and unaccountable police force that contributed to the problem of crime. But more importantly, it should be clear that this is a dangerous image. It is exactly this image of a state paralysed by liberal democratic constitutional restraints that has led many societies in Latin America to support a return to more repressive states (Hinton, 2006; Mainwaring, 2006). It is Uruguay, not Argentina and Brazil, that is exceptional in this regard.

State-based members of the legal complex, as we saw, are prone to cooperating in this re-creation of the repressive state. Non-state segments of the legal complex can more easily join forces with those individuals whose interests are harmed by this retreat from liberal rights protection and advocate for the preservation of a more democratic state. They can use existing laws to hold the state to its commitments, as CORREPI, the Centro Santo Dias and other Private Prosecutors do; they can educate and advocate to prevent an erosion of those commitments, as the CELS and others do. But so long as the dominant social consensus runs against political liberalism, they will be fighting a rearguard action. Their success is dependent on the existence of laws that protect their clients, and on the at least minimal cooperation of judges and prosecutors—state actors all. Their ultimate success,

---

[19] These are available at www.colabogados.org.ar/posicion/declaraciones.php.

then, hinges on persuading their fellow citizens that the moderate state is worth preserving. In the end, perhaps, Learned Hand was using only a little hyperbole when he said:

> Liberty lies in the hearts of men and women; when it dies there, no constitution, no law, no court can even do much to help it. While it lies there it needs no constitution, no law, no court to save it. [Judge Learned Hand, 21 May 1944, addressing the public in Central Park on the occasion of I Am An American Day].

REFERENCES

Abel, R (2004), 'Lawyers Legalizing Torture' in *Biennial European Conference of the Working Group on Comparative Studies of Legal Professions*. Berder, France.

Ames, B (2001), *The Deadlock of Democracy in Brazil* (Ann Arbor, Mich, University of Michigan Press).

Amnesty International (2005), *'They Come in Shooting': Policing Socially Excluded Communities* (New York, Amnesty International).

Barcellos, C (1992), *Rota 66: A História da Polícia que Mata* (São Paulo, Editora Globo).

Bastos Arantes, R (1999), 'Direito e Política: O Ministério Público e a Defesa dos Direitos Coletivos', 14 *Revista Brasileira de Ciências Sociais* 83.

—— (2000), 'Ministério Público e Corrupção Política em São Paulo' in MT Sadek (ed), *Justiça e Cidadania no Brasil* (São Paulo, Editora Sumaré).

Batista Cavalcanti, R (1999), *Cidadania e Acesso à Justiça* (São Paulo, Editora Sumaré).

Bayce, R (1996), *Informe Final Sobre Acceso a la Justicia* (Montevideo, Corte Suprema de la Nación).

Bell, DA (1994), *Lawyers and Citizens: The Making of a Political Elite in Old Regime France* (Oxford, Oxford University Press).

Brinks, D (2003), 'Informal Institutions and the Rule of Law: The Judicial Response to State Killings in Buenos Aires and São Paulo in the 1990s', 36 *Comparative Politics* 1.

—— (2008), *The Judicial Response to Police Violence in Latin America: Inequality and the Rule of Law* (New York, Cambridge University Press).

Cano, I (1999), 'O Papel da Justiça Militar na Investigação das Mortes de Civis Pela Polícia no Rio de Janeiro', 1 *Polícia e Sociedade Democrática* 1.

Cardia, NN, Adorno, S and Pinheiro, PS (1998), *Pesquisa Direitos Humanos e Democracia: Proposta de Intervenção na Formação de Profissionais do Judiciário, do Ministério Público e da Polícia no Estado de São Paulo, Brasil (Relatório Final)* (São Paulo, Núcleo de Estudos da Violência).

Chevigny, P (1995), *Edge of the Knife: Police Violence in the Americas* (New York, The New Press).

Dutil, C and Ragendorfer, R (1997), *La Bonaerense: Historia Criminal de la Policía de la Provincia de Buenos Aires* (Buenos Aires, Editorial Planeta).

Epp, C (2003), *The Rights Revolution* (Chicago, Ill, Chicago University Press).

Faria, JE (ed) (1988), *A Crise do Direito Numa Sociedade em Mudança* (Brasília, Editora Universidade de Brasilia).

—— (1994), 'Os Desafios do Judiciário', 21 *Revista USP* 46.

—— (1996), 'A Crise do Poder Judiciário no Brasil', 3 *Justiça e Democracia* 18.

FORES and Colegio de Abogados de Buenos Aires (1999), *Justicia y Desarrollo Económico (Trabajo Completo)* in CD-ROM with full report of investigation (Buenos Aires, Consejo Empresario Argentino).

Fucito, F (1997), 'El Perfil del Abogado en Ejercicio Profesional', *La Ley* 1997-E: 1568.

—— (1999), 'Abogados: Un Estudio Cuantitativo sobre los Abogados', *La Ley* 1999-E: 1032.

Garland, D (2001), *The Culture of Control: Crime and Social Order in Contemporary Society* (Chicago, Ill, University of Chicago Press).

Halliday, T and Karpik, L (eds) (1998), *Lawyers and the Rise of Western Political Liberalism: Europe and North America from the Eighteenth to Twentieth Centuries* (Oxford, Oxford University Press).

Helmke, G (2002), 'The Logic of Strategic Defection: Court–Executive Relations in Argentina under Dictatorship and Democracy', 96 *American Political Science Review* 291.

Hinton, M (2006), *The State on the Streets: Police and Politics in Argentina and Brazil* (London, Lynne Rienner Publishers).

Holston, J and Caldeira, TPR (1998), 'Democracy, Law and Violence: Disjunctions of Brazilian Citizenship' in F Aguero and J Stark (eds), *Fault Lines of Democracy in Post-Transition Latin America* (Coral Gables, Fl, North-South Center Press).

Karpik, L (1998), *French Lawyers: A Study in Collective Action, 1274 to 1994* (Oxford, Oxford University Press).

Larkins, CM (1998), 'The Judiciary and Delegative Democracy in Argentina', 31 *Comparative Politics* (July) 423.

Mainwaring, S (2006), 'The Crisis of Democratic Representation in the Andes', 17(3) *Journal of Democracy* 13.

—— Brinks, D and Pérez-Liñán, A (2001), 'Classifying Political Regimes in Latin America, 1945–1999', 36 *Studies in Comparative Development* (Spring) 37.

Mello de Camargo Ferraz, AA (ed) (1997), *Ministério Público: Instituição e Processo* (São Paulo, Editora Atlas SA).

Merryman, JH (1985), *The Civil Law Tradition: An Introduction to the Legal Systems of Western Europe and Latin America,* 2nd edn (Stanford, Cal, Stanford University Press).

Miller, J (2000), 'Evaluating the Argentine Supreme Court under Presidents Alfonsín and Menem (1983–1999)', 7 *Southwestern Journal of Law and Trade in the Americas* (Fall) 369.

Murilo de Carvalho, J (1997), *Lei, Justiça e Cidadania: Direitos, Vitimização e Cultura Política na Região Metropolitana do Rio de Janeiro* (Rio de Janeiro, Centro de Pesquisa e Documentação de História Contemporânea do Brasil, Fundaçao Getúlio Vargas).

O'Donnell, GA (1999), 'Polyarchies and the (Un)Rule of Law in Latin America: A Partial Conclusion' in JE Mendez, G O'Donnell and PS Pinheiro (eds), *The (Un)Rule of Law and the Underprivileged in Latin America* (Notre Dame, Ind, University of Notre Dame Press).

—— (2001), 'Democracy, Law and Comparative Politics', 36 *Studies in Comparative International Development* (Spring) 7.

—— Schmitter P and Whitehead L (eds) (1986), *Transitions from Authoritarian Rule* (Baltimore, Mld, Johns Hopkins University Press).

Paulina, I (1999), 'Queixe-Se Ao Promotor', *Veja* 16.

Pereira, A (2001), 'Virtual Legality: Authoritarian Legacies and the Reform of Military Justice in Brazil, the Southern Cone, and Mexico', 34 *Comparative Political Studies* 555.

Pereira da Silva, CA (1999), 'Novas Facetas da Atuação dos Promotores de Justiça: Um Estudo Sobre o Ministério Público e a Defesa dos Interesses Sociais', Doctoral Dissertation, Political Science, Universidade de São Paulo, São Paulo.

Prillaman, WC (2000), *The Judiciary and Democratic Decay in Latin America: Declining Confidence in the Rule of Law* (Westport, Conn, Praeger Publishers).

Scarponetti, P, Garay, Z, Méndez, M, Vivanco, A and Sorribas, P (2000), 'Desde la Ineptitud a la Corrupción ¿Qué Pasa con la Independencia del Poder Judicial?', *Ponencias del Congreso Nacional de Sociología Jurídica, 2–4 Noviembre de 2000* (La Plata, Buenos Aires, Universidad Nacional de La Plata).

——, ——, ——, —— and —— (2000), 'La Cultura Jurídica Interna y sus Posibilidades de Cambio, Frente a las Propuestas de Cambio Organizacional', *Ponencias del Congreso Nacional de Sociología Jurídica, 2–4 Noviembre de 2000* (La Plata, Buenos Aires, Universidad Nacional de La Plata).

Seligson, A (2002), 'When Democracies Elect Dictators: Motivations for and Impact of the Election of Former Authoritarians in Argentina and Bolivia', Doctoral Dissertation, Political Science, Cornell University, Ithaca, NY.

Skaar, E (2002), 'Judicial Independence: A Key to Justice—an Analysis of Latin America in the 1990s', Doctoral Dissertation, Political Science, University of California—Los Angeles, Los Angeles, Cal.

Verbitsky, H (1993), *Hacer la Corte: La Creación de un Poder Absoluto sin Justicia ni Control* (Buenos Aires, Ediciones Planeta).

Zaverucha, J (1999), 'Military Justice in the State of Pernambuco after the Brazilian Military Regime: An Authoritarian Legacy', 34(2) *Latin American Research Review* 43.

10

When the 'Political Complex' takes the Lead: The Configuration of a Moderate State in Chile

JAVIER A COUSO

I. INTRODUCTION

A DECADE AGO, IN their book on the role of lawyers in the rise of Western political liberalism, two of the editors of the present volume concluded by stating that the case studies contained in that volume had demonstrated that, historically, the basic elements of political liberalism have depended in various degrees on the action of the legal professions (Halliday and Karpik, 1997: 349). In this new project, which addresses the same issue in the context of a wider range of states (Western and non-Western, from the North and from the South, affluent and relatively poor), and with the help of a richer concept, the 'legal complex', the reader will find evidence that judiciaries, bar associations and legal academia have made important contributions to the emergence of state moderation and political liberalism throughout the world. These findings are significant, because they suggest that the legal complex has played an important role in furthering state moderation not only in countries with a long tradition of liberal thought and practice, but also in areas of the world which not long ago were deemed too different to adopt this political philosophy. The present chapter, however, deals with a country which seems to represent a deviant case in this regard, that is, one in which the legal complex was largely absent in the process of construction of a liberal political order, which was instead built around the 'political complex', that is, the practices and routines developed by interaction between the political party-system and the executive and legislative branches. The relevance of this particular case for the overall project is that the country in question, Chile, is a Latin American state often held as a successful model of political stability and adherence to the rule of law and political liberalism, thus providing an important counterpoint to the path followed by other countries (such as most Western European countries and the former colonies of the United Kingdom) where the legal complex, instead of being dragged toward political liberalism and state moderation by the political system, appears to have led the way to it.

The structure of the chapter is the following. First, there is a brief description of Chile's *political complex*. This is followed by a section tracing the historical emergence and main characteristics of Chile's legal complex. Then, the chapter analyses the way in which the legal complex reacted to the repressive regime led by General Augusto Pinochet, as well as with its aftermath. Finally, there is a section analysing whether or not the Chilean legal complex contributed to political liberalism and state moderation.

II. THE HISTORICAL TRAJECTORY AND CHARACTER OF CHILE'S POLITICAL COMPLEX

Bolivian sociologist René Zavaleta once said that Chile was the 'homeland of the state', meaning that this country has been defined by the centrality of its state (Zavaleta, 1974). Such characterisation coincides with that of historian Mario Góngora, who has persuasively argued that the state was the central force behind the construction of the Chilean nation, reversing a trend prevalent in other state-formation processes, where the nation was the entity which created the state (Góngora, 2003).Given this trajectory—and the closed relation between the modern state and legal forms—it should not be surprising to find that law has always played a rather fundamental role in this country, although not necessarily a liberal-enhancing one.

Like most countries in the American continent, Chile has a presidential-ist political regime, with a clear separation of powers between the three traditional branches of government. In terms of the actual performance of its political institutions, it is often celebrated as a successful example of democratic consolidation, after a 17-year-long military dictatorship. Such assessment can be found in a series of reports elaborated by non-governmental organisations such as The Freedom House,[1] Transparency International[2] and Human Rights Watch,[3] which have consistently ranked Chile among the top nations of the developing world in terms of clean and open democratic elections, respect for the rule of law, and relative lack of corruption in its public institutions. Furthermore, many students of Chile's

---

[1] See Freedom House, (2002).
[2] See Hodess, R (ed), (2003).
[3] In fact, Human Rights Watch recognised already in 1994 the remarkable improvement in the domain of respect for civil and political liberties in Chile:

> Under former President Aylwin's four-year 'transitional' administration, Chile took notable steps toward consolidating democracy, reestablishing civil and individual rights, and healing the wounds caused by decades of political strife and gross human rights violations under military rule.

See Human Rights Watch, (1994).

political economy point out that the high quality of its public institutions has been a critical factor underlying the remarkable economic performance of the country in the last decade and a half.[4]

Although most aspects of Chile's political complex are indeed worthy of praise, others fall short of the image of this country as a model of democracy and respect for the rule of law. This is the case with the poor record it exhibits concerning non-political speech (Human Rights Watch, 1998) and other liberal rights. These shortcomings, however, do not contradict the fact that in Chile there is quite a reasonable degree of government respect for the population's civil and political rights.

At this point, it should be noted that the consolidation of a moderate state in Chile cannot be accounted for without paying close attention to its history. Indeed, this country seems to fit rather well with path-dependence theories,[5] since some of the most prominent features underlying the moderate nature of its state institutions have deep historical roots, reflecting beneficial paths taken at critical junctures. The first historical factor that should be taken into account is Chile's relatively early completion of its process of state-formation, which was consolidated well before that of the rest of the former Spanish colonies in America, allowing the country gradually to introduce a working rule of law (Halperin-Donghi, 1993). In fact, as we shall see below, already by the mid-nineteenth century, Chile was widely perceived as the most successful of the newly independent Latin American republics. Such an accomplishment represented a surprise to most of its neighbouring countries, since Chile had been a rather backward region in colonial times which was nonetheless able to consolidate a stable political regime, while most of the new independent states of the region continued to struggle with anarchy, personalised rule, or even civil war for decades after their emancipation from colonial rule.

Although there is still controversy over what explains this early departure from the mainstream of the region, some have suggested that Chile's socially homogenous elite and relatively cohesive territory—which, at the time of its independence, was a 500 mile long strip of land spread between the Pacific Ocean and the Andes mountain range—enabled the new independent state to start the complicated effort of nation-building earlier and more successfully than other Latin American states, which were burdened by far less cohesive elites or by a larger geography (Collier and Sater, 1996; Bauer, 1975). While these features no doubt contributed to Chile's success in achieving political stability, there was an additional, critically important,

---

[4] Chile doubled its GDP in that period, while at the same time reducing the poverty rate inherited from the military regime from 45 per cent (in 1990) to 18 per cent (in 2004). See Ffrench-Davis (2004).

[5] Good works on path-dependence theory as applied to political analysis include Pierson (2000: 267) and Bridges (2000: 112).

factor: the early emergence of a tradition of de-personalised government, expressed in the strict respect by the most powerful office of the land (the executive power) of the limits set by the Constitution 1833 concerning the length of the presidential term.[6] This was all the more remarkable if we take into account that under the 1833 charter—which lasted until the early twentieth century, when it was replaced by the Constitution of 1925— (Guerra, 1929) the President concentrated an enormous amount of power, which effectively made him a 'monarch in republican robes', as it was once said. Indeed, in spite of the nominal existence of two other branches of government (Congress and the judiciary), during the first two to three decades since the introduction of the Constitution of 1833, the President ruled without any effective check, thanks to his power to select the members of the judiciary (even the justices of the Supreme Court), and through his manipulation of parliamentary elections, which gave him control of the legislative branch (Frühling, 1984).

In a development that still begs for an explanation, however, and in spite of the awesome power presidents had during their tenure, all the individuals who filled the presidential post after 1833 dutifully respected the rule preventing them from continuing in office after two consecutive five-year terms. Thus, each and every President who served during the period 1833–1924 felt compelled to give up their posts at the end of their terms, resisting the temptation to remain in power illegally, or to attempt to change the rules to their benefit. Although this may strike modern observers as a rather modest achievement, it nonetheless represented a truly remarkable accomplishment in the context of a region then characterised by personal rule and disregard for constitutional formalities, and struggling between the poles of anarchy and the rule of *caudillos* (strongmen).[7]

---

[6] The Constitution of 1833, which governed Chile's public law for almost 100 years—well into the twentieth century, until 1925—established a presidential term of five years, allowing for the reelection of the serving president. After the so-called *decenios* (decade-long terms), in which the first three presidents got 10-year terms, the constitution was eventually amended in order to prohibit the reelection of the presidents after their first five-year term, leading to a uninterrupted sequence of 11 five-year term presidents, from 1870 to 1925.

[7] Argentinean historian Tulio Halperin-Donghi stresses the fact that Chile's ability to combine political stability with depersonalised government became the source of attention—and even some envy—in Latin American intellectual circles, particularly among its neighbours:

> The Chilean government went on to acquire a depersonalized institutional stability that made it the envy of Spanish American intellectuals, especially those fleeing from Rosas (the Argentinean dictator). Young Argentine political refugees like Domingo Faustino Sarmiento and Juan Bautista Alberdi, who found newspapers, universities, and even occasionally the magistracy of conservative Chile open to them, became assiduous publicists of the Portalian order. Their idealized descriptions of Chile in the 1830s and 1840s, should be qualified, but they do reflect real achievements. Republican institutions quickly acquired a strength unheard of elsewhere in Spanish America.

See Halperin-Donghi (1993: 114).

The peaceful and regular transmission of the most powerful public office in time contributed to the emergence of a tradition of respect for other elements of the constitutional scheme which had been formally introduced by the 1833 Constitution, but not honoured in practice in the first two decades, such as the principle of the separation of powers. Thus, after some years of struggle to assert itself vis-à-vis the President, Congress eventually managed to become an effective check on the executive branch, a development which transformed Chile into a truly republican state, toward the mid-1860s.[8] The emergence of Congress as an effective check on presidential power provided the former with enough political salience to make the natural actors of legislative life (the Political parties) more relevant than ever before. Indeed, the new political context which emerged after the legislative branch asserted itself against the executive power represented an excellent breeding ground for the formation of a solid and competitive political party system, which later pushed to end the oligarchic nature of Chile's republican regime.[9]

Once established as crucial actors in the public sphere, the political parties made efforts to reach new social groups and then channel their grievances to the state apparatus, which in turn helped them gain even more relevance in Chile's social and political life. As a result of these processes, by the twentieth century the prominence achieved by the political parties in Chile was so overwhelming that it came to dominate much of what is now refer to as 'civil society' (ie, labour unions, non-governmental organisations, students' associations, and professional organisations).[10] Such politisation of society

---

[8] The new republican context was, however, not entirely assumed by the individuals elected to the presidency, which started to clash with the legislative branch over the boundaries of their respective powers. One of such conflicts eventually led to a civil war pitting the executive against the legislative branches, in 1891. After a short and bloody confrontation, the congressional forces eventually prevailed, inaugurating a 30-year period of congressional domination of the presidency. The impact of the new balance of power between executive and legislative branches further empowered the political parties as the central actors of the congressional politics. Although the de facto parliamentary regime came to an end 30 years later, when the Constitution of 1925 re-established a presidential regime, the final arrangement was a political regime in which Congress and the presidency had an equal standing, a setting which favoured the continuing protagonist role of political parties. For an account of Chile's civil war of 1891 see Vial (1981).

[9] The franchise was restricted to between 2 to 5 per cent of the adult male population for the first decades of the new republic: see Loveman (1988). The opening of the franchise to new social groups started first with the emerging middle class associated with the expansion of the state bureaucracy towards the turn of the century, spreading later to the working class constituted around the copper and nitrate industries and in the midst of the massive migration from countryside to the big cities in the first decades of the twentieth century.

[10] Arturo Valenzuela, in a groundbreaking work on the Chilean democratic system, describes the role of political parties in the country in the following way:

> Chile's party system was everywhere, not only determining the political recruitment process for important national posts but also structuring contests in such diverse institutions as government agencies, professional and industrial unions, neighborhood organizations, even local high schools.

See Valenzuela (1978: 3).

represents the downside of a political party system remarkable in its ability to channel the many conflicts experienced by Chilean society throughout its history as an independent state. Furthermore, the parliamentary arena—the preferred locus of party politics—infused in the political system a strong legalistic culture.

The configuration of a regime characterised by strong and disciplined political parties, which were deeply embedded in society and accustomed to dialogue and compromise among each other, provided an efficient tool for the management of the social turmoil which Chile's rapid industrialisation and urbanisation created in the first third of the twentieth century.[11] Party control of social movements was later enhanced by a political system which showed a remarkable ability to open the legislative branch to even the most radical parties, such as the Chilean Communist Party (Faúndez, 1988). The incorporation of parties representing the social labour movement to mainstream politics eventually contributed to the reduction of the pressure created by the great social inequalities which had given rise to them in the first place, through the gradual enactment of social reforms aimed at taming the most intolerable aspects of a very unequal society.[12] The institutionalisation of a political scheme in which social struggles were ultimately resolved by a process of dialogue and compromise among political parties contributed to the emergence of a fairly moderate regime (Moulian, 1993). Thus, it should not be very surprising that by the mid-twentieth century Chile was widely regarded as one of the most politically advanced liberal democracies in the world (Gil, 1966).

Although Chile's republican trajectory would be later interrupted by a rather brutal military regime, the fact remains that it enjoyed an almost uninterrupted republican rule for 140 years (from 1833 until 1973). Furthermore, the long-standing tradition of political stability and moderation which preceded the military coup of 11 September 1973 seems also to have been at work in the remarkably smooth process of re-democratisation which followed the defeat of the dictatorship in 1988. At the present time, although political parties remain central players in Chile's democratic system, their capacity to penetrate civil society has significantly declined, which in turn may explain the marked decline in party-affiliation among the population.

---

[11] The emergence of the so-called *cuestión social* (social question) in the first two decades of the twentieth century was at first dealt with by the government through police and military means, on occasion leading to the violent repression of strikers and their families. Eventually, however, the social demands of workers' organisations led to the expansion of the franchise and the creation of left-wing political parties who channel their demands through the formal political system.

[12] The most important institutional expression of this was the Constitution of 1925 (which replaced the century-old Constitution of 1833). This charter included a number of so-called *social rights*, such as the right to health care, to housing, to work, to education and so on. In the years following the passage of the constitution a number of labour protection statutes were approved, taming what until then had been an extremely orthodox liberal economic model.

Paralleling this trend, however, the larger *political complex* has become more rich and varied, thanks to the emergence of social organisations autonomous from the political parties which seek to influence public policy. Although this is still an incipient process, there are signs suggesting that in the near future the still solid political-party system of Chile will have to share its mediation of state–society relations with other groups (Rindefjäll, 2005).

To sum up this brief overview of the Chilean political complex, it can be said that—almost since its constitution as an independent state—Chile was able to institutionalise a state apparatus endowed with a political regime characterised by a reasonably de-personalised exercise of authority, which in time led to the configuration of an effective system of checks and balances, in which political parties became the key mediating bridge between civil society and the state.

III. CONSTITUTION, EVOLUTION AND CHARACTERISTICS OF CHILE'S LEGAL COMPLEX

Before describing the main aspects of Chile's *legal complex*, it may be helpful to note that, from a comparative law perspective, Chile is firmly rooted within what John Merryman famously called the 'civil law tradition' (Merryman, 1985). As in most countries belonging to this legal family, in Chile the source of the law is deemed to lie in written (positive) law,[13] with the 1855 Civil Code representing the paradigmatic example of it. As is also the case with other countries sharing this legal tradition, judicial precedent is not accepted as a valid source of law. This rejection of judge-made law comes from the influence that legal positivism had on Chile's foremost legal thinker—and drafter of its Civil Code—Andrés Bello, who already in the 1830s defended the notion that judges ought merely to apply the laws enacted by the sovereign power, instead of legislating themselves.[14] In consonance with this rather passive and mechanical role expected by the courts, Chilean judges have traditionally been extremely formalist in their adjudication, showing high deference to positive law, even if its mechanical application produces substantive injustice (Squella et al, 1994).

When it comes to analysing Chile's legal complex, the first complication is to date the time of its consolidation as a functionally autonomous domain. As we shall see below, this happened late in the process of state-formation. Indeed, although it is possible to identify institutions and actors bearing the same names we associate with the legal complex (such as courts or lawyers)

---

[13] Customary law is only allowed in commercial law, and only if it does not contradicts positive law.

[14] Bello's rejection of judicial precedent was also a result of having been a disciple of Jeremy Bentham, who among English jurists was notable for adherence to legal positivism. See Jaksic (2001).

well before emancipation from colonial rule, they had very little in common with what we now recognise as such. For example, although in colonial times there were bodies reminiscent of present day courts, they fulfilled both judicial and administrative tasks, working under the tight control and supervision of the central royal administration, all features which would shock contemporary notions of what a judicial body should look like.[15]

Something similar can be said of one of the other elements which constitute the legal complex, the legal academy. Indeed, although law teaching and writing dates back to colonial times—it was one of the few subjects taught at Chile's first higher education institution, the *Universidad Real de San Felipe*, introduced by the Crown in 1738—it lacked the professional orientation which would later contribute to the constitution of a legal academy properly speaking. In fact, law was then a discipline very much linked to philosophy and theology, and considered to offer a general intellectual training, not a professional one.

Finally, in the case of the bar, although it was first organised in the final decades of the colonial era, its status as a royal institution made it incapable of performing the defence of the corporate interest of lawyers and the liberalising role it had in other countries.

Given that during colonial times nothing like a legal complex was articulated, the task of forming one was left to the newly independent Republic of Chile, organised in 1818. Due to a series of factors that will be explained below in this chapter, however, the configuration of a legal complex took over a century to be completed, even though some of its elements were already in place in the second half of the nineteenth century. Starting with the judiciary, the crucial year was 1875, when it was able to attain a minimum of institutionalisation and autonomy from the executive power, thanks to the approval of the *Ley de Organización y Atribuciones de los Tribunales* (Law of Organisation of the Judiciary). In the case of the legal academy, its emergence and institutionalisation were made possible after the creation of the Law Faculty of the University of Chile (in 1860), which in turn contributed to the conformation of a critical mass of law teachers and commentators (Serrano, 1993). Finally, and regarding the last of the three basic actors which form the legal complex, the organised bar was introduced in 1925, after a series of failed attempts.

---

[15] As a student of the administrative structure of the Spanish empire overseas territories put it:

> [In the] Spanish imperial government ... There was never a clear-cut line of demarcation between the functions of various governmental agencies ... . On the contrary, a great deal of overlapping was deliberately fostered to prevent officials from unduly building personal prestige or engaging in corrupt or fraudulent practices.

See Sarfatti (1966: 30).

In order to have a better understanding of the Chilean legal complex, we now turn to the description of each of its basic elements.

(a) The Judiciary

Soon after the creation of the independent state of Chile, the authorities started to experiment with a series of constitutional charters aimed at organising the new republic.[16] In terms of the basic structure of the political regime, the model adopted was that of the United States of America, whose system of checks and balances was widely regarded as the most appropriate for Chile. In consonance with a separation of powers scheme, already in the Constitution of 1823, an autonomous Supreme Court was introduced.[17] In the following year, Congress aproved the *Reglamento de Administración de Justicia* (Regulation for the Administration of Justice), the first systematic attempt to regulate the functioning of the judiciary since the country's independence.[18]

At any rate, and in spite of the formal regulations established by the successive constitutional charters of the time, the political instability experienced by the country in its first decade and a half as an independent state made the judicial system an administrative mess. Judicial disarray was not, however, solely a function of political anarchy, but also the result of the disjunction between a system structured on a republican constitutional context but still working with colonial laws and procedures.[19] Indeed, for a number of decades after independence, the Chilean courts were left with the difficult task of administering justice under a complex mix of legislation,

---

[16] The constitutional charters were, in chronological order, the following: (a) *Reglamento Provisorio of August 14th 1811*; (b) *Convención of January 12th 1812*; (c) *Reglamento Constitucional of October 27th1812*; (d) *Reglamento para el Gobierno Provisorio of March 17th 1814*; (e) *Constitution of 1818*; (f) *Constitution of1822*; (g) *Constitution of 1823*; (f) *Constitution of 1826*; and (h) *Constitution of 1828*.

[17] The Supreme Court was then constitutionally recognised by Art 156 of the Constitution of 1823. Although this constitutional charter was derogated 2 years later, its clauses referring to the Supreme Court survived.

[18] The judicial clauses of the Constitutions of 1823 and 1828 continued in existence after the promulgation of the Constitution of 1833, as prescribed by Arts 2 and 3 transitorios of the latter. To the basic framework set up by these constitutional and legal norms we must add some minor reforms in 1843 and 1866. See Huneeus, 1880: 247).

[19] Edwin Borchard lists the following colonial laws as still having legal validity after independence of Chile. They include: (1) The ordinances and *Cédulas Reales'* (Royal Decrees) issued for America, and communicated by the *Consejo de Indias* (Council of the Indies) from May 1680 to the period of independence; (2) the *Recopilación de Leyes de Indias* (Collection of the Laws of the Indies); (3) The *Novísima Recopilación de Leyes de España* (New Collection of the Laws of Spain); (4) The *Leyes de Estilo* (Laws of Stylus); (5) The *Fuero Real* (The Royal Exemption); (6) The *Fuero Juzgo*; and (7) The *Siete Partidas*. See Borchard, 1917: 383, 385).

which included both laws enacted by the new republican authorities and colonial legislation.[20]

This chaotic scenario would only start to improve with the adoption of the Constitution of 1833, which for the first time introduced a measure of institutional stability in Chile. This new charter maintained the basic structure of the judiciary already set up by the constitutional charters of 1823 and 1828, adding a clause guaranteeing the non-interference of the other branches of government in judicial decisions. This provision, set out in Article 99 of the Constitution of 1833, declared that:

> The power to judge civil and criminal cases belongs exclusively to courts established by law. Neither the President of the Republic, nor Congress, can, in any case, exercise judicial functions, interfere with cases being tried by the courts, or review cases already decided by the courts.[21]

In spite of this solemn declaration, however, the judiciary maintained the same subordinated status it had had in colonial times, due to the power that the Constitution granted the President to nominate judges. The dependence of the judiciary on the executive branch would only end decades later (toward the 1870s), when Congress achieved enough institutional muscle to counterbalance the overwhelming political power of the President. Indeed, only after the legislative branch managed to gain itself enough autonomy from the executive, it eventually forced upon the latter legislation providing for the institutionalisation of the judiciary as a separate branch (Frühling, 1984). The incentive for Congress in this regard was the following: as the main body in charge of enacting legislation, it had a strong interest in making sure that the entities which would later adjudicate the laws of the land were impartial vis-à-vis the executive branch. This was accomplished through the already mentioned Law on Organisation of the Judiciary, which gave a systematic organisation and provided for continuing public funding to what had been until then a loose set of courts highly dependent on the executive branch, with poor territorial penetration, and lacking the professional staff characteristic of a modern judiciary (De Ramón, 1989).

---

[20] This appears to have been the same dilemma confronting the judiciary in other Spanish American countries. Indeed, as Jeremy Adelman's important work on the early republican era in Argentina shows, one of the reasons for the crisis in the justice system after independence derived from the clash between a new political regime centred around republican forms and rhetoric and a judicial sphere still anchored in the ways and forms of a radically different regime, absolutism, in which such cornerstone ideals of republicanism, such as equality before the law, did not exist. In fact, quite to the contrary, the legal and judicial practices under Spanish absolutism were premised on the critical role played by status in judicial procedures: see Adelman (1999).

[21] Transcribed from Huneeus, 1880: 235).

The next important step toward the constitution of a fully autonomous judiciary was the approval of the Constitution of 1925, which introduced a mechanism for the selection of judicial personnel where the top echelons of the judicial branch had a crucial role. The system consisted of the selection by the superior courts of a closed list of candidates which was only then presented to the executive power for its consideration. Although in the end the President decided who among those included in the list was to be appointed, he could only select names included by the courts, a process which greatly reduced presidential control of the judiciary.[22]

In its current form, the Chilean court system fits well with what Mirjan Damaska calls the 'hierarchical ideal of officialdom' (Damaska, 1986: 17). In consonance with this model, Chile's judiciary has a pyramid-like structure, with the Supreme Court holding tight control over lower courts. Also coinciding with Damaska's ideal-type, Chile's judicial branch is a highly disciplined bureaucratic body, in which personnel is recruited early in their professional life, and then spend the rest of their working lives slowly climbing the judicial hierarchy. The tight control exercised by the Supreme Court in every aspect of the work of the courts is particularly important concerning matters of judicial personnel, since the top court has the ultimate say in the processes of selection, evaluation and promotion of each of the members of Chile's judiciary. This feature reinforces the hierarchical nature of the Chilean judicial branch, which in turn reduces the 'internal independence' of judges—that is, their autonomy to rule without the fear of what their superior will think—who know that their chances of advancing their careers demands complete subordination to their superiors. One important consequence of this strong hierarchical control is that it creates powerful incentives in lower court judges to be deferential toward their superiors, an attitude which in turn contributes to a very conservative institutional culture in which judges are typically risk-averse, preferring the obscure and pacific professional life of a bureaucrat to the more challenging (but more risky) life of judges willing to engage in creative jurisprudence. In stark contrast with say, their Argentinean peers, the few Chilean judges who dare to break ranks with their superiors in jurisprudential matters soon get disciplined by the hierarchy (Hilbink, 2001).

---

[22] Although soon after the passing of the 1925 Constitution the authoritarian regime of Carlos Ibañez del Campo (1927–31) brutally intervened in the courts, the judiciary started a long lasting period of autonomy when democratic rule was reinstated in 1932 and which was fundamental for the constitution of its current character. However, this 'golden period' of professionalisation, institutional stability and independence from the political branches of government came at a price. The Chilean Supreme Court systematically refrain from actively using the power to declare legislation inapplicable which the Constitution of 1925 had given it. This period ended when the next authoritarian stage fell upon the country, in 1973, marking a new period of complete submission to the government.

While troublesome for the internal independence of courts and the development of a more responsive jurisprudence, the extremely hierarchical nature of the Chilean judiciary has, on the other hand, allowed it to develop a strong corporate identity and *esprit de corps*, which has in turn contributed to strengthening the external independence of the judiciary, that is, its autonomy in adjudicating vis-à-vis the other branches of government or powerful private interests. Indeed, the cohesion and corporate identity which characterise Chile's judicial branch allow judges—particularly those in the lower echelons of the hierarchy—to resist pressure from either the government or other powerful groups, with the confidence of having the support of the whole organisation behind them.

Confronted with the task of evaluating the impact that the judiciary has had in furthering political liberalism and state moderation in Chile, it should be noted that there are not enough historical data available to address this problem properly, at least with regard to the last decades of the nineteenth century and the first half of the twentieth century. This scarcity of historical evidence explains that while some scholars claim that (after its constitution as a fully autonomous branch in the 1870s) the judiciary did have a positive impact on the emergence of a liberal polity in the country,[23] others disagree.[24] The difficulty of assessing the role of the judiciary in moderating state behaviour in Chile is also apparent when one considers that, while constitutional law scholars have traditionally celebrated the liberalising role of the legal system, the revisionist social history which has emerged over the last two decades has emphasised the passivity of the courts during the dramatic instances of state repression of workers which characterised the first half of the twentieth century, leaving hundreds of workers dead or wounded (Centro de Investigaciones Diego Barros Arana and LOM Ediciones, 1998).

In the context of judicial passivity toward gross instances of state abuse, it was the political party system which eventually ended the conflict through the passage of social legislation aimed at improving, at least in part, the plight of Chile's emerging working class. Thus, in a dynamic which would characterise the rest of the twentieth century, the answer to social conflict came from political parties reaching compromises in the legislative arena, not from the courts.

The pattern of avoidance exhibited by the courts in the presence of conflicts with political ramifications was even more pronounced when the

---

[23] In the words of one of the handful of students of the historical evolution of the Chilean legal system, Hugo Frühling: '[t]he limitation on the presidential powers and the reaffirmation of the judicial role (that happened in the 1870s) went together with an enlargement of individual guarantees': see Frühling (1984:52).

[24] That was the assessment of Chile's foremost constitutional scholar of the nineteenth century, Jorge Huneeus (1880).

source of the problem was law itself. Indeed, due to the penetration which the ideology of the sovereignty of law had in the legal culture of Chilean judges,[25] the courts were typically passive in front of legislation undermining individual rights, as was the case with the so-called *Ley de Defensa Permanente de la Democracia* (Law of Permanent Defence of Democracy), passed in 1948, which outlawed the Chilean Communist Party under pressure from the United States.[26] This Bill was consistently upheld by the courts, until its derogation by Congress 10 years later. Something similar happened with the many national security laws approved throughout the twentieth century, aimed at controlling social unrest, which were also dealt with deference by the courts (Caffarena de Jiles, 1957). As these examples suggest, very rarely did the Chilean courts object to a law infringing constitutional rights, limiting themselves instead to checking the legality of administrative acts.

(b) The Organised Bar

The history of the bar in Chile started over 200 years ago, when a royal-sponsored iniciative created the *Colegio de Abogados* (Bar Association), the first organisation of lawyers in the country. In terms of its political impact, the fact that it was an institution created and tightly controlled by the Spanish Crown greatly reduced its liberalising potential. Then, with the collapse of the colonial era and the organisation of a new independent state, that first attempt to organise a bar association came to an end.

During the first decades of republican life, lawyers were few and isolated (Pérez Perdomo, 2004; De la Maza, 2002). As one of the few students of the legal profession in Chile has noted, this was a consequence of the mostly agrarian nature of the country's economy, which meant that the commercial sector was poorly developed, thus conspiring against the formation of a vibrant legal profession (Urzúa, 1992). Furthermore, the presence of a cohesive oligarchy which was able to exercise strong social control of its

---

[25] The ideology of judicial subordination to the law and its 'legitimate' source, the legislative power, had profound historical roots, dating back to the first decades of republican era. Indeed, as early as 1848 the Chilean Supreme Court, ruling on a petition to declare a law unconstitutional, explicitly declared that: 'no court has the prerogative of declaring any law promulgated after the introduction of the Constitution (of 1833) unconstitutional, depriving them through such declaration of their effects and legal force. Such a power, which by it own nature would be of a superior nature than that of the Legislator itself, since it could void its acts, does not exist in any tribunal whatsoever, according to our constitutional system. The supreme judgement of the Legislature, that the laws it passes are not in violation of the Constitution, leaves no doubt whatsoever about the matter.'
This statement by the Supreme Court was issued on 27 June 1848. See Huneeus (1880: 253).
[26] That was Law 8.987.

members also accounts for the small number of lawyers the country had at the time. In such a society conflict was dealt with by social control, not legal forms and lawyers. Another element which explains the insignificance of legal practice in Chile at the time was the small size of its state apparatus, a feature which started to change only toward the end of the nineteenth century.

Given the small numbers of lawyers at the time, it is not surprising that the first attempt to create a bar association (in 1862) was a resounding failure.[27] After that, it would take another half-century and the constitution of a substantial critical mass of lawyers until a new effort was made. Success came only after a long and gradual process, in which the creation of the first formal law firms (in 1905 and 1906) represented a crucial step. This development, complemented with the increase in the demand for lawyers which the expansion of the state apparatus brought about, eventually led to the inauguration of the first bar association in republican times -also labelled *Colegio de Abogados*- in 1925 (De la Maza, 2002: 14). By this point in history, the judiciary was fully organised and had already started to develop a strong corporate identity, and the legal academy had already acquired the shape that would characterise it until the end of the twentieth century. Although the bar association was meant to organise the members of what by then constituted a liberal profession, it got official state sponsorship in the form of a law recognising the *Colegio de Abogados* as the only bar association of the country. According to this regulation, only lawyers associated with the bar could legally exercise their profession. Moreover, the Bar Association was entrusted by law with the privilege of exercising the ethical control of the profession, which included the power to punish unprincipled lawyers by suspending or preventing them from the practice of law.

Even though there is a dearth of studies of the Chilean organised bar, it appears that (even during the twentieth century) it lacked the kind of autonomy necessary to play a role as a promoter of political liberalism. In fact, as was the case with other professional associations of the country, the organised bar was just another arena where the ubiquitous political parties competed against each other, which meant that the elections of the bar's board was organised along party lines. The partisan nature of the fight for control of the bar meant that its agenda was highly influenced by the political contingencies at any particular time, something which prevented this entity from developing a coherent agenda regarding the advancement of the rule of law.

The partisan nature of the Chilean bar was in fact so embedded in the organisation that it deepened during the political crisis which preceded the military coup of 1973, as well as during the military regime which

---

[27] The short-lived bar association was already dissolved by 1878 (De La Maza, 2002: 14).

followed it. Thus, during the tense three years of the Socialist administration of President Salvador Allende—in which the government on occasion overstepped its constitutional powers, which in turn led to a clash with the Supreme Court—[28] the bar could not agree upon a cohesive course of action, because it was profoundly divided along party lines.

Such inability to act coherently on behalf of the rule of law was again apparent during the first 10 years of the military dictatorship, when a bar almost completely under the control of supporters of General Pinochet threw itsr support behind a regime which represented the antithesis to Chile's old tradition of respect for at least the most basic elements of the rule of law. Continuing with this partisan pattern, only when the opposition to General Pinochet within the bar was able to rearticulate (around 1982–3) and eventually prevailed within its Board of Directors did it do something to oppose the patent violations of the rule of law characteristic of the military regime.

In the fifteen years since the return to democracy, although the politisation of the Bar has been less pronounced than in the previous decades, partisan politics have continued to play a role, which has prevented it from consolidating a strictly autonomous agenda.

(c) The Legal Academy

As stated previously in this chapter, university-level legal education started in Chile during the colonial era, with the incorporation of the *Universidad Real de San Felipe* in 1738. Law was one of the few subjects taught at the time, along with philosophy, theology, mathematics and medicine. As Serrano (1993) reports, legal education at the university was highly theoretical in nature, with a strong emphasis on Roman and Canon law, subjects consistent with the stated goal of training jurists, not litigantsGiven this reality, the teaching of the skills required by the actual practice of law was done by a separate entity, called *la Academia* (the academy). In any case, the fact that royal regulations required that individuals hold a university degree in order to practise law established a link between the university and the legal profession (Serrano, 1993: 168).

---

[28] Although Allende was a committed democrat, the narrow legislative space available to his government eventually led him to try to manipulate Chile's legal and constitutional framework in search of the opportunity to implement his radical programme of social and economic reform. This strategy was elaborated by Allende's top legal adviser, Eduardo Novoa Monreal, who introduced what came to be known as the *resquicios legales* (legal loopholes), which consisted in using long-forgotten legislation issued during a short-lived socialist regime in the 1930s, allowing the government to make what amounted to a de facto expropriation of privately owned industries just by executive decrees. This measure was later followed by Allende's refusal to order the prompt police enforcement of judicial injunctions against illegal takings of farms by radical groups , which in turn led to an unprecedented formal protest by the Supreme Court. See Faundez (2007).

With the demise of colonial rule, university-level legal education experienced a marked decline, amidst the process of organisation of the new republic which characterised the first decades of independent rule in the country. The disarray in which legal education was immersed during those years echoed the chaos experienced by the whole legal domain, where patches of colonial legislation survived amidst legislation approved by the newly independent state for many years. The decay of legal education would only end with the establishment of the University of Chile by the government in 1868. Indeed, thanks to the impulse created by the incorporation of this institution (the first university after independence), a vibrant debate started among jurists and public officials over the role of legal education. Whereas the few survivers of the old colonial university system wanted to reinstate the traditional education based on Roman, Canon, and Natural Law, Andrés Bello, Chile's foremost intellectual and the key jurist working on the drafting of the new Civil Code, disagreed profoundly, defending a radically different model of legal education, which, in his own words:

> Not only aims at the training of jurists, but also of men able to fulfill high functions in the (state) administration and in the legislature, and able to influence public opinion. Thus, not only trained in the strictly legal sciences, but also in the social and political ones, consistent with the new title of the section of the university which has been labelled 'Faculty of Law and Political Sciences'.[29]

Eventually, Bello's position prevailed, making the University of Chile a breeding ground for the country's most important jurists and practising lawyers, but also the place where most Chilean politicians got their university training.[30] Thanks to the boost which legal education received with the organisation of the Law Faculty of the Universidad de Chile, eventually the graduates from this school formed a sizable critical mass of legal academics, which in the last third of the nineteenth century started to produce a rather impressive intellectual production.[31] Later on, the legal academy consolidated with the gradual creation of new schools, starting with the introduction of the Law Faculty of the Catholic University of Chile (1889).

After this initial impulse, legal education progressed slowly, in terms both of quantity and quality. Concerning the former, it is interesting to note that for most of the twentieth century the number of law schools remained very low, reaching just five in 1980. From the point of view of quality, after a

---

[29] Andrés Bello, cited by Serrano (1993: 171).

[30] As Serrano put it: 'Lawyers became the prototype of the public man of the nineteenth century, because the state not only requiered bureacrats, but also ideologues capable of explaining the new political order'(Serrano. 1993: 177).

[31] Examples of such production include J Huneeus, *La Constitución ante el Congreso. Segunda i última parte* (Santiago, Imprenta de 'Los Tiempos', 1880), and M Carrasco Albano, *Comentarios Sobre la Constitución Política de 1833* (Valparaíso, Imprenta y Librería del Mercurio, 1858).

promising start the work of the legal academy experienced something of a decay during most of the twentieth century, due to the fact that the bulk of legal education was left to prestigious practising lawyers who spared some hours a week to teach one or two subjects in the law faculties. This scheme affected the quality of academic criticism of legislation and jurisprudence, since the overwhelming majority of the law professors were only part-time teachers and scholars, who were also highly conscious of the need to be careful in their criticism of the courts' jurisprudence, because they would have to argue cases in front of the very judges they criticised on academic grounds.

Quite ironically, the rather stagnant state of the Chilean legal academy would come to an end thanks to a policy decision made by the authoritarian regime of General Pinochet. This was the dramatic transformation of the country's higher education system implemented in the early 1980s by the neoconservative economic team of the regime, which allowed the private sector freely to open universities for the first time in the country's history (Lemaitre, 1990). The opening of a market for higher education led to a radical expansion of the number of law schools: from only five in 1980, to over 50 in 2004.[32] This proliferation of law schools eventually led to the gradual transformation of Chile's legal academy, due to the emergence of a critical mass of law professors whose only activity is legal teaching and research, something which by itself provoked an enormous change in legal education.[33] At this point it is important to note that before the proliferation of law schools and the emergence of a corpus of law professors solely dedicated to teaching law, the legal academy was reduced in Chile to a set of prominent practising lawyers who typically devoted a couple of hours a week to teaching and writing.[34] The trouble with this kind of law-teaching and writing was its amateurish nature, a characteristic which in turn prevented the legal academy from exercising a minimum of intellectual control on the quality of legislation and jurisprudence.[35] Such modest academic life did little to further or deepen political liberalism, as it has had in other latitudes through the denunciation of illiberal laws and jurisprudence.

In contrast to Chile's traditional legal academy, the one entering the scene since the 1980s resembles more that prevalent in developed nations of both

[32] Until 1981, the only law schools in the country were at: Universidad de Chile (1842); Universidad Católica de Santiago (1889); Universidad de Valparaiso (1911); Universidad Católica de Valparaiso (1928); and at Universidad de Concepción (1929).

[33] Among others, the following Law Schools now have full-time law teachers: Universidad Diego Portales, Universidad Adolfo Ibáñez; and Universidad de los Andes.

[34] In fact, the very reason most lawyers did teach law in that period was to enhance their law practice, due to the glamour associated with having a law teaching post. See Dezaley and Garth (2002).

[35] Indeed, criticism of the jurisprudential work of the courts has been traditionally scarce in Chile, due to the fact that the legal academy was composed of practising lawyers, who would have to appear before the same courts they commented upon in their academic work.

the common law and continental tradition, in which a set of full-time jurists exercise close control of the legislation and jurisprudence that parliaments and judges produce, through their academic work. Having said this, it is important to note that the transformation of Chile's legal academy is still an incipient process.

IV. THE CHILEAN LEGAL COMPLEX IN A TIME OF EXCEPTION (1973–90)

In the previous sections, we have characterised each of the elements of Chile's legal complex, in order to then evaluate their role in furthering political liberalism throughout the country's history. In this section, I address the way in which the legal complex dealt with the country's most tragic political episode of its independent history, the dictatorial regime led by General Augusto Pinochet, a period which for 17 years seemed to completely erase the long tradition of state moderation and political liberalism which the country had gradually constructed since the mid-nineteenth century.

The need to account for what appears as an anomaly in Chile's history stems from the sheer evil unleashed by the military coup which deposed president Salvador Allende on 11 September 1973. Indeed, in a sequence of events which is still the object of analysis by social scientists and historians (Stern, 2004), Pinochet's regime engaged in an unprecedented and shocking repression of dissidents, which included summary executions, 'dissapearences' and widespread torture. Such display of what Carlos Ninoonce called *radical evil* (Nino, 1996) cannot be dismissed as a mere accident in a study aimed at assessing the relationship between the legal complex and political liberalism in Chile.[36]

Given that the military coup of 1973 was directed against a Marxist President, at first the leaders of the coup emphasised the need to 'extirpate the Marxism from Chile', as one of the members of the military *Junta* put it at the time.[37] This rhetoric—which evidences the strong penetration of Cold War thinking among Chilean military men—provided the ideological backing to the systematic elimination of opponents that ensued.

In addition to the violent repression of opponents, the new government engaged in an institutional reshaping of the country which was unprecedented. In the words of a subtle observer writing at the time:

> Soon after the military coup, Congress was dissolved; a State of Siege was declared, suspending individual guarantees; municipal authorities were deposed, being replaced by municipal authorities designated by the Military Junta …

---

[36] Altough there had been a short autoritarian experience earlier in the 1920s (between the years 1927–31), that was nothing compared with the brutality which characterised the military regime led by General Pinochet.

[37] See *Decree Law* 77, 8 Oct 1973, quoted by Valenzuela (1991: 28).

Furthermore, the Constitutional Court was dissolved ..., all public employees were declared to be interim ..., with the exception of members of the judiciary and the *Contraloría General de la República* (Comptroller Office of the Republic), the political parties declared to be Marxist were dissolved, while the rest were declared to be in recess ... the universities were intervened by the Military Junta ..., the electoral register were declared void, and then incinerated .... The government passed a Law Decree authorizing the expulsion of individual from the national territory on political grounds ... elections within the unions were suspended, and the government adopted norms allowing it to deprive some political opponents of the Chilean nationality [Arriagada, 1974: 38-9].

As we can see from this dramatic description, the new regime adopted a 'take no prisoners' strategy, closing down or coopting any institution suspected of harbouring dissidence. Thus, for example, in its zeal to eradicate opposition, the regime took the extravagant measure of appointing military men to preside over each and all the universities of the nation.

Confronted with the radical rejection by the military of a republican tradition going back to the mid-nineteenth century, we face the following dilemma: How was it possible that a country could engage in the wholesale destruction of a century-old liberal tradition? What does the relative ease with which the military *Junta* managed to destroy Chilean democracy tell us about the true nature of the latter? What can we learn about the Chilean legal complex's relationship with political liberalism and state moderation from this dismal political experience?

These are hard questions to answer. In order to address them, it is useful to describe the way in which each of the elements of the Chilean legal complex reacted to the highly illiberal nature of the military regime.

Starting with the bar, the record of its role during the military regime shows very poor performance in advancing liberal values or moderating the many abuses of individual rights perpetrated by the government. Of course, a few individual lawyers did do a lot to defend human rights and to struggle for the return of democracy, but they did so in response to calls from the Catholic Church, which took the lead in the defence of the rights of the thousands of dissidents facing the repressive apparatus of the Chilean military regime.[38]

The bar's support of the military coup and its subsequent passivity vis-à-vis the gross human rights violations perpetrated by Pinochet's dictatorship reflect the lack of autonomy of a body then dominated by lawyers more

---

[38] The crucial role played by the Chilean Catholic Church in defending human rights during the military dictatorship was later recognised by a report of the Organisation of American States, which declared that:

In Chile, the work of defending the essential rights of individuals has, to a large extent, been possible because of the attitude of the Roman Catholic Church, which has taken the necessary measures for ensuring that this work can be carried on within its own structure.

See Organization of American States (1985: 241). See also Dezaley and Garth (2001).

concerned with their ties to the military regime than with the bar's formal commitment to the rule of law. This lack of autonomy from politics would continue when—toward the end of Pinochet's rule—the board of the bar turned to the control of lawyers representing the opposition parties, who then started to issue criticism of the abuses of the dictatorship. Such late-hour action, however, cannot be regarded as an instance of mobilisation in defence of liberalism by the Chilean organised bar, but instead as the natural consequence of the triumph within the bar association of lawyers belonging to the opposition to the military regime. In other words, the reversal of the Chilean bar's attitude toward the dictatorship reveals not the mobilisation of the legal complex on behalf of political liberalism, but rather the political capture by the opposition of a bar association which, throughout most of the military regime, showed no commitment to either liberalism or state moderation.[39] In the case of the few courageous lawyers who worked in defence of human rights during the military regime at the request of such an unlikely champion of political liberalism as the Catholic Church, they represented a tiny fraction of the country's bar who were completely alienated from it and who did not have any support from it.

If the role of the bar in fighting the abuses of the military regime was overall poor, that of the legal academy was even worse, since its political split along party lines meant that those academics who supported the military coup actively worked to expel their left-wing colleagues from the law schools—and soon after those of the centrist Christian Democratic Party, when this political group joined the opposition to Pinochet, (in 1974). The shocking behavior of an academic body which privileged partisan prejudice over loyalty to university values such as tolerance, freedom of thought, as well as liberal-constitutional principles, suggests that even before the military coup of 1973 the legal academy was extremely weak, lacking even the most basic cohesion around the basic features of the rule of law.

Finally, and going back to the role of the judiciary in dealing with Pinochet's dictatorship, it must be noted that ever since the day of the coup, the courts supported the military regime. Indeed, as Carlos Huneeus has noted, the close relationship between the judicial branch and the military started just days after the coup, when the new authorities recognised the

---

[39] The inability of the *Colegio de Abogados* to act as a truly autonomous body in defence of liberal values such as the rule of law and individual rights was in fact appalling. In the words of Ives Dezaley and Bryant Garth:

> Lawyers mainly supported the coup, and there was no autonomous human rights movement or discourse under which lawyers could gain any distance from politics. A petition circulated against the military coup in 1973, but it gained only twelve signatures.

See Dezaley and Garth, 2001: 358.

autonomy of the judicial branch.[40] Grateful for this decision by the military, the Supreme Court expressed its support to the new government in public, when its members attended the religious ceremony in which the *Junta* celebrated its triumph.[41]

The initial support expressed by the Chilean judiciary to the military regime established in 1973 would last for more than a decade into that repressive period, as it was established by an official report issued by the Organisation of American States in 1985, which in no ambiguous terms denounced the judicial system for its failure to protect human rights in Chile:

> During the period covered by this Report (1973–1985) the Judiciary in Chile has restricted its action in such a way that in many cases it has facilitated the transgressions of the Executive to the detriment of the rights of individuals (through) the renunciation by the Supreme Court of the exercise of the power of supervision of all courts operating in the territory of Chile, the merely formal application of the provisions issued by the government Junta and reluctance to carry out exhaustive investigations when what was involved was the verification of violations of human rights attributed to the security forces ... This serious self-limitation of the Supreme Court left persons who had been submitted to war-time military courts without recourse. The military court proceedings were characterised by extremely serious violations of the guarantees of due process.[42]

In this context of complacency vis-à-vis the military regime, the most serious failure of the Chilean judiciary was its unwillingness to respond to the thousands of habeas corpus writs filed by the relatives of political prisoners and the disappeared. The strongly hierarchical nature of Chile's judiciary—and the consequent weak internal independence of the judicial personnel in ranks located below the Supreme Court—ensured that the complacent attitude towards abuses of power by the authoritarian regime taken by the highest court of the country was followed by the lower courts. Crucial in this respect was the system of annual evaluation conducted by the superior courts of the lower judicial ranks, which allowed the Supreme Court throughout the military regime to discipline the few judges who dared to inquire into the

---

[40] Decree Law 1 stated: 'The Military Junta will guarantee the full efficacy of the faculties of the Judicial Power and will respect the constitution and the laws of the Republic, as far as the circumstances allows it': quoted in Huneeus, 2000: 110.

[41] See *ibid*, 230. Huneeus also notes that the public support of the Supreme Court was actually reiterated by the Court in the first public ceremony of 1974, when the Chief Justice of the Chilean Supreme Court, Enrique Urrutia, publicly expressed 'that in Chile human rights were being respected and denounced those who were voicing criticism of the state of public affairs in the country': *ibid*, 111.

[42] See Organisation of American States, 1985: 156–7. Adding insult to injury, some of the justices of the Supreme Court publicly complained that the enormous numbers of writs of habeas corpus overwhelming the courts were 'a nuisance' that was making it hard for the judicial branch to attend their regular business: see Matus, 1999: 248.

cases that the human rights groups persistently presented before the courts. True, on a few occasions a lower judge ventured into some of the human rights cases filed by the victims of disappearance, torture or exile, but by and large the Chilean judiciary ignored the gross human rights violation which characterised Pinochet's dictatorship.[43]

Even though the judiciary exhibited a rather appalling submission to what represented Chile's most violent regime in its history, in time it started to require the military regime to follow its own legislation. Such enforcement of existing legality—however authoritarian in nature—was consistent with the courts' traditional understanding of the rule of law which, contrary to liberal notions which include substantive fairness or constitutional values, was restricted to reminding political power of the need to obey its own norms.[44] This commitment with what constitutes a very thin notion of the rule of law (or, better said, rule by law), helped create what Robert Barros has labelled 'a dictatorship subject to rules' (Barros, 2000), a development which in time proved crucial to ending the dictatorship.

An example of the liberalising potential of even this weak form of the rule of law is the way in which the Chilean Constitutional Court dealt with a case which ultimately contributed to the demise of the authoritarian regime.

In 1981, the dictatorship had introduced a Constitutional Court endowed with the power of reviewing the constitutionality of bills approved by the government before their promulgation as laws. Of course, the notion of introducing such review in a dictatorial regime is odd, suggesting a facade rather than a genuine commitment to constitutionalism. In view of the important powers granted to the Constitutional Court, the military took great care in nominating jurists loyal to them. Thus, of the court's seven members, two were appointed by General Pinochet himself; two by the

---

[43] Among the few cases of which there is record of judicial concern for the fate of detainees by the military intelligence apparatus, the Supreme Court (defending its role during the dictatorship after the publication in 1991 of a report critical of its performance) mentioned its 10 March 1975 decision to 'prevent delays in the study of writs of habeas corpus' (although it did not specify what were those measures); a visit by then Chief Justice José María Eyzaguirre on 10 June 1976 to a couple of detention centres; the decision to investigate the circumstances surrounding the discovery of some human remains in 1978; and a discourse of the Chief Justice criticising a new criminal procedure code in 1979: see Huneeus, 2000: 113.

[44] Lisa Hilbink provides good examples of this. She writes that:

Freedom of expression and of the press was another area in which the courts did not allow the military government to stretch its own (limited) boundaries. For example, judges reminded the government that the Constitution prohibited prior censorship under a state of emergency (though it allowed it under a state of siege), and ruled that both the retraction of previous authorization for publication as well as the indefinite postponement of a decision on such authorization were unconstitutional. However, they also ruled that police harassment of journalists, in the form of covert infiltration of a reporting site, forced removal of journalists from a news scene, or seizure of journalistic equipment, did not constitute a violation of freedom of the press.

See Hilbink, 1999: 360.

government-controlled *Consejo de Seguridad Nacional* (National Security Council), and the other three by the Supreme Court, which—as we have seen—was sympathetic to the government. This appointment procedure ensured that each and every one of the members of the Constitutional Court was a supporter of the regime. The interesting element was, however, that four of its members did not belong to the judiciary, but were instead prestigious jurists with long years of experience in the practice of law and in academia. Such background would prove crucial later.

The case I am commenting on is Decision 33 of the Constitutional Court(issued on 3 October 1985), which dealt with a bill approved by the military *Junta* regulating a plebiscite which would take place in 1988, and which was set to confirm General Pinochet's rule as President of Chile for an additional term of eight years. The bill in question included a transitory clause prescribing that the Electoral Court would only start to function 'in the date of the first election of deputies and senators'.[45] That meant that the crucial plebiscite scheduled for 1988 would be held without an Electoral Court in place, something that would have allowed Pinochet to tamper with the election results, and which had no precedent in Chile's long democratic tradition.

In a dramatic four to three decision, the Court (led by Justice Eugenio Valenzuela, a prestigious lawyer with a vast experience in legal practice and law teaching) ruled that the bill under review was unconstitutional, because it did not allow for a clean and open election in the 1988 scheduled plebiscite. The surprising decision astonished the military regime. There, four lawyers with a long history of support for the military regime nonetheless ruled against it in a crucial matter.[46]

Confronted with this remarkable example of the liberalising potential of the legal complex, one has the impression that—more than a typical display of liberalism by a judicial body—the story of Chile's Constitutional Court in enhancing the return to democracy seems to represent the indirect influence of another aspect of the legal complex, that is, that of the legal culture working through a group of lawyer with professional integrity.

---

[45] The clause was Art 11, transitory of the Constitution of 1980.

[46] Robert Barros, commenting on this decision by the Tribunal Constitucional, writes:

Undoubtedly, the courts' 24 September 1985 ruling on the organic constitutional law regulating the Tribunal Calificador de Elecciones (TRICEL), the special electoral court, was the most consequential. The court struck as unconstitutional a transitory article that left oversight of the presidential plebiscite to an ad hoc electoral court and ruled not only that this plebiscite had to be supervised by the TRICEL but that the full electoral system specified in the main body of the text had to be in place for the plebiscite. This meant that the plebiscite would be constitutional only if it took place with electoral registries and independent oversight and counting. Like all of the court's rulings, this decision was final and not subject to appeal.

See Barros, 2000: 27–8.

To sum up this section on the role played by the Chilean legal complex in the most trying times in Chile history, Pinochet's dictatorship, we can conclude that its performance was at best poor. In fact, it is an indictment of the latter that the historically conservative Catholic Church did much more to further state moderation and political liberalism than the lawyers who were members of the bar, the judiciary or the academia.

V. THE RECOVERY OF POLITICAL LIBERALISM AND THE LEGAL COMPLEX (1990–2006)

The defeat of General Pinochet in the plebiscite of 1988 inaugurated a period of gradual recovery of Chile's liberal-democratic tradition, which, it can be argued, has only recently been completed, after the approval in 2005 of a constitutional reform that finally eliminated a set of 'authoritarian enclaves' left by the military regime's Constitution of 1980 (Garretón, 1999). Important elements of this reencounter of the Chilean political system with its long democratic tradition were the steps taken by the centre-left coalition which has ruled since 1990 to deal with the legacy of the unprecedented human rights violations perpetrated by the dictatorship (Zalaquett, 2000; Wilde, 1999).

In this transitional process towards accountability and full democratic recovery the driving force was—as in the past—the political party system and the executive and legislative branches, not the legal complex. Actually, as we shall see below, on occasion the legal complex worked against liberal democracy.

An important example of the liberalising role of the political complex in the aftermath of Pinochet's dictatorship was the introduction by the first democratic administration of Patricio Aylwin of a non-partisan commission in charge of investigating the circumstances surrounding the widespread human rights violations under the military regime. This commission, called the Truth and Reconciliation Commission (also known as the 'Rettig Commission') was introduced in 1990 as a response to the refusal of the judiciary to nullify an amnesty law inherited from the military regime which gave impunity to the perpetrators of gross human rights violations during Pinochet's dictatorship.[47] Although the Rettig Commission was not allowed to identify perpetrators or to press charges against them, it at least provided the first chance to establish the truth about what had happened during the military regime in relation to the human rights of dissidents. Furthermore, after the Report was issued (in 1991) the government proposed and got congressional approval of legislation aimed at compensating the victims. Finally, President Aylwin concluded his attempt to end impunity by publicly

---

[47] For an account of this process see Cavallo, A (1998).

requesting the courts to end their refusal to investigate human rights cases that have been amnestied.

While this process developed the legal complex was all but absent. Even though many of government initiatives eventually required legal assistance and advice, neither the bar nor the legal academy did much to address this fundamental issue in the early years of the transition. Even worse, the other component of the legal complex, the judiciary, reacted with anger to some of these initiatives, particularly when the Rettig Report issued a very critical assessment of the poor performance of the Chilean judicial branch during the military regime.[48] This corporate defence of its passivity exhibited by the judiciary during the military dictatorship eventually led the way to a gradual shift in the court's interpretation of the Amnesty Law (a statute passed by the military regime to protect their own people against criminal lawsuits for past human rights violations), in the direction of ending the impunity enjoyed by those who had been involved in the disappearances and illegal executions during the dictatorship. Although some socio-legal scholars have held this remarkable change in the courts' jurisprudence with regard to the Amnesty Law as an expression of a supposedly more liberal ethos of the new justices of the Supreme Court, it is more likely that this change reflected the will of the judiciary to be more in line with the prevalent social and political views with regard to this issue. In other words, the shift we have sketched does not represent an instance of judicially-triggered political liberalism, but instead the adjustment of the courts to a new political context.

The same conclusion applies to the handling by the Chilean courts of its most famous human rights case, that affecting General Pinochet himself. The political context just outlined explains why by October of 1998—seven years into the new democratic regime—Pinochet had remained untouched by legal actions against him. This inertia would, however, dramatically

---

[48] Confronted with such strong criticism of its performance during the military regime, the Supreme Court reacted, issuing a complete condemnation of the report, stating that it was 'passionate, reckless, and biased', and arguing that the Rettig Commission had concurred in an unacceptable intromission in adjudicative matters. Given the complete dismissal by the Supreme Court of the non-partisan Truth and Reconciliation Commission, President Patricio Aylwin rebuffed the judicial response by going on national television to declare that in his view the Chilean courts 'had shown a lack of moral courage in face of the vast human rights violation perpetrated by the military regime'. Unimpressed, the Supreme Court reacted by accusing the government of undermining the judiciary's independence and endangering the rule of law, while defending its trajectory during the military regime by declaring that the mission of the courts was just to obey the existing law, and not judge the justice or injustice of it which, in the case of its action under the authoritarian regime meant that they limited themselves to applying laws that made it impossible for the courts to defend human rights. Hiding under a supposedly strict adherence to legal positivism understood as a mechanical application of existing law, without concerning themselves with the fairness of it, the Supreme Court, sitting en banc, repudiated what they regarded as an 'attack on the independence and honor of the judiciary': see Correa, 1999: 281–315.

change in the most unexpected way, when General Pinochet was arrested by the British authorities in London in response to an extradition petition issued by a Spanish judge attempting to try him for crimes against humanity. The decision by the UK to arrest a foreigner for crimes committed in a third country stunned the legal community throughout the world and completely changed the social and political dynamic concerning Pinochet's impunity in Chile, eventually led to the loss of his senatorial immunity against prosecution and the subsequent filing of hundreds of criminal cases filed against the former dictator (Davis, 2003), a process which was only stopped by the natural death of the general on 10 December 2006.

VI. CONCLUSION

After describing the main characteristics of Chile's 'political complex', and analysing the historical evolution of the legal complex (including its response to the military regime of 1973–90 and its aftermath), I now turn to the assessment of the role played by it in furthering political liberalism and state moderation in Chile. Put in simple terms: can we say that Chile's legal complex contributed to the rise of political liberalism and a moderate state?

The answer to this question is twofold. On the one hand, the historical evidence shows that only rarely did the actors we identify with the legal complex—the courts, the bar and the legal academy—contribute to further political liberalism and state moderation in Chile. On the other hand, on occasion at least some elements of the legal complex took advantage of openings made possible by the political complex, and worked in support of political liberalism.

Another element which helps understand the dynamic of the emergence of state moderation and political liberalism in Chile is the fact that there the introduction of an effective system of checks and balances (a central aspect of political liberalism) not only preceded the configuration of the legal complex, but it actually contributed to its emergence, thanks to the creation of a truly independent judicial branch by Congress in 1875. Indeed, the configuration (toward the mid-nineteenth century) of a solid and competitive political party system in need of an impartial executioner of the deals and compromises reached in the parliamentary setting, eventually led Congress to force upon the President a law organising a truly autonomous judicial branch. Such a move was functional with the configuration that the Chilean political complex had acquired at the time, characterised by the channelling of social grievances to the state apparatus through the political-party system, which was also in charge of providing resolution to those through compromises expressed in the promulgation of statutory law. In this scheme, given that law represented the most solemn way in which political deals and compromises expressed themselves in, the expected role of the courts was that of impartial implementers of such formalised agreements among political parties. This explains the obsession exhibited by the Chilean judiciary with preserving its traditional deference to positive law, even after they were given powers of judicial review of the constitutionality of legislation. All the above suggests that the reasonable degree of individual freedom which Chileans have enjoyed during most of the last 150 years is largely a consequence of the limits which the country's vibrant political party system imposed upon the executive power.

Having said this, there are signs that things have started to change in recent years, to the point that it seems that at least portions of the legal complex—in particular the legal academy—appear to have acquired an unprecedented degree of autonomy from the political complex and a will more assertively to defend the basic tenets of political liberalism. If this trend continues, it could in time inspire the other elements of Chile's legal complex (the bar and the judiciary) to follow a similar path, something which in turn could be critically important if the country wants to avoid in the future the kind of brutal state repression characteristic of dictatorial regimes.

REFERENCES

Adelman, J (1999), *Republic of Capital. Buenos Aires and the Legal Transformation of the Atlantic World* (Stanford, Cal, Stanford University Press).

Arriagada, G (1974), *De la Vía Chilena a la Vía Insurreccional* (Santiago, Editorial del Pacífico).

Barros, R (2000), 'Dictatorship and the Rule of Law: Rules and Military Power in Pinochet's Chile', paper prepared for the *Conference on Democracy and the Rule of Law', Centro de Estudios Avanzados en Ciencias Sociales*, Instituto Juan March, (Madrid, 22–24 June).

Bauer, A Jr (1975), *Chilean Rural Society from Spanish Conquest to 1930* (Cambridge, Cambridge University Press).

Borchard, E (1917), *Guide to the Law and Legal Literature of Argentina, Brazil and Chile* (Washington, DC, Library of Congress).

Bridges, A (2000), 'Path Dependence, Sequence, History, Theory', 14(1) *Studies in American Political Development* 109.

Caffarena de Jiles, E (1957), *El recurso de amparo frente a los regímenes de emergencia* (Santiago, Imprenta San Francisco).

Carrasco Albano, M (1858), *Comentarios Sobre la Constitución Política de 1833* (Valparaíso, Imprenta y Librería del Mercurio).

Cavallo, A (1998), *La Historia Oculta de la Transición: Memoria de una época, 1990–1998* (Santiago, Editorial Grijalbo).

Centro de Investigaciones Diego Barros Arana y LOM Ediciones (1998), *A 90 años de los sucesos de la Escuela Santa María de Iquique* (Santiago, Universidad Arturo Prat de Iquique & Lom Ediciones).

Collier, S and Sater, W (1996), *A History of Chile: 1808–1994* (New York & Cambridge, Cambridge University Press).

Correa, J (1999), 'La Cenicienta se queda en la fiesta: El poder judicial chileno en la década de los 90' in P Drake and I Jaksic (eds), *El modelo chileno: Democracia y desarrollo en los noventa* (Santiago, LOM Ediciones).

Damaska, M (1986), *The Faces of Justice and State Authority. A Comparative Approach to the Legal Process* (New Haven, Conn, and London, Yale University Press).

Davis, M (2003), *The Pinochet Case: Origins, Progress and Implications* (London, ILAS).

De la Maza, I (2002), 'Los abogados en Chile: Desde el Estado al Mercado', 10 *Informe de Investigación* (Santiago, Facultad de Derecho de la Universidad Diego Portales).

De Ramón, A (1989), 'La Justicia Chilena Entre 1875 y 1924' in *Cuadernos de Análisis Jurídicos*, Vol 12 (Santiago, Chile, Editorial de la Universidad Diego Portales).

Dezaley, I and Garth, B (2001), 'Constructing Law Out of Power. Investing in Human Rights as an Alternative Political Startegy' in A Sarat and S Scheingold (eds), *Cause Lawyering and the State in a Global Era* (Oxford and New York, Oxford University Press).

—— and —— (2002), *The Internationalization of Palace Wars* (Chicago, Ill, and London, University of Chicago Press).

Facultad de Derecho de la Universidad Diego Portales (2004), *Informe Anual sobre la situación de Derechos Humanos en Chile 2004. Hechos del 2003* (Santiago, Ediciones Universidad Diego Portales).

Faúndez, J (1988), *Marxism and Democracy in Chile* (New Haven, Conn, Yale University Press).

—— (2007), *Democratization, Development and Legality: Chile 1831–1973* (Cambrige, Cambridge University Press, forthcoming).

Ffrench-Davis, R (2004), *Entre el neoliberalismo y el crecimiento con equidad: tres décadas de política económica en Chile* (Mexico City, Editorial Siglo XXI).

Freedom House (2002), *Freedom in the World 2001–2002* (New York, Transaction Publishers).

Frühling, H (1984), *Law in Society: Social Transformation and the Crisis of Law in Chile, 1830–1970*, PhD dissertation, Cambridge, Mass, Harvard University School of Law.

Garretón, MA (1999), 'Chile 1997–1998: the Revenge of Incomplete Democratization', 75 *International Affairs* 259.

Gil, F (1966), *Instituciones y Desarrollo Político de América Latina* (Buenos Aires, Banco Interamericano de Desarrollo).

Góngora, M (2003), *Ensayo histórico sobre la noción de Estado en Chile en los siglos XIX y XX* (Santiago, Editorial Universitaria).

Guerra, JG (1929), *La Constitución de 1925* (Santiago, Anales de la Universidad de Chile).

Halliday, T and Karpik, L (1997), 'Postscript: Lawyers, Political Liberalism and Globalization' in T Halliday and L Karpik (eds), *Lawyers and the Rise of Western Political Liberalism. Europe and North America from the Eighteen to Twentieth Centuries* (Oxford, Clarendon Press).

Halperin-Donghi, T (1993), *The Contemporary History of Latin America* (Durham, NC, Duke University Press).

Hilbink, L (1999), *Legalism Against Democracy: The Political Role of the Judiciary in Chile, 1964–1994,* PhD thesis, San Diego, Cal, University of California, San Diego.

—— (2001), 'Judges like Soldiers: Lessons for Judicial Reformers from the Literature on Military Reform in Latin America', paper delivered at the Annual Meeting of the American Political Science Association (APSA) San Francisco, 30 August–2 September.

Hodess, R (ed) (2003), *The Global Corruption Report* (Berlin, Transparency International).

Human Rights Watch (1994), *Unsettled Business. Human Rights in Chile at the Start of the Frei Presidency* (New York, HRW).

—— (1998), *The Limits of Tolerance. Freedom of Expression and the Public Debate in Chile* (New York, HRW).

Huneeus, C (2000), *El Régimen de Pinochet* (Santiago, Editorial Sudamericana).

Huneeus, J (1880), *La Constitución ante el Congreso. Segunda i última parte* (Santiago, Imprenta de 'Los Tiempos').

Jaksic, I (2001), *Andrés Bello: Scholarship and Nation-Building in Nineteenth-Century Latin America* (Cambridge, Cambridge University Press).

Lemaitre, MJ (ed) (1990), *La educación superior en Chile: un sistema en transición* (Santiago, FLACSO/CEP/CPU).

Loveman, B (1988), *Chile. The Legacy of Hispanic Capitalism* (New York and Oxford, Oxford University Press).

Matus, A (1999), *El Libro Negro de la Justicia Chilena* (Buenos Aires, Editorial Planeta).

Merryman, JH (1985), *The Civil Law Tradition* (Stanford, Cal, Stanford University Press).

Moulian, T (1993), *La forja de ilusiones: el sistema de partidos 1932–1973* (Santiago, FLACSO/ARCIS).

Nino, C (1996), *Radical Evil on Trial* (New Haven, Conn, Yale University Press).

Organisation of American States (1985), *Report on the Situation of Human Rights in Chile* (Washington, DC, General Secretariat, Organisation of American States).

Pérez Perdomo, R (2004), *Los Abogados de América Latina. Una Introducción Histórica* (Bogotá, Universidad Externado de Colombia).

Pierson, P (2000), 'Path Dependence, Increasing Returns, and the Study of Politics', 94(2) *American Political Science Review* 251.

Rindefjäll, T (2005), *Democracy beyond the Ballot Box: Citizen Participation and Social Rights in post-Transition Chile* (Lund, Lund Political Studies).

Sarfatti, M (1966), *Spanish Bureaucratic-Patrimonialism in America* (Berkeley, Cal, Institute of International Studies of the University of California at Berkeley).

Serrano, S (1993), *Universidad y Nación. Chile en el Siglo XIX* (Santiago, Editorial Universitaria).

Squella, A, Peña, C, Correa, J and Ruiz-Tagle, P (1994), *Evolución de la Cultura Jurídica Chilena* (Santiago, Corporación de Promoción Universitaria).

Stern, SJ (2004), *Remembering Pinochet's Chile: On the Eve of London 1998* (Durham, NC, Duke University Press).

Urzúa, R (1992), 'La profesión de abogado y el desarrollo: antecedentes para un estudio' in G Figueroa (ed), *Derecho y Sociedad* (Santiago, Corporación de Promoción Universitaria).

Valenzuela, A (1978), *The Breakdown of Democratic Regimes: Chile* (Baltimore, Mld, Johns Hopkins University Press).

—— (1991), 'The Military in Power: The Consolidation of One-Man Rule' in P Drake and I Jaksic (eds), *The Struggle For Democracy in Chile* (Lincoln, Neb, and London, University of Nebraska Press).

Vial, G (1981), *Historia de Chile* (Santiago, Santillana del Pacífico).

Wilde, A (1999), 'Irruptions of Memory: Expressive Politics in Chile's Transition to Democracy', 31 *Journal of Latin American Studies* 473.

Zalaquett, J (2000), 'La Mesa de Diálogo sobre Derechos Humanos y el proceso de transición política en Chile', 79 *Estudios Públicos* (Winter) 5.

Zavaleta, R (1974), *El Poder Dual* (Mexico, Editorial Siglo XXI).

11

Lawyers and Political Liberalism in Venezuela[1]

ROGELIO PEREZ PERDOMO

A S THIS ARTICLE is written, three well-known jurists are facing trial
in Venezuela: Cecilia Sosa, Allan Brewer Carias and Carlos Ayala
Corao. Sosa was the first female President of the Supreme Court of
Justice and former director of the Centre for Legal Studies at the Catholic
University Andres Bello. Brewer Carias is probably the internationally best
known Venezuelan jurist and former director of the Public Law Institute
at the Central University of Venezuela. Ayala Corao has been president of
the Inter-American Commission of Human Rights and is professor at the
Metropolitan University. All three are well known as legal scholars. They
have been accused of conspiracy in the attempted coup d'état that ousted,
for a short period of time, President Hugo Chávez, and that for a few hours
dissolved the National Assembly and the Supreme Court of Justice. Could
three distinguished jurists be implicated in an act so contrary to the constitution? If not, how can one make sense of the charges they face?

This chapter looks at this matter from a general perspective, trying to
explain the political role of the lawyers who are considered, in the field
of law, to be the intellectual elite of Venezuela, and analyse their relation
to political liberalism. We accept the definition of *political liberalism* in
terms of a moderate state that guarantees fundamental individual freedoms
(Halliday and Karpik, 2002, and the statement at the basis of this volume).
This is a notion clearly close to that of the *rule of law*, in the sense that the
rule of law imposes a check on state officials, defining their authority and
distributing their responsibilities in such a way that the power of some will
act to balance the power of others. The traditional expression was *constitutional government*, wherein government leaders are subject to a constitution that distributes powers, and enumerates and guarantees citizens' rights.

[1] I thank M Feeley, T Halliday, M Gómez and H Njaim for comments on early drafts. I also
thank A Ross and S Lemke for the English version.

The term *political liberalism* has the advantage of not requiring that the political project it promotes be fully realised. Thus, it is possible for liberal political groups to exist, even groups with access to power, in a country that does not function according to the rule of law or as a constitutional government.

One of the recurrent characteristics of the Venezuelan political system has been the predominance of the strong man who has governed the country with little attention to the constitutional and legal limits of his own power. The regimes where these strong men predominated could be identified as illiberal (Zakaria, 2003) and certainly do not fit into the model of political liberalism built in this volume. Soriano (1996) and other Venezuelan historians have proposed characterising as *political personalism* the regimes where the predominance of strong men weakens the power of the constitution and laws to frame the limits of political life. The term was proposed to avoid the debate over whether political leaders with great popular support, who have attained power through elections, should be defined as dictators. Political personalism would be the reverse of political liberalism.

Illiberal or personalist politics have not been a permanent characteristic of Venezuelan politics. In fact, in the twentieth century, the periods 1936–45 and 1958–98 were democratically stable, respectful of basic constitutional principles, even though we cannot say that everybody's rights were respected. In these periods, which span half a century, the regime's politics were closer to political liberalism in the sense that the Constitution, the Supreme Court and other courts moderate the exercise of power, the opposition and basic freedoms were guaranteed to people able to pay for lawyers.

One durable characteristic of Venezuela in the nineteenth and twentieth centuries was the importance of lawyers. They had a significant presence in the ministerial cabinets, parliaments and other organisations of government (Pérez Perdomo, 1981). Lawyers were also renowned public figures, making their opinions known through the media, and at times becoming part of the opposition, when allowed. The preeminence of lawyers was notable in liberal as well as personalist regimes. In the period 1958–98 the most politically liberal of Venezuela history, three of the six elected presidents were lawyers and two others law students who abandoned university studies because of political persecution.

This chapter first focuses on analysing the traditional role of lawyers in personalist regimes. The reason for this focus lies in the fact that lawyers, since the beginning of independence, were educated in the virtues of the constitutional government. Law school classes such as constitutional or administrative law have been dedicated to studying the characteristics and limits of public powers, the principle of legality and, in general, the submission of the functions of state to legal principles and rules. But despite this intellectual foundation, lawyers cooperated with personalist regimes that had little respect for the rule of law. The cooperation of lawyers, especially from

those who have a special distinction for being law professors or legal scholars, should be considered a dissonance that needs explanation. At issue in
this inquiry is how it is possible for distinguished lawyers, conscious of the
importance of the constitution and the virtues of the rule of law, to become
collaborators of dictators in the unravelling of constitutional government.

In the first years of the twenty-first century, under the presidency of Hugo
Chávez, Venezuela is living through a political revolution. The nature of
the change has been a subject of intense controversy among the Venezuelan
people and among analysts. However, it is beyond dispute that the regime
seeks the complete control of all powers by the President and perhaps the
erection of a socialist society, rather than strict compliance with the law and
the constitution. Its policies have affected important interests of business
and, more generally, the law of property. The political opposition eroded
systematically until the point where there is no opposition representative in
the National Assembly.

Secondly, this chapter will analyse how a group of lawyers have used the
judicial system or their own status as prominent jurists to resist the regime.
This is a new development in the political history of Venezuela, and we will
ask why it is happening now but not during previous personalist regimes.

I. LIBERALISM, THE STATE AND LAWYERS IN THE VENEZUELAN TRADITION

In Venezuela, as in other Latin American countries, the meaning of 'liberal'
in the nineteenth and beginning of the twentieth century had a resonance
that is distinct from the political liberalism that we discuss here (Pérez
Perdomo, 1991). Exploring this meaning briefly is indispensable to a better
understanding of lawyers' traditional role in the political system.

Spain, with which Latin American countries had colonial relationships
until the beginning of the nineteenth century, was an absolutist theocracy.
All political power was concentrated under the monarch, and he governed
by the grace of God. The Catholic Church was not separate from the monarchy. By virtue of patronage, the King was an elector of the bishops, and
the Church itself was an apparatus of public power that exercised important
economic, educational and police functions in addition to the spiritual ones
we consider today as the religious sphere. Independence posed the huge
difficulty of redefining the relationship between religion and politics. The
new states (or the new rulers) were the legal successors of the monarchy in
that they had sovereign power over what were colonial countries. In that
sense, they wished to exercise the power of control over the church based
on patronage, but clearly the rulers could not pretend that their power
came directly from God. At least theoretically, their power came from the
will of the people. Moreover, the new states were apparatuses with scanty

resources and weak social roots: they had neither a significant number of functionaries (civil servants) nor the resources to create civil and military institutions, while the church had a more stable bureaucratic apparatus and very substantial resources in its productive real estate.

As a result of independence, two groups or political parties emerged: the liberals and the conservatives. The conservatives were worried about maintaining order, and they saw the church as an ally towards this end. The liberals, on the other hand, saw the church as a significant obstacle to the freedom and modernisation of the country. The way to control and diminish the role of the church was to take away its functions, depriving it of its properties, and strengthening the state. Liberals in that sense were pro-state. In Venezuela, the liberals' dominance started in 1870 and the Catholic Church since then has lost most of its political and economic power. The weakening of the Catholic Church led to the loss of the sense of historical rivalry between liberals and conservatives. In fact, the liberal party and the conservatives ceased to exist. In the Venezuelan political vocabulary of the twentieth century, the expression *liberal* took on a connotation related to economic policy.

After independence, the study of law was reformed so as to correspond with the new function of educating the political elite. For this reason, the legal curriculum focused on constitutional law, administrative law, public international law, and principles of legislation. Disciplines such as political economy, which were considered useful in the formation of high civil servants, were also included. In fact, the top positions of the state tended to be filled by lawyers. Because there was not sufficient economic activity to support a true legal profession, the expectation of a recent college graduate in law was to find an appropriate position within the government. At the same time, because lawyers came from the upper social strata and were thought to have the knowledge required to run the state, low bureaucratic positions were inappropriate for them. The occupation as a lawyer was not lucrative during the nineteenth century and beginning of the twentieth and was a way to disguise a period of political disgrace or unemployment. As Gaitán Bohórquez (2002) pointed out in the case of Colombia, lawyers were *hosts of the state*. Although there were some conservative lawyers, especially immediately after independence, lawyers were mainly liberals (or pro-state) because of their association with the state. Because of their educational background it can be presumed they were in favour of the rule of law.

Holding an important job in the state apparatus posed several challenges for lawyers. Throughout the nineteenth century there were constant civil wars and the stability of the state was precarious (Pérez Perdomo, 1990). The *caudillos*, non-professional military leaders, controlled politics. Because lawyers felt obliged to involve themselves in politics, they inevitably collaborated with the *caudillos*. But in the first third of the twentieth century, lawyers allied themselves with the leaders who managed to defeat the *caudillos*.

These leaders consolidated their power over national politics and became know as the Andean dictators.[2]

Lawyers were temperamentally and professionally drawn to statecraft, so it was essential for them to reach agreement with those who held political power. For their part, the rulers—personalist, *caudillo* or dictator—needed the services of lawyers to lend their regimes the appearance of legality. Governing, after all, requires the drafting of laws, decrees, administrative acts, contracts and international treaties. For all these matters, lawyers were indispensable, especially for any ruler with a limited political culture and poor grasp of the intricacies of the law.

But just because lawyers and rulers enjoyed a symbiotic relationship did not mean either that their political behaviour followed the rule of law, or that the law provided only a thin decoration to cover actions that were in fact taken without any consideration of constitutional limits. The actual role of law and of lawyers adapted over time in response to changing situations: the balance of power within a given regime, the character of a given leader and the legitimacy of the constitutional and legal order.

Venezuela, like the rest of the countries of Latin America, faced serious difficulties in constructing a viable state in the early stages of independence. The power of the king came directly from God and the people who governed in the king's name were peninsular Spaniards. Independence removed from the scene not just the king but also his envoys who had managed the government. The town councils, or *cabildos*, were the only infrastructure of government that remained. They were important in the independence movement, but the bloody war that ensued practically eliminated the elites that had controlled the *cabildos*. The constitutions that followed this period did not satisfy the political appetites of the *caudillos*. As a result, with the exception of certain periods of relative stability, rebellion was the common way to participate in politics, and the constitution was merely the document to be rewritten according to the political times. The result: an important but subordinated role for jurists.

In 1899, the triumph of the 'liberal restoration' gave rise to the period of the so-called Andean dictators. This period, especially during the leadership of General Juan Vicente Gomez (1909–27), is very important because it ended the civil wars, unified political power, and the government gained control of the national territory. Gomez also left behind the image of the authoritarian and cruel ruler. Contemporary revisionist accounts of Gomez's regime do not deny his authoritarian government, but they point out that he surrounded himself with very distinguished intellectuals (Segnini, 1987), allowed for debate within the elite, and gave great attention to the creation

---

[2] Testimony to how that relation was produced can be seen in the Memoirs of Pedro Manuel Arcaya, one of the great jurists between the end of the 19th century and beginning of the 20th (Arcaya, 1983).

of legislation (Capriles, 1991). In sum, he was a 'liberal tyrant' (Caballero, 1993), who protected foreign property and investment, and established security and clear rules for the economic game.

Among his most important collaborators were Jose Gil Fortoul (1861–1943) and Pedro Manuel Arcaya (1874–1958), jurists and historians of recognised importance. Gil Fortoul was a diplomat, senator, minister, and acting President of the Republic when Gómez engaged in a military campaign (1913–14). Arcaya was a justice of the Federal Court, Attorney General, President of Congress, and Minister of Internal Affairs and Justice. Gil Fortoul (1890) was the author of *Constitutional Philosophy*, which reveals familiarity with the political philosophy and constitutional law of the time. Arcaya (1935) offers a detailed analysis of the Gómez political regime, in addition to numerous legal and historic works.

On the other hand, Gómez's regime was characterised by the severe treatment of prisoners, especially political prisoners. Torture, used as a means to obtain political information or simply as a way to punish opponents, has been well documented (Pocaterra, 1973, 1990; Pino Iturrieta, 1998). What motivated such distinguished jurists to cooperate with a regime that violated the proclaimed rights that they wrote in the national constitutions?

Situating their action in an epoch is important. Arcaya and Gil Fortoul had lived through the period of the civil wars of the second half of the nineteenth century. For them, Gómez was the country's pacifier, the promoter of peace and material progress. The feared alternative was to go back to the prior anarchy. Perhaps they knew of the prisons and the institutionalised torture,[3] but these negative aspects were no reason to deny the positive balance. Human rights were not an important consideration at the time. Not every lawyer supported Gómez, and many lawyers kept their distance because of the drastic methods he used to maintain order, and the limited play he allowed for legality and freedom. Some of them found refuge in the newly professional practice to keep themselves away from politics (ie Carlos Mendoza, in Pérez Perdomo, 1981: 394). Others were more daring: a work such as *Civilizacion y barbarie* (Salas, 1919) can be understood as an indirect criticism of Gómez's regime at a time when open opposition could have had huge personal costs. With some exceptions, lawyers were the collaborators of illiberal regimes.

---

[3] Arcaya (1935: 197) refers to criticisms of the Gomez regime, which identified him as a tyrant and pointed to the cruel treatment in the prisons. He explains that such criticisms were made up by Gomez's adversaries. According to Arcaya Gómez did not execute the people that rebelled against him and released them after a time in prison. On the other hand, Arcaya shows the positive balance of the pacification and the prosperity of the country, despite the world crisis that had recently existed at the time. This situation makes a contrast with Arcaya's memories of the long gone civil wars. For Gil Fortoul's praises to Gómez see the section 'discursos y palabras' from his Obras Completas (volume 5) (Gil Fortoul, 1956).

From 1936 onwards, political life followed constitutional channels and the governments could be considered moderate, except for the period 1945–57, which was one of political turbulence, followed by Pérez Jiménez's dictatorship (1952–7). Several important jurists collaborated with the dictatorship and no lawyer dared to use the legal system to oppose the government.

II. CHÁVEZ'S REGIME AND THE JURISTS

In 1998, the electoral triumph of Hugo Chávez marked a significant change within the modern Venezuelan political system. Since 1958, there had been a system that in the 1970s was seen as a model of democratic stability, while other Latin American countries were suffering under severe military dictatorships. In the 1990s, the main political parties had accumulated such a reputation for inefficiency and corruption that the Venezuelan people chose an outsider for President. Lieutenant Colonel Hugo Chávez had attempted a coup d'état in 1992 that was a military failure but a political success, in that it left the impression he was dedicated to ending the corruption, inefficiency and lack of personal security that had characterised the politics of the time. He promised a new beginning—to reestablish the republic by enacting a new constitution.

By means of consecutive referenda, the Venezuelan people gave him a blank cheque to call a constitutional assembly and approve a new constitution, which declared many rights and liberties and, at the same time, concentrated political power in the hands of the president. It established a multi-functional role for referenda. The subjacent model is a type of direct democracy with direct communication between the leader-President and the people (Njain, 2005). With these new instruments, Chávez has driven the republic to a close alliance with Cuba and several revolutionary groups in other countries, and hads initiated a movement that he and his party members call the socialism of the twenty-first century.

In practice, Chávez's regime borrows many elements from the nineteenth century, such as constant references to Bolivar and the liberal *caudillos*. The frequent conflicts with the Catholic Church and the seizure of rural properties are also vestiges of the nineteenth century. The regime also has twentieth century elements such as the extensive use of television as a means of communication, the use by the opposition of violent groups of people wearing red shirts to create nuisances at rallies, the occupation of empty urban properties and 'unproductive' factories. It also features innovative elements such as electronic voting machines, using programming code that is not in the public domain, and the use of the legal system and tribunals to harass the opposition.

The regime controls the National Assembly, the Supreme Court of Justice, the National Electoral Council, and all other public offices, but it allows a considerable, albeit decreasing, amount of freedom to the media and a certain amount of economic freedom. The regime has used law to grant Chávez great powers in these arenas and restrict freedoms. For example, the new legislation on social responsibility of the media has restricted television stations in transmitting news in which violence is shown under the rationale of children protection. Defamation legislation has been specially strengthened to protect public functionaries. A reform of the Penal Code has broadened and strengthened the punishment of political activity. In sum, the regime has many authoritarian characteristics and is not a representative democracy. The model is neither political liberalism, nor rule of law government.

What have been lawyers' reactions? Venezuela has about 100,000 lawyers (370 per 100,000 people) and, as in any society, there are lawyers for all political tendencies. On counting lawyers in Venezuela, it is important to note that a lawyer is simply anyone who has a registered law degree. No bar examination is required. Perhaps half or fewer of those with a registered title are lawyers who actually practise law. Additionally, there are about 40,000 law students, which guarantees that the number of lawyers will increase in future years and that there is a market for law books and legal journals.

Practising Venezuelan lawyers are grouped in professional bar associations called *colegios de abogados*. There is a *colegio* in every important city (especially in every state capital). Membership of a *colegio* is obligatory in order to practise law. There is also an entity in charge of coordinating the *colegios* called the *Federación de Colegio de Abogados*.

Neither the federation nor the *colegios* have played a politically important role. During the period of two-party democracy, the *colegios* were the battlefield for the political parties, but political control did not yield any advantage to the parties because the *colegios* did not play an important social role. Most probably, the *colegios'* governing boards are split politically, like the rest of Venezuelan society, but during the Chávez's years, the Caracas Bar Association—*Colegio de Abogados de Caracas*—the most populous and important of the country, has been controlled by lawyers from the opposition parties.[4] However, it has not played a role opposing (or supporting) the regime. To act against an authoritarian government is not an easy decision. As the state apparatus and an important part of the economy are controlled by the government, bar associations and many lawyers prefer to take a back seat in opposing the regime. Another explanation is that, giving the bar associations' lack of social prestige, it is probably not easy for them to catch the public eye.

---

[4] In the election of November 2005 two thirds voted for the opposition lists in the *Colegio de Abogados* of Caracas (Linares Benzo, 2005).

The practice of law has an intellectual elite made up of those who are university law professors and write articles in academic journals. Frequently, they are interviewed by the media on law-related political problems or they write opinion and editorial articles. We are interested in studying that group in particular because they are the ones who are more politically active and have opposed Chávez in the name of the law. Moreover, because the country has had a change in its constitution, and new laws of political importance have been passed, the members of this elite group have a professional responsibility to express themselves and take part in public debates.

There has not yet been a study of the legal publications and the positions taken by Venezuelan jurists in relation to Chávez' revolution. As a hypothesis, the works fall into two distinct periods. Because the new constitution was passed in 1999, analytical works published during 2000 and 2002 have focused on explaining and analysing the new role of the Supreme Court of Justice and other aspects of the new constitution. Since 2003, the publications have become more critical of the Chávez regime itself.

Along with scholarly production, there have been judicial claims and decisions that have attracted the attention of the media. For instance, when the municipal government of Caracas signed an agreement that allowed Cuban physicians to give medical assistance in Venezuela, the Medical Federation— the professional organisation of medical doctors—sought a court order paralysing the deal before the administrative high court (*Corte Primera de lo Contencioso Administrativo*). The court ruled by a majority vote that the agreement was illegal because it violated the Law on the Practice of Medicine. But the Politico Administrative Chamber of the Supreme Court of Justice overturned the decision, thus allowing Cuban physicians to practise medicine in Venezuela. As a backdrop to this legal dispute there was a political conflict. In each court, one could easily identify the judges willing to decide in favour of or against the government. Many political actions by the regime have generated significant legal battles.

The regime has taken action to ensure that judges were on its side. For instance, judges from the Administrative High Court, which tended to rule against the government, were dismissed, and the courthouse was occupied by the police for several months.[5]

The Supreme Court had serious internal disagreements, which prompted the publication of a new Supreme Court Organic Law (2004) that increased the number of justices, and provided for their appointment by a simple

---

[5] The Administrative High Court was occupied by the police because of an investigation into judges' corruption, but they were later dismissed for other reasons. In the end, none of the magistrates were tried for corruption and one of the magistrates was dismissed for signing the decision that, according to the Supreme Court, showed lack of knowledge of the law, was appointed justice of the Supreme Court. She was pro-government.

majority in the National Assembly (packing the Court). When the statute was published (in May 2004), the President of the Academy of Political Sciences (a distinguished senior lawyer himself), several law deans and well known law professors went to the Supreme Court and filed an unconstitutional action against the statue (Various Authors, 2004). This was a public act with the senior jurists crossing a line of soldiers who were 'protecting' the Supreme Court for the occasion. There was vast media coverage. The Constitutional Chamber never took any action on this case.

Several justices were pressured to retire and by December 2004, half of the justices were newly appointed by Chávez' people and the Supreme Court was solid on Chávez' side. The Supreme Court, which controls and supervises the judiciary, has overseen a purge of judges: about 500, or approximately a third, of the country's judges were dismissed. Although a variety of reasons were given for these dismissals, one imagines that a number of them reflect the government's lack of political confidence in certain judges, or an effort to punish judges for decisions that inconvenienced the government (Pérez Perdomo, 2005).

Lawyers who requested judicial nullification of a governmental act or attempted to stop such acts beforehand were aware that they might find themselves appearing before judges who could be fearful or partisans of the government, and that their demands were not likely to be given impartial consideration. When lawyers found judges ready to rule in their favour, they knew that, ultimately, the government had in place the mechanisms to block the ruling. Some lawyers have gone to international organisations and, occasionally, obtained favourable decisions from entities such as the Inter-American Commission of Human Rights and Inter-American Court of Human Rights, but these decisions have had little effect within the country.[6] Judges who ruled against the government knew that at the very least their jobs were in jeopardy. Their actions raise the question of how we can explain conduct that appears contrary to pragmatic rationality.

The answer lies in the expressive value of judicial actions. Lawyers who take such actions know that their stand is going to be noted in the news media and that it is going to be seen as an act of opposition to a government that has paid little attention to matters of legality. Certainly, legal action is a way publicly to declare opposition using the instruments of law, but the effect is not much different from a public protest featuring shouts of opposition to the government. Their motivations can vary. Many of those

---

[6] Both the Inter-American Court and Commission on Human Rights have ruled giving protection to several journalists, journals and television stations, ordering the government to act in accordance. The government has taken no action, but the rulings could have restrained it in the use of mobs to intimidate journalists. Intimidation has proceeded through the use of 'legal' means such as tax revisions, regulatory red tape and stiff legal sanctions for 'untrue' news or information on violent acts.

who assume such positions probably do it to affirm their legal values, and others simply to obtain public notoriety. But their protests must also be seen as an instrument of political opposition and require a good deal of courage. The judges who risk their positions engage in the same type of protest, but from a higher podium.[7]

As for the effects of this chapter, motivations do not matter. What matters is that this kind of judicial activity did not happen under similar political circumstances in Venezuela 50 years ago. Between 1945 and 1958, Venezuela was run by successive regimes from opposing sides of the political spectrum, but all of them violated the constitution and the rule of law. We have found no evidence in newspapers or in documents from the old Supreme Court—*Corte Federal y de Casación* at that time—that the legal system as been used, as it is now, as an instrument of opposition and defiance. Surely at that time there were lawyers who wished to promote their legal values, to participate in the political opposition, or simply to seek publicity for themselves, but they did not use the legal system as a means to express their opposition.

What has changed? One possible lawyer's answer is that the law has changed. Neither in 1945 nor in 1957 was there in Venezuela the *recurso de amparo*, nor had administrative and constitutional law developed enough to provide lawyers with the instruments to act. A lawyer who wanted to ask for protection against the actions of the 1945 Junta de Gobierno, or against the 1952 electoral fraud, or against the despicable actions by the National Security, would not have had adequate legal instruments to do so. He (there were very few women lawyers at that time) also would not have been able to complain to the Inter-American Commission of Human Rights or Inter-American Court of Human Rights because they did not exist.[8]

A sociolegal historian would attempt to explain the differences in lawyers' actions by pointing to the changes in the legal culture, the evolving social situation of the profession, and social changes in general. Around 1950, there were about 2,000 lawyers in Venezuela, and in occupational terms they functioned as arms of the state. Practising law independently was not very profitable, except for those who had a personal connection to businessmen. Because businesses were fundamentally connected to the state, any public political opposition meant professional suicide. It could also mean literal suicide, given the methods of repression at the time.

---

[7] Several lawyers who defend politically persecuted people or take constitutional and administrative action against the government have attained a kind of celebrity status. Judges' presence in the news tends to be more ephemeral. Perhaps the only exception is judge Monica Fernández who was dismissed or pressured to retire but became very active in an NGO (Foro Penal Venezolano) that monitors the use of courts for political persecution.

[8] The American Declaration of Human Rights was approved by the Organisation of American States in 1948, but the Commission and the Court started later and did not attain political importance until the 1980s.

In 2005 Venezuela, there are about 100,000 lawyers, and although many lawyers are still civil servant, lawyers are not identified mainly as hosts of the state but as servicing clients from the civil society. An act of public opposition, such as signing a petition to recall President Hugo Chávez or introducing a sanction against a ruling by the National Electoral Council, will make it impossible for a lawyer to hold a job in the public sector. But there are other job opportunities—in law firms, private companies or non-governmental organisations.

In the last 40 years of party democracy, lawyers became used to pursuing *amparos*[9] or other actions against the government, and, progressively, the Venezuelan adapted to these types of actions. In the 1990s, most of the significant public decisions were challenged in the courts. The Supreme Court obliged the government to change policies on mining and other matters. Even in 1999, the Supreme Court obliged Chavez to change the terms of the referendum on the reform of the Constitution. Since 2000, the conditions of the profession have become more difficult, but for lawyers there remains the habit or professional culture of using the law as a means to fight actions that are apparently against the constitution or the law. This new mentality on the part of lawyers may be even more important than the changes in law and legislation, although certainly they go together: the law changed because there was a progressive change of mentality, and at the same time the change in the law made easier the adoption of the new mentality.

Who were the actors? The lawyers willing to pursue judicial actions against government, against governmental organisations, or against government related agencies are numerous. Many do it within their 'regular' practice, for instance, representing oil workers who were fired on a large scale from the state's petroleum company as a result of the 2002 strike, or landowners who are seeking protection against an illegal occupation of an agricultural estate or an urban building. Although a case of this type may appear to be strictly professional, a pro-government lawyer will not take a case that will force him to confront the government's policies, because he or she will find herself subject to criticism for not remaining fully faithful to the revolution. Under these circumstances, to act as a lawyer against the government in politically related cases, even if the political relevance is minimal, the lawyer must be willing to be identified with the opposition.

There are also lawyers who are more specialised in politically related cases, such as those whose practice often entails seeking the nullification of a law, a decree or decision made by the National Electoral Council or a government agency. These lawyers act in their own name, as citizens, or as representatives of political parties or non-governmental organisations. These actions receive good media coverage and the lawyers involved have become political personalities who are interviewed in the press, radio and television.

---

[9] An *amparo* is an injuction paralysing any act about to infringe a constitutional right.

Finally, there are lawyers who do not necessarily practise before the tribunals, but instead express their opinion in the media or in public speeches detailing the unconstitutionality or illegality of the government's actions. Especially noteworthy has been the activity of law professors, especially law school deans, and the president of the Political Science Academy, who have given public statements or press conferences, which have generally been received as important news. They act individually, using scholarly publication, media opinion articles and interviews and public lectures, to state their positions, or collectively, giving a press conference or signing a legal petition to the Supreme Court. Some scholarly associations, like the association of professors of constitutional and administrative law, have been active in promoting protest documents.

III. THE EMPIRE'S COUNTERATTACK

Fifty years ago, those who opposed a dictatorship did not use the legal system and the government did not use it either. Gómez and Pérez Jiménez put their opponents directly in prison or forced labour camps as a means of repression, without establishing a penal process to do it. Of course, there were judges and tribunals, but they did not intervene in politically sensitive cases. Pedro Manuel Arcaya, an eminent jurist and also one of the most prominent intellectuals in Gómez's regime, could defend his actions as impartial and proper (Arcaya, 1983:87 ff) because they were not linked with the dirty work of Gómez's government. The legal system stayed at the margin of politics.

Hugo Chávez's government made extra-legal attempts to frighten the media and the opposition in 2001 and 2002, when armed *círculos bolivarianos* and the Bolivian Liberation Army were created, but soon Chávez realised that these groups had little effect, were opposed by many of his own supporters, as well as diminishing the international prestige of the government.[10] At present the strategy seems to have been abandoned. Instead, the government pretends to play according to the legal rules subjecting an increased number of people to criminal investigations on various charges. The strategy has led to the prosecution of several journalists and military personnel.

An example of legal persecution is the case of Súmate, an ONG specialised in electoral matters that has enormously helped the opposition in monitoring electoral processes and has pointed up important irregularities. As

---

[10] Some *círculos bolivarianos* were armed gangs that attacked journalists, newspapers, television stations or opposition demonstrations. When these groups acted, the police and the army stayed on the sidelines. They are now out of view, if they still exist. Now the government has a semi-military corps (*reservistas*) ready to enter into action if needed, but they are more disciplined and there is a known commander. On the other hand, there are people ready to squat or take over factories, but they are presented as spontaneous revolutionary people.

Súmate received US $50.000 from the National Endowment for Democracy (a foundation funded by the US Congress to promote democracy in the world), Súmate's leaders were indicted for treason, a grave felony under the Venezuelan Penal Code.

This strategy requires an increased control of the judicial system, especially over judges and the Public Ministry, and their increasing role in repression. This is not the place to touch on this matter, but the increasing numbers of journalists, retired military personnel, lawyers, human right activists, people of non-governmental organisations and political parties that have been tried, or are being tried, are a reflection of these policies. The international human rights organisations have been concerned with the repressive use of the judicial process.[11]

The criminal charges against the jurists mentioned at the beginning of this chapter are an example. Ayala Corao, Brewer Carías and Sosa are vocal members of the opposition. They have dedicated themselves to shedding light on the violations of the constitutional norms and human rights. They have written scholarly articles in law journals, but, more important in the eyes of the government, they have frequently appeared in the newspapers and on talk programmes in radio and television. Their relationship with the attempted coup d'état of 2002 is weak, if any, but this does not deter the prosecutors. There has been a reaction from law professors, including law professors' associations, and international organisations of jurists, but the bar associations have stayed silent.

In their trials, the issues and the evidence do not seem very relevant. To make a criminal case is a way to neutralise them, surely forcing them to exile themselves in order to avoid prison. To make them look like supporters of an intended coup d'état is a way to keep them silent: the purpose is to take away their legitimacy in speaking out in the name of the law.

REFERENCES

Arcaya, PM (1935), *Venezuela y su actual régimen* (Washington, DC, The Sun Printing Office).
—— (1983), *Memorias del doctor Pedro Manuel Arcaya* (Caracas, Librería Historia).
Caballero, M (1993), *Gómez, el tirano liberal. Vida y muerte del siglo XIX* (Caracas, Monte Ávila).
Capriles, R (1991), *Los negocios de Román Delgado Chalbaud* (Caracas, Academia Nacional de la Historia).

---

[11] As an example we take into account press releases from Human Rights Watch dated 8 July 2005: 'Court orders trial of civil society leaders'; 5 Apr 2005: 'Rights lawyer faces judicial persecution'; 24 Mar 2005: 'Curbs free expression tightened', all available at www.hrw.org, 05.11.05).

Gaitán Bohórquez, J (2002), *Huestes de Estado. La formación universitaria de los juristas en los comienzos del Estado colombiano* (Bogotá, Universidad del Rosario).

Gil Fortoul, J (1890), *Filosofía constitucional* (republished in *Obras Completas*, vol IV, 1956; Caracas, Ministerio de Educación).

—— (1956), *Obras completas* (Caracas, Ministerio de Educación).

Halliday, T and Karpik, L (1997), 'Politics Matter: a Comparative Theory of Lawyers in the Making of Political Liberalism' in T Halliday and L Karpik (eds), *Lawyers and the Western political liberalism* (Oxford, Clarendon Press).

Linares Benzo, G (2005), 'El Colegio de Abogados', *El Universal*, 20 November 2005, Caracas.

Njaim, H (2005), 'Democracia directa y autoritarianismo en la Constitución de 1999 y en la práctica política', Membership Lecture, Academia Nacional de Ciencias Políticas y Sociales, Caracas (not published).

Pérez Perdomo, R (1981), *Los abogados en Venezuela* (Caracas, Monte Ávila).

—— (1990), 'La organización del estado en el siglo XIX (1830–1899)', 14 *Politeia*, 349.

—— (1991), 'Liberalismo y derecho en el siglo XIX de América Latina', XX(2), *Sociología del Diritto* 81.

—— (2004a), *Los abogados de América Latina. Una introducción histórica* (Bogotá, Universidad Externado de Colombia) (English version: *Latin American lawyers. A historical introduction* (Stanford, Cal, Stanford Universitiy Press, 2005)).

—— (2004b), 'Reforma judicial, estado de derecho y revolución en Venezuela' in L Pásara (ed), *En búsqueda de una justicia distinta. Experiencias de reforma en América Latina* (Consorcio Justicia Viva).

—— (2005), 'Judicialization and Regime Change: the Venezuelan Supreme Court' in R Sieder, L Schjolden and A Angell (eds), *The Judicialization of Politics in Latin America* (London, Palgrave Macmillan).

Pino Iturrieta, E (1998), *Venezuela metida en cintura, 1900–1945* (Caracas, Universidad Católica Andrés Bello).

Pocaterra, JR (1990), *Memorias de un venezolano de la decadencia* (Caracas, Biblioteca Ayacucho).

Salas, JC (1919), *Civilización y barbarie,* 2nd edn, 1977 (Caracas, Centauro).

Segnini, Y (1987), *Luces del gomecismo* (Caracas, Alfadil).

Soriano de García Pelayo, G (1996), *El personalismo político hispanoamericano del siglo XIX. Criterios y proposiciones metodológicas para su estudio* (Caracas, Monte Ávila).

Various Authors (2004), *Acción de inconstitucionalidad vs la Ley Orgánica del Tribunal Supremo de Justicia* (Caracas, Editorial Concilium).

Zakaria, F (2003), *The Future of Freedom: Illiberal Democracy at Home and Abroad* (New York, WW Norton).

12

Contesting Legality in the United States after September 11

RICHARD L ABEL

I BEGAN STUDYING THE role of law in the struggle against apartheid in February 1989, a particularly dark moment for South Africa, when more than 30,000 were detained without trial and 1,000 were on hunger strike (Abel, 1995). The legal complex was extremely weak: no written constitution,, bill of rights, or judicial review; a supreme Parliament, dominated by the National Party for more than 40 years, which had appointed every judge; an almost entirely white bar that supported apartheid or was politically disengaged; the African National Congress (ANC) outlawed in 1960; Mandela and other leaders jailed for life soon thereafter; the media owned or censored by government. Yet law still made a difference. Courts granted migrant workers residence outside the 'homelands' and let their wives join them. The state lost all three 1980s treason show trials. Lawyers blocked forced removals of blacks and the grand apartheid scheme of making them citizens of 'independent' Bantustans. Lawyers defended the press against censorship and curtailed prison torture. They won recognition for trade unions, exposed government complicity in 'black-on-black' violence, and lowered sentences for conscientious objectors.

This experience informs the present inquiry into the fate of legality in the United States after September 11. I am interested in the core of political liberalism: freedom from arbitrary imprisonment and abuse. Along every dimension the American legal complex should be more protective of political liberalism: more than two centuries with a written constitution, bill of rights, and judicial review; two reasonably well balanced political parties, both of which have appointed federal judges to lifetime terms; a large, diverse, organised legal profession, which invented public interest law nearly a century ago; a recent explosion of pro bono legal services; a rich civil society (lauded by de Tocqueville two centuries ago), including many NGOs dedicated to legality; and an independent press. Yet legality is gravely endangered. The Bush Administration used the 'war on terror' to assert extraordinary executive powers. Checks within that branch have failed.

The Republican-controlled Congress has been acquiescent at best, often a cheerleader. NGOs, lawyers (including legal academics) and professional associations have vigorously defended legality. The media exposed reported outrages: Abu Ghraib, extraordinary rendition, abuse at Guantánamo, electronic surveillance. But with notable exceptions, judges have exhibited their political loyalties.

This chapter begins by documenting how administration lawyers constructed a legal framework for executive lawlessness. After briefly summarising the abuses this licensed, I examine two internal checks: courts martial and military investigations. Finally, I analyse how judges have dealt with assertions of legal right (through the June 2004 Supreme Court decisions). I conclude by assessing the fate of legality.

I. UNLEASHING EXECUTIVE POWER

Two weeks after 9.11 John C Yoo, Deputy Assistant Attorney General in the Department of Justice Office of Legal Counsel (OLC), wrote to Bush's Deputy Counsel describing the president's 'plenary constitutional power':[1]

> Force can be used both to retaliate for those attacks and to prevent and deter future assaults on the Nation ... to strike terrorist groups or organizations that cannot be demonstrably linked to the September 11 incidents, but that, nonetheless, pose a similar threat to the security of the United States ... .

Given 'the difficulty or impossibility of establishing proof to a criminal law standard (or of making evidence public) ... in the exercise of his plenary power to use military force, the President's decisions are for him alone and are unreviewable'. Two months later Bush issued an Executive Order asserting his power to detain anyone he had reason to believe belonged to al Qaeda or 'engaged in, aided or abetted, or conspired to commit, acts of international terrorism' or knowingly harboured such people.[2] Detainees would be tried only by military commissions, which could hear any evidence that had 'probative value to a reasonable person', even if hearsay. Accused could see evidence only 'in a manner consistent with the protection of' classified information. Assistant Attorney General Jay S Bybee declared that defendants had no right against self-incrimination in military commissions, and in courts the 'public safety' exception permitted introduction of information gained during intelligence gathering and military operations without regard to the Fifth Amendment.[3] Defendants could be convicted

---

[1] Yoo to Flanigan (25 Sept 2001), Memo 1 in Greenberg and Dratel, 2005.
[2] 66 FR 57831–36 (13 Nov 2001), Memo 2 in *ibid*.
[3] Bybee to Gonzales (26 Feb 2002), Memo 13 in *ibid*. That misrepresented *US v Bin Laden*, 132 F Supp 2d 168 (SDNY 2001).

and sentenced by a two-thirds vote, with an appeal only to Bush or his designate. Yoo and Patrick F Philbin (who held the same position) assured the administration that 'the great weight of authority' denied federal courts jurisdiction over Guantánamo.[4]

Ten days after invading Afghanistan the US Commander ordered that the Geneva Conventions (GC) applied to all detainees.[5] But Yoo and Robert J Delahunty (OLC Special Counsel) told the president that neither GC nor the War Crimes Act protected al Qaeda or the Taliban.[6] 'Any congressional effort to restrict presidential authority by subjecting the conduct of the U.S. Armed Forces to a broad construction of the Geneva Convention ... would represent a possible infringement on presidential discretion to direct the military.' '[I]t is clear that the President has the constitutional authority to suspend our treaties with Afghanistan' and should do so. '[C]ustomary international law ... does not bind the President ... because it does not constitute federal law under the Supremacy Clause ... .'

The first prisoners' arrival in Guantánamo in January 2002 accelerated policy-making. Following OLC advice, Defense Secretary Donald Rumsfeld wrote to the Joint Chiefs of Staff (JCS) that al Qaeda and the Taliban were 'not entitled to prisoner of war status for purposes of the Geneva Conventions' but would be treated 'humanely and, to the extent appropriate and consistent with military necessity, in a manner consistent with' their principles.[7] A week later White House Counsel Alberto R Gonzales wrote to Bush anticipating Secretary of State Colin Powell's objections.[8] The 'definitive' OLC memo 'preserves flexibility'. 'The nature of the new war ... renders obsolete Geneva's strict limitations on questioning of enemy prisoners and renders quaint some of its provisions ... .' Bush's determination that GC 'does not apply to al Qaeda and the Taliban eliminates any argument regarding the need for case-by-case determinations of POW status ... .' Powell wrote to Gonzales the next day that declaring GC inapplicable:

> will reverse over a century of U.S. policy and practice ... has a high cost in terms of negative international reaction ... will undermine public support among critical allies ... may provoke some individual foreign prosecutors to investigate and prosecute our officials and troops ... will make us more vulnerable to domestic

---

[4] Philbin and Yoo to William J Haynes, II, General Counsel, Department of Defense (28 Dec 2001), Memo 3 in *ibid*.

[5] Independent Panel to Review Department of Defense Detention Operations, Final Report, 908, 947 in *ibid* (hereafter Schlesinger). Indeed, although the Pentagon denied its existence, CENTCOM Reg 27-13 (7 Feb 1995) declared that 'should any doubt arise as to whether a person who has committed a belligerent act falls into one of the classes of persons entitled to EPW status under GPW Article 4, he shall be treated as an EPW until such time as his status has been determined by a Tribunal under GPW Article 5 and this regulation'.

[6] Yoo and Delahunty to Haynes (9 Jan 2002), Memo 4 in *ibid*.

[7] Memorandum for Chairman of the Joint Chiefs of Staff (19 Jan 2002), Memo 5 in *ibid*.

[8] Gonzales to Bush (25 Jan 2002), Memo 7 in *ibid*.

and legal challenge ... undermines the President's Military Order by removing an important legal basis for trying the detainees before Military Commissions [and] ... will be challenged in international fora ... .[9]

Powell urged Bush to 'determine that the Geneva Convention does apply to the conflict in Afghanistan, but that members of al Qaeda as a group and the Taliban individually or as a group are not entitled to Prisoner of War status under the Convention'. This offered 'the same practical flexibility'. The Legal Adviser to the JCS Chairman and many military lawyers agreed.[10] Attorney General John Ashcroft sided with Gonzales and the OLC.[11] If Bush determined that GC did not apply to the Taliban 'various legal risks of liability, litigation, and criminal prosecution are minimized' because this 'is fully discretionary and will not be reviewed by the federal courts'. Powell's alternative carried a 'higher risk of liability, criminal prosecution, and judicially-imposed conditions of detainment—including mandated release of a detainee'.

The next day William H Taft, IV, State Department Legal Adviser, tried to persuade Gonzales.[12] Application of the GC:

> is consistent with the plain language of the Conventions and the unvaried practice of the United States in introducing its forces into conflict over fifty years ... the position of every other party to the Conventions ... [and] UN Security Council Resolution 1193 ... . It demonstrates that the United States bases its conduct not just on its policy preferences but on its international legal obligations.

Gonzales should tell Bush that 'DOS lawyers do not agree that Afghanistan is a failed state, that a failed state is relieved of its treaty obligations, or that the GPW [Geneva Prisoners of War] may be suspended' and that a presidential determination obviating the need 'for further screening of any al Qaeda or Taliban detainees' was still 'being reviewed'. (Resigning in March 2005 after more than 30 years in government, President Taft's great grandson reiterated: 'There is no basis in the law of war, criminal law or human-rights law for such practices'. 'How our government treats people should never, at bottom, be a matter merely of policy, but a matter of law'.[13]) During these debates senior military officials also argued that GC should be followed 'without qualifications'.

But on 7 February Bybee wrote to Gonzales that, based on an Information Paper the day before by Rear Admiral LE Jacoby (Defense Intelligence Agency

---

[9] Powell to Gonzales (26 Jan 2002), Memo 8 in *ibid*.

[10] Schlesinger, above n 5, at 923.

[11] Ashcroft to Bush (1 Feb 2002), Memo 9 in Greenberg and Dratel, 2005.

[12] Taft to Gonzales (2 Feb 2005), Memo 10 in *ibid*.

[13] J Bravin, 'U.S. Mishandled Prisoner Policy, Ex-Adviser Says', *Wall Street Journal*, 5 Apr 2005, B9, available at www.ffhsj.com/bios/taftwi.htm.

Director), Bush had 'reasonable factual grounds to determine' that Taliban were not POWs.[14] The same day Bush brushed aside State Department reservations.[15] He accepted 'the legal conclusion of the Department of Justice' that GC did not apply to al Qaeda and claimed authority to suspend Geneva with respect to Afghanistan. While declining to do so, he declared the Taliban 'unlawful combatants'. But 'as a matter of policy, the United States Armed Forces shall continue to treat detainees humanely and, to the extent appropriate and consistent with military necessity, in a manner consistent with the principles of Geneva'.

The most notorious memoranda by Bybee (assisted by Yoo) narrowly defined torture by requiring specific intent to inflict unendurable pain and suffering.[16] Bybee invoked *laws defining entitlement to emergency medical care* to require 'permanent and serious physical damage' rising to 'the level of death, organ failure, or the permanent impairment of a significant body function'. 'Prolonged mental harm' had to last 'months or even years'. Psychotropic drugs had to 'substantially interfere with [the subject's] cognitive abilities, or fundamentally alter his personality'. Any threat of death had to be imminent. The statute implementing the Convention Against Torture:

> must be construed as not applying to interrogations undertaken pursuant to his Commander-in-Chief authority.... Congress may no more regulate the President's ability to detain and interrogate enemy combatants than it may regulate his ability to direct troop movements on the battlefield.

Furthermore, 'standard criminal law defenses of necessity and self-defense could justify interrogation methods needed to elicit information to prevent a direct and imminent threat to the United States and its citizens'.

The military promptly wielded its new power. On 11 October Guantánamo Commander Major General Michael E Dunlavey requested approval of interrogation techniques beyond the 17 authorised in the 1992 version of Army Field Manual 34-52 (Category I).[17] Category II techniques included: 'stress positions' for four hours, isolation for 30 days (extendable with approval), darkness, hooding, 20-hour interrogations, removal of all comfort items (including Korans), switching from hot rations to meals ready to eat (MREs) removal of clothing, shaving of facial hair, and 'using detainees' and individual phobias (such as fear of dogs) to induce stress'. Category III

---

[14] Bybee to Gonzales (7 Feb 2005), Memo 12 in Greenberg and Dratel, 2005.
[15] Memo 11 in *ibid*.
[16] Bybee to Gonzales (1 Aug 2002), Memo 14 in *ibid*; Yoo to Gonzales (1 Aug 2002), Memo 15 in *ibid*. They were 'released' by the government nearly a year later after being leaked: A Liptak, 'Author of '02 Memo on Torture: "Gentle" Soul for a Harsh Topic', *New York Times*, 24 June 2003, A1.
[17] Dunlavey to Hill (11 Oct 2002), Memo 17; Beaver to Dunlavey (11 Oct 2002), Memo 18; Phifer to Dunlavey (11 Oct 2002), Memo 19; Beaver to Dunlavey (11 Oct 2002), Memo 20, all in *ibid*.

required approval by superiors: threats of imminent death or severe pain to self or family, cold, 'misperception of suffocation', and 'mild, non-injurious physical contact'.

Lieutenant Colonel Diane E Beaver, a Staff Judge Advocate (SJA), explained that 'more aggressive interrogation techniques' were necessary because 'resistance strategies have become more sophisticated'. In the absence of 'established clear policy for interrogation limits and operations at GTMO ... interrogators have felt in the past that they could not do anything that could be considered "controversial"'. Category II and III methods were legal if done for 'an important governmental objective' and without specific intent to harm; but she urged 'legal review prior to their commencement'. General James T Hill, Southern Command (SOUTHCOM) Commander, forwarded this request to General Myers, Chairman of the Joint Chiefs of Staff, on 25 October because 'some detainees have tenaciously resisted our current interrogation methods'.[18] Hill believed the first two categories were 'legal and humane'. While uncertain about the third, especially death threats, he wanted 'as many options as possible at my disposal'. On 27 November Department of Defense General Counsel William Haynes advised Rumsfeld that he, Deputy Defense Secretary Douglas Feith, and General Myers favoured Category II and 'mild, non-injurious contact'. Rumsfeld approved these on 2 December, commenting: 'I stand for 8–10 hours a day. Why is standing limited to 4 hours?'[19]

Responding to concerns of the Navy General Counsel Alberto Mora, Rumsfeld rescinded this on 15 January 2003.[20] (An Air Force Staff Judge Advocate filed a 'Memorandum for the Record' that day expressing the concern of other SJAs about Guantánamo interrogation practices. Other SJAs consulted Scott Horton, chair of the human rights committee of the Association of the Bar of the City of New York (ABCNY). Rear Admiral John Hutson and Brigadier General James Cullen, both retired Judge Advocates General (JAGs), felt the practices would 'blacken the names' and 'stain the honor' of the military.)[21] Rumsfeld appointed a departmental working group, chaired by Air Force General Counsel Mary Walker, which 'relied heavily on the OLC'.[22] All four JAGs opposed some of the interrogation techniques as violating domestic civilian and military law and international customary

---

[18] Hill to Chairman (25 Oct 2002), Memo 16 in *ibid*.

[19] Haynes to Rumsfeld (27 Nov 2002) and Rumsfeld approval (2 Dec 2002), Memo 21 in *ibid*.

[20] 'Memo: Pentagon Concerned About Legality of Interrogation Techniques', *ABC News*, 15 June 2005.

[21] NA Lewis and E Schmitt, 'Lawyers Decided Bans on Torture Didn't Bind Bush', *New York Times*, 8 June 2004, A1; JG Meek, 'At War With Gitmo Grilling', *New York Daily News*, 13 Feb 2005, 20; B Herbert, 'We Can't Remain Silent', *New York Times*, 1 Apr 2005, A25.

[22] Schlesinger, above n 5, at 924; Rumsfeld to Haynes (15 Jan 2003), Memo 22; Rumsfeld to Commander, SOUTHCOM (15 Jan 2003), Memo 23; Rumsfeld to Walker (17 Jan 2003), Memo 24, all in Greenberg and Dratel, 2005.

law and treaties.[23] But the working group report on 6 March largely reiterated earlier OLC memos, recommending nine new techniques, including
hooding, mild physical contact, dietary and environmental manipulation,
sleep adjustment (not deprivation), false flag, and threat of transfer 'to a
third country that subject is likely to fear would subject him to torture or
death'.[24] Superiors could approve another nine, including isolation, 20-hour
interrogation, forced grooming, four hours standing, sleep deprivation for
four successive days, forced exercise, face or stomach slap, nudity, and
'increasing anxiety by use of aversions ... e.g., simple presence of dog without directly threatening action'. Interrogation should be 'conducted in close
cooperation with units detaining the individuals. The policies established by
the detained units that pertain to searching, silencing, and segregating also
play a role in the interrogation of a detainee'. The:

> decision whether to authorize a technique is essentially a risk benefit analysis that
> generally takes into account the expected utility of the technique, the likelihood
> that any technique will be in violation of domestic or international law, and vari-
> ous policy considerations.

Rumsfeld approved seven of the first nine for Guantánamo.[25]

Before the Iraq invasion, Special Operation Forces developed Standard
Operating Procedures for interrogations in Afghanistan, published in
February 2003. The 519th Military Intelligence (MI) Battalion assisted in
these interrogations and then took the procedures to Abu Ghraib in July
2003. In a memorandum that month, Captain William Ponce Jr, a Baghdad
headquarters Military Intelligence officer, wrote:

> The gloves are coming off, gentlemen, regarding these detainees. Col. Boltz
> [Baghdad MI chief] has made it clear that we want these individuals broken.
> Casualties are mounting, and we need to start gathering info to help protect our
> fellow soldiers from any further attacks.[26]

---

[23] Maj Gen Jack L Rives, Deputy JAG, USAF, to SAF/GC (5 Feb 2003; 6 Feb 2003); Rear
Adm Michael F Lohr, Navy JAG, to SAF/GC (6 Feb 2003); Brig Gen Kevin M Sandkuhler,
Marine Corps SJA to SAF/GC (27 Feb 2003); Maj Gen Thomas J Romig, Army JAG, to SAF/
GC (3 Mar 2003; 13 Mar 2003). Senator Lindsay Graham (Rep, South Carolina) had these
declassified and inserted in the Congressional Record during the Senate debate of amendments
to the National Defense Authorization Act Fiscal Year 2006 to subject detention and interrogation to law. Congressional Record S8794-96 (25 July 2005).
[24] Working Group Report on Detainee Interrogations in the Global War on Terrorism (6
Mar 2003), Memo 25 in Greenberg and Dratel 2005. A complete version was dated 4 Apr
2003, Memo 26 in *ibid*. Haynes rescinded it on 17 Mar 2005: J White, 'Military Lawyers
Fought Policy on Interrogations', *Washington Post*, 15 July 2005, A1.
[25] Rumsfeld to Commander, SOUTHCOM (16 Apr 2003), Memo 27 in Greenberg and
Dratel, 2005.
[26] 'Memo Appealed for Ways to Break Iraqi Detainees', *Washington Post*, 23 Aug 2004,
A12; R Bernstein, 'Reservist to Plead Guilty to Some Charges in Mistreatment of Iraqi
Prisoners', *New York Times*, 24 Aug 2004, A6; J Fleishman, 'Judge Demands Results in Prison
Probe', *Los Angeles Times*, 24 Aug 2004, A3.

At the request of Coalition Joint Task Force Seven (CJTF-7), JCS sent Guantánamo Commander Major General Geoffrey D Miller to Baghdad from 31 August to 9 September 2003. He brought Rumsfeld's latest order. Miller's 13 September report recommended 'a detention guard force subordinate to the JIDC [Joint Interrogation and Debriefing Center] Commander that sets the conditions for the successful interrogation and exploitation of internees/detainees'.[27] The next day, advised by his SJA Colonel Warren that he had inherent authority as Commander in a Theatre of War even though GC applied, Iraq Commander Lieutenant General Ricardo S Sanchez authorised a dozen techniques beyond the 1992 FM 34-52, five not even approved for Guantánamo. When CENTCOM disapproved, Sanchez replaced these on 12 October with an outdated 1987 version of FM 34-52, which allowed modification of 'lighting and heating, as well as food, clothing, and shelter'.[28] (The Schlesinger Report, below, noted that Abu Ghraib staff 'perceived pressure' for 'better intelligence' in autumn 2003 as a result of visits by Sanchez and Major General Barbara Fast (CJTF-7 Intelligence Director), Miller and a senior National Security Council staff member.[29])

Walker's task force had recommended *threatening* to transfer detainees to countries that tortured. In March 2004, Jack Goldsmith, Assistant Attorney General in the OLC, prepared a memo for Gonzales asserting legal authority for forced renditions.[30] Despite the GC prohibition on 'individual or mass forcible transfers', the US could render illegal aliens from Iraq under local immigration law and 'relocate' anyone 'to facilitate interrogation, for a brief but not indefinite period, so long as adjudicative proceedings have not been initiated against them'.

When the Department of Justice memoranda were leaked after Abu Ghraib, lawyers denounced them as 'extraordinary', 'just wrong', 'an argument I have never seen made before'.[31] Prominent legal academics agreed: Harold Koh (Yale's Dean and Clinton's Assistant Secretary of State) and Jack Balkin (Yale); Cass Sunstein (Chicago); Walter Dellinger (Duke; Clinton's

---

[27] Miller, Assessment of DoD Counterterrorism Interrogation and Detention Operations in Iraq (13 Sept 2003) in Danner, 2004, also in MG Antonio M Taguba, Article 15-6 Investigation of the 800th Military Police Brigade (Mar 2004), in Greenberg and Dratel, 2005 (hereafter Taguba).

[28] Schlesinger, above n 5, at 911–12, 925; Sanchez to Commander, CENTCOM (14 Sept 2003) in Taguba, above n 27, at 460.

[29] Schlesinger, above n 5 at 940.

[30] Goldsmith to Gonzales (19 Mar 2004), Memo 28 in Greenberg and Dratel, 2005.

[31] NA Lewis, 'Ashcroft Says the White House Never Authorized Tactics Breaking Laws on Torture', *New York Times*, 9 June 2004, A10; DG Savage and RB Schmitt, 'Lawyers Ascribed Broad Power to Bush on Torture', *Los Angeles Times*, 10 June 2004, A16; JC Yoo, 'With "All Necessary and Appropriate Force"', *Los Angeles Times*, 11 June 2004, B13; AM Dershowitz, 'Stop Winking at Torture and Codify It', *Los Angeles Times*, 13 June 2004, M5; A Liptak, 'Legal Scholars Criticize Torture Memos', *New York Times*, 25 June 2004, A14; A Liptak, 'How Far Can a Government Lawyer Go?', *New York Times*, 27 June 2004, §4 at 3; J Rosen, 'The Struggle Over the Torture Memos', *New York Times*, 15 Aug 2004, §4 at 5.

OLC head); Douglass Cassel (Northwestern); and Stephen Gillers (New York University). Watergate prosecutor Philip Lacovara remembered 'the first time I heard one of the Nixon tapes, when Nixon was giving a little primer on how to escape prosecution for perjury. "Just tell them you don't recall". Hutson (now Franklin Pierce Law Center dean) said lawyers advising the executive 'have to be right legally, and I think they have an obligation to be right morally ... they failed on both counts'.

Counterattacking, Yoo sought to divert attention from his legalisation of torture to the 'paroxysm of leaking ... classified memos'. 'Would you want the government to have open discussions about whether we could legitimately assassinate Osama bin Laden and what rules you'd have to follow?' He had done nothing more than 'ask the meaning of a publicly enacted law'. Was that 'politically incorrect'?

Conservatives supported him. Douglas W Kmiec (Pepperdine Law School) declared that '[o]ne of the most important functions of the O.L.C. is to be candid ... to ask the question of what authority the president has to confront the situation'. Charles Fried (Harvard; Reagan's Solicitor General) saw 'nothing wrong with exploring any topic to find out what the legal requirements are'. 'The lawyer's role is to answer only ... what does the law require?' not 'is it moral?' Geoffrey Hazard (Pennsylvania) called it 'very appropriate for lawyers' in government 'to think in concrete terms about what is meant by torture'. Indeed, Alan Dershowitz (Harvard) urged the US to follow Israel: 'Stop Winking at Torture and Codify It'.

In June the ABCNY Committees on International Human Rights and on Military Affairs and Justice supplemented the interrogation standards they had published before the Abu Ghraib revelations (ABCNY, 2004b). 'There is no blanket exception for so-called "unlawful combatants"'. They urged that SJAs advise the interrogators and monitor interrogations on site, a function that had been 'curtailed at the direction of senior officials'. In August nearly 300 lawyers (including 12 former ABA presidents, 11 ex-judges, seven former law school deans, four ex-Representatives, an ex-Senator and an ex-Governor) wrote an open letter to Bush, Cheney, Rumsfeld, Ashcroft and Congress.[32] The 'most senior lawyers in the Department of Justice, White House, the Department of Defense (DoD) and the Vice President's office have sought to justify actions that violate the most basic rights of all human beings'. The memoranda 'seek to circumvent long established and universally acknowledged principles of law and common decency'. 'The unprecedented and under-analyzed claim that the Executive Branch is a law unto itself is incompatible with the rule of law and the principle that no one is above the law.' Administration lawyers 'failed to meet their professional obligations'. Their 'ultimate client ... is not the President ... but

[32] 'Group Criticizes Rules on Prisoner Treatment', *New York Times,* 5 Aug 2004, A17, available at www.afj.org.

the American people'. A lawyer has a duty 'as an officer of the court and as a citizen, to uphold the law'. A few days later the American Bar Association House of Delegates (joined by several city and state bar associations) condemned renditions and 'any use of torture or other cruel, inhuman or degrading treatment'. 'The use of torture ... has brought shame on the nation and undermined our standing in the world.'[33]

In anticipation of Gonzales's confirmation hearing for Attorney General, the OLC acting chief replaced the August 2002 torture memorandum on 30 December 2004 (when Americans were distracted).[34] Torture was 'abhorrent both to American law and values and to international norms'. The memorandum repudiated the narrow definition. But Yoo and Delahunty remained true believers: 'the Geneva Convention makes little sense when applied to a terrorist group or a pseudo-state ... [and] will become increasingly obsolete'.[35] Yoo insisted that interrogators could use 'shouted questions, reduced sleep, stress positions ... and isolation', the purpose of which 'is not to inflict pain or harm, but simply to disorient'.[36] Two weeks later he asked: 'Why is it so hard for people to understand that there is a category of behavior not covered by the legal system?' Congress had no power to 'tie the President's hands in regard to torture as an interrogation technique' (Mayer, 2005). He insisted 'the public has had its referendum' on interrogation practices—the November 2004 election—'that's why we have elections, to approve policies or reject policies'. The Torture Act 'has never been interpreted by any court ... the administration did its best to try to come to some kind of understanding of what the statute meant'.[37] When three *Republican* Senators proposed to regulate detention and interrogation in Fiscal Year 2006 National Defense Authorization Act, Bush threatened a veto because this 'would restrict the President's authority to protect Americans effectively from terrorist attack and bring terrorists to justice'.[38]

---

[33] Greenberg and Dratel, 2005, at 1132; also available at www.abanet.org/media/docs/torturereport10b.pdf.

[34] Daniel Levin to Deputy Attorney General James B. Comey (30 Dec 2004) Re: Legal Standards Applicable Under 18 USC §§ 2340-2340A, available at www.usdoj.gov/olc/18usc23402340a2.htm.

[35] RJ Delahunty and JC Yoo, 'Rewriting the Laws of War for a New Enemy', *Los Angeles Times*, 1 Feb 2005, B11.

[36] J Yoo, 'Behind the "Torture Memos"; As Confirmation Hearings Near, Lawyer Defends Wartime Policy', *San Jose Mercury News*, 2 Jan 2005, 1P.

[37] 'Re-Securing the Homeland: Is the Patriot Act the Right Solution for Homeland Security?', Panel at Princeton University, 8 Apr 2005. Yoo had been harshly criticised for telling Jane Mayer several months earlier that the election was a referendum on torture.

[38] 'Detainee Rules May Lead to Veto', *Los Angeles Times*, 22 July 2005, A27; J White and RJ Smith, 'White House Aims to Block Legislation on Detainees', *Washington Post*, 23 July 2005, A1; E Schmitt, 'Cheney Working to Block Legislation on Detainees', *New York Times*, 24 July 2005, §1 at 15.

(a) Analysis

Power resists limits. To administration lawyers (another generation of the 'best and brightest'), law was imposed by critics, not intrinsically obligatory. David Addington (Cheney's counsel) was shameless: 'We think what we are doing is right—why should we stop doing it? If the courts tell us we're wrong, we'll stop then.' The administration claimed unprecedented power. Lawyers advising the military how to abuse detainees misappropriated the hired-gun ethic of the criminal defence lawyer. Lawyers denied personal accountability for their advice. They pledged loyalty to the president, not the people. They narrowed the definition of torture so that everything not forbidden was permitted. The very goal of rules was to encourage interrogators to push the boundaries.

Certain that its allies would always occupy the White House, the administration resolved to free the presidency from *any* legal restraint. Its lawyers pronounced that: the president's military discretion—which included every aspect of detention—could not be constrained by Congress (the War Crimes Act) or reviewed by the courts; the Constitution did not protect detainees or extend to Guantánamo; *no* international law protected al Qaeda or the Taliban; the president could unilaterally interpret and suspend treaties, unconstrained by customary international law. The administration constructed a 'legal' framework to immunise itself from possible war crimes trials. OLC lawyers advanced tendentious legal views as uncontroversial, even 'definitive'. The administration paid lip service to Geneva as a matter of *policy*, not legal obligation, and only 'to the extent appropriate and consistent with military necessity'. Confronted with the abuses of high-level Guantánamo detainees, Yoo replied:

> Sure, we are taking criticism from other nations, from human rights groups, and that's certainly a negative, but it has to be balanced against the positives that the United States can gain in intelligence from interrogating people, coercively ... it's a cost-balance decision that our policy-makers have to make ... and so far, I think, our political leaders in [*sic*] any rate have decided that that's the case.[39]

Law is retrospective, policy prospective. America used to respond to attacks; now it claimed the right to preempt them. Legal interrogation uncovers past crimes, and imprisonment punishes them; now government would anticipate and prevent terrorism. Geneva required an individual retrospective adjudication of prisoner of war (POW) status; Bush prospectively excluded al Qaeda and the Taliban.

There were dissenters within government. Powell argued enlightened self-interest while assuring Bush that legal forms would not reduce 'flexibility'. Taft was avowedly legalist. Military lawyers reminded the civilian about

---

[39] S Simon, *NPR's Weekend Edition*, 18 June 2005.

the Constitution. Retired JAGs launched a crusade; serving SJAs leaked information. Even Rice was anxious not to alienate allies; and the NSC legal staff were concerned about lawlessness. But the administration barely went through the motions of consultation. While Powell and Taft were writing memoranda, Rumsfeld had already decided. Gonzales made sure the president saw his own rebuttal before Powell's critique. And there were plenty of *apparatchiki* to carry out administration policy: Haynes, Walker, Beaver, Warren.

Almost all lawyers outside government were critical, especially academics and professional associations. They couched their opposition in terms of universals, not utilitarian policies: legal competence, law, morality, rule of law, natural law, common decency. But their protests had no visible effect. The administration had packed the Justice Department with Federalist Society ideologues committed to expanding executive power.

Yoo returned to Berkeley, Goldsmith was appointed by Harvard. Bybee was rewarded with an appointment to the Ninth Circuit before the scandal broke; Haynes's nomination was derailed by it. Gonzales became Attorney General despite it. Nominated to be his deputy (once again), Flanigan followed Gonzales's opportunistic attempt to distance himself from the OLC memoranda, calling their assertion that the president could override Congress 'sort of sophomoric'. 'The president is never above the law.'[40]

II. LEGALISING LAWLESSNESS

The first victims of arbitrary state power after 9/11 were immigrants, who enjoy few constitutional or other legal protections. Immediately after the attack police detained about 1,200 (mostly Muslim) men for immigration irregularities. The Absconder Apprehension Initiative prioritised 6,000 Arab and Muslim men out of the 300,000 outstanding deportation orders, deporting over 1,100. At least 50 were detained under material witness warrants.[41] The FBI summoned 8,000 for 'voluntary' interviews and required more than 80,000 others to register, 13,000 of whom faced deportation. Just before the March 2003 invasion the government detained all asylum seekers entering the country, and the FBI interviewed more than 11,000 Iraqi immigrants.[42]

---

[40] E Lichtblau, 'Justice Nominee Is Questioned on Department Torture Policy', *New York Times*, 27 July 2005, A16.

[41] E Lichtblau, 'Two Groups Charge Abuse of Witness Law', *New York Times*, 27 June 2005, A10; Human Rights Watch and ACLU, 2005.

[42] A Elliott, 'Caught in a Net Thrown for Terrorists', *New York Times*, 24 May 2005, A21; Bâli, 2005; Fine, 2003a, b.

The USA Patriot Act broadly curtailed civil liberties (Brasch, 2005; Brown, 2003; Etzioni, 2004; Sidel, 2004).[43]

The executive eagerly exercised its expanded power. The military detained more than 50,000 people abroad, primarily in Afghanistan and Iraq, and sent more than 700 to Guantánamo, where some remain more than five years later.[44] Interrogators used all the methods described above, whether or not authorised (Saar and Novak, 2005). The military and the CIA hid 'ghost' detainees from the International Committee of the Red Cross (ICRC).[45] More than 100 were seized abroad and forcibly 'rendered' to countries where they were tortured and sometimes killed.[46] Several dozen detainees died in custody, some murdered. Abu Ghraib is merely the best documented atrocity.[47]

Yoo denied any responsibility. 'It's a stretch to say that a very limited, tightly held memo somehow translated into orders that soldiers on the ground violated human rights. That's the difference between law and policy.'[48] The Abu Ghraib 'abuses had nothing to do with the memos defining torture ... nor the decision to deny POW protections to Al-Qaida or the Taliban'.[49] But it is not hard to connect the dots from the DOJ memos to Gonzales and Bush (White House), to Rumsfeld, Haynes, Walker, Hill and Myers (DOD), to Dunlavey, Beaver and Miller (Guantánamo), to Special Operations Forces in Afghanistan, to the 519th Military Intelligence Battalion (Afghanistan and Iraq), to Boltz, Warren and Sanchez (Iraq command), and to the requirement that Military Police guards engage in 'close cooperation' with interrogators.

---

[43] It was enacted on 26 Oct by votes of 98–1 in the Senate and 357–66 in the House.

[44] Department of the Army Inspector General, Report on Detainee Operations (21 July 2004), in Greenberg and Dratel, 2005, at 630, 632 (hereafter Mikolashek).

[45] E Schmitt and T Shanker, 'Rumsfeld Issued an Order to Hide Detainee in Iraq', *New York Times*, 17 June 2004, A1; D Jehl, E Schmitt and K Zernike, 'U.S. Rules on Prisoners Seen as a Back and Forth of Mixed Messages to G.I.'s', *New York Times*, 22 June 2004, A6; T Shanker and A Elliott, 'Rumsfeld Admits He Told Jailers to Keep Detainee in Iraq Out of Red Cross View', *New York Times*, 18 June 2004, A13; Meeropol, 2005.

[46] Mayer, 2005; D van Natta Jr. and S Mekhennet, 'German's Claim of Kidnapping Brings Investigation of U.S. Link', *New York Times*, 9 Jan 2005, A1; J Fleishman, 'Man's Claims May Be a Look at Dark Side of War on Terror', *Los Angeles Times*, 12 May 2005, A1 (K el-Masri); MK Stack and B Drogin, 'Detainee Says U.S. Handed Him Over for Torture', *Los Angeles Times*, 13 Jan 2005, A1; R Bonner, 'Detainee Says He Was Tortured While in U.S. Custody', *New York Times*, 13 Feb 2005, §1 at 1 (M Habib); 'Judge Says Agents of West Took Egyptian', *Los Angeles Times*, 20 May 2005, A13 (H Osama Nasr from Italy); S Grey and D Van Natta, 'Thirteen with the C.I.A. Sought by Italy in a Kidnapping', *New York Times*, 25 June 2005, A1. See Commission of Inquiry into the Actions of Canadian Officials in Relation to Maher Arar, available at www.ararcommission.ca/eng.

[47] Taguba, above n 27, at 405, 416–17.

[48] ML La Ganga, 'Scholar Calmly Takes Heat for His Memos on Torture', *Los Angeles Times*, 16 May 2005, A1.

[49] J Yoo, 'Behind the "Torture Memos"; As Confirmation Hearings Near, Lawyer Defends Wartime Policy', *San Jose Mercury News*, 2 Jan 2005, 1P.

III. INTERNAL CORRECTIONS

The military had two responses to abuses: courts martial and internal investigations. Its spokesmen endlessly repeated that '[t]he Army and Department of Defense have aggressively investigated all credible allegations of detainee abuse and held individuals accountable'.[50] But of the 367 investigations opened in the 3.5 years after the Afghanistan invasion, only 218 had been resolved: 105 with administrative punishments and just 35 after courts martial.[51] Abu Ghraib exemplifies this lenience. Only two participants received significant punishment: Staff Sergeant Ivan L Frederick II got eight years (out of a possible 18) after pleading guilty, and ringleader Specialist Charles Graner Jr got 10 (out of a possible 15).[52] This was not exceptional. At Camp Whitehorse outside Nasiriyah, Nagem Sadoon Hatab was handcuffed, hooded and badly beaten. Discovered two days later covered in excrement and unable to stand, he was dragged outside to be

[50] J Hendren, 'Pentagon Files Reveal More Allegations of Abuse in Iraq', *Los Angeles Times,* 25 Jan 2005, A1; NA Lewis, 'A.C.L.U. Presents Accusations of Serious Abuse of Iraqi Civilians', *New York Times,* 25 Jan 2005, A11.

[51] D Jehl and E Schmitt, 'U.S. Military Says 26 Inmate Deaths May Be Homicide', *New York Times,* 16 Mar 2005, A1; 'U.S. Counts 108 Deaths in Custody in Iraq, Afghanistan', *Los Angeles Times,* 17 Mar 2005, A7; M Mazzetti, 'Army Finds Evidence of Homicides', *Los Angeles Times,* 26 Mar 2005, A3; D Jehl, 'Pentagon Will Not Try 17 G.I.'s Implicated in Prisoners' Deaths', *New York Times,* 26 Mar 2005, A1; SL Myers, 'Why Military Justice Can Seem Unjust', *New York Times,* 6 June 2004, §4 at 3; M Davey, 'An Iraqi Police Officer's Death, a Soldier's Varying Accounts', *New York Times,* 23 May 2005, A1; A Salvato, 'Soldier Says Killing of Iraqi Was Self-Defense', *New York Times,* 24 May 2005, A20.

[52] R Bernstein, 'Reservist to Plead Guilty to Some Charges in Mistreatment of Iraqi Prisoners', *New York Times,* 24 Aug 2004, A6; J Fleishman, 'Judge Demands Results in Prison Probe', *Los Angeles Times,* 24 Aug 2004, A3; J Fleishman, 'Judge Gives Prosecutors a Deadline in Abuse Case', *Los Angeles Times,* 25 Aug 2004, A8; R Bernstein, 'Abuse Judge May Give Immunity for Testimony by Officers', *New York Times,* 25 Aug 2004, A11; 'Prison Abuse Figure Blames "Secret Services"', *Los Angeles Times,* 30 Aug 2004, A6; M Morin, 'GI Pleads Guilty to Iraq Jail Charges', *Los Angeles Times,* 21 Oct 2004, A1; RA Oppel Jr, 'Sergeant in Abu Ghraib Case Pleads Guilty to 8 Counts', *New York Times,* 21 Oct 2004, A12; E Wong, 'Trial Date Set for Another Reservist in Prison Abuse Case', *New York Times,* 22 Oct 2004, A8; M Morin, 'GI Gets 8-Year Sentence After Guilty Plea in Abuse Scandal', *Los Angeles Times,* 22 Oct 2004, A4; 'G.I. Accused of Prison Abuse in Iraq Faces Military Trial', *New York Times,* 10 Jan 2005, A1; K Zernike, 'Central Figure in Iraq Abuse Goes on Trial', *New York Times,* 11 Jan 2005, A1; RA Serrano, 'Guard Enjoyed Beating Iraqis, Three Testify', *Los Angeles Times,* 11 Jan 2005, A10; TR Reid, 'Case Against Soldier Is Presented', *Washington Post,* 12 Jan 2005, A3; RA Serrano, 'Guard Was "Primary Torturer," Prisoner Says', *Los Angeles Times,* 12 Jan 2005, A10; K Zernike, 'Detainees Describe Abuses by Guard in Iraq Prison', *New York Times,* 12 Jan 2005, A1; K Zernike, 'Plea Deal Is Set for G.I. Pictured in Abuses in Iraq', *New York Times,* 30 Apr 2005, A1; 'Reservist Pleads Guilty in Prison Abuse, Cites Peer Pressure', *Los Angeles Times,* 3 May 2005, A15; R Blumenthal, 'Judge Tosses Out Abuse Plea After the Ringleader Testifies', *New York Times,* 5 May 2005, A1; L Hart and RA Serrano 'Abu Ghraib Guilty Plea Is Dismissed', *Los Angeles Times,* 5 May 2005, A1; R Blumenthal, 'Private Will Face New Charges Over Abuse of Prisoners in Iraq', *New York Times,* 6 May 2005, A10; K Zernike, 'Behind Failed Abu Ghraib Plea, a Tale of Breakups and Betrayal', *New York Times,* 10 May 2005, A1; 'Soldier Gets Closer to Abuse Retrial', *New York Times,* 25 May 2005, A6; 'England Gives Up Right to Hearing', *Los Angeles Times,* 25 May 2005, A31.

cleaned but forgotten and later found dead. Charges against six Marines were dropped; one pleaded guilty and was demoted; the ringleader got 60 days' hard labour and a demotion.[53] Manadel al-Jamadi died in CIA custody two hours after being beaten by Navy SEALs. Nine of the 10 accused were handled administratively.[54] Lieutenant Andrew K Ledford was charged with assault, dereliction of duty, filing a false report, and conduct unbecoming but acquitted after three hours of deliberation.[55] After M Sayari died in Afghanistan, four Special Forces soldiers were charged, but only one even administratively punished.[56] Captain Rogelio Maynulet was charged with murdering Karim Abid Ali Haleji.[57] Apparently accepting the defence of a mercy killing, the jury convicted of only assault with intent to commit voluntary manslaughter. Although he faced 10 years, the prosecutor

[53] T Perry, 'Trial Begins for Marine Accused of Beating Iraqi Prisoners', *Los Angeles Times*, 25 Aug 2004, B5; T Perry, 'Reservists' Testimony Details Sleep Deprivation at U.S. Facility in Iraq', *Los Angeles Times*, 28 Aug 2005, B6; T Perry, 'Officer's Trial in Abuse of Iraqi Inmate Is Delayed', *Los Angeles Times*, 17 Sept 2004, B8; T Perry, 'Marine Convicted of Assault', *Los Angeles Times*, 3 Sept 2004, B1; C LeDuff, 'New York Marine Convicted of Assaulting Iraqi Prisoners', *New York Times*, 3 Sept 2004, A9.

[54] '4 Navy SEALs Charged with Iraq Inmate Abuse', *Los Angeles Times*, 4 Sept 2004, A3; E Schmitt, '4 Navy Commandos Are Charged in Abuse', *New York Times*, 4 Sept 2004, A6; T Perry, 'A Navy SEAL Is Cleared of Abuse Charges', *Los Angeles Times*, 28 Oct 2004, A3; S Shane, 'Navy Drops Charges Against Commando in Abuse of Prisoners', *New York Times*, 29 Oct 2004, A10; NA Lewis and D Jehl, 'Files Show New Abuse Cases in Afghan and Iraqi Prisons', *New York Times*, 18 Feb 2005, A8; 'Hearing to Begin in Iraqi Abuse Case', *Los Angeles Times*, 20 Mar 2005, B4; T Perry, 'Navy SEAL Goes on Trial in Death of Iraqi Prisoner at Abu Ghraib', *Los Angeles Times*, 24 May 2005, A12; D Cloud, 'Seal Officer Hears Charges in Court-Martial in Iraqi's Death', *New York Times*, 25 May 2005, A6; T Perry, 'CIA Operative Testifies He Saw SEAL Beating Iraqi Prisoner', *Los Angeles Times*, 25 May 2005, A32; T Perry, 'SEALS Instructed to Treat Prisoners Well', *Los Angeles Times*, 26 May 2005, A29; DS Cloud, 'Seal Officer's Trial Gives Glimpse of C.I.A.'s Role in Abuse', *New York Times*, 26 May 2005, A12; T Perry, 'Navy Lieutenant Denies Assaulting Iraqi Prisoner', *Los Angeles Times*, 27 May 2005, A31; T Perry, 'SEAL Officer Not Guilty of Assaulting Iraqi', *Los Angeles Times*, 28 May 2005, A35.

[55] T Shanker, 'Army Says Up to 28 G.I.'s Could Face Afghan Abuse Charges', *New York Times*, 15 Oct 2004, A12; J Hendren and M Mazzetti, 'Army Implicates 28 U.S. Troops in Deaths of 2 Afghan Detainees', *Los Angeles Times*, 15 Oct 2004, A13; D Jehl, 'Army Details Scale of Abuse of Prisoners in an Afghan Jail', *New York Times*, 12 Mar 2005, A1; L Hart, 'Afghan Detainee's Leg Was "Pulpified"', *Los Angeles Times*, 23 Mar 2005, A18; L Hart, 'Soldier Facing Trial in Death of Prisoner Wins Round', *Los Angeles Times*, 4 Apr 2005, A13; T Golden, 'In U.S. Report, Brutal Details of 2 Afghan Inmates' Deaths', *New York Times*, 20 May 2005, A1; T Golden, 'Army Faltered in Investigating Detainee Abuse', *New York Times*, 22 May 2005, §1 at 1; 'Jail Term for Soldier in Abuse Case', *New York Times*, 23 May 2005, A10; 'World Briefings', *New York Times*, 5 Aug 2005, A10; T Golden, 'Abuse Cases Open Command Issues at Army Prison', *New York Times*, 8 Aug 2005, A1.

[56] J Hendren, 'Pentagon Confirms Detainee Deaths After Disclosure', *Los Angeles Times*, 14 Dec 2004, A3.

[57] J Fleishman and R Salman, 'U.S. Soldier on Trial for Murder', *Los Angeles Times*, 9 Sept 2004, A3; 'U.S. Officer Calls Killing an Act of Mercy', *New York Times*, 9 Sept 2004, A14; 'Soldier Defends His Killing of Iraqi as "the Honorable Thing"', *Los Angeles Times*, 31 May 2005, A4; 'Military Panel Convicts Soldier', *Los Angeles Times*, 1 Apr 2005, A8; 'Convicted GI Will Not Serve Time', *Los Angeles Times*, 2 Apr 2005, A5; 'Army Officer Convicted in Iraqi's Death Is Freed', *New York Times*, 2 Apr 2005, A5.

sought three and the judge gave none. A soldier who pleaded guilty to killing a severely wounded Iraqi teenager 'to put him out of his misery' was sentenced to three years.[58] When Specialists Charley Hooser and Rami Dajani were 'joking around' about shooting someone, Dajani handed Hooser a pistol. Thinking it had been cleared of ammunition, Hooser shot their translator in the head, killing her. For 15 days they told investigators she had shot herself. Hooser received three years and Dajani 18 months.[59] Second Lieutenant Ilario G Pantano was charged with the premeditated murder of two Iraqis during a vehicle check. The military accepted the preliminary hearing recommendation to drop the charges.[60]

If law is the state's reason for exercising power, courts martial are profoundly lawless. The military offers no explanation for dismissing complaints. Administrative penalties remain secret. Trial transcripts are not readily available. And judges do not explain sentences. Most Abu Ghraib accused claimed to have followed orders, and their lawyers sought to question superiors up to Rumsfeld. But we will never be able to evaluate those claims since all but Graner pleaded guilty. Was lenience a pay-off for not fingering those higher up? There are obvious parallels between soldiers and police.[61] Society entrusts both with our highest value—security—conferring exclusive authority to use deadly force while rewarding arrests and body counts. It wants both to do our dirty work out of sight and then punishes a few caught transgressing ambiguous boundaries, often because the actions are recorded, as at Abu Ghraib and the Rodney King beating.

The military did no better prospectively. In response to Sanchez's request for an expert assessment of detention and interrogation, Major General Donald J Ryder, Army Provost Marshall General, visited Iraq from 13 October to 6 November 2003 and reported on the latter date. He observed:

> Military Police, though adept at passive collection of intelligence within a facility, do not participate in Military Intelligence-supervised interrogation sessions. The 800th MP Brigade has not been tasked to change its facility procedures to set the conditions for MI interviews, nor participate in those interviews.

[58] E Wong, 'Trial Date Set for Another Reservist in Prison Abuse Case', *New York Times*, 22 Oct 2004, A8; 'Soldier Convicted in Teen's Death', *New York Times*, 15 Jan 2005.

[59] E Wong and C Hauser, '2 G.I.'s Guilty in Iraqi Co-Worker's Death', *New York Times*, 23 Jan 2005, §1 at 10.

[60] M O'Donnell, 'Marine Charged With Murder in Iraqis' Deaths', *New York Times*, 11 Feb 2005, A17; J DeSantis, 'Hearing Begins for Marine Accused of Killing 2 Iraqis', *New York Times*, 27 Apr 2005, A12; J DeSantis, 'National Briefing South: North Carolina: Accused Marine Is Praised', *New York Times*, 29 Apr 2005, A19; J DeSantis, 'Prosecution Presses Murder Case Against Marine', *New York Times*, 1 May 2005, §1 at 20; J DeSantis, 'Call to Drop Murder Case Against Marine', *New York Times*, 14 May 2005, A9; J DeSantis, 'Marine Cleared in Deaths of 2 Insurgents in Iraq', *New York Times*, 27 May 2005, A18; D Zucchino, 'Marine Cleared in Killing of 2 Iraqi Detainees', *Los Angeles Times*, 27 May 2005, A18; 'North Carolina: Officer to Resign', *New York Times*, 3 June 2005, A18.

[61] The classic account of the latter is Skolnick, 1966.

On 13 January 2004 Specialist Joseph M Darby anonymously slipped under the Criminal Investigation Division (CID) door a CD of abuse photographs copied from Graner's computer.[62] Six days later Sanchez asked CENTCOM to investigate.[63] On 31 January the Coalition Commander appointed Major General Antonio M Taguba, a career officer, who submitted a briefing on 3 March and the written report on 9 March. It was classified Secret/No Foreign Dissemination but reported by Seymour Hersh on *The New Yorker* website on 30 April (Hersh, 2004).[64] Contrary to Ryder, Taguba found that MI and CIA interrogators 'actively requested that MP guards set physical and mental conditions for favorable interrogation of witnesses'.[65] MPs 'had received no training in detention/internee operations' before deployment and 'few, if any, copies of the Geneva Conventions'.[66] He recommended criminal inquiries into the culpability of MI and contract employees and discipline and criminal investigation of superiors: Brigadier General Janis L Karpinski (Commander, 800th MP Brigade), Colonel Thomas M Pappas (Commander, 205th MI Brigade), and Lieutenant Colonels Jerry L Phillabaum (Commander, 320th MP Battalion) and Steven L Jordan (former director, JIDC).

On 10 February the Acting Army Secretary instructed the Army Inspector General to conduct 'an assessment of detainee operations in Afghanistan and Iraq'.[67] He appointed Lieutenant General Paul T Mikolashek, a career officer, whose 21 July whitewash was replete with excuses and denials.[68] Soldiers:

> are conducting operations under demanding, stressful, and dangerous conditions against an enemy who does not follow the Geneva Conventions. They are in an environment that puts a tremendous demand on human intelligence, particularly, at the tactical level where contact with the enemy and the people are most intense.

He 'discovered no incidents of abuse that had not been reported through command channels'. There were the 'only' 94 cases of confirmed or possible abuse among more than 50,000 detainees; nearly half 'occurred at the point of capture, where soldiers have the least amount of control of the environment'. 'Officially approved' interrogation policies and practices

---

[62] Schlesinger, above n 5, at 926.

[63] Sanchez to Commander, CENTCOM, in Taguba, above n 27, at 469.

[64] CBS already had the photographs (though not the report) but delayed disseminating them at the request of Gen Myers, who claimed the information would endanger Coalition soldiers fighting in Fallujah and Najaf, as well as hostages. But once CBS learned that Hersh was not caving in to Pentagon pressure, Dan Rather broadcast the photographs on *60 Minutes* on 28 Apr 28: D Remnick, 'Introduction' in SM Hersh, *Chain of Command: The Road from 9/11 to Abu Ghraib* (New York, HarperCollins, 2004) at ix, xviii; Schlesinger, above n 5, at 926–7. The Taguba Report was released only on 8 June.

[65] Taguba, above n 27, at 417–18.

[66] *Ibid*, 419.

[67] Brownlee to Inspector General (10 Feb 2004), in Mikolashek, above n 44, at 631.

[68] *Ibid* at 632–5, 637, 649, 657, 726–8.

'generally met legal obligations', and 'no confirmed instance of detainee abuse was caused by the approved policies'.

— the overwhelming majority of our leaders and soldiers understand the requirement to treat detainees humanely and are doing so.
— we were unable to identify system failures that resulted in incidents of abuse. These incidents of abuse resulted from the failure of individuals to follow known standards of discipline and Army Values and, in some cases, the failure of a few leaders to enforce those standards of discipline.

Law of War training devoted just 36 classroom minutes to 'the principles, spirit and intent of the Hague and Geneva Conventions ... and the laws of war requiring humane treatment of prisoners of war' and 'did not differentiate between the different classifications of detainees, causing confusion concerning the levels of treatment'. A 'command climate that encourages behavior at the harsher end of the acceptable range of behavior towards detainees may unintentionally, increase the likelihood of abuse'. 'In a few cases, the perception ... that Other Governmental Agencies (OGA, a euphemism for the CIA) conducted interrogations using harsher methods than allowed by Army Regulation, led to a belief that higher levels of command condoned such methods'. Senators reacted predictably. Jack Reed (Democrat, Rhode Island) accused the report of 'reinforcing the conclusion that there are five or six aberrant soldiers'. Jeff Sessions (Republican, Alabama) complained: 'We want our soldiers right up to the limit of what they legally can do to obtain good intelligence to help save lives'.[69]

Two weeks after the Abu Ghraib exposé, Rumsfeld appointed two former Defense Secretaries (Schlesinger, chair, and Brown), a former Representative and a retired Air Force General to review DoD Detention Operations.[70] Their 24 August report began: '[t]he events of October through December 2003 on the night shift of Tier 1 at Abu Ghraib prison were acts of brutality and senseless sadism'.[71] But they 'were not part of authorized interrogations nor were they even directed at intelligence targets'. Like Mikolashek, Schlesinger emphasised that more than 50,000 detentions had produced only 66 substantiated cases of abuse, a third 'at the point of capture or tactical collection point, frequently under uncertain, dangerous and violent circumstances'. 'No approved procedures called for or allowed the kinds of abuse that in fact occurred'. They rejected the International Committee of the Red Cross's insistence that the US follow GC Protocol 1. To 'grant legal protections to terrorists equivalent to the protections accorded to prisoners of war ... would undermine the prohibition on terrorists blending in

---

[69] E Schmitt, 'Army Report Says Flaws in Detention Did Not Cause Abuses at Abu Ghraib', *New York Times*, 23 July 2004, A9.

[70] Rumsfeld to Schlesinger *et al.* (12 May 2004), in Schlesinger, above n 5, at 961.

[71] *Ibid*, at 909, 911–12, 914–16, 921, 945, 948–53.

with the civilian population', and 'interrogation operations would not be allowed'. They recommended clarification of the status and treatment of detainees 'consistent with U.S. jurisprudence and military doctrine and with U.S. interpretation of the Geneva Conventions'. 'Well-documented policy and procedures on approved interrogation techniques are imperative to counteract the current chilling effect the reaction to the abuses have had on the collection of valuable intelligence through interrogations'.

The report advanced many explanations. The 'legal resources of the Services' Judge Advocates General and General Counsels were not utilized to their full potential' in developing detention policy; this might 'have avoided the policy changes which characterized the December 2, 2002, to April 16, 2003 period'. Furthermore, 'the augmented techniques for Guantánamo migrated to Afghanistan and Iraq where they were neither limited nor safeguarded'. Schlesinger believed that 'CJTF-7's determination that some of the detainees held in Iraq were to be categorized as unlawful combatants' illustrated Justice O'Connor's observation in *Hamdi* (below) that 'the Government has never provided any court with the full criteria that it uses in classifying individuals' as enemy combatants (ECs).[72] Guantánamo had a 'high ratio of approximately 1 to 1 of military police to mostly compliant detainees', whereas 'in Abu Ghraib the ratio of military police to repeatedly unruly detainees was … at one point 1 to about 75'. The report blamed lack of 'proper training, leadership and oversight' and 'the predilections of the non-commissioned officers in charge', noting that the 72nd MP Company, which had opened Abu Ghraib in July, was 'a very strong unit that kept tight rein on operational procedures at the facility' and 'called into question the interrogation practices of the MI brigade regarding nakedness of detainees'. In 'nearly 10 percent of the cases of alleged abuse, the chain of command ignored reports of those allegations. More than once a commander was complicit.' The report criticised Sanchez but acknowledged that at one point CJTF-7 had only 495 of its 1,400 authorised staff. It seconded Taguba's disciplinary recommendations and anticipated more from the Jones/Fay inquiry (below).

A SOUTHCOM secret investigation of Guantánamo abuses produced only a six-page summary on 19 June.[73] This confirmed that 'immediate reaction forces' punched and kneed detainees, tied them to gurneys, left them naked for days, and used pepper spray in the cells. Some teams were all women, although devout Muslims could not touch women other than their wives. But the report found no systematic abuse.

---

[72] As late as May 2004 Yoo maintained that 'if an Iraqi civilian who is not a member of the armed forces, has engaged in attacks on Coalition forces, the Geneva Convention permits the use of more coercive interrogation approaches to prevent future attacks': J Yoo, 'Terrorists Have No Geneva Rights', *Wall Street Journal* 380, 26 May 2004, A16.

[73] 'Secret Report Questions Guantánamo Tactics', *New York Times*, 2 Feb 2005, A14.

On 31 March Sanchez appointed Major General George R Fay to investigate misconduct by the 205th MI Brigade. When Sanchez seemed to be a possible target, Lieutenant General Anthony R Jones was added. Only 171 of the several thousand pages were released in late August.[74] They identified 44 alleged incidents involving 54 people: physical abuse, use of dogs, humiliating and degrading treatments, nakedness, photographs, simulated sexual positions, isolation, sleep deprivation, exposure to heat and cold, and failure to safeguard detainees and report abuse.

Fay found that the Office of the SJA had given Rumsfeld's 16 April memorandum to Captain Fitch (Command Judge Advocate), who 'copied [it] almost verbatim onto a document entitled CJTF-7 Interrogation and Counter-Resistance Policy' and sent it to the 519th MI Battalion, which added the use of dogs, stress positions, sleep management, sensory deprivation and yelling, loud music and light control. Sanchez promulgated this on 14 September. Although CENTCOM ordered it to be withdrawn, the 12 October replacement miscited GC IV Article 5 for the proposition that 'detainees engaged in activities hostile to security of coalition forces had forfeited their Geneva Convention rights of communication'. The memorandum retained the superseded *1987* Field Manual 34-52 language. '[I]nterrogators, with their section leaders' knowledge, routinely utilized approaches/techniques without obtaining the required authority'. 'Concepts for the non-doctrinal, non-field manual approaches and practices clearly came from documents and personnel in Afghanistan and Guantánamo.' Pappas 'perceived intense pressure for intelligence from interrogations', which 'was passed ... to the interrogators and analysts operating at Abu Ghraib'. 'Local CIA officers convinced Col. Pappas and LTC Jordan that they should be allowed to operate outside the established local rules and procedures.' 'According to Col Pappas, MG G. Miller said they, GTMO, used military working dogs, and that they were effective in setting the atmosphere for interrogations'. (Miller denied this.) A team from US Army Intelligence Center in Arizona visited Abu Ghraib for two weeks in October. One member 'related several stories about the use of dogs as an inducement ... explained that detainees are most susceptible during the first few hours

[74] Maj Gen George R Ray, AR 15-6 Investigation of the Abu Ghraib Detention Facility and 205th Military Intelligence Brigade, in Greenberg and Dratel, 2005, at 1018; Lieut Gen Anthony R Jones, Investigation of the Abu Ghraib Prison and 205th Military Intelligence Brigade, in *ibid*, at 987; E Schmitt, 'Abuses at Prison tied to Officers in Intelligence', *New York Times*, 26 Aug 2004, A11; 'Latest Report on Abu Ghraib: Abuses of Iraqi Prisoners "Are, Without Question, Criminal"', *New York Times*, 26 Aug 2004, A11; A Elliott, 'Perilous Conditions Led Up to Abuses at Baghdad Prison', *New York Times*, 26 Aug 2004, A1; D Jehl, 'Some Abu Ghraib Abuses Are Traced to Afghanistan', *New York Times*, 26 Aug 2004, A11; RA Serrano, 'Pentagon Cites Widespread Involvement in Prison Abuses', *Los Angeles Times*, 26 Aug 2004, A1; G Miller, 'CIA Spurned Prison Rules, Report Says', *Los Angeles Times*, 26 Aug 2004, A1; M Mazzetti, 'Prison Abuse Reports May Insulate Bush From Blame', *Los Angeles Times*, 26 Aug 2004, A7.

of capture' and suggested that a civilian interrogator 'could take some pictures of what seemed to be guards being rough with prisoners ... so he could use them to scare the prisoners'. During visits to Abu Ghraib on 9–12 and 21–23 October, the International Committee of the Red Cross saw and heard of abuses, which it reported on 6 November. Major O'Kane prepared an analysis on 25 November; a 4 December meeting discussed the reports and response, which Karpinski signed on 24 December. The ICRC was denied access to eight detainees during subsequent visits on 4–8 January and 14–18 March.

Fay offered various explanations: inadequate command; lack of unit cohesion caused by mixing personnel from many sources; 'intense pressure they felt from ... CENTCOM, the Pentagon, and DIA for timelier actionable intelligence'; inconsistent doctrine; ineffective training; mutual ignorance and uncertain authority between MP and MI; reliance on 'instinct'; and use of contract interrogators. The GTMO and Arizona training teams 'validated the use of unacceptable interrogation techniques'. The Army 'allowed CIA to house "Ghost Detainees"', whom they detained and interrogated 'under different practices and procedures which were absent any DoD visibility, control, or oversight'. 'ICRC recommendations were ignored by MI, MP and CJTF-7 personnel'. Indeed, 'there seemed to be a consensus ... that the allegations were not true'. He found evidence for charges against Pappas, Jordan, Captain Carolyn Wood (519th MI Battalion Commander), two other officers, 17 soldiers, and five civilians.

Jones basically concurred. No 'policy, directive, or doctrine caused the violent or sexual abuse incidents'. Rather, 'misinterpretation as to accepted practices or confusion occurred due to the proliferation of guidance and information from other theaters of operation' and 'individual interrogator experiences'. 'Inaction at the CJTF-7 staff level may have also contributed to the failure to discover and prevent abuses before January 2004'. The 'chain of command above the 205th MI Brigade was not directly involved in any of the abuses'. Although Sanchez and Wojdakowski 'failed to ensure proper staff oversight', 'CJTF-7 Commander and staff performed above expectations'.

Vice Admiral Albert T Church, Navy Inspector General, reported in March 2005, releasing only 21 of 368 pages.[75] His 'key findings' were that 'no policy ... condoned or authorized either abuse or torture. There was no linkage between the authorized interrogation techniques and the abuses that in fact occurred'. Only 70 of the 187 allegations were substantiated: 38 were minor, and a third occurred at the point of capture when 'passions often

[75] M Mazzetti, 'Lack of Oversight Led to Abuse of Detainees, Investigator Says', *Los Angeles Times*, 9 Mar 2005, A10; E Schmitt, 'New Interrogation Rules Set for Detainees in Iraq', *New York Times*, 10 Mar 2005, A1; E Schmitt, 'Official Declines to Pin Blame for Blunders in Interrogations', *New York Times*, 11 Mar 2005, A8; G Miller and J Hendren, 'No Need for CIA Abuse Probe, Republican Says', *Los Angeles Times*, 11 Mar 2005, A11.

run high'. '[W]e have nonetheless identified a number of missed opportunities in the policy development process'. First, 'with hindsight I think guidance should have been issued to Afghanistan and Iraq either by the Central Command or higher authority'. Secondly, interrogation techniques at Guantánamo were approved over the objections of senior military lawyers.

In an unreleased report, Army Inspector General Lieutenant General Stanley E Green cleared Sanchez, Fast, Warren and Wojdakowski of any responsibility. Fast was promoted to head the Army Intelligence Center (whose training team had encouraged the Abu Ghraib abuses).[76] Sanchez was made commander of the Army V Corps in Germany, losing his chance at a fourth star and command of SOUTHCOM.[77] Karpinski was demoted to colonel—for concealing in her promotion application a conviction for shoplifting a $22 bottle of perfume from the Post Exchange (PX) several years earlier.[78] (On a radio talk show three months later she claimed to have seen a memorandum authorising aggressive interrogation, signed by Rumsfeld with a handwritten note: 'Make sure this happens'.)[79] Pappas received a written reprimand and $8,000 fine.[80] Wojdakowski became head of the Army infantry training school at Fort Benning, Georgia. Warren was nominated for brigadier general. General Horner, a member of the Schlesinger panel, called him a 'hero' and 'straight shooter' for acknowledging his mistakes.[81]

In December 2004 the American Civil Liberties Union (ACLU) disclosed confidential FBI memoranda graphically describing abuses agents had witnessed in Guantánamo from early 2002 to May 2004.[82] SOUTHCOM Commander General Bantz J Craddock assigned Brigadier General John T

---

[76] E Schmitt, 'Former Intelligence Officer Clear in Iraq Abuse', *New York Times*, 12 Mar 2005, A7.

[77] E Schmitt and T Shanker, 'Posts Considered for Commanders after Abuse Case', *New York Times*, 20 June 2005, A1.

[78] E Schmitt, 'Four Top Officers Cleared by Army in Prison Abuses', *New York Times*, 23 Apr 2005, A1; J White, 'Top Army Officers Are Cleared in Abuse Cases', *Washington Post*, 23 Apr 2005, A1; RA Serrano and M Mazzetti, 'General Demoted Over Prison Scandal', *Los Angeles Times*, 6 May 2005, A20; 'General Who Ran Prison Is Demoted', *New York Times*, 6 May 2005, A10.

[79] 'Rebuilding in the Gulf: Did Rumsfeld Order Abu Ghraib Rough Stuff?'. *WorldNetDaily.com* (3 Aug 2005).

[80] E Schmitt, 'No Criminal Charges for Officer at Abu Ghraib Interrogations', *New York Times*, 12 May 2005, A11; RA Serrano, 'Abu Ghraib Intelligence Chief Is Reprimanded', *Los Angeles Times*, 12 May 2005, A15.

[81] E Schmitt, 'Army Moves to Advance 2 Linked to Abu Ghraib', *New York Times*, 29 June 2006, A19, available at www.intel-dump.com/posts/1121522295.shtml, last visited 18 July 2005.

[82] NA Lewis, 'F.B.I. Memos Criticized Practices at Guantánamo', *New York Times*, 7 Dec 2004, A18; RA Serrano, 'Guantánamo Abuse Detailed in FBI Letter', *Los Angeles Times*, 7 Dec 2004, A14; RA Serrano, 'FBI Agents Complained of Prisoner Abuse, Records Say', *Los Angeles Times*, 21 Dec 2004, A1; NA Lewis and D Johnston, 'New F.B.I. Files Describe Abuse of Iraq Inmates', *New York Times*, 21 Dec 2004, A1; K Zernike, 'Newly Released Reports Show Early Concern on Prison Abuse', *New York Times*, 6 Jan 2005, A1; Unnamed FBI agent, Memo to Marian Bowman, Legal Counsel, FBIHQ (27 Nov 2002) (some interrogation techniques unconstitutional or violate torture statute).

Furlow to investigate.[83] When it appeared that Major General Miller might be implicated, Craddock added Lieutenant General Randall M Schmitt. Their March 2005 preliminary report confirmed some charges,[84] but the July final report (only partly published) pulled its punches.[85] Of the nine FBI allegations (out of 24,000 interrogations) they found two unsubstantiated, five substantiated but authorised, and only three substantiated but unauthorised (short-shackling detainees to the floor, duct taping a detainee's face to quieten him, and threatening a detainee and his family). They concluded that though interrogating Mohammed Al-Qahtani (allegedly the missing twentieth hijacker) for 20 hours on 48 of 54 consecutive days and sexually humiliating him was 'abusive and degrading ... no torture occurred; detention and interrogation operations were safe, secure, and humane'. They recommended that the Special Team Chief be disciplined and Miller admonished, but General Craddock decided that Miller had violated no law or policy. The Pentagon reiterated that it 'remains committed to the unequivocal standard of humane treatment for all detainees, and [al-Qahtani's] interrogation plan was guided by that strict standard'.[86]

Quis custodiet ipsos custodes? Especially when some culprits are military police! The record does not inspire confidence in self-regulation. After three weeks in Iraq the Army Provost Marshall General declared that MPs had no role in preparing detainees for interrogation—although Miller had just brought that practice from Guantánamo and Army Intelligence Center trainers seconded it. Officers at Abu Ghraib disregarded abuse complaints by soldiers and the ICRC. Had Graner and his groupies not bragged about and photographed their crimes nothing might have happened. Only Specialist Darby blew the whistle, forcing the Army to realise that truth would out. It classified Taguba's report Secret. The military persuaded CBS to postpone broadcasting the photographs, but Hersh could not be silenced. The dozen subsequent reports remained mostly secret (like some legal memoranda).

---

[83] CJ Williams, 'Inquiry Ordered Into Alleged Guantánamo Prisoner Abuse', *Los Angeles Times*, 6 Jan 2005, A15; 'New Chief for Guantánamo Probe', *Los Angeles Times*, 1 Mar 2005, A19.

[84] NA Lewis and E Schmitt, 'Inquiry Finds Abuses at Guantánamo Bay', *New York Times*, 1 May 2005, §1 at 23; RA Serrano, 'Report Details Discipline for Guantánamo Abuses', *Los Angeles Times*, 7 May 2005, A13.

[85] Lieut Gen M Schmidt and Brig Gen J Furlow, DCR USSOUTHCOM Directed AR 15-6 Investigation into Detainee-Abuse Allegations at Guantánamo Bay, Cuba; M Mazzetti, 'General Rejects Call to Penalize Ex-Guantánamo Prison Chief', *Los Angeles Times*, 13 July 2005, A11; DS Cloud, 'Guantánamo Reprimand Was Sought, an Aide Says', *New York Times*, 13 May 2005, A16; J White, 'Abu Ghraib Tactics Were First Used at Guantánamo', *Washington Post*, 14 July 2005, A1; NA Lewis, 'Report Discredits F.B.I. Claims of Abuse at Guantánamo Bay', *New York Times*, 14 July 2005, A17; M Mazzetti and S Bodzin, 'Senators Hear of "Degrading" Interrogations', *Los Angeles Times*, 14 May 2005, A14; A Zagorin and M Duffy, 'Inside the Interrogation of Detainee 063', *Time*, 20 June 2005.

[86] 'Guantanamo Provides Valuable Intelligence Information', No 592-05 (12 June 2005), available at www.dod.mil/releases/2005/nr20050612-3661.html.

Taguba was unusually candid, naming offenders and urging serious punishment. Secrecy may have made him less defensive. But once the news was out
the military reverted to type: cover your ass. It endlessly repeated the mantra:
our policy (not law) is to treat detainees humanely; abuses are investigated and punished. Every other report offered the same litany of excuses:
battlefield pressures, enemy disregard for the law of warfare, inadequate
staffing, poor training, organisational deficiencies, confusing guidance, and
'few' abuses given the number of detainees. Demonising the enemy—from
Bush's 'axis of evil' to the military's facile condemnation of 'bad guys'—
made abuses more acceptable. Senator Trent Lott (Republican, Mississippi)
expostulated: 'Interrogation is not a Sunday-school class. You don't get information that will save American lives by withholding pancakes'.[87]

Some reports did attribute abuses to superiors' pressures for intelligence
but found those legitimate. As Senator Jeff Sessions (Republican, Alabama)
explained: 'We want our soldiers right up to the limit of what they legally
can do to obtain good intelligence to help save lives'. Each group pointed
at another: the FBI in Guantánamo at MI, MPs in Abu Ghraib at MI, the
military at the CIA, and the CIA at Special Forces. Every report depicted the
Abu Ghraib night shift as unique. Indeed, its infantile gratuitous, sexualised
cruelty let the military trumpet condemnation while distracting attention
from and obscuring connections with the pervasive abuses. Investigators
sharply distinguished between culpable foot soldiers and blameless superiors even though the military command structure makes deniability difficult.
Lieutenant General Jones explicitly exculpated Major General Sanchez,
who lost his promotion but probably for other reasons. Karpinski was disciplined for an extraneous offence. Craddock rejected the Schmidt/Furlow
recommendation that Miller be admonished. Fast was promoted and
Warren nominated for promotion.

The reports hedged the relationship between policy and practice (which
Mikolashek emphatically denied). Schlesinger regretted that military lawyers had been insufficiently involved (actually systematically excluded).
Several reports decried doctrinal deficiencies but insisted that the problem was not too little law but too much, leaving soldiers confused. The
Schmidt/Furlow finding that treatment was 'degrading and abusive' but
not 'torture or inhumane' perfectly echoes the pilpul (sharp reasoning) in
Bybee's August 2002 memorandum. No one was responsible for promul-
gating bad policies, which passively 'migrated'. 'Interrogation techniques
intended only for Guantánamo *came to be used* in Afghanistan and Iraq.'[88]
Schlesinger declared that '[w]ell-documented policy and procedures on

---

[87] 'All's Fair', *New York Times Magazine*, 20 June 2004, 15. He seems to have assumed
that his idealisation of Strom Thurmond had been forgotten: see Abel, 2003, 'Lott's Life: Don't
Look Back, The Politics of Respect' (2003) 5 *Rutgers Race & The Law Rev* 269.
[88] Schlesinger, above n 5, at 941 (emphasis added).

approved interrogation techniques are imperative to counteract the current chilling effect the reaction to the abuses have had on the collection of valuable intelligence through interrogations'. Rather than setting limits, doctrine should embolden interrogators to test the margins. No one questioned the administration's expansion of its powers. Indeed, Schlesinger explicitly embraced 'U.S. jurisprudence and military doctrine and ... U.S. interpretation of the Geneva Conventions', rejecting the ICRC recommendation to extend POW protection to unlawful combatants.

IV. JUDICIAL CHALLENGES TO DETENTION

A Federal Public Defender petitioned for habeas corpus on behalf of Yaser Esam Hamdi, captured in Afghanistan and sent to Guantánamo but transferred to the Norfolk Naval Brig because he had been born in Louisiana.[89] The Fourth Circuit reversed District Judge Doumar's order granting Hamdi unrestricted access to his attorney:[90]

> The order arises in the context of foreign relations and national security, where a court's deference to the political branches of our national government is considerable ... where as here the President ... act[s] with statutory authorization from Congress, there is all the more reason for deference.

At the next hearing the District Court 'expressed concern over possible violations of Hamdi's rights as an American citizen' and

> questioned the government's most basic contentions regarding the ongoing hostilities, asking 'with whom is the war I should suggest that we're fighting?' and 'will the war never be over as long as there is any member [or] any person who might feel that they want to attack the United States of America?'[91]

Ignoring these questions, the government moved to dismiss, filing an affidavit by FBI Agent Michael Mobbs declaring Hamdi an Enemy Combatant. At the Fourth Circuit's direction, Doumar held a hearing in which:

> the court asserted that it was 'challenging everything in the Mobbs' declaration' and that it intended to 'pick it apart' 'piece by piece.' The court repeatedly referred to information it felt was missing from the declaration, asking 'Is there anything in here that said Hamdi ever fired a weapon?' The court questioned whether Mr. Mobbs was even a government employee and intimated that the government was possibly hiding disadvantageous information from the court.

[89] *Hamdi v Rumsfeld*, 294 F 3d 598 (4th Cir 2002) (*Hamdi I*).
[90] *Hamdi v Rumsfeld*, 296 F 3d 278 (4th Cir 2002) (*Hamdi II*).
[91] *Hamdi v Rumsfeld*, 316 F 3d 450 (4th Cir 2002) (*Hamdi III*) (Wilkinson J).

Finding that the declaration 'falls far short' of supporting Hamdi's detention, Doumar ordered the government to present evidence in camera so he could determine whether Hamdi was a prisoner of war.[92] Otherwise 'this Court would be acting as little more than a rubber-stamp'.

Although Doumar certified for appeal only the narrow question 'whether the Mobbs Declaration, standing alone, is sufficient as a matter of law to allow a meaningful judicial review of Yaser Esam Hamdi's classification' as an EC, the Fourth Circuit chose to address 'any issue fairly included within the certified order'. If 'deference to the executive is not exercised with respect to military judgments in the field, it is difficult to see where deference would ever obtain'. It rejected Hamdi's GC claim for a hearing on his status because the Convention was not self-executing. Holding that lawful and unlawful combatants was 'a distinction without a difference, since the option to detain until the cessation of hostilities belongs to the executive in either case', it dismissed the petition:

> To transfer the instinctive skepticism, so laudable in the defense of criminal charges, to the review of executive branch decisions premised on military determinations made in the field carries the inordinate risk of a constitutionally problematic intrusion into the most basic responsibilities of a coordinate branch.

Any 'evidentiary hearing or factual inquiry' would 'entail an unacceptable risk of obstructing war efforts'. '[C]essation of hostilities would seem no less a matter of political competence than the initiation of them'.

Two judges dissented from the denial of a rehearing en banc.[93] Luttig felt Hamdi should not be bound by his *father's* concession that he had been seized in a foreign combat zone. Motz said the panel 'has seriously erred'. This was:

> the first time in our history that a federal court has approved the elimination of protections afforded a citizen by the Constitution solely on the basis of the Executive's designation of that citizen as an enemy combatant, without testing the accuracy of the designation.

The panel's 'rubberstamp of the Executive's unsupported designation lacks both the procedural and substantive content' of meaningful review. The 'experienced' district judge 'has courageously attempted to provide the meaningful judicial review that the Constitution mandates, however unpopular the case'. Judge Wilkinson justified his earlier opinion. 'There was extensive review of every legal challenge to Hamdi's detention'. 'To start down this road of litigating what Hamdi was actually doing among the enemy or to what extent he was aiding the enemy is to bump right up against the war

---

[92] *Hamdi v Rumsfeld*, 243 F Supp 2d 527 (ED Va 2002).
[93] *Hamdi v Rumsfeld*, 337 F 3d 335 (4th Cir 2002) (*Hamdi IV*) (without opinion).

powers of Articles I and II'. '[T]here is value to having the United States state under oath its reasons for the detention of an American citizen … . To go further, however, would be folly'. Judge Traxler also defended the opinion he had signed. The 'Judiciary became compelled, by the nature of war and by dint of the separation of powers we are required to safeguard and honor, to give deference to the Executive to determine who within a hostile country is friend and who is foe'.

Shortly before Judge Doumar found the Mobbs declaration 'little more than the government's "say so"', District of Columbia Judge Kollar-Kotelly dismissed habeas corpus petitions by Rasul and al Odah because Guantánamo was 'not part of the sovereign territory of the United States', which 'merely leases an area of land for use as a naval base'.[94] Any rights they might have under international law 'are for the military and political branches to determine'. The DC Circuit affirmed.[95] Because 'aliens outside the sovereign territory of the United States' lacked constitutional rights, 'no court in this country has jurisdiction to grant habeas relief'.

When his plane landed in Chicago on 8 May 2002, Jose Padilla was arrested on a material witness warrant issued by the Southern District of New York (SDNY) to secure his testimony before its grand jury.[96] After he was transferred to New York his lawyer moved to vacate the warrant. But on Sunday, 9 June, two days before the motion was to be heard, the government notified the court ex parte that President Bush had declared Padilla an Enemy Combatant and the DoD had moved him to the Naval Brig in South Carolina. The government denied him contact with his lawyer and submitted a redacted Mobbs declaration (and an unredacted one under seal). Rumsfeld told the press on 12 June:

> [O]ur interest really in his case is not law enforcement, it is not punishment because he was a terrorist or working with the terrorists. Our interest at the moment is to try and find out everything he knows so that hopefully we can stop other terrorist acts.

SDNY Judge Mukasey found jurisdiction over Rumsfeld, 'who was charged by the President in the June 9 Order with detaining Padilla'. Mukasey felt his 'discretion under the All Writs Act should be exercised in favor of permitting [Padilla] to consult with counsel in aid of his petition and, in particular, in aid of responding to the Mobbs Declaration', which Mukasey called 'gossamer speculation'. After the Fourth Circuit decided *Hamdi* the government moved to reconsider *Padilla*, submitting declarations by Defense Intelligence Agency Director Jacoby.[97] But Mukasey noted that 'the prospect of courts

[94] *Rasul v Bush*, 215 F Supp 2d 55 (DDC 2002).
[95] *Al Odah v United States*, 321 F 3d 1134 (DC Cir 2003).
[96] *Padilla v Bush*, 233 F Supp 2d 564 (SDNY 2002).
[97] *Padilla v Rumsfeld*, 243 F Supp 2d 42 (SDNY 2003).

second-guessing battlefield decisions' in *Hamdi* 'does not loom in this case'. He reiterated that:

> unless [Padilla] has the opportunity to make a submission, this court cannot do what the applicable statutes and the Due Process Clause require it to do: confirm ... that because his detention is not arbitrary, the President is exercising a power vouchsafed to him by the Constitution.

The Second Circuit (Judges Parker and Pooler) affirmed:[98]

> The Constitution's explicit grant of the powers authorized in the Offenses Clause, the Suspension Clause, and the Third Amendment, to Congress is a Powerful indication that, absent express congressional authorization, the President's Commander-in-Chief powers do not support Padilla's confinement.

The Non-Detention Act's 'plain language' prohibited 'all detentions of citizens'. The dissenter believed Bush could detain but agreed Padilla needed counsel to exercise his habeas corpus right. 'Certainly, a court could inquire whether Padilla continues to possess information that was helpful to the President in prosecuting the war against al Qaeda'.

In Spring 2004 the ABCNY Committee on Federal Courts issued a report on detainees.[98a]

> The holding of persons incommunicado in this country, without charges, indefinitely, based solely on the executive's decision, has nothing in common with due process as we know it. ... these detentions are alien to America's respect for the rule of law. Until now, no court has ever sustained the assertion of such unilateral detention powers by a President ... .

The Supreme Court decided all three cases on 28 June 2004. In *Rasul*, Justice Stevens found that 'by the express terms of its agreements with Cuba, the United States exercises "complete jurisdiction and control" over the Guantánamo Bay Naval Base, and may continue to exercise such control permanently if it so chooses'.[99] Scalia dissented. This 'novel' holding 'contradicts a half-century-old precedent on which the military undoubtedly relied'. The Court had sprung 'a trap on the Executive'. 'When does definite detention become indefinite? How much process will suffice to stave off jurisdiction?' This 'monstrous scheme in time of war, and in frustration of our military commanders' reliance upon clearly stated prior law, is judicial adventurism of the worst sort'.

Rehnquist summarily told Padilla to file in South Carolina.[100] Stevens objected that the case 'raises questions of profound importance to the

---

[98] *Padilla v Rumsfeld*, 352 F 3d 695 (2nd Cir 2003).
[98a] ABCNY, 2004a.
[99] *Rasul v Bush*, 124 S Ct 2686 (2004).
[100] *Rumsfeld v Padilla*, 124 S Ct 2711 (2004).

nation'. Because the jurisdictional rule 'is riddled with exceptions ... this is an exceptional case that we clearly have jurisdiction to decide'. '[W]e should not permit the Government to obtain a tactical advantage as a consequence of an *ex parte* proceeding'. Rumsfeld's decisions 'have created a unique and unprecedented threat to the freedom of every American citizen':

> At stake in this case is nothing less than the essence of a free society. Even more important than the method of selecting the people's rulers and their successors is the character of the constraints imposed on the Executive by the rule of law. Unconstrained Executive detention for the purpose of investigating and preventing subversive activity is the hallmark of the Star Chamber. Executive detention of subversive citizens, like detention of enemy soldiers to keep them off the battlefield, may sometimes be justified to prevent persons from launching or becoming missiles of destruction. It may not, however, be justified by the naked interest in using unlawful procedures to extract information. Incommunicado detention for months on end is such a procedure. ... if this Nation is to remain true to the ideals symbolized by its flag, it must not wield the tools of tyrants even to resist an assault by the forces of tyranny.

Hamdi produced four opinions. Writing for a plurality, O'Connor said 'due process demands that a citizen held in the United States as an enemy combatant be given a meaningful opportunity to contest the factual basis for that detention before a neutral decisionmaker'.[101] The Authorization for the Use of Military Force (AUMF) satisfied the Non-Detention Act's requirement that detention be 'pursuant to an Act of Congress' but did not authorise 'indefinite detention for the purpose of interrogation'. Hamdi could be detained as an Enemy Combatant only if he were 'part of or supporting forces hostile to the United States or coalition partners' and 'engaged in an armed conflict against the United States'. '[R]espect for separation of powers and the limited institutional capabilities of courts in matters of military decision-making in connection with an ongoing conflict' did not require courts to test the categorisation of ECs by a very deferential 'some evidence' standard. This would '*condense* power into a single branch of government. We have long since made clear that the state of war is not a blank check for the President when it comes to the rights of the Nation's citizens' (citing *Youngstown*, a case disregarded by every OLC memorandum).

The Fifth Amendment required a balancing. On one side were 'the most elemental of liberty interests', which were not 'offset by the circumstances of war or the accusation of treasonous behavior'. On the other were the 'weighty and sensitive governmental interests in ensuring that those who have in fact fought with the enemy during a war do not return to battle

---

[101] *Hamdi v Rumsfeld*, 124 S Ct 2633 (2004).

against the United States'. The Constitution 'recognizes that core strategic matters of warmaking belong in the hands of those who are best positioned and most politically accountable for making them'. But 'it is during our most challenging and uncertain moments that our Nation's commitment to due process is most severely tested; and it is in those times that we must preserve our commitment at home to the principles for which we fight abroad'.[102]

Emphasising the separation of powers, Souter concurred that 'deciding finally on what is a reasonable degree of guaranteed liberty whether in peace or war … is not well entrusted to the Executive Branch of Government, whose particular responsibility is to maintain security'. *Ex parte Endo* held that 'in interpreting a wartime measure we must assume that [its] purpose was to allow for the greatest possible accommodation between … liberties and the exigencies of war'. He therefore read the Non-Detention Act 'broadly' to 'require clear congressional authorization before any citizen can be placed in a cell'. The AUMF did not suffice. Its 'focus is clear, and that is on the use of military power'. It 'never so much as uses the word detention'. Hamdi 'would … seem to qualify for treatment as a prisoner of war under the Third Geneva Convention', which incommunicado detention violated. Even the USA Patriot Act 'authorized the detention of alien terrorists for no more than seven days in the absence of criminal charges or deportation proceedings'. Souter also quoted *Youngstown*: 'the President is not Commander in Chief of the country, only of the military'. We 'are heirs to a tradition given voice 800 years ago by Magna Carta, which, on the barons' insistence, confined executive power by the "law of the land"'.

Scalia in dissent went even further. 'The very core of liberty secured by our Anglo-Saxon system of separated powers has been freedom from indefinite imprisonment at the will of the Executive'. '[C]riminal process was viewed as the primary means—and the only means absent congressional action suspending the writ—not only to punish traitors, but to incapacitate them'. That 'the Executive lacks indefinite wartime detention authority over citizens is consistent with the Founders' general mistrust of military power permanently at the Executive's disposal'. Even if the AUMF satisfied the Non-Detention Act, Hamdi would be entitled to habeas corpus. 'If civil rights are to be curtailed during wartime, it must be done openly and democratically, as the Constitution requires, rather than by silent erosion through an opinion of this Court.' Hamilton had warned that war:

> will compel nations the most attached to liberty, to resort for repose and security to institutions which have a tendency to destroy their civil and political rights. To be more safe, they, at length, become willing to run the risk of being less free.

[102] 'Enemy Prisoners of War, Retained Personnel, Civilian Internees and Other Detainees', Army Reg 190-8, §1-6 (1997).

The view 'that war silences law or modulates its voice ... has no place in the interpretation and application of a Constitution designed precisely to confront war and, in a manner that accords with democratic principles, to accommodate it'.

Only Thomas felt 'this detention falls squarely within the Federal Government's war powers, and we lack the expertise and capacity to second-guess that decision'. '*[J]udicial* interference in these domains destroys the purpose of vesting primary responsibility in a unitary Executive'. He quoted Holmes: 'When it comes to a decision by the head of the State upon a matter involving its life, the ordinary rights of individuals must yield to what *he* deems the necessities of the moment'. Due process 'requires nothing more than a good-faith executive determination'. 'I do not believe that we may diminish the Federal Government's war powers by reference to a treaty and certainly not to a treaty that does not apply'. In any case 'Hamdi's detention comports with the laws of war, including the Geneva Convention (III)'. The government could detain Hamdi 'not only to prevent him from rejoining the ongoing fight' but also 'to gather critical intelligence'. Access to counsel 'would often destroy the intelligence gathering function'. It seemed 'quite likely that, under the process envisioned by the plurality [opinion], various military officials will have to take time to litigate this matter'. This would 'probably require the Government to divulge highly classified information to the purported enemy combatant, who might then upon release return to the fight armed with our most closely held secrets'. Thomas ridiculed the plurality's balancing approach: '[b]ecause a decision to bomb a particular target might extinguish *life* interests, the plurality's analysis seems to require notice to potential targets'.

The (conservative) Washington Legal Foundation assailed the Court's 'bald assertion of judicial imperialism'.[103] 'At the urging of radical legal activists' the Court had 'issued several sweeping decisions which extended new rights to enemy combatants and opened up the federal courts to a terrorist litigation explosion'. WLF shared Thomas's fears: 'Are we about to see dedicated American battlefield commanders hauled into courts to give testimony?'. 'Imagine if our troops had to deal with such legal intrusions in World War II. We'd be a bilingual country today, speaking German and Japanese'. The JCS Chairman had warned that detainees 'would gnaw through hydraulic lines in the back of a C-17 to bring it down'. WLF commented: 'Maybe they don't need to go to the trouble. America's activist lawyers are determined to get them on a flight back home—seated in first class'.

At its August 2004 meeting the American Bar Association (ABA) House of Delegates unanimously approved without debate a resolution urging

---

[103] Washington Legal Foundation, 'A Pause for Foresight', *New York Times*, 26 July 2004, A17 (advertisement).

Congress and the President to ensure all military commission defendants access to civilian lawyers.[104] The chair of the ABA panel on Enemy Combatants declared 'we must defend those whom we dislike or even despise. The world will be watching'. But earlier that month the National Association of Criminal Defense Lawyers advised members it would be unethical to represent detainees with whom the lawyer could not communicate confidentially.[105] The outgoing president said 'civilian lawyers should not legitimize this sham proceeding'. Eugene R Fidell, founder of the National Institute of Military Justice, maintained that 'the process has been discredited'.

(a) Analysis

If administration lawyers used law to unleash executive power and the military failed to punish or prevent lawlessness, the judiciary at least gave law a voice. Lower courts unquestioningly accepted the administration claim that they lacked jurisdiction over Guantánamo until Justice Kennedy demolished it.[106] Some judges eagerly embraced the OLC assertion of untrammelled executive power over military policy broadly defined. If 'deference to the executive is not exercised with respect to military judgments in the field', wrote Wilkinson, 'it is difficult to see where deference would ever obtain'. Traxler concurred: the 'Judiciary became compelled, by the nature of war and by dint of the separation of powers we are required to safeguard and honor, to give deference to the Executive'. But Doumar refused to 'rubber-stamp' government decisions, demanding to know 'with whom is the war ... that we're fighting?' and 'will the war never be over ...?' Criticising her colleagues' 'rubber-stamping of the Executive's unsupported designation', Motz praised Doumar for having 'courageously attempted to provide the meaningful judicial review that the Constitution mandates'. Mukasey also felt compelled to determine if 'the President is exercising a power vouchsafed to him by the Constitution'. Justice Souter did not want to 'permit the Government to obtain a tactical advantage as a consequence of an *ex parte* decision' to spirit Padilla out of New York. But Scalia denounced his brethren for 'spring[ing] a trap on the Executive' by finding jurisdiction over Guantánamo. And Thomas parroted the OLC memoranda: the war powers allowed the president to make 'virtually conclusive factual findings' and

---

[104] JD Glater, 'A.B.A. Urges Wider Rights In Cases Tried By Tribunals', *New York Times*, 13 Aug 2004, A18.

[105] The struggle against apartheid engendered fierce debate about whether judges should resign if they could not protect the rule of law: Wacks, 1984.

[106] *Coalition of Clergy v Bush*, 189 F Supp 2d 1036 (CD Cal 2002), aff'd, 310 F 3d 1153 (9th Cir 2002).

'quite obviously' detain anyone. Several Justices invoked *Youngstown*, the Court's most famous decision on executive power, which the OLC memoranda scrupulous overlooked.

Several Justices declaimed paeans to liberty: 'the essence of a free society', 'the hallmark of the Star Chamber'; we 'must not wield the tools of tyrants' (Stevens in *Padilla*); 'the state of war is not a blank check for the President' (O'Connor in *Hamdi*); 'heirs to a tradition given voice 800 years ago by Magna Carta' (Souter in *Hamdi*); 'the very core of liberty'; nations must resist the 'tendency to destroy their civil and political rights' (Scalia in *Hamdi*). Scalia concluded his *Hamdi* dissent by declaring that '*inter arma silent leges*' 'has no place in the interpretation and application of a Constitution designed precisely to confront war and, in a manner that accords with democratic principles, to accommodate it'. The Court's stirring rhetoric may explain why Kollar-Kotelly (who initially bowed to the government claim that she lacked jurisdiction) subsequently repudiated her dictum that detainees' rights were 'for the military and political branches to determine', expressed sympathy for those 'detained virtually incommunicado for nearly three years without being charged with any crime', and called it 'an understatement' that their ability to challenge detention without access to counsel was 'seriously impaired'.[107]

Judges deployed the full panoply of rhetorical tropes. Scalia naturally invoked original intent (all the way back to Blackstone and the 1350 Statute of Treasons). Thomas paraded horrors: 'various military officials will have to take time to litigate this matter', freed Enemy Combatants would 'return to the fight armed with our most closely held secrets', the military would have to warn bombing targets. The Washington Legal Foundation indulged in even greater hyperbole: first-class air travel for terrorists, an occupied America speaking German and Japanese. Attorney General Ashcroft warned that 'second-guessing of presidential determinations in these critical areas of treaties can put at risk the very security of our nation in a time of war'.[108]

Judicial polarisation became *ad hominem*. The Fourth Circuit ridiculed Doumar, whose 'instinctive skepticism, so laudable in the defense of criminal charges', carried 'the inordinate risk of a constitutionally problematic intrusion into the most basic responsibilities of a coordinate branch' when applied to 'military determinations made in the field'. Accused by Judge Motz of having 'seriously erred', her colleagues criticised her and Judge Luttig for dissenting from the en banc denial of a rehearing. Justice Scalia's *Hamdi* dissent was typically scathing. O'Connor had

---

[107] *Al Odah v US*, 346 F Supp 2d 1 (DDC 2004).
[108] 'Remarks by Attorney General John Ashcroft at the Federalist Society for Law and Public Policy Convention', *Federal News Service* (12 Nov 2004), available at www.fnsg.com.

invoked *Mathews v Eldridge*, which involved '*the withdrawal of disability benefits!*'[109] 'Having distorted the Suspension Clause, the plurality finishes up by transmogrifying the Great Writ', displaying a 'Mr. Fix-it Mentality' intended 'to Make Everything Come Out Right'. O'Connor replied in kind. Scalia relied on overruled cases, 'does not explain', 'ignores the context', 'refers to only one case', which 'suffers from the same defect', and 'can point to no case or authority'. Scalia's *Rasul* dissent was even more acerbic. A claim that *Braden* overruled *Eisentrager* 'would not pass the laugh test'. The Court's 'carefree' decision was 'breathtaking', its treatment of Guantánamo 'a wrenching departure from precedent'. Ashcroft sneered at 'theories generated by academic elites, foreign bodies, and judicial imaginations'.

Judges split over basic legal questions. Were the GCs self-executing? Did they protect ECs? Did Bush's classification of ECs satisfy Article V's requirement of a competent tribunal? Did international law give justiciable rights to individuals or political arguments to nations? Did separation of powers demand judicial deference or review? Could the military detain to interrogate or only to keep fighters off the battlefield? Did Congress intend the Non-Detention Act to cover *these* detentions? O'Connor found that the AUMF expressed the necessary intent to detain, but Souter objected that it 'never so much as uses the word detention'. Several judges were troubled by the prospect of indefinite detention in a Global War on Terrorism with no foreseeable end. Ninth Circuit Judge Tashima warned that 'the war on terrorism threatens to destroy the very values of a democratic society governed by the rule of law'. Interned during World War II, he warned: 'It's happening all over again'.[110]

Judges disagreed about the standards for evaluating government evidence. Wilkinson found 'value in having the United States state under oath its reasons for the detention of an American citizen'. But Doumar dismissed the Mobbs declaration as 'little more than the government's "say so"', and Mukasey was equally sceptical: 'before Padilla achieved his current status as a suspected terrorist, he was a criminal, and criminals are people with whom this court has at least as much experience as does Admiral Jacoby, and perhaps more'.[111]

How can we understand these disagreements? Although none of the more than 150 amicus briefs was cited, they represent public affirmations about legality. The few filed on behalf of the government by conservative public interest law firms (Washington Legal Foundation, American Center for Law and Justice) were outnumbered at least 10 to 1 by government

---

[109] 124 S Ct 2633, 2672 (emphasis in original).

[110] S Hymon, 'Rights a Victim of Terror War, U.S. Judge Says', *Los Angeles Times*, 7 Nov 2004, B3.

[111] *Padilla v Rumsfeld*, 243 F Supp 2d 42, 52 (SDNY 2003).

critics. Some of the latter were predictable: civil liberties, civil and human rights, legal aid, criminal defence, liberals and radicals. (Detainees may not have welcomed support from the Freedom Socialist Party and Spartacist League, nor government that of anti-immigrant groups.) Unitarians and Quakers predictably defended detainees; more surprising was support for Muslims from the Churches of Christ and Reform Judaism (though a Jewish group also filed for the government). Amici invoked different kinds of authority. Some claimed expertise in law, national security and history. Law professors for detainees outnumbered those for government more than 20 to 1. Briefs appealed to government experience, especially in the military and foreign service. Signers wrote as present or former political office-holders: current members of Congress, former members who had sponsored the Non-Detention Act, and retired judges. Some recalled personal suffering: Fred Korematsu and other Japanese Americans interned during World War II, Asian Americans, ex-POWs, Medal of Honor recipients, Hungarian Jews. Others appealed to internationalism: UK and EU parliamentarians, humanitarian organisations, foreign correspondents, international legal groups (including participants in international criminal courts). There were a few anomalies: the Cato Institute (Republicans dedicated to 'individual liberty, free markets, and limited government') opposing the Bush administration; the Rutherford Institute joining the ACLU, its traditional adversary in church–state issues. Perhaps most striking were those that rarely took partisan positions on government actions: retired judges, bar associations (ABA, ABCNY, Beverly Hills), and state governments (on both sides).

Judges' politics made a difference.[111a] Republican appointees to lower courts were more likely to support government, Democratic to support detainees.[112] (Indeed, the government chose certain venues because of their conservative judges (and juries): the Eastern District of Virginia, the Fourth Circuit.) But the exceptions are more interesting. Doumar and Mukasey were strong conservatives appointed by Reagan. Indeed, Mukasey had earlier sentenced Muslim terrorists to long prison terms. But both seemed protective of the judicial role, which charged *the judges* with evaluating evidence. Hence Doumar was sceptical of the Mobbs declaration and Mukasey convinced he could evaluate an ex-convict's credibility better than

[111a] Dunne, 1899; Schubert, 1959.
[112] Ruled against or for government by part of appointing president

	Against	For
Republican	9	4
Democrat	1	6

$p = 0.057$ (one tailed test $p = 0.029$).

some Vice Admiral. Luttig dissented on the narrow ground that Hamdi could not be bound by a statement by his father, to whom he could not talk. Although George W Bush elevated Parker to the Circuit Court, Clinton had appointed him to the District Court. Parker's father invalidated the price controls of Nixon, who had appointed him; Parker was one of the very few African Americans at Yale College and Law School before affirmative action. And again the issue was narrow: whether Rumsfeld could strip the court of jurisdiction by spiriting Padilla out of New York on a Sunday without notifying his lawyer. Garland, a Clinton appointee, joined a decision rendering the Supreme Court's *Rasul* opinion meaningless. But after clerking for Friendly and Brennan (both liberals), Garland spent most of his career prosecuting high profile cases (including the Oklahoma City bombing) and defending corporations. Roberts was first interviewed by Gonzales for the Supreme Court six days before oral argument in *Hamdan*, again by Cheney, Andrew Card and Karl Rove while his Circuit Court panel was deliberating, and by Bush the day it gave judgment.[113]

But the Supremes rule. Some of their behaviour was entirely in character: liberals in *Rasul* ruling that the US exercised 'complete jurisdiction and control' over Guantánamo, a holding conservatives castigated as 'judicial adventurism' (although O'Connor and Kennedy sided with the former); conservatives evading Padilla's petition, angering liberals; the positions of Souter, Ginsburg and Thomas in *Hamdi*. The real surprises are the other *Hamdi* opinions. O'Connor's plurality opinion, signed by Rehnquist and Kennedy, resoundingly endorsed legality. While conceding on hearsay and burden of proof, it still threatened the Combatant Status Review Tribunals and military commissions. Scalia's dissent is the most striking. Originalism led him to defend habeas corpus. Even such limited autonomy from politics provoked the Washington Legal Foundation to denounce some of its favourite Justices as 'radical legal activists' engaging in 'judicial imperialism', and Ashcroft to condemn the 'growing tendency of the judicial branch to inject itself into areas of executive action that were originally assigned to the discretion of the president in the Constitution'.

V. THE RESILIENCE OF LEGALITY

Legality has suffered severely in the United States since 9.11, despite a host of determined, capable, well-resourced champions. Law's first defence is always its obligatoriness. But Addington cynically declared that the administration would stop 'only if the courts tell us we're wrong'. Dismissing

---

[113] J VandeHei, 'Judge Heard Terrorism Case As He Interviewed for Seat', *Washington Post*, 17 Aug 2005, A4.

history (because the US confronted a 'new paradigm') and hubristically confident that Republicans would always occupy the White House, the Bush administration was determined to expand executive power at the expense of courts and Congress. The American hegemon was openly contemptuous of the international community. Administration lawyers used law to construct a domain of lawlessness. They demanded unaccountable trust. Their client was the president, not the public. They claimed the commander-in-chief's untrammelled battlefield discretion in a GWOT without end. They displayed no fidelity to due process: the treatment of detainees implicated policy, not law. And they denied responsibility for abuses flowing from those policies.

Legality had defenders within the executive, but they never prevailed. Policy-makers and lawyers in both the State Department and the National Security Council advocated respect for international law, based on enlightened national interest. Lawyers throughout the military—General Counsels, JAGs and SJAs—exhibited a professional attachment to established legal institutions and procedures but were disregarded by the White House and Defense Department. Superiors ignored egregious misconduct until a single foot soldier blew the whistle with photographic evidence graphically documenting inexcusable abuses. Despite the terrible impact on public opinion (domestic but especially foreign), Abu Ghraib was a gift to the administration—portrayed as an aberration that became a lightning rod, drawing attention away from the routine execution of illegal policies. The exemplary sentences of just three ringleaders distracted from pervasive lenience towards the many others who mistreated, even killed, prisoners. Like other forms of professional self-regulation (lawyers, doctors, police), military justice is intended to protect service members from punishment (precisely why the administration insisted on military commissions for the Guantánamo detainees). Although a few investigations blamed superiors, no heads rolled. The military (and executive) instinct for secrecy concealed from the public much of the information uncovered by investigations and courts martial.

That left it to courts to redeem legality after the fact. At least they listened to arguments, which encouraged more than 150 amicus briefs—hybrids of legal advocacy, assertions of extra-legal authority, and moral witness. Unlike executive and legislature, the judiciary must give reasons for actions. Unfortunately, this just confirmed the cynicism of critical legal theory that for every argument there is a plausible counter-argument. Judges disagreed about the most fundamental questions. Politics explains most of that partisanship: the appointee's party, amici's ideology. But the exceptions were revealing. Political liberalism outweighed ethno-religious loyalty (to both Judaism and Protestantism); libertarianism trumped political affiliation (the Cato and Rutherford Institutes). Even politically conservative judges felt obligated to evaluate evidence. Republican appointees defended due process and preferred limited government. Lifetime tenure and the judicial role fostered independence. Yet almost four years after 9.11 courts have not released a single detainee. Faced with a determined executive and a complicit or complacent legislature in the world's only superpower, the rest of the legal complex—lawyers, legal academics, professional associations, judges and NGOs—could do little to protect political liberalism.

REFERENCES

Abel, RL (1995), *Politics by Other Means: Law in the Struggle against Apartheid, 1980–1994* (New York, Routledge).

—— (2003), 'Lott's Life: Don't Look Back, The Politics of Respect', 5 *Rutgers Race & The Law Rev* 269.

ABCNY (Association of the Bar of the City of New York), Committee on Federal Courts (2004a), *The Indefinite Detention of 'Enemy Combatants': Balancing Due Process and National Security in the Context of the War on Terror* (New York, ABCNY).

—— Committees on International Human Rights and on Military Affairs and Justice (2004b), *Human Rights Standards Applicable to the United States' Interrogation of Detainees* (New York, ABCNY).

Bâli, AU (2005), 'Scapegoating the Vulnerable: Preventive Detention of Immigrants in America's "War on Terror"', presented at the annual meeting of the Law & Society Association, Las Vegas.

Brasch, W (2005), *America's Unpatriotic Acts: The Federal Government's Violation of Constitutional and Civil Rights* (New York, Peter Lang).

Brown, C (ed) (2003), *Ashcroft and the Assault on Personal Freedom* (New York, New Press).

Danner, M (2004), *Torture and Truth: America, Abu Ghraib, and the War on Terror* (New York, New York Review Books).

Dunne, FP (1899), *Mr. Dooley in the Hearts of his Countrymen* (Boston, Mass, Small Maynard).

Etzioni A (2004), *How Patriotic Is the Patriot Act? Freedom versus Security in the Age of Terrorism* (New York, Routledge).

Fine, GA (DoJ Inspector General) (2003a), *The September 11 Detainees: A Review of the Treatment of Aliens Held on Immigration Charges in Connection with the Investigation of the September 11 Attacks* (Washington, DC, DoJ IG).

—— (2003b), *Supplemental Report on September 11 Detainees and Allegations of Abuse at the Metropolitan Detention Center in Brooklyn, New York* (Washington, DC, DoJ IG).

Greenberg, KJ and Dratel, JL (eds) (2005), *The Torture Papers: The Road to Abu Ghraib* (New York, Cambridge University Press).

Hersh, SM (2004), 'Torture at Abu Ghraib', *The New Yorker*, 5 October.

Human Rights Watch and ACLU (2005), *Witness to Abuse: Human Rights Abuses under the Material Witness Law since September 11* (New York, HRW and ACLU).

Mayer, J (2005), 'Outsourcing Torture: The Secret History of America's "Extraordinary Rendition" Program', *New Yorker,* 14–21 February, 106.

Meeropol, R (ed) (2005), *America's Disappeared: Secret Imprisonment, Detainees, and the 'War on Terror'* (New York, Seven Stories).

Remnick, D (2004), 'Introduction' in SM Hersh, *Chain of Command: The Road from 9/11 to Abu Ghraib* ix (New York, HarperCollins).

Saar, E and Novak, V (2005), *Inside the Wire: A Military Intelligence Soldier's Eyewitness Account of Life at Guantánamo* (New York, Penguin Press).

Schubert, GA (1959), *Quantitative Analysis of Judicial Behavior* (Glencoe, Ill: Free Press).

Sidel, M (2004), *More Secure, Less Free? Antiterrorism Policy and Civil Liberties after September 11* (Ann Arbor, Mich, University of Michigan Press).

Skolnick, JH (1966), *Justice Without Trial* (New York, John Wiley).

Wacks, R (1984), 'Judges and Injustice', 100 *South African Law Journal* 266.

Part Four

Europe

13

Politicising Law to Liberalise Politics: Anti-Francoist Judges and Prosecutors in Spain's Democratic Transition*

LISA HILBINK

U NTIL THE LAST two decades of the twentieth century, elements of
political liberalism were weak and ephemeral in Spain. While aspirations for and/or lip-service to liberalism were a constant feature
of nineteenth and twentieth century Spanish politics (Carr, 1980), violence,
instability and 'the absolutist temptation' (Malefakis, 2003: 90) prevailed.
Despite the promulgation of numerous constitutional texts that provided
for varying measures of political liberalism, law remained a mere tool of
whomever held power, 'employed for the maintenance of public order and
the assurance of political power, not for the protection of constitutional
or human rights or to provide for limited government' (Beirich, 1998:
5). Although the basic structure of the administration of justice remained
continuous across time (Toharia, 1975), and authoritarian rulers respected
judicial independence in cases that were not politically sensitive (Toharia,
1974–5), 'a judge's role was extremely restrictive' and the court system
remained in 'complete servility to the other parts of government' (Beirich,
1998: 54 and 53). Citizens thus had no recourse when state officials
violated fundamental rights.

* I would like to thank Matthew Johnson, Ana Belén Benito Sánchez and Marcela
Villarrazo for their invaluable research assistance on this chapter, as well as Victor Ferreres,
Thomas Hilbink, Ignacio Sánchez Yllera, three anonymous reviewers, and the editors of this
volume for their most helpful suggestions and corrections. I also thank the Graduate School
and the Centre for European Studies of the University of Minnesota, and the Woodrow Wilson
School at Princeton University, for funding research and travel for the project, as well as the
American Bar Foundation and the Oñati Institute for Law and Sociology for making this
volume possible.

Today, all this has changed. Spain is widely hailed as one of the most stable and robust liberal democracies on the planet (Przeworski, 1991; Pérez-Díaz, 1993; Linz and Stepan, 1996; Encarnación, 2003). As Encarnación (2003: 62) notes, since 1982, the Freedom House scores for respect for political and civil rights in Spain 'have been virtually indistinguishable from those of older and presumably more mature democracies such as Italy, France, and Germany'. The 1978 Constitution, upheld by a respected Constitutional Court (Beirich, 1998) and supported by a widespread 'constitutional patriotism' (Pradera, 2003), effectively structures and limits the exercise of state power. And, as in the rest of Latin Europe, 'judges are today not only more institutionally independent from the political branches but also much more likely to assert their independence when on the bench' (Guarnieri, 2003: 235).

Intrigued by this dramatic change, numerous scholars have analysed Spain's transition to liberal democracy (eg, Carr and Fusi, 1979; Maravall, 1982; Pérez-Díaz, 1993; Linz and Stepan, 1996; Encarnación, 2003). Only a few, however, have focused explicitly on the place of legal actors in the transition (eg, Beirich, 1998; Poblet, 2001). This chapter draws on these latter works, as well as on the author's primary research, to shed light on the role of the legal complex in advancing political liberalism in late twentieth century Spain. In particular, it focuses on the activities of a group of judges and prosecutors who organised in the later years of the Franco regime under the name *Justicia Democrática* (Democratic Justice).[1] These jurists[2] mobilised to promote all three elements of political liberalism as defined in this volume: (1) judicial independence aimed at the moderation of executive power; (2) greater autonomy for civil society in the form of free speech, press, association and assembly; and (3) guarantees of basic civil rights, such as bodily integrity, due process and equal treatment under law. Not only did they protest abuses of these liberal principles under the Franco regime, but they also advanced reforms to enhance them both before and after the transition to democracy. To do so, however, they openly challenged traditional, positivist understandings of the judicial role as passive, bureaucratic and apolitical, calling on their colleagues to pursue a more assertive (and openly political) defence of liberal and democratic norms. While they invoked their professional experience, responsibility and standing to justify and enhance the impact of their actions, they eschewed the notion that law could or should be completely separate from politics. Otherwise put, they

---

[1] The group dissolved after the transition and regrouped into two separate organisations, *Jueces para la Democracia* (Judges for Democracy) and *Unión Progresista de Fiscales* (Progressive Union of Prosecutors).

[2] The group also included judicial secretaries, essentially full-time clerks who are also part of the judicial hierarchy and who often go on to fill judicial offices later in their careers. For the purposes of this chapter, I include them in the category of 'judges'.

sought to politicise law—in the sense of defining it in terms of substantive political commitments—in order to liberalise politics.

I should make clear that the argument I will advance in this chapter is *not* that Spaniards have the members of *Justicia Democrática* to thank for the high level of political liberalism they enjoy today. *Justicia Democrática* (JD) was part of a much larger movement for democratisation, which emerged within a particular national and international structural context, and benefited from an arguably singular combination of *virtú* and *fortuna* (O'Donnell and Schmitter, 1986; Sanchez, 2003). It would thus be folly to pretend that this small group of legal professionals was the primary agent of political liberalisation.

Instead, what I aim to explain here is how and why the judges and prosecutors associated with JD were willing and able to take stands against the Franco regime and to use their professional training and standing to contribute to the transition to political liberalism. As I will establish below, the historical-institutional context was in many respects highly unfavourable for the development of such activism among judges and prosecutors. Participants in JD had to take tremendous personal and professional risks to advance their cause. What, then, were the conditions that inspired and permitted their collective action, and contributed to the realisation of their goals?

Borrowing from the social movement literature in political science and sociology, I frame my argument in terms of three factors: political opportunities, cultural framings and mobilising structures (McAdam, McCarthy and Zald, 1996).[3] First, I follow other analysts of the Spanish transition to democracy (eg, Pérez-Díaz, 1993; Encarnación, 2003) in highlighting the important changes in the structure and policies of the Franco government that increased opportunities for liberals to exert influence and pressure on the regime. The opening of Spanish society to freer exchange (economic and otherwise) with Western Europe and an increased tolerance of intellectual debate during the 1950s and 1960s gave critics within and outside the state access to a wider set of ideas and more room to discuss them publicly. This, in turn, encouraged and supported a redefinition of the proper role of law and courts in public life, away from the narrow and instrumental conception of the past and toward a substantive linkage of law to liberal principles. This reframing took place gradually and was diffused to a new generation of university students during the 1960s and 1970s. The most vocal advocates of this new conception were left-leaning Catholic academics, but the general idea of a more independent, fully competent, and rights-oriented judiciary was also supported by economically liberal

---

[3] For other studies of legal actors working as part of social movements see Scheingold (1998); Bisharat (1998); Shamir and Ziv (2001); and TM Hilbink (2006).

technocrats employed by the Franco regime and other actors with training and exposure to debates in European democracies. The members of JD were thus motivated by and able to appeal to a liberal orientation that was widely shared among the youthful legal and political elite that forged the transition.

What ultimately enabled the judges and prosecutors of JD to organise collectively to advance political liberalism was not, however, a strong organisational alliance with a robust and ideologically unified bar (Halliday and Karpik, 1998; Feeley, 2002), or with any other members of the legal complex. Rather, these judicial actors relied on ties to and support from clandestine political parties, progressive clergy, sympathetic media outlets, and the Council of Europe. It was primarily these entities, and not other members of the legal complex, that emboldened them to act and enhanced the efficacy of their efforts. Moreover, it was the very fragmented nature of Spanish society, including of the legal profession, that facilitated the emergence of JD. It is no mere coincidence that the group emerged in Catalonia, whose geographic and cultural distance from Madrid provided a setting conducive to dissent and oppositional mobilisation.

Once the balance tipped in favour of anti-Franco forces, and the transition to democracy was underway, the relative importance of JD faded somewhat. The 1978 Constitution, drafted by political party leaders with strong legal credentials (ie, other members of the legal complex), provided guarantees for both judicial independence and secure jurisdiction (Gor, 2003), and gave a privileged place to fundamental rights (Bereijo, 2003). The members of JD continued, nonetheless, to keep discussion about judicial independence and judicial rights protection alive. By forming *Jueces para la Democracia* and *Unión Progresista de Fiscales*, they have maintained outlets for like-minded colleagues to voice professional concerns and opinions, to build professional solidarity, and to offer a constant reminder to their brethren of the crucial, and unquestionably political, role they are called to play in the maintenance and deepening of a liberal democratic regime.

The chapter proceeds in six parts. In Part I, I offer a brief overview of the failed efforts to institutionalise liberalism in Spain during the nineteenth and twentieth centuries, along with a discussion of the contours and role of the judiciary in that period, and particularly under Franco. In Part II, I describe the formation and actions of JD in the later part of the Franco era, highlighting their contributions to Spain's transition to political liberalism. I then turn to the development of my argument regarding the structural and ideological conditions (Part III) and the organisational factors (Part IV) that account for the willingness and ability of JD participants to act collectively in the cause of political liberalism. In Part V, I offer a brief discussion of JD's role during and since the drafting of the 1978 liberal-democratic Constitution. Part VI concludes.

I. HISTORICAL AND INSTITUTIONAL BACKGROUND: DEBASED LIBERALISM AND DOCILE COURTS

According to at least one scholar of Spanish history, the term 'liberal' has its origin in early nineteenth century Spain, when it was used to describe 'a group of radical patriots', who fled to Cádiz from the Napoleonic invasion of 1808 and drew up a Constitution that enshrined the separation of powers, equality before the law, freedom of property and contract, and 'the revolutionary doctrine of the sovereignty of the people' (Carr, 1980: 1). This proud liberal moment proved to be fleeting, however, as traditional monarchist forces prevailed within two years. Ferdinand VII returned to the throne and immediately nullified the 1812 Constitution.[4] In subsequent decades, liberal principles reappeared in multiple constitutional documents, but were ignored, perverted, or trampled in practice. Conservative clericalists fought every push for liberalism, throwing the country into no fewer than five civil wars (Payne, 1967: 2).

The frictions were intensified by Spain's regional divisions, which fueled opposition to centralist, anti-clerical liberals. Liberals theorised that the state could recognise and protect only the rights of individuals, not the rights of corporate institutions, such as the church, or the rights of the regions as separate entities with distinct customs and interests (Carr, 1966: 60–8). This was unacceptable to wide swathes of Spain's primarily Catholic, agrarian, and provincially-identified society. Moreover, the liberals disagreed amongst themselves: while both the 'Progressives' and the 'Moderates' believed in economic individualism and the need to protect property, the Progressives were stronger critics of the church than were the Moderates, and argued for the expansion of the suffrage in order to promote more equitable economic development (Carr, 1966: 162–3). 'Within this fractured polity, the only institution to exhibit any cohesion or efficacy throughout the [nineteenth and twentieth] centuries [was] the military', which intervened regularly to reconcile the contending parties by force (Beirich, 1998: 49).

In 1868, Progressives staged the 'Glorious Revolution', which called for national sovereignty, secularism, universal suffrage, the division of powers, a declaration of rights, and a jury system. These principles were enshrined in Spain's first democratic Constitution, that of 1869, but the Progressive revolutionaries could not control the centrifugal forces they unwittingly set loose (Carr, 1980: 6–7). In 1873, radical democrats declared Spain's First Republic, which was to include internally self-governing provinces. After eight months, the country was on the verge of disintegration, and the army stepped in once again to impose unity and order (Carr, 1966: 342).

---

[4] Indeed, determined to 'crush liberalism', the king 'reintroduced the Inquisition to destroy "the disastrous mania of thinking"' (Beevor, 2006: 7).

Spooked by this chaotic interlude, liberal oligarchs (including numerous lawyers) partook in a conservative reaction which led to the restoration of the Bourbon monarchy and a long stretch of stability from 1874 to 1917 (interrupted briefly by the so-called 'Cuban Disaster' of 1895–8). The new king, Alfonso XII, succeeded in cultivating good relations with the army, the church, and the civilian political elites (Carr, 1966: 355–6). A new Constitution provided for a constitutional monarchy, with an elected parliament and, until 1890, restricted suffrage. Two elite parties, the Conservatives and the Liberals, alternated in power through a carefully controlled (and electorally manipulated) system in which the monarch served as the moderator (Carr, 1980: 8–11; Beirich, 1998: 50). The system produced stability until the turn of the century, when leftist and regional independence movements emerged and challenged the legitimacy of the arrangement. The oligarchic parties quarrelled and splintered, and in the midst of increasing social conflict, the military intervened to install (and later remove) the corporatist dictator, Primo de Rivera.

The military's removal of Primo de Rivera provided the opportunity for a variety of leftist and regional parties to unite in the cause of republicanism. When they proclaimed the Second Republic in 1931, they directly challenged the pillars of the late-nineteenth century state: the monarchy (they demanded the king's abdication); the army (they called for reform to eliminate its political power); liberal economics (they called for redistribution and workers' rights); centralism (they advocated regional autonomy); and the church (they demanded secular education) (Cowans, 2003: 147–51). But in the five years that followed, there proved to be no consensus on whether, in what form, and with what speed such social and institutional reforms should proceed. As political parties fragmented and polarised and social and political tensions mounted, the military intervened on the side of the social conservatives, the propertied classes, and the idea of a unified and centralised state.

In the bloody civil war that ensued (see Beevor, 2006), and the repressive regime of General Franco that followed, liberalism appeared to have all but died in Spain. Although the Francoist leaders were 'obsessed' with dressing the regime in rule of law clothing (Poblet, 2001: 57), Franco never accepted any institutional limits on his power. While he decreed seven fundamental laws during his rule, providing the regime with the trappings of constitutionalism, the laws were developed to strengthen and legitimise the status quo, and thus stressed the role of the 'Roman Holy Church', the 'unity among men and lands of Spain', and the 'organic representation' of the people (Díaz-Plaja, 1970: 330–3). Moreover, what freedoms and guarantees they gave with one hand, they took away with the other. For example, the 1942 Constituent Law of the Cortes created a parliament, but gave it only the power to approve laws presented by the executive. Franco retained the authority to legislate by decree and to dismiss dissenters and critics. The 1945 *Fuero de los Españoles* (a purported 'bill of rights'), for its part, bestowed Spaniards with a battery of liberal rights, but put greater emphasis on corresponding duties and allowed for the suspension of rights without justification (Angoustures, 1983: 161).

It should be noted that the Franco regime's concern for keeping up legal appearances, as well as a more sincere desire to provide a legal framework to support economic development, led it to respect the formal independence of the judicial system.[5] Rather than intervene in the judicial process to manipulate outcomes, Franco's strategy, which sociologist José Juan Toharia argues is typical for authoritarian governments,[6] was to restrict the scope of jurisdiction for ordinary courts, channelling any politically sensitive cases into 'special' courts under his direct control (Toharia, 1975: 198; Andrés Ibáñez, 1988: 66).[7] Franco could thus claim, quite legitimately, that the regular judiciary was independent,[8] and surveys from late in his regime show that most lawyers, even those on the Left, agreed this was so (Toharia, 1975: 198, 192).[9]

The effectiveness of this strategy was enhanced by the traditional quiescence of the judiciary, which derived from its longstanding institutional structure and ideology (Beirich, 1998: 66). Judges in Spain had 'never administered justice in the name of the people, but always in the name of the King, the Head of State, the State' (Toharia, 1975: 26). The adoption of the Napoleonic model in the nineteenth century continued the pattern from the *ancien régime*, by which the judiciary was a tightly controlled bureaucracy designed to serve the central power. Judges were never authorised to exercise any real discretion or independent power, but were expected to maintain 'an attitude of blind submission and obedience' to the sovereign will as embodied in the law (Toharia, 1975: 26–7; Poblet, 2001: 65–6). The 1870 Organic Law of the Judiciary established that:

> The Tribunals and Courts are not allowed to dictate rules or dispositions of a general character that have as their object the interpretation of the laws.... Neither can they approve, censure or correct through the use of general dispositions the laws applicable to the case at hand. Their attributions are limited to resolving those recourses placed before them [Article 2, Organic Law of the Judiciary, cited in Beirich, 1998: 54–5].

---

[5] As Poblet (2001, 80) puts it, 'Nothing better guarantees the legitimacy that the war-issued regime seeks than the institutional framework it has at hand.'

[6] This strategy had also been used by the Restoration governments, the Primo de Rivera dictatorship, and even the Second Republic (see Beirich, 1998: 57–8 and 64).

[7] The most notorious of these was the Tribunal for Repression of Masonry and Communism, which later became the Tribunal of Public Order. The scope of military jurisdiction was also broadened significantly.

[8] The 1956 Law of the Fundamental Principles of the Nationalist Movement declared that 'All Spaniards have a right to an independent judicial system that is free of charge for the needy', and that 'the Christian ideal of social justice ... will inspire policy and laws' (Cowans, 2003: 236–7).

[9] As one founding member of *Justicia Democrática* (JD) put it, under Franco 'ordinary judges had the sad luxury of being *limpios en el limbo* (clean but kept apart)' (Mena interview, 2004).

In a word, the judge, as any good civil servant, was expected to be 'apolitical', or strictly 'professional'.

To encourage this professionalism, entrance into the Spanish judiciary was (and is still) achieved through a state-administered examination, both written and oral, which candidates take after completing law school. This exam, established in 1869, is known as the *Oposición*, and involves the memorisation of some 400 subjects. Aspirants for both judicial and prosecutorial posts take the same examination and choose their track afterwards. To prepare for the exam, candidates must study for several years under the tutelage of acting or retired judges, people who can (hence) heavily influence their understanding of the judicial role. Those with the best scores on the *Oposición* get their first choice of entry-level posts after an additional obligatory period of study in the judicial school.[10] Because judicial aspirants must forego any kind of remunerative work for several years to receive this professional training, the system clearly favours those who come from a comfortable economic background.[11] This could be mitigated by permitting lateral entrance into the judiciary, which was done from 1869 to 1905,[12] but a 1905 law all but abolished this possibility by allowing it only in cases where there were no aspirants from the *Oposición*. The judiciary thus became a very closed, corporatist body (Toharia, 1975: 38; Andrés Ibáñez, 1988: 18).

Discipline and promotions within the Spanish judicial hierarchy were controlled (until 1980) by members of the country's highest court, the *Tribunal Supremo* (TS), who used their power to 'exercise explicit ideological control' over all judges (Andrés Ibáñez, 1988: 42). A 1952 law made it obligatory for every hierarchical superior to provide an annual report on the 'honesty, intelligence, work ethic, professional aptitude, tact, discretion, public and private conduct, and [when relevant] management' of each of his subordinates (Andrés Ibáñez, 1988: 67). These secret reports were then transmitted to the Ministry of Justice and used by the Judicial Council

[10] The original judicial school was established in 1950 in Madrid, but was 'plagued with internal disputes from the very beginning' and 'did not achieve ... the transmission of substantive technical and professional knowledge' (Poblet, 2001: 87). A new school, in Barcelona, took its place in 1996.

[11] This was evident in Toharia's early 1970s study, which showed that 67 per cent of judges were upper and upper-middle class (Toharia, 1975). This varied, though, by region. Mena (interview, 2004) noted that in Barcelona, which industrialised earlier than most of Spain and was thus more affluent, law school graduates interested in making a lot of money could easily do so in private practice. Those who went into the judiciary, then, tended to so out of a sense of vocation. Many of them were following a family tradition, which he claimed gave them a sense of professional dignity and pride, but also tended to make them rather risk-averse. As he noted, 'I think the majority of judges and prosecutors were indignant about what was happening under Franco, but didn't want to take risks, get mixed up in problems.'

[12] Until 1905, one quarter of judicial posts were reserved for lateral entrance (Toharia, 1975: 37).

(essentially a subdivision of the TS) to decide who qualified to appear on the lists of three nominees for vacancies in higher ranks (including the TS itself).[13] The process was complemented by reports from the *Inspección de Tribunales*, a group composed of the president of the TS and 10 magistrates (that is, judges who had already been promoted once) that were nominated by the president of the TS and approved by the Ministry of Justice. This group conducted 'periodic, routine inspection of the nation's courts' aimed primarily at 'preventing than really correcting irregularities'. In the name of professionalism, the judicial elite thus exercised 'formidable social control' over their subordinates and gave the judiciary a clearly quietist and conservative orientation (Toharia, 1975: 59–60).

The 'notable absence of a critical spirit' among judges (Andrés Ibáñez, 1988: 66) was enhanced, of course, by the general context of repression during the Franco years (1936–76). To guarantee their strict loyalty to the state, all judges were prohibited from belonging to political parties and unions.[14] While there was only a small (less than 10 per cent) purge of judges following the civil war (Fernández Viagas, 1982: 66),[15] 50 per cent of all vacancies in the public administration, including the judiciary, were reserved for 'ex-combattants' (Toharia, 1975: 196–7). Moreover, from 1938 to 1964, upon taking office judges were required to swear 'unconditional adhesion to the Caudillo of Spain [Franco]', and then, from 1964 on, 'absolute loyalty to the Head of State [and] strict fidelity to the basic principles of the National Movement' (Andrés Ibáñez, 1988: 61).

This, then, was the unlikely context in which JD emerged. While the Spanish judiciary had survived the country's turbulent political history largely unchanged in structure and function, and while judges and prosecutors enjoyed respectable levels of formal independence and professionalism, they had no constitutionalist or democratic tradition upon which to draw to support any assertions of 'positive independence' (Simpson, 1989: 147; Widner, 2001: 41). Moreover, the judiciary of the 1960s was a closed, elitist bureaucracy, controlled from the top by a 'coopted gerontocracy' (Toharia, 1975: 59). It was a body characterised by conformity, conservatism, and submission to the executive, in which the dogma of judicial apoliticism and

---

[13] Only the president of the Supreme Tribunal was selected directly by the executive (Toharia, 1975: 58).

[14] It was, however, routine for judges temporarily to leave the judiciary for other posts in the Francoist state apparatus, without loss of seniority, and often return to plum posts in the upper judicial ranks (Andrés Ibáñez, 1988: 65).

[15] In a personal interview, José Juan Toharia noted that a purge was not necessary in a system constructed to be 'person proof' (Toharia interview, 2002). Note, however, that Poblet's figures, drawn from a study by Mónica Lanero, show that a much higher percentage of judges (37 per cent) and prosecutors (42 per cent) were affected by the purge, even if most of these were ultimately restored, with or without sanction, to their offices (Poblet, 2001: 83–4).

neutrality reigned (Andrés Ibáñez, 1988). As the late President of Spain's Constitutional Tribunal, Francisco Tomás y Valiente, once noted:

> The system wanted conformist judges, and it got them. The system practiced positivistic, acritical law and produced judges more jealous of the appearance of being apolitical than an effective independence. The result was not a norm of corruption; rather it was the predominance of an obedient judge, often competent, highly cognizant ideologically of the regime, apolitical and highly conscious of his position in the Administration of Justice, but not a true judicial power [cited in Beirich, 1998: 69].

In sum, neither the professional training and incentives of individual judges, nor the broader historical or institutional context in which they operated, were conducive to judicial mobilisation in defence of liberalism. And yet, as I explain in the next section, such mobilisation did occur.

II. EMERGENCE AND ACTIONS OF *JUSTICIA DEMOCRÁTICA*

In previous work, I have analysed the role of the judiciary in the politics of Chile, a country whose cultural heritage comes from Spain and whose political history, in some ways, parallels that of Spain.[16] The institutional structure and ideology of the Chilean judiciary were almost identical to those I have just described for Spain, and it is precisely to those factors that I have attributed the refusal of Chilean judges to take stands in defence of liberal-democratic principles, before, during and after the Pinochet regime. Because high court judges controlled the careers of their subordinates, and because judicial professionalism had long been equated with apoliticism, Chilean judges had neither the professional understandings nor the incentives to assert themselves in public law cases (L Hilbink, 2003; L Hilbink, 2007). To the extent that Chile has enjoyed political liberalism in the past or present, it is decidedly not because of the vigilance and assertiveness of the country's judges (see Couso, this volume).

Given that Spanish judges operated in a very similar institutional setting, under a similar authoritarian regime, and had even fewer historical resources upon which to draw (in terms of constitutional and democratic traditions) than did their Chilean counterparts (see Couso, this volume), it is quite surprising that a group of Spanish judges (even a minority) was willing and able to organise collectively to defend and promote a transition to political liberalism. In this section, I draw on both written and oral accounts of the

---

[16] Although their 19th-century political histories were actually quite different, with Chile enjoying long periods of political order and stability, as well as gradual and genuine democratic development (see Couso, this volume), there were many parallels between the Franco regime and the Pinochet regime (some quite intentional), as well as the leftist governments that preceded them.

origins and actions of this group of judges during the 1968–78 period, offering specific examples of the ways in which they drew on their professional expertise, experience and standing to advance the liberal cause. I reserve an analysis of how and why this was possible for subsequent sections.

According to its founders, *Justicia Democrática* (JD) had its origins in clandestine meetings of the mid-1960s, in which a handful of judges and prosecutors began discussing 'problems of justice, politics, and citizens' dignity' (Chamorro, 1989: 8). In the beginning, they met in very intimate groups of two or three individuals, being very careful to include only those they felt they could trust completely, those 'who knew how to keep quiet' (Mena interview, 2004; Doñate interview, 2004). In 1968, inspired by the student and worker revolt in France, a slightly larger group of 10–20 jurists formed an informal association in Barcelona. However, they proceeded cautiously, since 'it didn't escape anybody that conditions within the corporatist judicial structure were not favourable to such adventures, nor were dissonant voices that...staked out attitudes of resistance from the juridical field looked upon kindly' (Marín Gámez, 2003: 336–7).

The earliest protagonists of the movement were from families who had suffered directly under Francoism, members of the clandestine Communist and Socialist parties. However, all interviewees emphasised that as the organisation developed it became very plural. The initial nucleus expanded to include other Marxists, Christian Democrats, Christians for socialism, liberal democrats and Catalan nationalists, all united around the idea of promoting democracy, of 'breathing democratic air' (Jiménez Villarejo interview, 2002; Mena interview, 2004; Doñate interview, 2004). The leftists in the group recognised that they could never hope to create a socialist society without democracy, so they focused on the problem of how to advance democratisation, both within the judiciary and in society as a whole (Carmena interview, 2002). In addition to a new Constitution, the recognition of political parties, and basic rights, they agreed on the need for judicial reform. Improving the administration of justice was inseparable from broader democratisation.

In 1971, this varied group of individuals officially formed the illegal association, JD, with the primary objective of creating a democratic consciousness and current within the administration of justice (Peris Gómez, 1989: 7). As noted above, the organisation sprouted in Barcelona and then spread to other major cities and regions, becoming a nation-wide network by 1974. The group acted on two fronts: within the judiciary and in the fight against the dictatorship in general. They struggled to eliminate both judicial and prosecutorial submission to the government, and to support popular action by refusing to prosecute when people were exercising their human rights (see, eg, Burgos, 1998). They also sought to prosecute abuses of power, so as to expose what was going on, and to distance themselves from the government (Jiménez Villarejo interview, 2002). Though specific lower court records documenting this activity are difficult to access, the judicial action taken by various members of the group against members of the political police for violations of criminal procedure was apparently significant enough to elicit a reaction from the regime in 1974, in the form of amendments to the Law of Criminal Procedure and the creation of a special jurisdiction (*fuero*) to protect the police (see Andrés Ibáñez, 1988: 70).[17]

Perhaps the most important contribution that JD made to the anti-Francoist struggle was the distribution of a series of clandestine documents, which, with a 'high level of technical rigor' but in 'precise and accessible language', brought to light the government's extensive rights abuses and outlined the many ways in which 'the judiciary was being used to legitimate the repressive measures that were ever more necessary for the maintenance of the regime' (Andrés Ibáñez, 1988: 71). The documents also proposed specific legislative reforms aimed at enhancing formal rights protection and bolstering the authority and likelihood of judges to uphold these. The first of these publications, entitled *El Gobierno y la Justicia en 1971*, was published in early 1972, and three more followed annually in its mould (all reprinted in Justicia Democrática, 1978).

One of JD's primary strategies in these documents was to invoke the liberal aspects of the country's positive legal texts, which the Franco regime had either left intact and sought to circumvent in practice, or promulgated itself in an attempt to put on a liberal face for the outside world (Fernández Viagas, 1982: 82). For example, *El Gobierno y la Justicia en 1971* denounced the government's December 1970 suspension of Article 18 of the *Fuero de los Españoles*, which had been on the books since 1945 and prohibited preventive detention beyond 72 hours.[18] The document argued that although this merely formalised an established government practice of detaining suspected subversives without charge for months on end, the move constituted a direct affront to legal principles and to the professional integrity of the judiciary, whose raison d'être was to protect such principles (Justicia Democrática, 1978: 22–3). In the group's second publication, *Justicia y Política 1972*, it emphasised that the preamble to the *Fuero de los Españoles* declared the guiding principle of the state to be 'respect for the dignity, integrity, and liberty of the human person' and that its central Articles promised citizens the 'rights to liberty of expression, correspondence, abode, assembly and association, security, habeas corpus, due process, nationality, and petition'. Because the *Fuero* was a

---

[17] During this period, the regime often used formal modification of the laws as a means to avert and silence criticism from a growing opposition across society. See, eg, Zaragoza, 1975.

[18] The suspension followed on the heels of the Burgos trials, in which 6 members of the armed Basque nationalist movement, ETA, were sentenced to death for the 1968 assassination of a police inspector. The trials rallied the opposition and marked a major turning point for the anti-Francoist resistance (Poblet, 2001: 104).

fundamental law, they argued, it took precedence over any particular laws, and the judiciary was bound to interpret all norms in the juridical order in terms of its spirit. Should the government issue dispositions that violate the fundamental law, they argued, judges should rule these laws null and void (Justicia Democrática, 1978: 78–9).

The documents also dissected the regime's repressive legislation and, appealing to the democratic aspirations of Spanish society, called for reforms to liberalise specific areas of law. For example, the 1971 document focused on the need to reform the penal code and the military justice code, which were 'lacking in the most elementary procedural guarantees' and were 'a constant source of legal insecurity'. The group denounced the criminalisation of autonomous political association, restrictions on labour organisation, and the creation of 'offences against Catholicism'. It also highlighted the 'constant clamor' in Spanish society for 'the abolition of the death penalty and for the amnesty of innumerable political crimes' (Justicia Democrática, 1978: 34–42). In the document covering 1972, the group offered a technical analysis of the importance of criminal procedure guarantees, arguing for stricter adherence to existing rules and the introduction of others, such as oral procedure, in order better to protect the rights of the accused (Justicia Democrática, 1978: 81–102).

At the same time, the publications railed against the escalating levels of repression that the regime mounted against the growing mobilisation of civil society. In the 1972 document, they critiqued the 'aberrant' legal conditions at the nation's universities, in which 'part of the professoriate assumes inappropriate police functions and the other part suffers the exercise of these functions or is forced to "cooperate" in this exercise' (Justicia Democrática, 1978: 130). They urged their colleagues to consider whether or not they could, in good conscience, participate in the prosecution of student dissent and protest. In the same publication, they voiced their alarm at the rise in repression against the working class: 'While as jurists, any attack on the individual rights of citizens concerns us, as judges we are particularly concerned that ... even as workers are succeeding in having their legal rights recognised, there exists a greater limitation of their rights in the extrajudicial sphere' (Justicia Democrática, 1978: 132). They noted, thus, that 'legal reforms were not enough', that the only way to secure workers' rights was through 'an absolute change of socioeconomic and political structures'. However, in the mean time, they encouraged their colleagues in the labour courts to give special weight to the vulnerability of workers, and to consider their responsibility as judges to 'make and live a liberalising law (*Derecho Liberalizador*)' (Justicia Democrática, 1978: 152–3).

Another key demand running through JD's clandestine publications was for greater respect for judicial independence, without which judges could never 'respond to the public's demand for justice' (Fernández Viagas, 1982: 82). To achieve this, they insisted repeatedly on the restoration of a full scope of jurisdiction for the ordinary courts, which the regime had severely restricted through the assignment of political crimes first to military courts and later to special courts, such as the Tribunal for Public Order—created in 1963—and the *Juzgados de Peligrosidad Social* (Social Danger Courts)—created in 1974. They also called for a relaxation of the hierarchical control within the judiciary, which subjected lower-ranking judges and prosecutors to regular, and clearly politically-inflected, reviews by their superiors. This system, which favoured subjective 'merit' over seniority, meant that lower-ranking judges did not enjoy full independence, since the system could be (and was) used to intimidate them into submission (Justicia Democrática, 1978: 55–9, 160–74, and 246–7).

Perhaps boldest of all, however, was JD's open critique of those judges whom they viewed as 'complicit in the regime's arbitrariness'. They repeatedly chided their colleagues, and especially their superiors, for 'remaining silent' in the face of 'serious events that affected the function and the good name' of the judiciary (Justicia Democrática, 1978: 74–5 and 187). Each of their clandestine publications carried the same message: 'the judiciary is not politically innocent and its members must become conscious of the reach and the political implications—by action or by omission—of their own behavior' (Andrés Ibáñez, 1988: 72). To redeem the institution, they advocated a more critical approach to legal interpretation, underscoring the (liberal) political commitment that the judicial vocation entailed:

> The jurist, especially the judge, cannot fall into the temptation of taking shelter in the imperatives of a juridical positivism and applying norms that have nothing to do with legality. For, aside from the fact that what the reigning political regime exhibits as legality has not emanated from any representative legislative organ, one should not forget that positive Law (*Derecho positivo*) is not exclusively made up of laws (*leyes*), but also of general principles of Law (*Derecho*), which must inspire any honest interpretation. These principles derive from a set of norms of civilisation, based in respect for individual rights and the *judicial* guarantee of their exercise and protection, at all times, in the face of excessive uses of power, especially when that power is regressive, violent, and destructive of the very foundation of collective life [Justicia Democrática, 1978: 69].

Moreover, they maintained that 'the function of the judiciary does not consist only in reading what is written, but rather in verifying what has taken place'. Judges had a duty, JD insisted, 'to remove the mask of the law' that gave cover to the Franco regime, exposing the illiberal—and anti-legal—reality that lay beneath it (Justicia Democrática, 1978: 65). In response to the charge that in promoting such ideas they were fomenting the politicisation of the judiciary, JD argued forthrightly:

> The judge cannot be an automaton. The judge is a citizen like everyone else. And he has, like everyone else, the right to demand propriety and justice in the handling of public decision making…. He does not become improperly politicised in

demanding this. By contrast, he who is complicit in a situation of raw and unjust power, who tolerates it, permits it, and sanctions it, does politicise himself and dirty himself. He who is politicised is he who requests silence and adulation, discipline and servility to power, he who calls the independent judge 'red,' the judge who wants to be clean and honest 'subversive,' the judge who defends and speaks of the fundamental rights of man 'stupid' [Justicia Democrática, 1978: 186].

Not surprisingly, the judicial leaders implicated in such statements were not pleased, and a number of known JD participants thus suffered reprisals from their institutional superiors. For example, two young public prosecutors involved in JD, José María Mena and Carlos Jiménez Villarejo, were forcibly transferred to remote posts, where the government hoped they would be isolated and silenced (Jiménez Villarejo and Fernández interviews, 2002). Their annual evaluations stated that both men's performance was tarnished by their 'rebel character' and their 'sympathy' and 'communion' with 'elements disaffected with the National Movement' (cited in Poblet, 2001: 102). Mena was accused of fomenting rebellion in the judiciary, participating in the organisation of the Catalan Assembly, prosecuting crimes against workers, and investigating torture. He was thus transferred to a tiny town in the Pyrenees, 100 miles from Barcelona, in the province of Lérida.[19] As Mena himself explained, 'The word from Madrid was, "Tell them not to complain, because they should really be in another place," meaning in prison!' (Mena interview, 2004).

In 1976 and 1977, JD began attracting significant national media attention, particularly from the national daily *El País*, thereby introducing the group into the consciousness of the broader Spanish public. In 1976, for example, the press reported on the case of Plácido Fernández Viagas, a high-ranking judge from Seville and member of JD who was suspended by his superiors for three months without pay for participating in an unauthorised demonstration (Andrés Ibáñez, 1988: 74).[20] In January of 1977, when the group held its first (still clandestine) congress, a major debate erupted in the press over the group's publication of two documents, one of which took a strong stand against 'the false and self-serving apoliticism of the judicial function which has been used as an instrument for the docile application of fascist legality' (cited in Andrés Ibáñez, 1988: 77). Thus by the time of the formal transition to democracy, it was public knowledge that the judiciary was no longer a monolithic, conservative body (Andrés Ibañez, 1988: 20).

---

[19] This was Mena's second forced transfer; his first was to Barcelona from Tenerife (Canarias), where he had stirred up trouble by trying to prosecute violations of labour protection laws (Mena interview, 2004).
[20] This was surely a pretext, since it had long been known in Andalucía that Judge Fernández refused to sanction the detentions of workers and students arrested for exercising their rights to assembly, expression or strike (Burgos, 1998).

III. CONDITIONS FOR JD'S MOBILISATION:
OPPORTUNITIES AND FRAMES

As should be clear from the preceding section, JD participants took great personal and professional risks in order to protest the illiberalism of the late Franco regime and demand liberal reforms. It would have been far safer and easier for them simply to play along with the regime right through to the end, to maintain a distance from the political fray, and to take refuge in traditional conceptions of judicial neutrality and independence. This is certainly the path their counterparts in Chile and many other places chose, as did the majority of their colleagues. What were the factors, then, that encouraged and enabled JD members to organise and speak out collectively? In this section, I explain how developments in the wider political context, or 'opportunity structure', opened the door for a redefinition, or 'cultural (re-)framing', of the role of law and courts in political life—a redefinition that both inspired and strengthened JD's determination to act.[21]

As Pérez-Díaz (1993) and others (eg, Poblet, 2001) have argued, Spain's political and institutional transition was greatly facilitated by the profound cultural/ideological transformation that preceded it. This transformation began in the 1950s, and was made possible by policy changes of the Franco regime. The first key change was Franco's decision to promote Catholic segments of his coalition at the expense of Falangists. The second, and related, change was the abandonment of an autarchic model of development in favour of trade with and investment from Western Europe, as well as the construction of a welfare state. And following on these was a softening of repression against liberal, social-democratic and socialist critics, who were able to air their opinions more freely in university settings and, to some extent, in print.[22] The result of these policies was that ideas and resources poured into Spain from Europe, influencing an entire generation of Spaniards who came of age in the late 1950s and 1960s (Johnston, 1991: 81; Pérez-Díaz, 1993). Among the professional spheres most influenced by this influx of European ideas was that of law.

During the 1940s, fascist legal thinkers, committed to 'the spread of work by [thinkers such as] Carl Schmitt' dominated Spanish legal academia

---

[21] Due to space limitations, I do not explore the specific differences between the Spanish and Chilean cases in this chapter, though such a comparison is part of my larger work in progress.

[22] I do not mean to imply here that there was a seamless and benevolent liberalisation carried out by the Franco regime. Communists and Basque separatists continued to be dealt with heavy-handedly, there were numerous crack-downs at the universities in the 1960s and early 1970s, and, the regime remained fierce and resilient enough to endure until after the *Caudillo*'s death. Indeed, numerous scholars have emphasised how uncertain the transition to democracy appeared when it was happening, and how important specific decisions of enlightened and pragmatic statesmen in both the regime and the opposition were to its success. My point here, then, is simply to highlight the developments that favoured the mobilization of liberal sectors in the early 1970s.

(Poblet, 2001: 52). With the defeat of the Axis powers in World War II, however, Franco needed to seek international ideological support from elsewhere, and the logical place to turn was the Catholic Church. He moved swiftly to fill important posts in the state and in universities with Catholic activists (Poblet, 2001: 55), and with their help negotiated a Concordat with the Vatican in 1953 (Carr and Fusi, 1979: 29). The Concordat confirmed and expanded the public status of the Church in Spain, with Franco promising that the country would become 'the West's spiritual reserve' (Poblet, 2001: 55). Catholic intellectuals and administrators were thus wellplaced to diffuse the ideas and debates that emanated from the (universal) church during the decades that followed (Pérez-Díaz, 1993: 144).

There were two main groups of Catholic activists that exercised influence and advanced reforms in the 1950s and 1960s: academics of a Christian-democratic persuasion committed to the autonomy of intellectual activity and the advancement of social justice, and technocrats associated, at least early on, with the socially conservative group *Opus Dei*, who believed that the adoption of market economics would bring prosperity and social peace (Pérez-Díaz, 1993: 147). The former group was most influential in civil society, while the latter group worked within the state.

'In the fifties, the liberal Catholic intellectuals were a force of the first order on the Spanish cultural horizon' (Pérez-Díaz, 1993: 147). Many of them came out of the ACNP (*Asociación Católica Nacional de Propagandistas*), which had been founded by a Basque Jesuit in 1909, and sought to place Catholics in all spheres of power. In 1951, Franco chose an ACNP activist and professor of legal philosophy, Joaquín Ruiz Giménez, to be his Minister of Education. Ruiz Giménez supported the intellectual ferment within the Catholic intelligentsia, appointing liberal-minded figures as rectors of the universities at Madrid and Salamanca. These figures sponsored regular discussion groups, into which they brought progressive French Catholic thinkers like Jacques Maritain and Pierre Teilhard de Chardin to offer lectures, and welcomed the participation of local Marxists and secular-humanists (Carr and Fusi, 1979: 29 and 112–13; Arango, 1995: 266). In 1956, however, when their defence and exercise of academic freedom was blamed for contributing to a student uprising at the Complutense University of Madrid, a number of these liberals lost their official posts (Carr and Fusi, 1979: 147–8). While their weight within the regime thus diminished, the standing and influence of these liberal Catholics in civil society only increased in the years that followed (Pérez-Díaz, 1993: 148).

Subsequently, *Opus Dei* technocrats gained the upper hand in the administration, where, in the late 1950s, Franco let them take over economic policy. Most of these individuals were newcomers to the political scene, and, like their ACNP counterparts, they believed they were divinely called to serve their society. Their approach, however, was to act from within the regime, working to render state policies more effective and society

more content and stable.[23] To do this, they promoted a turn away from
economic nationalism and toward open markets (Carr and Fusi, 1979:
54; Encarnación, 2003: 87). They wanted desperately to integrate Spain
into the new European Economic Community, which rejected the country's
application for membership in February of 1962 on political grounds (Carr
and Fusi, 1979: 175).[24]

Many of the *Opus Dei* administrators were trained in law, including the
group's leading light, Laureano López Rodó, who was a professor of administrative law (Carr and Fusi, 1979: 36–7). They believed that the key both
to rendering their Development Plans effective and, ultimately, winning
the legitimacy necessary to merit membership in the EEC was constructing
and developing an *Estado de Derecho* (understood in purely formal terms)
(Carr and Fusi, 1979: 41). To this end, they convened a commission of
technical legal experts to help draft the regime's legislation, especially its
administrative laws, during the 1950s and 1960s (Pita, 2003: 462). These
individuals consciously and openly worked to create what they referred to
as 'anticipatory constitutional law', which they hoped would, in the not too
distant future, bring Spain up to European legal standards (Poblet, 2001:
57–8). They did this in part through reinvigorating the *Consejo de Estado*
(Council of State) and the administrative courts, whose competencies the
Franco regime had previously curtailed significantly. The permanent staff of
the Council of State, composed of the country's 'most influential public law
jurists,—most of whom were not *Opus Dei*, and quite a few who identified
with a more moderate wing of the ACNP (Ortega interview; Rubio interview)—, elaborated a normative doctrine that gradually overtook the previous view that 'political decisions always prevailed over the basic elements
of the rule of law' (Poblet, 2001: 95). This emboldened the ordinary courts,
including the Supreme Court, which by the early 1970s had no compunc-
tion about ruling against the central public administration in a majority of
administrative law cases (Poblet, 2001: 98).[25]

---

[23] Much like the conservative liberals of the 19th century, then, they held that market-led
economic development would serve to pacify those unhappy with the regime and render calls
for radical change unattractive. They were modernisation theorists par excellence (Rubio
interview).

[24] Interestingly, the rejection came at the urging of a number of the ACNP intellectuals
exiled in Europe after 1956 and insistent that Spain not be granted membership of the EEC
until it democratised (Rodríguez de Lecea, 1985: 325).

[25] It is important to note, however, that the Supreme Court put up no challenge whatsoever
to the regime's diversion of politically-sensitive cases to military and ad hoc courts, nor did
it challenge the anti-liberal decisions of those courts. Bastida (1986) analyses the decisions
of Spain's Supreme Court from 1964–74 on appeals of decisions rendered by the Tribunal of
Public Order (known as the 'TOP'), a special court created by Franco in 1963 to handle 'political crimes' (eg, propaganda, illicit association and public disorder). He shows that although
more than 80 per cent of the TOP's decisions were reviewed by the Supreme Court, the latter
overturned only one of the TOP's decisions in one case. In the rest, the Court accepted and
reinforced the illiberal reasoning of the TOP.

Meanwhile, Joaquín Ruiz Giménez broke with the regime and became the 'leading spirit of the only critical magazine of the time, *Cuadernos para el Diálogo*'. Inspired by the progressive encyclicals of Pope John XXIII, *Cuadernos* began with a Christian-Democratic orientation, but 'gradually, with the collaboration of Marxists and opposition intellectuals, it became more democratic and less Christian'. From its founding in 1963 through the transition, the publication played a crucial role in 'educat[ing] Spanish opinion in democratic ideas [and] keep[ing] up a continuous process of criticism of the regime, undermining its moral credibility and denying its legitimacy' (Carr and Fusi, 1979: 31, 152 and 167; see also Rodríguez de Lecea).

Among the topics the *Cuadernos* editors took on was the role that law and courts should play in society. Denouncing 'what officialdom wanted to present as a Rule of Law', the publication set out 'to rescue eighteenth-century doctrines on liberty and democracy [with their emphasis on] civil and political rights', as well as 'to make explicit the new historical sensibility with respect to economic and cultural rights' (Gimbernat, 1985: 366, 348). In the early 1970s, the magazine published a series of articles arguing that legal professionals, as intellectuals and as jurists, had an obligation 'to seek the realisation of Law (*Derecho*), and not just automatic compliance with the law' and 'to constitute a social guarantee' of the human person 'before the absolute power of the State' (Cuadernos para el Diálogo, 1970c; Peces-Barba, 1970; Castellano, 1972). The editors supported what they identified as 'the growing understanding among jurists that the training they receive in university classrooms and in subsequent professional practice has not been given for their own benefit, but rather in order to offer to society ... a [means of] protection and juridical control' (Cuadernos para el Diálogo, 1970a). In addition, multiple contributors argued for reforms to bring Spain's criminal procedure in line with the rest of Europe, to grant the judiciary greater independence and restore the full scope of its jurisdiction, and to establish a genuine rule of law (*Estado de Derecho*) (Castellano, 1972; Cuadernos para el Diálogo, 1974a and 1974b; and Gil-Robles, 1975). Justicia Democrática drew directly on such articles to support some of the arguments in their clandestine documents (see, eg, Justicia Democrática, 1978: 24, 35 and 130).

Both the progressive intellectuals in civil society and the moderate to conservative technocrats in the state thus contributed, in different ways and with different emphases, to the redefinition of the proper role of law and courts in public life.[26] As I have explained, they were able to do this thanks

---

[26] As Johnston (1991: 66) explains, the emergence of a new frame involves 'the mobilization of new meanings' regarding 'what is just and unjust' and 'the spread of new definitions of what is possible' in terms of 'appropriate avenues to rectify the situation'. This is precisely what took place within the wider juridical community in Spain during the 1950s and 1960s.

to policy changes of the Franco regime, changes from which they not only benefited, but to which, more importantly, they further contributed. Both groups served as conduits of liberal and democratic ideas coming from outside Spain's borders, and both argued for the importance of keeping those borders open. Pragmatist that he was (Malefakis, 2003: 101), Franco permitted this, and in the spheres where ideas mattered most, namely the university and the press, a new generation of leaders absorbed and came to identify with European norms (Ortega interview; Rubio interview). As Pérez-Díaz (1993: 148) explains, the influx of ideas from Europe expanded through 'travel abroad, books brought in from outside, a network of book-shops, publishers, university magazines, informal gatherings, experimental theater, film societies, student unions, and political organisations', such that 'from the sixties on, the content of debates among a large minority in Spanish university circles became increasingly homogenous with that of European universities, and its evolution continued on a par with it'.[27]

These factors emerged strongly in first-hand accounts from participants in *Justicia Democrática*. They underscored how political struggles in the universities in the late 1950s helped raise the political consciousness of some would-be lawyers and judges (Mena interview, 2004). By 1968, the universities became 'spaces of great politico-cultural effervescence' (Andrés Ibáñez interview, 2004). From this point forward, the traditional scholastic, positivist methods of legal training lost favour, such that within a decade, the change in the nature of law school training had undergone an 'awesome transformation' (Andrés Ibáñez interview, 2004). Gradually, civil servants, such as judges and professors, began to feel comfortable discussing demo-cratic alternatives (Toharia, 1975), and by the 1970s, the growing mobili-sation of civil society gave them the confidence to start expressing publicly some dissent (Andrés Ibáñez, 1988: 69). As one participant put it, 'change was in the air and there was a great sense of confidence among the activists' (Carmena interview, 2002).

It is important to emphasise, however, that it was not simply structural changes that explain the mobilisation of this new generation. To understand both the goals they shared and the depth of their commitment to working for their realisation, it is necessary to take into account the religious origins of and support for them (Johnston, 1991: 71; Pérez-Díaz, 1993: 156). The profound ideological changes within the Catholic Church, backed by the papacy in the Vatican II sessions (1962–5) and put into practice by Jesuit priests and other Catholic leaders in Spain (including the liberal intellectu-als discussed above), inspired and lent confidence to the 'generation of dissent', offering them a combination of 'religious authenticity with a com-mitment to the struggle for justice and freedom' (Pérez-Díaz, 1993: 162–3

---

[27] On this point see also Johnston, 1991: 70–1.

and 157; see also Johnston, 1991: 67–81).[28] Thus, the members of *Justicia Democrática,* though very diverse in their specific ideological orientations, could coalesce around the notion of professional 'mission', 'duty' or 'social responsibility' (found throughout Justicia Democrática, 1978), and be confident that the appeal to such notions would resonate far beyond the confines of their organisation (Cuadernos para el Diálogo, 1970a and 1970c; Peces-Barba, 1970; Doñate interview, 2004).

IV. CONDITIONS FOR JD'S MOBILISATION: ORGANISATIONAL ALLIANCES AND SUPPORT

While the preceding section sheds light on the structural and ideological changes that made the idea of organising judges around the cause of political liberalism conceivable, these are not sufficient to explain how and why *Justicia Democrática* participants were able to act collectively, and quite successfully, on their convictions. Even with the liberalisation described above, oppositional political organisation was extremely difficult. 'The right of public meeting was closely controlled by the Ministry of the Interior and its agent in the provinces, the Civil Governor. Public meetings of more than twenty people had to have governmental permission, while an agent of the government could attend and could dissolve it if he saw fit' (Carr and Fusi, 1979: 45). Moreover, those in charge of the careers of judges and prosecutors, namely the judges of the Supreme Court, had proven themselves loyal to the principles of the regime (Bastida, 1986), or at least unwilling to question the regime's repression of dissent.[29] Thus, as Beirich (1998, 218) notes, 'even if a judge disliked the authoritarian system and wanted to exercise independence, they would not be able to do so for fear of having their careers destroyed'.[30]

In this section, then, I argue that what ultimately rendered the judges and prosecutors of *Justicia Democrática* willing and able not just to contemplate and discuss the need for political liberalism, but actually to mobilise collectively in defence of liberal principles, was organisational support from political parties, liberal clergy, sympathetic media, and access to European institutions. Although sectors of the bar also mobilised around similar causes during the same period, JD had no explicit alliance with and did not

---

[28] As Gimbernat puts it, the mission of *Cuadernos para el Diálogo* was 'very explicitly about changing the political orientation of Spanish Catholicism', so as to synthesise it with that which had always been portrayed as its opposite, namely liberalism (1985, 345 and 352).

[29] See n 25 above.

[30] In 1977, eg, following JD's first and only congress, the president of the Supreme Court ordered the chiefs of police throughout the country to conduct an immediate investigation to identify which members of the judiciary were members of the association (Andrés Ibáñez, 1988: 78).

coordinate any specific actions with them. While they were aware of and drew confidence from the public statements and actions of their colleagues in legal practice, JD's actions should not be understood as part of a movement that grew out of and was fuelled primarily by solidarity with a unified bar. Rather, JD was the judicial instantiation of a much broader movement in Spanish civil society, to which liberal-minded sectors of many professions (ie, doctors, teachers, engineers, architects, artists, as well as lawyers) contributed in whatever ways they could (Zaragoza, 1975).

As noted in section II above, JD was born out of intimate meetings between judges and prosecutors in Barcelona in the late 1960s, and formed an official, albeit clandestine, association in 1971. Around this same time, a group of Madrid lawyers created their own discussion group, known as the *Círculo de Estudios Jurídicos*, to debate legal and political difficulties that they encountered in their professional lives (Poblet, 2001: 255). Many of their concerns, which found echo in the clandestine documents of JD, were aired in the pages of *Cuadernos para el Diálogo* (Cuadernos para el Diálogo, 1970a, 1970b and 1970c; Castellano, 1972). In June of 1970, these lawyers participated in the fourth National Congress of the Spanish Bar, held in León. It was the first such meeting since 1953, and it was described by one participant as 'the Vatican Council II of the advocacy' (Poblet, 2001: 256, citing Albert Fina). The Congress produced a list of demands that included guarantees for the rights of detainees, the abolition of the death penalty, the restoration of political rights, the dismantling of special jurisdictions, and the independence of the judiciary. This presentation of demands irked the government, which moved in various ways to reassert control over the bar associations (and all professional associations) in the years that followed (Zaragoza, 1975; Poblet, 2001: 255–7).

The mobilisation of this sector of the bar did not go unnoticed by *Justicia Democrática*; indeed, they referenced it in their first clandestine publication (Justicia Democrática, 1978: 34). However, in interviews, the founders of the movement did not mention links with the bar to be essential to their own organisational capacity and success, nor did sources on opposition lawyers' activism mention such links (Zaragoza, 1975; Poblet, 2001).[31] Instead, JD veterans underscored the importance of personal ties to two sets of organisations: the clandestine political parties and the progressive wing of the Catholic church.

As noted above, the founders of JD were individuals affiliated with the Communist and Socialist parties, many of whom had lost family members to the Nationalist forces in the civil war. Thanks to their party ties and experience, the founders 'had the capacity, knew the technique' for operating

---

[31] Fernández Asperilla notes that parallel movements emerged in two other pillars of the Franco regime at this time: the church and the military, and links all of these to the general 'awakening of civil society' that took place in the 1970s (1995, 67–8).

a clandestine group (Doñate interview, 2004). As Encarnación (2003: 93) notes, the Communist party, in particular, was at the forefront of the anti-Francoist movement in Spanish civil society, helping to organise groups across the political opposition, from students and workers, to women, and (in this case) to judges. Moreover, JD began in Barcelona, where a well-coordinated democratic resistance was well underway by the early 1970s (Johnston, 1991), offering JD regular contact with and support from the Catalonian leftist parties (Marín Gámez, 2003: 338–9).

Also essential to the group's organisation and survival was support, moral and physical, from sympathetic clergy. The Franco regime had granted the church the right of assembly and freedom from state censorship, which meant that it was in a position, when clergy were so inclined, to provide protective cover to oppositional organisation (Johnston, 1991: 57). As Judge Antonio Doñate put it:

> One thing is clear: during our clandestine period, if it hadn't been for the help of the Catholic Church, our capacity to respond would have been far weaker. We didn't have the capacity to disseminate our clandestine programs, because the risk was enormous. Keep in mind that we printed our publications in the abbey at Montserrat. One of the meetings of the Democratic Assembly of Catalonia, which united the entire clandestine political opposition, took place in the abbey at Montserrat! We had a very fluid dialogue with sectors of the Church. They supported us in a variety of concrete ways [Doñate interview, 2004].

As another example, JD prosecutor José María Mena reported that after his transfer to the small village in the Pyrenees, he arranged a secret meeting on the border with a Catholic bishop, who also happened to be the co-prince of Andorra, in which he secured his help in pleading for the release of political prisoners (Mena interview, 2004).

These examples also indicate the significance of geography to JD's emergence. It is not coincidental that Barcelona was the organisation's birthplace. Catalonia had a long-standing resentment and mistrust of Madrid's centralising control, as well as a strong sense of cultural distinctiveness and solidarity. As previously noted, judges were just one sector of a much larger anti-Francoist movement that developed in Barcelona in the mid to late 1960s (Johnston, 1991; Marín Gámez, 2003: 337), whereas the democratic opposition in the rest of the country remained 'deeply divided until 1976' (Carr and Fusi, 1979: 164). Though JD had some contacts outside Catalonia, the relations were limited at first, since interpersonal trust did not extend much outside the region.[32]

---

[32] As one interviewee put it, the 'madrileños have a distinct sociology; they are very Latin, with a tendency to shout out everything in the bars' (Mena interview, 2004).

Barcelona was also within driving distance of the French border, intensifying the influx of wider European ideas that was affecting all of Spain by this time and facilitating international contacts (Johnston, 1991; Pérez-Díaz, 1993; Marín Gámez, 2003; Doñate interview, 2004; Mena interview, 2004).[33] In the early 1970s, for example, JD members, largely individually and on an informal basis, began making contacts with sympathetic judges in France and Italy, where similar groups (*Syndicat de la Magistrature* and *Magistratura Democrática*) had already formed (Mena interview, 2004; Andrés Ibáñez interview, 2004). With help from these groups, JD's publications were disseminated both to the European media and to European Community institutions. JD's 1973 report, for example, trumpets the fact that the document covering the previous year received press coverage in both France (*Le Monde*) and Britain (the BBC) (Justicia Democrática, 1978:72). And one of the group's veterans emphasised that:

> we knew our annual reports were followed and analysed in the Council of Europe, which naturally energised us to keep going forward, because we knew that was a source of big political pressure, and we knew our reports could carry great weight there. They represented a voice from within the judiciary itself—ours wasn't an analysis by a particular political party interested in demonstrating that nothing was working, but rather a view from inside of what we saw happening, and this collective voice had great value in that platform [Doñate interview, 2004].

In sum, while JD members were able to seize on opportunities presented by the softening of the Franco regime, and while they drew inspiration from the broader cultural change that occurred within Spanish society, including in the legal profession, during the 1960s and 1970s, what ultimately made their mobilisation feasible and effective were their alliances with or access to political parties, clergy, domestic and foreign media, and the Council of Europe. Not only did these entities offer JD the organisational resources that they otherwise lacked, but they also lent the group's cause publicity and weight. Hence this group of 'delinquent judges' (Justicia Democrática) was able to contribute in a unique way to Spain's transition to liberal democracy.

---

[33] As Johnston (1991: 71) explains, for the Catalonian-based resistance:

France was a beacon of intellectual freedom. Books by French writers and philosophers ... were often smuggled across the border, read, and discussed. These books were about democracy, nationalism, socialism, and socially conscious Catholicism—subversive topics prohibited by Francoist censors. Anticipating the Second Vatican Council by ten years, the French worker-priest movement merged a Christian concern for the poor with progressive issues and leftist politics that also resonated among university students and younger clergy.

V. JD'S ROLE IN THE TRANSITION TO AND CONSOLIDATION OF DEMOCRACY

Despite the mobilisation of civil society that took place in the early 1970s, Spain's formal transition to democracy was very much a transition from above, in which elite actors from the regime set the terms for regime change and negotiated a series of pacts with the opposition. Unlike in some other pacted transitions, however, where the outgoing leadership sought to preserve illiberal controls on the new regime, the key players from the Franco regime, particularly King Juan Carlos I and Adolfo Suárez, actively promoted liberal-democratic values and principles. Not only did Suárez invoke the sovereignty of the people to promote the Law of Political Reform,[34] but in April of 1977, two months before the elections for the constituent assembly, he took the bold step of legalising the Spanish Communist Party. In so doing, he proclaimed:

> I do not think that our people wants to find itself fatally obliged to see our jails full of people for ideological reasons. I think that in a democracy we must all be vigilant of ourselves, we must all be witnesses and judges of our public actions. We have to instill respect for legal minorities. Among the rights and duties of living together is the acceptance of the opponent (cited in Linz and Stepan, 1996: 97).[35]

A liberal tone was thus set for the transition, and almost all parties to the constitutional negotiations embraced it.

The *lingua franca* of the negotiations themselves, meanwhile, was the language of law, a language that was useful since 'it provide[d] all the shared ambiguities ... required to bridge the gaps between old and new generations' (Poblet, 2001: 19). On the outgoing regime side, Torcuato Fernández-Miranda, president of the *Cortes* (the legislative assembly), proved to be a key figure in taking the regime 'from the law to the law' (Poblet, 2001: 31). Fernández-Miranda was a trusted Franco-era minister, who had also worked as a professor (*catedrático*) of public law in the 1960s and was preceptor to none other than (then Prince) Juan Carlos. By the time of the transition, Fernández-Miranda held that 'it would be absurd [if] Spanish society, in spite of the changes that have taken place within it, should continue for ever to wear the juridical clothes of [Franco's] Fundamental Laws' (Carr and Fusi, 1979: 221). He thus drafted the Law of Political Reform, and backed the strategy, publicly articulated by Suárez, of urging the *Cortes*

---

[34] In approving the Law of Political Reform, the Francoist *Cortes* endorsed the transition to democracy and essentially voted themselves out of existence. In urging his colleagues to vote for the law, Suárez argued, 'The future is not written because only the people can write it' (Linz and Stepan, 1996: 95).

[35] King Juan Carlos, for his part, was responsible for appointing the moderate Suárez in the first place, and came out strongly in defence of the new democratic regime following the attempted military coup in February of 1981.

to approve the reform so as to avoid a 'vacuum of legality' (cited in Linz and Stepan, 1996: 95).

Once free elections had been held (in June of 1977) and the new democratic Parliament convened, then, the drafting of the new Constitution commenced immediately. Preparation of the document was delegated to a seven-member subgroup of the Constitutional Commission, five of whom (Manuel Fraga, Miguel Herrero de Miñón, Gregorio Peces-Barba, Miquel Roca and Jordi Solé Tura) were or had been university law professors, one (Gabriel Cisneros) a public servant, and one (José Pedro Pérez-Llorca) a diplomat (Poblet, 2001: 32).[36] Herrero de Miñón was a former member of the Council of State, and saw his role as incorporating the previous work of that organ into the new democratic regime. In his memoirs, he stated, 'We framers of 1978 were able to consecrate such general principles as legality, hierarchy, publicity, non-retroactivity, security, [and] accountability ... thanks, in large part, to the legal doctrine the Council of State had elaborated in the previous decades' (cited in Poblet, 2001: 59). Such principles were shared by his colleagues on the Left, such as Peces-Barba, who cited the influence of Joaquín Ruiz Giménez, among others, on his constitutional proposals (Poblet, 2001: 61). Reflecting on the process 25 years later, both men highlighted the tacit consensus of Spanish society at the time of the framing around the need for 'a Constitution similar to the European Constitutions, containing recognition of fundamental and social rights, a formula for [federal] autonomy ..., and a system of parliamentary monarchy' ('Peces-Barba y Herrero de Miñón ...,' 2003: 7).

There was thus broad agreement among the framers of the 1978 Constitution that the new regime must be grounded in liberal-democratic principles, and hence there was strong support across party lines for both fundamental rights protection and judicial independence (Bonime-Blanc, 1987: 72; Bereijo, 2003; Gor, 2003).[37] What the parties disagreed on was how judicial independence should be defined and secured. Representatives from the Right (the UCD and the AP) called for the complete separation of the judiciary from politics, thus requiring those holding judicial offices to sever any political ties they had. Representatives from the Left (PSOE, PCE, MC and PNV), however, echoed the argument put forward by *Justicia Democrática*: no citizen, including a judge, could be above politics, nor should he or she be deprived of the fundamental right of political association (Bonime-Blanc, 1987: 79–80).

---

[36] I thank Victor Ferreres for the correction to this information.

[37] The 1978 Constitution protects a full battery of civil, political and social rights in Chaps. II–IV. Very significantly, it also established the Constitutional Court (Arts 159–165) as an institution separate from the ordinary judiciary, granting it both abstract and concrete review powers. For a thorough examination of the role of the Constitutional Court in the Spanish transition to democracy, see Beirich (1998).

This argument was one of many that had been articulated in resolutions of JD's first and only congress, held in January of 1977. Reiterating a point made repeatedly in their clandestine publications, the congress officially concluded that the group 'rejected the supposed apoliticism of the judicial function that has been used as a docile instrument for applying fascist legality [and] emphasised that, on the contrary, the judiciary maintains at all times a function of indisputable political transcendence for the society that it serves' (Fernández-Viagas, 1982: 139–40). They thus insisted that judges be guaranteed their right to political association and unionisation, and they resolved that the judiciary have its own governing organs, elected by all members of the institution. Moreover, they proposed a number of ways that the judiciary should be subjected to 'democratic control', among these jury trials, class actions, and various mechanisms of public transparency. As in the past, they insisted on unified jurisdiction, and called for abolition of the death penalty and the criminalisation of torture. Finally, they demanded an end to legal discrimination between men and women, and committed themselves to promoting 'an application of the law that tends toward the democratic development of society' (Fernández-Viagas, 1982: 141–3).

The constitutional text of 1978 embodied many, but not all, of these proposals. Article 117 abolished all special jurisdictions (except military, whose jurisdiction was minimised) and prohibited exceptional tribunals. Article 125 provided that 'citizens may exercise popular action and participate in the administration of justice through the institution of the jury'.[38] Article 15 banned torture and abolished the death penalty. Article 14 guaranteed equality before the law, prohibiting 'discrimination for reasons of ... any ... personal or social condition or circumstance', and Article 32 secured 'matrimonial equality' for men and women. In addition to guaranteeing the publicity, non-retroactivity and security of legal norms, Article 9 (on the rule of law) declared it to be 'the responsibility of the public powers to promote conditions so that liberty and equality of the individual and groups he joins will be real and effective; to remove those obstacles which impede or make difficult their full implementation, and to facilitate participation of citizens in political, economic, cultural, and social life'. Although Article 127 declared that judges, magistrates and prosecutors, 'while on active service, may not hold other public positions or belong to political parties or unions', it left 'the system and modalities of professional association of judges, magistrates, and prosecutors' to be determined by ordinary law. Moreover, Article 122 provided for the formation of the *Consejo General del Poder Judicial* (CGPJ, or General Council of the Judiciary) to manage internal governance of the institution. This body, modelled after Italy's *Consiglio Superiore della Magistratura*, was charged with nomination, promotion and discipline of

---

[38] Juries were not introduced, however, until 1995, and there is broad dissatisfaction among legal experts about their functioning.

judges. Its creation responded to JD's longstanding demand that vertical control within the judiciary be relaxed. The Constitution mandated that the CGPJ be composed of 21 members: the president of the Supreme Court (*de oficio*), eight 'lawyers and jurists of recognised competence with more than fifteen years of professional experience' appointed by 3/5 majorities in the parliament (four by the House and four by the Senate), and 12 members chosen from among all ranks of judges in active service, whose selection was to be determined by the (subsequent) Organic Law of the Judiciary.

Witnessing the codification of many of their demands, and unable to agree on what form the group could and should take after the transition, JD dissolved and its members integrated into the *Asociación Profesional de la Magistratura* (APM), the corporatist professional body that carried over, in large part, from the Franco era.[39] Within the APM, however, they found the climate to be very hostile. The conservative majority seemed determined to silence them. Although the progressives were able to secure support from 30 per cent of the magistrates attending the 1979 APM congress (Andrés Ibáñez, 1988: 23), the conservative APM leaders, in consultation with the conservative UCD government,[40] decided that the judicial representatives to the CGPJ would be chosen by majority vote, thereby denying voice to the progressive minority in the new 'self-governing' body.[41] Moreover, the judicial elite successfully fought to establish a 15 per cent threshold for the formation of a separate judicial association (which might force the adoption of a proportional system for the CGPJ elections). This percentage was just out of reach for the progressive faction, whose official membership was in the 10–12 per cent range.

The group's fortunes changed, however, when the Socialists (PSOE) decisively won the 1982 elections. Aware that the Socialists might seek a radical restructuring of the laws governing the judiciary,[42] the APM leadership

[39] The very existence of the APM in the new regime was a victory for the JD activists, for they had strongly advocated for the formation of a judicial union of some sort (Justicia Democrática, 1978: 314).

[40] The (conservative-controlled) parliament finally passed an Organic Law on the Judiciary that went into effect in 1980, replacing the 1870 statute that had governed the judiciary until that time. It provided that the 12 judicial members of the CGPJ would be appointed by other magistrates and judges, as in Italy.

[41] Subsequently, judicial appointments continued to follow a conservative ideological pattern, though disciplinary action was not used in the intimidating, ideologically-controlling way it had been in the past (Andrés Ibáñez, 1988: 42).

[42] This was indeed the case, since 'the new PSOE government felt very strongly that the justice system should reflect, to some extent, the new and overwhelming majorities in the Parliament', and that 'a common sentiment at the time was that the only institution that still needed to be reformed was the judiciary' (Beirich, 1998: 226). In 1985, they reformed the (1980) Organic Law on the Judiciary and made a key change to the selection of CGPJ members: the 12 judicial appointees were no longer to be elected by the judges themselves, but chosen from among the judicial ranks by the parliament. This was and remains hugely controversial, even among JpD members, since it established formal political control over the judicial appointment, promotion and disciplinary body. However, when the parliamentary opposition challenged the constitutionality of the new organic law in 1986, the Constitutional Court upheld it (see Beirich, 1998: 227–31).

suddenly decided to permit the existence of *corrientes* (ideological currents) within the association itself. The progressive judges, composed by this time of 'a generic, moderate Left, independent [and] difficult to classify' (Andrés Ibañez, 1988: 25), thus regrouped to form *Jueces para la Democracia* (JpD).[43]

The founding documents of JpD established as the group's mission: 'to work for a judicial organisation that is truly functional to the superior values of the constitutional order: "liberty, justice, equality, and political pluralism"'. In particular, they committed themselves to fulfill the duty set out in Article 9.2 of the Constitution (cited above), that is, to help render citizens' liberty and equality 'real and effective'. This task, the JpD reasoned, required a new type of judge, independent from power and 'committed to the reality of the polis', who would take care 'to avoid allowing the coercive instruments that they handled in a social context of inequality to function as a factor of legitimation and even expansion of that inequality'. JpD thus called on their colleagues to 'interpret existing legislation in a manner that allows space for the just demands of broad social sectors that rarely have had the opportunity to be recognised within the judiciary'. As a means to this end, they pledged to work for the 'democratisation of the judicial career', recovering space for internal and external criticism of judicial performance.[44] Since its formation, JpD and its sister organisation for prosecutors, the *Unión Progresista de Fiscales* (UPF),[45] have continued to attract the explicit support of only a minority of eligible professionals, about 10–15 per cent. Nonetheless, they have had a disproportionate influence on institutional reform of the judiciary, facilitated particularly by their close ties to the PSOE (Spanish Socialist Party). For example, they promoted and won (in 1985) a reform to allow lateral entrance to the judiciary, as an alternative to the *Oposición*. Today, 75 per cent of judicial posts are filled through the *Oposición* and 25 per cent through lateral entrance. This is important because, as mentioned above, the *Oposición* system is conservatising, since after law school aspirants must devote three more years to studying and preparation (without remuneration), and so they must have a certain level of financial independence. The lateral entrance possibility opens the door to people who could not afford to go through the *Oposición*—and this has thus allowed individuals more sympathetic to the views of the JpD to join the judicial ranks (Comas and Andrés Ibáñez interviews, 2002). Moreover,

---

[43] Within a year, another *corriente*, Francisco de Vitoria, formed, as a self-proclaimed 'third way' alternative between the conservative majority faction and the JpD. Their main objective is to 'modernise' the judiciary, that is to render it more rapid and efficient through an increase in resources (Andrés Ibañez, 1988: 29).

[44] Available at www.juecesdemocracia.es/asociacion/autobiografia.html.

[45] Information on this latter group is available at www.upfiscales.com.

in recent years, JpD has been very active in promoting the idea of the administration of justice as a public service. Several interviewees stressed that the organisation's principal goal today is trying to bring judges and courts closer to society, to meet the needs of average citizens. In cooperation with the CGPJ, they have thus conducted broad surveys on public perception of the judiciary. With support from the former Centre-Right government, they were authorised to conduct 'user surveys' in the nation's courts, and to target reforms around the responses to those. Arguing that the judiciary exists for the consumers—the citizens—rather than as an arm of the state, the JpD are thus very focused on improving their accessibility, transparency and accountability to the citizenry (Comas, Carmena, and Toharia interviews, 2002).[46] As Mena (interview 2004) stated, 'I think we have been successful at bringing justice closer to the citizenry, making it less hateful than it was'.[47]

VI. CONCLUSION

Spain provides a remarkable example of a society that, after centuries of cycling between instability and absolutism, experienced, in the late twentieth century, a transition to a robust political liberalism. It thus offers an important testing ground for theories regarding the sources of political liberalism, including that which drives the collective project of this volume: under what conditions and in what ways will actors in the legal complex contribute to the construction and/or defence of political liberalism? The analysis in this chapter points to three main conclusions.

First, it demonstrates that a given society may have a longstanding tradition of legal professionalism and an independent judiciary without the institutionalisation of political liberalism. For decades, and arguably centuries, members of Spain's legal complex were unwilling and/or unable to mobilise collectively to advance the cause of political liberalism. Some actively cooperated in legitimising illiberal norms and policies, but most were perfectly content to perform their professional function, whether private or public, in a narrow or passive manner, ignoring or consciously eschewing any substantive political commitments (Poblet, 2001: 309). This is not a phenomenon unique to Spain (see, eg, L Hilbink, 2007). Indeed, as Judith Shklar (1985: 209) famously put it, 'legalism as an ideology is compatible with political

---

[46] For an analysis of the results of several years of these surveys see Toharia, 2001.

[47] There are, it should be noted, plenty of critics of the JpD (and its sister organisations), who would challenge the notion that their influence, at least post-1978, has been positive. The author is currently engaged in research designed to provide an empirically-informed assessment of the impact Judges for Democracy groups have had in Spain and other civil law countries.

attitudes and institutions which are not even remotely liberal, or even civilised'. In and of themselves, 'neither the autonomy of the judiciary ... nor the prevalence of rules ... produce[s] ... freedom [or] decency'.

Secondly, and relatedly, the Spanish experience suggests that legal professionals will only be equipped and inclined to work for political liberalism if their professional training and socialisation instills in them a sense of vocation, or professional duty and mission, to uphold and defend liberal principles. Spanish legal professionals, including JD members, were important protagonists of the transition to political liberalism in Spain, but they only became so thanks to a shift in the understanding of the appropriate role of law and courts in public life. This ideological change happened gradually, as liberal ideas and commitments were transmitted through various elements of the Catholic Church and via trade with and tourism from the European Community. The Franco regime's reliance on the church for much of its legitimacy and its desire for the economic benefits of European integration consigned it to acceptance of these cultural influences, which were spread through universities, the media and other intellectual circles. Hence, many legal professionals, particularly those who came of age between the late 1950s and the early 1970s, absorbed and came to identify with a politically liberal conception of their role—that is, one which made their primary responsibility to citizens and society, rather than to the state. This reconceptualisation motivated the judges and prosecutors of *Justicia Democrática* to challenge the traditional framing of adjudication as 'apolitical' and to urge their colleagues to fulfill their duty to promote and defend liberal-democratic principles.

Thirdly, and finally, the Spanish case indicates that, regardless of their level of professional commitment, jurists alone, and particularly judges, cannot construct or defend a liberal regime. While they may understand it as their special duty to protect citizens from the abuse of state power, or to advance other moral principles embodied in domestic or international legal texts, ultimately they cannot do so without alliances or constituencies outside the legal complex (see Widner, 2001: 35–7, and Della Porta, 2001: 15). This is perhaps especially true in authoritarian contexts, where such alliances will be central to the success of oppositional activity. To be sure, connections to and support from political and religious groups and institutions, as well as to the domestic and foreign media, directly enabled *Justicia Democrática*'s mobilisation in Spain. While parallel mobilisations took place within the bar, it was not collaboration within the legal complex that lent JD's actions strength and effectiveness; rather, it was cooperation with politically like-minded actors from a variety of professional backgrounds that explains their success. In more than one sense, then, the liberalisation of politics in Spain involved—indeed, required—the politicisation of law.

REFERENCES

(a) Written Works

Andrés Ibáñez, P (1988), *Justicia/Conflicto* (Madrid, Editorial Tecnos).

Angoustures, A (1983), *Historia de España en el Siglo XX* (Barcelona, Ariel Historia).

Arango, ER (1995), *Spain: Democracy Regained* (Boulder, Colo, Westview Press).

Bastida, F (1986), *Jueces y Franquismo* (Barcelona, Editorial Ariel).

Beevor, A (2006), *The Battle for Spain: The Spanish Civil War 1936–1939* (New York, Penguin Books).

Beirich, HL (1998), 'The Role of the Constitutional Tribunal in Spanish Politics (1980–1995)', PhD Dissertation, Purdue University.

Bereijo, AR (2003), 'Los derechos fundamentals en España', *El País Extra: La Constitución del XXI*, 6 December, 20.

Bisharat, G (1998), 'Attorneys for the People, Attorneys for the Land: the Emergence of Cause Lawyering in the Israeli-Occupied Territores' in A Sarat and S Scheingold (eds), *Cause Lawyering: Political Commitments & Professional Responsibility* (New York, Oxford University Press).

Bonime-Blanc, A (1987), *Spain's Transition to Democracy: The Politics of Constitution-making* (Boulder, Colo, Westview Press).

Burgos, A (1998), 'La Soledad de Plácido Fernández Viagas', *El Mundo de Andalucía*, 28 February, available at www.antonioburgos.com/memorias/1998/02/memo022898.html.

Carr, R (1966), *Spain 1808–1939* (Oxford, Oxford University Press).

—— (1980), *Modern Spain, 1875–1980* (Oxford, Oxford University Press).

—— and Fusi Aizpurua, JP (1979), *Spain: Dictatorship to Democracy* (London, George Allen & Unwin).

Castellano, P (1972), 'Abogados en Tension', 102 *Cuadernos para el Diálogo* (March) 42.

Chamorro, JV (1989), 'Antonio Carretero y Justicia Democrática', 8 *Revista de Jueces para la Democracia* (December) 8.

Cowans, J (ed) (2003), *Modern Spain: A Documentary History* (Philadelphia, Penn, University of Pennsylvania Press).

Cuadernos para el Diálogo editorials:

(1970a) 'Congreso de Abogados', 79 *Cuadernos para el Diálogo* (April) 7.

(1970b) 'La Función del Abogado en el Momento de la Detención', 79 *Cuadernos para el Diálogo* (April) 6.

(1970c) 'La Abogacia en Vanguardia', 80 *Cuadernos para el Diálogo* (May) 8.

(1974a) 'Proyecto de Ley de la Justicia', 124 *Cuadernos para el Diálogo* (January)15.

(1974b) 'El Proyecto de Ley de Bases de la Justicia', 130 *Cuadernos para el Diálogo* (July) 15.

Della Porta, D (2001), 'A Judges' Revolution? Political Corruption and the Judiciary in Italy', 39 *European Journal of Political Research* 1.

Díaz-Plaja, F (ed) (1970), *La Posguerra Española en sus Documentos* (Madrid, Plaza and Janés).

Encarnación, OG (2003), *The Myth of Civil Society: Social Capital and Democratic Consolidation in Spain and Brazil* (New York, Palgrave MacMillan).

Feeley, M (2002), 'The Bench, the Bar, and the State: Judicial Independence in Japan and the United States', in M Feeley and S Miyazawa (eds), *The Japanese Adversary System in Context: Controversies and Comparisons* (London, Palgrave Macmillan).

Fernández Asperilla, AI (1995), 'El Resurgir de la Sociedad Civil y la Aparición de Disensiones en el Aparato del Estado: El Caso de Justicia Democrática (1970–1978)' in J Tusell (coord), *Historia de la Transición y Consolidación Democrática en España (1975–1986)* (Madrid, Alianza), i.

Fernández Viagas, P (1982), *Togas para la Libertad* (Barcelona, Editorial Planeta).

Gil-Robles y Gil-Delgado, J (1975), 'Desiguales ante la Justicia', 143 *Cuadernos para el Diálogo* (August) 19.

Gimbernat Ordeig, JA (1985), 'El Pensamiento Político y los Derechos Humanos' in J Ruiz-Giménez (ed), *El Camino Hacia la Democracia: Escritos en 'Cuadernos para el Diálogo'* (Madrid, Centro de Estudios Constitucionales), ii.

Gor, F (2003), 'Un modelo judicial lastrado por la política', *El País Extra: La Constitución del XXI*, 6 December, 22.

Guarnieri, C (2003), 'Courts as an Instrument of Horizontal Accountability: The Case of Latin Europe' in JM Maravall and A Przeworski (eds), *Democracy and the Rule of Law* (New York, Cambridge University Press).

Halliday, TC and Karpik, L (eds) (1998), *Lawyers and the Rise of Western Political Liberalism: Europe and North America from the Eighteenth to Twentieth Centuries* (New York, Oxford University Press).

Hilbink, L (2003), 'An Exception to Chilean Exceptionalism?'in SE Eckstein and TP Wickham Crowley (eds), *What Justice? Whose Justice? Fighting for Fairness in Latin America* (Berkeley, Cal, University of California Press).

—— (2007), *Judges beyond Politics in Democracy and Dictatorship: Lessons from Chile* (New York, Cambridge University Press).

Hilbink, TM (2006), 'The Profession, the Grassroots, and the Elite: Cause Lawyering for Civil Rights and Freedom in the Direct Action Era' in A Sarat and S Scheingold (eds), *Cause Lawyers and Social Movements* (Palo Alto, Cal, Stanford University Press).

Johnston, H (1991), *Tales of Nationalism: Catalonia, 1939–1979* (New Brunswick, NJ, Rutgers University Press).

Justicia Democrática (1978), *Los Jueces contra la Dictadura: Justicia y Política en el Franquismo* (Madrid, Tucar Ediciones).

Linz, JJ and Stepan, A (1996), *Problems of Democratic Transition and Consolidation: Southern Europe, South America, and Post-Communist Europe* (Baltimore, Mld, The Johns Hopkins University Press).

Malefakis, E (2003), 'Democracy in Spain: Two Paradigms' in TK Rabb and EN Suleiman (eds), *The Making and Unmaking of Democracy: Lessons from History and World Politics* (New York, Routledge).

Maravall, JM (1982), *The Transition to Democracy in Spain* (New York, St. Martin's Press).

Marín-Gámez, JA (2003), '*Vale más un buen juez que una buena ley*: Apuntes a propósito de la corriente Justicia Democrática, en el XXV aniversario de la Constitución española de 1978', 70 *Revista Poder Judicial* 329.

McAdam, D, McCarthy, JD and Zald, MN (eds) (1996), *Comparative Perspectives on Social Movements: Political Opportunities, Mobilizing Structures, and Cultural Framings* (New York, Cambridge University Press).

O'Donnell, G and Schmitter, PC (1986), *Transitions from Authoritarian Rule: Tentative Conclusions about Uncertain Democracies* (Baltimore, Mld, The Johns Hopkins University Press).

Payne, S (1967), *Politics and the Military in Modern Spain* (Stanford, Cal, Stanford University Press).

Peces-Barba Martínez, G (1970), 'La Misión del Abogado', 83–84 *Cuadernos para el Diálogo* (August/September) 19.

'Peces-Barba y Herrero de Miñón claman contra los profetas de la catastrophe', *El País Extra: La Constitución del XXI*, 6 December, 7.

Pérez-Díaz, VM (1993), *The Return of Civil Society: The Emergence of Democratic Spain* (London, Harvard University Press).

Peris Gómez, M (1989), 'Antonio Carretero Pérez: Recordando a un juez Demócrata', 8 *Revista de Jueces para la Democracia* (December) 6–7.

Pita Brocano, C (2003), 'La Constitución Española de 1978: El Consenso', XXI *Anuario de la Facultad de Derecho* 453.

Poblet Balcell, M (2001), 'Spanish Legal Culture: Between State and Society', PhD Dissertation, Stanford University Law School.

Pradera, J (2003), 'El espíritu de la letra constitucional', *El País Extra: La Constitución del XXI*, 6 December, 12.

Przworski, A (1991), *Democracy and the Market* (New York, Cambridge University Press).

Rodríguez de Lecea, T (1985), 'La Trayectoria de la Revista' in J Ruiz-Giménez (ed), *El Camino Hacia la Democracia: Escritos en 'Cuadernos para el Diálogo'* (Madrid, Centro de Estudios Constitucionales), ii.

Sanchez, O (2003), 'Beyond Pacted Transitions in Spain and Chile: Elite and Institutional Differences', 10(2) *Democratization* 65.

Scheingold, S (1998), 'The Struggle to Politicize Legal Practice: A Case Study of Left-Activist Lawyering in Seattle' in A Sarat and S Scheingold (eds), *Cause Lawyering: Political Commitments & Professional Responsibility* (New York, Oxford University Press).

Shamir, R and Ziv, N (2001), 'State-Oriented and Community-Oriented Lawyering for a Cause: A Tale of Two Strategies' in A Sarat and S Scheingold (eds), *Cause Lawyering and the State in a Global Era* (New York, Oxford University Press).

Shklar, JN (1985), *Legalism: Law, Morals, and Political Trials* (Cambridge, Mass, Harvard University Press).

Simpson, AWB (1989), 'The Judges and the Vigilant State', 4 *Denning Law Journal* 145.

Toharia, JJ (1974–5), 'Judicial Independence in an Authoritarian Regime: The Case of Contemporary Spain', 9 *Law and Society Review* 475.

—— (1975), *El Juez Español: Un Análisis Sociológico* (Madrid, Editorial Tecnos).

—— (2001), *Opinión Pública y Justicia: La Imagen de la Justicia en la Sociedad Española* (Madrid, Consejo General del Poder Judicial).

Widner, JA (2001) *Building the Rule of Law* (New York, WW Norton).

Zaragoza, A (1975), *Abogacía y Política* (Madrid, Cuadernos para el Diálogo).

(b) Interviews

Andrés Ibáñez, Perfecto, Magistrado del Tribunal Supremo, Member of JpD, and Founding Member of JD, 11 June 2002, Madrid.

Andrés Ibáñez, Perfecto, Magistrado del Tribunal Supremo, Member of JpD, and Founding Member of JD, 20 July 2004, Madrid.

Camacho, Antonio, Fiscal del Tribunal Superior de Justicia de Madrid and Spokesman for UPF, 13 June 2002, Madrid.

Carmena, Manuela, High Court Penal Judge in Madrid, Member of JpD, 11 June 2002, Madrid.

Comas D'Argemir, Montserrat, Vocal, Consejo General del Poder Judicial, Member of JpD, 10 June 2002, Madrid.

Doñate Martín, Antonio, Judge in Barcelona and Professor at Judicial School, 21 July 2004, Barcelona.

Fernández, José María, Judge in Barcelona, Member of JpD, 13 June 2002, Madrid.

Jiménez Villarejo, Carlos, Fiscal Jefe de Anticorrupción, Founding Member of JD, 12 June 2002, Madrid.

Mena, José María, Fiscal Jefe de Catalunya, Founding Member of JD, 14 July 2004, Barcelona.

Ortega Álvarez, Luis, Catedrático de Derecho Administrativo, U Castilla-La Mancha, 23 January 2007, Madrid.

Rubio Llorente, Francisco, Presidente del Consejo del Estado, 30 January 2007, Madrid.

Toharia, José Juan, Catedrático de Sociología, U Autónoma de Madrid, 10 June 2002, Madrid.

14

Lawyers and Statist Liberalism in Italy

CARLO GUARNIERI

T HE ITALIAN LEGAL complex seems to be characterised by a rather high level of fragmentation, exemplifying the traditional state of 'balkanisation' of legal professions in the civil law tradition: lawyers, judges and law professors form different groups, exhibiting an increasingly distinct cultural and political outlook. The last decades have confirmed the important role played by the legal complex in Italian politics and society, although with a slow but steady decline of the influence played by the academic doctrine, and a corresponding ascent of the role of the judiciary. Italian legal liberalism shows a basic ambiguity, due to the traditional importance given to the role of the state, sometimes at the expense of the protection of individual rights. Today, this ambiguity is fuelled by the strong role entrusted to public prosecution in the fight against organised crime and political and business corruption: a policy that can claim some significant success but whose implementation seems to be pursued also at the expense of the dispute-resolution function of the judicial process.

I. THE LEGAL COMPLEX: THE STRUCTURE

In Italy, as in most civil law countries, the legal professions are composed mainly of three groups:[1] attorneys, magistrates (that is, professional judges and prosecutors[2]) and law professors (Merryman, 1985). Therefore, in order to analyse the legal complex, at least all three categories have to be considered.

---

[1] Another important group are the notaries. However, they do not seem to have played a visible role in elaborating legal liberalism. On Italian notaries see Santoro (1998).

[2] The term follows French usage. Other European countries use different terms: *Richter v Staatsanwalt* or *Juez v Fiscal*. As is well-known, English magistrates are lay judges.

Contemporary legal professions in Italy took shape after the unification of the country in 1861. Although the influence of the past cannot be denied, the main traits of the system are the product of decisions taken in the years just after unification (Tacchi, 2002). For example, the structure of the bar was regulated by a statute in 1874 and has remained substantially unchanged since then. The 1874 statute foresaw for each local court[3] a council elected by all members of the local bar. The council was in charge of selection—in order to practise law it was, and still is, necessary to go through a professional examination—and discipline.

As for Italian law professors, as in Germany they were high civil servants and enjoyed high prestige and influence. The liberal period (1861–1922) saw the academic doctrine expanding its authority.[4] From the end of the nineteenth century the so-called 'scientific school' began to exert great influence. Following similar development in Germany, the school predicated a 'scientific', value-free, study of law, understood, according to the principles of legal positivism, as the product of parliamentary statutes and executive decrees and regulations. However, there was no strong separation between attorneys and law professors. Many academics practised law, especially in the highest courts: the court of cassation and the Council of State.[5] Actually, they were part of the upper stratum of the legal profession. However, the bar seemed extremely fragmented, from both social and territorial points of view (Siegrist, 1994).

More or less until the end of the nineteenth century, the judiciary remained strongly connected to the political class. The process of unification was not without problems in Italy: in the first decade, the problem of dealing with a veritable breakdown of civil order in the South was a crucial challenge for the new political class. Peasant revolts had political and, above all, social implications: opposition to the unification and support for the old rulers mixed with demands for agrarian reform. The situation led the government, backed by almost all the liberal political class, to exert a strong influence on the judiciary. Its powers, following the French, Napoleonic tradition, were extremely wide.[6] However, the purges of magistrates of the old states allowed the appointment of a personnel strongly associated to the liberal movement and therefore to the new political class.

---

[3] *Tribunale*: there were at the time 284 of them. Today they are 166.

[4] For analysis of academic doctrine see Merryman (1965 and 1985) and Monateri (2003).

[5] Between 1875 and 1923 there were 5 courts of cassation, at least in civil matters: Turin, Florence, Rome, Naples and Palermo. After 1923, only the court of Rome survived. As in France, in Italy the Council of State is the highest administrative court.

[6] France had traditionally influenced the kingdom of Sardinia—to which also Piedmont and Liguria belonged—which was the leading partner in the process of unification. Sardinia's juicial setting was more or less completely adopted by Italy.

Moreover, again following the French tradition, prosecutors and judges formed a unified corps (and they still do). Although judges and prosecutors were somewhat separated until the 1890, that year a reform completely merged the two groups and, by establishing public competition after university as de facto the only way of recruitment, brought about a growing bureaucratisation of the judicial career.[7] Therefore, from the end of the century the judiciary began to distance itself from the bar. Rare were the appointments of experienced attorneys to the bench: between 1904 and 1999 no attorney was ever appointed! Therefore, the Italian case well exemplifies the 'balkanised' state of the legal professions in civil law countries (Merryman, 1985).

The impact of Fascism on the structure of legal professions should not be overvalued. At least until the middle of the 1930s the regime followed an authoritarian rather than totalitarian path, attempting at repressing political participation and opposition rather than at mobilising the masses for its political goals. In addition, the attitude of the regime toward the bar was to some extent ambivalent: on one hand, the role of lawyers in the criminal process was regarded with suspicion, as being in opposition to the repressive aspirations of the regimes, on the other, law was a typical middle-class profession and the regime had its mass support in the middle classes. However, between 1926 and 1933, the autonomy of the bar was strongly curtailed: the local councils were no longer elected but appointed by the government. In addition, many attorneys were expelled, although the regime was unable wholly to 'fascistize' the profession.[8]

On the whole, Fascism did not represent a sharp break in the development of Italian public bureaucracies, to which the judiciary can be assimilated (Guarnieri, 1995). The process of bureaucratisation of the judiciary went on: the role of the hierarchy was strengthened but there were no political appointments, no radical change in the rules governing the career and political interference with the ordinary judiciary was kept to a minimum. The political goals of the regime were achieved by instituting politically-controlled special courts and increasing the powers of the police. Unlike in Nazi Germany, the judicial corps was not politically penetrated but, with few exceptions, kept substantially a low profile during the whole of the fascist period.[9]

---

[7] Shortly said, unlike professional common law judiciaries, a bureaucratic judiciary tends to recruit its members just after university: therefore, they are trained mostly inside the organisation (Guarnieri and Pederzoli, 2002).

[8] The number of practising attorneys at the time has been estimated to be at least 25,000. We have no precise data about expulsions: the well-known anti-fascist historian Salvemini spoke of more than 2,000 (Olgiati, 1996; Tacchi, 2002: 450).

[9] As a rule, the judiciary in authoritarian regimes plays a minor role in politics. Political repression is usually entrusted to special politically-appointed courts or dealt with directly by the police or other security forces. The ordinary judiciary is only marginally involved in the policies of the regime and usually retains a modest degree of independence, like the judiciary in Spain under the Franco regime (Toharia, 1975).

The influence of the academic doctrine remained strong. Prestigious law professors—also of anti- or no fascist persuasion—were appointed in the law commissions in charge of writing the new codes.[10] Much the same can be said for administrative law: the Council of State, under the leadership of Santi Romano (another respected jurist) tried to preserve the traditional value of legal certainty and to narrow the margins of administrative discretion (Melis, 1995).

In this context, it is not surprising that the return of democracy did not mean a radical change in the structure of the legal professions: the *status quo ante* was swiftly restored. For example, in 1944 the election of the bar councils was reinstated and in 1946 judicial guarantees of independence were reinforced, more or less restoring the pre-fascist status of the judiciary. However, in the long run Italy experienced a remarkable change in the structure of its judicial system.

Following the new republican Constitution of 1948, judicial power has dramatically expanded. Judicial guarantees of independence have been strengthened, giving way in 1959 to a form of self-government through the Higher Council of the Judiciary. Constitutional review—that is, judicial review of legislation—has been instituted and entrusted to a special constitutional court, although ordinary courts play a significant role in filtering cases of constitutionality to the court.[11] The traditional career has been de facto abolished by entrusting all promotions to the Higher Council which, since 1975, has been mainly elected by the very magistrates it should evaluate.[12]

The growing autonomy of the judiciary, together with the dismantling of the traditional career has brought about a slow decline of academic influence. Academic doctrine had already lost its traditional cohesion during the fascist period (Tarello, 1988; Monateri, 2003). Today, since merit is no longer a criterion for judicial promotion, academic assessments of judicial decisions has lost much of its value.

In the post-war period, the bar has not been able to confront the growth of judicial power. Its quantitative expansion—attorneys today are estimated to be around 155,000[13]—has been coupled with increasing fragmentation.

---

[10] This is especially true for the Civil Code and the Code of Civil Procedure (Olgiati, 1996: 133 ff).

[11] Ordinary courts have the authority to refer laws to the constitutional court in order to evaluate their constitutionality. In Italy, unlike in Germany and Spain, citizens cannot access the court directly (Stone, 2000).

[12] Today, promotions are based, at least de facto, on seniority. That is, after a definite period of time, magistrates are evaluated for promotion by the Higher Council which tends to promote almost all candidates, also because the law allows an indefinite number of promotions. Magistrates promoted but not able to fill a position corresponding to their rank can continue to perform their previous functions but enjoy the salaries attached to the new, higher rank (Zannotti, 1989; Guarnieri, 2003).

[13] See 'Il Sole-24 Ore', 12 Sept 2005. According to a recent survey of the Council of Europe, in 2002 in Italy there were 128,000 practising lawyers.

The role of the local bar councils—and of the national bar council (*Consiglio Nazionale Forense*)—has been limited. Many associations have developed in the post-war period, divided along professional and political lines (Cipriani, 1998: 902–4). Also the role of the bar in political institutions has declined. In the liberal period (1861–1922), attorneys were very well represented in the parliament: between 28 and 42 per cent of deputies were lawyers (Malatesta, 2003: 100). After 1946 their number has declined: in the 1950s they were around 20 per cent, but in the 1990s they fluctuated between 11 and 14 per cent of the parliament (Verzichelli and De Michelis, 2004: 152).

Only recently, the political activism of lawyers seems to have resurfaced, although in a different form. This time, the representation of attorneys' immediate interests seems to be more important: as we are going to see, they have played a role in the reform of the criminal process and are still deeply involved in its implementation.

Summing up, in the long term, the Italian legal complex seems to be characterised thus:

— the legal professions are rather fragmented, with low interchanges, a growing role of the judiciary and strong tensions between the bench and the bar (unlike in common law countries);
— the bar depends on the state for its prerogatives, although the state has never been able really to control the professions (with the partial exception of the fascist regime);
— the academic doctrine, at least until recently, has played an important role, for example influencing judicial decisions. However, Italian law professors seem to have identified themselves with the state much less than their German colleagues;[14]
— lawyers have always played a role in politics: attorneys—and law professors—in the parliament and law professors in advising the executive and the administration. Recently, also magistrates have entered the political arena.[15] As we are going to see, the result has been a growing politicisation of the legal complex.

II. VARIETIES OF POLITICAL LIBERALISM

As we have seen, the Italian legal complex is extremely fragmented. Therefore, it is difficult to speak of unified attitudes, although some common traits can be ascertained. We will try to present a general outline of the

[14] It could be argued that this attitude is due to the apparent higher propensity of Italians law professors to practise law.
[15] In 1996 27 magistrates were elected in the parliament, although in 2001 the number fell to 14.

political ideologies prevailing inside the legal complex.[16] Especially because their ideologies are easier to detect, we will concentrate on judges and law professors. Magistrates not only speak with their decisions but, in Italy, are organised in union-like groups, producing a lot of public statements. As for law professors, although in Italy they have been traditionally devoted to a kind of value-free legal science, their ideology can also be detected without much difficulty. However, recently also attorneys have become more vocal, having developed some union-like activities.

It is impossible to understand the traits of legal ideologies in Italy without taking into account the historical context in which they have developed. As we have seen, Italy emerged late as a unified state. The first decades after unification were characterised by strong opposition to the new liberal state. On one hand, there was deep disappointment in the lower classes—especially peasants—for the increasing tax burden and for the lack of an agrarian reform. On the other, the powerful Catholic Church—hit by the loss of its temporal power—was boycotting the new state. Therefore, the legitimacy of the new political order seems to have been rather weak and the risk of succumbing to foreign threats (eg Austria) always real.

Legal professions were strongly influenced by this context. Lawyers had played an important part in the *Risorgimento*: defending the new, liberal state was most important to them. Therefore, when it seemed necessary, they supported military justice and state of siege in order to suppress the insurgency in the South (Martucci, 1980). At a more abstract level, legal doctrine found in positivism a useful tool. Positive law, and therefore legislation, became the main object of legal study. Citizens' rights depended on legislation, that is on statutes: they were the product of the state's will. Outside the state, there were no rights.[17] Positivism was coupled with individualism. Following a tradition going back to the French revolution, intermediary groups were distrusted: nothing had to disturb the direct relationship between the citizen and the state. On the other hand, this relationship had to be governed by legal rules, actually by statutory rules, according to the principles of continental rule of law, better defined as 'rule of legislators'.[18]

Later in the century, legal doctrine devoted itself to analysing legislation, in a 'scientific' way, in order to extract the concepts and rules of legal science. This effort was made in order to assist the parliament in enacting legislation. However, the trust in the reasonableness of legislators was

---

[16] Relying in large part on the work of historians and lawyers: Rodotà (1995); Melis (1995); Sbriccoli (1998); Ferrajoli (1999); Grossi (2003); Monateri (2003); Fioravanti (2004).

[17] However, the Civil Code—a product of legislation but incorporating the principles of legal 'science'—had de facto, at least for a while, a quasi-constitutional status (Rebuffa, 1993).

[18] See Sartori (1987: 321 ff) distinguishing between rule of law and rule of legislators.

high: Parliament was the assembly of those competent enough to perform the legislative function.[19] Italian doctrine developed itself as a unique mix of French and German influences (Monateri, 2003) but it was characterised by the search for a pure, value-free, legal science, in any case by an effort at reducing—or hiding—the political implications of legislative choices. This effort pushed the doctrine to a high level of abstractness and increasingly to disregard the concrete implementation of legal rules.

From the end of the nineteenth century, Italian legal doctrine was characterised by a strong statist flavour. In a few words, one of the most significant traits of statist liberalism is that it tends to assume the moral primacy of the state over society: the state is looking after the public interest, while society is the place where sectional, particularistic interests tend to prevail (Panebianco, 2004: 165 ff). Therefore, it should not be surprising that Italian legal doctrine could accommodate itself without much strain to the Fascist regime. As we have seen, many legal scholars, although of liberal persuasion, were able to survive during the regime. The key was statism and the version of rule of law we have already discussed. Actually, this sort of legalism was a way to somewhat reduce the regime's arbitrariness and to check abuses of power. However, at least in a first phase—until the mid-1930s—the regime was able to present itself as the restorer of the 'true spirit' of the *Risorgimento*: a strong state, that is a strong executive, capable of suppressing the 'mischief' of political factions but ruling according to the tradition of Italian—that is, Roman—law. The totalitarian wing of the regime, advocating developments similar to Nazi Germany—*Freirecht*, *Führerprinzip* or similar—was in the minority. Only the racial laws of 1938 marked a clear break with tradition. But still in 1942 the Civil Codes enacted in that year were heavily influenced by traditional liberal doctrine. Also the judiciary more or less fitted this picture: most magistrates, without openly opposing the regime, tried to insert the Fascist 'revolution' into the tradition of the Italian state. The attempt was made easier by the fact that special courts, staffed with politically appointed judges of fascist faith, were in charge of political crimes.[20]

The return of democracy marked a break with the past, especially at the constitutional level. The Constitution of 1948 was the product of three main political camps, each with its strong ideology, encompassing the entire political spectrum, with the obvious exception of fascists. The liberal camp, much weaker than in the past, was still influential, especially because of the hold it had on the universities. However, it was divided between those willing only to restore the old order—for example, the traditional preeminence

---

[19] See the attitude of Vittorio Emanuele Orlando, a prominent constitutional lawyer, who filled important political positions in pre-fascist Italy (Fioravanti, 2004).

[20] See the testimony of Jemolo, a distinguished antifascist Catholic jurist (Guarnieri, 2003: 94).

of the parliament—and those, worried about another lapse into some form of dictatorship, stressing the need of strengthening judicial independence and of introducing judicial review of legislation along the lines suggested by Hans Kelsen. The Marxists—that is socialists and communists—were strongly influenced by the myth of the popular will, incarnating itself in an all-powerful representative assembly on which all other institutions had to depend. Therefore, they favoured a weak executive—only in charge of 'executing', that is mechanically applying, statutes enacted by the parliament—and were distrustful of judicial independence and, above all, judicial review: Togliatti, the powerful leader of the communist party, at the Constituent Assembly defined judicial review 'an oddity'. However, at the end, the Left decided to accept many of the judicial checks, especially under the pressure of the Christian Democrats, the Catholic party, the most important group in the Assembly. Catholics had travelled a long way since the time they had opposed unification. They have elaborated a critique of the pre-Fascist state, pointing out its excessive centralisation and the lack of true guarantees. Judicial review—along Kelsen's prescriptions—became one of their key demands, skillfully elaborated by a group of young jurists, who later became very influential in Italian culture and politics (Fioravanti, 2004).

The influence of leftist and Catholic ideologies left other marks on the Italian Constitution. It is a 'long' Constitution, modelled to some extent on that of Weimar, introducing a wide set of social rights.[21] The principle of equality was extended to include—at least the perspective of—substantial equality:

> all citizens are equal ... It is the duty of the Republic to remove all economic and social obstacles that, by limiting the freedom and equality of citizens, prevent full individual development and the participation of all workers in the political, economic, and social organization of the country [Article 3].

The 'inviolable rights' of man were recognised (Article 2) but also as performed inside 'social formations'—that is groups—and together with the 'inescapable duties' of solidarity. The result has been the introduction of a group—or corporatist—dimension in the Italian constitutional setting. Therefore, notwithstanding the introduction of judicial review, the protection of individual rights in Italy by courts has been somewhat attenuated by the influence of group, corporatist or solidarity considerations.

During the Cold War the political tensions contributed to somewhat 'freeze' the progressive aspects of the Constitution. But in the late 1950s the *garantiste* part of the Constitution came to be implemented and, especially since the end of the 1960s, the influence of leftist legal doctrines grew.

---

[21] See Arts 29–47.

Above all, the attitude of the judiciary changed. Some magistrates began to develop a new definition of their role. Traditionally—and Fascist experience had even reinforced this propensity—judges interpreted their role as that of an executor: the *bouche de la loi*. Especially since 1964,[22] some have begun to advocate a more activist definition, interpreting the law with an eye at implementing directly the long list of rights inserted into the Constitution or in any case calling more often upon the Constitutional Court to adjudicate. Moreover, judges—as a group and as individuals—began to appeal directly to public opinion and, after 1969, some of them decided to see the working class and the parties of the Left as their reference group. Although initially the majority of magistrates saw these developments with increasing apprehension, in the following decades activist attitudes spread all over the corps. In any case, public opinion has become one of the most important points of reference of the judicial corps (Morisi, 1999: 145; Guarnieri, 2003; Vauchez, 2004). The development was welcomed, at least at the beginning, by most academic lawyers and also by many attorneys, especially on the Left, who saw in an activist judiciary a potential ally in their fight for implementing civil rights.

III. A CRUCIAL ISSUE: THE REFORM OF THE CRIMINAL PROCESS

The reform of the criminal process has been one of the major political issues of recent decades, involving all the actors of the legal complex: law professors, magistrates and attorneys, at least those of the criminal bar.

At the beginning, the return to democracy only marginally affected the constitutional rights of Italian citizens. The attitude of the ordinary judiciary, especially of the highest court—the Court of Cassation—was extremely conservative. In the wake of establishing the new Constitutional Court, the Constitution of 1948 allowed ordinary courts the power to review the constitutionality of statutes in individual cases, but the Court of Cassation was able to keep untouched most of fascist legislation restricting civil and political rights and, in any case, allowing the executive wide discretion in regulating the way they could be exercised (Rodotà, 1995; Guarnieri, 1995; Ferrajoli, 1999). Things began to change only after 1956, when the new Constitutional Court was instituted. In the following decade, the court, composed mostly of non-career judges,[23] played a crucial role in dismantling

---

[22] In that year *Magistratura Democratica*, a group of progressive, left-wing magistrates, was founded.

[23] Two thirds are attorneys and law professors appointed by the parliament and by the president of the republic. The remaining third is elected by the highest ordinary and administrative courts.

448 Carlo Guarnieri

most of fascist legislation, although its activity was resisted by the Court of Cassation. The Court of Cassation was ideologically conservative and, above all, jealous of the fact that the Constitutional Court impinged on its traditional prerogative of deciding the 'true' interpretation of the law. But lower court judges were happy to free themselves from the control of higher judges by asking the Constitutional Court to adjudicate on the constitutionality of fascist legislation. At the end, a sort of alliance between lower ranking judges, the Constitutional Court, academic doctrine and a group of civil rights attorneys was able to report a victory in the fight (Merryman and Vigoriti, 1967). The 1970s, thanks to this alliance and to the fact that the Left was more and more influential in the political system, saw a general reinforcement of civil and social rights: divorce, family, abortion, labour and health were all subject to reforms, often supported by judicial decisions, enlarging the content of citizens' rights. Only in the 1980s the trend seems to have subsided, because of the decline of the Communist party and increasing budget constraints (Rodotà, 1995).

Many of the constitutional decisions of the first decade (1956–66) concerned the rights of the accused in the criminal process and brought about a substantial improvement of his position. However, the discussion on the reform of criminal justice went on. The Italian traditional setting, influenced by French, Napoleonic reforms, was characterised by a two-phase process: the pre-trial investigation, entrusted to the instructing judge with the aid of the public prosecutor, was patterned along the century-long inquisitorial tradition; in a subsequent phase, the public trial was organised in a more triadic, accusatorial way, usually with a panel of judges—or in some cases a mixed court, with lay and career judges—adjudicating between prosecution and defence (Guarnieri, 1995). This structure was criticised by the criminal bar and the prevailing academic doctrine, which was able to pinpoint its illiberal traits, and since the early 1960s a reform came to be envisaged. However, in the 1970s, the need of fighting terrorism—and later organised crime—delayed the enactment of the reform and led to a reinforcement of the power of instructing judges and prosecutors and to their growing influence on police forces. After the defeat of terrorism, the ensuing expansion of judicial prerogatives pushed a large part of the academic doctrine again to support a reform of the criminal process along accusatorial lines. At the end of the 1980s the pressure succeeded, also because part of the political class was weary of the growing power of the judiciary, and a new Criminal Code—drafted under the strong influence of the American model (Amodioe Selvaggi, 1989; Langer, 2004)—was enacted.

The case of the new Italian Code of Criminal Procedure is an interesting example of the influence of the legal culture and of the distribution of strategic resources on the implementation of legal norms (Langer, 2004). The new code abolished the instructing judge and shifted the task of instructing the case to the public prosecutor. However, although the code had foreseen many limitations to the powers of the prosecutor, understood to be only one of the parties to the case, under the pressure of the judiciary[24] a series of Constitutional Court decisions brought about a strong reinforcement of its prerogatives. Building on the newly discovered principle of the need of 'economizing the means of evidence'[25]—in practice a variation of the traditional truth-seeking function of the trial of the civil law tradition—the court substantially restored to the prosecutor many of the traditional powers of the instructing judge, making it easier for the prosecution's dossier to be taken into consideration as evidence at the trial, even though it contained proofs obtained *inaudita altera parte* and therefore in violation of the adversary principle.

What followed was a long confrontation between the parliament, trying to strengthen the individual rights of the defendant, and the Constitutional Court, weakening those rights through its emphasis on the primacy of the search for truth at trial.[26] In 1999, a constitutional amendment was voted in order to insert into the Constitution the principle of the accusatorial trial: the move was—rightly—understood as a reaction by the political class to the jurisprudence of the Constitutional Court. In 2001, a law seems to have settled the issue, substantially in favour of the defendant's rights.[27]

On the other hand, the ordinary judiciary—which from the beginning was somewhat divided on the virtues and vices of the new code—has become very critical of the reform, considered to be inadequate for fighting organised crime and corruption as well as financial scandals.[28] Academic doctrine was at the beginning supportive of the reform, but today it seems increasingly divided: some share the view of the Constitutional Court, and of most magistrates, that the criminal process has become too complex, as a result of too many guarantees enshrined in it, to become practically unworkable. Therefore, they are also critical of the 1999 constitutional amendment.[29] The division has been made deeper by the growing politicisation of the issue. Especially since 2001, a strong conflict has erupted between the judiciary and the centre-right government led by Berlusconi, himself famously on trial on multiple charges of corruption and false accounting. In this conflict most

---

[24] Judges came to send to the court all sort of objections on the constitutionality of the reform.

[25] *'Non dispersione dei mezzi di prova'*. For these developments see Fabri (1994); Grande (2000); Amodio (2004); Pizzi e Montagna (2004); Vogliotti (2004); and Panzavolta (2005).

[26] Between 1992 and 1999 the court several times declared uncostitutional parts of the new Code of Criminal Procedure as well as the attempts by the parliament at overruling court's decisions.

[27] As a rule, statements taken by the prosecutor *inaudita altera parte* cannot be taken into consideration as evidence at trial. However, there are exceptions to the rule.

[28] See, eg, Spataro (2002). The recent *Parmalat* case has further supported this view.

[29] See, eg, Grevi (2000); and Riccio (2000). An important role in this discussion has been played by Franco Cordero, a very influential criminal law professor, with his articles in the daily *La Repubblica*, strongly criticising Berlusconi's judicial policies.

leftist academic lawyers have sided with the judiciary, while lawyers on the Right tend to support Berlusconi's claims of being politically persecuted.

However, the bar—and especially criminal lawyers[30]—seems to have been consistent in supporting the aims of the reform. For example, the criminal bar is presently very critical of the fact that in Italy, as in France, judges and prosecutors belong to the same corps.[31] According to this view, such a setting harms the impartiality of judges and radically undermines the guarantees of the defendant. On the other hand, the judiciary and a large part of academic doctrine argue that splitting the judiciary would endanger judicial independence, since it will certainly become the first step in the process of abolishing the independence of prosecutors. In addition, some argue that separating prosecutors from judges will cut off the former from the so-called 'culture of the jurisdiction', that is a culture that defines the role of the prosecutor as a truth-seeker, akin to the role of the judge.[32] On this basis, a recent government reform—aiming at fostering a (moderate) separation between the two roles—has been strongly criticised.

A similar alignment can be traced out in the case of the so-called European arrest warrant and of the creation of a European judicial space in which judges and prosecutors could act beyond traditional national borders (Bargis, 2004). On one hand, the judiciary—supported by a large part of the academic doctrine and by most leftist parties—is supporting the change, claiming that the new judicial space is the inevitable consequence of the process of European unification and it is necessary in order effectively to fight organised crime and terrorism. On the other, criminal attorneys are very critical of the way the judicial space is being constructed, pointing out the risks it brings to the individual rights guaranteed by the Italian Constitution. This attitude is supported by the Right, a part of which is radically opposed to any diminution of national sovereignty in this field,[33] a fact that has caused a serious delay in the implementation of the provision.

IV. FIGHTING TERRORISM, ORGANISED CRIME AND CORRUPTION

Behind the debate on criminal justice reform lies the long familiarity of Italy with organised violence. Italy experienced a long season of political

---

[30] The *Unione Camere penali italiane* (UCPI, the main association of criminal lawyers) has become increasingly vocal in its support of the new accusatorial system.

[31] But, unlike in France, Italian public prosecutors enjoy the same guarantees of independence as judges (Di Federico, 1998).

[32] A traditional way of defining this role is to underline the duty of the prosecutor to pursue 'justice'. From here comes the definition of the public prosecutor as 'an organ of justice' (Guarnieri, 1984).

[33] This is the position of the Northern League, a member of which filled the Justice portfolio in the Berlusconi Cabinet between 2001 and 2006.

terrorism in the 1970s. That decade was characterised by all sorts of terrorist attacks, carried out by different organisation of both extreme left and extreme right. The period culminated, in 1978, with the kidnapping and killing of Aldo Moro, who was at the time president of the Christian Democrats and in the past had often been Prime Minister. The fight against terrorism was led, especially after the middle of the 1970s, by the judiciary, that is by prosecutors and instructing judges.[34] Actually, anti-terrorism activity had important and long-lasting effects on the judicial system.[35] A new drive toward increasing coordination between judicial offices developed. Traditional systems of coordination, based on hierarchy, proved themselves to be slow, cumbersome and in the last analysis ineffective in order to confront terrorist activities, often brought about by organisations with wide territorial ramifications. New, direct, face-to face relationships developed between prosecutors and instructing judges of different territorial offices, overcoming the traditional, bureaucratic, channels. Although these relationships were not foreseen by the law, they were supported by public opinion, anxious at getting results in the anti-terrorist fight. In this development a crucial role was played by the abolition of the traditional career—bringing about a decline of the power of higher ranking magistrates—and by the growing significance of the Higher Council of the Judiciary, which increasingly played a coordinating role, in any case legitimising the new practices.

Another important change was the growing influence of the judiciary—prosecutors and instructing judges—on police forces. Traditionally, prosecutors and judges did not interfere directly with police investigations. Often they just waited for the police to provide them with the evidence in order to start a prosecution. However, some initial police failings and the urgent need to confront the mounting threat of terrorism pushed the judiciary to take a more proactive stance and therefore increasingly directly to lead investigations. In this way, magistrates were able to improve their investigative skills and to exert a growing influence on police forces: a development that later would have had significant consequences (Vogliotti, 2004).

The fight against terrorism was carried out, at least in part, through 'spontaneous' adaptation of the system, although with the support of some special legislation. The project of reforming the criminal process in an accusatorial way was postponed, pre-trial detention was lengthened and the powers of prosecutors and instructing judges were somewhat reinforced. Above all, lenient sentences were provided for those who were willing

[34] We have to take into account that at that time the criminal process was still organised on a semi-inquisitorial pattern.
[35] A detailed and interesting analysis of the corresponding evolution of the conceptions of the judicial role can be found in Vauchez (2004).

to collaborate (the so-called *pentiti*): especially by providing information about terrorist activities and by giving evidence against other members of the organisation. These provisions were extremely effective in bringing down terrorist organisations, providing judicial investigations with enough evidence to ensure a conviction at trial.

In any case, the judicial fight against terrorism was strongly supported by public opinion and main political parties. After some initial hesitation, the Communist party supported the hard line against terrorism, whatever its ideological inspiration. The party was also strongly in favour of entrusting the judiciary with the task, since it was suspicious of police forces, traditionally under governmental, that is Christian Democrat, influence. On the contrary, the judiciary was at the time manifesting a more diversified political outlook: among the most visible anti-terrorist magistrates many were directly or indirectly affiliated with leftist judicial groups. Therefore, allowing the judiciary to play a significant role in the fight against terrorism was for the Communist party a sort of guarantee against possible governmental abuses and a means to exert some influence on the way investigations were carried out. Therefore, only minor civil rights groups—and in part the smaller Socialist party—were left to object to the substantial entrusting of investigative, prosecutorial and judicial functions to the same body. The need to deal with the terrorist emergency was considered to be more important by most political and social groups (including the majority of academic lawyers). As a result, after some initial wavering and although no formal political responsibility was foreseen, the judicial system adapted itself to the need of confronting the terrorist challenge and its response has been rather effective, although it is difficult to give an accurate estimate of possible infringements of civil rights of defendants.

At the beginning of the 1980s, as terrorism began to decline, a new danger began to challenge the Italian political system: organised crime (Lupo, 1993). The judiciary—or at least part of it—took the initiative to confront the threat, and it is not surprising that the methods developed in the fight against terrorism were quickly applied to organised crime. Often, magistrates already active against terrorist organisations moved into the new field. In this fight, an even more significant role was played by *pentiti*, partly because of the great difficulty in obtaining other forms of evidence in the field of organised crime.[36] Also in this case, an important role was played by coordination: for example, departing from traditional practice— and to some extent also from the law—and in order to improve their investigative capacity— for example by sharing information—instructing judges began to work in groups. On the other hand, in the case of organised crime political support for judicial investigations was less strong. For example, it

---

[36] The role of the mafia in intimidating witnesses is well-known.

seems that only after the killing in Palermo of a top anti-terrorist official, General Dalla Chiesa, did the Christian Democrats support the strengthening of the judicial and police forces in Sicily. In any case, while the national leaders seemed to have supported judicial activities, local party bosses were often much more timid, due to the fact that criminal organisations were able to exert a significant pressure at the local level. However, thanks also to the effort of Giovanni Falcone,[37] in 1991 a national anti-mafia prosecution office was established (DNA: *Direzione nazionale antimafia*) with the task of coordinating specialised units working at the local level: an important step, in the context of the strong decentralised setting of public prosecution in Italy.[38] The result has been, also in this case, at least a partial success. Although today many are lamenting a decline of effort in the fight against the mafia—and although the problem of organised crime in Southern Italy needs, without doubt, a long term strategy—recent analyses of the anti-mafia policies have underlined their effectiveness (La Spina, 2005).

The strong investigative capacity acquired by the judiciary in the 1970s and 1980s was exploited, in the 1990s, in order to pursue political corruption. The new Code of Criminal Procedure in 1989 abolished the instructing judge and entrusted all the investigation to the prosecutor, whose powers we have seen later enlarged by the Constitutional Court. Therefore, prosecutors—and many of them were instructing judges before 1989—were able to employ their powers and skills, as well as their good relationships with police forces, strongly to pursue cases of political corruption and of illegal party financing.[39] We do not need to analyse here in full all developments. However, judicial actions, enjoying the strong support of public opinion and in connection with a deep political and economic crisis,[40] were substantial in bringing about the breakdown of the traditional political class: in a few months, all governing parties were almost obliterated. Thus, a strong anti-judicial sentiment has developed in this political camp, which has been in large part absorbed into Berlusconi's new political party. On

---

[37] Falcone, as instructing judge in Palermo, was able to prepare the first great mafia trial in the 1980s. After being for a while deputy chief prosecutor, in 1990 he was appointed head of the criminal division of the Ministry of Justice. He was killed by the mafia in 1992.

[38] After the war, the traditional powers of the Ministry of Justice were first, in 1946, curtailed and later, in 1959, abolished. Therefore, in Italy there is no national coordination of public prosecution, with the exception of the powers—not to be overvalued—of the DNA. It is normally assumed that the principle of compulsory prosecution—enshrined in the Constitution—is capable of ensuring consistency and impartiality. Therefore, the institution of the DNA was strongly criticised by many lawyers and magistrates (Di Federico, 1998).

[39] However, there were some significant differences in the zeal of different prosecutorial offices (Colajanni, 1996).

[40] Judicial investigations began to hit the political class only after the 1992 parliamentary elections when the governing parties suffered a serious loss of votes. They developed later in connection with a serious financial crisis (Guarnieri, 2003).

the other hand, also on the Left, although basically unscathed by the investigations, some doubt developed about the new power of the judiciary.[41] After *Mani pulite* ('clean hands', as the anti-corruption investigations of the 1990s were baptised), the distrust of the political class toward the judiciary has become, although to a different extent, a permanent trait of the Italian political landscape.

The Twin Towers attack, in 2001, again inserted terrorism in the political and judicial agenda. Immediately after the attack, the Criminal Code was modified in order to make it capable of fighting new forms of international terrorism. The result has not been wholly satisfying: for example, at the beginning of the 2005, a judge in Milan acquitted a group of defendants—belonging to an alleged terrorist Islamic organisation—pointing out the ambiguity of the definition of 'terrorist organisation' and introducing a distinction between 'guerrilla' activities—which in a war situation need not to be punished—and terrorism. The decision has been strongly criticised by the government and by the prosecution, and also by other judges.[42] However, the fight against Islamic terrorism, although still in its infancy, can introduce an element of division inside the judiciary. On the one hand, many prosecutors in charge of terrorist cases, having fought in the past against Italian terrorism, organised crime and political corruption, tend to apply the same zeal in the new fight. On the other, some judges seem to show a certain 'understanding' for the reasons of defendants, often illegal immigrants and/or Arabs fighting against US military intervention in Iraq.

On a long term perspective, Italian criminal justice seems to have been rather effective in the fight against terrorism and organised crime. After some initial failures, Italian terrorist organisations have been substantially dismantled.[43] As for organised crime, although it is far from been definitively smashed, it has been contained and its terrorist wing heavily hit (Paoli, 2003; La Spina, 2005). The case for political and administrative corruption is mixed. The 1990s have been characterised by a wave of criminal prosecutions against political corruption. However, the perception of its presence in Italy is still rather widespread (Di Nicola, 2003), and at the same time many prosecutions have been overturned or circumscribed at trial (or on appeal).

[41] A strong criticism of judicial investigations on corruption is in Fasanella and Pellegrino (2005). Pellegrino was, in the 1990s, an influential MP for the Left: he was chairman of the parliamentary commission in charge of the decision of lifting the immunity to MPs under judicial investigation.

[42] See the decision of the judge of Brescia, who was entrusted with the task of adjudicating on a case in which the same organisation as in the Milan proceedings was accused.

[43] The last significant terrorist act was the killing in Bologna in March 2002 of Marco Biagi, a labour law professor. Today, all the perpetrators have been sentenced.

In all these events the judicial system, although with some tensions, has shown a remarkable degree of adaptation, often going beyond formal legal rules. A part of the judiciary has been able to direct a de facto restructuring of the system. In this process it has been supported by part of the political class—especially, but not exclusively, on the Left—and by the media. Also academic doctrine has been, on the whole, supportive of these developments. The only real opposition has come from the criminal bar, the most affected by the expansion of judicial power: its effectiveness has increased with time. In fact, as we are going to see, as a result of the way the judiciary has dealt with political corruption, criminal lawyers have found allies in the political class, especially on the Right. It goes without saying that the transformation of the criminal system—with wide powers entrusted to public prosecution and the extensive use of conspiracy crimes[44]—has often been made at the expense of the rights of the defendant (Di Federico and Sapignoli, 2002), although in recent years the balance between prosecution and defence has been to some extent re-established.

V. PERSPECTIVES

Taking as points of reference the cases analysed by Halliday and Karpik (1997), Italy can be considered a variant of the French model. Lawyers tend to have a role in politics: in the pre-fascist period they were well represented in the parliament and tried to appeal to the public, although often with limited success. Recently, in the struggle for a new accusatorial criminal trial, they seem to have become more vocal as a group. But they have to confront the strong influence of the judiciary, which in recent decades has often been more effective in appealing to the public (Pizzorno, 1998; Della Porta, 2001; Newell, 2005).

As for their relationship with the state, although their monopoly is publicly sanctioned, attorneys are rather autonomous. State interference has been limited—with the exception of fascism, of course—and in any case the capacity of the Italian state to interfere with corporate autonomy must not be overstated. Italy has never had a corps of civil servants similar to that of France or Germany. The power of the bureaucracy tends to be negative, capable of stopping or delaying reforms rather than introducing change or in any case taking initiatives (Melis, 1995). After fascism, the setting of the

---

[44] Moreover, at least one of them is derived from a decision of the Court of Cassation, broadening the crime of mafia conspiracy by recognising the so-called *concorso esterno in associazione mafiosa* (external participation in a mafia organisation: that is, abetting the mafia without being a veritable mafia affiliate). This crime, although not openly foreseen in the criminal code, has been very effective in bringing about the conviction of many 'external' supporters of the mafia, like politicians, businessmen or professionals.

Italian political system has been rather polycentric—with different power centres pitted one against the other—and the electoral reforms of the 1990s have only slightly affected the situation.[45]

This polycentric setting seems to reflect itself also inside the legal complex. The rise of judicial power is, without doubt, the most important institutional change of the republican period. This power is mainly due to the strong guarantees of independence but, at least in the criminal field, also to the fact that magistrates are allowed to perform two of the crucial roles of the criminal process—judge and prosecutor—and that prosecutors have gained a growing influence on police forces.[46] However, the roots of judicial power have to be traced in the evolution of the political system (Guarnieri, 2003). The influence of the authoritarian past and the distrust between the political forces led to introducing judicial review and strong judicial independence into the Constitution. Since the late 1950s, the decline of Christian Democratic power and the pressure of the Left opened the way for the implementation of the Constitution. After having initially distrusted the judiciary, the Left, having no expectations of rising to power, has become a strong advocate of judicial power. In the meanwhile, the judiciary has gained a high capacity of exerting pressure on the political class.[47] However, the relationships of the judiciary with politics are characterised by some ambiguity. Magistrates are divided in several groups, competing against each other for appointing their affiliates to top positions in the judiciary.[48] Judicial factions have tended to reinforce their positions by building alliances with sectors of the political class. In this way, at least until the 1990s, political parties have been able somewhat to contain the power of the judiciary.

Moreover, we have seen that the relationships between the bar and the bench have to be considered problematic.[49] The 1990s have seen a sort of political mobilisation by the criminal bar in support of the reform of the criminal process. The new assertiveness of criminal lawyers has further deepened the traditional gulf. Today, attorneys in politics seem to align

[45] In 1993, in the wake of a deep political crisis, a new, quasi-majoritarian electoral law was enacted. The result has been the formation of two political coalitions—Left and Right—which since then have alternated in power (Guarnieri 2007).

[46] You must also to take into account the principle of compulsory prosecution which, especially because of the way it is currently interpreted, makes prosecutors in practice unaccountable for their discretion (Di Federico, 1998).

[47] The Italian case fits, at least in part, hypotheses put forward in other contexts by Ramseyer (1994) and especially by Ginsburg (2003).

[48] Two thirds of the Higher Council's members are magistrates. They are directly elected by the corps and belong to its main factions. The remaining third is composed of attorneys and law professors appointed by the parliament, usually along party lines.

[49] The significance of this relationship for judicial independence has been pointed out by Feeley (2002). In Italy, the judiciary seems to have in some way substituted the bench with the political class, but with the limits pointed out in the text.

themselves in large part with the *Alleanza nazionale*, the traditional, conservative 'post-Fascist' Right.[50] However, many prominent criminal attorneys have been elected to Parliament in *Forza Italia*, Berlusconi's party. Some of them, often involved in the defence of the Prime Minister, play important roles in the Chambers.[51] As we have already pointed out, the conflict on judicial issues has become politicised. However, the Italian bar is divided not only on party lines but also according to the different functions performed (eg criminal vs civil) and suffers from the extreme fragmentation of the profession, as reflected in the number of different associations.

The tensions we have seen characterising in recent decades the legal complex erupts out of a basic disagreement between its main actors concerning the respective significance of the need of social defence and that of protecting individual rights in the criminal process. Traditionally, social defence, easily interpreted as 'law and order', that is support for the status quo, was an issue put forward by the political Right[52] and by conservative magistrates and law professors. In the 1950s and 1960s this group was increasingly confronted by a broad alliance made of attorneys, law professors and young judges, which much contributed to the liberal role played by the Constitutional Court in those years. Since the 1970s, criminal threats like terrorism, organised crime and, later, political corruption have complicated the scene: the judiciary effectively organised the fight, with the bar reduced to playing the traditional role of assisting increasingly unpopular defendants. As for academic doctrine, on the whole, it joined the judiciary in the fight against the state's enemies. Today, we seem to witness a development by which the theme of social defence has been taken over and reinterpreted by the judiciary, or at least part of it: the task of the criminal process is to protect the weak, the less privileged, especially from the attacks of organised and corporate crime and to fight tax fraud in order to recover resources for the welfare state. Therefore, this task does not need to be obstructed by too many formalities and, in any case, by an excessive preoccupation for the rights of defendants, who often have disproportionate legal and monetary resources at their disposal: the rights of victims must also be taken into account.[53] It is interesting to note that recently one of the main issues

[50] In the parliament elected in 2001, 14.5 per cent of parliamentarians were attorneys. The percentage rises to 27.1—the highest—for *Alleanza Nazionale*, the one-time fascist party, today mainly composed of traditional, conservative notables from the South (Verzichelli and De Micheli, 2004: 152). In *Forza Italia*, Berlusconi's party, lawyers are 19 per cent of the parliamentary groups.

[51] In 2001, the presidents of the Justice committees of both Chamber and Senate were criminal attorneys. One of them was—and still is—the main Berlusconi defence attorney.

[52] See the Criminal Code drafted by the fascist Justice minister Rocco (Sbriccoli, 1998: 528–34).

[53] The review 'Micromega', very influential in some leftist milieux, has been extremely vocal on these points, often giving voice to the more militant wing of the judiciary.

emphasised by *Magistratura Democratica*, the traditional faction of left-wing magistrates, has become court delay and the effective implementation of judicial decisions.[54] This stand has been contested by criminal lawyers, although traditional leftist civil rights lawyers are today in a difficult position.[55] As for academic doctrine, it tends to oscillate between the two positions, although the need of social defence—especially when reinterpreted as defence of the weak—seems to be more intensively felt. As a consequence, the traditional preoccupation of the Left for the rights of defendants—often considered to be underdogs or in some way victims of social and economic discrimination—has been circumscribed. Paradoxically, defendants' rights have become a Right issue, not least because of the prosecutions started against its leader, Berlusconi. However, the new attitude of the Right—in any case not without internal dissents and contradictions—seems to have been brought about by the distrust of the judiciary, where leftist propensities are considered to be prevailing.[56]

All in all, Italian legal liberalism seems to be characterised by some ambiguity, especially in the field of criminal justice. Borrowing from the well-known distinction of Damaska (1986), it seems that in the legal culture the policy-implementation function of the criminal process is still dominant. Adversary settings are supported only because of short-term interests, likely to be abandoned, should the context change. Often, the dilemma between individual rights and social defence is 'solved' through formalistic formulae, relying on linguistic artifacts: usually claiming that we can—and must—have the better of the two, at least on paper, since the practice is usually different.[57] However, the influence of the statist tradition—maybe with a corporatist flavour—is still important. Rights are recognised to the extent to which they can be traced in some written document: a statute, the Constitution, an international Declaration. Therefore, textual analysis remains important and linguistic manipulations are always possible: for example, as we have seen, the Constitutional Court has supported prosecutorial powers by 'discovering' into the Constitution the principle of 'economizing the means of evidence'.

Summing up, the statist version of liberalism prevailing inside the Italian legal complex—in large part related to the late and difficult unification of

---

[54] See, eg, Nunziata (2003) as well as the congress of the group in Palermo in May 2005.

[55] Eg, as we have seen, the criminal bar is strongly in favour of radically separating judges and prosecutors and some well-known leftist attorneys play an important role in it.

[56] In this way the *securitaire* trend has been somewhat checked!

[57] Recently, one of the most influential Italian legal philosophers, Ferrajoli (2001: 32), maintained that, in order to fight corruption and clientelism, the implementation of fundamental rights—including social rights—should be freed from bureaucratic discretion and made 'free, compulsory and even automatic'. No word has been added about the way this prescription can be actually implemented.

the country—is not particularly supportive of a strong form of political liberalism. However, after the negative experience of fascist authoritarianism, in the first phase of the Republican period, the legal complex played an important role in the implementation of the political and civil rights of the 1948 Constitution. Later, the rise of strong criminal challenges to the democratic state was confronted especially by the judiciary which since the 1970s has come to play a leading role in the fight. However, in the 1990s the growing role of the prosecution in the criminal process led to a sort of counter-mobilisation on the part of the criminal bar, supported also by the discontent judicial investigations on corruption had generated in the political class. The picture that emerged is of a legal complex rather fragmented, although its very fragmentation has become, not without cost,[58] a sort of check on abuses, coming from judicial or political powers.

REFERENCES

Amodio, E (2004), 'The Accusatorial System Lost and Regained: Reforming Criminal Procedure in Italy', 52 *American Journal of Comparative Law* 489.

Amodio, E and Selvaggi, E (1989), 'An Accusatorial System in a Civil Law Country: The 1988 Italian Code of Criminal Procedure', 62 *Temple Law Review* 1211.

Bargis, M (2004), 'Il mandato d'arresto europeo dalla decisione quadro alle prospettive di attuazione', 35 *Politica del diritto* 49.

Cappelletti, M (1989), *The Judicial Process in Comparative Perspective* (Oxford, Clarendon Press).

Cipriani, F (1998), 'La professione di avvocato' in L Violante (ed), *Legge Diritto Giustizia* (Torino, Einaudi) 883.

Colajanni, N (1996), *Mani pulite?* (Milan, Mondadori).

Damaska, M (1986), *The Faces of Justice and State Authority* (New Haven, Conn, Yale University Press).

De Micheli, C and Verzichelli, L (2004), *Il Parlamento* (Bologna, Il Mulino).

Di Federico, G (1998), 'Prosecutorial Independence and the Democratic Requirement of Accountability in Italy', 38 *British Journal of Criminology* 371.

Di Federico, G and Sapignoli, M (2002), *Processo penale e diritti della difesa* (Rome, Carocci).

Di Nicola, A (2003), 'Dieci anni di lotta alla corruzione' in M Barbagli (ed), *Rapporto sulla criminalità in Italia* (Bologna, Il Mulino) 109.

Fabri, M (1994), 'Theory Versus Practice in Italian Criminal Justice Reform', 77 *Judicature* 211.

Fasanella, G and Pellegrino, G (2005), *La guerra civile* (Milan, Rizzoli).

---

[58] Eg, court delay in Italy has become so persistent as to push the Council of Europe to decide continuously to monitor the state of the Italian judicial system. Among its causes one has to mention the extreme complexity of the procedure, due in large part to a growing legislation designed to curb judicial discretion and to the weak role played by the Court of Cassation in rationalising the legal system.

Feeley, MM (2002), 'The Bench, the Bar and the State' in M Feeley and S Miyazawa (eds), *The Japanese Adversary Process in Context. Controversies and Comparisons* (London, Palgrave Macmillan).

Ferrajoli, L (1999), *La cultura giuridica nell'Italia del Novecento* (Bari, Laterza).

—— (2001), *Diritti fondamentali* (Bari, Laterza).

Fioravanti, M (2004), *Costituzione e popolo sovrano* (Bologna, Il Mulino).

Ginsburg, T (2003), *Judicial Review in New Democracies* (Cambridge, Cambridge University Press).

Grande, E (2000), 'Italian Criminal Justice: Borrowing and Resistence', 48 *American Journal of Comparative Law* 227.

Grevi, V (2000), 'Spunti problematici sul nuovo modello costituzionale di "giusto processo" penale', 31 *Politica del diritto* 423.

Grossi, P (2003), *Prima lezione di diritto* (Bari, Laterza).

Guarnieri, C (1984), *Pubblico ministero e sistema politico* (Padua, Cedam).

—— (1995), 'L'ordine pubblico e la giustizia penale' in R Romanelli (ed), *Storia dello Stato in Italia* (Rome, Donzelli) 365.

—— (2003), *Giustizia e politica. I nodi della Seconda Repubblica* (Bologna, Il Mulino).

—— (2007), *Il sistema politico italiano* (Bologna, Il Mulino).

—— and Pederzoli, P (2002), *The Power of Judges* (Oxford, Oxford University Press).

Halliday, T and Karpik, L (eds) (1997), *Lawyers and the Rise of Western Political Liberalism* (Oxford, Clarendon Press).

Langer, M (2004), 'From Legal Transplants to Legal Translations: The Globalization of Plea Bargaining and the Americanization Thesis in Criminal Procedure', 45 *Harvard International Law Journal* 1.

La Spina, A (2005), *Mafia, legalità debole e sviluppo del Mezzogiorno* (Bologna, Il Mulino).

Lupo, S (1993), *Storia della mafia* (Rome, Donzelli).

Malatesta, M (2003), 'Per la storia sociale dell'avvocatura: tradizione e trasmissione' in G Alpa and R Danovi (eds), *Un progetto di ricerca sulla storia dell'avvocatura* (Bologna, Il Mulino) 89.

Martucci, R (1980), *Emergenza e tutela dell'ordine pubblico nell'Italia liberale* (Bologna, Il Mulino).

Melis, G (1995), 'L'amministrazione' in R Romanelli (ed), *Storia dello Stato in Italia* (Rome, Donzelli) 187.

Merryman, JH (1965), 'The Italian Style: the Doctrine', 18 *Stanford Law Review* 39.

—— (1985), *The Civil Law Tradition* (Stanford, Cal, Stanford University Press).

Merryman, JH and Vigoriti, V (1967), 'When Courts Collide: Constitution and Cassation in Italy', 15 *American Journal of Comparative Law* 665.

Newell, JL (2005), 'Americanization and the Judicialization of Italian Politics', 10 *Journal of Modern Italian Studies* 27.

Monateri, G (2003), 'Export of the Rule of Law: The Weak Law: Contaminations and Legal Cultures', 13 *Transnational Law & Contemporary Problems* 575.

Morisi, M (1999), *Anatomia della magistratura italiana* (Bologna, Il Mulino).

Olgiati, V (1996), 'Law As an Instrument of "Organizational Totalitarianism": Fascist Rule over Italian Lawyers', in A Podgorecki and V Olgiati (eds), *Totalitarian and Post-Totalitarian Law* (Aldershot, Darmouth) 123.

Panebianco, A (2004), *Il potere, lo stato, la libertà* (Bologna, Il Mulino).

Panzavolta, M (2005), 'Reforms and Counter-reforms in the Italian Struggle for an Accusatorial Criminal Law System', 30 *North Carolina Journal of International Law and Commercial Regulation 577.*

Paoli, L (2003), 'Il crimine organizzato' in M Barbagli (ed), *Rapporto sulla criminalità in Italia* (Bologna, Il Mulino) 275.

Pizzi, WT and Montagna, M (2004), 'The Battle to Establish an Adversarial Trial System in Italy', 25 *Michigan Journal of International Law* 429.

Pizzorno, A (1998), *Il potere dei giudici. Stato democratico e controllo della virtù* (Bari, Laterza).

Ramseyer, JM (1994), 'The Puzzling (In)dependence of Courts: A Comparative Approach', 23 *Journal of Legal Studies* 721.

Rebuffa, G (1993), *La funzione giudiziaria* (Turin, Giappichelli).

Riccio, G (2000), 'Istanze di riforma e chiusure ideologiche nella soluzione del problema italiano del pubblico ministero', 31 *Politica del diritto* 451.

Rodotà, S (1995), 'Le libertà e I diritti' in R Romanelli (ed), *Storia dello Stato in Italia* (Rome, Donzelli) 301.

Santoro, M (1998), *Notai* (Bologna, Il Mulino).

Sartori, G (1987), *The Theory of Democracy Revisited* (Chatham, Chatham House).

Sbriccoli, M (1998), 'Caratteri originari e tratti permanenti del sistema penale italiano (1860–1990)' in L Violante (ed), *Legge Diritto Giustizia* (Turin, Einaudi) 487.

Siegrist, H (1994), 'Profilo degli avvocati italiani dal 1870 al 1930. Omogeneità istituzionalizzata ed eterogeneità reale di una professione classica', 8 *Polis* 223.

Spataro, A (2002), '1999–2002: La riforma della giustizia penale in Italia, dal Governo dell'Ulivo a quello del Polo', 5 *Giornale di storia contemporanea* 235.

Stone Sweet, A (2000), *Governing with Judges* (Oxford, Oxford University Press).

Tacchi, F (2002), *Gli avvocati italiani dall'Unità alla Repubblica* (Bologna, Il Mulino).

Tarello, G (1988), *Cultura giuridica e politica del diritto* (Bologna, il Mulino).

Toharia, JJ (1975), 'Judicial Independence in an Authoritarian Regime: the Case of Contemporary Spain', 4 *Law & Society Review* 475.

Vauchez, A (2004), *L'institution judiciaire remotivée. Le processus d'institutionnalisation d'une « nouvelle justice » en Italie (1960–2000)* (Paris, LGDJ).

Vogliotti, M (2004), 'Les relations police-parquet en Italie: un équilibre menacé?', 58 *Droit et Societé* 453.

Zannotti, F (1989), *La magistratura un gruppo di pressione istituzionale* (Padua, Cedam).

Postscript

15

Political Lawyers

LUCIEN KARPIK

Sociologist A: How do you explain that lawyers are much more committed to the building or the defence of civil rights than any other profession?

Sociologist B: How could you make such a statement! Look around. Politically, when they are not conservative, lawyers are indifferent. I don't see your point.

Sociologist A: But in a number of countries they are taking risks in defending people whose civil rights are threatened.

Sociologist B: And so what! They represent only a tiny fraction of the profession and moreover they are only doing their job, as business lawyers are doing theirs.

Sociologist A: Don't you think that something has been inherited from the period when legal professions were parts of the conflicts over political liberalism through which our individual freedoms have been established?

Sociologist B: I can only remark that as you couldn't sustain your thesis for the present you have switched to the past. I don't know too much about the past but I'll bet that they were like they are everywhere today and like other professions are: mainly driven by material intests.

TEN OR 15 years ago such a discussion would have been commonplace. Attorneys would have been almost exclusively linked to the market. It is within that theoretical situation that a comparative project was launched on the specific relationships between attorneys and political liberalism in four western countries: France, Great Britain, Germany and the US. It brought together historians and sociologists and looked at attorneys' specific political involvements, if any.

Since the eighteenth century, western lawyers have been activist in the creation, defence and development of individual rights. Such a general proposition should be linked to three others: through legal-political battles against the authoritarian state, lawyers have participated in the construction of the collective representation of a society divided into the state and civil society; they have been among the main builders of the liberal state; and, finally, through their commitments, individual rights have become more or less strongly incorporated into their professional bodies. Affinities between attorneys and basic freedoms are a historical reality.

Of course, variations existed across countries/periods. The English bar was the least offensive as its autonomy preceded the development of the modern state but that did not prevent barristers, alone or in small groups, from defending individual rights through legal-political involvements even against the Bar Council's power. The French bar was the most radical: its fight on behalf of individual rights and against the absolute monarchy began very early. The American bar had to bring together absolute individual rights and the development of a federal state. German lawyers faced an authoritarian state and chose to act via proceduralism. Thus, the four countries' attorneys, sometimes from a very early date, have been activists in the transformations through which liberal regimes have replaced authoritarian regimes.

Fighting for freedom. This book brings together contributions that deal with legal actors' action on individual rights in authoritarian as well as in liberal countries/periods. In this volume, the same issues are at stake as in the previous book and the same socio-historical point of view has been maintained. The main differences are twofold: the inquiry bears on countries dispersed on several continents; and as a legal actor, the *legal complex* replaces attorneys, at least partially. The combination of continuity and of novelty is not without risks. Why should countries located on other continents confirm an interpretation elaborated for countries that were part of the same history? Why should the legal complex behave like attorneys? Why should a very heterogeneous universe exhibit the same characteristics as a rather homogeneous one?

Since the general framework and results were presented in Chapter 1, the Postscript will concentrate on four goals: to look closely and critically at the notion of 'political liberalism' and identify the conditions under which it may become the basis of lawyers' international comparison; to reflect further on the general classification of forms of action by legal actors; to expand the explanation of the diversity of actors/forms of action that are treated by the contributions; and, finally, to elaborate on the distinction between 'political lawyers' and 'cause lawyers', as this distinction should help deal with peculiar political transformations of contemporary societies as well as help develop the theory of political commitments by legal actors.

I. POLITICAL LIBERALISM: WHICH ONE?

Sociologist A: Your 'results' seem to me quite fragile.
Sociologist B: Why?
Sociologist A: Because you are linking together actors that belong to different countries, different periods, different political regimes, different judicial systems.

Sociologist B: Isn't this the rule for doing comparisons? Or shall we only compare what is similar?

Sociologist A: Don't be sarcastic! You may build these comparisons under the condition that the term of comparison is the 'same' or at least the 'same enough'. And that is not the case.

Sociologist B: You're rather elliptical. What are you thinking about?

Sociologist A: About 'political liberalism', 'individual rights', 'basic freedoms', 'first generation rights'—all those notions that are supposed not only to designate the same reality but whose meaning is also supposed to be shared by your actors.

Sociologist B: So what?

Sociologist A: These requirements are far from being respected

Sociologist B: But definitions have been proposed and the views that mobilise the actors in the different countries have been presented.

Sociologist A: I am still not convinced. Why should I believe that the nineteenth century's reality will still exist today? Why should I accept that in Latin America, Middle East, Asia or Western Europe political liberalism would have the same meaning! Don't you think that with time and space, the content and the scope of the individual rights have been modified or more properly transformed ? Aren't you only playing with words?

Sociologist B: If you think so, maybe I have some additional work to do. So let's begin (again) what you call a 'demonstration'. Let us look carefully at what is common and at what is different in the political orientations of the legal complex.

Across political regimes, political philosophies and social sciences histories, the notion of political liberalism has taken a wide variety of meanings. That is true for its legal and political contents as well as for its concrete implementations. Even if its definitions are restricted to those suggested by contemporary social scientists, the multiplicity of meanings will remain great.

Two definitions will be used. On the one hand, a general definition has been constructed through a critical discussion with other theories. It combines three characteristics: basic individual freedoms, the moderate state and civil society (Halliday and Karpik, 1997: 15–54). On the other hand, a specific definition which is also one of main results of our research links actors and orientations of action: *attorneys/legal complex mobilise themselves only for individual rights.*

These rights include mainly freedom of speech, of thought, of assembly, security rights, property rights and the right to justice and due process of law. With some exceptions lawyers have not fought outside this universe. Looking at lawyers' vocabulary, one may remark that civil rights are their home. They were, and still are, the bearers of 'basic freedoms', of 'individual rights', of 'civic professionalism (Halliday, 1987), of a liberal political culture. The link between western lawyers and political liberalism is not general but specific: they have defined themselves by a *restricted conception of political liberalism.*

How general is this proposition? Does it apply to extra-European countries? And to the contemporary period? On the meaning of political liberalism, some diversity exists between the contributions. Thus the task is twofold: to formulate a positive definition that is shared by all and to identify the issues that are found in one or another country and that are to be excluded from the general analysis as they do not belong to the framework of political liberalism. At the end, one should get an elaborated common conception of political liberalism.

(a) The Relevant Universe of Rights

The particular political liberalism of attorneys/legal complex is incompletely described by a simple list of individual rights. That usual presentation does not help to understand the peculiar affinities existing between basic freedoms and legal actors. Clarification comes from the successive investigation of the first generation's rights and the judiciary.

1. First Generation Rights

Political liberalism is conveniently defined by reference to succeeding generation rights. The classical formulation comes from TH Marshall who distinguished civil, political and economic rights and related them respectively to the eighteenth, nineteenth and twentieth centuries. First 'the rights necessary for individual freedom', then 'the right to participate in the exercise of political power', and finally social rights—'*the* whole range from the right to a modicum of economic welfare and security to the right to share to the full in the social heritage and to live the life of a civilized being according to the standards prevailing in the society' (Marshall, 1965). This three-generation rights schema *lays* out a harmonious evolution as new rights are added to old ones even if Marshall did not hide the fact that this process would be conflictual but, at least implicitly, evolution and civilisation were moving together.

This analytical and historical scheme is both expressive and convenient. These reasons explain its general use. Nevertheless, from our point of view, it presents one shortcoming: the inclusion of 'political rights'. Usually, in contemporary classifications, political rights are rightly excluded because they belong to another universe. Consequently, in this evolutionary schema, social rights directly follow civic rights. Although it may look logical, this succession does not work for attorneys/legal complex: *in the past as today, they stick to the first-generation rights.* And as social rights were outside their goals, Continental attorneys were (and still are) considered conservative.

When we look at the extra-European countries/periods presented by our national studies, the results seem slightly different. Basic freedoms everywhere are exclusively orientating legal actors with the two exceptions of Korea and Taiwan: '[i]n the Korean case, explicit focus on the machinery of national repression in the form of the National Security Act was a crucial fulcrum for mobilisation, reflecting demand for a classic "negative liberty". Yet activists were also engaged in calls for socio-economic rights and redistribution .... The ultimate concern of the Taiwan activist lawyers is for national "self-determination," which fits uneasily into the traditional binary framework' (Ginsburg, this book).

An interpretation could be that the formation of the legal complex began late, that it could only be effective by making alliances with other professions, social movements and political parties, and it did not separate the fight for individual rights from the conquest of political power. Therefore the legal complex had to take into account the claims and goals of its allies: social rights in Korea, social rights and national self-determination in Taïwan. Such an evolution may happen in other countries. But for the author this combination of civic and social rights is unique and should be explained by the history of North East Asia and the working of 'capitalist authoritarianism'. In this perspective, Korea and Taiwan appear as exceptions. And what was right for Western European countries holds for the other countries: *the conception of restricted political liberalism is everywhere orienting the action of attorneys and the legal complex.* Now the real test will be to check in a few years if the legal complexes in Korea and Taiwan, and especially the bar associations, have maintained that diversity or if they have rejoined the orientations of the legal complex observed in other countries.

2. The Judiciary

The list of first-generation rights does not really show the characteristics that are particularly meaningful to legal actors' orientations and powers. To identify them, one has to distinguish between *legal citizenship* and *judicial citizenship* and the specific rights linked to each of them: those which protect the individuals from state arbitrariness and those which give access to and control over a powerful weapon, the judiciary.

Attorneys and the legal complex are not only legal actors but also judicial actors. They have the skills, the functions and the powers that give them a very peculiar position in relationships with the judiciary. That distinguishes them from all other actors. They have privileged access to the tool that is able to transform through legitimate violence, formal rights into real rights. This position does not explain their political orientations but it makes clear one of the sources of their authority and influence on the state as well as on civil society.

3. History

By dealing with this distinction between two types of citizenship it becomes possible to show, as TH Marshall himself remarked, that the succeeding generations rights scheme is not the only possible evolution, that another history *can* exist within each category of rights.[1] In the case of basic freedoms, it works along *three* principles of action. First, with the composition of individual rights that varies across countries ; Secondly, with the degree of reality of the so-called 'universal' rights, whose universality varies according to the extent of slavery, serfdom, racism, xenophobia and sexism within society, and to the extent of racism, xenophobia or sexism within the legal professions. Thirdly, with changes in the judiciary that may affect its autonomy as well as its access, especially through legal aid. Thus restricted political liberalism displays numerous differences the general explanation of which is still to come.

(b) Limits of Political Liberalism

In some contributions in this book, the label of political liberalism is associated not only with individual rights but also with other political issues like corruption (Italy), national self-determination (Taiwan, Turkey), the relative position of religion and politics (Turkey, Israel), or democracy (Egypt, Hong Kong). Shall we include them in the universe of restricted political liberalism or not? Do they belong to that comparison or not?

We need a rule. We can use external criteria or internal criteria. With the first one, unless we find that the relevant political issue is linked to individual rights in a rather large and growing number of countries, it will not be included. The relation will be considered as contingent, peculiar to the country/period. With the second one, the decision is based on the comparison of meanings of political issues. In this perspective we want to know if the democratic question and if the religious question are components of restricted political liberalism.

1. Political Liberalism and Democracy

TH Marshall and other authors have considered that democracy should succeed to individual rights. This thesis was supported by historical and logical arguments. But as the French Revolution showed clearly, these two principles are far from being spontaneously compatible. On the contrary, at that time, they were opposite forces. And logically they are.

As a matter of fact, by itself democracy does not contain any limit to state power, and thus it may give birth to despotism which equals the end of individual rights. And individual rights, when they are considered as absolute, do not allow the state to impose a general interest upon particular interests. To put it differently, the logic of individual rights is to protect the citizen, to

---

[1] 'First, when the institutions on which the three elements of citizenship depended parted company, it became possible for each to go its separate way, travelling at its own speed under the direction of its own peculiar principles': Marshall (1965: 80).

resist state arbitrariness, where the logic of democracy is to participate, to govern. One is 'negative' and is supposed to gather all those, whatever their characteristics, who feel frightened by the state and whose similitude creates, from that point of view, a united body, namely, the *public*. The other is 'positive' and contains partisan commitments and conflictual diversity.

Attorneys/legal complex have fought and are still fighting for basic freedoms but not for democracy. If one takes the central issue of democracy, which is universal voting, in nineteenth century Europe, attorneys were strongly committed toward political liberalism but they did not care about a suffrage based on property qualification, or a suffrage that excluded women. Today, it is not by chance that one may find political liberalism without democracy (Hong Kong)[2] and democracy without political liberalism (Egypt). The same perspective explains that liberal democracies are based on delicate and unstable compromises, and even in mature democracies the compatibility between both principles is not spontaneously smooth.

Freedom and democracy do not go together easily: they belong to two different and contradictory worlds. As the relationship with basic freedoms is the same for social rights and democracy, one may wonder if the two last notions should not be linked together if they do not belong to the same universe which, as such, is outside the political liberalism of the attorney/legal complex.

2. Political Liberalism and Religion

Are issues like the headscarf ban for women part of individual rights? Do they belong to the restricted conception of political liberalism, and accordingly should lawyers, logically, have a peculiar view of them? I do not have an automatic answer, but as this issue and its equivalents will become more frequent, as attorneys and the legal complex will have to deal with them, it seems useful to propose some preliminary remarks from the analyst's point of view.

In a liberal society people are opposing each other when they disagree on individual rights; in a *proto-liberal society*, people oppose each other on behalf of the same individual right. Therefore, the battle is ambiguous and the real stakes may remain hidden for a long time. The headscarf ban conflict in Turkey confronts the government, the parliament, the judiciary and the lawyers, all of them supporting the law that forbids women to wear

---

[2] 'It [Hong Kong] shares the core values and rights of a liberal state—protections against the arbitrary exercise of power (such as arbitrary arrest and detention) habeas corpus, due process, the right to silence, to public trial and to legal representation, as well as the core freedoms, such as freedom of speech and freedom of association associated with the moderate state. But it is not a "liberal democracy", has never had universal suffrage nor a representative government' (Jones, this book, 109).

headscarves at universities with some lawyers and a large fraction of people who are asking for more tolerance (Arslan, this book). The common reference of both sides is freedom of conscience, but the more it is invoked the more the intensity of the conflict is increasing.

The roots of that conflict go far into the past, to the Renaissance at least, to the thirteenth century for some historians, when European societies slowly transformed themselves by the extension of the 'individual'. The major steps of this evolution were habeas corpus in England (1679), the American (1787) and the French Constitutions (1789). Whether individuals rights were linked to God or to Nature did not change the central difficulty that arose from human beings considered as individuals necessarily equipped with absolute and inalienable rights. Who could organise them? Limit them? How could a political body govern itself?[3]

From Hobbes to Tocqueville and even later two central notions emerged—*individual sovereignty* and *representation*—and a general reasoning that can be elaborated. When individuals are sovereign their consent is necessary for organising individual rights. And this process requires representatives acting by laws. That general argument concentrates a wealth of conflictual issues. Nevertheless, in its generality, it was usually accepted because *the process was immanent*: nothing external to the collectivity of individuals could intervene. Nothing was superior to law. It was the end of a history where God was above society and when the Church tried to control simultaneously the religious and the temporal powers. Political liberalism was the product of the emancipation of politics from religion. It is not secularisation which was at stake but the autonomisation of the political sphere. For political liberalism to prosper, religion had to be maintained outside politics. Of course, the concrete balance between people's sovereignty and religion will vary according to countries and periods.[4] But what was and still is common is the autonomy of the political sphere.

On the headscarf ban, history gives us two contradictory teachings. As the Kemalist regime has adopted the principle of the separation between politics and religion it is not surprising that in Turkey lawyers will be on the side of the government and the institutions. One may say that the legal

---

[3] 'We hold these truths to be self-evident: That all men are created equal; that they are endowed by their Creator with certain unalienable rights; that among these are life, liberty, and the pursuit of happiness': American *Declaration of Independence*, 1776; 'The aim of all political association is the preservation of the natural and imprescriptible rights of man. These rights are liberty, property, security, and resistance to oppression': French *Declaration of the Rights of Man and of the Citizen*, 1789.

[4] For the USA see de Tocqueville: and 'In the United States religion exercises but little influence upon the laws and upon the details of public opinion; but it directs the customs of the community, and, by regulating domestic life, it regulates the state': and 'Religion in America takes no direct part in the government of society' (de Tocqueville, 1997).

complex is defending individual rights as they are organised by law. This position is in line with the history of political philosophy. But one may also say that the demand for enlarged rights to conscience is in line with the diversity of compromises found in liberal societies. Those are the roots of difficulty for the analyst who does not want to take sides but who is looking nevertheless for a way to study that reality. The same difficulty will arise with all issues belonging to a protoliberal society or protoliberal arena. Ambiguity is the rule. What shall we do with it?

I recall that we are 'only' dealing with a preliminary question: does this issue belong to the universe of individual rights? The positive answer is the very condition that justifies a peculiar involvement of the legal actors as legal actors and, as a consequence, the choice of including this issue in the analysis. With a negative answer, lawyers are like other citizens and the issue is no more relevant for this study. But it is not easy to identify the nature of the conflict as it may be considered a limited–reform and it is often presented like this or, on the contrary, it may be considered as a step to extend the position of religion in society. Is it a reform or a revolution?

The ambiguity comes from the fact that no clear answer can be given because it is the future that will give its real meaning to the present. In economics that is called *uncertainty on quality*. A large number of goods and services cannot be completely known before they are bought as is the case for a used car, for the visit to a doctor or the choice of a novel. In such a case the market *will* necessarily disappear (Akerlof, 1970: 488–500). This issue is not marginal: it is one that has created a major crisis in neoclassical theory. Before this analysis, economic actors were supposed to sell and buy products, and afterwards we find that they are selling and buying *promises*. But the exchange of promises *necessarily* requires that actors *trust* each other (Karpik, 2007). The same is true in the realm of politics. It is because trust does not exist that conflict is always on the verge of bursting out. Those who want to maintain the primacy of politics do not want the balance between politics and religion to be changed through this issue; those who want only that specific reform do not understand that they cannot have it as it is for them an enlargement of individual freedoms. The ambiguity of the issue is not attached to the content's issue but to the high degree of distrust between social actors.

Coming back to the relevance of this issue for lawyers' ideology one may now present the elements of the choice. One may say that the legal complex is defending individual rights as they are organised by law, and its adversaries are defending freedom as it is required by God. The conflict in other European countries has not been very different. Usually, it is the first conception that is understood as the very condition of political liberalism. But that situation is more complicated. It is the ambiguity of the issue that gives rise to extreme reactions.

Under uncertainty, those who want to protect politics' autonomy will rigidly defend the present balance in fear of opening Pandora's box; those who want that reform will push it strongly as the reason for a refusal look weak. For the first one, the same vocabulary, the same reference to freedom, and more precisely to freedom of conscience are hiding the discontinuity between two superior principles: politics' autonomy as an expression of people's sovereignity and God's will. Adversaries are not sharing the same political paradigm. Although they are part of the same country they belong to two antagonistic worlds, to two different conceptions of the relationships between religion and politics.

If he does not want to take sides even involuntarily, the analyst has to understand the reasons for the conflict and to make a detour in order to study distrust and its causes. It is there and nowhere else that fundamentally lie the reasons for a problem that has been transformed into an issue. I will stop here and leave the reader to make his or her decisions on what should be done about including or excluding the topics of the analysis. I just wanted to lay out some arguments about a tricky question for sociological analysis.

* * *

To compare countries/periods about legal actors' orientations toward basic freedoms two conditions must be satisfied. First, and by definition, all the countries/periods where attorneys or legal complex are strictly subordinated to the political rulers have to be excluded. That is the case for Venezuela (before 1936), Japan (before 1870), Egypt (before the nineteenth century), Hong Kong (before 1840?), Spain (before 1973), China and Taiwan (before 1912), Korea (before 1970). Secondly, issues like corruption, national self-determination, democracy, the balance between religion and politics and so on must also be excluded as not belonging to the lawyers' conception of political liberalism. Under these two conditions, the content of the conception of restricted political liberalism can be defined. And through its diverses concrete expressions, it *everywhere orients the actions of attorneys/legal complex.*

II. LIBERAL COMMITMENT OF ATTORNEYS AND OF THE LEGAL COMPLEX

Sociologist A: You have shown the similarities of action between attorneys in four western countries. It is easy to understand such a result. Political liberalism was born and has developed in these countries. And lawyers have shared the same history. But how could anyone think of extending a model rooted in Europe to countries whose histories, cultures, religions, political institutions are very different?

Sociologist B: Don't you think that the passion for individual rights could have been transmitted through very diverse channels and could have become a commun political framework?

Sociologist A: Even so, it does not mean that we have to disregard what makes countries unique realities. Not to recognise that requirement would amount to committing the sin of ethnocentrism or sociocentrism. Moreover, what seems all the more unbelievable is that not only lawyers but also judges, law professors even civil servants will be part of this history! Do you really think, for example, that judges would anywhere join lawyers for the defence of civil rights? Aren't they everywhere the sword of the State?

Sociologist B: Well instead of expressing doxa, perhaps we should look at the concrete reality and analyse it!

Sociologist A: You're right, of course. Nevertheless I maintain my scepticism.

The restricted conception of political liberalism is compatible with numerous choices. These are our 'units of analysis': the diverse combinations of countries/periods and forms of action presented by the contributions. To describe and explain this diversity, one has to combine actors and orientations toward basic freedoms.

(a) Attorneys, Lawyers and the Legal Complex

Depending on the level of generality, one find three categorisations in the contributions. The most specific contains different legal professions: attorneys, judges, prosecutors, law professors, and civil servants considered as jurists. The notion of 'lawyer' is an intermediary notion as its meaning oscillates between attorney alone and the whole of legal professions; thus its use allows the possibility of switching between a specific and a general comparison. Further, with 'legal complex' a new concept has been added. It has been coined not only to avoid the tiresome list of legal professions but also to formulate some new theoretical problems. As soon as it was presented, it became an integral part of our collective vocabulary. Two reasons may explain that 'success'. The first is that 'legal complex' is a catchword: it gathers all the legal professions without the ambiguity linked to the notion of lawyers and therefore it is helpful for exchange as well as for writing. But, something else is at work. 'Legal complex' is a *structural notion*. It is not defined by the sum but by the systematic relationships of legal actors. It is varying in its composition, interelationships, causes and effects. Comparison does not happen any more between each legal actor but between *structured relationships of actors*. As a consequence it means that legal complex is not an abstract model or an ideal type; it is a formal notion that, on one hand, invites one to look beyond the attorneys and, on the other hand, requires one to look to the structural relationships between the legal actors and actions. It is all the more useful when it is linked to a methodological point of view and to tools that permit one to deal directly, and over the different studies, with relationships. It opens new possibilities of interpreting reality.

Consequently, the analysis has to identify patterns of relationships between the component of the legal complex in order to explain the diversity of their forms of action. As the contributions show clearly, the authors' strategies have been to conciliate structural relations and methodological flexibility, to maintain the possibility of switching between the legal complex and its components. Quantitative data would have encouraged the use of particular statistical methods; qualitative data bring with them a specific point of view and peculiar modes of reasoning.

To describe and explain the diverses legal actors' orientations toward basic freedoms, the analysis deals mainly with the attorney and the legal complex. Ultimately, attorneys eventually act alone against all other actors. This was the dominant model in the past in Continental Europe. The legal complex, by definition, brings together several legal actors defined by their relationships.

(b) Models of Action

To identify the different models of action found in the contributions, we constructed a classification by combining two dimensions: the types of actors—attorneys and the legal complex—and three orientations toward basic freedoms: hostility, passivity and support. This yielded a typology of four relevant models of action: (1) hostility of the legal complex toward basic freedoms; (2) passivity of the legal complex toward basic freedoms; (3) attorneys' support of basic freedoms; (4) legal complex support of basic freedoms.

1. Hostility of the Legal Complex Towards Basic Freedoms

Activist attorneys/legal complex are not necessarily leftists. They may support authoritarian regimes that violate the very basis of political liberalism, as was the case for Nazi Germany (Ledford, 1997), Japan during the militarisation period (1930–45), and at least partially for Italy (1926–45) (Guarneri, this book). Such an involvement would seem to demonstrate that the thesis on the generality of affinities between political liberalism and lawyers is false. Before jumping to that general conclusion one should at least identify the conditions under which such an orientation becomes dominant, as was the case with Pinochet's Chile (1973–91).

How can one explain that, with some exceptions, the legal complex took the side of a regime not only hostile to basic freedoms but a regime that used criminal means in order to eliminate political opposition and 'undesirable' people? This question amounts all the more to an enigma as Chile represents a country which, compared to other Latin American countries long plagued by numerous dictators, has had a long history of being a moderate state. Even if the laws that restricted the state's power opened some free expression to civil society, respected individual rights and political parties were not written in the constitution, they were respected in practice. Moreover, the same tradition seems to explain the smooth process of re-democratisation which followed the defeat of the dictatorship (Couso, this book). Among Latin American countries, logically Chile was the least predisposed to the *rightist extremism of the legal complex*. How can we explain the sudden rupture with a history of moderation and public free expression that nevertheless remains strong enough spontaneously to reappear after the end of the dictatorship?

Several causes have been identified: the strong hierarchical structure of the judiciary, and as a consequence the limited autonomy of the judges, a tradition of neutrality embedded in professionalism, the late creation of the bar and therefore the fragility of its liberal tradition, and the strong influence of political parties that divided the legal profession and weakened its solidarity. (Couso, Hilbink, this book). Although impressive, these causes do not completely explain Chile's 'political anomaly' (Couso). Something more general must have played a role that may have worked not only on Chile but on other countries too.

My proposed line of analysis is based on the distinction between a class logic and a professional logic. Every lawyer belongs to both. In a liberal democracy, the professional logic is strong and autonomous enough to organise lawyers' or judges' professional life. With Pinochet, all of a sudden the class logic replaced the professional logic. Rightly or not, the Allende government and more generally the spread of communist actions in Latin American countries had created 'great fears', a sense of a global threat to the symbolic and material interests of the middle and small bourgeoisies. I am not saying that the reasons for these fears really existed; we are not taking sides between the different historical interpretations; it is enough to observe that these fears (manipulated or not) did exist, that they were collective, and that they become the roots of a *civil war*. From the sixteenth century religion wars to the contemporary civil wars, for example, in Ireland we know too well that civil wars are ferocious, bloody and lasting. In what members of the legal complex considered an extreme situation, the professional logic tended to disappear: attorneys, judges, prosecutors and law professors, with few exceptions, reacted mainly as members of a bourgeois class ready to support every means in order to maintain their world conception and their symbolic and material interests.

Chile shows the conditions under which class belonging will dominate professional principles. The proposition is general. Political cleavages are volatile and social identities are unstable. When a political regime is on the way to being brutally and radically changed, threatened legal professions may convert themselves into radical principles of action. The oscillation between class primacy and professional primacy may exist everywhere. It may help to understand the very conditions under which the political liberal orientation can be converted into its contrary.

2. *Passivity of the Legal Complex Towards Basic Freedoms*

The notion of 'silence', presented by Barzilai (this book) as the notion of passivity or 'non-decision',(Bachrach, 1962)[5] is both useful and ambiguous. Silence refers to situations where an otherwise talkative and active actor has become quiet and passive. Such a change may result from fear, as was at least partially the case in Italy (1926–45) or in Japan (1930–45). It may also be the product of a voluntary choice as in Israel (since 1980), Brazil and Argentina (since 1980). In these cases, silence equals a self-censured voice. But to become meaningful, this passivity presupposes that a prior commitment had existed or it still exists, but on non-security issues. Even lasting passivity is thus considered as contingent and provisional, and as such it has to be related to an 'exceptional' cause.

In *Israel*, attorneys' 'silence' or passivity is remarkable by comparison with their past behaviour and with present behaviour on non-security issues. Between the 1960s and the 1980s attorneys have taken sides publicly: '[o]ther lawyers have become prominent members and leaders of NGOs that have focused on litigation for human rights in the occupied territories and civil rights in Israel in its pre-1967 borders' or, more precisely, lawyers got involved in 'affirmative action for minorities, gender equality in military service, torture, prohibitions on unification of Palestinian families, civil supervision over the security services, military actions in the occupied territories, political appointments, budget allocations, political partisan corruption, the status of Arabic language, land distribution, the status of internal Palestinian refugees and unrecognized Palestinian villages, religious conversions, and civil marriage'. Thus, 'by the 1980s individual rights and the moderate state had extended', and during the same period the bar had become stronger and more prestigious (Barzilai, this book).

But silence already surrounded the 'Jewish state' question and it will after the 1980s be extended to individual rights. It is not easy to understand why the legal complex qua legal complex should take a specific position on the 'Jewish state'. After all, the general problem of a nation's fundamentals has nowhere been part of political liberalism, but, of course, the contrary is true with individual rights: for them, passivity has replaced activism. The justification is well-known: it is *national security*. I will come back to this later.

In Brazil (since 1980) and Argentina (since 1980) the threat to civil peace has been the product of delinquency. This danger has become a collective reality and an obsession. It has transformed the relative weakness of the state in a crucial political issue. In the past as today, everywhere the state's first duty is to create and maintain security. When it is too weak to achieve that goal some unexpected actions may happen. When streets are

[5] S Bachrach, 'Two Faces of Power' (1962) 56 *American Political Science Review* 947–52.

dangerous, when civil kidnapping is becoming a job, when drug criminals are openly selling in the streets, when criminals control some urban areas, other means of security are replacing official institutional ones. In the cases of Brazil and Argentina this alternative means of security was police killing delinquents in the streets.

As the main pressure in favour of that practice has been coming from civil society, prosecutors and judges, as well as a large majority of attorneys, have agreed, at least implicitly, not to prosecute criminal policemen. The only opposition has been coming from private prosecutors acting on behalf of victims and from ideological lawyers belonging to specific organisations (Brink, this book). Their number and their efficacy have been limited. The legal complex by its passivity has demonstrated its (provisional) support for illiberal practices that seem necessary to maintain social order.

It is usual to distinguish between external and internal national security. But this distinction, especially with the new forms of terrorism, is not really helpful. When danger seems to dominate everywhere, when war is at stake, when it threatens the nation's independence or the nation's social order, when national security is on the top of national priorities, when it is invoked by the government in order to defend people even by violating individuals rights, by people who wanted to be protected by every means, *activist lawyers may become passive lawyers.* The silent lawyer is the product of war. But this proposition does not express any mechanical determinism. Even war, and the dangers linked to war, are a matter of interpretation. Thus, in Urugay, the rates of crime have been as high as those in Brazil and Argentina. Nevertheless, the government has been much more moderate in dealing with insecurity, it has defended legality, police killing has been opposed by the legal complex and strongly repressed by judiciary (Brink, this book). In comparable situations, the legal complex may not always act in the same fashion.

Silence is the product of the contradiction between the defence of basic freedoms and the necessities of national security. Such a position can only appear solid if the public discourse of the state can silence the media and the public as a way to express their consent. Under these conditions the passivity of the legal complex will dominate. This is the case for Israel, Brazil and Argentina. It was also the case, for a short period after September 11, in the US and Great Britain.

3. Support of Basic Freedoms by Attorneys

The attorney model has characterised Western Continental Europe and it may also be found in Japan (1870–1930 and since 1960), in the US after 2001, in Hong Kong after 1997, in today's Turkey on individual rights, in Egypt between the late nineteenth century and 1952, and in today's China. This model of action is dispersed over countries, historical periods and political regimes. My comparison will concentrated on Japan and the US.

We can also add present day China although we are aware that the decision to put a totalitarian country in that category may look arbitrary. Some reasons are conducive to this solution and they will be presented.

In *Japan*, before the Meiji period, law, judiciaries and 'citizens' did not exist: all power was controlled by a strong administrative state. During the Meiji period, with foreign experiences, with the debate on individual rights, the judiciary became autonomous and the attorneys did so too. Among attorneys, more and more chose to work as private lawyers instead of as usual joining the public careers within the justice system. Being despised they turned against the state. For this and other reasons, it was the beginning of the bar action to increase its autonomy and that of the judiciary, its capacity for collective action and to develop an 'anti-government ethos' (Feeley and Miyazawa, this book).

If the bar was quickly autonomous, if it remained cohesive for a long period, its capacity to influence the state especially by litigation was limited by its small size and by the judges' timidity. Even if they fought the government's persecution of the political opposition and helped the development of political life before and after the militarisation of the regime, even if they got some help from civil society, it is the long persistence of action that explains lawyers' influence and effects on state moderation.

In the *USA*, after September 11, the country which has often been considered as the most liberal, in order to defend itself against any strike from terrorists quickly produced a radical change in legality especially with the Patriot Act (2001). As it was a time of war and as he was the Commander-in-Chief of the Armed Forces, President Bush unilaterally suspended the application of several fundamental national and international laws, treaties or constitutional principles. The executive became, legally, a discretionary power. Legally it could put people in jail and detain them indefinitely without counsel and a judge; legally it could order the use by the army of an enlarged and legalised system of torture; and still legally, after having abrogated the Geneva Conventions, it could deal with prisoners as it wished (Abel, this book). Because the US is a democracy, the President could legally, by invoking national security requirements, erase some of the very fundaments of political liberalism.

How is it possible that a nation defined by a strong Supreme Court and by a long history of political liberalism could so quickly, so radically, and so easily get rid of some of the most central achievements of the Founding Fathers? How could it happen that more than two centuries after the 'Bastille', the most symbolic expression of arbitrary power has re-emerged in the US? And how could it be that attorneys, law professors, bar associations, and even lawyers within the Army, quickly and publicly defended fundamental civil liberties and yet had so little influence, at least at that time?

Parallel to attorneys' public involvement in the defence of individual rights, the amazing reality has been the development of a large and public disagreement among judges, including the Supreme Court, over the executive's limits. One may look at it as the expression of a democratic debate, but as it lasted several years it gave the executive the chance to act without any control. As a result hundreds of US citizens have been and still are detained indefinitely by discretionary decisions. Perhaps, this apparent paradox may open the way to some explanation. Clearly, the political-legal issue that was at stake is a difficult one as it deals with national security. Clearly too, here, lawyers and the bar associations were not silent. And *the result was the same* as with passive attorneys: the government acted without control. Two main causes may begin to explain this situation.

First, the long, complex, public debate between judges looks awkward. In a war against terrorism, when uncertainty dominates, it is authentically difficult to construct the right balance between freedom and rights, to establish the right proportionality between the danger and the loss of individual rights. But it is the dilemma that any government which is conducting a war has to meet. Efficacy does not necessarily require arbitrariness, and therefore in a democracy some control has to play on government. The centre of the controversy was the Supreme Court as the central potential counter-power at that time. But President Bush's policy shows clearly that the state had been concentrating such a vast amount of skills, information, justifications, discipline, and experts that he was able, as long as some trust stills existed, to construct the reality he wanted the others to believe in. The disorganisation of the judicial system has all the more been one of the consequences as it was amplified by political partisan cleavage within the judiciary (Abel, this book). In other words, the government demonstrated that it has the means to construct the reality that will both protect its secret moves and get the people's consent. Illiberal activities easily took the form of legality[6]. One should not forget, of course, the hubris of President Bush. But its expressions would have been less 'remarkable' without the concentration of such vast resources, technologies and expertise.

To summarise, in the US since 2001, the attorney's model of action shows two main characteristics: (1) when judges are divided, when civil society is weak because people are frightened or indifferent, when mass media have forgotten their critical tasks, at least provisionally, the executive can become an arbitrary power; (2) By the same token these conditions explain why attorneys and law professors who alone rose to defend basic freedoms were almost not heard.

Today as yesterday, in *China*, justice is subordinated to the state/Party and individual rights are usually ignored. The rebirth of attorneys happened

---

[6] 'The Supreme Court has finally and decisively rejected the Bush administration's outrageous claim that the President has the power to jail people he accuses of terrorist connections without access to lawyers or the outside world and without any possibility of significant review by courts or other judicial bodies': Dworkin (2004).

late, in 1982, and its development has been slow. To defend his clients an attorney has to defend himself against the state and the local officials, as all of them are inclined to abuse and to ban litigation. To be an attorney is therefore a risky function that may bring you to be fined, to be beaten, to be put in jail, and even to be killed. No protection should be expected from bar associations as they are controlled by public authorities, from the judges as they are under the control of the Party, or from a civil society divided on the issue of criminals getting an attorney's help before the court. Defence therefore should be what it is expected to be within a totalitarian regime. And China should be put in another category.

But several practices do not fit this representation (Halliday and Liu, this book). First, although attorneys' commitment to the defence of clients is threatened by the state, the Party, local authorities, prosecutors, judges and police, and even if they do not receive much help from civil society, nevertheless this defence of rights does exist. We cannot measure its scope, but it is large enough not to be ignored. Secondly, a large number of attorneys are participating in a national forum on the internet, showing a substantial de facto freedom of speech, some solidarity, the formation of a common culture, and a demonstration that they do have some individual and collective autonomy. Thirdly, since the 1970s and especially with the 1996 Criminal Procedure Law, the formal rights of defendants and of attorneys have been substantially increased, at least, officially. Fourthly, civil society is changing and the development of the market favours the ascendancy of the rule of law, the increase in the influence of the court even if it plays more in favour of commercial court than criminal courts.

The reality is kaleidoscopic. Nevertheless a tentative picture of the attorneys' behaviour can be drawn. To defend individual rights, attorneys usually alone, occasionally with the bar association or the press, have been opposing the state and regional officials, sometimes at great risk. Through these individual conflicts, through the collective action expressed by the debate on the internet, they have been simultaneously constructing the function of attorneys as a profession that should be ready to meet the opposition of the prosecutors, of the police, of the judges, of the Party and public officials, in order to defend individuals against the abuses of the state and all powers and by invoking the official law they have also begun, very slowly, to push toward a more moderate state. Moderation here begins with the respect of the rule of law (Halliday and Liu, this book).

Because they are risky, all these forms of action by Chinese lawyers explain what some lawyers describe as the 'spirit of sacrifice'. But how does it come about that so many attorneys can be defined by such a moral characteristic? Is the profession recruiting lawyers on the criterion of a 'spirit of sacrifice'? In fact, Chinese lawyers are part of a collective evolution in which they are playing their part. The attorney model of action is

inseparable from the extension of more liberal laws, the extension of proceduralism, from their readiness to take seriously western lawyers' model
of restricted political liberalism and of their self-representation as the only
weapon that may help individuals to fight against abuses of state/party
power. That topic will be dealt with again at the end of this analysis.

If China globally is a totalitarian regime, locally, with the attorney's model
of action, it shows a quite surprising reality that explains why China has
been put in this category of model of action. Although it is at its very beginning, although it may one day or another be wiped out, the attorney's model,
and with it some individual rights, does exist. Within certain limits.[7]

* * *

For almost a century in Japan, for the US since 2001 and for today's China,
the attorney model of action expresses very different realities. The Chinese
attorney's model shows a birth, the US attorney's model helps to discover
that even in mature democracies, even with attorneys' mobilisation, basic
freedoms can be lost at least provisionally, and, finally, the influence of the
Japanese attorney's model of action, should be studied over a long period.
This diversity should not hide the fact that *the passion to defend basic
freedoms* in several forms has been shared by all these actors. This characteristic converts them into political actors.

4. Support of Basic Freedoms by the Legal Complex

The legal complex model of action includes Korea (since 1980), Taiwan
(since 1980), Egypt (since 1970), Venezuela (since 1958) and Spain (since
1970). It represents different configurations of relationships among legal
actors. In all cases the legal complex includes at least judges and attorneys
whose lines of action are either parallel or functionally cooperative. With
this minimal structure as a common characteristics, the qualification and
explanation of the forms of action stem from the influence of the judicial
decision and that justifies the distinction between the Constitutional Courts
and ordinary courts. Within each category forms of action by the legal complex will vary (among other causes) according to the degree of civil society
mobilisation.

---

[7] It would be too easy to have before hand the Chinese profession's history. It was the
fantasm of the professionalisation thesis. But probably it will be a hybrid between the self-
governed profession that we know and another form, perhaps not too far from the one that
existed in France between the 13th century and almost the end of the 17th century. This professional form of organisation may be called 'the state bar'. During that period, among other
features, lawyers were beaten and it took a long time to make that habit disappear; they were
under the control of the state and the judges and nevertheless they managed to get autonomy
as well as professional and social recognizance: Karpik (1999: 15–35).

Thus the diversity of the legal complex forms of action is ordered according to the combination of these two dimensions: first, attorneys and judges of Constitutional Courts with strong civil society mobilisation, as in Korea and Taiwan ; secondly, attorneys and judges of Constitutional Courts with weak civic society mobilisation, as in Egypt; thirdly, attorneys and judges of ordinary courts and strong civil society mobilisation, as in Spain; and, finally, attorneys and judges of ordinary courts and weak civil society mobilisation, as in Venezuela. I will examine successively the legal complex around the Constitutional Courts and the legal complex around the ordinary courts.

	Constitutional Court	Ordinary Courts
Strong Civil Society mobilisation	Korea Taiwan	Spain
Weak Civic Society mobilisation	Egypt	Venezuela

The constitutional court/legal complex model of action is characterised by three countries: Korea, Taiwan and Egypt. By comparison with other models of action, it does not deal with individual cases but with individual laws and therefore the litigation strategy, if judges and attorneys try to rebuke individual rights' violations by the state, represents a direct threat not only to the government but to the political regime itself. Compared to other models of action, the stakes are the highest, the conflicts are the most intense and the effects according to the degree of mobilisation by civil society may be the most radical.

In *Korea* since 1980, the legal complex involved judges, attorneys and academics, it became the leading part of a composite social and political movement based on numerous civic organisations that expressed a civil society strong mobilisation. Political action was directed against repression but also more largely to democratic reforms. Therefore, the litigation strategy was only a part of the collective movements. In *Taiwan* since 1980, the general process has been the same but the legal complex has been more oriented toward direct political opposition than to litigation. In both countries the movement was as much democratic as liberal and the legal complex was embedded in social and political movements. As a result, the authoritarian regimes were abolished (Ginsburg, this book).

Egypt differs from Korea and Taiwan because of weaker mobilisation by civil society. After Nasser's presidency, a period of a more vivid political life began. Against torture, against indeterminate periods of detention, and against other violations of individual rights, a litigation strategy as well as demands of judicial independence arose around the Constitutional Court, its judges and attorneys. To which one should add academics and, in the 1990s, human rights associations helped financially by foreign funding. This opposition lasted because the political regime was sophisticated and could accept official legal losses, as long as a parallel judiciary subordinate to the state kept working. Once the conflict became dangerous in the eyes of the government it did not take much time for it to reduce the strength of a divided and weakened bar, to replace activist judges and to assault the human rights associations. International help could not compensate for the lack of citizen mobilisation due to a repressive state. Thus, with a weak civil society, the state prevailed over the legal complex (Mustapha, this book). We may tentatively conclude that *when attorneys and judges of the Constitutional Courts share the same political orientation this model of action can be victorious or defeated according to the degree of civil society mobilisation.*

The ordinary court model of action is exemplified by two countries: Spain and Venezuela. It differs from the Constitutional Court model, because the litigation stakes are less important, and from the attorney model by the scope of the civil society mobilisation.

In Spain, activist lawyers existed during the Franco regime *and* a fraction of them were involved in the litigation strategy as were *some* judges, but *the judges* were also committed to more global political ends. Although they shared the same ends and knew each other's commitment both groups acted in a parallel way. One could follow legal actors' practices to defend citizens against arbitrary decisions violating basic freedoms, but in that case what became crucial for the fight in favour of individual rights was a more global democratic movement that brought together the Catholic Church, the university, the communist party, fractions of the press and of professions, legal professions of course, to which one should add a multiform European aid. The notion of law played a central role in the claim against arbitrariness, as a willingness to respect individual rights and as the common language in the building of a liberal democracy (Hilbink, this book).

In *Venezuela*, in the past, whatever the regime, a 'symbiotic relation' existed between lawyers and rulers. Human rights and, more generally, legality were not part of their ethos. In 1958 a democratic period began that was characterised by the rise of judicial autonomy, by judges ready to take decisions against the government and by attorneys who pursued judicial trials against the government. Since the 1998 elections, an authoritarian regime has been established. It met and fought opposition from the legal complex which was opposing litigation against violations of human rights, by repeated purges of judges and judicial harassment of attorneys, legal professors, journalists, civic associations members. As in Spain at the end of the Franco regime, the legal complex is embroiled in a general political battle whose stake is the nature of the regime. But compared to yesterday's Spain, the civil society of Venezuela looks relatively weak (Perdomo, this book).

* * *

The analysis of the conception of political liberalism shared by lawyers all over the world, and the analysis of the universe of attorney/legal complex forms of action in relations with political liberalism, have given results that are recalled briefly here.

1. Lawyers are acting everywhere according to a restricted conception of political liberalism. This conception is organised around a strong link between basic freedoms and judicial action. That does not foreclose in one country or another, in one period or another, the enlargement of this restricted point of view to other political issues. But such a change, as it is peculiar, does not mean that the concept of political liberalism has to be modified.

2. Activist lawyers' orientations toward basic freedom can be negative, passive or positive.

3. Whenever the attorney/legal complex models of action are dominated by a social class logic and not by a professional logic, the probabilities are high that they will be hostile to basic freedoms.

4. Whenever national security is at stake, attorneys and legal complex that otherwise would have been politically committed could remain passive.

5. Lawyers positively oriented towards basic freedom belong to three categories: the attorney model, the Constitutional Court legal complex model and the ordinary courts legal complex model. They differ among themselves not by their issues but by the actions of the judiciary, by their forms of action, by the conflict intensity, by civil society mobilisation and by their possible results.

6. The attorney model of action deals with the attorney alone. Their repertoire contains the moves within a conflictual space delineated by the court transformed into a forum and by the political arena being transformed into an *agora* where the public is supposed to arbitrate. According to the political regime and their own commitment, their action can take different forms: a 'heroic' one punctuated by risky conflicts with the state (France, China) as well as a 'dull' one because results are only coming with repeated pressures (Japan) with other variants in between. Whatever the forms of action, the results will vary according to the degree of public mobilisation but usually they are piecemeal, specific, reformist.

7. The constitutional legal complex model of action deals at least with judges and lawyers who are sharing the same political orientations and in a voluntary or involuntary way are cooperating to limit state action by nullifying laws. The conflictual space is delineated by the moves between the court being transformed into a forum and the political arena transformed into an area of the political power conquest. According to the political regime and the degree of mobilisation the confrontation may become intense, and the legal complex

may be joined by a growing number of actors (Korea, Taiwan) or on the contrary it may be excluded and silenced (Egypt). The conflict may end up either in a regime crisis or a severe repression.

8. The ordinary court legal model of action deals with judges and attorneys who are sharing the same political orientations but do not cooperate. This mutual autonomy can last because they are the components of a global movement that claims individual rights reforms as well as democratic reforms. It is the degree of civil society mobilisation that will make the difference (Spain, Venezuela).

9. The notion of legal complex is not only relevant, it is also a fruitful one. As we faced a bewildering diversity of countries and periods, it helps to look at the data, to organize them. With it has become possible to distinguish between the attorney model of action and the legal complex models of action which encompasses Hostility, Passivity and Support of basic freedoms. Used as ideal types, these models help to describe and explain the diversity of the reality. And with the degree of civil society mobilisation, it has also become possible to identify the cause that makes the difference between victory and failure. It should be clear that there is nothing mechanically determinate in these conflicts and their results: without that uncertainty nothing would have happened.

III. BACK TO THE GENERAL CONCEPTION OF POLITICAL LIBERALISM

The analysis of the concrete forms of action of the legal actors, whether they are positively, passively, or negatively oriented toward individual rights, has shown again and again that the building of the state is a by-product of the action on behalf of political liberalism, that civil society is omnipresent but it cannot be really understood without the notion of spokesman, that globalisation exerts a diversified influence and that the attorney's action remains partially enigmatic.

(a) About the Building of the State

In a liberal society the state is supposed to be moderate. Moderation here is not conceived as the product of individual decisions but as the result of a constructed institutional architecture the measure of which can only be relative. Nevertheless it is also inhabited by some ideal where individual rights are protected and the separation of powers is working. That achievement may be only provisional. Unfortunately, we do not have precise studies on the transformations of the state under the influence of the judicial system that could help to figure out the different effects of the different forms of action.

Besides the state's primacy that is found during the long periods of traditional subordination of the judiciary, besides also the passivity of the legal complex, lawyers are acting on the state. With the attorney model, the action is mainly a piecemeal evolution punctuated by litigation, debates, political crises, law reforms. Moderation covers a large number of changes from the judiciary's autonomy, the bar's self-government, the lawyer's independence to the progressive elaboration of a jurisprudence that protects individuals against the state. With the legal complex models one may find the same picture, but the enlargement of the comparison to new countries shows that moderation is often established through radical crisis, when the authoritarian state is replaced by a liberal democratic state. Whatever the forms of change the tasks remain to identify not only the number and types of institutions, rules, judicial decisions but also to inquire about national and historical diversity.

(b) Does Civil Society Exist Without Spokesmen?

The notion of civil society is central to this theory. It has been criticised for its abstraction; for its emptiness. It does not say anything about society's structure, inequality, class structure or genre. One could plead that these and other omissions are the very reasons to have it and to keep it.

The division between the state and civil society is not the result of the analyst's inventiveness but the product of history. It is a collective representation of society that appeared long ago as a means to show by a radical simplification where the main danger lies for individuals, for those who belong to the *Public*. Wherever and as long as the state concentrates great discretionary power, this division is not only meaningful, it is also politically and, thus, theoretically useful. As long as distrust of the state is strong, this dichotomy will remain useful for the very same reasons. By itself it transforms the relationship between Behemoth and individuals into a problematic reality. The notion may look poor but it is powerful because it compels us to think globally about the state's limits. It is a necessary notion in general but it is all the more so in the present study as *the restricted political conception of political liberalism is based on the representation of a divided and fearful society.*

Civil society or its equivalent, the Public, is an amorphous reality. Nevertheless it is often characterised by significant features. It is more or less lively, more or less supporting or opposing, more or less indifferent, frightened or enthusiastic, more or less demanding or refusing. But paradoxically it does not speak or act by itself: it has to be represented. To exist, the public needs a spokesman. To be a spokesman is to act on behalf of the public. And to be considered as a spokesman after talking and acting, one has to be considered as such by other spokesmen. And to be trusted and followed.

Even if it is not explicitly mentioned, the spokesman is there because concretely it is the mechanism to explain lawyers' influence on others. With few exceptions, attorneys do not belong to large professions. Moreover, they are neither at the top of the social hierarchy nor members of the wealthy elite. How can we explain that this political conception of the attorney/legal complex action is so largely present in the world? How shall one explain that attorneys are so often ready to oppose authoritarian powers? How shall one understand the gap between their relatively small symbolic and material resources and their influence? And the fact that they so often win?

Two answers may be given. The first one is that their power results from the use of the judicial system. It is this powerful institution which is working on their behalf. That explanation is true but only partially. It meets some strong limits particularly in authoritarian regimes when the state wants to silence such a small minority of opponents. It usually has the tools to do it.

The second reason lies in the fact that the *representative has power that is given to him by the represented*. The notion of representative is central to attorneys' professional craft. In the past, it had extended from the client to the Public to get (or try to get) more influence. On this basis, yesterday as today lawyers are trying to be recognised as the spokesmen of the public. Under specific conditions, this conversion explains that a fraction of the bar could represent the whole bar and a fraction of lawyers could represent part or the whole public.

It is of course not that simple. One needs here a theory of the spokesman. Without developing it, it may be summarised like this: (1) lawyers claim to speak for the public; (2) the public is merely a figure of political speech; (3) political action, spokesmen and the public are intimately linked; (4) for the spokesman, credibility is central; (5) popularity, influence and power are the yardsticks of the success of the public spokesman (Karpik, 1999: 75–86 and 131–134). The conversion works more or less. As a result the individual or collective power will be small or great, solid or fragile, continuous or unstable.

(c) Economic, Ideological and Professional Globalisation

Globalisation has become multiform. One has to distinguish even crudely between the economic, the ideological or political, and professional globalisation. Their nature, rhythms and effects are different. The first one exerts the strongest and the more continuous effects, the second influence is more discontinuous, the last one, although the least visible, is probably in the long term quite powerful.

Economic globalisation produces contradictory effects. As an ideal type form of evolution one may consider that when the market is growing in a country (1) business lawyers are becoming more numerous and, as they are less politically oriented than criminal lawyers, the balance of the bar will change toward political neutrality; (2) but the global number of lawyers will grow too and more resources will go to political commitments; (3) as a result the bar will become more divided; (4) but so long as the political

orientation deals with basic freedoms it could be accepted by business lawyers unless it meets radical opposition from the political power. Economic
globalisation is not univocal although it favours probably more restriction
than an increase toward political action.

Ideological globalisation can take opposite forms: during the 1970s the
fight against communism and in favour of economic liberalism was dominant in Latin American countries and explains the multiplication of dictators and the brutal assault on political liberalism. In the two last decades
human rights ideology has become dominant, intervening through diverse
organisations such as international financial fundings, Council of Europe
(Spain), Court of Rights (Turkey), International Courts (Vénézuela), creating new political and financial solidarities and favouring the fight to expand
basic freedoms. One finds concrete examples of these forms of intervention
in the contributions. But this global influence is not really global, and when
it exists it does not necessarily produce the same results. In politics, one step
does not supercede other steps: the past is always ready to become our present again. It is the difference with the economic. That explains why apparently similar causes acting on different national histories, various political
regimes, unequal civil society mobilisation will produce different effects.
Even with the convergent actions of what may be called the 'human rights
institutions', success and failures have to be analysed country by country.

Professional globalisation is not new: foreign professional models began
to move from one country to another centuries ago. With them, knowledge, forms of organisation, conceptions of defence and more generally
the past of the legal profession were transferred with the English, German,
French, American, Japanese professional models, from countries to countries, and, of course, in the process they were re-interpreted. These moves
are known. But it is useful to insist on two intangible realities which
have shown a surprising general powerful influence. On one hand, the
restricted view of political liberalism the limitations and unity of which
have facilitated its transferability, and, on the other hand, a *moral conception* of the profession, an ideal definition of the legal profession's duty.

Taken together, globalisation exerts probably a stronger influence than
in the past. But its effects vary according to the causes, their contents, their
distribution and their re-interpretation by the different countries. The economic ones are more continuous, and the second and the third will heavily
depend on the ways the different countries will choose to integrate them.

(d) Why Do They Care?

The moral conception of the attorney opens several questions. How is it
that lawyers doing their work, which sometimes means opposing arbitrary
power, are ready to take risks and sometimes extreme risks? Why are they

not more neutral? More cautious? Of course, risk varies with countries, with periods, with individuals. Depending on the countries/periods/issues, they will be few or numerous, they will be isolated or be part of collective action. In every case, the question remains.

The intervention of the legal complex gives us one partial answer based on the observation that judges can take the same risks as the attorneys (Spain, Egypt). They will do it because of their political commitment. But it is a partial explanation especially as these actors occupy high positions and often are partly protected by public opinion and by foreign intervention. Something more primitive, more general is at stake. It combines restraints from power and courage from lawyers.

Quite often, the strong state will accept attorney activism. It will not use its full power against it. It is true for today and even more true for the past. More than three centuries ago lawyers' willingness to fight (although they were 'nothing' as they said) was amazing and, facing lawyers' opposition, the French absolute monarchy usually restrained severely the use of its powers. It looks like an enigma. But now, with China or other countries the enigma is even more amazing. Although Chinese lawyers are isolated, without public expression, without help, they are ready to engage in conflict to defend individual rights of private persons even if that may lead to fines, jail or death. And the state that could easily suppress that profession not only does not do it but on the contrary gives the attorneys by the use of the internet a surprising degree of autonomy and free speech. Here two complementary questions may be asked: why does the state take so long a time before it uses force when it uses it? And where does lawyers' courage comes from?

The tentative answer that I will not develop is that even if they are adversaries, the state and the attorneys, without necessarily knowing it, share a common conception of the institution of justice. It is not so much that lawyers as persons are 'respected'; it is defence as an integral part of the judicial system that is needed. Unless the state is strong and authoritarian enough to forget the benefits associated with justice—civil peace—it is very rational to establish and to keep as long as possible the continuity of justice. And for attorneys, justice as an institution brings with it an ideal conception of the function of lawyers.

Justice by itself is a public good, a universal common good. It is the belief in its value and in the rule of law that is perhaps everywhere at the source of radical professional commitment. If Chinese lawyers are ready to make a sacrifice it means that, at least in their minds, even when they are isolated, they are playing on a collective stage. What looks to others like a sacrifice is perhaps for them a militant act: they are not victims but combatants. It is the paradox of justice that at the same time it puts limits on state action and it radicalises the conception of the attorneys' duty.

IV. POLITICAL LAWYERS[8]

Sociologist A: How could you limit your analysis to those lawyers that usually are only involved in the restricted political liberalism? Don't you know that politics can take other forms?
Sociologist B: I have remarked on that diversity already!
Sociologist A: Well that doesn't seem the case. You should read the books published by your excellent colleagues on cause lawyers.
Sociologist B: I have read them.
Sociologist A: So why don't you call the lawyers you studied 'cause lawyers'? Is it because you are jealous that the authors coined a fortunate notion?
Sociologist B: Not at all.
Sociologist A: So why?
Sociologist B: Because I think that the lawyers studied here are not cause lawyers.
Sociologist A: But 'cause lawyers' is a very general term and should encompass all lawyers oriented toward 'morality and politics'.
Sociologist B: I know that and nevertheless I maintain my affirmation.
Sociologist A: Well you have to explain yourself because you're becoming more and more obscure.

How shall we characterise the attorneys/legal complex in this book? The task is so not much to differentiate them from conventional lawyers as to distinguish them from 'cause lawyers'. For all contributors to this book it would have been readily possible to apply the characteristics of cause lawyers to the legal actors: 'moral and political commitments', 'political actors whose work involves doing law', 'they tend to see client service as a means to their moral and political ends' (Sarat and Scheingold, 2004: 2,3,7). Nevertheless the notion has rarely been used by the contributors. Not because that literature was unknown but because something resisted that assimilation. It is this difficulty that I wish to make explicit and elaborate.

The term *cause lawyers* has been coined because nothing existed in English with the exception of the public interest lawyer to designate lawyers committed to moral and political goals. But what is true for English is not necessarily true for other languages. For example, French ignores 'cause lawyers' but has known for a long time the term *avocat politique*. It first appeared in the second half of the eighteenth century and it has been widely used since then. Are these two terms equivalent? Or equivalent enough to be mutually translated into each other? One general meaning is the same: all these lawyers are *engagés*, committed, activists. But beyond that point some important differences do exist.

Let us call 'political issues' those that belong to the conception of restricted political liberalism and 'cause issues' that bring together all the other issues. They are of course much more diverse as they include human rights, feminism, right-to-life, civil rights and civil liberties, anti-death penalty, environment, property rights, anti-poverty, social rights, right-wing, immigration practice, police violence, rights of minorities, landlord–tenant conflict and so on (Sarat and Scheingold, 2004: 3). The list keeps growing as new issues are rising on the legal-political stage. The most obvious differences between them lie in historical roots and in territorial distribution.

Historically, if individual rights litigation has appeared in the eighteenth century to spread everywhere, cause issues have mainly flourished since the 1960s in the US, since the 1970s in France with the first feminist movement's strong involvement in an abortion trial and they have also but more slowly spread elsewhere in the world. Thus, the history of cause issues is only half a century old, whereas it is three centuries old for political issues. It makes some difference.

All of the issues can be found all over the world. But the distribution is strongly unequal. Cause issues are more numerous in the most advanced countries, those which combine wealth and individualism because their number and their diversity follow the multiplication of subjective rights. The distribution of political issues should obey the opposite rule as they will be found especially in authoritarian states. To sum up, political issues are related to the central and old conflict between the state and civil society where basic freedoms have to be established, defended or restored, cause issues are much more numerous and diverse in the most advanced countries.

The two categories of issues are the basis of the distinction between 'political lawyer' and 'cause lawyer'. Usually, lawyers do not cross from one universe to the other: they are not interchangeable. The lawyers' differences can be shown about the resources, the construction of judicial issues and the relations with the bar.

First, as they belong to a long history, political lawyers are characterised by numerous resources, including especially a voluminous political philosophy, a repertoire of forms of action and a privileged position within the liberal state. By comparison, the cause lawyers' symbolic, technical and financial resources are more limited especially for the new causes when they have literally to create from scratch their philosophical and moral arguments, then build a repertoire of efficient forms of action, to gather allies and money and to conquer public position.

Secondly, the construction of judicial and political issues shows one central difference. For political lawyers, no justification is needed: to defend individual rights has become self-evident. Everywhere they feel like the descendants of an old and glorious history even if several variants may exist. On the contrary, no cause lawyer can take the cause he is defending for granted in such a way that is considered by everybody from the public as important and legitimate. Especially if the cause is rather new. The cause lawyer's first task—and it is by no means easy—will be to implement a persuasion strategy for the public, for the mass media and of the judge.

Moreover, as the issues may belong to very different categories like abortion rights and environmental issues, the shared collective meaning of the political cal lawyers will not be found between the cause lawyers. This difference leads into a system of differences between the lawyers' work.

Thirdly, and contrary to cause lawyers, political lawyers belong to a shared tradition that is, at least in the liberal democracies, part of the *bar's collective identity*. Quite often the fight for freedom and the expansion of the bar have gone together. With time, individual rights have been linked to the collectivity, and their defence has become part of their identity. Even if the real orientations and mobilisation toward basic freedom within the bar are quite diverse, even if business lawyers are much less interested in the defence of basic freedoms than are the clients of individual lawyers, the first type of lawyer will accept and even support action in favour of individual rights because the defence of liberties has become the counterpart of the special status of the profession. Even if their economic standards and prestige status are lower than those of business lawyers, political lawyers belong to the same collectivity. Usually they have their share of professional power because they bring to the bar the legitimation that all lawyers need. For these reasons they will get support from some fraction of the bar if needed, they will also have easier access to organised political forces and to the state. By comparison, cause lawyers are marginals. It takes time and success to change that position.

* * *

Political lawyers and cause lawyers do not share the same issues, the same history, the same references and they share only partially the repertoire of forms of action. They do not occupy the same position in the bar; they do not receive the same solidarity. Their relationships with history, with political philosophy, with the state, with civil society are different. They make up two different groups.

All are activist lawyers, but the differences between political lawyers and cause lawyers are great and systematic. No good reason exists to mix them for analysis. And there is at least one good reason to separate them: to elaborate a better theory. The argument is not that one notion will replace the other: we need both of them to elaborate that theory. To come back to this book, it should be now quite clear *that the contributions deal only with political lawyers*.

V. CONCLUSION

The distinction between political lawyers and cause lawyers is all the more crucial as it also expresses the transformations of society. In the last decade, cause issues have become more diverse and more numerous, bringing together more people, raising the interest of the mass media and, at the same time and for other reasons, political issues have remained remarkably lively. The first one is linked to the progress of individualism and the second to the permanent, if sometimes potential, state's danger. Both are everywhere but unequally present or developed.

Cause lawyers have all the more attained a more visible position than before 2000, at least in the mature countries, individual rights seem to have become old fashioned and political lawyers less mobilised, less visible. But these democracies have rediscovered that we never get rid of the task of defending basic freedoms. More generally liberal societies are never as liberal as we may think. And a larger number of countries are still trying to become liberal democracies. We are not at the point of getting away from politics. It was one of the conclusion of the previous book several years ago (Halliday and Karpik, 1997: 366–70); it can only be reiterated perhaps more strongly this time.

Political lawyers are there because basic freedoms have to be established, and when one has them they have to be defended. Outside that universe cause lawyer issues are becoming more numerous and they are spreading over a larger number of countries. Political lawyers and cause lawyers at least for the time being manifest the two embodiments through which rights may be established, extended, defended. At least, whenever they do not feel themselves threatened in the continuity of their profession, and whenever they do not have to choose between freedom and security.

These intertwined histories express a more complex society. They point the ways to elaborate a theory of lawyers' political action that could accommodate simultaneously political lawyers and cause lawyers. In the meantime, the task is to continue the development of each theory.

REFERENCES

Akerlof, GA (1970), 'The Market for Lemons: Qualitative Uncertainty and the Market Mechanism', *Quarterly Journal of Economics* 488.

Bachrach, S (1962), 'Two Faces of Power', 56 *American Political Science Review* 947.

Dworkin, R (2004), 'What the Court Really Said', 51 *New York Review Books* (August) 12.

Halliday, TC (1987), *Beyond Monopoly. Lawyers, State Crises, and Professional Empowerment* (Chicago, ll, University of Chicago Press).

Halliday, TC and Karpik, L (1997), 'Politics Matter: A New Framework for the Comparative and Historical Study of Legal Professions' in TC Halliday and L Karpik (eds), *Lawyers and the Rise of Western Political Liberalism* (Oxford, Oxford University Press).

Karpik, L (1999), *French Lawyers. A Study in Collective Action, 1274 to 1994* (Oxford, Oxford University Press).

—— (2007), *L'économie des singularités* (Paris, Bibliothèque des Sciences humaines, Gallimard).

Ledford, KF (1997), 'Lawyers and the Limits of Liberalism: the German Bar in the Weimar Republic' in T Halliday and L Karpik (eds), *Lawyers and the Rise of Western Political Liberalism* (Oxford, Oxford University Press) 349.

Marshall, TJ (1965), *Class, Citizenship and Social Development* (Garden City, NY, Anchor).

Scheingold, S and Sarat, A (2004), *Something to Believe In: Politics, Professionalism, and Cause Lawyering* (Stanford, Cal, Stanford University Press).

Tocqueville, A de (1997), *Democracy in America* (trans Henri Reeves, ?place, Vir, University of Virginia Press) Book 1, chapter 17, available at http://xroads. virginia.edu/~HYPER/DETOC/religion/ch1_17.htm.

Index

www.ingramcontent.com/pod-product-compliance
Lightning Source LLC
Chambersburg PA
CBHW060126280326
41932CB00012B/1433